Governing
Urban
America

GOVERNING URBAN AMERICA

CHARLES R. ADRIAN
Professor of Political Science
University of California, Riverside

CHARLES PRESS
Professor of Political Science
Michigan State University

FOURTH EDITION

McGraw-Hill Book Company
New York   St. Louis   San Francisco   Düsseldorf   Johannesburg
Kuala Lumpur   London   Mexico   Montreal   New Delhi   Panama
Rio de Janeiro   Singapore   Sydney   Toronto

The quotation from St. Clair Drake on page 31 is reprinted by permission of DAEDALUS, Journal of the American Academy of Arts and Sciences, Boston, Mass., Fall, 1965, *The Negro American*.

The quotation from Scott Greer on page 506 is from URBAN RENEWAL AND AMERICAN CITIES, by Scott Greer, copyright © 1965, by The Bobbs-Merrill Company, Inc., reprinted by permission of the publishers.

Governing Urban America

Library of Congress Catalog Card Number 70-37086
07-000445-5

1234567890KPKP798765432

This book was set in News Gothic by University Graphics, Inc., and printed and bound by Kingsport Press, Inc.
The designer was Emilio Squeglio.
The editors were Robert P. Rainier and Ellen Simon.
Peter D. Guilmette supervised production.

CONTENTS

PREFACE

A textbook that achieves a fourth edition must have a group of people loyal to it, and we wish to acknowledge our debt to those who have used the book over these many years. In particular, we extend our thanks to those who have offered helpful comments and suggestions. Through such assistance, we are enabled to make improvements with each edition.

We find it interesting to make comparisons with previous editions. The first one came off the press in August 1955. It sought to retrieve municipal government for political science students by emphasizing that "the process of urban government is primarily a *political* process" and by treating it as part of an urban culture. After this political approach was found acceptable, the second edition expanded on these themes and added greater emphasis to the influence upon the political process of the pattern of urban decentralization that characterized the 1960s.

With the third edition, the senior author was joined by a coauthor. This 1968 edition added chapters on the politics of education and of civil rights and liberties. Earlier, there had been little research done by political scientists on public education, and civil rights and liberties had been thought of as a matter for the Federal courts.

While preserving the relative brevity of the text, we now add material on the politics of poverty and the ghetto and also pay attention to the changes taking place in the now-aging suburbs. We hope that instructors and students will find the additions to their liking. We have, of course, sought to maintain the flavor and character of the earlier versions.

Charles R. Adrian
Charles Press

Governing
Urban
America

PART 1 THE URBAN POLITICAL PROCESS

At all levels of government in a democracy, the decision process is one of negotiation, accommodation, compromise, and the achievement of proximate rather than ultimate goals. The end result of the process is a public policy that seldom completely satisfies anyone, but leaves relatively few of the politically aware completely dissatisfied. And this is true whether one perceives government as "pluralistic" (in which there are so many ideas and interests involved in the process that no single set can dominate) or "elitist" (in which a dominant class rules in its own interests). Even a ruling elite must compromise its internal conflicts. The first part of this book, then, deals with the process by which ideas and interests are converted into urban public policy.

A THE SETTING

CHAPTER 1 THE SPRAWLING METROPOLIS

The college student of today is by all odds likely to spend his lifetime in an urban community. This textbook is designed to help him gain a better understanding of the operation of city government. Particular stress is laid throughout the text upon the issues in city politics that are political in nature, that is, issues that are controversial and possess alternatives in the public policy process. As such, these issues may require the ordinary citizen to make a choice and take a stand, either at the polls or as a member of an interest group.

The possible approaches to the study of political institutions are many. In this book, the emphasis is placed upon a study of the *political process* with the objective of supplying to the reader a method that will provide him with *a tool for the analysis of political events* that affect him and his society. No attempt is made to supply details concerning the thousands of urban communities in the United States. Such information is available in the nearest library and in the material in the footnotes, which list ample citations. Neither is there an effort made to outline a set of ethical norms for the reader's guidance, since analysis requires an objective or amoral examination of relevant data if understanding of politics is the goal. A word of warning, however: Although we have tried to avoid introducing our preferences, values—the beliefs one holds dear—are an essential ingredient in the decision-making process of politics. When one votes, or joins a group that seeks to influence governmental policy, or otherwise takes political action, he uses his sense of values of what is right or wrong, good or bad, in deciding what to do. At such times, personal values are of critical importance. However, to introduce one's personal preferences into an analysis of the political process is to blur the image; this we have tried to avoid doing. But no reader should assume that "one choice is as good as another" or that "no matter what I do, things will turn out the same anyway." The analysis in this book does not imply or justify such conclusions.

THE CITY AND THE URBANITE

The City Today. American city government has changed rapidly in the present century. Unlike most state and county governments, cities have undergone extensive alteration of their structure, and they are attempting to furnish the services demanded by contemporary society. Most city political machines and bosses have disappeared. The remaining ones are adopting policies more appropriate for the environment they now find themselves in. Blatant corruption and spoilsmanship have given way before the need for governmental services performed by technical specialists.

The realities of government in the contemporary American city are not well understood by the typical citizen. The folkways and folk tales of Americana saddle city government and city politicians with a stereotype that has little basis in fact. The stereotype does, however, have a *historical* basis.

The Public Attitude toward City Governments. Nearly everyone has at one time heard of the famous comment by the British political scientist James Bryce, who called "the government of cities the one conspicuous failure of the United States." That statement was made more than sixty-five years ago. Yet many Americans think of it as being appropriate today. Partly for this reason, citizens have developed a cynicism regarding municipal governments, especially the governments of the larger municipalities that make up the core cities of metropolitan areas. It is worthwhile, therefore, to inquire into the following causes, which formerly resulted in corrupt and incompetent city government.

1. *Rapid Growth of Cities.* In the first place, difficulties in achieving confidence in city government are partly a product of the rapidity with which the American city grew after the Civil War. This nation was predominantly an agricultural one until (roughly) the last half of the nineteenth century, and its democratic traditions were oriented toward the frontier and the farm, not toward the city. The same traditions do not necessarily fit each of them equally well. Furthermore,

effective *democratic* government is built largely upon a sound foundation of customs, attitudes, and traditions that require time to build and to work into the normal behavior patterns of a society. A nation of farmers cannot overnight discover methods for the effective government of industrial cities. Furthermore, when blossoming cities of the nineteenth century had added to their populations shiploads of immigrants, ignorant of the customs, laws, beliefs, and even language of an adopted country, the problems of government became vastly more complex. In recent times, most core cities have declined in population but have continued to add large numbers of new residents unused to urban ways, particularly Negroes and whites from economically marginal areas of the rural South.

2.   *City as Creature of State.* A second factor is to be found in the position of the city as a creature of the state. With minor exceptions (to be discussed in Chapter 7), the relationship of a city to the state in which it is located is the relationship between a child and its parent. A city can perform only those functions authorized for it by state law. These functions generally apply in (1) matters in which the city acts simply as the agent of the state and (2) matters of local concern. An example of the former is the protection of the public health; of the latter, the provision for transit service. American courts historically have given a very narrow interpretation to the powers of cities. This approach has been based on the theory that, if in doubt, power belongs to the sovereign state and not to one of its corporate subdivisions. The result has been that the state legislature—in the past dominated by small-town merchants and lawyers who were inexperienced in city social patterns—has often not given the city the power needed to deal with local problems. This situation has sometimes led to dissatisfaction, cynicism, and a tendency on the part of the public to look elsewhere for the solution of the problems of the city. The typical citizen, casually interested in politics and law, is not concerned with *why* the city cannot perform a function felt to be needed—he wants it done, and if the city cannot do it, he will look for another unit of government that can and will.

The state-imposed limitation upon the power of the city to tax has especially restricted the actions of city governments. American cities have been, and still are, overwhelmingly dependent upon a levy that was designed to fit the needs of a frontier society—the general property tax. Because legislatures have not been anxious to allow cities to use other types of taxes, municipalities often have found that their limit of services renderable comes at whatever point the property tax seems to reach a psychological saturation point. Again, the impatient and annoyed citizen is likely to turn to the state or national government for a service for which the city "has no money."

Picayunish control over local matters has been carried to such an extent by many state legislatures that cities have sometimes been given almost no opportunity to decide any important matters for themselves. This type of action by the lawmakers turns the legislature into an *administrative* overseer of city government. Although the practice appears to be on the decline today, it continues in many states, giving the citizen the impression that the really important decisions are made, not in the city hall, but in the state capital and that, therefore, city government is not of sufficient consequence to rate his attention. Such supervision by the state government has also had its adverse effect upon the municipal officeholder, whose creativity becomes dulled and discouraged by being constantly told that he is in danger of exceeding his authority. When his powers are interpreted narrowly by the courts and he must go to the legislature whenever he wishes to make a departure from customary policy, the city official begins to orient his job toward the annotated statutes and the opinions of the attorney general instead of toward economic and sociological demands. The ordinary citizen, impatient with legalism, is likely to view the plight of the harassed official without sympathy. The explanations he hears will sound to him like excuses for inaction.

3. *Financial Weakness.* A third item discouraging citizen faith in city government has been its financial weakness. During the Great Depression that began in the fall of 1929, municipalities, supported by a tax base often deceivingly inflated by the artificial real estate boom of the 1920s, found themselves financially unable to meet the suddenly enormous costs of the public welfare load, the costs of the municipal payroll, or the costs of the interest upon bonded indebtedness.[1] The phenomenon of a municipality nearly or actually bankrupt in a time of great public need is well remembered by millions of persons alive today. The story has passed into American folklore. It does not enhance the prestige of our cities. The almost unending financial crises of the 1960s and 1970s have not helped to improve the image.

4. *Corruption.* A fourth consideration has been the persistency with which American cities have been plagued with varying degrees of corruption. It was long a veritable tradition in our larger municipalities and has affected a great many of our cities of any size at one time or another in history. Corruption may enter city government, in the first place, as a result of the commonplace lack of interest in the operations of the city which permits lax administration. Dishonesty and irregularities breed a greater lack of interest and a cynicism

---

[1] On the impotence of municipal government during this period, see David A. Shannon (ed.), *The Great Depression,* Prentice-Hall, Inc., Englewood Cliffs, N.J., 1960, chap. 3.

which allows for more of the same. Another cause stems from circumstances which demand that city officials enforce formally enacted laws that do not accord with the prevailing public mores. Examples of this may be found in the case of liquor prohibition during the 1920s and of gambling today.[2] Such anomalies place city officials in positions of great temptation, yet the same citizens who drink illegal liquor or insist upon gambling will be among those who will censure public officials who do not enforce the law. Individual Americans expect tougher moral fiber in their public officials than they themselves possess.

Corruption is far less widespread and certainly less overt today than it was formerly. Yet, in 1959, a number of Chicago policemen were found to have been operating as part of a burglary gang. At about the same time, in New York, a variety of charges were made alleging maladministration or corruption in connection with a slum-clearance program, the inspection of meat retailers, and the purchasing of salt for snow removal. A borough president was charged with having accepted a large gift from a real estate operator who was doing business with the city. In 1970, a former mayor of Newark and other local officials were convicted on charges of corruption.

5. *Decay.* Confidence in municipal government has waned as increasing numbers of citizens have come to view core cities as areas of decay. The flight to the suburbs cannot, of course, be attributed to the crime-in-the-streets issue alone, but threats to personal safety have become a part of the widely held image of cities as areas that provide unpleasant and unattractive living surroundings. City government, despite its relative weakness as an agency for social control, has been viewed by many citizens as somehow responsible for the aspects of urban life they disapprove of, while the services it has provided have been taken for granted, with little curiosity as to how they are made possible.

6. *Apathy.* Finally, however, whenever our cities have not been governed in a fashion that satisfies the high expectations of most citizens, the cause may be found in general public apathy. The ordinary citizen is a busy person with many demands upon his time. As a consequence, he must budget his interests—and municipal government has rated a low priority. This has been true in part because the city dweller has viewed his local government as one that performs primarily routine service functions. Who, he wants to know, can become interested in such prosaic problems as the supplying of water, the maintenance of streets, the disposal of sewage? Are these

---

[2] The effect of organized crime upon our cities will be examined in chap. 16; the influence of the old-time boss as a "broker of privilege" will be considered in chap. 6.

not routine matters to be handled by civil servants? Why should he concern himself? Many advocates of the reform movement of a few decades ago advanced the misconception that municipal government is nothing more than the application of the principles of "good business management" from which the politician ought properly to be excluded.[3] Undoubtedly, city governments exist primarily to render services to patron-citizens. These services, however, are often far from routine, and the existence of alternative approaches to public policy offers the basis for lively citizen participation in genuine political issues. In the 1960s, issues of fluoridation, annexation, open occupancy, the integration of public facilities, and the unionization of local employees have destroyed the image of city governments as being unconcerned with public policy matters. Much of this book will be taken up with the consideration of nonroutine political issues in urban functions.

Until recent decades, citizen interest was often at low ebb because middle-class citizens thought they could not be connected (or at least not openly) with city administrations that were often under the control of a boss or a machine or were cooperating with professional criminals. It was uncommon for a representative of the community elite to become involved in municipal politics prior to the advent of the reform movement in the 1880s, which helped to make that sort of thing respectable. Even today, many persons still believe that city politics is corrupt and hence to be shunned by good citizens. Such viewpoints severely cripple the efforts of city governments.

The high-mobility characteristic of contemporary American city dwellers, combined with their extreme heterogeneity, has militated against most people's having a sense of belongingness in the community. This in turn has resulted in a low degree of civic pride and morale, which produces lack of interest in the local political process. Irvin S. Cobb once said, "There is this to be said for New York City: it is the one densely inhabited locality—with the possible exception of Hell—that has absolutely not a trace of local pride." Mr. Cobb to the contrary notwithstanding, the same problem exists in most large cities.

Another aspect of low citizen interest may be found in factors related to the phenomenon that the psychologists call identification. The individual, in his fantasies—in his daydreaming—tends to associate himself with the heroic, the "important" things in life. The dramatic, glamorous activities of the national government attract the layman, appeal to his imagination, and help him to form opinions about controversial matters on this level of government, but the

[3] This movement, its ideology, and its results will be reviewed in chap. 2.

commonplace problems of health and of police and fire protection will have much less appeal. When the President of the United States discusses problems over the radio and television and asks for the assistance and support of the citizen, the individual is flattered. If, however, the mayor of the city appears on the television screen to talk to the citizenry about the daily problems of the municipality, the response of the citizen is not likely to be the same. Unless the mayor is an unusual individual, the citizen is likely to switch to another channel. His mind, busy with a thousand attractions calling for attention, can be directed only toward those things that are "important" or "interesting."

Many factors have, therefore, combined to produce the cultural image of municipal government that exists today. Of all of them, however, the most important is the failure of the lay citizen to take an interest in the government that is the most intimate, the most observable, and the closest to him of all the coercive agents of society.

METROPOLITAN PANORAMA

Cities come in all sizes and shapes. Some are large, some are small. No two are exactly alike. We can speak of statistical averages and "typical" cities, but we can only approximate what we would find if we were to give an intensive examination to any one city. An impressionistic glance may, however, furnish a few generalizations which can be examined in greater detail as we proceed farther on in this text.

What, then, are the characteristics of the metropolis? It is a smoky, grimy sea of television aerials, noisome slums, bright neon signs, impatient traffic, mammoth factories with fantastic productive capacity, manicured suburbs desperately seeking to imitate a fond memory of a county-seat town in grandfather's day. It is a Champaigne fair of conflicting cultures where thousands of human beings live in close proximity to other thousands whom they dislike in one degree or another because—though they would not so state it—their values and cultural habits do not coincide. For the human being dislikes what he fears, he fears much that he does not understand, and there is much in the modern city that he does not understand. It is a land of coolness in a nation of supposedly friendly people, where *émigrés* from rural places find an absence of the primary social relationships to which they are accustomed, and where people, in the midst of the greatest possible variety of activities, may lead basically dull lives, although they seek to hide that fact from their own consciousness.

The City Hall. The people of the city have little interest in their local government and treat it with a lack of respect which, in their opinion, is its due. Somewhere downtown in an area lacking adequate parking space—as is the entire city, for that matter—is the city hall.

The city administration is headed by the mayor, who is quite likely to be a man of broad smiles, firm handshakes, and modest talents. There are probably several other elective administrative officials—most of them glorified bookkeepers or file clerks, but the voters insist upon electing them.

The members of the city council are perhaps somewhat more difficult to classify. Depending upon the city, a few or even perhaps most of them may be men chosen from the business and industrial world who often are more concerned with the interests of the groups that selected them to run for office than with the public interest. The council is apt to include in its membership one or more representatives of organized labor, who similarly are primarily concerned with labor interests. Usually it includes several lawyers, often those who are politically ambitious and who would use membership in the council as a stepping-stone to higher political careers. It is not uncommon for lawyers to run for the council in the hope that the prestige and public notice gained will advance them in their profession. Realtors are ubiquitous in city government and watch over the decision-making machinery on behalf of all realty interests; also, the realtor who is elected to the council is given a bonus in free advertising. A number of political hacks may serve on the council: men who know nothing but the art of politics and to whom defeat would threaten starvation.

Although the citizen may pay little attention to local politics, he is quite likely to consider himself a competent "Monday morning quarterback." He is quick to offer criticisms of state and national officials, and he is even more convinced of his competence in evaluating problems of municipal government. Furthermore, since municipal officials are close at hand, it is much easier for the citizen to make his complaints known at that level.

The Urban Personality. American cities, for the most part, have a dull monotony about them. To be sure, there are exceptions. There is only one Boston, New Orleans, New York, Atlantic City, San Francisco, or Washington.[4] But the typical city has little to distinguish it as a personality. It has failed to develop its own individuality, to exploit latent traditions, to use its every opportunity to make the community a place where life is richer because of its own particular

[4] Constance McLaughlin Green, *American Cities in the Growth of the Nation* (Harper Colophon Books, Harper & Row, Publishers, Incorporated, New York, 1965), looks at the history of sixteen cities; Anselm Strauss, *Images of the American City* (The Free Press of Glencoe, New York, 1961), looks at American opinions regarding rapid urbanization.

attributes. In the past, the local politicians and most pillars of the community have been too busy in a frenetic world to concern themselves with such an expendable as local color.

Chaotic Development. Inadequate planning and weak land-use controls are endemic, for the concepts of individual initiative and individual use of one's own property have been interpreted to mean a right to damage property values of others indiscriminately and to destroy the physical beauty and utility of an area. This result has been praised by some as providing a diversity that makes cities fascinating,[5] but it is not liked by urban planners or land economists. Inefficient land use is especially common on the fringe of the city. Although the suburbanite has taken a deep interest in land-use controls—they represent a major governmental technique for molding the community to suit his image of a desirable life style—much damage has usually taken place before a planning commission is established and controls made effective.

The City Is a Playground. From the hinterland for miles around, people flock to the city when they seek recreation and relief from the chores of everyday. The informal amusement patterns of rural America have given way to commercialization. In the metropolis, any kind of recreation demanded by its hordes of people will be furnished by someone. In a day when people feel more than ever the need for escape from the humdrum, gambling serves as a way out for increasing numbers. Except for operations at the gaudy track laid out in the suburbs, this business is illegal, to be sure, but it is controlled by a syndicate of gangsters who welcome its illegality. This same syndicate is likely to be involved in furnishing other illegal services: prostitution and narcotics. Illegal occupations produce enormous problems for the police—and city officials receive no sympathy from a public that simultaneously demands law enforcement and illegal services.

The City Is a Magnet. In comparison with the rural life that once dominated America, contemporary city life produces more crime, especially of the organized and professional type, more neurotics, more psychotics, more lung cancer (possibly because of the greater amount of hydrocarbon irritants in its polluted air), greater extremes of wealth and poverty, more social and economic interdependence and hence more insecurity, more juvenile delinquency, more wrecked marriages, more suicides, and more deaths per thousand people.

---

[5] Jane Jacobs, *The Death and Life of Great American Cities,* Random House, Inc., New York, 1961.

Why, then, do increasing numbers of people come every year to the metropolis? And why do those who are already there only *talk* about giving up the struggle and taking "a little place in the country"? Because there is in the city a greater freedom for individually chosen behavior patterns; greater tolerance of diversity (but only in the more crowded parts of the city); more and better schools at all educational levels; a greater variety of entertainment mediums; far more institutions of fine art—libraries, museums, theaters, art cinemas, symphony orchestras, and the ballet; more wealth; and a much greater opportunity for advancement in accord with the American pattern of values.

The city contains greater extremes of wealth and poverty than does the country, but for most people it means the prospect for a higher standard of living. It suggests more material things and more of an opportunity for "the good life." The older pattern has been reversed: Ours is now a society based largely upon urban life styles, with the rural dweller more and more imitating the ways of the urbanite. The contemporary American dream is housed among the millions in our cities.

THE SMALL TOWN: URBAN ANOMALY

Village and small-town life has been a traditional part of America, honored in memory and song and satirized in novel and poem. The town has its origins as a service center for a small rural area. Throughout much of the nation, shopping villages were originally spaced close enough together to allow any farmer to reach one by horseback or buggy within a reasonable length of time, perhaps an hour. County seats were generally situated so that they were not more than a day's buggy ride from the farthest farmer. They were larger than ordinary trading places, since they contained the incipient bureaucracy of government, the offices of lawyers who dealt with that bureaucracy on behalf of clients, livery stables, hotels, and other establishments catering to the citizenry that found it necessary or desirable to visit the seat of government.

The ordinary country town contained a general store, repair shops, a physician and a veterinarian, a weekly newspaper, a bank, a school, and a church or two. If the community was large enough, it also served as a market. With the coming of the automobile and telephone, this pattern began to change. By the 1950s, the general store had come more to resemble the corner grocery of the city or, in larger towns, had become a supermarket (which is, in fact, a reconstitution of the old general store, except that modern merchandising techniques have been added and the traditional function as a news and gossip center has declined). The physician found he could make more money and serve more people by moving into the nearby city. The weekly newspaper, in the face of high labor and newsprint costs, was beginning to disappear. The bank had become a branch of a city institution or had disappeared. The school now represented the consolidation of a great many formerly rural districts with an elaborate system of school bus routes. The churches continued to perform some, though not all, of their traditional functions. The population was made up of locally employed persons, a considerable number of retired farmers, and a new element—the commuters. Many persons, either because of a preference for the small-town life or because of shortages in low-cost housing in the cities, have taken up residence in the town but may drive up to 25 miles and more each day to their jobs in the city. Townsmen themselves commute to city jobs.

Small-town Politics. Politically, the villages and towns tend to be, throughout the nation, centers of conservatism. Most of them are one-party communities, either Democratic or Republican, depending upon local traditions. Although their governments provide some basic community services in the areas of water, sewage disposal and sewerage, police and fire protection, the small community remains a center of opposition to the social-service state. Lacking experience in the social problems of large cities or in living together with cultural groups having different values from their own, its citizens tend to be intolerant of proposed state or municipal legislation dealing with problems that do not exist or exist in minor ways in their communities. To them, the fact that such problems exist in large cities is taken to be evidence of the degeneracy or moral inferiority of urban life. This attitude cannot be ignored as quaint but harmless, however. Representatives from small towns, until the mid-1960s, dominated most state legislatures, which are the agencies that control the powers exercised by large city governments.[6]

Yet the town is itself a political, economic, and social problem. Its difficulties stem from several things: the declining farm population which produces a declining market; the preference of many farmers for the more specialized and hence more expert services in the nearby city, now easily available by modern auto and good roads; the lack of opportunity in the town, while our culture emphasizes the desirability of opportunity, with the resultant draining off of the most able young people; extreme conservatism in a day when many attitudes which this produces do not fit into the value

[6]Charles Press and Charles R. Adrian, "Why Our State Governments Are Sick," *Antioch Review,* 53:100–120, June, 1964.

systems learned in the consolidated schools and on television by young people; and finally, current highway department practices of bypassing practically all towns, thus cutting off the transient business that had earlier helped to sustain them. The small town is an urban place and its life style is no longer as different from that of the large city as it once was, but it is still different—and its governmental and social problems are different.

Consensus and Inaction in Springdale. Springdale, a rural village in upstate New York, was studied by two sociologists who wanted to see how the villagers were accommodating to life in mass society. The community offers some not atypical examples of small-town life. Its politics differs radically from that of the metropolis. The large city is often the scene of strident and undisguised political conflict, but in the village:[7]

> . . . politics is conducted on the principle of unanimity of decision. In two years of observation of village board meetings in Springdale, all decisions brought to a vote were passed unanimously. The dissent, disagreement, and factionalism which exist in the community are not expressed at board meetings. Through a process of consultation prior to an official meeting and by extended discussion involving the entire group during the meeting itself, a point is reached when it seems reasonable to assume that everyone will go along with the proposed action. Only then, as a final parry, will someone suggest that a motion be made to propose the action.

Although the large city is the scene of constant experimentation, the arena in which new social-service activities of government are launched and in which a highly professional bureaucracy administers complex programs, the pattern in the village is totally different:

> Although the principle of unanimity of decision is almost a requirement in Springdale politics, few items of business outside of routine and legally required action ever reach the decision-making stage. It is an outstanding characteristic of village government that it does not initiate new undertakings and new projects. . . . It is a common complaint among all groups in the community that the village board does nothing.

Grand Plans and Grass Roots in Suburbia. Although great variety is the characteristic of urban politics in America, there are some common patterns. The small-town dweller wishes to avoid decisions and opposes new or expanded programs, but the suburbanite looks

[7]A. J. Vidich and Joseph Bensman, *Small Town in Mass Society*, Princeton University Press, Princeton, N.J., 1958.

to his local government to provide many of life's amenities. (See Table 1-1.) The person living in a large city has a feeling of isolation from the political process and tends to be apathetic, but the suburbanite feels close to his government and is likely to believe that he and his neighbors can run it on a grass-roots basis. In fact, one characteristic of suburbia is the resident's[8]

> ... acceptance of an obligation for extensive civic participation on the part of the lay constituency. ... On the local level civic interest may express itself in the citizen's inclination to undertake the supervision of the local bureaucracy directly, or in his suspicion of the role of the professional political leader. Here the image of resurrected grass-roots democracy commits the citizen, theoretically, at least, to a do-it-yourself brand of politics, in which as many issues as possible, simple and complex, require his personal sanction, and the acceptable elected official is the part-time amateur, taking his term in office just as he once led the community chest drive.
> Finally ... there is a belief that the individual can and should arrive at his political convictions untutored and unled; an expectation that in the formal process of election and decision-making, a consensus will emerge through the process of right reason and by the higher call to the common good.

TABLE 1-1. Dissatisfaction with Local Governmental Services (In percent)

Number of Services with Which Dissatisfied	Dayton	Suburban Zone	Outer Zone
None	45	20	32
One	26	24	20
Two	16	23	29
Three or more	13	33	14

Note that suburbanites and exurbanites desire the services that the core city already has.
Source: John C. Bollens and others, *Metropolitan Challenge,* Metropolitan Community Studies, Inc., Dayton, Ohio, 1959, table 47. Used by permission.

Summary Statement. The village, small city, core city, and suburb differ from one another in many ways. But they are all urban areas, and they share many characteristics, problems, and issues. This book will be concerned with their similarities and their differences.

[8] Robert C. Wood, *Suburbia: Its People and Their Politics,* Houghton Mifflin Company, Boston, 1959, pp. 156–157. By permission of the Houghton Mifflin Company.

THE COMING OF THE CITY

Meanings and Usages. Nothing much can be learned concerning the nature of an area simply because it is called a city. The term itself descends from the Latin *civis* (citizen) and was restricted in England to application to cathedral towns. Other urban areas in England were known as boroughs—a term used today in the city of New York and to some extent in Connecticut, New Jersey, Minnesota, and Pennsylvania. The word *town* is from the Anglo-Saxon *tun,* a homestead surrounded by a hedge or other fence, from Old High German *zûn,* a hedge. *Borough* is from the Anglo-Saxon *burh,* a fortified town. Today, in the four states named above, it represents an incorporated area occupying a position between that of a city and a village. The five administrative subdivisions of New York are also called boroughs. *Village* is from the Italian and Latin *villa,* meaning originally a farm or country house. The term *municipality* is from the Latin *municipium,* which referred to certain Italian towns that enjoyed special privileges under Rome. In the United States today, and in this book, the term is popularly used interchangeably with *city* or *village.* A city in the United States is a legal, not a sociological, concept. City limits may be greater or smaller than the *de facto* urban area. In most states, a city may or may not be larger than the largest villages in the state. Villages may be tiny rural trading centers, or they may be sizable urban areas, as in the case of several of Chicago's large suburbs. There may or may not be meaningful legal differences between cities and villages. In this text, what is said to apply to cities will also generally apply to villages as well. As a matter of fact, the smaller urbanized areas of a state may legally be called villages (as in Minnesota) or towns (as in Iowa). The smallest rural unit of government is usually the township—except in New England, where it is a unique institution and is called a town. To add to the confusion, however, the township does not exist at all in most states, but in some metropolitan areas it has been permitted to become virtually a city. In states where this trend has not developed, the existing township—sometimes using its full 36 square miles—has often been the basis for an incorporated village or city.[9] In Minnesota, townships are legally (although not popularly) known as towns; and around some of our cities they have become urbanized and constitute virtually another form of city government (for example, in Michigan, New Jersey, and Pennsylvania).

The largest urban communities are often popularly (although not legally) known as metropolitan areas (from the Greek *meter,* mother,

---

[9] Thomas F. Hady and Clarence J. Hein, "Congressional Townships as Incorporated Municipalities," *Midwest Journal of Political Science,* 8:408–424, November, 1964.

and *polis,* city-state). These "mother-cities" are ordinarily made up of an agglomeration of cities, villages, townships, special districts, and other units that may total several hundred in number. In the United States, these sociologically cohesive units are virtually never treated as legal units; the metropolitan area is almost never a single city.

The student should be warned, therefore, against any hasty conclusions concerning the meaning of the terms usually used in connection with urban areas. Without a standard terminology, he must be prepared to adapt his understanding of terms to conditions prevailing locally. For purposes of this text, an urban area is conceived of as a sociological community wherein the individuals are engaged primarily in diversified nonagricultural pursuits and where distinctive, nonrural patterns of behavior prevail. A city, village, borough, or (sometimes) town is a legally described region which seldom coincides with the actual urban area.

Urbanization of the Western World. The city in western civilization is primarily a product of the industrial revolution. To be sure, cities existed in Europe before 1770 (roughly the time of the beginning of the revolution), but they were chiefly capital or trading centers. In 1550, Paris, both a trading center and a great seat of government, was, according to William B. Munro, the largest city in Europe, and its population did not exceed 300,000. Mighty London was a village during the Middle Ages, having only about 40,000 people as that period came to an end. It grew very rapidly in the sixteenth and seventeenth centuries as Britain became the trading center of the rising new economic world. By the time of the American Revolution, it had become the largest city in Europe, with a population of around three-quarters of a million people.

With the rise of a machine technology, steam power, and the factory system, cities grew at phenomenal rates. Europe and America, predominantly rural from prehistoric times, rapidly became urbanized. In the United States, there were only small towns at the time of the Revolution. They were growing, however, and they continued to grow. From the turn of the nineteenth century, cities expanded at an ever increasing pace. Between 1820 and 1840, the number of people engaged in manufacturing increased by 127 percent. Between 1840 and 1850 alone, America's urban population increased by nearly 50 percent.

After the construction of railroads, the heavy influx of foreign investment and the Civil War (1861–1865), urban growth, which earlier had occurred on the East Coast and especially in New England, spread into the Middle West. The rise of the great corporations and the never-ending developments in technological knowledge continued to raise the American *standard* of living even as it changed the American *mode* of living. Immigrants who before had hurried to the rich clay loams of the Middle Western farm belt now remained in New York, or Cincinnati, or Chicago to become a commodity called "labor" in the factory, the steel mill, or the stockyard. The children of country bumpkins yearned to become city slickers and hurried off at the earliest opportunity to what was often their disillusionment. And they continue to do so today.

The City Today. The population of cities doubled between the beginning of the Civil War and 1900. In the next quarter of a century, it doubled again. By 1920, over one-half (51.2 percent) of the American people were living in cities.[10] The percentage in 1960 was around 70 and continues to climb. We live in an urban nation. The American farmer is no longer a member of the dominant group in our society. His cultural patterns and sets of values are rapidly being replaced by new ones more in keeping with our own, rather than our parents' or grandparents' world.

In 1970, nearly two-thirds of the American population lived not merely in urban but in the 233 *metropolitan* communities. Approximately one-fourth of it lived in the twelve largest metropolitan areas. About 220 counties hold over one-half of the nation's population. The other half is scattered over 2,800 essentially rural counties.

The population of the United States reached 205 million by census-counting time in 1970. This represented an increase of about 25 million in a ten-year period. All of that increase was urban, for the population that earns its livelihood from working the soil declines each year as it has—interrupted only by the years of the Great Depression—since shortly after the beginning of the century. The gain was highest of all in the suburbs.

It was the very largest cities that generated the greatest suburban population increases, but the moderate-sized metropolitan areas (those between one-half million and one million people) grew more rapidly than did any other size community. The huge cities (except Los Angeles) generally lost population as people continued to show

---

[10] For statistical purposes, the U.S. Bureau of the Census classifies cities as incorporated places with 2,500 or more inhabitants. Legal definitions differ from this in the various states.

In the censuses of 1960 and 1970, the Bureau defined urban, as distinguished from rural, areas as (1) places of 2,500 inhabitants or more incorporated as cities, boroughs, or villages; (2) the densely settled urban fringe, whether incorporated or unincorporated, around cities of 25,000 or more (the limits of this area determined more or less arbitrarily, based upon physical features); (3) unincorporated areas of 2,500 inhabitants or more outside of the urban fringes; and (4) towns of 2,500 or more except in New England, New York, and Wisconsin.

The Bureau has also undertaken to define large urban places. "Standard metropolitan statistical areas" contain at least one city of 50,000 or more population. The nucleus of the area is the county or counties containing the core city or cities. Contiguous counties are included in the area if they are densely settled by nonagricultural workers and are socially and economically integrated with the core city. For technical criteria, see U.S. Bureau of the Census, *Standard Metropolitan Statistical Areas*, 1959.

a preference for suburban life styles. New York remained the nation's largest city, although its population declined as it had a decade earlier. So did Chicago's. The Los Angeles metropolitan area remained the second largest in the nation, having passed the Chicago area in 1960. The greatest increases, as had been the case a decade earlier, took place along the Pacific and Gulf of Mexico coasts and in the areas near the Great Lakes. The nation, with nearly 70 percent of its population crowded into only about 6 percent of the area of the fifty states, had indeed become metropolitan.

The Urban Region. Only seven of the fifty states contain no metropolitan areas. These are Alaska, Idaho, Montana, Nevada (which is, however, 70 percent urban), North Dakota (the least urban state, with about 35 percent), Vermont, and Wyoming. Elsewhere, of course, it is around the metropolises that the population continues to cluster. In fact, these areas are growing into one another so that Charlton F. Chute has found it advantageous to define "urban regions." These consist of two or more contiguous standard metropolitan statistical areas. The greatest of these is the eastern seaboard region, which stretches for 600 miles from the vicinity of Haverhill, north of Boston near the New Hampshire border, to the southernmost suburbs of Washington, in Virginia, from the Atlantic Ocean to the Appalachian foothills. Forty-one million people, about 20 percent of the national total were concentrated in this vast region in 1970. A French geographer has called the area a "megalopolis"—seeing it as a new kind of densely urbanized and suburbanized area containing a dozen or more metropolitan areas with two focal points, Boston and New York. This kind of gigantic urbanized region, he believes, will become the characteristic type of settlement in the late twentieth century.[11] Other megalopolises are well developed already, one from Milwaukee to Pittsburgh, and another in the West running from Santa Barbara to south of the Mexican border.

In all, eighteen urban regions contain about 40 percent of the nation's population. Because the complexity as well as the cost of government increases disproportionately with density, it can be expected that these will be the areas where governmental problems will continue to make their greatest challenge.[12]

The Negro Leaves the Farm. American Negroes are descended from persons who were brought to the New World as slaves. Their ancestors labored on plantations in the South, and nearly all of them were rural dwellers. After the Civil War, most Negroes remained

---

[11] Jean Gottman, *Megalopolis: The Urbanized Northeastern Seaboard of the United States,* The M.I.T. Press, Cambridge, Mass., 1961.
[12] See Charlton F. Chute, "Today's Urban Regions," *National Municipal Review,* vol. 45, June and July, 1956.

in the deep South, becoming sharecroppers on land subdivided when the great plantations were broken up. Their number increased with each census, but a lower economic standard, leading to a higher death rate, combined with an almost all-white immigration, caused the percentage of the population, which had been nearly 20 percent Negro in 1790, to drop to 14 percent in 1860 and to about 10 percent in 1930. The percentage rose to about 12 percent in 1970.

Even before slavery was abolished, some movements of Negroes out of the South took place. However, as late as 1900, only 10 percent of the Negro population lived in the North. The big change, the one that brought economic opportunity to the poverty-ridden Negro sharecropper, was the demand for his labor in the urban factory. The first great demand for this purpose came during World War I, when a shortage of factory hands caused an imbalance in supply and demand of labor. It was the younger, more adventuresome who first made the long trek to Chicago, Detroit, or New York. The word they sent back was that one could make far more money in less time under better conditions of labor in a factory than in the almost hopeless atmosphere of the tenant farm. As early as 1914, Henry Ford created a sensation when he offered a $5-a-day minimum wage. He also established a quota for Negro employees.

The young man in a Chicago rooming house, listening to the words of encouragement offered by the precinct worker for Mayor "Big Bill" Thompson's machine, did not write home about the terrible housing conditions, what would happen when employment dropped off, or the unscrupulous gougers who often acted as real estate men or retail merchants in the burgeoning South Side "Black Belt." Nor did he emphasize the bitter loneliness of the culturally marginal man—the man who was reared according to the values of one culture, in this case, that of the Southern Negro tenant farmer, but who moves to an area applying a different set of cultural values, in this case, those of a Northern industrial urban community. To him, a job in the city meant, for the first time, the possibility of entering into the competitive struggle for upward mobility and an increase in status position that had long been a typical pattern of activity for other Americans.

Recent Developments. After World War I, only the Great Depression served temporarily to stop the urbanization of the Negro. Every other important economic and political consideration—the closing of the gates to immigrants (1924), the mechanization of agriculture (after about 1920), World War II (1941–1945), and the prosperous years after 1945—encouraged the movement to cities. In the decade following 1940, 3 million Negroes made the rural-to-urban change.

By 1950, 27.6 percent of the Negro population lived in the North and nearly 60 percent of the total was urban, for Southern Negroes also moved into Southern cities. This percentage has continued to climb.

In 1970, the percentage of the Negro population located in urban areas was very nearly as large as that of the white population. In the years following the beginning of war preparations about 1940, the nonwhite growth in urban population was far greater than that on the farm. In cities of over 50,000, the nonwhite population increased at a rate five times that of the white population.

By 1970, one person in four within the city limits of Chicago was a Negro; in Detroit, the proportion had reached nearly one in three. But the growth of nonwhite suburban population has been very slow. Therefore, because Negroes tend to concentrate in the core cities and because their rate of urbanization is much faster than that of the white population, we may expect that they will become the dominant racial or ethnic group in the core cities of many metropolitan areas in the coming decades. This will likely mean dramatic changes in the political patterns of those cities, with black majorities on the council and a black mayor in city hall soon a probability in such cities as Chicago, Baltimore, Detroit, and St. Louis. It is a matter for speculation as to the effect that such developments will have upon metropolitan-area government, intergovernmental relations, partisan conflicts in state legislatures, the suburban movement, interracial friction, and a host of other political and social matters.

The Effects of Physical Mobility. Ours is a nation of seminomadic people. Opportunity for advancement, the necessity for going to the job that will not come to the individual, the practice of businesses and industries that operate over the entire nation or over even larger areas, to send men from assignment in one city to assignment in another while moving up the organizational ladder—all contribute to this mobility. As William H. Whyte, Jr., has said, "The man who leaves home is not the exception in American society, but the key to it."[13] In the postwar years, one-fifth of the population has changed place of residence each year. Some people move more often than the average, of course, and there are still Americans who are born, live, and die in the same house; but every five years, about one-half of the people in the United States change their places of residence. Most of these moves are within the same county, although about 5 percent of the total population annually moves to a different

---

[13] William H. Whyte, Jr., *The Organization Man,* Anchor Books, Doubleday & Company, Inc., Garden City, N.Y., 1956, p. 297.

county within the same state and another 5 percent moves to a different state.

Why Do People Move? To some extent, people move to escape unemployment. Some people shuttle back and forth between their childhood town or farm and the city several times during a lifetime as it suits their momentary needs or whims. But, for the most part, moves are made as the result of, or in search of, economic advancement. Whether it is the Southern sharecropper moving into the Northern city to become a factory worker or the son of a clerk becoming an "organization man" and a middle-class suburbanite, the result is viewed by the migrant as another step toward the fulfillment of the great American dream of continued opportunity.

SOME CHARACTERISTICS OF URBAN LIFE

The urban dweller, and especially the middle-class suburbanite, of today is motivated in the direction of pleasing others—particularly strangers and near strangers. He is afraid of the cold, impersonal world in which he finds himself. He desires power, prestige, and security. But these are hard to find in the metropolis. Yet they seem to be fundamental human needs. What is modern man to do?

Urban Classes. It has always been popular among tellers of the great American myth to say that this nation is lacking in classes, that all are equal, that anyone can do anything that his ability and determination dictate. Less romantic sociologists point out that while we have a good deal of mobility between classes, the classes do, indeed, exist. Some sociologists would go further and say that, because of the inferior social position of the Negro, America has both a class and a caste system, although the rapid postwar changes in the status of Negroes have encouraged a trend away from caste status.

A social class is a division of society in which individuals are recognized as belonging to a certain social-status group. These people have a sense of *belonging* to one another and of being separate from others. A social caste exists when the status position of the individual in society is determined by birth and cannot be changed by any personal efforts made by the individual. In the same sense just given, a class can be said to exist only in a given small or middle-sized community; on a nationwide basis, the middle class and working class are more statistical aggregations than self-conscious classes,[14] although some behavioral differences continue to exist.

America has no national class structure for several reasons, the

[14] Arnold W. Green, *Sociology,* 4th ed., McGraw-Hill Book Company, New York, 1960, chap. 10.

three most important being (1) because our nation has always had a great deal of mobility, with much movement up and down the status ladder; (2) because the nation has, until after World War I, had a population made up largely of recent arrivals with widely varying national backgrounds; and (3) because of the egalitarian influence of the frontier which discouraged class-differentiated behavior for many decades. Under these circumstances, "the emergence of fairly uniform classes over an extended geographic area, such as are clearly discernible in England," never took place.[15]

Class systems, within a particular locality, are based upon relative wealth, occupations, education, manners, mode of life, and such things as membership in an "old family" or a recent-immigrant family. But migration and mobility and the distribution of material things throughout all except the lowest income tiers have tended to have a leveling effect upon American manners and way of life.[16]

Social Role and Social Status. The continuing trend in America—and this among many other things distinguishes the American from the European way of life—is away from status determined by class position, even within the local community, to status determined by occupation. In other words, one's social function has become more important than one's class position.

The structure of the American economy itself discourages the development of a clear-cut class system, and some social critics regard this as desirable. American business management, as compared with that of Belgium, France, or Italy, allows far more room for advancement in ranks and access to managerial status.[17] Decision making in business is more decentralized in America, and businessmen are much more conscious of *expanding* industry as against merely retaining control over it. Management of business in much of Europe tends to be concerned with security, which encourages working classes to look in the same direction, thus making business enterprise static. The European system does not, by its nature, work toward raising the standard of living and improving the health of the economy, as the American system does.[18] It does, however, tend to perpetuate existing class patterns.

Social Striving and Political Conflict. Sociologists find that social mobility remains high in America but that the prestige of white-collar work is diminishing. This will perhaps have a tendency to accentuate the traditional political struggle between the lower

[15] *Ibid.*, p. 181.
[16] *Ibid.*, chap. 11.
[17] See C. H. Coates and R. J. Pellegrin, "Executives and Supervisors," *Social Forces,* 35:121–126, December, 1956.
[18] See F. H. Harbison and E. W. Burgess, "Modern Management in Western Europe," *American Journal of Sociology,* 60:15–23, July, 1954.

middle class and the working classes. The former have long been the most insecure group in society, clinging desperately to identification with higher-status groups and seeking to differentiate themselves from workers. Yet, in their struggle, they have been faced with a continuing improvement in the lot of the workingman. This situation has made the lower-middle-class member a particularly sympathetic reactor to the nostrums of the demagogue. Current trends would seem to indicate possible increasing friction along the rough edge between the middle classes and the working classes.

Social striving in America is not along class lines alone. If it were, classes would be far more important and more identifiable. Instead, this type of behavior is related to three categories: social class, wherein the individual seeks to become identified with a particular group within his community; occupational success and prestige, wherein Americans tend to give recognition to individuals upon the basis of a culturally recognized hierarchy of jobs and the income and other perquisites connected with the job; and, finally, economic and political power which may exist in varying degree independently of class or occupation.

Various public opinion polls have been conducted to show the rank order of jobs. These always show that certain positions involving responsibility for human life, such as those of physician or airline pilot, rate very high in prestige. Performing such a social role will gain the individual much social deference, regardless of his family background or of class behavior patterns. So far as power is concerned, it is often accompanied by a certain general type of occupational classification, and the economically powerful, in particular, tend to have high-class positions. But a Jewish merchant of great economic and political power in a community will have lower status than a non-Jew in an equivalent position. A Negro politician may possess great power but low social prestige. The son of an Irish immigrant might become a city boss so powerful as to be able to hamstring the business activities of the economic chieftains, but he would not be received as a social equal in the very "best" homes of the city.[19]

Politics and Classes. Politically, a class or caste system is an important determinant of strategy or tactics of campaigning. Politicians appeal to Negroes, the foreign-born, Jews, Puerto Ricans, Americanized Mexicans, homeowners, renters, and other socially or economically identifiable groups. These appeals may be basically harmless or they may arouse virulent intergroup prejudices.[20] Because

[19] See chap. 5 on community power.
[20] For examples of the latter, see Carl O. Smith and Stephen B. Sarasohn, "Hate Propaganda in Detroit," *Public Opinion Quarterly*, 10:24–52, Spring, 1946; Forest Frank, "Cincinnati Loses P.R.," *National Municipal Review* (now *National Civic Review*), 46:534–535, November, 1957.

of the prestige factor (which in turn has economic repercussions that affect, for example, property values), many political battles—in the city council chamber, in the mayor's office, on the campaign platform—are fought over the issue of what the sociologist calls "invasion," that is, a new type of people, institution, or activity moving into an area of the city. Much social, and hence political, tension is caused when a rapid increase in Negro population, as in Chicago and Detroit, forces rapid invasion. The question of intended policy, expressed or implied, toward invasion has been important in postwar mayoralty campaigns in Detroit, especially in 1945 at the height of the housing shortage, but also in the 1949 contest when opponents of change in residential patterns won easily, and in 1961, when Negroes formed a coalition with middle-class businessmen to elect a mayor sympathetic to their problems. The question sometimes takes the form of policy toward proposed public housing units. Should they be built only after tearing down existing slums, or should vacant areas be used where there may be alterations of the character (and hence the property values) of existing communities?

Tensions may also result from counterinvasions, as in the case of the reexpansion of Boston's Beacon Hill into the surrounding slums or the white "colonial restoration" of the largely Negro Georgetown section of Washington, D.C., in the 1930s. Residential areas may be invaded by commerce and industry, which also causes resentment and political strife, because it, too, threatens property values. So-called "improvement associations" have been established in many urban neighborhoods, chiefly to protect property values. Often these organizations exist primarily to keep lower-status groups out of the area. In the past, they and subdivision developers have had legal assistance in the form of "restrictive covenants" in deeds to property. Such covenants prohibited conveyance of the land to specified groups of persons (e.g., Negroes, Jews, persons of the yellow race) for a certain number of years, or permanently. In 1948, however, the United States Supreme Court, taking note of the fact that the United States Constitution prohibits a state from denying "to any person within its jurisdiction the equal protection of the laws," declared all such provisions unenforceable.[21]

Many improvement associations have broader interests. Nearly all of them concern themselves with threats of commercial and industrial invasion, and many of them spend much of their time on the little things (good street lighting, prompt repair of chuckholes, countless stop signs, etc.) that interest the people of the neighborhood. Chicago's Commission on Human Relations, the Commission

[21] *Shelly v. Kraemer,* 334 U.S. 1 (1948).

on Community Relations in Detroit, and similar groups in other cities have encouraged a new type of improvement association designed to further tolerance and understanding and to help all groups in a neighborhood to seek to make it a happier dwelling area.

Hearings before city councils or appeal boards on the rezoning of an area often conceal interclass or interracial conflicts behind ostensible arguments concerning property values. A public or cooperative multifamily housing project which is to be nonsegregated is likely to become a political issue. Opponents may not state their real objection but may advance other arguments, such as a complaint that the proposed project will destroy the single-family-homes character of the neighborhood. If the apartments were designed to rent to restricted clientele at $200 a month, the community attitude might be much different.

Invasion by a different class may even cause the established residents of an area to encourage their own law-enforcement officers to violate the law. In the Cicero riot of 1952, where a well-educated, middle-class Negro family attempted to move into a lower-middle-class all-white suburb of Chicago, not only did many members of the community encourage unlawfulness on the part of spectators, especially of impressionable teen-agers, but they actually encouraged the chief of police to refuse to extend the protection that the law grants to all peaceful persons. Refusal of the police to perform their duty when it involves the rights of members of minority groups is an old, though now a gradually more uncommon, story.

The problem of social prestige may appear in many different ways. In Park Forest, Illinois, for example, it arose in connection with the building of a swimming pool. (In keeping with the argot of suburban Americana, it was called an "Aquacenter.") A municipal pool was first discussed, but this might have required the admission of people from adjoining Chicago Heights, a community of less prestige and one, furthermore, that contains a large number of Negroes. The alternative, finally accepted, was a private pool. But this produced fears of a first step toward social stratification of the all-new suburb. Even though pool fees were set very low, many appeared to fear that their very existence was a move toward the creation of an unwanted country-club set.[22] In both Park Forest and Levittown, classlessness does not extend to the admission of Negroes, and in Levittown, Pennsylvania, there were open demonstrations during 1957 against a Negro family's moving in.

Life styles differ by social class, and these differences include habitual differences in attitudes toward community responsibilities.

[22] Whyte, op. cit., pp. 343–344.

Thus, two political scientists found that persons in upper income groups "vote against their self-interests narrowly conceived" on many occasions. They conclude that voters in some income and ethnic groups (particularly Jews) are more likely than voters in others to take a "public-regarding" rather than a narrowly self-interested view of things—that is, to take the welfare of others, especially that of "the community," into account as an aspect of their own welfare. They conclude that in every American subculture there exists a general notion of how much a citizen should be expected to sacrifice for the sake of the community, as well as a definition of what constitutes "community welfare."[23]

Impersonalization of Life. Cities are based upon a money economy. Many business relationships are impersonal and devoid of sentiment, in contrast with these same activities in rural and small-town situations. In the apartment-house areas of the city, one is lost in anonymity, having casual contacts with many persons rather than intimate contacts with a relatively few. One is judged by what he can do, not by what he is—by his reputation rather than by his character. So relationships among people are brief and stylized. People are cool toward one another, quick to take advantage, and, in the view of many ruralites, callous and hardhearted.

In the small town and on the farm, society is subjected to social controls characterized by *primary*—that is to say, close and personal—relationships. Some of these exist in crowded portions of cities, too, but to a much smaller degree. *Secondary* relationships and controls predominate there, and these are impersonal, fragmentary, and ephemeral. Social distance—the degree of relative lack of intimacy that one person has with another—is much greater. Urban society, therefore, becomes organized more formally, through more laws, than is the case in rural areas. The political process becomes more important in the city.

Urban behavior patterns have immediate effects upon the political institutions of the community. The rural society (and, to a considerable extent, suburbia) is policed largely by its system of primary social controls. Gossip and community opinion strongly discourage deviations from accepted values. The back-fence tattler may be a nuisance, but she is also a protectress. Crime rates are low, and there may not be a professional law-enforcement officer within 30 miles or more. This is not so in the heart of the city. The near absence of most primary controls means that crime rates in cities are higher; mores must be enforced by policemen and by more

[23] James Q. Winson and Edward C. Banfield, "Public-regardingness as a Value Premise in Voting Behavior," *American Political Science Review*, 58:876–887, December, 1964. Quotations from p. 885.

laws instead of by gossips and community opinion; the courts are kept busier settling civil disputes; bigger government is necessary to reach more people in a more formalized, institutionalized manner. **Rootlessness.** High physical and social mobility have been characteristics of American society from early colonial times. From the point of view of participation in democratic government, high mobility is of consequence in that large numbers of migrants fail to identify themselves with their adopted communities.[24] Their civic pride is likely to be nonexistent. There is no loyalty to the city as an institution or as "home." If the migrant happens to live in a suburb, he may not even know whether it is actually an independent unit of government. Politically, this means that elections will be ignored. Government will be left in the hands of others—and the others may be grossly unrepresentative of the interest of the newer arrivals.

The Transient as a Community Participant. Vast suburban growth has created special problems in the matter of rootlessness and a lack of belonging. The values of the middle class call for individual participation in political, social, and civic activities. Yet members of this group often lack the deep roots that at once command and, at the same time clear the way for, the assumption of local social responsibilities. Still, if nearly everyone in a community such as Levittown or Park Forest is a newcomer, some way must be found to get people to serve on city councils, on planing commissions, on united community fund boards. Thus, we come to the question:[25]

> Are the transients a rootless people? If by roots we mean the complex of geographical and family ties that has historically knitted Americans to local society, these young transients are almost entirely rootless. They are very much aware of the fact; surprisingly often they will bring up the home town, and though they have no intention whatsoever of going back, they dwell on what they left behind.

Whyte, in his examination of Park Forest, found that there was indeed a good deal of apathy toward community problems in a new town made up entirely of persons who were rootless in the traditional sense. But he also found that many residents took up the real issues of providing for schools and public services because of a feeling of a need for "ties more meaningful than those of bridge and canasta and bowling."[26]

[24] See Robert C. Angell, "The Moral Integration of American Cities," *American Journal of Sociology*, vol. 57, July, 1951, part 2; Basil G. Zimmer, "Participation of Migrants in Urban Structures," *American Sociological Review*, 20:218–224, April, 1955; Basil G. Zimmer, "Farm Backgrounds and Urban Participation," *American Journal of Sociology*, 61:470–475, March, 1956.
[25] Whyte, *op. cit.*, p. 318. There is a Levittown on Long Island and others in New Jersey and Pennsylvania, each built on a mass-production basis after World War II in an area which was previously open country. Park Forest is a similar suburb south of Chicago.
[26] *Ibid.*, pp. 325–327.

Trade Unionism. The factory worker, like the middle-class organization man, is also faced with the problem of establishing some kind of roots in lieu of the traditional type. He, too, is accommodating himself to the new American way of life. A study of Detroit automobile workers, for example, found that the great bulk of them (82 percent) are American-born, in contrast to the factory worker in Andrew Carnegie's steel mills or to Jurgis Rudkus, the Lithuanian who slaved in the stockyards of Chicago at the beginning of the present century.[27] Over one-half of them (52 percent) had immigrant fathers, however. Most automobile workers are living in towns where they did not grow up, and they are to some degree culturally marginal. The home-ownership level of 59 percent is high, almost as high as that of Detroit in general (65 percent), but much lower than that of the middle-class and upper-working-class suburban dwellers. (In Chicago, a preautomobile-age city of apartments, home ownership is only 30 percent and would be lower than that for factory workers. Detroit, like many other industrial cities, is, however, a postautomobile-age city consisting principally of one- and two-family homes. Home ownership in most types of suburbs averages about 90 percent.)

One-fifth of Detroit automobile workers grew up on farms, another one-fourth in small towns. Only 44 percent were raised in large cities. Two-thirds of them are the only breadwinners in their families. One-half of them are church members, but factory workers seem to be quite inactive in church groups, fraternal organizations, veterans groups, neighborhood associations, and parent-teacher associations—a matter of considerable importance so far as social and political representation of interests is concerned.[28]

In suburbia, neighbors and business peers are the mainstays of social relationships, since organization-man families are often forced to live far from any of their relatives. Residents of the core city, including factory workers, find that relatives are more important than are next-door neighbors. Unskilled workers probably migrate more to areas where relatives have already located than do middle-class persons. The latter have less of a choice of destination, being required to go where their skills are demanded. In Detroit, 89 percent of core-city working-class couples have relatives living in the same neighborhood. Two-thirds of the couples see their relatives once or twice a week at least, and over one-fourth see some relative nearly every day. Family gatherings at weddings, funerals, birthdays, and holidays are important. Of the people who see relatives once or

[27] In the novel by Upton Sinclair, *The Jungle*, The Viking Press, Inc., New York, 1906.
[28] Arthur Kornhauser, H. L. Sheppard, and A. J. Mayer, *When Labor Votes*, University Books, Inc., New York, 1956, pp. 26–28.

twice a week, more than one-half see neighbors less than once a month.[29]

Core-city residents are thus less neighborhood-oriented than are suburbanites, though they seek to maintain primary relationships of some kind. When relatives live within driving distances, they are likely to concentrate their social activities upon them (and upon the impersonal aspects of urban recreational activities), thus emphasizing traditional family ties in preference to amalgamation into the impersonal community and its activities. This difference between core-city and suburban dwellers may have important effects upon the pattern of politics in the community and upon political participation. It should be noted, however, that persons with family ties are probably more likely to develop an interest in the community than are isolated persons.

Trade Unions in Politics. In contrast to the frantic, reformist periods of the 1930s, trade unionism became an accepted part of the American way of life after World War II. By no means are all members of unions enthusiastic over the necessity of membership, and collective security by way of the union runs counter to American values of individualism, but only the wistful consider it even remotely possible that unions will not remain a significant social and political force in America. The day when working-class people had no voice, or only the voice of the political machine, in local politics is gone. (See Chapter 5.)

By 1960, union members and their immediate families made up one-third of all the eligible voters in the United States. In urban industrial centers, over one-half the potential voters are now in this category.[30]

In municipal elections and in the consideration of legislation pending before city councils, the working class, represented by the professional bureaucracy of the trade union, will continue to make its position known and its votes felt.

THE GHETTO

Although in the nineteenth century nearly all people in an urban area lived within the core city, the present-day pattern is very different. The suburban movement has tended to leave the core with little but specialized governmental, business, and professional activities—and the poor. Some large cities have virtually no middle-

[29] Survey Research Center, University of Michigan, 1955, report of the Detroit Area Study. See also Joel Smith and others, "Local Intimacy in a Middle-sized City," *American Journal of Sociology,* 60:276–284, November, 1954.
[30] Kornhauser, Sheppard, and Mayer, *op. cit.,* p. 261.

class residents left within their boundaries. Even many of the better-paid members of the working class (particularly the "hard hats") have moved to suburbia. Indeed, at the beginning of the 1970s, a majority of suburban residents in metropolitan areas were blue-collar rather than white-collar workers.

The core cities are, thus, becoming the home of the poor, of the lowest status Americans. The area they occupy is often called a "slum," a term of uncertain origin but probably bestowed unsympathetically by middle-class persons. Another term often used is "ghetto," an Italian word first used to indicate the section of a city occupied by poor Jews. It was later brought to the United States and gradually became a synonym for slum and not restricted to Jews. The term "ghetto" is most used by scholars and middle-class persons who are concerned about the "urban problem," but it is not the term used by ghetto residents. Much of the ghetto today consists of blacks and browns (Puerto Ricans and Mexican-Americans). Blacks often refer to "the community." Some, satirically, talk of the "plantation" or, bitterly, of the "concentration camp." Spanish-speaking Americans use the term "barrio," which is something of an irony since it literally means "open country," of which there is very little in the slums. (The term is also used to indicate any area where Spanish-speaking people live, irrespective of their wealth or poverty.)

The slums are not uniform in character. Housing and living conditions vary greatly within them, and on their edge, there is often to be found a middle-class area of better homes occupied by blacks or browns. And there are many American sub-cultures.

The ghetto is a study in contrast. There is the warm support of a sense of community and the terror of a police raid. There are delightful ethnic foods combined with the too frequent use of every type of dangerous drug. There is fear, hate, joy, and despair.

Throughout American history, the ghetto has been occupied by the most recent urban arrivals, so that almost every ethnic group has served its time in the ghetto. Some fine books have been written by persons who began in the slums, became successful, and as older persons recall the pains and pleasures of their youthful ghetto life.[31] That life and its concerns have always been far different from that of the well-off person living on the fringe of the city or in the suburbs. The black sociologist, St. Clair Drake, has given us a bit of the character of the contemporary black slum portrayed in the following word picture.[32]

[31] For example, Harry Roskolenko, *The Time That Was Then: The Lower East Side, 1900–1914*, Dial Press, New York, 1970.
[32] St. Clair Drake, "The 'Ghettoization' of Urban Life," *Daedalus*, 94:1168–1193, Fall, 1965.

The character of the Black Ghetto is not set by the newer "guilded," not-yet rundown portions of it, but by the older sections where unemployment rates are high and the masses of people work with their hands—where the median level of education is just above graduation from grade school and many of the people are likely to be recent migrants from urban areas.

The "ghettoization" of the Negro has resulted in the emergence of a ghetto subculture with a distinctive ethos, most pronounced, perhaps, in Harlem, but recognizable in all Negro neighborhoods. For the average Negro who walks the streets of any American Black Ghetto, the smell of barbecued ribs, fried shrimps, and chicken emanating from numerous restaurants gives olfactory reinforcement to a feeling of "at homeness." The beat of "gut music" spilling into the street from ubiquitous tavern jukeboxes and the sound of tambourines and rich harmony behind the crude folk art on the windows of store-front churches give auditory confirmation to the universal belief that "we Negroes have 'soul.'" The bedlam of an occasional brawl, the shouted obscenities of street corner "foulmouths" and the whine of police sirens break the monotony of waiting for the number that never "falls," the horses that neither win, place, nor show, and the "good job" that never materializes. . . . The spontaneous vigor of the children who crowd streets and playgrounds . . . and the cheerful rushing about of adults, free from the occupational pressures of the "white world" in which they work, create an atmosphere of warmth and superficial intimacy which obscures the unpleasant facts of life in the overcrowded rooms behind the doors, the lack of adequate maintenance standards, and the too prevalent vermin and rats.

The relationship of the people to their local government and their public policy concerns are very much different in the ghetto from those of the suburbs. An inquiry among ghetto residents would surely indicate that many of them are concerned about such things as welfare policies preeminently. Most city governments have only a limited welfare function today, and changes that seem to be needed in welfare policies probably will have to come at the Federal government level. But certainly the inquiring, "bossy" social caseworker has become increasingly a symbol of scorn and hatred which probably carries over to other government workers.

Slum dwellers are also concerned about police policies. Most middle-class citizens had no contact with the police before the coming of the automobile age, excepting perhaps to ask directions. But such is not the case in the ghetto where policemen (mostly white) with working-class backgrounds are called upon to enforce laws reflecting middle-class values upon people, many of whom do not accept the middle-class notion of the legitimacy of the law and of the policeman's activities.[33] But, contrary to a popular notion, ghetto residents do worry about crime quite as much as do middle-class citizens, and they are anxious to be protected by the police.[34] Ghetto residents also worry about their health and that of their children, even though they may not inform themselves of available facilities. Some slum dwellers are concerned about the quality of education their children are getting in the ghetto schools, accepting the traditional American emphasis upon education as a way toward upward mobility; but others seem to place little emphasis upon education, and the drop-out rate in the ghetto is high.[35] Many residents cannot afford automobiles and hence are concerned about public transportation facilities. Factories have moved to the suburbs, which is convenient for the white-collar workers but not for the unskilled worker living in the old core city. As transportation facilities decline, so do the prospects for the slum dweller of getting to work. As a result, welfare rolls increase and morale in the ghetto declines still further.

Many of the governmental concerns of the suburbanite are of little or no importance in the ghetto. The suburbanite worries about such things as taxes, commuter highways, school curriculum, smog, the fluoridation of water, and the aesthetics of the city and suburb. Although schools are a mutual interest, the concerns about them are vastly different. The others are often seen as irrelevant or beyond the poor man's ability to influence.[36] Even as to taxes, there may be little concern in the ghetto. Persons with little education also tend to have little information about the tax system, and it is probable that the typical slum dweller pays far more in taxes than he realizes, for the relative burden upon him is heavy, particularly in the case of the retail sales tax and the general property tax (which the slum landowner passes on to him as a part of his costs in calculating his rent).

The middle-class suburbanite and the ghetto dweller are both very much concerned about one aspect of urban government policy, which is that of land uses and controls. The suburbanite is more interested in protecting the value of his property than in anything else, but both he and the ghetto dweller share in concerns about possible changes in the character of their neighborhoods. The breaking up of a neighborhood by running a limited-access highway

---

[33] See chaps. 16 and 17, below; and Burton Levy, "Cops in the Ghetto: A Problem of the Police System," in Louis H. Masotti and Don K. Bowen (eds.), *Riots and Rebellion*, Sage Publications, Inc., Beverly Hills, Calif., 1968, pp. 347–358.
[34] See *Newsweek*, Aug. 22, 1966.
[35] See chap. 19, below, and Marilyn Gittell (ed.), *Educating an Urban Population*, Sage Publications, Inc., Beverly Hills, Calif., 1967.
[36] *Ibid.*

through it or by construction of an urban-renewal project can have serious economic and psychological consequences for slum dwellers. Such changes may break up important neighborhood patterns, force changes in school attendance, or make it more difficult or impossible to get to work. Throughout its history, urban renewal has resulted in fewer homes that the poor can afford to rent, and black leaders sometimes refer to urban renewal bitterly as "Negro removal." Some urban-renewal projects may have been undertaken in order to discourage Negro residency in that particular city, but the main reasons blacks are so much affected by it is that they usually occupy the poorest housing in the city.

A few final observations about the ghetto should be made:

1. The most obvious indication of a ghetto is to be found in the low quality of its housing. Much of it consists of small, overcrowded apartment houses, called tenements, or of what were once large family homes that have now been broken up into many apartments. Not all ghettos give one the initial impression of being what they are. The Watts area of Los Angeles, for example, requires further investigation before one can be certain that it is, in fact, a ghetto. But housing in all such areas of our cities shares one important characteristic: it declines in quality through time. This is partly so because of the continuing migration of rural people into the ghettos, assuring the landlord of customers and hence no need to make his property more attractive to prevent it from standing vacant. Another important reason is to be found in the characteristics of the general property tax.[37] Since the tax is based upon the value of the land and building rather than upon its income-producing ability, any improvements by the landlord—by the logic of the tax—should result in an increase in his tax assessment. It is therefore to his advantage to let the property run down, though not to the point where the building might be condemned for occupancy. But even if threatened with that, the slum landlord can usually count on his own tenants coming to his support; for if they were forced to move out, they might have no suitable place to which to move, at least at the same amount of rent. In Great Britain and in other countries, local taxes are based upon the income of the property or its equivalent. Such a plan forces the landlord to pay his fair share of taxes and does not penalize him for improving his property. This may be a factor in the Scandinavian countries, much poorer than the United States, having no slums. However, there are probably also cultural differences. Much of the

---

[37] See chap. 14, below.

American middle class is relatively unconcerned about slums and ghetto life. Americans are accustomed to ghettos, for they have existed throughout the history of the nation.

2. Not only is the ghetto an area of low income but its retail prices tend to be higher than are those in suburbia. The resident is thus at a double disadvantage. This pattern prevails for at least three reasons. One is that the ghetto dweller typically has less transportation mobility than does the suburbanite. The slum shopkeeper has something of a captive customer. Secondly, shoplifting and other forms of petty thievery are common and probably occur much more often than they do in the suburban shopping center, thus raising costs of business which are passed on to the consumer. Finally, vandalism and riots are more common in the ghetto than elsewhere, and as a result insurance rates may be ten or more times higher than in a middle-class area.

3. The ghetto of today is generally in a weaker political position than it was two or three generations ago. During the time of the political bosses and machines, the ghetto was organized on a ward, precinct, and even block basis, often with a professional block or precinct worker serving as a connecting link between the needs of the ghetto dweller and the political organization.[38] Only in Albany and Chicago do such linkages with the city hall remain. The changes that have taken place in the years especially since the Great Depression have further alienated the ghetto dweller from his urban government. Few professional political workers exist any longer in the ghettos. Political organization between elections may be almost nonexistent. The reform movement desire for small city councils, preferably elected at large, often results in no ghetto representation on the council at all and with that body reflecting overwhelmingly middle-class values.[39] In the 1880s and 1890s, city councils were typically much larger than they are today and were almost always, in large cities, elected by wards. This guaranteed that each ghetto area would have some direct representation on the council; and, to further reinforce this, ward boundaries were often drawn along ethnic and racial lines. Furthermore, although the bosses and machines cooperated closely with businessmen, they were dependent for votes primarily in the ghetto areas; and they had means for making certain that the vote was turned out on election day. Today, with no such spur, the ghetto resident is likely to be apathetic about municipal elections unless some salient event has given them extraordinary visibility in some particular year.

[38] See chap. 5, below.
[39] See chap. 9, below.

The general isolation of the urban poor from their local government was taken cognizance of in the Economic Opportunity Act of 1964. That Act provided that, in carrying out its various programs, the Office of Economic Opportunity should involve the "maximum feasible participation" of the poor. Although most Congressmen probably thought this was no more than a homily, some of the supporters of the bill intended it to be taken literally. Since the Act coincided with the emergence of a new type of young black and brown leadership in many ghetto areas, this provision was given an unusual amount of attention. But political participation is a complex matter; and a group of essentially apolitical people cannot be molded and integrated into a political system simply by holding public meetings or establishing advisory boards, or even through well planned confrontation politics. The effect of this provision concerning participation appears to have been minimal. In cases where more radical activists have sought to invoke it, their activities have probably been dysfunctional for the causes of the poor.[40] Furthermore, as soon as the program got under way, local political leaders took steps to prevent political control from slipping out of their hands into those of the ghetto leadership. Indeed, the net result was to reinforce prevailing political patterns rather than to bring about major changes.[41]

The ghetto is the home of millions of Americans and of almost as many social and economic problems. Many, perhaps most of the issues of domestic social policy in the 1970s will center on this part of the metropolis. Many of the problems that have been overlooked or ignored since the time when ghetto residents became virtually excluded from the urban political process with the decline of the political machine will confront decision makers. How the nation will cope with them cannot accurately be predicted, but it is safe to say that the issues can never again be entirely dropped from the agendas of national, state, and local governments.[42]

SUBURBIA

The American city today is much more than an entity existing within legally described boundaries and headed by a single government. It is actually a sociological complex consisting of a central sector, a blighted and decaying older portion, newer sections of a principally residential character, and, beyond the legal limits but

---

[40] See J. David Greenstone and Paul E. Peterson, "Reformers, Machines, and the War on Poverty," in James Q. Wilson (ed.), *City Politics and Public Policy,* John Wiley and Sons, Inc., New York, 1968, pp. 267–292; Donald Von Eschen, Jerome Kirk, and Maurice Pinard, "The Conditions of Direct Action in a Democratic Society," *Western Political Quarterly,* 22:309–325, June, 1969; Harlan Hahn, "Ghetto Sentiments on Violence," *Science and Society,* 33:197–208, Spring, 1969.
[41] Greenstone and Peterson, *op. cit.*
[42] For further reading, see Jack R. Van der Slik (ed.), *Black Conflict with White America,* Charles E. Merrill Publishing Co., Columbus, Ohio, 1970; and Alan Shank (ed.), *Political Power and the Urban Crisis,* Holbrook Press, Inc., Boston, 1969.

an intrinsic part of the community, the suburbs. A "suburb" may be defined as a community beyond the legal boundaries of the core city but lying within its economic and sociological limits and with a population at least partially dependent for a livelihood upon the core city.

Some sections within core cities are still relatively undeveloped and assume some, but not all, of the characteristics of the suburb. The movement toward the urban fringe is overrunning both types of areas.

Why Move to the Suburbs? What is behind the centrifugal force that is pushing our urban population toward the periphery of the community? No doubt the increasing size of the urban population is itself a factor, for additional population is likely to require increasing area. But this alone is not a sufficient reason to explain the great suburban movement since the end of World War II.

Rather we should ask: What do most American people want out of life? Where, and under what conditions, can their desires best be fulfilled?

A summary of the findings of social-psychological research into these questions has been reported as follows:[43]

> The goal which, if reached or reasonably approximated, will fulfill the basic needs of the urbanite is a community that will combine some qualities of both small town and large city. Neither, in its present form and at the current stage of cultural development, satisfies all of the fundamental human requirements. The small town provides ample opportunity for companionship and friendship, for easy access to local services, and for certain forms of security. On the other hand, it may fall short of fulfilling man's need for recognition and variety of experience. The large city does provide insurance against boredom, affords wider opportunity for choice of occupation, freedom from unwanted interference with one's personal life, and permits one to identify himself with the city's greatness or, at least, bigness. Nevertheless, it may fail to meet other basic social needs of man. The city can be a very lonesome place. It can thwart natural human friendliness. It can breed suspicion and misunderstanding. It often has dissolved long-established values as to behavior while putting nothing comparable in their place.

The suburb, many middle-class urbanites believe, is the best available compromise, especially if the medium-sized city is not a possible choice. In addition to allowing the urbanite to keep *some* of the best of both the large city and the small town, there are other

[43] William L. Slayton and Richard Dewey, "Urban Redevelopment and the Urbanite," in Coleman Woodbury (ed.), *The Future of Cities and Urban Redevelopment,* University of Chicago Press, Chicago, 1953, p. 367. By permission of the University of Chicago Press.

subjectively determined values held by Americans today that add to the attractiveness of the suburb. Studies show that people want to own their homes, that they want single-family dwellings, and that they want more space than is available within built-up cities at a cost they can afford. They want to avoid, or at least reduce, dirt, noise, congestion, traffic, and taxes. They want vegetable gardens and rosebushes. They want a private play yard for the children.

People want better government than they think they are getting in the core city. They want "services without politics." The suburbanite talks of the desirability of a council-manager government, which the large city, as a rule, does not have. A "better, more honest" government is something that many think is available in the suburb, although this is much less important than are many other factors. Neighborliness, the reestablishment of some of the primary controls of the rural and small-town society, is something that many yearn for. A suburban address is also a symbol of higher prestige than the typical core-city address, and this fact does not escape many urbanites, for social climbing is very important as a source of recognition in an impersonal society.

The suburb keeps within hailing distance of the variety of scene and activity, of job opportunities, and of accessibility to multiple and specialized services that people want from the large city. Most people would like to have nearby a corner grocery for last-minute shopping (the supermarket for the large weekly shopping list may be some distance away), a drugstore, a playground, and a grade school. Other services, entertainment media, and places of work may be considerable distances away, for the automobile, people believe, will take them there within the limits of a tolerable amount of sacrifice. The commuting time and effort, within present value systems, is not too great a price to pay for the advantages of not living near the manufacturing or business districts.[44]

What Makes Suburban Living Possible? A brief answer might be simply this: modern techniques of transportation and communication. To the extent that a decentralization of industry is also a factor, the availability of highly mobile sources of power in the form of electricity has also been important. Together with prosperity after World War II, the Federal government's policy of aiding purchasers of new homes through a loan guarantee to the mortgage holder has been another important factor. The Veterans Administration and the Federal Housing Authority have thus been substantial contributors to the suburban movement by making low-interest mortgages a

[44] This section draws heavily upon Slayton and Dewey, op. cit., part III. The empirical research justifying the above statements is there summarized and cited. See also William Dobriner (ed.), The Suburban Community, G. P. Putnam's Sons, New York, 1958.

possibility for large numbers of middle-class and upper-working-class families who could not otherwise have afforded homes of their own.

World War I brought an acceleration in the rate of urbanization in the United States. People began to look for additional space to occupy. They found it outside of the city proper. They also found that a prewar novelty, the automobile, had now become commonplace. In fact, it had become a necessity for members of the middle class, and Henry Ford was building a "poor man's" car in the famous Model T. There were suburbanites and commuters before the 1920s, to be sure, for those were the days of the electrified interurban lines and commuter trains were operated by the railroads out of the largest cities, but it was the coming of the automobile that made suburban living as it is known today a possibility.

Modern methods of communication also contributed to the suburban movement. Without the effective, inexpensive telephone service of today, few would isolate themselves from the core city. The telephone is used to obtain services rapidly, for the employer in town to contact his employee in his suburban home, for the husband at work downtown to call home, and for all to keep in contact with relatives and friends in other parts of the city even when many miles of crowded highways separate them.

Without the automobile and the telephone, it is possible that the present-day value patterns previously discussed would never have evolved. Even if they had, it is certain that few would have been able to take advantage of them.

Other technological developments also played important though lesser parts in the growth of suburbia. In particular, the electric water pump and the septic tank made possible urban-style homes beyond the water mains and sewers of the city. Before their development, land developers and home builders often had to convince the city council and sometimes the voters that a certain area should be annexed, for only by taking the development into the city could urban services be obtained. These two developments also made it economically feasible to build homes of moderate price on lots larger than the common 35- or 40-foot lots of the nineteenth century.

The Image of Suburbia. Although suburbia has been the sought-after home of Americans now for a generation and hence must meet many social and psychic needs of people in numerous social categories, it has also been one of the most criticized aspects of America. The criticism has come chiefly from intellectuals; and, indeed, suburbia was perhaps their favorite target prior to the war in Indochina and the rediscovery of the problems of the poor and of the environment.

Scott Donaldson has concluded that the suburb "has been the

victim of a critical onslaught of monumental, and largely nonsensical, proportions."[45] Some of this criticism has tended to ignore the long-time characteristics of the American culture. Suburbia is accused of conformity, for example, by critics who ignore the fact that most people in any milieu at any time in history have essentially been conformists and that this is an important device for social stability. The materialism of suburbia is also a long-time characteristic of the general American culture. Some of the criticisms have been made by persons emotionally committed to a rural society and are really directed against a metropolitan-industrial society rather than simply suburbia, which is the symbolic villain. Donaldson suggests, relying upon Freud, that perhaps the harsh criticism is the result of feelings of guilt and ambivalence. The suburb represents the pursuit of personal happiness and satisfaction, but our consciences tell us that we also have a responsibility to be concerned for all mankind, much of which is not comfortable or secure. Suburbia is the symbol of America's cultural success and of her sense of guilt over it.

Rate of Suburban Growth. Since about 1950, most cities of under 50,000 people—indeed, even very small communities—have seen the bulk of their growth take place in the suburbs. It seems likely that nearly three-fourths of the population growth since 1950 has taken place in urban areas outside core cities of all sizes. This figure is a reflection of the fact that core cities now are largely built up and— in most states—find it difficult to annex new territory.

Increases in suburban populations have not been uniform throughout the country, of course. The greatest gains have been made around the perimeter, and especially along the Great Lakes, the Gulf of Mexico, and the Pacific Ocean. Some areas have lost population not only at the core but for the metropolitan area as a whole. This happened particularly in regions having difficulties in readjusting their economic bases as the result of changing manufacturing or mining patterns. New England, which has lost some of its former economic base, particularly in textiles, to the South, and Pennsylvania's depression-ridden coal fields are examples.

TYPES OF SUBURBS

Suburbs may be of many types. They are difficult to classify, and it is probable that most of them will include characteristics of more than one of the following types: first of all, "dormitory" suburbs,

---

[45] Scott Donaldson, *The Suburban Myth,* Columbia University Press, New York, 1969, p. 1. Donaldson offers a critical review of the literature on suburbia, drawing upon both the social sciences and fiction.

especially built up on undeveloped land for the purpose of absorbing the overflow from the city; second, industrial suburbs; third, suburbs, or *enclaves,* that have become completely surrounded by the core city; fourth, recreational suburbs; fifth, communities that were once independent, autonomous municipalities, probably serving as marketing towns, and that have been overrun by a metropolitan community; last, the heterogeneous suburbs that serve many purposes and for that reason cannot be classified readily.[46]

The Dormitory Suburbs. The residential suburbs are primarily living places for persons who work within the core city or the industrial suburbs. There may be very little community spirit and almost nothing to give the area a sense of community. Its boundaries may well be determined by following main traffic arteries.

Industrial Suburbs. Industrial suburbs usually center on large manufacturing establishments. They may have a relatively independent existence from the core city.

From the turn of the century until World War II, a slow, rather persistent diffusion of industry took place within the major areas of industrial concentration. It appears to be continuing, especially in the Middle Atlantic, East North Central, and Pacific industrial regions.

Industries are leaving the core cities, not primarily because of being squeezed out but rather in response to positive factors. Suburbs offer some hope of lower taxes; they offer cheaper land, a vital consideration since a properly laid-out, healthful, physically attractive factory needs a good deal of room; they offer better parking facilities for workers; they bring the factory nearer the workers' homes; they eliminate the need to bring large semitrailer trucks into the heart of the city, for the factory can be located near important highway intersections; and they aid in reducing congestion on the commuter highways and in the central portion of the core city.

In addition to a pattern of diffusion for some industries in our larger manufacturing cities, there has also been a certain amount of dispersion of industry. Smaller cities are acquiring more industries and becoming more important economic units.

Enclaves. Some American cities have grown so rapidly that they have quite literally swallowed up their suburbs. Independent suburbs on the urban fringe may remain approximately static in area for years. The core city may then surround them on all sides, making something of a mockery out of their independent legal status, and their suburban appellation.

---

[46] See Leo F. Schnore, "The Social and Economic Characteristics of American Suburbs," *Sociological Quarterly,* 4:122–134, Spring, 1963.

Recreational Suburbs. This type of suburb probably seldom exists by itself, and the term should be taken to mean places where people go to play, to escape. Sometimes there is a lake or the sea near the core city. Beaches, dance halls, and picnic places are built up, with perhaps a carnival or amusement-park area included.

Some suburbs become havens of gambling establishments and houses of prostitution.[47] This is sometimes the result of advance knowledge that these localities will not enforce the law strictly. They may be across a county or state line or, in the case of some, such as Tijuana and Windsor, across an international boundary. Racetracks, because they require a great deal of room for the physical plant and for parking space and because they cause dust and a good deal of noise both day and night, are nearly always located in a suburban area which is (at least at first) not heavily populated.

Formerly Autonomous Communities. Not only does the core city sometimes swallow up its suburbs, but it may sometimes draw into its economic and sociological (but rarely into its *political*) orbit communities that were once independent of it, that were created for, and developed as the result of, factors other than those that created the core city.

RESIDENTIAL SUBURBS

Among the residential suburbs, certain patterns have begun to emerge. Although the wealthy were generally the first to move out of the central city, they were rivaled by the working people of some communities. In any case, all income levels of people are suburbanites today, and collectively they behave somewhat differently in relation to their governments than do their economic peers in the central city. We might note some of the types of residential suburbs here, keeping in mind, however, that a great many of them contain mixed groups. Although the goal of Americans seems to be to reduce social conflict by moving into a suburban area where people share one's income level, beliefs, and life styles, it is not always possible to achieve complete homogeneity among the various groups.

The Wealthy Suburb. Before the beginning of the present century, wealthy Americans began to move out to fringe-area "estates" where they built large homes that were manned by armies of servants. They reached their offices in the central city by using commuter trains. The early developments along the main line of the Pennsylvania Railroad outside of Philadelphia demonstrate this type of

---

[47] See James A. Maxwell, "Kentucky's Open City," *The Saturday Evening Post,* Mar. 26, 1960, pp. 22ff. The story of Newport, Ky., recreational suburb to Cincinnati for three generations.

phenomena. Today, the suburbs of the wealthy are likely to have smaller lots—perhaps half an acre—but 10-acre and larger areas are still to be found in many of them. The large lots required by zoning ordinance discourages efforts of lower-income people to move into the area and guarantees the pristine charm of quasi-rural living.

Here the homes are all individually designed by architects. Services may be of a luxury type—in one "estate" suburb of Cleveland, the police once delivered the milk. Many such suburbs have "city parks" that are exclusively for residents and are actually country clubs administered by the suburban government. In some cases, the wealthy do not want ordinary city services—street lights, curbs and gutters, paved streets—because these things remind them of urban life, not of the gentlemanly country living they seek to imitate. Around the largest cities, many of the wealthy seek to locate on the outer fringe, far from the core, where open land is still available and where the leisure implied by great distance from the hub assures high status. These people even have a special term for themselves— the *exurbanites.*

The government of these suburbs is often a triumph of amateurism of a sort that the business executives living there would never permit in their own firms. Some wealthy suburbs have professional city managers, but the key administrator—the clerk, or supervisor, or mayor—may be a local resident who lives in one of the several modest enclaves that are likely—perhaps through historical accident —to exist. The necessary, full-time, nonprofessional, nonelective persons, such as clerical help and street-maintenance men, may not live in the suburb at all. The people in the city hall are likely to be obsequious in their relationships with the great men for whose homes they provide services.

The elected council and school board will probably be made up of both men and women from among the wealthy residents. They will seek to establish policies that fit their objectives: No invasion of lower-status families or groups, and a school system that will allow their children to gain admission to the most prestigious preparatory schools and universities. Some of them will be concerned about metropolitan-area government generally and about the pattern of change in the core city—after all, they are frequently landowners or members of the top bureaucracies of core-city business and manufacturing firms. As "organization men" of corporations, they have been told that they have a responsibility to take part in public affairs, to be concerned about metropolitan-area problems, and to help make their organizations "good citizens." As a result:[48]

[48] Norton E. Long, "The Corporation, Its Satellites, and the Local Community," in E. E. Mason (ed.), *The Corporation in Modern Society,* Harvard University Press, Cambridge, Mass., 1960, p. 210.

> An . . . executive will inveigh against the jurisdictional mess of
> his metropolitan area in a staff-ghosted speech that repeats
> uncomprehendingly the clichés of current municipal reform. This
> activity is good corporate citizenship, the more so as the execu-
> tive hasn't the foggiest idea as to how the changes he advocates
> will help his company, though doubtless in all honesty he thinks
> they will. It is difficult for the corporation executive to avoid a
> kind of ritualistic do-gooding when he embarks on the unfamiliar
> role of city father.

The wealthy suburbanite is likely to play some kind of role in
core-city politics as well as in the community where his home is
situated. He is not so likely to be as concerned about suburban
independence as are lower-income persons because he believes that
he can probably influence core-city policy, should his area be annexed
or a supergovernment created, while the more typical suburbanite
fears that annexation means loss of influence over matters—particularly school and land use policies—that he considers really important. Yet the high-income suburbanite—perhaps especially his
wife—will not approve of metropolitan-area changes that may result
in significantly lessened influence for him over the policies of the
government that serves his place of residence.

The Middle-class Suburb. This is the home of the average-income
person, the white-collar worker, the picture window, the charcoal
grill, and the power mower. It is here that preoccupation with property values and social acceptance has helped mold a distinctive
contemporary American life style. The homes here are mass-produced, the number of different models that the builder has to offer
depending generally on the cost level of the area's homes. The people
in the mass-produced houses follow the fashions in mass culture and
mass leisure. They are not innovators; they do not want to solve the
world's problems, or even those of their own metropolitan area.
Social conflict is not, to them, a challenge to be met through the institutions of democratic government—they seek to avoid conflict
by living in homogeneity with those who share their goals. There is
no place in their lives for experimentation with the admission of
lower-status ethnic or racial groups, with seeking meaning in life
through a concentration on one's personal resources. The suburbanite "is attuned to others but never to himself."[49] In David Riesman's
words, "he is other-directed, not inner-directed, as were his grandparents."

These people have helped bring back a revival of interest and
confidence in local grass-roots government, an interest that rarely

[49] Robert C. Wood, *Suburbia: Its People and Their Politics,* Houghton Mifflin Company, Boston,
1959, p. 6.

exists in rural communities which are governed by consensus, low-tax ideologies, and the avoidance of innovation; and a confidence that is not often to be found in the government of the core city, with its impersonal professional bureaucracy and strife-ridden politics.

The middle-class suburbanites, then, have a life style with a special view, including a special view of politics:[50]

> Deeply concerned with the quality of schools, conscious of their new status, suburbanites are inclined to "care" about local affairs—zoning regulations, recreational plans, garbage collection, school curricula, street paving—in an especially intense way. As the logical converse of their apathy toward strong party affiliations, suburbanites approach the politics of the community on the basis of individual preferences; they are, more and more frequently, nonpartisan, sharply distinguishing their local public preferences from their views of national and state affairs.

The Workingman's Suburb. The stereotype of urban America, sometimes reflected in careless writing by social scientists and journalists, is of a decaying core city, occupied largely by lower-status persons, with a middle-class and upper-class suburbia of the affluent. While this is generally the pattern around the largest cities and some of moderate size, it is by no means always the case. In the South and Southwest, in particular, the relatively new core cities will likely contain most of the more expensive housing, with low-quality housing being found mostly in the unincorporated fringe area. In California and Arizona, this tendency is accentuated by the practice of cities to annex large areas of undeveloped land in order to control its eventual use and to make it a buffer against the working-class suburbs. In the nation as a whole, suburbs differ from core cities significantly only in percentage of nonwhites (the difference is less in the South and West), proportion of families with children at home, proportion of broken families with children, and proportion of single persons not living at home (except in the West).[51] Some of the other socioeconomic measurements show no locational differences. (See Table 1–2.)

The suburb of the hourly rated unskilled or semiskilled worker usually consists of mass-produced single-family homes which have less variation than those of the middle-class types described above. They are built of siding that is less expensive than that of brick or stone, the lots are small—possibly no larger than the minimum established by law—and the traditional gridiron pattern of streets may

[50] *Ibid.,* p. 153.
[51] Advisory Commission on Intergovernmental Relations, *Metropolitan Social and Economic Disparities,* Report no. A-25, 1965.

TABLE 1-2. Central City and Suburb, Comparisons on a Nationwide Basis

	Central Cities	Suburbs
Percent of persons over 24 with less than 12 years of education	57	56
Percent of families with children under 18	54	62
Unemployed persons as percent of labor force, 1960	5	4
Percent of nonwhites, 1960	15	7
Percent with income under $4,000	29	26
Percent with income over $15,000	4	4
Percent of broken families with children under 18	10	5
Percent of single persons not living with their families	10	5

Source: Advisory Commission on Intergovernmental Relations, *Metropolitan Social and Economic Disparities*, Report no. A-25 (1965).

be used rather than the loops, cul-de-sacs, and curves that typify the neighborhood of the organization man. Low cost, not aesthetics, is the concern of the developer. These are the homes that are often spoken of as America's next slums, but because of individual ownership and a concern for resale value, they have generally been well cared for and continue to have a satisfactory appearance.

There are other working-class suburbs, too, however. Many of these were first developed in the 1920s and were located at the end of the streetcar line. Some are built around amusement parks which the transit company built before World War I in order to attract customers and to give core-city dwellers somewhere to go on a summer Sunday. Others center around a lake or stream and consist largely of summer cottages that were converted for year-round living by desperate factory workers during the Great Depression. These tiny old homes, on lots now below the legal minimum size, create health and roadway problems. Many of them are occupied by retired factory workers. All the residents want to enjoy the status of home ownership and they imitate some, but not all, of the patterns of Babbittville, which is nearby. One would find breezeways and charcoal grills, for example, but also an ancient car under repair in the backyard—a situation that would generate a call to the police or the planning commission in a middle-class suburb—and a tavern on the corner. (The organization man does his drinking at home or in a private country club.)

The working-class suburb is quite likely to be unincorporated. It is cheaper that way, and the residents must look for ways to save money so as to preserve their status as homeowners in time of economic difficulties—and in order to spend money on luxuries in imitation of the middle class. If the county or township administers the area, part of the cost of governmental protection and services may, through the property tax, be transferred to residents in wealthier areas, and costly services are less likely to be demanded of a more distant government than one's own municipal organization. If the area is incorporated as a separate municipality, less participation in government is likely than is the case in the middle-class suburb. The residents may be skeptical of the council-manager plan or other forms of professionalization, and they will expect taxes to be low. Services will be few: Septic tanks are preferred to sewage disposal systems, state parks to municipal parks, inexpensive gravel to hard-surfaced roads, open ditches to curbs and gutters. Building codes will place few limitations on the builder and will probably, in any case, not be rigidly enforced. Many new residents may build their own homes. The educational system will probably have a pronounced vocational cast to its curriculum. The area as a whole will view with hostility potential annexation to the core city or the imposition of a metropolitan-area supergovernment. Both threaten to expand services, raise the caliber of the existing ones to a professional level (more expensive than what exists), and deprive the residents of such access to government as they may now have. These are marginal homeowners, and they do not want to fall below the margin. The great majority of them may have one or two parents who were born on a farm and have fond memories of childhood.[52]

Although many studies immediately after World War II seemed to confuse middle-class with working-class suburbs and often assumed that the working-class people who did move to the suburbs would take on the protective coloration of the middle class, we now have enough information to know that some of the early assumptions are incorrect. In general, suburbia is developing in the same general pattern as did the older core cities. That is, it has wealthy, middle-class, working-class, and industrial areas, but instead of being under a single government, each tends to be separately incorporated, although some life styles may share a single government in the form of the county or special districts. In general, working-class people in suburbia tend to continue their older life styles. They are still less interested in voluntary organizations than are members of the middle class, they retain their Democratic political allegiance, are less interested in politics than are members of the middle class, and are relatively less interested in churches and civic activities. But they are conservative as to tax policies and less likely to support expanded local services if paid for by property tax revenue.[53]

[52] Charles Press and Clarence J. Hein, *Farmers and Urban Expansion*, U.S. Department of Agriculture, 1962.
[53] Bennett Berger, *Working-class Suburb: A Study of Auto Workers in Suburbia*, University of California Press, Berkeley, Calif., 1960; and Frederick M. Wirt, "The Political Sociology of American Suburbia," *Journal of Politics*, 27:647–666, August, 1965.

Racial and Ethnic Suburbs. Specialization is a characteristic of American culture and it is applied, as with almost every other aspect of our lives, to residential suburbs. The larger the metropolitan area, the more suburbs are specialized by racial, ethnic, and religious criteria. In a city of around 100,000, there are not enough Italian-Americans or Jews, say, to make possible separate suburbs, or even segregated neighborhoods, or to make economically feasible the ethnically specialized land developers, builders, and realtors one finds arcing the large cities. Negroes have had the least opportunity of all to move to the suburbs, not only because of the policies of realtors and home sellers but also because of their low-income position.[54] Still, during the 1960s, some 800,000 additional blacks became suburbanites. If blacks had moved into suburbia at the same rate as whites, the figure would have been twice as large, but it indicates that blacks are following the same pattern as have earlier ethnic groups.[55] It is no longer accurate to speak of the "lily-white suburbs."

The Choice of a Suburb. How do people select a suburb in which to locate when they move from the core city or from some distant community?[56]

> This out-movement follows what might be called the "homogeneity principle," that is, like kinds of people tend to segregate themselves: the rich, religious or ethnic groups, white-collar workers, etc. This tendency is reinforced by the practice of building houses in large blocs within a fairly narrow price range, which results in economic segregation.
>
> Also, institutions locate or relocate in certain areas. For instance, the building of a synagogue in an already Jewish residential area multiplies the attraction of this area for more Jewish people. The suburban parish does the same for Catholics—even more so when the church buys up considerable residential land around its new church structure and sells it largely to Catholic home builders.

The objective of minimizing conflict within the suburb threatens America's traditional emphasis upon fair play and equality. How, then, do suburbanites rationalize their practices of segregation? They do so in two ways, principally: (1) by arguing that nearly all persons are happier if they live among people like themselves and if

---

[54] See Edward C. Banfield and Morton Grodzins, *Government and Housing in Metropolitan Areas,* McGraw-Hill Book Company, New York, 1958; and Albert I. Gordon, *Jews in Suburbia,* Beacon Press, Boston, 1959.
[55] *The New York Times,* July 12, 1970.
[56] Governor's Study Commission on Metropolitan Area Problems, State of Michigan, *Final Report,* Lansing, Mich., 1960. The senior author served as chairman of the commission.

there is as little friction as possible of the sort that results from a clash of values and (2) by arguing that the "ghettoization" of the suburbs "protects property values."

A sensation was caused in 1960 when the attorney general of Michigan—with one eye on reelection prospects, perhaps—publicly revealed the techniques used in the wealthy Grosse Pointe suburbs of Detroit in order to control the land use, life styles, and ethnic composition of the area. For each person who wanted to buy in one of the suburbs involved, the local property owners' association and the realty board had an investigation conducted by a private detective. The detective filled out a standard form; for most people, 50 percent was a passing grade. The questions asked dealt with such things as level of education, place of birth, and church membership. But the realtors also inquired into whether the family's life style fitted that of the Grosse Pointes or perhaps more closely resembled that of some cultural subgroup—in particular, whether the applicant spoke English without an accent, whether his friends were primarily from the mainstream of American culture rather than from an ethnic group, whether the men of the family dressed in conservative or flashy style, and whether they were swarthy or fair-skinned. Persons of, or descended from, certain cultural subgroups had to have more than 50 points: Italian-Americans, for example, had to have 65, and Jews 85. Negroes and Americans of Oriental descent apparently could not qualify at all.

This technique for segregation is probably more formalized and elaborate than one would find in most suburbs, but the process takes place through one means or another. When asked how the system could be justified, one broker explained that the "fears and prejudices" of the *buyers* made the system necessary. He said they "prefer congenial neighborhoods where their investment is likely to be secure."[57]

The standard argument that homogeneity protects property values requires some examination, and it has received this in a study of 10,000 real estate sales in areas that were changing from all-white to mixed Negro and white.[58] The findings indicated that the odds were 4 to 1 against property values declining when Negroes began to buy into an area. Even when values did go down, as they did in 15 percent of the cases studied, the decline was modest, nearly always less than 9 percent. The reason for restrictive land-

[57] Norman C. Thomas, *Rule 9: Politics, Administration and Civil Rights,* Random House, Inc., New York, 1966.
[58] Luigi Laurenti, *Property Values and Race,* University of California Press, Berkeley, Calif., 1960.

use and realty practices is not usually just to guard against a perceived threat to property values but also to maintain the social homogeneity of the area—and for this purpose local control, that is, suburban rather than metropolitan-wide government, is a powerful aid. Regardless of the statistical data, many a suburbanite would agree with the businessman in the Chicago suburb of Deerfield who said, "I've put everything I have into my home here and I don't want to lose it to a bunch of do-gooders," and with another man who complained, "We're all mortgaged up to here. And although we've got most of our money tied up in our homes, we don't expect to live in them really very long."[59]

American suburbanites and their little governments which seek to preserve values and life styles on a parochial basis are hence a source of political conflict by the very techniques they use in seeking to minimize conflict. The Balkanized pattern of suburban America is not designed to help solve the national problem of racial and group conflict.[60]

PROBLEMS OF THE CORE CITY

The centrifugal movement of population and industry to the periphery of the urban area has caused a multitude of problems for both the core city and the suburbs. Some of these problems are severe and seem to be chronic.

Race Relations. The issue of racial relations is one of the most important facing the core city of metropolitan areas today. Whites who remain poor continue to be among those who are prejudiced against the newer and darker migrants to the city. Blacks and browns, in turn, have basic areas of conflict between themselves. As the core city becomes increasingly dominated by new types of political leaders—with black mayors and a black majority of the council soon to become commonplace in many of the largest of them—relationships between the core city and the affluent suburbs will become increasingly sensitive. Although there is no research evidence on the subject, it seems very likely that the deterioration of the core city has resulted at least in part from the failure in the first quarter of a century after World War II to work out a satisfactory relationship between or among the races. This problem was deliberately not faced up to by many who looked at the problems of the metropolis in the 1950s and 1960s. Thus, a major and expensive study of the

[59]Wilma Dykeman and James Stokely, "'The South' in the North," *The New York Times Magazine,* Apr. 17, 1960, pp. 8ff.
[60]On this last point, see Wood, *op. cit.,* part III.

Cleveland metropolitan area almost totally ignored the problem of interracial relationships, even though common knowledge suggested that this was the most fundamental issue confronting the area.[61]

Declining Tax Base, Rising Costs. Money has been a major problem to the core cities of metropolitan areas in all the years following World War II. Even after the exodus of many middle-class residents and of much of business and industry, the core city continued to have a solid base of tax support in the valuable businesses and industries that could not or, for some reason, chose not to move outside the core. But even though these cities retained sources of taxable wealth, the problems confronting them were greater than the taxable resources permitted them by suburban- and rural-oriented legislatures. As a result, every large city in the United States has now for decades suffered from a serious shortage in financial resources. Mayors of such cities have been faced with the problem of trying to secure from reluctant and suspicious legislatures, or from an often unenthusiastic Congress, the funds needed to try to cope with the ever-expanding problems of an aging city with a largely impoverished population.[62]

Ghetto Problems. The cities are faced with a host of problems mentioned above in connection with the ghetto. In particular, they are confronted with those related to public welfare, even if they are no longer basically responsible for that function. They are also generally responsible for trying to find a suitable means of public transportation and to provide adequate protection against crime. And they are asked to perform services beyond their capabilities, particularly functions in the areas of housing, health, mental hygiene, and education that can realistically be financed only by the state or national levels of government.

Threats to the Central Business District. The traditional "downtown" areas of cities, the central business district (CBD), has been undergoing a gradual decline in value and social usefulness in the years since 1945. Its streets are congested, it has inadequate parking facilities, it lacks off-street loading facilities, it is not compactly organized for shopper convenience, its land remains highly valued—often, perhaps, overvalued—and is hence difficult to redevelop, it is usually owned by a great many persons—many of them nonresidents—who often cannot agree on policies of renovation. And the area is gener-

[61] For a partial exception, but not part of the official reports, see Richard A. Watson and John H. Romani, "Metropolitan Government for Metropolitan Cleveland," *Midwest Journal of Political Science,* 5:365–390, November, 1961.
[62] This trend was anticipated many years ago. See Harvey E. Brazer, "The Role of Major Metropolitan Centers in State and Local Finance," *American Economic Review,* 48:305–316, May, 1958.

ally old in appearance, unattractive, and lacking in an architecturally integrated design.[63]

The importance of the central business district has changed rapidly with the coming of the automobile as a family car and with the great expansion of population in metropolitan areas. One of the most dramatic movements away from dependence upon the central business district has been seen in Los Angeles, where the pattern is perhaps only slightly more exaggerated than is the case in the typical community. In 1930, about three-fourths of the retail sales for the metropolitan area took place in downtown Los Angeles. By the end of World War II, this figure had been cut to one-half. After that, it dropped precipitously. It was down to 18 percent in 1960, and was still falling. By that date, Los Angeles had no central business district worthy of that name. Neither did many communities of moderately large size.

Yet the CBD is an area carrying an enormous investment. The Cleveland CBD, for example, is estimated to be worth at least 750 million dollars in land and buildings. Many of the "metropolitan area studies" that have been so popular in the postwar years have probably been inspired by those who fear the results of the pattern of decline that is evident in the CBD. They wish to put a stop to this trend and hope that an integrated government and area-wide land-use controls will lend them a hand. In many cases, city fathers have sought to correct the CBD situations that are making suburban living and trading alternatives so much more attractive. At best they can hope only to diminish the rate of decentralization. They cannot stop it.

Subsidization of the Suburbs. In addition to its decreasing tax base, the core city has been forced in most states to subsidize the suburbs. As the tax base declines, the amount and number of subsidies increase. There are at least two ways in which the core city is forced to help the suburbanite pay for his governmental services: by furnishing services of the city free or below cost; and by paying a disproportionately large share of state and county taxes in return for a disproportionately small share of their services.

The core city furnishes services free to suburbanites in many ways. Whether it likes it or not, it builds streets to carry people into the city each morning and back to the dormitory towns each evening. After the morning rush hour is over, it must be prepared to handle another miniature rush hour as the shoppers come into the city. The city pays for the repairs on the highways that deteriorate rapidly under the pounding of an ever increasing traffic load. The city hires extra policemen to handle the nonresident traffic.

[63]*Horizons*, 3:1, June, 1956. John Rannels, *The Core of the City*, Columbia University Press, New York, 1956.

Some core cities are required by state law—the legislature is likely to listen more sympathetically to suburban pressure groups than to those of the metropolis—to furnish fire protection, water, sewage disposal, or other facilities to the suburbs at less than cost. Chicago has tried unsuccessfully since 1904 to get permission from the legislature to charge a differential rate to suburbs, for example.

The core city also subsidizes the urban fringe through the payment of a disproportionate share of the county taxes. The county is traditionally a rural unit of government. In many urban communities it performs almost no functions within the core city. There are some important exceptions to this, but for the most part the county collects most of its taxes within the city and spends them outside, particularly in unincorporated areas. The inequity is increased by the fact that core-city properties are sometimes assessed at a higher rate than are those in suburbs.

The large cities also pay most of the state taxes since, in spite of losses to the suburbs, they remain centers of concentration of wealth. Yet the state tends to spend most of its money in the rural and suburban areas, expecting the large cities to finance most of their functions themselves. The state police, for example, will often lend assistance to the amateurish efforts of suburban policemen but seldom operate within the core city. Health, education, highway, welfare, and other state functions may be provided more generously outside the large cities than inside them. Grants-in-aid by the state usually give preference to the lesser-populated local governments. And state governments, by and large, have done little to assist core cities with the problems of housing, public transportation, jobs for the poor, or area-wide planning and land-use controls.

In the frontier tradition of America, we have developed an area, used it for individual and social profit; and then, as the efficiency of the area has declined, we have abandoned it with its problems and moved on to newer, more promising places. Such, to a considerable degree, has been the fate of the core of our metropolitan areas. Yet, the core cities with their housing areas for the poor and their central business districts still serve a useful social purpose and therefore cannot be abandoned.

PROBLEMS OF THE SUBURB

The politically atomized pattern of contemporary American suburbia results from the fact that this was a rural nation in the days when laws of annexation and attitudes toward large cities were developing. In those days, rural and urban life styles were sharply distinguished. Legislatures have for the most part kept the traditional legal separation unchanged. As a consequence, the boundaries of a city are almost always artificial and arbitrary and have nothing to do with economic and social realities. The entire community is an organic whole, despite its legal compartmentalization, and most suburbs are based on a metropolitan economy and social system.

The Demand for Independence. Although less than 7 percent of the American population in the early 1970s lived on farms and less than one-third of the people lived in rural areas or in towns of under 10,000, the traditional American attachment to the soil remains important. The tendency to live in cities, particularly in metropolitan areas, where the wealth and opportunities are primarily to be found, is great. But Americans continue to romanticize the life styles of the communities from which they or their parents came. In 1966, 49 percent of the persons interviewed in one survey indicated that they would prefer to live in a small town or on a farm if they could choose to live anywhere they wanted to in the United States.[64] Even in cities of one-half million people or more, nearly 50 percent of the residents would prefer to live somewhere else: in the suburbs, in a small town, or on a farm. Of those interviewed, only 22 percent thought a city the best place to live. For vast numbers of metropolitan Americans, retreat to a suburb with a legal wall around it is the most feasible way to approximate the idyll of small-town life.

Why do people want "their own" little suburb? A major reason is surely a desire to own their own homes, however heavily mortgaged. Because the cost of home ownership is increased by core-city taxes levied in order to provide urban services, suburbanites hope to be able to afford to own a home by keeping taxes low. Because many suburbanites may feel that they literally cannot continue to afford a home in their current price category if costs increase, they will fight anything that threatens higher costs, including taxes. This attitude, therefore, produces hostility toward annexation. It may also produce opposition to the incorporation of the suburb, for incorporation symbolizes increased taxes and the threat of being required to accept urban service costs.

Another significant reason deals with the common belief that the core city is run by professional politicians, is expensive to operate, and is strife-ridden. The first of these is regarded as bad because it violates the Jacksonian value of government by neighbors. The second runs counter to the citizen's use of his home as a status symbol which causes him to prefer a larger home to additional services. The last violates a desire for a sense of community, a consensus of values. The core city is made up of many ethnic and racial groups, a variety

[64] Gallup poll, published Mar. 23, 1966.

of subcultures. The one-class, one-culture, one-group tendency in individual suburbs appeals to the desire of the citizen to minimize
social tensions and conflicts.

Government in the suburb is also likely to be more personal. One
may more easily come to know the suburban officials personally or by
reputation. The city hall is more personalized and humanized than
in the core city. All these features are regarded as desirable by the
typical suburbanite.

The Desire for Access. A psychological factor that has contributed
to the Balkanization of the suburbs is the desire of citizens to have
access to the decision-making centers of local government. As urban
life became more impersonal with the growth of population and as
the old-fashioned political machine, which had served as an access
point to great numbers of citizens, declined, the feeling of isolation
and of frustration on the part of the urbanite must have increased.
The reform-period practice of electing all councilmen at large contributed to the curtain that the ordinary citizen saw as being dropped
between himself and those who decided things that mattered. But
in the suburb he found a reestablishment of the close relationships
that symbolized democracy on the frontier. In the suburb, the citizen
did not necessarily participate more by voting or attending meetings,
and he did not make a greater effort to know his governmental officials, but he regained the comfortable feeling that goes with the
thought of having influence over government decisions and of having
officeholders who share one's social values.

To the urbanite of today, the concept of community is, in any case,
a vague one. Certainly he feels only the most tangential loyalties to
the metropolitan areas as a whole. There are few regional institutions. To the typical citizen the only reality is the family and the neighborhood, so "regional problems find no vehicle for their solution and
the capacity to look ahead, to plan rationally, to awake a regional
consciousness is lost."[65]

Because of his narrow scope of vision and narrow loyalties, the
typical suburbanite knows little of the structure or physical limits of
his local government, to say nothing of the metropolitan area as a
whole. The local government to him is good, not because he has an
emotional loyalty to it, but because through it he has influence and
access in relation to governmental services, whereas through any
type of regional government he does not.[66]

---

[65] Robert C. Wood, "Metropolitan Government, 1957: An Extrapolation of Trends," *American Political Science Review,* 52:111, March, 1958. On this section, see also his *Suburbia, op. cit.;* and Banfield and Grodzins, *op. cit.*
[66] Basil G. Zimmer and Amos H. Hawley, "Local Government as Viewed by Fringe Residents," *Rural
Sociology,* 23:363–370, December, 1958, provides partial verification.

The Desire for Local Control. Over which governmental functions does the suburbanite wish to retain control for himself and his neighbors? In which service areas is diversity positively preferred to uniformity? An attitude survey would probably show that suburbanites feel that some services are more important than others in terms of the way in which policies will affect the character of their neighborhoods. Among the areas where local retention of control is most wanted would probably be the following: land use, garbage and rubbish collection, police policies, maintenance of residential streets, and education.[67]

Local wishes may call for luxury services, for minimal services, or for some level in between. Wealthy people do not want to be forced into a single mold by the creation of one legal entity for the whole area because they can afford, and often wish to have, luxury services which core-city government would not be likely to provide.

In contrast, one finds in modest suburbs a violent dislike and fear of the core city. In these areas, residents can barely afford to own their homes. They want minimal services because they fear that even a small increase in costs through "unnecessary" services, for example, might force them out of the homeowning category with all its prestige and psychological satisfaction. To these people, joining the core city would mean buying a package of services that they feel they can do without and cannot afford. People in between these two extremes recognize that additional services are symbols of status and that they cost money. They are usually willing to pay extra taxes for extra services, but they generally believe that these services can be secured more cheaply by incorporating the area than by becoming annexed to the core city.[68]

It should be clear why residents of different types of suburban areas would want to control the above functions. Low-income neighborhoods may want to haul their own rubbish to the dump. Well-to-do people may prefer twice-a-week collection from the back door while the core city offers only once-a-week service from the front curb. Local control of educational services is desired because of the great expense of this item, its importance to the future of their children, and the importance of the school plant as a status symbol. Low-income areas and areas of older people may want minimal services in education out of cost considerations. But the size and luxury

[67] Oliver P. Williams, Harold Herman, Charles S. Liebman, and Thomas R. Dye, *Suburban Differences and Metropolitan Policies,* University of Pennsylvania Press, Philadelphia, 1965, offers supporting data.
[68] For partial verification of this paragraph, see three articles by Basil G. Zimmer and Amos H. Hawley, "Home Owners and Attitude toward Tax Increase," *Journal of the American Institute of Planners,* 21:65–74, Spring, 1956; "Property Taxes and Solutions to Fringe Problems," *Land Economics,* 32:369–376, November, 1956; "Approaches to the Solution of Fringe Problems," *Public Administration Review,* 16:258–268, Autumn, 1956.

of the school auditorium and, especially perhaps, of the swimming pool (if any) have become important symbols in contemporary suburbia. To have decisions about these policies left to the impersonal bureaucracy of a large-city school system would be undesirable to suburbanites of low and high income alike. Land-use policies, which by the logic of the planning profession are the most region-wide in character of all policies, are vitally important to the suburbanite. The ethnic, industrial, and commercial balance is of the greatest concern to him. He wants races, classes, and occupations segregated. He wants to be personally acquainted with, or to feel that he can influence, those who sit on the planning commission so that they will not change the land use in his area (except to his advantage). The professional bureaucracy of the core city with its impersonal dedication to the principles of planning does not spell an improved community to him; it spells loss of control and potential disaster for him as a homeowner.

TABLE 1-3.   Citizen Participation and Ability to Name Leaders (In percent)

Types of Participants	Local Leaders			
	None Named		Two or More Named	
	Dayton	Rest of County	Dayton	Rest of County
Actives	40	40	31	23
Casuals	38	52	18	10
Nonvoters	61	76	11	4

Note that suburbanites *do not* necessarily have a better knowledge of local leaders than do core-city dwellers. Similar findings have been reported from other metropolitan areas.
Source: John C. Bollens and others, *Metropolitan Challenge,* Metropolitan Community Studies, Inc., Dayton, Ohio, 1959, table 46. Used by permission.

The Control of Functions of Marginal Importance. In addition to the services named above, certain other services are regarded by the suburbanite as being important enough so that local retention of control over them is preferred. These include police, fire protection, mass transportation, and public housing. To the suburbanite, police protection has a highly elastic demand curve.[69] He does not view it

---

[69] So it would seem from the figures in Seymour Sacks and others, *Metropolitan Cleveland: A Fiscal Profile,* Metropolitan Services Commission, Cleveland, 1958.

as being vitally important. In a suburb that has rarely had a case of murder, rape, or arson, arguments for a metropolitan police force make little sense indeed. If a difficult case should come along, the county sheriff or the state police would provide the needed extra help. Fire-protection costs can be reduced in the suburbs by using volunteer help—there is usually a waiting list of persons wanting to join the company—and suburbanites seem not to mind paying higher fire-insurance premiums than do core-city residents. Furthermore, without a metropolitan fire-protection system, the suburbanite can avoid helping to pay for the expensive equipment needed to guard the high-rise buildings and warehouse areas of the core city. Suburbanites, with one, two, or more cars in the family, would rather not help subsidize a public transportation system designed primarily for the lower-income residents of the core city. And to the suburban homeowner, public housing is regarded with suspicion and as something that might better not exist at all.

There are certain areas where the suburbanite might not object strongly to region-wide administration of services. These would probably include functions or portions of functions where professionals in the field are popularly expected to make basic policy—and the average citizen therefore views the activity as not involving "politics," at all.[70] Examples include public health, garbage and sewage disposal, water supply, and police crime laboratories and communications systems. In these areas, the suburbanite feels no strong need to control policy, but he is not willing to spend more than a minimum amount, in the typical situation, for the service. With few multifamily dwellings, restaurants, or public assembly places in his suburb, he is likely to think of health as a matter for the family physician (many suburbs spend nothing on public health); he may favor disposing of sewage in the raw state into the nearest stream if no one stops him; and he will insist that a well is cheaper than a municipal system, so long as the pump brings forth unpolluted water.

Amateurism. In the midst of specialists of every type, many of the suburbs try to get along with untrained amateurs. On the other hand, the governmental operations of suburbs are simpler than are those of large cities, and fewer skills are required.

Lack of Services. "Taxes are lower in Perambulator Park," the real estate advertisements proclaim; they are less likely to mention that they are lower in part because few services are provided. The absence of many urban services may be accounted for in a variety of ways. Suburbanites may think they cannot afford some services or

[70] Roscoe C. Martin and Frank J. Munger, *Decisions in Syracuse,* Indiana University Press, Bloomington, Ind., 1961.

may prefer to perform them individually. They may regard them as not worth the cost. Many services are more expensive in the suburbs than in the core city because of the lesser density of population. This applies particularly to sewerage, storm drainage, street paving and maintenance, street lighting, water supply, garbage collection, and sewage disposal.[71]

Lack of Cooperation. Suburbs tend to become intensely jealous of their independence, and—encouraged by local officeholders—they attribute ulterior motives to all suggestions of cooperation with the core city or even with other suburbs. This attitude is likely to decrease coordination and lead to inefficient use of plant and equipment.

Unequal Tax Bases. The accident of boundary lines contributes to the creation of suburbs with highly unequal financial facilities for supporting local government. There may be wealthy suburbs alongside of a core city that is desperately in need of more taxable wealth to support its services—which are used by residents of that suburb. Other suburbs may be very poor, even though they are located in the heart of a prosperous urban area. This is true, for example, of middle- or lower-income suburbs with no industry. Often the suburbs most needing services are among those least able to afford them.

Some inequities are being partly relieved by the transfer of some functions to special districts, the county, or the state; by increasing use of state and Federal grants-in-aid with built-in formulas to consider relative need; by state-shared taxes; by forcing the commuter to pay some of the cost of his use of services of other local units of government through the application of earnings taxes or through his payment of state and local taxes; and by a broadening of the tax base so that even poor suburbs that have not attracted industry are having their property-tax income increased somewhat through the diversified location of offices, salesrooms, medical clinics, supermarkets, shopping centers, and other commercial establishments.[72] But these trends are being partially offset by the decline in the relative average value of new construction in suburbs as they become increasingly the home of all classes.

Rising Costs. Fringe-area taxes may begin at what appears to be a much lower level than those of the core city, but the suburban buyer can be assured that they will increase at a rapid pace. The major portion of one's property-tax bill goes toward the support of schools, and in contemporary suburbia, one school-bond issue has followed another with little respite. Each issue raises taxes. As

---

[71] John K. Galbraith, *The Affluent Society,* Houghton Mifflin Company, Boston, 1958, pp. 251–264.
[72] Wood, "Metropolitan Government, 1957," pp. 113–115.

population density increases, furthermore, the need for other urban services increases. Each new service must be paid for by additional taxes.

Water and sewage systems must be installed. Soon neighbors want to have the street paved and a storm sewer laid. Street lights become desirable. Fire and police service may have to be expanded. The sewage-disposal problem, enormously expensive and nearly always ignored as long as possible, must be solved.

All these problems fall upon the mortgage- and debt-ridden suburbanite. Many of them were never faced by the subdivision developer. He has, in any case, long since disappeared from the area. In desperation, the citizens seek solutions through special districts, incorporation, new state legislation, or, more rarely, annexation to an existing municipality.

Problems of the Metropolitan Area. The problems listed above generally are those of either the core city or of the suburbs. But there are also matters of concern to the metropolitan area as a whole. Unsafe sewage-disposal practices in any part of the area may endanger health in another part. Economics may dictate a collective effort to secure additional water supplies from a distant lake or mountain stream. Traffic-flow patterns for the entire area are necessarily interrelated. Land-use practices in any one section will affect those in other sections. Smoke and noise nuisances pay no more attention to legal boundaries than do disease germs.

These are some of the collective problems. There is little agreement as to which are the most important, and they probably differ from one metropolitan area to another according to local values and existing service levels. The greatest problem of all, perhaps, is "the inability of metropolitan residents to reach any substantial degree of consensus as to what should be done . . . about the generally recognized issues of their common life—government organization, finance, blight and redevelopment, schools, race relations, land use control, and so on."[73]

Closing Statement. Some of the characteristics of American life and the values that guide our decisions concerning governmental policies have been presented in this chapter. The issues of policy raised in connection with various functions of government will be developed in more detail in the appropriate later sections of the book.

[73] Coleman Woodbury, "Great Cities, Great Problems, Great Possibilities?" *Public Administration Review,* 18:332–340, Autumn, 1958. Quote from p. 339.

SELECTED
READINGS

Banfield, Edward C.: *The Unheavenly City,* Little Brown and Co., Boston, 1970. (A critical examination of the assumptions concerning urban blight and poverty.)

Berger, Bennett: *Working-class Suburb,* University of California Press, Berkeley, Calif., 1960. (Auto workers in California.)

Burgess, E. W., R. E. Park, and R. D. McKenzie: *The City,* The University of Chicago Press, Chicago, 1925. (A classic study.)

Dobriner, William (ed.): *The Suburban Community,* G. P. Putnam's Sons, New York, 1958. (Readings by leading social scientists.)

Dobriner, William M.: *Class in Suburbia,* Prentice-Hall, Inc., Englewood Cliffs, N.J., 1963. (Social classes in Levittown, N.Y.)

Dollard, John: *Caste and Class in a Southern Town,* 3d ed., Doubleday & Company, Inc., Garden City, N.Y., 1957. (A study of social status in the South.)

Donaldson, Scott: *The Suburban Myth,* Columbia University Press, New York, 1969. (Argues that suburbia has been "grossly and unfairly maligned." A review of works on suburbia.)

Douglass, H. Paul: *The Suburban Trend,* Appleton-Century-Crofts, Inc., New York, 1925. (An early study by a sociologist.)

———: *The Little Town,* The Macmillan Company, New York, 1927.

Drake, St. Clair, and H. R. Cayton: *Black Metropolis,* Harcourt, Brace & World, Inc., New York, 1945. (A classic study of Chicago's Negro community.)

Fraser, John: "The Impact of Community and Regime Orientations on Choice of Political System," *Midwest Journal of Political Science,* 14:413–433, August, 1970. (Some empirical evidence on the importance of a sense of community.)

Gans, Herbert J.: *The Levittowners: Ways of Life and Politics in a New Suburban Community,* Pantheon Books, Random House, Inc., New York, 1967.

Gottmann, Jean: *Megalopolis,* The M.I.T. Press, Cambridge, Mass., 1961. (A study of the Northeastern seaboard urban region by a famous French geographer.)

Green, Constance McLaughlin: *The Rise of Urban America,* Harper & Row Publishers, Incorporated, New York, 1965. (History of sixteen cities in various parts of the nation.)

Grodzins, Morton: *The Metropolitan Area as a Racial Problem,* The University of Pittsburgh Press, Pittsburgh, Pa., 1958. (The social and economic implications of multiracial metropolitan areas.)

Handlin, Oscar: *The Newcomers: Negroes and Puerto Ricans in a Changing Metropolis,* Harvard University Press, Cambridge, Mass., 1959.

Hirsch, Werner Z. (ed.): *Urban Life and Form,* Holt, Rinehart and Winston, Inc., New York, 1963. (Nine papers by outstanding urbanists of various disciplines.)

Howard, Ebenezer: *Garden Cities of Tomorrow,* The M.I.T. Press, Cambridge, Mass., 1965. Originally published, 1898, as *Tomorrow: The Peaceful Path of Reform.* (His description of the "town-country magnet," pp. 50–57, is very similar to the Slayton-Dewey quotation in this chapter.)

Johnson, Keith, and others: "Suburbia: The New American Plurality," *Time,* Mar. 15, 1971. (A questioning of stereotypic assessments. Includes the findings in a Louis Harris opinion poll of suburban attitudes.)

Laurenti, Luigi: *Property Values and Race,* University of California Press, Berkeley, Calif., 1960. (Traces effects of Negro movement into previously all-white areas.)

Long, Norton E.: "The Corporation, Its Satellites, and the Local Community," in E. E. Mason (ed.), *The Corporation in Modern Society,* Harvard University Press, Cambridge, Mass., 1960. (The "corporate citizen" encourages harmless do-gooder activities by its executives.)

Mumford, Lewis: *The City in History,* Harcourt, Brace & World, Inc., New York, 1961. (Reviews the place of the city in human society through 5,000 years. Highly opinionated.)

Orleans, Peter, and W. R. Ellis, Jr. (eds.): *Race, Change, and Urban Society,* Sage Publications, Inc., Beverly Hills, Calif., 1971. (Includes bibliography on race and cities.)

Petersen, E. T. (ed.): *Cities Are Abnormal,* University of Oklahoma Press, Norman, Okla., 1946. (Unfavorable criticisms of cities as social institutions.)

Rossi, Peter H.: *Why Families Move,* The Free Press of Glencoe, New York, 1956. (A study of inducements for the suburban movement.)

Schlesinger, Arthur M.: *The Rise of the City,* The Macmillan Company, New York, 1933.

Schlesinger, Arthur M., Jr.: *The Age of Jackson,* Little, Brown and Company, Boston, 1945. (An account of the coming of industrial society to America.)

Schmandt, Henry J., and Warren Bloomberg, Jr. (eds.): *The Quality of Urban Life,* Sage Publications, Inc., Beverly Hills, Calif., 1969. (Emphasizes current conditions and trends.)

Schnore, Leo F.: "The Socio-economic Status of Cities and Suburbs," *American Sociological Review,* 28:76–85, February, 1963. (Suburbs have higher socioeconomic status in larger and older urban areas than do core cities, but the opposite is the case in newer, smaller urban areas.)

Seeley, John R., and others: *Crestwood Heights: The Culture of Suburban Life,* Basic Books, Inc., Publishers, New York, 1956.

Slayton, William L., and Richard Dewey: "Urban Redevelopment and the Urbanite," in Coleman Woodbury (ed.), *The Future of Cities and Urban Redevelopment,* The University of Chicago Press, Chicago, 1953. (A major early study of slum redevelopment problems and prospects.)

Strauss, Anselm: *Images of the American City,* The Free Press of Glencoe, New York, 1961. (A sociopsychological interpretation of how Americans have reacted to rapid urbanization.)

Vidich, A. J., and Joseph Bensman: *Small Town in Mass Society,* Princeton University Press, Princeton, N.J., 1958.

Warner, Sam B.: *Street Car Suburbs,* Harvard University and The M.I.T. Press, Cambridge, Mass., 1962. (The early suburban movement was made possible by public transportation.)

Warner, W. Lloyd, and others: *Social Class in America,* Science Research Associates, Inc., Chicago, 1949.

Weber, Adna F.: *The Growth of Cities in the Nineteenth Century,* Columbia University Press, New York, 1899.

White, Morton, and Lucia White: *The Intellectual Versus the City,* Harvard University and The M.I.T. Press, Cambridge, Mass., 1964. (A review of criticism of American cities from Thomas Jefferson to Frank Lloyd Wright.)

Whyte, William H. Jr.: *The Organization Man,* Anchor Books, Doubleday & Company, Inc., Garden City, N.Y., 1956. (Contains a vigorous criticism of suburbia.)

Willbern, York: *The Withering Away of the City,* University of Alabama Press, University, Ala., 1964. (Explores various political implications of the urbanization movement.)

Wirth, Louis: "Urbanism as a Way of Life," *American Journal of Sociology,* 44:1–24, July, 1938. (A seminal statement, although no longer fully accepted by social scientists, of urban life styles as unique compared with rural.)

Wood, Robert C.: *Suburbia: Its People and Their Politics,* Houghton Mifflin Company, Boston, 1959.

Zorbaugh, Harvey: *The Gold Coast and the Slum,* The University of Chicago Press, Chicago, 1929. (A classic study of Chicago's socially mixed near-North Side.)

CHAPTER
2 LOCAL GOVERNMENT IDEOLOGY

Ideas make a difference in politics. So do emotions. The effective politician knows how to mix the two in the proper proportion. He seeks to find the ideas that will make the most effective type of appeal in a given situation. He knows, too, that the typical citizen often responds more readily to an emotional appeal than he does to a closely reasoned argument. Since this is the case, the politician becomes interested in ideas as *weapons.* They become devices through which people can be manipulated. Ideas are stated in terms that reflect existing value patterns of society. They are repeated with variations and elaborations; they are tied together with clichés that are already well established in their ability to produce a desired response; and through skillful reiteration, ideas are distilled until they become slogans or proverbs that produce a conditioned response in the individual who is exposed to them. But it must be remembered that politicians, in seeking to influence people, are limited and restrained by the existing value structure, and they cannot move effectively except within that structure.

An understanding of ideas, attitudes, ideals as goals, and cultural values is important not just to the politician seeking to sway the minds of citizens, however. To know something about these concepts is vital to anyone who would wish to understand the political process. The materials in this chapter, then, are some of the most important analytical tools that are necessary for the citizen to make a meaningful analysis of the political events which take place about him and which affect him as a participant as well as an observer of politics.[1]

THE FRONTIER PRECEPTS OF JACKSONIAN DEMOCRACY

The British Colonial Background. It was an agricultural nation that declared its independence from the mother country in 1776. Only about 3 percent of the people lived in nonrural communities, and there were not more than twenty-four incorporated municipalities in all thirteen of the new states.[2] The city having the largest number of people living within its legally defined area was New York, which, fourteen years later, in the first census of the United States, claimed a population of 33,131. The urban area, including suburbs, with the largest number of inhabitants was Philadelphia with 42,444. Today, the United States possesses hundreds of cities of that size or larger, and an urban area in the 30,000 to 40,000 population class is often summarily dismissed as a "small city."

These few figures are cited to indicate that there was little *need* for Americans of the late eighteenth century to devote their time to the development of a theory of urban government. As a matter of fact, the cities and villages of the time used a government structure modeled upon a system that had been familiar to the colonists in their native England. There was no separation of powers between the legislative and executive branches. The council possessed virtually all power. It was headed by the *mayor,* who had no veto power and practically no executive power. His task was to preside over meetings of the council as one of its members and to perform the ceremonial functions of the city. He was appointed, usually for one year, by the colonial governor, by the council as a whole, or by the aldermen. In a very few instances he was elected, under the complex suffrage rules then prevailing. Another appointed officer was the *recorder,* who held his post for an indefinite period. He was a member of the council, a member of the local court,[3] and served as the corporation

---

[1] For a more elaborate development of ideology than is offered here, see Charles R. Adrian and Charles Press, *The American Political Process,* McGraw-Hill Book Company, New York, 2nd ed., 1969, chap. 6.

[2] In New England, urban and rural areas alike (including Boston) were ruled by the same unit of government, the *town.* In its pristine form, the town was a form of direct democracy, with the town meeting serving as the policy-making body. At this time, New England had no legally described villages or cities.

[3] The court was usually made up of the mayor, the recorder, and the aldermen (but not the common councilmen). Jurisdictions varied but usually covered misdemeanors in violation of state law and of municipal ordinances. Powers of a justice of the peace were also included. From this court came the term *recorder's court,* which we still find in North Carolina for minor courts, in the city of Detroit for the major criminal trial courts of the city, and in other places in the United States.

counsel (city attorney). In addition to these two, the council was made up of *aldermen* (distinguished citizens of the community who were usually selected by the common councilmen from their own membership) and *councilmen*. The latter were the only members of the city government to be elected directly by the "people"—i.e., by the eligible electors.[4] Furthermore, nearly one-third of the boroughs (the English term for an incorporated municipality and the one generally used in the United States in the early years) were "close corporations" in which no popular elections at all were held. In these cities, the original charter named the members of the council, and vacancies were filled from time to time by surviving members of the body.

The city actually had a plural executive. Administrative supervision was exercised and minor appointments were made by the council as a whole, by committees of the council, or by the municipal court.

This plan, largely removed from the supervision or participation of the common citizen, remained in effect without basic change for the first few decades after independence. (In England, this same fundamental structure is in use today. It has been made operable under modern conditions by the installation of permanent, professionally trained department heads, a competent civil service, and an extension of voting privileges on the principle of universal suffrage.) That alterations might be expected was presaged, however, in one change that took place at the time of the Revolution. Under colonial rule, no charter could be made or amended without the consent of the city or village. With the cessation of British rule, control over charters passed from the Crown to the state legislatures, rather than to the logical successor, the governor, for executives fell into disrepute during the Revolution. Since the legislatures appear to have assumed that their powers were plenary and unrestricted (excepting in a few cases of state constitutional limitations), the trail was opened for domination of the city government from the state capital—a phenomenon that characterized nineteenth-century American city government.

This potential for domination probably would never have been developed—the British tradition of local self-government being to the contrary—were it not for the evolution in the early decades of the nineteenth century of a genuinely American ideology of government.

---

[4] To find out who was eligible in a rather complicated system, see Kirk H. Porter, *A History of Suffrage in the United States,* The University of Chicago Press, Chicago, 1918. For more recent research indicating that voter eligibility was less restricted than was formerly believed, see Robert E. Brown, *Middle-class Democracy and the Revolution in Massachusetts,* Cornell University Press, Ithaca, N.Y., 1955, chaps. 1–5.

This ideology came out of the everyday experiences of the American frontiersman, and, as such, it was pragmatic rather than introspective, functional rather than universal; and it was applied to state, county, township, village, and city governments alike. We usually refer to its rather unsystematic precepts by the use of the term *Jacksonian democracy.*

Jacksonian Theories and City Government. The rustic idyll that was the America of the dreams of Thomas Jefferson began to disappear as an actual possibility well before that statesman had completed his days on earth. Jefferson firmly believed that democracy, if it were to be successful, must find its strength in the individual farmer working in soil that he could call his own. To him, local government was to "emerge as the paramount center of power" in the entire political system, more important than the states or the national government, but local government was to be rural government.[5] Jefferson had no direct knowledge about large cities (except for what he had seen in Paris), but he was an insatiable reader, and what he read about them did not please him. His opinion was stated trenchantly in *Notes on Virginia* (1782): "The mobs of great cities add just so much to the support of pure government, as sores do to the strength of the human body." So long as he lived, he urged that the United States remain an agricultural nation.

But the cities came anyway, and with them the urban proletariat that Jefferson thought spelled doom for democracy. With the rise of the city came also an ideology for its proper government. That ideology came via Jefferson and the frontier to the rising urban centers, where it was embraced by the workingman. It was an attitude toward government taken by those who labored on the farm and in the city alike; it was an ideology of a rapidly growing nation, constantly pushing westward, founding new towns, building up old ones through the rise of a new industrialism; it was a viewpoint of a people constantly in debt, yet perennially optimistic as they realized, or at least hoped for, the unearned increment of increasing site value of land; and it was the thoughts of the common man about a nation that was now his own and that no longer belonged to an oligarchy of propertied aristocrats. Together, these made up the political ideology of Jacksonian democracy which provided a rationalization for city government that survived nearly intact the remainder of the nineteenth century and is still important in our thinking today. Its general principles are not difficult to summarize.

[5] Anwar Syed, *The Political Theory of American Local Government*, Random House, Inc., New York, 1966, p. 51.

Jacksonian Principles. Probably antecedent to all others in importance was the concept of *government by the common man.* Government existed not for a privileged class but for the general citizen. Any one man was equal to any other man. Jefferson had said so in 1776, when the country was controlled by an aristocracy; now the words were to be taken quite literally, although only the visionary extended the concept beyond the *white* man in the 1820s. If this were the case, then it followed that any man was as good as any other man in a public office—no special qualifications were needed, no special training, nothing other than status as a human being willing to serve the community.

Out of this concept came the principle of *universal manhood suffrage.* It followed logically from egalitarianism; it was necessary to the development of Jacksonian thought; and, furthermore, it was the natural result of the effect of inertia upon the already existing trend. There were property requirements to vote. These appear to have been quite easily met in rural areas—nearly 90 percent of the adult white males of Massachusetts could vote at the time of the Revolution—but their continued existence might have created a disfranchised urban proletariat. With the Democrats seeking the support of urban workingmen, restrictions on the suffrage disappeared almost completely in the two decades following the first election of Andrew Jackson to the Presidency (1828).[6] Thenceforth, the general public possessed the potential for the control of government in its own interests.

Universal manhood suffrage made it possible for any man to run for office, to get support from all classes of people, and to be elected. Jacksonians were not greatly concerned with the education, background or experience, or private calling of a candidate. It might be noted in passing that this viewpoint made a career as a professional politician, or even as a political hack, legitimate.[7]

Following from the above, Jacksonians believed that public office-holders, as servants of the people, should hold their mandates directly from the people. It was therefore held desirable to elect public officials rather than to appoint them. Gradually this came to mean the election of virtually all top-level officers, thus imposing upon Americans the unique institution of the long, or "bedsheet,"

[6] See Brown, *op. cit.,* chaps. 1–5; and Walter Hugins, *Jacksonian Democracy and the Working Class,* Stanford University Press, Stanford, Calif., 1960.
[7] The frequently used term *political hack* may be said to refer to the individual who has never "made good" at anything else, who is a perennial office seeker, and who depends for a livelihood upon scraps from the political table. His competence and public faith in him are questionable. The term *professional politician* is here used to refer to a person who secures his livelihood from political jobs, but whose competence is assumed or has been demonstrated.

ballot. To further ensure proximity to the people, a short term of one or two years in office and rapid turnover of personnel was advocated. In the small village or city, government could be *personal,* and the long ballot was therefore of little handicap to the casual voter, for he probably knew all or most of the candidates either personally or by reputation. Similarly, although rapid turnover of personnel meant inexperienced officeholders, this was no great problem where government was on a neighborly basis and administration was simple and nontechnical.

The movement toward the direct public oversight of officeholders through the use of the ballot was begun when the office of mayor was made elective. This was initiated in Boston and St. Louis in 1822 and spread rapidly throughout the nation. It was but a start, however. The Detroit charter of two years later not only made the office of mayor elective but, in true frontier spirit, added the other city administrative offices to the list. This idea spread less rapidly than did that of the elective mayoralty, but gradually along the frontier the council was deprived of its power to appoint administrative officials. Some or all of the following became elective in various cities: the offices of tax collector or city treasurer, clerk, assessor, and city attorney, and, somewhat later, the myriad posts on the various boards and commissions that became a part of city government.

The rise of the independent board or commission for administrative purposes came about gradually as a protest against inadequacies in the performances of council committees as administrative overseers. It also reflected the growing distrust of city government and the desire to take certain functions "out of politics" by setting up independent commissions—sometimes appointed by state officials—to administer them. The New York charter of 1830 replaced the committees with single officers or boards (still, however, appointed by the council). In 1849, New York made these offices elective, and a similar plan was applied in Cleveland in 1852. After the Civil War, the use of the independent board and commission gained headway rapidly, and throughout the remainder of the nineteenth century this was the general practice. While the use of multimember boards did not originate in the springtime of Jacksonianism, it was a direct and logical outgrowth of its tenets.

Deterioration of Responsible Self-government in the City. By the time of the Civil War, a system of city government based on Jacksonian principles had matured. It is usually referred to as the "weak-mayor" plan. It dominated the last half of the nineteenth century, and even now it is found in more cities and villages in America than is any other structural form.[8] Its characteristics included a mayor who usually had a veto power but who was weak administratively; a large council that dominated the scene, performing both legislative and administrative functions; a long ballot with many elective administrative officials, each independent of the others; numerous elective or appointive (but almost unremovable) boards and commissions; many ex officio positions; and an extreme deconcentration of both legislative and executive responsibilities.

Legislative Domination. During this period state legislatures tended to control the profitable or politically important aspects of city government. This they did in a variety of ways: by reserving the power to grant public utility franchises for gas, water, electricity, and street railways; by granting special act charters to specifically named cities, amendable only at the legislatures' discretion; by removing many local powers from a city if it fell to the control of a party not in a majority in the state legislature; by direct state administration of particularly patronage-laden local functions through special commissions (so-called "ripper" legislation); and by many other techniques. After about 1850, special legislation (i.e., legislation affecting exclusively a specifically named city) became so common that in many states its consideration took up more of the legislature's time than did legislation directed at the state as a whole. In many instances it had the effect of making the legislative delegation from each city a veritable supercouncil, far more powerful than the members of the formal council.

Political differences between the state legislative majority and the largest cities of the state led to reduction in the degree of local self-government in many cities. As early as 1861, Chicago was Democratic while the legislature was Republican; this resulted in a struggle for control of the city that has lasted intermittently ever since. Similar differences caused trouble between the city of New York and the state, between Boston and Massachusetts, and between St. Louis and Missouri. A feud within the party resulted in the temporary abolition of self-government for Pittsburgh and other Pennsylvania cities in 1901. In 1879, the Alabama legislature actually abolished Mobile, and Memphis suffered the same fate in Tennessee. In the latter case, the city had become bankrupt and the creditors applied pressure on the legislature to help them save their investments.

Special commissions controlled by the governor or legislature to take control of police, health, and other functions of cities became

---

[8] A detailed examination of structures of city government will be made in chap. 6.

common after 1850. At various times, the police departments of New York, Chicago, Boston, Detroit, Baltimore, and St. Louis, among others, were removed from local control. It should not be assumed that the legislature was never motivated by any other desire than to secure control of luscious patronage pastures; often municipally controlled departments were so corrupt that citizens rushed to the legislature asking that certain functions be transferred to state control with the hope, at least, that a change might be effected.

Legislatures often were not beyond paying out the city taxpayers' money for the benefit of favored businessmen. Note, for example, the elaborate set of city buildings erected for Philadelphia in 1870 by the state legislature without consulting the citizens of the city—but with the uninvited bill being turned over to them. Individual legislators in those days were far more often guilty of questionable ethics and of sheer venality than is the case today. Members were frequently in the pay of railroads, land speculators, liquor interests, and the like. Gas, electric, street railway, and other franchises were sometimes virtually auctioned off by legislators to the highest bidder. Public faith in the state legislature as the guiding authority for cities could not be great under such circumstances. The city boss and machine, a phenomenon of the new industrial city, operated under a value system similar to that of the legislators.[9]

Reaction to State Control. Protests and reactions to this situation were prompt in coming. However, reforms proved to be much easier to suggest than to make effective. As early as the 1820s, specific provisions were written into constitutions granting voters in cities certain privileges, such as the power to choose their own principal officers. Special legislation—the most direct technique of state control—was prohibited by the Ohio constitution of 1851. Similar provisions are found today in most of the state constitutions. A further development in the effort to free the city from control by the state legislature came with the provision for constitutional home rule in the Missouri constitution of 1875. Home rule refers to the right of the voters of a city (or their representatives on a charter commission or city council) to frame, adopt, and amend their own city charters, as distinguished from the practice of having this done for them by the state legislature.[10]

These attempts often met with frustration. The courts commonly permitted legislatures to continue to enact special legislation, so long as it was thinly disguised as general legislation. Constitutional

[9] For the city boss and machine, see chap. 3.
[10] See chap. 5.

home rule, likewise, did not of itself establish autonomous and effective self-government in cities.

While these experiments were failing to provide urban self-government, the unwieldy, uncoordinated, complicated, weak-mayor system was becoming increasingly ineffective as a form of government for America's rapidly growing cities. Something more was needed.

THE INHERENT RIGHT OF LOCAL SELF-GOVERNMENT

A Romantic Legalism. Under the theory of home rule, advanced in protest against legislative control of local affairs, the community has an inherent right to rule itself on local matters without interference by the state. The doctrine enjoyed but a brief life as a *legal* theory; yet overtones of the concept were felt in American thinking long before Judge Thomas M. Cooley of Michigan first expressed his often-cited dictum, and they are still felt today whenever the "rights" of city governments as against state control are argued by citizens at civic-association, council, charter-commission, and other meetings of a similar nature.

The lay citizen, arguing for a "right" of the city to control local affairs, is not likely to give a closely reasoned argument for his view, but the crux of it is likely to hold that there are three levels of government in the United States and that each has certain areas of exclusive control. The legal argument is somewhat more sophisticated, but it comes to the same thing. In 1871, Judge Cooley, asserting that local self-government was a matter of "absolute right," gave a historical argument augmented by some concepts from the eighteenth-century natural-rights philosophers. The historical argument holds that local self-government was well established as an Anglo-American tradition long before an American state was created and that this practice was transferred to American municipalities through the common law. Unless the state constitution specifically turned over control of local government to the states, the argument ran, it remained as it had long been established. Writers sought to show that the principle of local self-government predated the establishment of the kingdom of England, that it had, in fact, been the greatest contribution to government of the Angles and Saxons before William the Conqueror, and that its origins were to be found in the democracy of the ancient German tribes in the days before that part of Europe fell under the influence of Rome.

The argument as presented by Judge Cooley was actually an obiter dictum—that is to say, his remarks were not absolutely necessary, since he had already settled the case before him upon other, more conventional, grounds. His viewpoint suited the spirit of the times, however, and was cited by judges at one time or another in California, Indiana, Iowa, Kentucky, Michigan, Nebraska, and Texas. The doctrine, however, never became established, for the courts generally followed the opposite principle: that the state is supreme and the city is its creature. Indeed, the doctrine of the inherent right of cities to home rule was a wistful, fanciful notion based upon weak legal reasoning and largely manufactured by judges who were sympathetic to local self-government.

Actually, local government in England is not, and probably never has been, independent of the central government. Since the days of William I, there certainly has been no question but that any "rights" that cities may have are actually privileges extended by the Crown. Sovereignty over the former colonies passed from the British Crown to the American states, which have since retained such powers as were not relinquished to the national government. And as for any "rights" of cities existing under the common law, all judges, and most certainly the scholarly Thomas M. Cooley, knew that the un-written common law is automatically superseded by any contrary provisions in statute or constitutional law. More important, there is no natural cleavage to separate local from state powers. Probably all "local" concerns have within them some element of statewide interest, and state powers must often be administered, when it comes to detailed application, in specific local areas. The definition of "local" concerns is therefore not natural at all, but a fairly arbitrary legalism that has historically been determined in the United States by the state legislatures and the state courts.[11]

Short-lived as was the legal protest, a legacy remains in the widespread belief among Americans that the municipality has, or should have, a "right" to rule itself in local matters without detailed supervision by the state.

PREMISES OF THE MIDDLE-CLASS BUSINESSMAN: THE EFFICIENCY AND ECONOMY MOVEMENT

The Organization of Protest. Determined but poorly organized amateurs began their efforts to reclaim city government from the boss and political machine as early as the 1870s. They lacked experi-

---

[11] The principal legal case is *People of Michigan ex rel. LeRoy v. Hurlbut,* 24 Mich. 44 (1871). A supporting argument is given in A. M. Eaton, "The Right of Local Self-government," *Harvard Law Review,* 13:441ff.:570ff.:638ff. The reasoning in the Cooley doctrine is effectively rebutted in H. L. McBain, "The Doctrine of an Inherent Right of Local Self-government," *Columbia Law Review,* 16:190ff.:299ff., March and April, 1916.

ence and organizational skills and were often politically naïve. The movement, like its Jacksonian predecessor, was pragmatic, unsystematic, and loosely coordinated. It had no single intellectual leader and was not part of a general ideology, although it did have definite Hamiltonian overtones. Its strength was centered in the middle-class businessman with aid coming from a handful of academicians. The businessmen had a particular motivation for action. They paid a large portion of the taxes to city governments that were not noted for cautious expenditure of public funds, and they lived under their own code of civic obligations.

The difficulties which confronted reformers were at first almost overpowering. Political machines, often headed by a well-known boss, resisted by using any technique that would destroy or discourage the neophytes. The machine was usually well organized, with an army of precinct workers and large numbers of voters who were obligated to it, and hence was generally able to defeat any attempts at reform. The minority of businessmen who turned reformers were in a particularly vulnerable position. A strong political machine in control of the city government had many weapons at hand to injure those who dared to oppose it, as, for example, increasing the assessment of their properties, refusing them permits and licenses, or harassing them through overadministration of fire, health, or other city codes.

Many industrialists and businessmen refused to cooperate with reformers because they followed a belief popular among their kind that it was cheaper to buy off the machine than to fight it. The reformers were also confronted by a public that was almost completely cynical regarding the possibilities for honesty in municipal government, and they had to fight that greatest of all opponents of change, public apathy.

Attitudes and Antidotes. Nevertheless, reforms took place. Some were the result of political accidents and compromises, such as the adoption of constitutional home rule in the Missouri constitutional convention of 1875. Others were the result of organized pressures upon the state legislatures, as in the case of the New York and Massachusetts acts of 1883 establishing civil service for all cities in those states. A nationwide organization, the National Civil Service Reform League, had been organized in 1877. In that same year, the report of a governor's commission in New York condemned the use of national political parties in municipal elections, giving an opening wedge to the concept of election without party designation, an idea that became a favorite of reformers.

In answer to demands for a more modern type of city government, a version of the "strong-mayor" plan was put into effect in Brooklyn in 1880 and Boston in 1885. This plan is one in which the council is restricted to a sharing of the legislative power with the mayor, while the entire administrative structure is integrated under the control of the mayor, who is also a powerful policy maker. By an *integrated* administrative structure, we mean one in which all administrative authority and responsibility is in the hands of a single individual or body. The administrative structure is arranged so that each employee or officer is in theory responsible to some one superior who in turn must answer to his superior, until ultimately department heads are each responsible to a single chief executive.

After about 1820, many cities imitated the American national government by adopting a bicameral (two-house) council and mayoralty appointments subject to council approval. This trend was later abandoned. The strong-mayor plan, however, was thought by reformers to be a much more workable, systematic approach to the problems of city government than was the weak-mayor plan, for the latter had not been conceived of for use in the larger cities of an industrial age. Although varying considerably in detail from one city to another, the strong-mayor plan met with the approval of an increasing number of state legislatures during the 1890s and today is the plan generally used in America's largest cities.

The reform movement developed through organizations on the local level. The Municipal Voters' League was formed in Chicago in 1896, and before long such groups, supported by and made up chiefly of local businessmen, began to appear in nearly all large and medium-sized cities, although they were, of course, not all of equal effectiveness. They were characteristically known as "voters' leagues," "citizens' leagues," "taxpayers' associations," "nonpartisan reform committees," "committees of 100," or similar titles.

An important effort to coordinate these local groups was made through the National Municipal League, which was formed in 1894. This organization became the center, and a veritable symbol, of the movement. In its "model" charters and laws, its booklets and pamphlets, it made available to local groups ammunition that included all the most recently developed reform favorites. It became an effective and respected leader of the struggle.[12]

Another key step toward effective organization was taken with the creation of a Bureau of Municipal Research in New York in

---

[12]The story of the League is told, largely from its own viewpoint, in Frank M. Stewart, *A Half Century of Municipal Reform*, University of California Press, Berkeley, Calif., 1950; see also Richard S. Childs, *Civic Victories*, Harper & Row, Publishers, Incorporated, New York, 1952; and Alfred Willoughby, "The Involved Citizen, A Short History of the National Municipal League: 1894–1969," a 75th Anniversary edition of *National Civic Review*, 58: 519–564, December, 1969.

1906. Dozens of imitations appeared in other cities in the next decade and after.[13]

The municipal research bureaus were often formed with the thought that attempts to elect reform administrations were doomed to failure and that the best way to secure improvement in the administration of cities would be to work with city officials, furnishing them with research data. The bureaus were privately financed. They concentrated upon problems of finance and administration.

More organizations followed: the Proportional Representation League (to further the plan designed to give every significant interest group or political party representation in proportion to its voting strength at the polls); the National Popular Government League (to secure the public ownership of local utilities[14] and to urge the adoption of the *initiative, referendum,* and *recall*[15]); the National Short Ballot Organization (to end the "bedsheet" ballot); taxpayers' leagues (sometimes chiefly to protect the interest of the largest taxpayers); local government committees of chambers of commerce; many different women's clubs; and the League of Women Voters (which does not confine its activities to reform or to local affairs). By the early years of the twentieth century, reform was still largely in the hands of amateurs, but it was now effectively organized and the amateurs were experienced in politics.

Institutions of Reform. Practical results of "reform" began to be made evident. The commission plan of city organization appeared in Galveston in 1901; shortly received the endorsement of many reformers; and in the next few years, it spread rapidly throughout the nation wherever the movement was effective. This plan, which provides for elected commissioners (usually five) who serve collectively as the legislative body and individually as heads of administrative departments, was regarded as an improvement over the weak-mayor system, especially in providing for a shorter ballot and for some semblance of an integrated administrative structure, but it contained fatal defects which caused it to pass into eclipse after about 1917. It was succeeded by the council-manager (or city-manager) plan, which got its start about 1908. The latter is characterized by a governmental structure that places legislative power in a small, preferably lay, council and administrative authority under a professional manager who is appointed by and answerable to the council.

The reform movement also generally included the initiative,

---

[13] Norman N. Gill, *Municipal Research Bureaus,* American Council on Public Affairs, Washington, D.C., 1944.
[14] Public ownership of public utilities was neither socialistic nor radical in concept. It was merely an attempt to eliminate racketeering or gouging private organizations in this area by adopting the standard European practice of public ownership.
[15] These terms are defined on pp. 161–166.

referendum, and recall, although some conservatives at first feared that they would serve the causes of radicals. The *initiative* (which allows the voters themselves to enact legislation or amend city charters without resort to the legislative body) was first authorized by city charter in San Francisco in 1898. This charter also provided for the *referendum* (which requires popular approval, under certain conditions, of acts of the legislative body before they become effective). The *recall* (removal of an elective public official from office by a vote of the people prior to the expiration of his term) seems to have been authorized first by the Los Angeles charter of 1903.[16] In an attempt to write a "model" reform charter, and apparently under the assumption that if a little medicine is good, a lot of medicine is better, reformers in Des Moines combined the commission plan with the initiative, referendum, and recall (1907). For some years the "Des Moines plan" symbolized reform. (As a word of caution to the zealot who may wish to devise an "ideal" solution and then dogmatically defend it as a permanent panacea, it might be noted that in 1949 Des Moines abandoned the "Des Moines plan" and adopted a council-manager form of government.)

During their heyday—the first and second decades of the present century—reformers sponsored other organizational and procedural changes: preferential voting, such as the Bucklin and Ware systems, which did not become popular; reapportionment of urban representation in state legislatures; "model" plans of budgeting, accounting, contract procedures, election procedures, and bond issuing; the direct primary election system of nomination for city officers; and a shorter ballot. Underlying nearly all reform efforts were two basic assumptions: (1) that the political party and elected officials were not to be trusted, and (2) that the principle of "efficient business management" could and should be applied to city government. The muckraker at the turn of the century had shown the low moral tone to which the professional politician of the day had descended, and the reforming businessman wanted no part of it in his city.[17] In contrast, he viewed the structure of the private corporation and the "business methods" of the nineteenth century with pride and respect. He made famous the assertions that "there is no Democratic way to lay a sewer and no Republican way to pave a street," and that running a city is simply a matter of applying the "principles of good business management."

---

[16]See chap. 4 for more details.
[17]The most famous muckraker was Lincoln Steffens. See his *The Shame of the Cities,* McClure, Phillips & Company, New York, 1904, which originally appeared as a series of magazine articles; and his *Autobiography of Lincoln Steffens,* Harcourt, Brace & World, Inc., New York, 1931.

An Appraisal. The reform movement made a contribution to local self-government by recovering a certain amount of responsibility, by replacing the checks and balances of Jacksonian democracy with a more modern system of centralized leadership, and by reestablishing at least a modicum of public respect and confidence in local government. However, it did some damage, too. It placed a misleading overemphasis upon forms and structures of government. It led people astray in its constant preaching to the effect that there are few, if any, partisan issues in city government—that it is a mere matter of "efficient business management." Not only was this concept false, it also did a great deal to discourage interest in local politics.

The reform movement failed, for the most part, to make local government in large cities more representative of a cross section of the community.[18] The old-style politician was rather thoroughly repudiated, true enough, but the balance of power in government was not fundamentally altered. The business community continued to dominate city government. Formerly it had had to do this indirectly, through the machine. Now a new type of control grew up. Businessmen began to participate directly in government. Control of the voter was now achieved, not through the traditional devices, but through control of the media of mass communication. Nonpartisan elections, in particular, made it easy for the conservative business interests to run the city government.

The movement—and especially what is left of it today—has in most places become closely associated in the minds of workingmen and labor leaders with the business community and its interests. Workingmen and labor leaders know that the reformers have produced a more efficient type of government, but they feel that it is often more concerned with saving taxpayers' money than with solving the problems of the community. This situation is partly responsible for the manner in which organized labor has turned to the national government for legislation.

Many of the "citizens' action" groups and bureaus of municipal research (there are exceptions) have changed a good deal from their original character and purpose. A generation ago these groups had life, ideas, and a set of goals planted in the future. Today, many of them have become tools of large taxpayers who want attacks on municipal taxes and essentially on municipal government itself. In seeking to minimize city-government services and expenditures,

[18] The failure of the movement to include a "solid basis in mass support" was pointed out many years ago by John A. Vieg, "Advice for Municipal Reformers," *Public Opinion Quarterly,* 1:87–92, October, 1937.

they have in effect become organizations *opposing* municipal government.

CURRENT THEORIES OF CITY GOVERNMENT

The City and the New Deal. The worst depression in the history of the United States began in the autumn of 1929 and did not actually end until the country began preparing for war about a decade later. The election of 1932 produced a huge protest vote that resulted in (1) the election of Franklin D. Roosevelt and (2), as it proved, the New Deal. The New Deal attempted to do at least two things simultaneously: to combat the Depression and to effect social reforms. It developed programs for almost every area where extensive demands for improvement were heard: social security for the aged and dependent; farm-price supports; slum clearance; soil conservation; protection for organized labor; emergency "make-work"; and a host of others.

The farmer, worker, banker, small businessman—almost everyone, in fact—began turning to the national government for whatever aid they felt was needed. The states and cities were bypassed, either because their financial resources or their legal authority was hopelessly inadequate, because they were unwilling to tackle the problems, or because the scope of the problems was so broad that they could be handled adequately only by the national government.

However, some effort was made by the New Deal to utilize local agencies. PWA projects (such as new city halls, water standpipes, sewerage systems, bridges, even public housing units) were determined upon the approval of recommended plans submitted by local governments. Perhaps the most outstanding case of New Deal reliance upon municipalities came as a result of the United States Housing Act of 1937.[19]

Contemporary Theory for the Sprawling Metropolis. Municipal self-government faces a problem of finding a satisfactory contemporary niche for itself. The preceding brief review of American theory indicates that the concepts of the Jacksonian frontiersman and the resulting institutions (such as the weak-mayor system and the city boss) are not appropriate for an industrialized, urbanized, specialized, technological society. The legal theory of an "inherent right" of local self-government is quite dead though the yearning for local control by smaller units within the larger metropolitan whole is clearly not dead. The efficiency and economy movement

---

[19] See chap. 18 for a closer look at housing.

did much to modernize local government. But its modernity was that of fifty years ago, before the advent of either powerful organized labor or the social-service state. The movement never had a strong base in mass support, and its institutions have not often included in their membership a cross section of the general public.

The trend has not been toward abandoning municipal government as meaningless but rather toward blending its activities into those of the state and national governments. This is true for both suburbia with its variety of subunits crying out for some degree of area-wide coordination and planning and also for the central city whose slums, crime, and poverty are seen as problems of the whole of American society. In the areas of health, highways, education, welfare, recreation, and others, the cities and villages have increasingly worked in cooperation with the higher levels of government. They have come closer together, not only through the use of grants-in-aid, but also because modern means of transportation and communication have ended community isolation, and because much contemporary policy making tends to be dominated by the values and goals of professional administrators—professionals who increasingly man the bureaucracies at all three levels of government and who share the concepts of what constitutes preferred school administration, sanitation programs, highway plans, and the like. The municipality has not ceased to be a decision-making center, but it no longer makes its decisions alone, and the decisions that emerge are increasingly based on the policy goals of professional administrators rather than of amateur grass-roots leaders.

How do today's urbanites view city government? What do they consider to be its proper functions? There are probably many images of local government. Few of them have been identified, but one study has tentatively isolated the following images:[20]

1.   *The City as an Instrument of Community Growth.* Those who see the municipality in this guise believe that it has a duty to help the community to expand in both population and wealth. This is the "boosterism" that is traditional in America, stemming from the frontier notions that growth is progress, bigness is goodness, and that a community must expand or die. The merchant, banker, newspaper editor, chamber of commerce manager, and city bureaucrat all stand to gain from growth, and they are all likely to see the city government's highest duty as that of furthering it. This viewpoint is typically found in the smaller middle-sized cities and sometimes

[20] This material borrows from Oliver P. Williams and Charles R. Adrian, *Four Cities,* University of Pennsylvania Press, Philadelphia, 1963.

in blue-collar or even white-collar suburbia, where financial diffi-culties have spotlighted the need for growth of an industrial tax base.

2. *The City as the Provider of Life's Amenities.* In a wealthy nation with a high standard of living, Americans are conscious of themselves as conspicuous consumers. Their status in an impersonal society is symbolized in large part by the consumption items they can afford. To an increasing extent—above all in suburbia—govern-ment is viewed as an agency for providing not merely the necessities of life, but for adding to the comforts of urban living. Supporters of this image of municipal government reject growth as the highest goal, or sometimes as any goal at all. They often prefer the smallness of the suburb to the growing metropolis, the expenditure of funds in residential neighborhoods to outlays benefiting Main Street.

3. *The City Government as a Caretaker.* This is the view of the small-government, low-tax advocate. He sees government at all levels as best when it survives at a minimal level, providing only those functions that are ancient or—from his viewpoint—essential. Mu-nicipalities may patrol the streets against thieves and purify the water supply, but they should not seek expansion of functions into new areas. The advocate of caretaker government believes that the private allocation of personal resources is invariably to be preferred to governmental allocation. The caretaker philosophy appeals par-ticularly, not only to the person who prefers minimal government at all levels, but to retired persons on fixed incomes, to the marginal homeowner who can barely afford to keep himself in that prestigeful category, and to the person whose neighborhood already has a full quota of local services and is better supplied than are the poorer neighborhoods or the newer areas of the community. The bypassed rural trading center and the overextended and marginal suburb most often have citizens reflecting this view.

4. *The City as Arbiter of Conflicting Interests.* Those who hold to this view do not see local government as having a single dominant mission, but rather they consider it an umpire with responsibility to allocate the scarce resources of the community in such a way that all interested groups get a share. The self-conscious minority-group leaders, seeing no prospect for controlling the local government by themselves or in an effective coalition, are likely to take this point of view, as did the traditional political boss. The psychic or numerical majority can realistically advocate a concept of the "gen-eral good" or the "public interest," but a permanent minority can only seek access, and a set of rules that will help to guarantee it for them. Such a view is most frequently found in the large city,

particularly among minority ethnic groups concentrated in one area of the city.[21]

All these images, and no doubt others, probably exist in any community simultaneously. Rarely would a community larger than a small town demonstrate such total agreement that a single type would stand in unrivaled control over the minds of policy makers. In most cases, a variety of images serve as frames of reference for officeholders and for citizens as they vote on referendum matters. These ideas about the proper role of municipal government serve to channel the kinds of decisions that are made and the way in which they are made in the contemporary American city.

[21] For an illustration of the community-growth theory, listen to almost any talk by a chamber of commerce manager. For the caretaker idea, see A. J. Vidich and Joseph Bensman, *Small Town in Mass Society,* Princeton University Press, Princeton, N.J., 1958. The interest in amenities in Park Forest, Ill., is described in William H. Whyte, Jr., *The Organization Man,* Anchor Books, Doubleday & Company, Inc., New York, 1956. The arbiter function in "Paper City" is outlined in Kenneth W. Underwood, *Protestant and Catholic,* Beacon Press, Boston, 1957.

SELECTED READINGS

Abcarian, Gilbert, and Sherman M. Stanage: "Alienation and the Radical Right," *Journal of Politics,* 27:776–796, November, 1965. (Right-wing extremists suffer from political alienation and adopt a well-defined political style.)

Banfield, Edward C.: *The Unheavenly City,* Little, Brown and Company, Boston, 1968. (A slashing attack on the assumptions made by liberals concerning the causes and cures of poverty and racial tensions.)

Brown, Robert E.: *Middle-class Democracy and the Revolution in Massachusetts,* Cornell University Press, Ithaca, N.Y., 1955. (Reviews and revises theories about colonial democracy.)

Childs, Richard S.: *Civic Victories,* Harper & Row, Publishers, Incorporated, New York, 1952. (A statement of ideology by a leader of the efficiency and economy movement.)

Cox, Harvey: *The Secular City,* The Macmillan Company, New York, 1965.

Dahlberg, Jane S.: *The New York Bureau of Municipal Research,* New York University Press, New York, 1966. (Covers the work of a pioneer agency that connected academia with reform.)

Donaldson, Scott: *The Suburban Myth,* Columbia University Press, New York, 1969. (Argues that intellectuals have unjustly and inaccurately portrayed life in suburbia.)

Gelfant, Blanche: *The American City Novel,* University of Oklahoma Press, Norman, Okla., 1954. (Analyzes works of novelists who write about the city "as a distinctive and peculiarly modern way of life that has shaped the writer's vision and influenced the forms of his art.")

Hugins, Walter: *Jacksonian Democracy and the Working Class,* Stanford University Press, Stanford, Calif., 1960.

Long, Norton E.: *The Polity,* Rand McNally & Company, Chicago, 1962. (Includes a criticism of the efficiency and economy ideology, pp. 165-175.)

Look, May 16, 1967 issue. (A special issue devoted to life in suburbia.)

Lowry, Ritchie P.: *Who's Running This Town?* Harper & Row, Publishers, Incorporated, New York, 1965. (An examination of small-town ideology.)

Lyford, Joseph P.: *The Talk in Vandalia,* Harper Colophon Books, Harper & Row, Publishers, Incorporated, New York, 1964. (The ideology of an Illinois town of 5,500 where "the main strength of the past has become a problem for the future.")

MacDonald, Dwight: "Cit," *The New Yorker,* Aug. 22, 1953. (A profile of George H. Hallet, Jr., longtime proponent of proportional representation.)

Nisbet, Robert A.: *Community and Power,* Oxford University Press, New York, 1962. (Formerly titled *The Quest for Community.*)

Schlesinger, Arthur M., Jr.: *The Age of Jackson,* Little, Brown and Company, Boston, 1945. (A background picture of the era when ideas for governing the industrial city developed.)

Sherman, Richard B. (ed.): *The Negro and the City,* Prentice-Hall, Inc., Englewood Cliffs, N.J., 1970.

Steffens, Lincoln: *Autobiography of Lincoln Steffens,* Harcourt, Brace & World, Inc., New York, 1931. (By the most famous muckraker.)

————: *The Shame of the Cities,* McClure, Phillips & Company, New York, 1904.

Stewart, Frank M.: *A Half Century of Municipal Reform,* University of California Press, Berkeley, Calif., 1950. (A history of the reformist National Municipal League.)

Syed, Anwar: *The Political Theory of American Local Government,* Random House, Inc., New York, 1966. (Many of the elements of the ideology of local self-government, attributed in this text to the Jacksonian period, are here traced back to Jefferson.)

Underwood, Kenneth W.: *Protestant and Catholic,* Beacon Press, Boston, 1957. (Ideological conflict in a New England community.)

Vidich, A. J., and Jerome Bensman: *Small Town in Mass Society,* Princeton University Press, Princeton, N.J., 1958. (Ideology in an upstate New York village.)

White, Morton, and Lucia White: *The Intellectual versus the City,* Mentor Books, New American Library of World Literature, Inc., New York, 1962. (The intellectual tradition of suspicion of cities through the centuries.)

Whyte, William H., Jr.: *The Organization Man,* Anchor Books, Doubleday & Company, Inc., New York, 1956. (The community ideology of the corporate white-collar worker.)

Williams, Oliver P., and Charles R. Adrian: *Four Cities,* University of Pennsylvania Press, Philadelphia, 1963. (Contemporary images of the proper function of city governments.)

Wood, Robert: *Suburbia,* Houghton Mifflin Company, Boston, 1959. (A theory concerning the appeal of suburbia.)

B THE
POLITICAL
MACHINERY

CHAPTER
3 ELECTED OFFICIALS AND COMMUNITY LEADERS

Politics is the catalyst that changes citizens into public officials and individual wishes into public policy. It is essential to democracy. On the local scene it operates largely in the same manner as it does for state and national governments. A chief difference has been that more of the major political actors do not make a full-time career of politics. Otherwise only the emphasis and the relative balances of forces are changed.

THE NATURE OF THE POLITICAL PROCESS

Politics as Demand and Supply. In order to have an understanding of the nature of the political process, it is necessary to be able to picture it not as the principal purpose of a certain type of human activity but rather as a *by-product*. Human life in Western culture is a struggle for power, prestige, and security. Some people, in their search, turn to politics and attempt to secure these values through governmental action. They become the relatively small group of politically active citizens. The general public, politically passive on most issues, may occasionally express itself on policy choices through elections or an aroused public debate that may spread out into community conflict. More frequently a collection of specialized publics or clientele groups seeks services from government in order to help themselves. Or, alternatively, they seek to *prevent* government from launching certain types of services if they feel that their goals can be reached by some other type of activity.[1]

The politician, then, is a person who in his pursuit of a successful political career seeks to determine what some portion of the public is asking of government and to make this available to them if possible. (As a leader, he may also seek to determine what the general public or specialized publics potentially may want and seek to "sell" it to the voters.) Since the individual normally has a certain amount of choice in selecting public officers and is free to join various groups that exert pressure upon government, government is to some degree responsible to the people—the essential characteristic of a democracy.

The Role of Ideology. The political process occurs within the boundaries set by the currently popular ideologies. For many years questions of water and air pollution were largely off the local agenda, since the ideology then current argued that such questions should be beyond the sphere of governmental policy. In the same way, questions which once might have been considered properly on the local agenda, such as the proper length of women's skirts or the wearing of shorts, are no longer considered by most citizens as within the sphere of governmental action. Decision makers thus largely choose policies consistent with current ideological beliefs, but this allows considerable latitude, particularly today when it is believed by many that pressing problems are subject to amelioration or solution if government applies scientific knowledge to them.

Politicians, Influentials and Citizens. In every city some public officials set the tax rate, decide which streets will be paved, how marijuana laws will be enforced, and who the new park will be named for. Such governmental decisions are controlled by political officeholders—those politicians who are successful in getting elected. In making such public policy, the political official allocates the scarce resources of power, prestige, and security to some citizens often at the expense of others. Thus, the student of politics wants to know: how are these policy decisions made and what are the effects? This chapter begins the examination of the first question. Later chapters examine the second.

---

[1] See the writings of Harold Hasswell, especially *Psychopathology and Politics,* The University of Chicago Press, Chicago, 1930; and *Power and Personality,* W. W. Norton and Company, Inc., New York, 1948.

Sometimes public officials in making policy decisions follow largely their own policy or career goals. Often they are influenced and even may be coerced by others. It is the aspect of influence and power relations that properly has most concerned the students of local politics.

Democratic theory assumes the primary influence will be by the general public. We will examine in greater detail this influence in a later chapter. At this point we emphasize only that political participation involves both material and psychic costs, and this fact is related to the degree and type of political activity that one can expect from any citizen. Citizens have other matters to concern themselves with rather than whether an expressway will be built and, if so, where and how it will be constructed. Just the costs of gaining the information required to make an intelligent decision are often greater than most citizens wish to pay. Note also that some citizens are clearly advantaged in that because of education or position in the community, the costs of getting information about the proposed expressway are less. Also some are advantaged by being better able to pay the costs of participation or may actually have to pay less. Not everyone can take off from work and attend a daytime civic meeting or even take time off to vote when lines before the polling booth may be shortest. Not everyone can afford the risks of running for office, or being elected, or taking the time off from a regular job that such election may require.

The general citizen thus is limited in how much and when he will wish to participate in influencing the policy decisions officials make. The whole body of citizens cannot sit as a continuous town meeting to discuss every issue as it arises. The individual must depend on representatives, knowing that the cost even of influencing these very often may be high. But the citizens as a whole do reserve for themselves judgment of the results of official decision making (that is the power to throw the rascals out and possibly throw new rascals in) and the right to intervene as individuals or groups where they feel their own interests are directly affected.

Thus, commonly, the officials face a united and aroused general public rather rarely. More frequently they deal with a number of specialized constituencies and interest groups. In this chapter we are concerned with the political official himself, and then with those citizens whose social or economic status may give them such control over political resources that officials will consult them on major policy. Such citizens are seen by some as a local political elite or power structure. In the chapters that follow, we examine urban interest groups and then the influence of the general public.

THE URBAN ELECTED OFFICIAL

Urban politics differs most markedly from national politics in the degree to which it is politically unprofessionalized. In large cities, a few offices, notably the mayor's and sometimes the city council, are held by men who make politics a full-time career. Here one finds such pros as Mayor John Lindsay of New York: once a Congressman, prominently mentioned for Governor, Senator, or even Vice President or President. More commonly the mayor, even in middle-sized cities, and councilmen, even in large cities, are filling their public offices at the same time that they are running a local shoe store or are a middle-level executive at the local Thingemabob plant. The overwhelming number of urban elected officials are political amateurs. They seek no career in politics.

In American folklore, in newspaper editorials, in magazine articles, in political campaigns, and in suburban gossip, it has been common to picture the nineteenth-century city boss and machine as if they were a contemporary phenomenon. To many citizens, the boss and his ward heelers are the epitome of the professional politician. It is thus perhaps appropriate to begin a discussion of political office-holders by examining this type of political professional.

The Machine Type of Political Professional of the Past. It is not uncommon even today to hear the phrase "boss-ridden cities." Actually, the boss and machine performed a necessary social function in their day, but they have outlived their usefulness and have been disappearing from the American scene. William Marcy Tweed of New York, "Ed" Flynn of the Bronx, "Big Bill" Thompson of Chicago, "Doc" Ames of Minneapolis, "Abe" Ruef of San Francisco, and a host of others have left the front pages of the newspapers and are taking their place in the history books, where they will become a romantic, if not exactly an honored, memory.

There is probably no need to describe in detail the method of operation of the old-time machine. A few points should be made concerning it, however.

In the first place, the machine did not exist *in spite* of society. It existed because it filled a real need. It served as a highly effective, if inefficient, system of social welfare. To the poor in the slums of cities, the machine provided needed services: It found jobs, or tided the family over during periods of unemployment; it buried the dead; it cared for widows and orphans; it organized youth activities; it provided a multitude of neighborhood social functions; it contributed to the churches of poor neighborhoods; it provided bail bonds and legal advice; it furnished assistance in finding housing and tried to help tenants talk their landlords out of rent increases. It provided literally hundreds of services, the need for which was not recognized by much of the middle class.

Secondly, the machine was a product of universal suffrage, perhaps its first important manifestation. The services provided were offered in the expectation that the recipients would cast their ballots in support of the machine. If the ordinary worker in the slum had not been enfranchised, as he was in the 1830s and 1840s, the pattern of urban politics during the remainder of the nineteenth century would have been quite different from what it was.

Thirdly, the machine raised the great amounts of money that were needed for the services it provided (and often for the personal profit of its leaders) by acting as a broker for the city's services. It raised most of its money from businessmen and industrialists, and owing to the then-current belief that it was cheaper to buy off the machine than to fight it, the business community often worked hand in glove with the machine.

The organization raised its money in a great variety of ways. It made available, for a price, building permits, all types of licenses, utilities franchises, and ordinances that might be helpful to a business. Sometimes it resorted to simple blackmail or the shakedown racket. Much money was made through contract rebates. Contracts were granted to a firm that was working closely with the machine with the understanding that part of the profit would be returned to the machine. Municipal employees were very commonly assessed part of their pay, and other funds could be raised from the purchase of land by inside members of the organization for resale to the city. It was this type of profiteering that was made famous as "honest graft" by George Washington Plunkitt of Tammany Hall. It was Plunkitt who stated the code of the more sincere organization worker when he said, "If my worst enemy was given the job of writin' my epitaph when I'm gone, he couldn't do more than write 'George W. Plunkitt. He Seen His Opportunities, and He Took 'Em.'"[2]

The Decline of Bossism. Opportunities, as seen by Plunkitt, began to fade away as the effects of the reform movement came to be felt. The decline of the boss and machine began to accelerate after World War II, in particular, and by 1950, the boss and machine in almost every American city had been either destroyed, badly mangled, or profoundly modified in its pattern of behavior.

There were many reasons for this. Since World War I, there has

[2] See the fascinating profile by William L. Riordon, *Plunkitt of Tammany Hall*, Doubleday & Company, Inc., Garden City, N.Y., 1905.

been a steady decline in the percentage of foreign-born in American cities, and it had been to the needs of this group that machines had particularly appealed. Blacks and other rural-to-urban migrants likewise became less subject to machine control after they became more sophisticated in urban ways. Another factor was the high employment after 1940, which allowed large numbers of people to escape the extreme poverty that had forced them to be partly dependent upon the machine.

The general adoption of the officially printed secret ballot made it more difficult for the machine to stuff ballot boxes, falsify election returns, or conduct other election frauds. Lincoln Steffens tells us that the voting lists of Philadelphia at the beginning of the century were padded "with the names of dead dogs, children and non-existent persons." Success in such practices has become increasingly difficult in recent years. Yet it was not so very many years ago—in 1936—that the *St. Louis Post-Dispatch* won a Pulitzer prize for uncovering 45,000 false registrations in that city. Charges that the candidate of the party or faction not in power has been "counted out" in close election contests because the in-group controlled the election machinery continue to be heard today, and it is reasonable to expect that not all of them are unfounded.

The reform movement in general damaged machine government by helping to arouse potential members of opposition groups and by rallying businessmen to fight the machine instead of buying it off. The rise to power of organized labor and the growing independence of black leaders have upset the traditional balance of control in many cities.

Lastly, and perhaps of greatest importance, a modern and professionalized approach to the problems of social welfare has taken away from the political machine its principal means for achieving loyalty and support. The development of government control of such functions as workmen's compensation, unemployment compensation, old-age pensions, old-age insurance, Medicare, and their administration by professionally trained civil servants, rather than by political hacks, proved a mortal wound to the old-time machine.

Machines in Decay. Beginning with the reform movement around the beginning of the century, an entire procession of machine defeats has paraded across the front pages of the newspapers of the nation. The one-time organizations in St. Louis, Minneapolis, and San Francisco are long dead. The once-powerful Republican machine in Cincinnati was defeated and permanently modified by reform efforts in the elections of 1924 and those that followed. The castle of Thomas J. Pendergast and his Democratic machine in Kansas City came crashing down in 1939 and today lies in ruins.[3] Tammany Hall in New York has been losing ground since the 1932 Seabury investigation of the James J. Walker administration. It was greatly weakened during the long period when its enemy, Fiorello H. La Guardia, served as mayor.[4] Tammany has undergone considerable modification, and today, despite the fact that reformers still denounce it in each campaign, operates with a far more modern concept of politics than it did in former years, and is only a shadow of its old self.

By the time of World War II, bosses and machines were thoroughly outmoded. Nearly all those that remained were liquidated during the period of postwar readjustment. The Republican machine of Philadelphia, which had enjoyed uninterrupted control of that city since shortly after the Civil War, lost important ground in the election of 1949 and was thoroughly routed in 1951, when it lost control of the mayor's office and of a majority of the council to a reform Democratic group.[5] The old Democratic Kelly-Nash machine, now under Mayor Richard J. Daley, still held control of the city of Chicago in 1971. Despite much criticism from many sources, a serious scandal in the police department in 1959, and harsh criticism during the 1968 Democratic National Convention, the Kelly-Nash organization is regarded as having brought Chicago politics closer to prevailing urban patterns in the years after World War II. The same is true of the organization of Daniel P. O'Connell of Albany, New York. By 1971, its leader had spent fifty years in politics without losing a city-wide election and was then 85 years old.

James Michael Curley of Boston long ruled that city by building up a Robin Hood legend about himself. He was known as a builder of schools, a provider of jobs, and a man who got things done. He was strongly supported by the great bulk of the minority ethnic groups in the city and was so effective in personal contacts that in 1945, 10 percent of his supporters claimed to know him *personally*.[6] Yet in 1949, a reform group called the New Boston Committee defeated him, elected a mayor, and took control of the council. In the next election, Curley again lost.

[3] Miniature portraits of some of the more recent city machines are painted in John Gunther, *Inside U.S.A.*, Harper & Row, Publishers, Incorporated, New York, 1947.

[4] See the views of La Guardia in his article, "Bosses Are Bunk," *The Atlantic Monthly*, 180:21–24, July, 1947. On New York, see Wallace S. Sayre and Herbert Kaufman, *Governing New York City*, Russell Sage Foundation, New York, 1960.

[5] See James Reichley, *The Art of Government: Reform and Organization Politics in Philadelphia*, The Fund for the Republic, New York, 1959; Joseph D. Crumlish, *A City Finds Itself: The Philadelphia Home Rule Charter Movement*, Wayne State University Press, Detroit, Mich., 1959.

[6] Jerome S. Bruner and S. J. Korchin, "The Boss and the Vote," *Public Opinion Quarterly*, 10:1–23, Spring, 1946. See also J. M. Curley, *I'd Do It Again*, Prentice-Hall, Inc., Englewood Cliffs N.J., 1957; Joseph Dinneen, *The Purple Shamrock*, W. W. Norton & Company, Inc., New York, 1949; and a fictionalized life of a Curley-like boss, Edward O'Conner, *The Last Hurrah*, Little, Brown and Company, Boston, 1956.

In 1940, Dayton D. McKean wrote that the Hague machine in Jersey City "is so nearly perfect that other machines may be measured against it."[7] Yet Hague's candidate was defeated in 1950 and in succeeding elections, although the destruction of his machine did not signal the rise of a reform administration, as happened in many other cities. In Memphis, Edward H. Crump managed to keep an effective machine together until his death in 1954. But like so many who exercise power for a long time, he had made no adequate provision for a successor, and in the following year his heirs were not even able to field a candidate for mayor.

There can be no doubt that the nineteenth-century machine system has outlived its usefulness. In some cities, party organization is still viable, though less effective than it once was. A study of Gary attributed about 5 percent of the presidential vote in 1956 to precinct organizational activities.[8] Another study of New Jersey counties found party organization on the decline but still important as broker between citizens and government, particularly in black and Puerto Rican areas.[9] Some of the techniques of old-style machines have been adopted by a few organizations of a new suburban, middle-class type, such as those in Dearborn, Michigan, under Orville L. Hubbard and, for many years, in Nassau County, New York.[10]

The Political Professional of Today. The mayors of most large and a few middle-sized cities and sometimes a few of the councilmen devote full time to their professional political careers. Some, like Mayor Carl Stokes of Cleveland, moved into the job from the state legislature. Some were promoted from the council. Samuel Yorty of Los Angeles and John Lindsay of New York left Congress to take their jobs. A few like Jerome Cavanaugh of Detroit held no previous major office. In a few large cities, ways are still found to make the job of councilman a political sinecure in the style of the old-time machine. In most this is not the case.

Today's elected professionals depend on public relations more than on political organization. This has meant that they must be careful about their impact on public opinion through newspapers, radio, and television, being as concerned about their "image" as any Senator or presidential hopeful. At the same time, they are required to have a sophistication about urban policy problems. They are supposed to initiate programs to deal with such conditions as

---

[7] Dayton D. McKean, *The Boss: The Hague Machine in Action,* Houghton Mifflin Company, Boston, 1940.
[8] Phillips Cutright and Peter H. Rossi, "Grass Roots Politicians and the Vote," *American Sociological Review,* 23:171–179, April, 1958.
[9] Richard T. Frost, "Stability and Change in Local Party Politics," *Public Opinion Quarterly,* 25:221–235, Summer, 1961.
[10] E. E. Malkin, "Dearborn's Madcap Mayor," *Coronet,* 44:66–70, September, 1958; and a case study on Hubbard in the first two editions of this book.

urban blight, racial conflict, crime, and pollution. No longer can they run on the good government platform of "I will manage the local sewage plant in a more efficient and businesslike way than Torkelson." More is expected of the new breed of urban political professionals.

In Chapters 10 and 11 we detail some of the characteristics of this modern type of urban official. Here let us only note a phenomenon increasingly associated with them. They are dependent on the civil service professional within city government as well as the expert outside. Through professional organizations and panels of national urban groups, the mayors and even councilmen meet technically trained experts including many from universities. It is common for even professional politicians viewed by the general public as close to the old boss system mold, such as Mayor Daley of Chicago, to have as their assistants university trained aides or professors on loan from a nearby university. (Daley turned to the universities for the head of his police department.) Governing a big city is no longer a task that can be wholly trusted to political amateurs or political hacks.

The Amateur Politician. Politics dominated by amateurs means participation by those who can afford to take time off from their jobs, by the bored, and by those with free time on their hands. For these, costs of participation are relatively less. In suburbia, housewives tired of the routine of diapers and chauffeuring may, through the League of Women Voters or some other local organization, become active in politics and finally candidates for the council. The retired businessman is often attracted to the part-time political office and often makes a major contribution to his community through such service. But most of the amateur officials are likely to be local businessmen who are particularly concerned with the decisions made by their local city councils since they may intimately affect business on Main Street and in the shopping center.

Running for local public office, even for those who can afford it, is not all gravy, however. A Los Angeles *Times* reporter drew this composite picture of Candidate X, based on interviews with a number of amateur civic-minded citizens running for office: Two men running for positions on the Board of Education had amateur staff members who passed out a press release with misspelled words. But most such candidates had few supporters to help their campaign. They had no one to drive them about, write statements for them, put up lawn signs, or collect money. Rather they went themselves door-to-door by foot. The reporter described one candidate's gripe: "After I walked up the longest driveway in the world, the woman of the house said, 'I'm busy, can't you come back tomorrow?'" But that was the least of his trouble. "The dogs are terrible. Walk up to the door, ring, and the dogs start barking." Sometimes citizens have their own messages. "I handed one guy a brochure and he gave me a Bible," said Candidate X. Publicity was also a big problem. There were 122 candidates for council and television does not have enough time for them all. One candidate wanted to make a major statement. A small, local radio station offered him 15 seconds. He pleaded with the manager, saying the statement was complex and he needed more time. The manager relented, boosted it up to 40 seconds but would run it only once during the day. Getting money was difficult, the best sources being hard headed, unemotional contributors who did not want to waste a dime. Local businessmen and city employee groups, for example, usually give only to the incumbent because he usually wins. The reporter summed it up: "It all adds up to a difficult task. 'It's like swimming the Pacific Ocean' said Candidate X."[11]

A distinguishing feature of urban politics in cities where most politicians are pursuing other careers for their livelihood is the relative absence of the notion of conflict of interest. The local suburban businessman may sit on the Board of Review (which reviews grievances on local assessment of property for tax purposes) and see nothing wrong with participating in a decision concerning a bank or business with which he is associated. Not only is this not regarded as questionable but it may be positively defended on the basis that he has a greater knowledge about such matters than does the average citizen. Thus zoning boards may be dominated by the realtors, or councils deciding on parking lots and one-way streets may be controlled by local businessmen.

But a politics by amateurs also has some advantages, particularly if combined with professional civil service management of the day to day administration. The amateur does occasionally raise new issues and does often identify with the consumer of government services. Many such citizens have rendered great service for what are basically minimal returns. Chapters 8 and 9 on urban executives and the city council further discuss these contributions.

LOCAL COMMUNITY LEADERS: A POWER STRUCTURE?

Not enough is as yet known about those who are viewed by their fellow citizens as "leaders" of the community. Leadership is an intrinsic part of group existence, and community leaders may through

---

[11] Bill Boyarsky, "Race for Local Office, A Job of Pure Drudgery," Los Angeles *Times*, Mar. 17, 1971.

their influence with political officials actually make the decisions. Furthermore, group action generates power. Those who take a positive interest in any problem are likely to have a considerable advantage over those who are passive and apathetic. And, of course, those who feel they have the most at stake are also likely to be the ones who become the most active in political decision making.[12]

But it is also possible that persons who appear to be policy leaders, even to the extent of seemingly dominating the decisions of those holding public office, are really only verbalizers. That is, they merely say, as symbolic leaders of the community, the things that are already widely believed in the community. If this is the case, the same policies might have resulted whether or not these persons had taken any action in seeking to have policies developed. Leading bankers, merchants, realtors, and chamber of commerce secretaries in small towns or middle-sized cities are certain to have their remarks given considerable publicity through newspapers, radio, and television, and may thus seem to be real leaders. Merchant princes and bankers are sometimes listened to because they are natural leaders or because of the deference they receive as a result of their prestigeful positions. But their preferences as to public policy may be forestalled, for example, by implacable resistance from workingmen responding to a labor leader. This leader's own status position will probably be a modest one, and his technique not one of oppressive coercion but merely of pointing out to the union membership the consequences for them of a proposed line of action.

If community leaders had nearly absolute control, there would probably be consensus and little community conflict—only a disgruntled few would resist. In many cases, however, leaders have to do more than take a position. They must launch a selling campaign and must overcome opposition from competing leaders. A small amount of knowledge and drive—with a purpose—can sometimes project a relatively low-status person into a leadership position. He finds power in the community unused and seeks to exploit it. When he does so, his action spurs dominant leaders into counterattack. A conflict ensues that may not only get out of control for the initiators of action but may bring back memories of countless old (and often irrelevant) conflicts from the community's past.

[12] See Robert S. Lynd, "Power in American Society as Resource and Problem," in Arthur Kornhauser (ed.), *Problems of Power in American Democracy,* Wayne State University Press, Detroit, Mich., 1957, pp. 1–45; Robert and Helen Lynd, *Middletown,* Harcourt, Brace, New York, 1929; and Talcott Parsons, *Structure and Process in Modern Societies,* The Free Press of Glencoe, New York, 1960, chap. 6. A good bibliography of power-structure studies may be found in Robert O. Schulze and Leonard U. Blumberg, "The Determination of Local Power Elites," *American Journal of Sociology,* 63:290–296, November, 1957; and Charles Press, *Main Street Politics,* Institute for Community Development, Michigan State University, East Lansing, Mich., 1962.

Power Elites or Pluralism. The most continuous debate that has concerned students of local governmental decision making is whether the elected public officials respond primarily to the actions of a few persons of wealth and status or whether a pluralist situation exists in which political decision makers compete with each other as well as responding to a variety of specialized group pressures.

The boss and the political machine became a local governmental prototype of elite rule. Enterprising newsmen, like the turn-of-the-century muckraker Lincoln Steffens, showed that the boss was often part of or cooperated closely with an elite of wealth. As we have noted, however, some students have also argued that the boss was at the same time able to respond to citizen needs of immigrants so that the elitist view is an oversimplified one in this case.

In the 1920s, the first notable sociological study of community decision making, that of Robert and Helen Lynd, argued that in Middletown (Muncie, Indiana) the pattern of elite influence was somewhat less crude than boss rule but just as effective. Local government was viewed as dominated by the owners of the major local industry, and its officials were encouraged to do nothing about issues of concern to the public. Students of today holding this view argue that questions important to the average citizen are excluded from the local government's agenda in many communities, so that what these city governments do is largely inconsequential. Thus, it is argued that when city councils do not take action on such pressing problems as local air and water pollution, residential segregation of blacks, or the conditions of housing in the local slums, it is because an elite behind the scenes does not want them to and stops them either by direct action or by its control over the opinions being expressed in the local newspaper, church pulpits, etc. Such latter control is described as the mobilization of bias in the community.

Other students examining specific public decisions, as for example Robert Dahl in his study of New Haven, Connecticut, found that the members of the local economic elite had not participated greatly in shaping decisions which made major changes in the community and spent considerable amounts of local tax funds. Among such actions examined were those on urban renewal and public education. His study suggests that significant political action was being taken on major problems because political officeholders hoped to make a reputation and to carve out a further career in politics. Lack of political action of local government, where it occurs, is explained by students sharing Dahl's views less as the result of elite influence as of the absence of a structured political competition, the influence of specialized interests, or even the acquiescence or concurrence of local majorities which are not concerned with the problems of local air and water pollution, the effects of residential segregation of blacks, or the conditions of housing in local slums.

An additional explanation of the pattern, a view from which our own analysis has borrowed heavily, is that of Norton Long. He argues that local politics and policy is less the result of conspiracy or plan on the part of either community influentials or officeholders than it is a by-product of the uncoordinated acts of many persons. He sees it resulting from many individuals each pursuing private interests and no one concerned about what the overall result will be.[13]

At this point the battle among scholars is joined. The major agreement is on two facts: that relatively few citizens participate actively in local politics and this is particularly true of those who earn substandard wages or have low educational attainment, and secondly, that different patterns of elite or pluralist influence may exist in different types of communities. No student espousing one view, however, has ever found a community operating as those of the other view would claim it does. (Perhaps this is because of a difference in unarticulated assumptions about power. Those using an elitist analysis assume that the elites rule strictly in their own interests and "exploit" nonelites. Pluralists make no such assumption.)

Major Findings of Community Studies. The student examining his own urban area might keep in mind the following points in regard to the political power structure as it exists or is supposed to exist:

1.   Some economically powerful leaders, in particular the managers and top executives of local plants of nationwide corporations, may refuse to become involved in community activities of any kind not directly affecting the company, lest enemies are unnecessarily made. Thus some of the persons who, because of great economic power, might be expected to be important decision makers exert little or no influence on decisions regarding community public policy.[14] Heads of locally owned firms, on the other hand, are likely to be both active and powerful locally.[15]

2.   Power structures may not necessarily be constructed in the shape of pyramids, although some studies have found such shapes.[16]

[13] Norton E. Long, "The Local Community as an Ecology of Games," The Polity, Rand McNally, Chicago, 1962.
[14] See Peter H. Rossi, "Community Decision-making," Administrative Science Quarterly, 1:415–443, March, 1957; Robert O. Schulze, Economic Dominance and Public Leadership, University Microfilms, Ann Arbor, Mich., 1956; Robert O. Schulze, "The Role of Economic Dominants in Community Power Structure," American Sociological Review, 23:3–9, February, 1958; Harry M. Scoble, "Leadership Hierarchies and Political Issues in a New England Town," in Morris Janowitz (ed.), Community Political Systems, The Free Press of Glencoe, New York, 1959. Middle, as distinguished from top, management is likely to be active, however, especially in the suburbs, according to William H. Whyte, Jr., The Organization Man, Simon and Schuster, Inc., New York, 1956. The activities of these men are less likely to be interpreted as official company policy.
[15] See city "Alpha" in Williams and Adrian, op. cit., as an example.
[16] See the Mills and Hunter studies, op. cit.

It is quite possible to have power structures that do not lead to a few top leaders but instead have a polynucleated structure with various leaders, each of whom is powerful in some particular area of public policy but not in all such areas. In other words, there may be functional specialization, so that a man who is very influential in deciding questions dealing with, say, traffic-flow patterns, may have much less to say about housing policies and may not be consulted at all relative to the introduction of a new recreation program.

3. Some studies show that there are a few people who are very much interested in, and influential over, virtually all important decisions made in regard to public policy. These are the top members of the power elite. It is possible, even probable, that no such small clique of general leaders exists in the largest cities[17] simply because of the great complexity of social organization that exists in such large governmental units. In such cities, the leaders in various areas of community policy making seek their own goals, with imperfect coordination of their efforts with those of other leaders seeking other goals. Communication—keeping other leaders and the public informed—becomes increasingly imperfect as the size of community increases. To the public, interest groups, as such, become more visible than the individual leaders as the size of the city increases.

Some evidence indicates that community power complexes were once more nearly monolithic than they are today. With the decline of home-owned industry and the entrance into political activity on an effective basis of racial, ethnic, and labor groups, the community power complex has become increasingly competitive in character.[18]

4. Policy leadership should not be confused with policy invention. The studies made so far tend to show that leaders need not themselves be creative in finding solutions to social needs. Their job is to assess proposals as to their degree of adequacy as solutions and then to push for the adoption of those found most acceptable. New ideas in meeting problems are most likely to come from persons with exceptional technical knowledge of a particular subject, persons who may be in the bureaucracies of private business, government, the universities, or elsewhere. Their names are commonly little known to the general public and sometimes even to the person who serves as symbolic leader for the promotion of the ideas they have put forth. Thus, when the headlines read "Banker Lauded in Presenting New Parking Plan" or "Mayor Torkelson Announces Plan to Renew Business District," the prestigeful persons mentioned in the stories are

[17] See, for example, Martin Meyerson and Edward C. Banfield, *Politics, Planning and the Public Interest,* The Free Press of Glencoe, New York, 1955, which is a case study of public housing policy formulation in Chicago in the years following World War II, or N. E. Long, "The Local Community as an Ecology of Games," *American Journal of Sociology,* 64:251–261, November, 1958.
[18] Ruth McQuown, William R. Hamilton, and Michael P. Schneider, *The Political Restructuring of a Community,* Public Administration Clearing Service, University of Florida, Gainesville, Fla., 1964.

merely playing out their particular social roles. The anonymous men who actually thought up the plans in the first place will probably not even be mentioned in the story.[19]

5.   Governmental officials may once have been tools of the economic leadership group, but they are becoming increasingly important centers of power in their own right, and this is especially true as government plays an ever greater role in the lives of citizens.[20] In earlier times, government was simple and performed few functions. With business institutions overwhelmingly important by comparison, business leaders sometimes used officeholders as their front men. This is less likely to happen today, and many important community leaders themselves now become councilmen and mayors. Local politicians today generate demand, mobilize support, and otherwise serve as leaders, as power centers.

6.   The top members of the power structure may be powerful because they come from high-status families to whom deference has always been paid by other residents of the community or because they are newspaper editors. But they are most likely to be powerful because they are spokesmen for interest groups and have ability to bring some of the weight of the group to bear upon political institutions. One's place in the power structure reflects (except perhaps in small cities and towns where individuality remains especially important) the relative overall strength of the group for whom the leader is a spokesman.

7.   Members of what has been called the community power complex do not necessarily make up a monolithic power group.[21] They may, in fact, be badly divided internally into two or more factions. In some cases, the editor of the local newspaper, the real estate board, and commercial and industrial leaders may be arrayed against racial, ethnic-group, and organized-labor leaders. As the middle class moves out of the core city into the suburbs, the latter grouping is likely to increase in power, thus encouraging a split between the community economic and political leadership.

The exodus of the middle class to the suburbs in the last generation has altered the power structure of core cities. In one city:[22]

The top leaders of 1954 or their immediate successors in the same positions continued to dominate decision-making in 1961. However, the top group was no longer monolithic, but more var-

[19] See Peter H. Clark, *The Businessman as a Civic Leader,* The Free Press of Glencoe, New York, 1960.
[20] See Parsons, *op. cit.,* on this point.
[21] Delbert Miller and William H. Form, *Industry, Labor and the Community,* Harper & Row, Publishers, Incorporated, New York, 1960.
[22] David A. Booth and Charles R. Adrian, "Power Structure and Community Change," *Midwest Journal of Political Science,* 6:277–296, August, 1962.

iegated than was the case seven years before. Also, given roles appeared, in some cases to be more important than the particular incumbent. . . .

A further conclusion is that decision-making in the community is shared between two antagonistic groups, neither in complete control. The dominant group in the power structure cannot legitimize its decisions on public policy without the approval of an electorate-based veto group in the council, a group with only small membership in the top power complex.

8. Community power cannot be considered independently of power at the state and national levels. The important decisions affecting communities are not made in the community alone. All three of the traditional levels of government and all three of the traditional branches of government are involved in policy development. A prosperous community in which most persons are employed in locally owned industry may be relatively more independent than is the community which has most of its labor force employed in absentee-owned industry and business.[23]

9. Many vital decisions are not made by government at any level. Furthermore, "a comparatively small portion of the attention and involvement of most Americans" is devoted to governmental activities.[24] This means not only that many decisions are made by power structures of nongovernmental social institutions but also that those who feel strongly enough about the desirability of achieving a particular public policy and who are willing to invest time, money, social capital, and other resources are likely to find that they are not challenged by other citizens.

In a study by Robert V. Presthus, 52 percent of the organizations identified in one community and 28 percent of those in another participated in the major decisions of the community; however, 90 percent of these organizations had been active in only one decision each.[25]

In a small industrial city, politics was commonly viewed as being of less importance than other activities, particularly business. Political leaders were found to be selected from the middle level of economic positions. Persons of higher economic status felt that the political game was not worthwhile, and persons in lower positions did not possess enough information to play the game effectively.[26]

[23] See Robert V. Presthus, *Men at the Top*, Oxford University Press, Fair Lawn, N.J., 1964; and city "Alpha" in Williams and Adrian, *op. cit.*
[24] York Willbern, *The Withering Away of the City*, University of Alabama Press, University, Ala., 1964, chap. 5; Robert A. Dahl, *Who Governs?* Yale University Press, New Haven, Conn., 1961, chaps. 24–26.
[25] Presthus, *op. cit.*, pp. 432–433.
[26] Paul A. Smith, "The Games of Community Politics," *Midwest Journal of Political Science*, 9:37–60, February, 1965.

10. Professional administrative specialists and "influentials" are both necessary for decision making. In a study contrasting professional administrators with members of the community power structure not associated with bureaucratic positions in city government (influentials), the influentials ranked higher in socioeconomic status, were involved in more policy issues, and were far more willing to be involved in taking positions in local elections. Even so, the two groups were frequently involved in close working relationships and hence were interdependent to a considerable degree.[27]

11. In early community power studies, the assumption seemed to be made implicitly that power was inexhaustible in the hands of those who, for one reason or another, held it. More recent studies seem to imply that the use of power is costly, that is, that power is one form of social capital and can be exhausted if used improvidently. Because power is exhaustible, those who hold it probably choose not to make use of it unless they believe that the input-output ratio is efficient, that is, unless they believe the payoffs are worth the costs.

12. One of the difficulties in identifying a power structure results from the fact that participants in community decision making may be involved either overtly or covertly. Those who are openly involved are relatively easy to identify, but some may be powerful figures, even though they are not actors on the community stage. These may be individuals who enjoy high status in the community or who, because of their economic or political positions, are feared by others. This results in *anticipatory behavior.* That is, the decision makers *assume* that these persons are potentially actors in the decision-making process and that it is necessary to accommodate to their particular interests, as the other leaders view them, if they are not to become active in the process and veto proposed policies of other actors. The "richest man in town," or a leading banker, or a major manufacturer, or any other person viewed as potentially powerful may, hence, remain out of the political arena by having his expectations discounted in advance. The possibility always exists that they are overdiscounted and, for the researcher, it is extremely difficult to determine who such actors are and whether the allowance made for their potential power is exaggerated or not.

13. The community roles that are viewed by the culture as being important and hence deserving of a place in the community power complex are well known as the result of the large number of studies by sociologists and political scientists. Almost all power structure studies include the following leaders: the editor or the publisher of

[27] M. Kent Jennings, "Public Administrators and Community Decision Making," *Administrative Science Quarterly,* 8:18–43, June, 1963.

the local newspaper, a leading banker or two, the heads of the two or three largest manufacturing firms, the heads of the major central business district retail firms, the manager of the local chamber of commerce, the mayor, and one or possibly two councilmen, but never a majority of the council. In addition, the head of the realty firm that handles most of the central business district property will often be included.

Among those who are seldom mentioned in a study of reputational elites are ethnic and racial leaders, the manager of the leading television or radio station, and labor leaders. These persons probably are not included in the reputational power elite because they lack legitimacy, that is, the respondents do not view them as having a *right* to be included in the community power structure and hence they are not listed.

In an attempt both to simplify the determination of local power elites and to overcome the prejudice against persons who are not viewed by the upper middle class as having a right to a place in the power structure, two sociologists have developed a simplified method of determining the local power leaders.[28] They have assumed that the actual leaders in a community cannot be hidden from knowledgeable people, an assumption also made by the political scientist, Robert A. Dahl. Using this assumption, they have found it possible to construct a profile of the local power elite by asking any two leaders in the following seven areas to list the persons whom they regard as having most power and influence: persons from business, the clergy, the communications media, education, financial institutions, organized labor, and the black community.

14. An important aspect of political power lies in the ability of the powerful to control the community agenda. Leaders may decide not to act relative to an issue that some people in the community would like to have placed on the agenda, or they may decide not to decide. That is, they may implicitly accept some item of social concern as having at least a marginally legitimate place on the agenda, but they may decide to do nothing about it. Even beyond this, they may decide to engage in nondecision making. Thus, "When the dominant values, the accepted rules of the game, the existing power relations among groups, and the instruments of force, singly or in combination, effectively prevent certain grievances from developing into full-fledged issues which call for decisions, it can be said that a nondecision-making situation exists."[29] Thus, community leaders may decide not to develop a new municipal park, or they may decide not to make a decision this year concerning the imposition of a municipal

[28] Miller and Form, *op. cit.*
[29] Peter Bachrach and Morton S. Baratz, "Decisions and Nondecisions," *American Political Science Review,* 57:632–642, September, 1963.

income tax, or the school superintendent may decide not to call to the attention of civic leaders the fact that certain practices in the school system do not represent sound professional practice. (He may decide that the costs resulting from the conflict that would follow would do the school system more harm than good.)

Public Awareness of a Political Power Structure. In both the small-town and middle-sized city cases mentioned above, there was evidence that many citizens were not aware of the identity of the most influential persons in the community when it came to policy leadership. The extent of this specific problem was inquired into in a study made in Detroit.

Before answers are given to the question: Who runs Detroit? it should be pointed out that Detroit city government has been dominated almost without interruption from the time of World War I by the businessmen of the community, members of the board of commerce, the downtown merchants, and the real estate groups in particular. This is accomplished through a community of interests with the daily newspapers, whose control of the principal means of local communication is all important in a system of nonpartisan elections. Detroit political parties are weak, and there are no political bosses in the traditional sense. The labor unions, despite the huge membership of the United Automobile Workers, have been weak in local politics. Jews and blacks until recently have had little representation in either the legislative or the administrative branch of city government. (The first black was elected to the council in 1957.) Organized racketeering has not been influential in Detroit government for many years.

The answers to the question: Who runs Detroit? were classified as follows:[30]

Answer	Percent
No special group: "the public," don't know, etc.	42
Special groups named:	
Businessmen, industrialists, the rich	18
Labor unions, organized labor	11
Politicians, political bosses	11
Jews	6
Blacks	5
Racketeers, gamblers, underworld	2
Others	5
Total, special groups	58

[30] Reprinted from Arthur Kornhauser, *Attitudes of Detroit People toward Detroit,* Wayne State University Press, Detroit, Mich., 1952, pp. 13–15. This is a summary of a longer, more technical study, *Detroit as the People See It,* Wayne State University Press, Detroit, Mich., 1952. By permission of the Wayne State University Press.

The survey showed interesting variations of response among different population groups. The better educated were most convinced that special groups "really run the city." Only 30 percent of those who went beyond high school named no groups that had most influence, while 50 percent of people with eighth-grade education or less named no particular groups. High school and college graduates and the upper socioeconomic groups almost never named Jews or blacks. It is significant that the more education a person had, the more likely it was that he would be able to name the influential groups. Although this particular survey did not attempt to measure the ability of respondents to name specific individual leaders, it does give some idea of the relative ability of citizens in a large city to assess the actual power relationships that exist, as against the tendency that exists in some personality types to ascribe power to those who are distrusted or feared.

Closing Statement. In this chapter we have examined two aspects of the local policy-making process: the impact of the elected public official and of the community leader and influential. Both have important parts in the drama of community decision making, and they will reappear in the later chapters on the functions of government.

SELECTED
READINGS

Agger, Robert E., Daniel Goldrich, and Bert E. Swanson: *The Rulers and the Ruled,* John Wiley & Sons, Inc., New York, 1964. (A major empirical and theoretical study of community power.)

Bachrach, Peter: *The Theory of Democratic Elitism, A Critique,* Little Brown and Company, Boston, 1967. (A critique of pluralist theory as found in the writings of Dahl and Polsby.)

Bachrach, Peter, and Morton S. Baratz: *Power and Poverty, Theory and Practices,* Oxford University Press, New York, 1970.

Banfield, Edward C.: *Political Influences,* The Free Press of Glencoe, New York, 1961. (A study of Chicago politics, where decision making is found to be too decentralized for a general power structure to be identified.)

Clark, Peter H.: *The Businessman as a Civic Leader,* The Free Press of Glencoe, New York, 1960.

Clark, Terry (ed.): *Community Structure and Decision Making, Comparative Analysis,* Chandler Publishing Company, San Francisco, 1968.

Curley, James M.: *I'd Do It Again,* Prentice-Hall, Inc., Englewood Cliffs, N.J., 1957. (Autobiography of a famous boss.)

Dahl, Robert A.: *Who Governs?* Yale University Press, New Haven, Conn., 1961. (Includes a criticism of the reputation approach to power and concentrates upon decision-making participants. This study strongly influenced community politics research.)

Gosnell, Harold F.: *Machine Politics: Chicago Model,* The University of Chicago Press, Chicago, 1937.

————: *Negro Politicians: The Rise of Negro Politics in Chicago,* The University of Chicago Press, Chicago, 1935. (Relationships between Negroes and the Kelly-Nash machine.)

Greene, Lee S. (ed.): "City Bosses and Political Machines," *The Annals of the American Academy of Political and Social Science,* 353: entire issue, May, 1964. (An appraisal, by several authors, of contemporary municipal politics.)

Hunter, Floyd: *Community Power Structure: A Study of Decision-makers,* The University of North Carolina Press, Chapel Hill, N.C., 1953. (A watershed in the study of communities.)

Jennings, M. Kent: *Community Influentials: The Elites of Atlanta,* The Free Press of Glencoe, New York, 1964. (Atlanta, about a decade after Hunter, is not found to be homogeneous in its goals or structure.)

Kaufman, Herbert, and Victor Jones: "The Mystery of Power," *Public Administration Review,* 14:205–212, Summer, 1954. (Criticism of Hunter. This review article had a strong impact on urban politics research.)

Long, Norton E.: *The Polity,* Rand McNally & Company, Chicago, 1962. (See especially, "The Local Community as an Ecology of Games.")

McKean, Dayton D.: *The Boss: The Hague Machine in Action,* Houghton Mifflin Company, Boston, 1940.

McQuown, Ruth, William R. Hamilton, and Michael P. Schneider: *The Political Restructuring of a Community,* Public Administration Clearing Service, University of Florida, Gainesville, Fla., 1964. (Especially important for its examination of the influence of university faculty members upon a community.)

Merriam, Charles E.: *Chicago: A More Intimate View of Urban Politics,* The Macmillan Company, New York, 1929.

Meyerson, Martin, and Edward C. Banfield: *Politics, Planning and the Public Interest,* The Free Press of Glencoe, New York, 1955. (A study of politics and group activity in housing policy development for Chicago.)

Miller, Delbert, and William H. Form: *Industry, Labor and the Community,* Harper & Row, Publishers, Incorporated, New York, 1960. (Sees the "community power complex" as being frequently competitive and lacking in shared values. A major study by sociologists.)

Munger, Frank J., and others: *Decisions in Syracuse,* Indiana University Press, Bloomington, Ind., 1961. (A study in community decision making.)

Polsby, Nelson W.: *Community Power and Political Theory,* Yale University Press, New Haven, Conn., 1963. (Statement of pluralist position.)

Press, Charles: *Main Street Politics,* Institute for Community Development, Michigan State University, East Lansing, Mich., 1962. (A summary and evaluation of power analysis; digests many articles.)

Presthus, Robert V: *Men at the Top,* Oxford University Press, Fair Lawn, N.J., 1964. (A comparative study of two small cities, using both reputational and decision-making research techniques.)

Riordan, William L.: *Plunkitt of Tammany Hall,* Doubleday & Company, Inc., Garden City, N.Y., 1905.

Vidich, A. J., and Joseph Bensman: *Small Town in Mass Society,* Princeton University Press, Princeton, N.J., 1958. (An anthropological study of a New York village.)

Wildavsky, Aaron: *Leadership in a Small Town,* The Bedminster Press, Englewood Cliffs, N.J., 1964. (A study of Oberlin, Ohio, finds a pluralistic pattern of leadership and greatest influence with those who specialize in a functional area.)

Williams, Oliver P., and Charles R. Adrian: *Four Cities,* University of Pennsylvania Press, Philadelphia, 1963. (A comparative study of community politics in four middle-sized cities.)

Wood, Robert C.: *Suburbia: Its People and Their Politics,* Houghton Mifflin Company, Boston, 1959. (A theory of suburban politics.)

CHAPTER
4 URBAN
INTEREST
GROUPS

Public policy affects different segments of the general public in differing ways. Those whose ways of making a living are most intimately affected are most likely to band together in an attempt to shape such policy. In an urban setting, groups formed for other purposes, particularly those related to business and professional concerns, move readily into the political arena in an attempt to influence policy makers.

An interest group differs from a political party chiefly in that it does not seek to capture offices for its members but rather attempts to influence public policy. It also differs from most political parties in the United States in that it is made up of persons with basically the same interests and viewpoints—it is normally much more ideologically cohesive than is a political party in this country.

It is these specialized and relatively well-organized interests that we examine in this chapter noting their potential effect on urban policy making.[1] We also examine those potential groups whose interests are also affected but who are generally disorganized because they have few resources for influencing the local policy maker.

[1] A basic discussion of interest groups is David B. Truman, *The Governmental Process,* Alfred Knopf, New York, 1951. See also Mancur Olson, Jr., *The Logic of Collective Action,* Harvard University Press, Cambridge, Mass., 1965.

They may turn to protest activity since conventional channels to policy making seem closed. We conclude with a discussion of community conflict.

Is Group Action Democratic? Much has been said of the evil influences and dangers of pressure groups in politics. It has even been suggested by some critics that they be legally abolished or stringently controlled. Most such suggestions are, however, naïve. If we had a system of two or more political parties, each standing upon a definite platform of proposed action to which the parties could be held, interest groups, or at least their lobbying activities, could be greatly reduced.[2] Such is not the case in the United States, however, and especially not so in urban areas, many of which are nonpartisan or have long been dominated by one major party. Neither is it practical to say that a public official can determine the viewpoints of a cross section of the citizenry simply by noting the comments of those he happens to contact personally—not in any but the smallest villages, at any rate. And only the naïve or foolhardy would suggest that the officeholder should be elected with no promises to the public and then be entrusted to use his own free will and best judgment in doing as he sees best "for all the people" while in office. He must constantly be reminded of the nature of the shifting viewpoints of his constituents.

Interest groups are not only not evil, they are an absolute necessity in a democracy. They serve the purpose of marshaling individual opinions, organizing them, and presenting them in a skillful way to the proper governmental officials. Individual interest groups no doubt do sometimes go beyond the bounds of the mores of society, do fail to give an accurate picture of the interests, desires, and aspirations of their individual members, and do act otherwise irresponsibly. But they also face some checks on their activities.

The Effectiveness of Groups. It is a mistake to visualize all groups as operating with machinelike efficiency in influencing policy. Some groups are kept in check by a counterpressure group. For example, the local radio stations and newspapers compete for the same advertising dollars and are apt to be skeptical of each other's claims. In this fashion, some of the potential dangers of the organized power of one group is neutralized by the watchful eye of the opposing group. And each watcher is also watched. But for some groups, few organized counter groups are active. The radio station and newspaper

---

[2] *Lobbying* consists of seeking to influence legislative and administrative officials in a variety of ways so that their actions will be favorable to the group doing the lobbying. Lobbyists are also frequently in charge of the dissemination of propaganda to the general public.

may be owned by the same corporation. No general interest group representing the consumer's interest exists and none is likely to. Thus groups often are only held in check by such counter forces as community ideology, public officials and political candidates, and public opinion as educated by the news media.

Interest groups are also kept in check by their own ineptness and lack of full support of their membership. Group members sometimes belong to opposing groups and are cross pressured. The business-man who is a member of the Methodist Church may find the local Chamber of Commerce to which he belongs backing an enterprising businessman wanting to put in a deep-fry chicken and hamburger stand next to the house of worship. One of his groups or both are likely to receive his reduced support. But even in the absence of cross pressures, full mobilization of group membership is difficult.

Groups are made up of individuals seeking private goals. As soon as the group becomes larger than a dozen or so, and even some-times in these small groups, the internal conflicts begin to handicap those wishing to act collectively. The most serious handicap is that individual members find it to their advantage to reduce their own costs by cutting down participation. Thus the businessman who does not make a financial contribution to the fund created to bring new industry to Pottsville benefits as much as other Pottsville merchants if the campaign is successful but saves himself the contribution. In this case, social pressure from other merchants, if the group of merchants is small, may force him to contribute anyhow. Other groups, such as labor unions or the local bar or medical associations, can also force participation by coercion or by providing special side benefits. Without these techniques potential members would find they could get the benefits of the association without paying any of the cost.

This dodging of participation costs by group members means groups seldom operate at peak efficiency and can probably never depend on the full support of their membership. The fund drive may flop, only a few dozen or so may appear for the massive rally at city hall after the rumor goes out that trouble is expected, or only a handful of the total membership turns out for the mass meet-ing even if door prizes and entertainment are provided.

Action on behalf of the group is thus most probable where special benefits accrue to the group leader. A common method of achieving this is by hiring a professional to act on behalf of the group (the Urban League director or the Chamber of Commerce secretary). It also occurs when an individual member is crucially affected by the decisions and finds it worth his while to pay the costs of leadership (the realtor whose subdivision is under fire by the newspaper). Also a relatively unknown citizen with political ambitions may seize leadership of a group on an issue and pay the costs in order to advance his own political career. Other such leaders have emerged when their ideological commitment was unusually high as for example the relatively little known minister who became leader of the Birmingham bus strike—Martin Luther King, Jr. Thus while groups may not act at 100 percent efficiency, their impact on specific policies may be high because of an active leadership.

Characteristics of Groups. Several things should be kept in mind in classifying these interest groups. Some of them are especially created for the single purpose of lobbying; to others, lobbying is only a sideline. Some are temporary organizations created for a special problem; others are permanent groups. Some, in large cities and in state and nation at any rate, are always present and lobbying at the seat of government; others do not lobby except when a matter of particular importance to the group is under consideration.

Interest groups are constantly realigning their forces as expediency demands. It should not be assumed that politics is simply business versus labor, or that businessmen always work together, or that various groups operate in fairly permanent alignments. The *fluidity* of the pressure-group system is one of its most prominent characteristics.

Businessmen often line up on opposite sides of an issue, for example. Downtown merchants might lobby before a city council for one-way streets, since this would help hurry traffic to the place where their stores are located, but neighborhood-shopping-area merchants oppose one-way streets, since these reduce accessibility to their locations. Downtown and neighborhood-shopping-area merchants alike may favor municipally owned parking lots, but realtors are quite likely to oppose them. Labor unions frequently come into conflict with one another before legislative or administrative bodies. Jurisdictional disputes and the long-standing conflict of interests between the railroad brotherhoods and the teamsters' (truckers') union are examples. Businessmen and labor leaders work together on many matters. Ours is a dynamic system. (See Figure 4-1.)

Organized and Unorganized Groups. If all groups in society were equally well organized and equally effective in presenting their sides of issues, the process of determining public policy through compromise among the various interests involved would be highly satisfactory, indeed, nearly as perfect a device for democratic policy

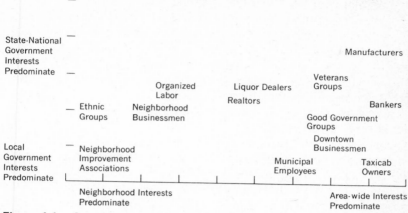

Figure 4-1. Group interests are multidimensional. Two aspects are shown here.

making as human society could achieve. Not all groups have their interests equally well protected, however. The less verbal members of the working class are not so likely to have their views expressed before councils as are members of the most prestigeful groups in society. They are certain to be accorded less deference when they speak. In terms of status, inside connections, funds for spreading propaganda, and other factors, there are vast differences in the relative power of groups.

It should not be assumed, however, that a group is necessarily strong because it is well organized or weak because it is unorganized. A well-organized and vigorously active group may, for example, have its relative strength reduced through the gerrymandering of the city council. Some unorganized groups are very weak politically (e.g., ex-convicts); others are very strong (e.g., the elderly). In a democracy, virtually all groups are free to organize and to lobby, but the ability of the members of a group to understand the techniques of doing this varies greatly, and their political resources also vary widely. The result is a weakening of the representativeness of a politics based upon the summation of vector forces.

The Techniques and Motivation of Groups. Not only do groups vary according to their degree of organization, but they also vary according to the techniques they use and the level of motivation they have for political participation.

Techniques might be said to vary according to the way in which the groups fit into the system of cultural values. One group may be able to "get away" with something that would produce highly unfavorable publicity for another. The medical association feels impelled to act within the public image of dignity which it has created for itself; a labor union can safely be more free-swinging in its behavior. A conservative group may be able to make recommendations concerning the election of nonpartisan judges with newspaper approval; a liberal group may be criticized by the same newspaper for "interfering" if it does the same thing.

There are many bases for the political motivation of groups. Many organizations, for example, seek to use the sanctions of the state to support their own battles against other interests. Either labor or management can benefit in their struggles by having governmental officials or legal provisions supporting one side. In other cases, one might make the generalization that *the political activity of any group is proportionate to its stake in the marginal definition of legality and of law-enforcement levels.* Thus, the middle-management bureaucrat in private industry is not intensely involved in politics, except by choice, because his job and his way of life are well within the bounds of accepted behavior. He is not likely to be in trouble with the law, nor is his welfare especially dependent upon its decisions. Similarly, the professional bank robber is not politically active because his job is so far outside the law that he cannot possibly hope to secure governmental sanction for his activities. But those on the edge of legality, where economic survival depends on marginal definitions, are the ones with the greatest stake in political decisions, and they make the maximum investment in the political process. Thus, a racetrack owner must be politically active because his business is just barely acceptable as legitimate by American values. The electric-utilities executive is similarly highly motivated, because his rate structure is determined through the governmental process. The corner druggist is deeply concerned over traffic-flow patterns. A decision to prohibit parking near his store may wipe out his margin of profit.

The pattern of marginality varies over time. Prostitutes, and public servants holding office by political appointment, were once highly active in politics. Neither group is apolitical today, but their activities have diminished as the prostitute has moved outside the pale, while the merit system, by extending protection to civil servants, has moved public employees away from the margin toward stability and acceptance. On the other hand, blacks who once thought they could not make economic or social progress through political action now find that they can. As a result, they have changed their behavior pattern from almost total political apathy to intense activity. Americans vote, lobby, issue propaganda, or otherwise take part in the process of politics according to their level of motivation. This, in turn, varies according to whether the individual's activities are well within the norms of society and of established public policy or whether decisions on public policy that may affect the individual are of a sort that are unpredictable but of immense importance to his social or economic welfare.

Groups and the Public Interest. When any group announces a policy position, it seeks explicitly or implicitly to associate its stand with the public interest. In fact, virtually every politically active individual or group claims to be acting in the public interest. Critics of the stand taken by a particular group, on the other hand, not uncommonly complain that interest groups are selfish and that they ought to act in the public interest. With everyone thus borrowing the term, it becomes useless as an analytical tool. Yet it is a basic part of the folklore of democracy to say that public policies as they are adopted are, or ought to be, in the public interest. As such, the concept may serve a useful function in encouraging compliance with the law, which in turn is an important device for achieving a stable society. It is also useful as a symbol to remind legislators and administrators that no matter how many groups they may have listened to before making a decision, other groups and citizens who are unrepresented or underrepresented before them will also be affected by the decision.

As one writer on the subject has said:[3]

> Instead of being associated with substantive goals or policies, the public interest better survives identification with the process of group accommodation. The public interest rests not in some policy emerging from the settlement of conflict, but with the method of that settlement itself, with compromising in a peaceful, orderly, predictable way the demands put upon policy.

URBAN INTEREST GROUPS

Interest groups operate in basically the same pattern on the national, state, or local level. To be sure, there may be differences in the relative balance of power of the various groups. On the national and state level, for example, agricultural groups tend to be among the more powerful. Liquor lobbyists tend to be more powerful

[3] Frank J. Sorauf, "The Public Interest Reconsidered," *Journal of Politics*, 19:616–639, November, 1957. Quotation from p. 638.

before state and local bodies than before the national government. Real estate groups and downtown merchants tend to be extraordinarily powerful in city politics.

Good-government Groups. The so-called "good-government groups" are among the few that restrict most of their organized efforts to the local scene. These groups have been mentioned above in connection with the reform movement.[4] Examples of them include the Citizens League of Pawtucket, the Richmond Civic Association, the Municipal League of Spokane, the Cleveland Citizens League, the Citizens Union of New York City, Citizens Action of Grand Rapids, the New Boston Committee, the Worcester Citizens Plan "E" Association, and the Hartford Citizens Charter Committee. While many of these groups date back to the reform era, new ones continue to be formed and old ones become inactive.

In general, these groups lobby for the lowest possible taxes and the greatest possible value from each tax dollar. They often seek to promulgate the basic aims of the reform movement, such as the council-manager plan, a professional civil service, performance budgeting, municipal home rule, and nonpartisan elections. They are interested in "good government" as such, usually with no immediate personal benefits expected except in the belief that the changes they advocate will save taxpayer dollars. Some members belong to these groups as something of a hobby; others consider it to be a civic obligation. The groups often work in close cooperation with municipal research bureaus (such as the Citizens' Research Bureau of Milwaukee, the St. Louis Governmental Research Institute, and the Cleveland Bureau of Governmental Research).

Because these groups are interested in keeping taxes low through keeping city expenses down, they often find themselves arrayed against labor unions in struggles for higher pay for city employees, the extension of old services, the assumption of responsibility for new services by the city, or a change or increase in the city tax structure. While these groups were considered "progressive" and forward-looking during the apogee of the reform movement in the 1920s, quite a few of them are today aligned with the largest taxpayers on the side of conservatism. Others, however, continue to be primarily interested in studying municipal issues and advancing rational attitudes toward them.

These "leagues" and "unions" often follow the practice of making recommendations concerning initiative and referendum propositions at each election and of endorsing a slate of candidates on a nonpar-

4 See pp. 76–77.

tisan or bipartisan basis. These recommendations receive much newspaper publicity in many cities, including New York, Chicago, and Detroit, for the groups often enjoy the open support of at least some of the newspapers. The effect of these endorsements varies greatly, however, depending upon the degree of political organization, local traditions, and many other factors. The Detroit Citizens League is far more effective, for example, than the Municipal Voters League of Chicago. Some groups do not make recommendations for voting but do give their opinions as to whether or not each candidate is qualified for the office he seeks.

An example of a good-government group that has existed for a long time is the Citizens Association of Kansas City. It has dominated the recruitment and election of councilmen in Kansas City from the time it was organized in 1941 until the present, with only the period between 1959 and 1963 as an exception. During the four-year interval, a group oriented much more toward working-class values and opposed to the council-manager plan controlled the city. This was a period of confusion and inaction in local politics, and it continued until a majority slate with Citizens Association backing regained control of the council. The association has been attempting to broaden its base through participation of a diversity of local group members and representatives of various life styles. One of the difficulties that led to its temporary eclipse in 1959 was that it had been viewed as exclusively a middle-class, do-gooder organization.[5]

Related to the above type of group are various other middle-class clubs and endeavors. Women's groups, particularly the League of Women Voters, often work for good government per se. The League prepares a voter-information sheet in many cities. Being nonpartisan, the League usually has a prepared set of questions on current issues which it submits to candidates. The questions are generally not "loaded" (the League *does* sometimes endorse certain policies—for example, perhaps, the council-manager plan, or a four-year term for elective officials), and the answers are printed verbatim (unless, of course, the candidate is too long-winded). The Parent-Teachers Association (PTA) is also a powerful group, much more interested in the affairs of the school board, of course, but where its interests overlap with those of the city, the PTA may lobby before the council or the voters, if a referendum is involved.

Improvement Associations. In many cities, virtually every neighborhood shopping area has an association for the safeguarding and furthering of the interests of the businessmen operating in that

[5] Stanley Gabis, "Leadership in a Large Manager City: The Case of Kansas City," *The Annals of the American Academy of Political and Social Science*, 353:52–63, May, 1964.

community. Likewise, in many sections of the city, similar groups will be found for the various residential subdivisions. These groups serve many purposes. If the city is growing or shrinking in size, they fight to keep property values high. If the city or neighborhood is losing population, the slackening of demand for homes demands diligence in order to save as much as possible of the homeowners' investment. If the city is increasing in size, older neighborhoods are constantly undergoing transition in character. In this case the association fights—usually without ultimate success if there is real demand for space—to keep Jews or blacks or Chicanos or some other socially unwanted group out of the area.

These groups often appear before the council or administrative officers of the city, for they have almost countless bases for making such contacts. They are interested in every proposed rezoning of the area, since this has a direct effect upon property values. They do not want commercial or industrial areas nearby; they want the factory eight blocks upwind to stop making all that smoke and noise; they want more stop signs in the neighborhood ("Trucks are using our street for a through street."); they want the chuckholes repaired immediately (though this must not result in a tax increase); they want the patrol car to drive past the house more often at night (but "Look at all the money the police want to run that lousy department for next year!"); and they want only single-family dwellings in the neighborhood if such has been the previous character of the area.

The improvement associations also serve other functions. Americans seek to lessen insecurity by joining together with others who feel as they do, and the neighborhood civic association gives the individual another club to add to his list. There are also offices to be filled, and Americans like to be presidents or vice-presidents of almost anything. They will appoint a committee at the first excuse, and neighborhood associations present a multitude of reasons for appointing committees: to "investigate the situation on 81st Street," or to "see the police chief." The associations also help to satisfy the urban dweller's longing to restore the primary relationships characteristic of the small town and rural community, for most of these groups are limited to a fairly small, truly neighborly area. If the group is made up primarily of homeowners, as a suburban group is, or if it is a businessmen's association, the organization also affords an opportunity to identify oneself more closely with these socially honorific classes. Members of neighborhood associations are fond of talking about the rights and responsibilities of homeowners and taxpayers, and members of a businessmen's group remind one another that they are indeed businessmen and hence the mainstays of the American economy. In fulfilling these psychological needs for prestige, the improvement associations, like many other pressure groups, serve a useful social function beyond that of exerting political pressure alone.

Taxpayers' Groups. As something of a cross between the good-government groups and the business groups in the community, there are often organized "taxpayers' leagues" of one title or another. In general, they stand for lower taxes and fewer government activities and services and have their support in the more conservative business community—the large taxpayers. They often publish propaganda based upon either real or pseudo research on taxation, budgeting, and borrowing policies. Their membership is normally not large, and their influence on government varies greatly from place to place. Some of these groups have broader interests, more in the nature of the good-government groups.

Business Groups. So many business groups exert pressure upon government that they would probably overshadow and overpower all the others if it were not that they spend so much of their time opposing one another. There is an organization equipped to lobby for every business interest in the city. To name only some of them: there is often an association of downtown merchants, representing the owners, or in a large city probably the managers, of the large stores downtown. These people would obviously have numerous interests. They pay much of the general property tax of the city and so have an interest in tax rates; they want ample parking spaces, paid for, if possible, from taxes and not from their own pockets; they want freeways that will bring people downtown to shop and will discourage the development of competing neighborhood shopping areas.

The small businessman, especially in the village or small city, sees his gross income as fairly fixed. His expansion prospects are poor. For this reason, he thinks in terms of cutting costs and sees taxes as one of his fixed costs. To him, additional taxes will not produce commensurate benefits but will only diminish his possible profits. He becomes, therefore, a supporter of a low-tax ideology.[6] In middle- and large-sized cities, the more prosperous, expansion-minded merchants of the central business district are likely to be advocates of boosterism—and of tax levies to support its aims of a bigger and better city—but the neighborhood small businessmen are likely to have views similar to those of the village merchant

[6] See A. J. Vidich and Joseph Bensman, *Small Town in Mass Society*, Princeton University Press, Princeton, N.J., 1958, chap. 5.

and to see the large downtown businessmen with their ideas of constant growth as a threat.

The large retailers have political problems, too. They must constantly be on the alert against all kinds of threats to their profits, many of which the ordinary citizen would not even think of as being political in character. For example, the mighty and prestigeful Fifth Avenue Association of New York City once took a large advertisement in the *New York Times* in order to urge the mayor to veto an ordinance which would permit a Loyalty Day parade on a regular business day. The city council was anxious to oblige the veterans' groups, but the great shops along the avenue pointed out that this particular expression of patriotism would cost them 1 million dollars in sales.[7]

The downtown merchants and property owners are of tremendous influence both in determining the outcome of elections and in setting policy afterward. In middle-sized cities without political machines they are often the dominant group, and even in large cities they wield great power. In Detroit and Los Angeles, for example, their influence is pervasive, although it is kept unpublicized and *sub rosa* by choice.

If a political machine exists, these groups must use a somewhat different approach. The traditional arrangement was for the dominant merchants and manufacturers to permit the machine's politicians to operate the city government and to control its patronage, in return for guarantees of nonharassment and assistance in commercial and industrial expansion.

General Business Groups. The chamber of commerce is interested at the local level, as at the state and national, in tax rates, labor legislation, and other matters that affect business activity and costs. In quite a few cities, the chamber serves as the principal spokesman for business before the council and city officials. Often it acts in lieu of a downtown property association and exerts the same type of pressure.

The so-called "service clubs," the Rotarians, Lions, and Kiwanians, are basically for businessmen, but their interests are not primarily political and they are not likely to act in this capacity, except perhaps in connection with a summer playground program or some such community service project.

Banks. Banks and related financial institutions are important interest groups for several reasons. First, they are businesses and have the interests of businessmen. Secondly, bankers being among

---

[7] *The New York Times,* Apr. 22, 1958.

the most respected of all businessmen, their views are likely to be taken into the bosoms of other businessmen, who then present them as their own. Furthermore, because the banker decides who is to be permitted to borrow money and under what conditions, he may in dozens of subtle or open ways influence the thinking, or at least the behavior, of other businessmen. Thirdly, bankers have a direct stake in local legislation affecting public utilities, in which banks have a pecuniary interest, and in bond issues and sinking funds, since banks act as brokers in servicing these. Banks are also interested in public policies that may affect businesses to which they have loaned money; hence they are interested in such matters as business regulation, taxation, zoning, and housing.

Utilities. Public utility companies in a great majority of cities are today dependent upon a state body for determining rates and service, but they also have many local interests. They must guard against movements to place their utility under public ownership; they are often dependent upon the goodwill of the city administration in order to extend or restrict the area covered by their services; and since the city is responsible for the public safety, the city's interpretation of what is safe or adequate equipment is of vital interest.

Contractors. The city has the power of inspection over all sorts of construction. The building, plumbing, lighting, and other codes are hence of great interest to contractors, as is the manner in which these are enforced.

Businessmen who are particularly desirous of procuring public contracts are, of course, unusually interested in the political scene. Some businesses, such as road-grading and -surfacing companies, depend for most of their work upon public contracts, and they can be expected to seek to do their utmost to influence both elections and policy decisions.

Taxicabs. Taxicab owners (and their drivers' unions) also play an important role in municipal politics. The city council normally determines the number of taxi licenses to be issued and decides the question of who is to get them. The council can thus make or break any given company. Furthermore, both the owners and the drivers are interested in *restricting* the number of licenses below that of actual need—so that they may charge monopoly rates. The driver and his union are as interested in keeping down competition as is the company itself.

In almost every American city, taxicab rates are high (especially if one includes the tip, which is really a hidden portion of the charge), and the number of cabs available is greatly restricted. This is a direct result of pressure-group activity upon the council and is an illustration of the council acting in the interest of the organized few rather than the unorganized many.

Taxicab companies, and often their drivers, find it necessary to pick candidates and support them in municipal campaigns. Those who bet on the winning candidates will have the lion's share of the licenses for the next term of office, while those who are wrong will get the crumbs. Taxicab companies also seek ordinances against "jitneys" and urge strict enforcement of these ordinances.

The Professions. Professional organizations have a stake in government. Some of them, such as medical and dental groups, are more important as lobbyists before state and national governments, but others, and particularly the city or county bar association, are also active locally. The bar association is interested in city government for a variety of reasons. Lawyers make up a large portion of the candidates for public office and are likely to view this field as a private hunting ground. Lawyers and their organizations look upon themselves as singularly responsible for guarding the law and its traditions. They are particularly concerned over the modern tendency to use administrative tribunals rather than law courts in the settlement of many public matters, since the former need not always be made up of lawyers and do not necessarily use the traditional processes of the courts of law. Lawyers, furthermore, often consider themselves to be trained in the problems of public policy formulation and peculiarly qualified to comment upon them, even though the law is not a social science and most lawyers have had very little training in sociology, economics, psychology, or even political science.

Real Estate Groups. The local real estate board and other similar groups have a special interest in local government. The city zoning ordinance and building code are of the greatest interest to them; the city tax rate is important, because the general property tax is the major source of city revenue; the cost of paving streets, curbs, gutters, and sidewalks is a factor in the selling of homes; public housing is anathema to them. Builders and real estate speculators are often among the most influential groups before a city government, and this is particularly true in suburban areas in a period of expansive home building. A builder may often contribute to the campaign funds of *all* candidates for office in a modest-sized suburb, especially if he is the large assembly-line type of "project" builder. There are often conflicts before the city council between project builders and improvement associations representing subdivisions of individually built homes, and also between homeowners and large real estate companies interested in the development of commercial and industrial properties.

Liquor Interests. Time was, near the beginning of the century, when the two most powerful groups in most cities were the public utilities and the liquor interests. Since then, there has been a considerable decline in the power of the liquor and beer industries. Prior to prohibition, licensing of beer and liquor stores was largely a local function, making the interests of these occupations in city government obvious. Of course, there was also the question of the attitude the local police would take toward laws dealing with closing hours, selling to minors, selling on Sunday, engaging in such socially disapproved but financially profitable sidelines as the narcotics trade and prostitution, and the like. During prohibition, the liquor industry continued (with public approval) quite unabated. In order to do so, it was necessary for purveyors to buy off local governments whose officials were in a position to work an easy shakedown racket. Bootleggers in many instances virtually captured whole city governments, even in very large cities, as when the Capone gang dominated Chicago in the 1920s. Today liquor interests are less powerful in most cities, but they still exercise considerable influence, especially where the law and local mores are not in accord. The policing of the liquor industry, now largely in the hands of state government, has relieved city officials of some of the problems and temptations that existed before prohibition.

Illegal Occupations. The gambling, prostitution, and narcotics businesses are almost everywhere illegal, but they operate to some degree in most of our larger cities, as well as in many smaller places. They may be beset by peace officers from all three levels of government, but they persist because they are profitable, and they are profitable because of the highly inelastic character of the demand for their services. Because they are illegal, they must be particularly concerned with politics. Where they cannot purchase protection, they seek to establish a pale wherein their operations are allowed by either tacit or explicit arrangement. Failing this, or as a preferable substitute, they may seek to operate in a suburb if the core-city administration is especially hostile. The narcotics trade is probably the least thriving of these businesses, for, despite the cravings suffered by the drug addict that will make him go to any extreme in order to obtain supplies, Federal-government officers have long sought to exterminate the trade, usually, although not always, with the cooperation of state and local peace officers. On the other hand, gambling and prostitution are likely to be with us for some time to come.

Newspapers. As has often been pointed out, newspapers tend to be conservative influences in the community because big business is conservative and newspaper publishing, at least of the large-city dailies, is big business. It is also true that newspapers which are moderate on national and international questions may become much more conservative, or even reactionary, on matters of local politics. A daily which accepts the existence of labor unions when discussing national labor law may speak of unions in the same terms it might have used in the nineteenth century when discussing local politics. Physical proximity and the immediacy of the economic interest involved may be factors in producing this phenomenon. A further consideration is that businessmen are dependent on the city government for all types of permits, licenses, favors, and sympathies, in order to operate freely and successfully. A government controlled by labor or by unsympathetic liberals is a frightening specter to most businessmen and hence to newspaper editors.

Newspapers often work together with good-government groups and give them much free publicity. They may even print their press releases on the front page as news stories and not mention that it is partisan propaganda of an interest group. In many cities, newspapers have been important forces in support of local governments that reflect middle-class values.

Reasons for the Importance of Newspapers. The overall effect of the opinion of a newspaper editorial board would probably not be great if the publication's effect were limited to its editorial opinions. Probably only a tiny percentage of newspaper readers pay any attention to the editorials, and those who do for the most part agree with them already. Yet a newspaper can be very influential in many different ways. It can influence individual opinion by emphasizing or burying an item; by distorting the relative importance of the various facts involved in a story; by choice of location for the story; by choice of adjectives and adverbs; by phrasing of headlines; by its use of cartoons (picture editorials that reach far more people than do the ordinary ones). A newspaper that would not permit the "loading" of a story on a national matter may make its stories during a local election into veritable editorials. It may play up the speeches and pictures of Candidate Twitingham and bury those of Candidate Torkelson on page 37. Individual newspapers may vary greatly in their use of these available weapons. Some seek to give balanced attention to all events. Others, for example, the Hearst newspapers, normally pay relatively little attention to local issues, being more concerned with the national and international scene. A locally owned newspaper is more likely to give space to local issues (and to take sides) than is one that is chain-owned or one whose editorial policy is determined by a person who lives elsewhere.

In many cities, especially large ones, limited-circulation weekly newspapers may be of more influence in elections than are the large downtown dailies. These newspapers are usually aimed at a definite clientele: residents of a suburb or of a neighborhood area in the core city, foreign-language-reading members of an ethnic group, members of a labor union, blacks, Catholics, or Jews. Since they emphasize the interests of particular groups, they are able to call specific candidates or issues to the attention of the voter and to discuss them in terms of his interests.

The suburban and neighborhood newspapers are especially influential since they are not viewed as "commercial" or "partisan." Because they reflect the interests and values of the neighborhood, they are thought of rather as agents of "community welfare and progress."[8]

Radio and TV. Radio and television are important media in large cities for reaching voters and people to be propagandized over local issues. In the days before television, radio was not too successful for conveying ideas concerning local matters. People would listen to the President, but not to the mayor, and almost certainly not to a local labor leader or the president of the local chamber of commerce, unless the issue were of the most unusual importance. Television, with a hypnotic quality lacking in radio, is able to catch the eye and thought of citizens where radio failed, but it is too expensive for most local candidates. Radio and television managers offer editorials on local issues but do not appear to have great influence.

Organized Labor. Probably no event in the present century is likely to have so great an effect upon the future pattern of urban government as the coming to power of organized labor. Especially important as a long-range factor was the rise after 1937 of the Congress of Industrial Organizations (CIO) with its organization of the unskilled and semiskilled workers and its fresh supply of imaginative, able, and ambitious leaders. The full effect of organized labor as a political-action group has never been felt at the local level because labor leaders have preferred to devote their resources to the election of governors and members of the two houses of Congress. Labor-union

[8] Morris Janowitz, *The Community Press in an Urban Setting*, The Free Press of Glencoe, New York, 1952.

membership, furthermore, is less united on local issues than it is on those at the state and national levels. Ethnic and racial jealousies and status strivings are most clearly manifested at the local level and sometimes involve loyalties stronger than those of the union. Although the leaders deliver the votes quite well on national, and even state, matters where they can convince members that they have a real and immediate stake, there has been less success in convincing them that local politics is of equal importance to the labor movement.

At the present time, "unions have a long way to go before they achieve a community position equal to that of older and better established groups."[9] To date, they have not been willing to devote a major share of their political-action funds to the local level. In addition, labor efforts to win local elections are quickly criticized as "partisan" and "aimed at the advantage of a small minority" in the conservative press. This makes the task the more difficult.

Labor groups have always had some effect upon urban politics in the largest cities, but the coming of the CIO with its definite social consciousness made a great difference. The older craft unions of the AFL were interested primarily in what is called "business unionism" —the highest possible wages, best possible working conditions, shortest possible hours. Few of them had developed a social ideology. The AFL sought essentially to achieve a monopoly of skilled labor and to make its people better and more prosperous members of the middle class. The CIO, on the other hand, sought to inculcate into its members the idea that the working class has a set of interests to pursue that are different from those of the business-oriented middle class. It was therefore to be expected that they would seek to challenge the business community for control of city government. After the merger of the two great unions into the AFL-CIO in 1955 and the establishment of a political arm—the Committee on Political Education (COPE)—the CIO ideology of political action came to dominate the new organization, and vigorous action in municipal politics was made a part of its program.

The Goals of Labor. Organized labor has a whole list of wants it desires from government, and a large number of them result in a conflict with other interest groups. Labor expects that the many services it demands be financed on an ability-to-pay theory of taxa-

---

[9] For a case study of one union local (of the United Steelworkers) in one city (probably Gary), see Joel Seidman, Jack London, and Bernard Karsh, "Political Consciousness of a Local Union," *Public Opinion Quarterly,* 15:692–702, Winter, 1952. The quotation is from this study. See also William Form, "Organized Labor's Place in the Community Power Structure," *Industrial and Labor Relations Review,* 12:526–539, July, 1959.

tion, rather than on a benefit theory. This brings labor into conflict with those who are expected to foot the bill. Labor is more interested in services than in the tax rate. Many workingmen feel that the burden of the general property tax is of no concern to them because they do not own homes. This assumption is fallacious, since the renter pays the property tax as part of his rent. It does, however, affect his attitude.

The considerable increase in the rate of ownership of homes by members of the working classes since the end of World War II, as a result of liberal financing provisions of the Veterans Administration and the Federal Housing Authority, is likely to change his attitude in time. Many workingmen, especially in the skilled trades, have today become members of a new middle class of suburbanites quite different from the traditional. They are sometimes called the "blue-collar" class. Though these people tend to be Democratic in state and national politics, they are likely to assume the conservative characteristics of homeowners in the nonpartisan politics at the local level. Some students of politics see such an emerging "hard-hat," blue-collar constituency as exerting great future influence.

Labor is also interested in such things as a subsidized public transportation system—in contrast to the businessman's views on a pay-as-you-ride system, preferably privately owned. It wants public housing with low rentals, perhaps an FEPC ordinance (although some of its members will oppose the leadership on this), and high wages for city employees, all of which are likely to run it into various conflicts with business, good-government, and other middle-class groups. Labor leaders also want to control the city administration, if possible, partly in order to ensure a sympathetic police force in the event of strikes or other labor disturbances. They well remember the time, not long ago, when the local police department was often considered available to any manufacturer for strikebreaking purposes.

The flight to the suburbs, led by members of the middle class, is changing the position of organized labor in core cities. In a larger and larger number of cities, labor will elect mayors and a majority of the council in future years; in many it already does so. Labor is also serving a special function as the social institution that is providing members of various ethnic groups with a base for political action. In the Ohio steel-manufacturing city of Lorain, for example, the multiplicity of ethnic groups had long produced mutual jealousy and suspicion which prevented effective political action. As a result, middle-class residents controlled the town, though they were a small minority. After 1937 and the unionization of the steel mills, the United Steelworkers of America succeeded in bringing the ethnic groups together by superimposing a sense of labor identity upon the ethnic sense that had long prevailed. The result was political control of the community by the combined groups.[10]

Municipal Employees. Employees themselves are organized into pressure groups and can exert influence on the administration and council for matters that interest them, particularly wages, hours, and conditions of labor. Because many employees belong to labor unions that have close association with the other AFL-CIO unions of the city, they are in a position to bring up reinforcements from these other unions at important times.

City employees may also be members of professional organizations such as the International City Management Association, the Civil Service Assembly of the United States and Canada, and the American Society of Municipal Engineers. Purely local unions also commonly exist, either because they are old, respected, and powerful, or because unions with national affiliations are discouraged by local public policy. Examples include the Milwaukee Government Service League and the Detroit Police Officers' Association. These groups occasionally compete when new groups of employees begin to organize. Unionization has advanced particularly rapidly among school teachers where competition between the NEA (National Education Association), a professional group, and AFT (American Federation of Teachers), affiliated with the AFL-CIO, has been intense in some communities.

In some cities, the municipal employees band together for political action, seeking to eliminate from the council members who will not support their demands regarding wages, hours, and conditions of labor. If they have the aid of the regular labor unions of the city, and if other organized political activity is not strong, municipal-employee unions may even succeed in electing a slate of councilmen that constitutes a majority of the council.[11]

The Politics of Equality. Although there is no logic from a theoretical standpoint in having democratic representation on the basis of racial or ethnic groups and no particular reason why such groups should be separated from one another in such a manner as to require them to act as interest groups, such is nonetheless the case. Minority groups find that they are beleaguered and feel the need to protect themselves from further encroachment by an unsympathetic dominant group in society. Blacks, Jews, Chicanos, and sometimes Poles, Ital-

---

[10] James B. McKee, "Status and Power in the Industrial Community," *American Journal of Sociology,* 58:364–370, January, 1953.

[11] For one example, see city "Delta" in Oliver P. Williams and Charles R. Adrian, *Four Cities,* University of Pennsylvania Press, Philadelphia, 1963.

ians, or Irish groups find that by banding together they can seek protection in the law.

A study that examined municipal elections in Newark and compared these nonpartisan elections with the partisan elections for the state legislature found that party identification was unimportant to the typical voter as he considered candidates for office. Ethnic affiliation, on the other hand, was extremely important; hence, social cleavages were accentuated by the viewpoints of the voters. This was, of course, in contrast to the goal of municipal reformers who, by the adoption of the nonpartisan ballot, hoped to eliminate party, ethnic, and class considerations in municipal elections.[12]

Minority groups are interested in such things as FEPC, the protection of their equal right to civil service jobs, equal police protection and treatment, and a fair share of housing. Minorities often vote in blocs in political campaigns, resulting in such situations as that in New York where the mayor, the controller, and the president of the council must always be of different ethnic or racial groups. For a well-balanced city-wide ticket, these positions must be apportioned with no more than one each to an Italian, an Irishman, a Jew, or a black. A similar recognition of political realities may be found in many cities where identifiable groups are important.

For pressure purposes, many organizations represent these people. Blacks, for example, may be represented at council hearings by the National Association for the Advancement of Colored People as well as by the local Urban League. The NAACP has been more active politically than has the League, which has been interested mainly in making more jobs, more economic opportunities, available to blacks. Both are potent organizations, especially in large cities, even though they are now considered by many blacks to reflect an old-fashioned approach. Many blacks now respond to an appeal quite different from that of these groups.

The effectiveness of the new type of leadership is reflected in the way that it has made a sub-culture, suffering under a tradition almost totally lacking in a concept of political participation, suddenly and significantly aware of the identity of white-supremacy candidates as against those who are more favorably disposed toward black interests. Black sophistication in politics is growing both in the South and in the Northern industrial cities where, in earlier years, the black was often a pawn completely manipulated by the adroit politician and almost totally without his own political leadership.

---

[12] Gerald Pomper, "Ethnic and Group Voting in Nonpartisan Municipal Elections," *Public Opinion Quarterly*, 30:79–87, Spring, 1966.

Some research[13] seems to indicate that attitudes toward direct black participation in the political process are not merely a function of economic concern, but may vary according to different cultural values within the same economic framework. These values, of course, tend to change with time. This offers the possibility that Southern values which seemingly have been changing over recent decades may, through further movement in the direction of permissiveness and tolerance, change enough to permit the development of a genuine universal system of suffrage in the relatively near future.

In every community that has more than a few blacks, a black leadership and power pattern develops, just as is the case in cities which continue to have identifiable ethnic groups. In a study of one Southern city, blacks rated themselves and were rated by others along a radical-conservative continuum. Black leaders, as rated by other black leaders, were predominantly liberal in their views on public policy questions. There were more conservatives than radicals, but the conservatives, although still considered powerful, were no longer important in decision making. Relative to the issue of school desegregation, liberal leaders were found to predominate by a 6 to 1 ratio over conservatives, and by 3 to 1 over moderates. The most powerful black leaders, in the view of both minority leaders and the general citizenry, were rated as liberals and were active in all phases of desegregation.[14]

The pattern of black leadership has changed greatly since about 1950:[15]

> Conservatives are no longer powerful leaders in Crescent City. In the past these compromise leaders often held their positions because they were acceptable to the white community. They believed that the interests of the Negro could best be served by adjusting to the authority of the whites. Some may have feared reprisals if they failed to cooperate with white leaders in controlling the minority community.
>
> They were acceptable to other Negroes, not only because accommodation was regarded as the most practical policy, but because they also had prestige in their own right within the Negro social structure. This type of race leader was powerful in Crescent City through the 1930s and early 1940s. . . .
>
> Today the suggestion that a Negro is unduly susceptible to white influence has meant loss of power. . . .

[13] See John H. Fenton and Kenneth N. Vines, "Negro Registration in Louisiana," *American Political Science Review*, 51:704–713, September, 1957.
[14] M. Elaine Burgess, *Negro Leadership in a Southern City*, The University of North Carolina Press, Chapel Hill, N.C., 1962, chap. 7.
[15] *Ibid.*, pp. 180–181.

Conservative leaders still remain the most acceptable to a segment of Crescent City's white leadership. By and large, however, the white leaders by-pass the conservative leader, for they know he no longer wields power in the Negro community.

TABLE 4-1.   Race-leader Peer-group Classification

Type of Leader	Radical Percent	Liberal Percent	Moderate Percent	Conservative Percent
Power nominees*	6.5	54.8	19.4	19.3
Power leaders*	9.1	72.7	18.2	

* Power nominees were persons believed by three groups of informants to be the most powerful or influential. Power leaders were those individuals who actually played the most active role in community issues.
Source: M. Elaine Burgess, *Negro Leadership in a Southern City,* The University of North Carolina Press, Chapel Hill, N.C., 1962, p. 178.

In a period of rapid economic, political, and social change, the black community is badly divided concerning the question of desirable techniques. Older black leaders fear that irresponsible individuals may gain power and thus weaken the entire movement toward equality of opportunity and status. Younger blacks fear that the movement may lose its militant spirit. Similarly, there is no agreement on tactics. Younger activists prefer use of the economic boycott and the sit-in; older, more conservative blacks prefer private negotiations, the traditional approach to relations with the dominant whites.[16]

Religious Groups. Virtually all religious and church-related organizations represent political forces. Perhaps the only exception would be those sects that are opposed to political action. Since a religion—any religion—is based upon some kind of faith or set of beliefs, it is to be expected that political and social questions will be interpreted in the light of these moral value scales and viewpoints taken in accord with them.

In almost any important councilmanic hearing, ministers, priests, rabbis, or leaders of religious lay groups will be found testifying for their members. Because Catholics tend to be concentrated in cities and because the Church is disciplined and dogmatic, its views are often particularly powerful and effective. The Church has dozens of lay organizations that act as pressure groups. Protestants are less well organized, but may be equally active, especially through local

[16] Jack L. Walker, "Protest and Negotiation," *Midwest Journal of Political Science,* 7:99–124, May, 1963.

ministerial associations. Methodist groups may work for a policy of restricting the number of retail liquor permits; Quakers may be interested in the humane treatment of prisoners in the local work-house; a group of ministers may lobby for an FEPC ordinance.

Ministerial associations may be interested in matters related to public health, welfare, housing, and other matters. They are especially likely to be concerned with public policies relative to vice, racetracks, liquor sales, and juvenile delinquency. In Underwood's "Paper City," Catholic priests were concerned about policies that affected the parochial schools, religious practices in public schools, public health clinics if they provided birth-control information, gambling, and problems related to alcoholism. The politicians, he found, "tend to look upon either Roman Catholic or Protestant moral interests chiefly as those of one more organized group to be anticipated, managed, and met."[17]

Veterans. After each war, veterans—at least many of them—organize themselves into interest groups. They are particularly powerful because, unlike ordinary groups, they have no organized opposition, no counter-pressure group. It is not easy for a politician or another interest group to oppose the interests and demands of a well-known veterans' group. In local politics, returned servicemen are interested in such things as tax exemptions, civil service preferences on job certification, "patriotism," taxicab licensing, liquor permits for their clubhouses, and all other types of licensing, with an eye toward privileges for veterans.

The largest and most powerful veterans' groups on the local as well as the national scene are the American Legion and the Veterans of Foreign Wars, both of which have members who served in the two world wars and in the Korean and Vietnamese conflicts. Products of World War II, such as the Amvets and the AVC, are smaller and less powerful. There are also groups that represent two special interests simultaneously, such as the Catholic War Veterans and the Jewish War Veterans.

Low-income Groups and Protest. Until the 1960s, no efforts were made to politicize large-city impoverished groups as such. Now new forces are operative. One is that of Federal administrators seeking to activate the poor through participation in poverty-board elections. Their efforts have not been notably successful, with sometimes less than 6 percent of the potential voters participating. Social workers and other professionals have, with perhaps greater success, worked with such groups. Saul Alinsky and his Industrial Areas Foundation

---

[17] For more on churches and local politics, see Kenneth W. Underwood, *Protestant and Catholic*, Beacon Press, Boston, 1957, especially chaps. 18–20. Quotation is from pp. 319–320.

have developed specific techniques for organizing in low-income areas.[18]

The problem of organizing the poor is complicated first by their lack of political resources such as wealth, organizational skills, or leadership experience.[19] Their major resource is in effect threats of violent action or of peaceful disruption. Thus instead of going through the conventional channels of influence, they may have a greater probability of influencing public officials through militant protest activity, including rioting, sit-ins, "trashing," or picketing. In doing this successfully, the leaders of low-income groups must concentrate on three constituencies.

Their first constituency is the low-income citizenry itself. We have already noted the problems of mobilizing and keeping a group together. These problems are maximized when individual members see the costs and risks of participation as high and the probability of success low. This is the case for low-income citizens, for they must come to meetings in their limited free time. They lose work time to engage in protest activities and sometimes may risk losing their jobs as well. They have few funds for even small group expenditures. Finally they have generally experienced failure in most other activities and have come to expect it to be the result of all activity.

The other constituencies are the communications media, and other groups within the community who, out of sympathy or to end protests, may act on behalf of the low-income citizens. Placating and managing each of these four constituencies (including the public officials) involves the leader in tensions and unresolvable conflicts. Michael Lipsky concludes that the positive results of protest activity are likely to be some symbolic action by officials rather than material rewards that low-income citizens can directly experience. Such symbolication is taken to satisfy the third parties motivated on behalf of low-income groups and because basic changes require large-scale costs for the community. The negative results of symbolic payoffs are disillusionment by low-income citizens and their reaching the conclusion that the benefits of protest are not worth the cost. The most rational course for individuals such as themselves, they may decide, is to lapse into political apathy or perhaps criminal activity.

Given symbolic responses that result in few perceived changes, low-income groups are also likely to turn from militant to moderate political leaders and from public to private goals. They will settle

[18] Saul D. Alinsky, *Reveille for Radicals*, The University of Chicago Press, Chicago, 1945, is the story of one of the earliest and best-known poverty workers. See also Charles Silberman, *Crisis of Black and White*, Vintage Books, Random House, 1964, chap. 10.
[19] See especially Michael Lipsky, "Protest as a Political Resource," *American Political Science Review*, 62:1144–1158, December, 1968.

for leaders and acts that at the very best promise only small incremental gains. The result overall is that low-income citizens are likely
to be unrepresented or poorly represented in the local group struggle, despite bootstrap organizing à la Alinsky. Some see the only hope
for change as commitment of large-scale resources by state and
national governments.

COMMUNITY CONFLICT[20]

Controversy occasionally divides a community so sharply that its
citizens behave like two warring factions in open conflict. Groups
within the community are pressured by contestants to join one side
or the other on an emotionally charged issue, and bitterness per-
meates much of the decision-making process. In recent years, such
conflicts have developed over any number of events: civil rights
(school integration, restaurant sit-ins, and other demonstrations, or
a riot over the movement of a Negro family into a previously all-white
neighborhood); the conduct of the school system; a change in zoning
practices; the status of the city manager; charges of communism,
generally directed at libraries or schools; a strike, or threat of one,
in a local industry. A long series of smoldering bad feelings may
suddenly burst aflame, as when permanent residents of a resort
community vent their dislike of summer transients. Most commonly
a feeling of suspicion, resentment, or frustration precedes the conflict. Citizens already feel some degree of discontent. This discontent
need not be over local issues. The conduct of the war in Vietnam may
be as significant as the threat of large-scale local apartment building.
The issue that erupts is generally one that persons can see as symbolic of a radical change in the life style of the community. Its symbolic nature makes it one to which extremist groups of the right or
left are readily attracted.

Serious and prolonged conflicts most commonly occur in small- or
medium-sized cities or suburbs; few sweep big cities, though, as the
Watts riots indicated, they may occur in a section of the metropolis.
It appears that a relatively high level of community identification is
necessary. Persons must feel deeply and be willing to act passion-
ately for an issue to catch fire. In suburbia, particularly, conditions
are often ideal for such strife, because many residents hold images
of the ideal community. When one set of images clashes with another,
conflict may become serious.

The way a community handles a traumatic struggle seems to affect
its handling of future controversy. In some cities, the conflict leaves
the community divided into antagonistic groups for many years, and

[20] James Coleman, *Community Conflict*, The Free Press of Glencoe, New York, 1957.

every new controversy is likely to follow the old cleavage lines. In other cities, the clash may have been resolved by a massive show of force, and there is evidence that other controversies that follow are handled the same way. Likewise, those communities that resolve their conflict by discussion, compromise, and adjustments are likely to handle other conflicts the same way. Communities thus seem to create patterns of handling frustrations, just as individuals do.

Community conflicts often follow similar patterns. An event touches the lives of groups of citizens in different ways. It poses an issue which citizens see as potentially resolvable at the community level if some community action is taken. It may well be a national issue. (One community, for example, decided to bar all books mentioning the Communist leader Lenin from its library.) The kinds of cleavage that form within the community are naturally related to the kind of battle lines that potentially exist. The issue may divide along economic, racial, ethnic, or religious group lines, or simply pit old against new residents; or subdivision against rural-life-style residents. A public housing or private development in an older neighborhood is capable of creating a sharp feeling of cleavage.

In a number of cases, conflict has been touched off by outsiders who either visit the community, as did civil rights and some anti-civil rights demonstrators, or who write widely circulated publications which activate local residents. The latter technique has been widely used by radical right groups. Where city or school administrators have few contacts with citizens or where a segment of the community is alienated from what they see as "the establishment," an issue can be easily found. At the beginning, the sides are likely to be composed of a small group of activists against those who defend the status quo, with the large majority of the community neutral and largely uninterested in getting involved. When suspicion among groups or general feelings of frustration already exist, the conflict can most easily spread. If it does, specific issues give way to general ones, new and different issues are introduced, and disagreement changes to antagonism. Associations between factions wither and, within groups, intensify. New leaders emerge, many of whom have only tenuous ties to the community. Lack of previous community involvement is an advantage at this stage since it permits greater freedom of action. These leaders often try to intensify the battle, drive out moderates, and draw established organizations to their side. As the controversy proceeds, more dependence is placed on word-of-mouth communication, and an insatiable demand for news develops. Rumors and the air of conspiracy abound (for example, the rumors of police beatings of blacks or black killings of whites during ghetto riots).

The way the conflict is resolved depends on the political and social arrangements that previously existed. A tradition of tolerance of diverse views may permit a community to ride out the issue. Individuals tend to respond in terms of their previous group associations, but group-association leaders frequently want to resolve the difficulty with compromise, lest the conflict tear apart their groups, for group memberships often overlap. Thus, the leaders of a church group with both strikers and nonstrikers in its membership will attempt to dampen open conflict and seek compromise in a labor-management clash. Those who least have attachments to community groups are most likely to want to release aggressions, often through violent action. Prestigeful groups and persons become important in determining the course of the conflict at this stage.

Closing statement. Struggles like those described above are relatively rare in most communities. More generally, an occasional controversy occurs, but less than one-quarter of the citizens become very intimately involved, and differences are settled by some form of compromise. For most communities, it appears that officials make most decisions with the acquiescence of the large body of citizens. Desires of the more important interest groupings are anticipated; lobbying tends to occur on minor points, such as zoning changes; and the policy that results is a blend of administrative and political points of view. Political parties are weak or absent. The same description might fit the politics of larger cities, except that parties and interest groupings are frequently better organized and more active.

SELECTED
READINGS

Alinsky, Saul: *Reveille for Radicals,* University of Chicago Press, Chicago, 1945.

Banfield, Edward C.: *Big City Politics,* Random House, Inc., New York, 1965. (A study of many of the nation's largest cities.)

Coleman, James: *Community Conflict,* The Free Press of Glencoe, New York, 1957. (A monograph of 26 pages that is incisive in its analysis.)

Crain, Robert, and others: *The Politics of Community Conflict, The Fluoridation Decision,* The Bobbs-Merrill Company, Inc., Indianapolis, 1969.

Crain, Robert: *The Politics of School Desegregation,* Aldine Publishing Company, Chicago, 1968.

Holtzman, Abraham: *Interest Groups and Lobbying,* The Macmillan Company, New York, 1966.

Janowitz, Morris: *The Community Press in an Urban Setting,* The Free Press of Glencoe, New York, 1952.

Lipsky, Michael: *Protest in City Politics, Rent Strikes, Housing and the Power of the Poor,* Rand McNally & Company, Chicago, 1970.

Lowi, Theodore J.: *At the Pleasure of the Mayor,* The Free Press of Glencoe, New York, 1964. (The patronage decisions of the mayor of New York are influenced both by clients directly and by interest groups.)

McConnell, Grant: *Private Power and American Democracy,* Alfred A. Knopf, Inc., New York, 1966.

Metropolitan Applied Research Center: *A Relevant War Against Poverty,* Metropolitan Applied Research Center, New York, 1968.

Olson, Mancur: *The Logic of Collective Action,* Harvard University Press, Cambridge, Mass., 1965. (An economist views interest-group behavior.)

Pennock, J. Roland, and John Chapman (eds.): *Voluntary Associations,* Atherton Press, Inc., New York, 1969.

Rogers, David: *The Management of Big Cities,* Sage Publications, Inc., Beverly Hills, Calif., 1971. (Looks at political power, inter-governmental relations, and, especially, urban interest groups as they affect policy.)

Salisbury, Robert H. (ed.): *Interest Group Politics in America,* Harper & Row, Publishers, Incorporated, New York, 1970.

Sayre, Wallace S., and Herbert Kaufman: *Governing New York City,* Russell Sage Foundation, New York, 1960. (An analysis of the groups that are important in New York policy making.)

Truman, David B.: *The Governmental Process,* Alfred A. Knopf, Inc., New York, 1951. (The principal work on political-group theory.)

"Unofficial Government: Pressure Groups and Lobbies," *The Annals of the American Academy of Political and Social Science,* vol. 319, September, 1958.

Wilson, James Q.: *Negro Politics: The Search for Leadership,* The Free Press of Glencoe, New York, 1960. (Negro politics in the 1950s.)

Zeigler, Harmon: *Interest Groups in American Society,* Prentice-Hall, Inc., Englewood Cliffs, N.J., 1964. (A summary of interest-group theory.)

CHAPTER
5   VOTERS
AND
ELECTIONS

Probably the simplest, most common, and ultimately most important *direct* contact the typical citizen has with his city or village takes place when he steps into the booth and exercises his privilege of voting. Unlike voting in national-government elections, the local suffrage offers a chance to make a choice for many offices (in most cities), in addition to numerous proposed charter amendments, bond issues, and referred and initiated municipal ordinances.

THE ELECTORATE

Who Is Eligible? Time was when more persons were eligible to vote in state than in municipal contests. As a matter of fact, some American cities in the colonial period were "close corporations" where no one at all, not even the wealthiest men, enjoyed the suffrage. Until after World War II (1945), Great Britain had one set of suffrage laws for parliamentary elections and another, less universal, set for municipal voting. In the case of the latter, occupancy as owner or tenant had traditionally been a prerequisite for voting in local contests. In Canada, voting restrictions for municipal elections are still generally greater than for other elections.

Today, with but a few exceptions, the right to vote in American municipal elections is determined by eligibility to participate in state elections. The usual prerequisites include American citizenship, a minimum age, soon to be eighteen in all states, a minimum period of residence in the state, county, and polling district, and registration. Other requirements are sometimes added.

Special Local Requirements. During the Great Depression, Arizona, Michigan, Montana, Nevada, Texas, and Utah provided that only property-tax payers could vote on questions of direct appropriation of public money or the issuance of bonds. By property-tax payers are meant property owners, of course. Contrary to popular misunderstanding, a renter pays just as much in property taxes as an owner, although it is hidden in the rent. There may well be a *psychological* difference between owner and renter when it comes to taxation, but there is no *economic* difference. One study indicated that the Michigan law prevented more than one-half of the Detroit electorate from voting on such issues during the Great Depression.[1] A very few states make, or are constitutionally permitted to make, an actual distinction between eligibility for municipal, as against general, elections. But all these provisions are unusual, are seldom resorted to, and are far off the course being steered by contemporary democratic theory. The almost universal rule is that persons who are eligible to vote in national and state elections may also vote in municipal elections.

VOTING AND NONVOTING

Political scientists have considerable information as to the kinds of people who vote, those who do not, and why they do not. Reasonably confident generalizations can be made.

Apathy on Election Day. In comparison with the people of such democracies as Great Britain and the Scandinavian countries, Americans take their voting responsibilities lightly. Only about one-third of the eligible voters are in the habit of going to the polls regularly. The turnout for state elections is ordinarily much smaller than that when the nation chooses a chief executive, and local elections usually produce the smallest of all. It is not uncommon for the vote in municipal elections to drop to less than one-fourth of the qualified voters. Even the New England town meeting does not appear to inspire citizens to participation. In one study, a town meeting was analyzed in which 700 citizens were qualified to take part. Only 110 did so, a participation figure of 15.7 percent.[2]

The extent of voting varies in different sections of the country, and even between different governmental units in the same section.

[1] Donald S. Hecock and Harry A. Trevelyan, *Detroit Voters and Recent Elections,* Detroit Bureau of Municipal Research, Detroit, Mich., 1938.
[2] From an article by Andrew Nuquist, reported in Roscoe C. Martin, *Grass Roots,* University of Alabama Press, University, Ala., 1957, pp. 60–61.

Each community has its own tradition of participation or nonpartici-pation. Sometimes a matter of particular interest will bring out a larger vote for a local election than was the case in the preceding presidential vote. The degree to which the electorate is organized, or to which organized groups are active in campaigns, influences the size of the turnout. In almost all jurisdictions and at all levels of government, the primary election is of considerably less interest than the general election. (Exceptions are to be found in one-party areas.)

One voter-participation study found that in the average city of Los Angeles County between 1935 and 1952, voter turnout at the average state and national election amounted to 77.2 percent of the registered voters. For the average municipal election, however, the figure was only 41.1 percent of those registered.[3]

The study indicated that participation did *not* vary inversely with the size of the municipality. The city of Los Angeles ranked twenty-sixth out of the forty-five cities in local elections but ranked lower in state and national contests. Tiny Avalon had a very good record, but San Marino, only slightly larger, had the poorest of all records in local elections. Some cities had good records in state and national elections but poor ones in local elections, and vice versa.

The study found that there was no correlation between distance from the core city and amount of voter participation. It was found, however, that predominantly Republican cities had better voting records than did those that were predominantly Democratic. (The municipal elections themselves are nonpartisan in California.) But wealthy communities did not necessarily have good records in *local* elections. Beverly Hills, for example, had next to the poorest record.

Among the important conclusions of the study were these:[4]

1. . . . People tend to vote *against* candidates and proposi-tions rather than for them. . . . People attend city council meet-ings more often to protest than to affirm some proposed action.
2. . . . Voter turnout is dependent upon the degree of *opposi-tion* that can be generated in the minds of voters.
3. . . . There is a sizable number of citizens who consistently participate in state and national elections, but *never vote* in mu-nicipal elections.
4. . . . Percentages of the registered electorates remain fairly *constant* in each city for almost all municipal elections. This may be contrasted with the somewhat more erratic percentages found in voting for state and national offices. . . . *There is a small core of citizens in each city who sustain municipal government.*

[3] L. W. O'Rourke, *Voting Behavior in the Forty-five Cities of Los Angeles County,* Bureau of Govern-mental Research, University of California, Los Angeles, 1953.
[4] *Ibid.,* chap. 2. Italics added.

Apathy and the Duty to Participate. Although the doctrine of grass-roots democracy calls for vigorously active participation in the political process and in the assumption of public office as a duty to the community, the fact is that in America there is frequently a great deal of difficulty in getting public positions filled. Not only may no competition exist for the jobs, but sometimes no one will even allow himself to be drafted.

The small town, the suburb, and the school district often present scenes, not of strident conflict, but of citizens urging other citizens to accept jobs that need to be done. These are positions that carry considerable prestige but involve the budgeting of much of what would otherwise be leisure time for the individual.[5]

In the case of bond-issue referendums, genuine disagreement may be generated, and hence more interest, but even when money is involved, the community may be essentially agreed as to how it should be used. The principal reason for apathy in municipal elections, in fact, is likely to be a pervasive consensus; that is, there may be widespread agreement in the community as to the kinds of persons who are wanted in public office, as to expenditure levels, and as to public policies. Under such circumstances, little incentive exists for any but the most conscientious voter to go to the polls.

Many other reasons are to be found, of course, for the absence of a contest in a local election, and hence for low interest levels. Some of them include:

1. The incumbent is sometimes so popular that other potential candidates have little or no chance to unseat him. He is hence unopposed.
2. In strongly one-party cities with partisan elections, there may be a contest in the primary election of the major party, but the second party can expect to have difficulty in getting candidates to run.
3. The formal political process may not be the effective process of decision making. That is, the important decisions affecting the community may be made outside of government, and public offices are therefore of little importance in the view of the ordinary citizen. A long tradition in America advocates keeping as many issues as possible "out of politics," because the political process is not trusted. Furthermore, community leaders may prefer to negotiate privately among the various interests centering around a controversy, keeping control out of public officials' hands—and outside the reach of the voter. Thus businessmen may agree among themselves on the amount of money to be devoted to port development and present a packaged plan to the council for its ratification. Land-use policies may be controlled in a similar way.

[5] See Martin, *op. cit.*, pp. 60–62.

4. The ruling political group may be so strong (as in Chicago much of the time) that no one thinks it worthwhile to oppose it.

Lack of competition for office reduces the importance of both the primary election or other nominating device and the final election. Absence of genuine conflict contributes to apathy.

Futility and Nonvoting. Even so, we may ask why voter turnout is so low. Why should 28 percent of the interviewees in a representative sample in the 1952 presidential campaign—one in which interest was generally regarded as having been high by American standards—be willing to state openly that they were "not much interested" in the contest?[6] Why should 32 percent of those interviewed say that it would make no difference whether the Democrats or Republicans won the election and another 40 percent think it would make only a small difference?[7]

Part of the answer seems to be furnished by a study made in Detroit.[8] A representative sample of persons was asked these questions: Do you feel that there is anything you can do to improve the way the city is run? What do you feel you can do? *More than one-half the people declared that they can do nothing.* One-third could suggest only voting. Only one person in twelve believed that he could exert influence by means of personal criticism or by joining in group action.

In another study, one-third of the members of the United Automobile Workers agreed that "people like me don't have any say about what government does."[9] These sentiments were especially strong among persons who had feelings of estrangement from society, or feelings of personal futility, or who were generally pessimistic. Persons who felt they could not influence governmental policy also, not surprisingly, tended to be nonvoters. On an authoritarian-democratic scale, they tended more toward the authoritarian position in personal values. A similar attitude of futility was to be found before the 1945 election in the city of New York when one-third of those eligible to vote told pollster Elmo Roper that "no matter which of the candidates is elected, the city will be run about the same."[10] Similar findings have been reported in Philadelphia and Boston.[11] In the latter

[6] Angus Campbell and others, *The Voter Decides,* Harper & Row, Publishers, Incorporated, 1954, p. 34.
[7] *Ibid.,* p. 38.
[8] Arthur Kornhauser, *Attitudes of Detroit People toward Detroit,* Wayne State University Press, Detroit, Mich., 1952, p. 28.
[9] Arthur Kornhauser, H. L. Sheppard, and A. J. Mayer, *When Labor Votes,* University Books, Inc., New York, 1956, pp. 198–200.
[10] Elmo Roper, "New York Elects O'Dwyer," *Public Opinion Quarterly,* 10:53–56, Spring, 1946. For a later study reporting similar findings, see the impressionistic reporting in F. J. Cook and Gene Gleason, "The Shame of New York," *The Nation,* Oct. 31, 1959, entire issue.
[11] James Reichley, *The Art of Government: Reform and Organization Politics in Philadelphia,* The Fund for the Republic, New York, 1958; Murray B. Levin, *The Alienated Voter: Politics in Boston,* Holt, Rinehart and Winston, Inc., New York, 1960.

city, the favorite in the 1959 mayoralty election apparently was defeated because he was perceived by many voters as the leader of a group of powerful politicians, businessmen, and others who wanted to run the city in their own interest. This reaction "was particularly strong because many voters in Boston felt politically powerless."[12] His opponent won, not for the positive qualities in his personality, record of experience, or campaign promises, but because people wanted to vote *against* the favorite. Furthermore, of those who helped elect John F. Collins as mayor, 57 percent thought he would be "no better than his opponent." They could only *hope* that he would come closer to the wanted image. Furthermore, they did not expect Collins's policies to differ fundamentally from those of the man he defeated.

They may have been quite right. Elections do not usually decide issues in America; the interaction of interest groups does that, and the election is only one part—perhaps a relatively minor part—of the political process.

Just how serious is our high percentage of nonvoting anyway? The chances are that its dangers have been greatly exaggerated. Although feelings of voter "alienation"—of frustration and impotence—are reported in studies of large-city politics, these feelings seem much less common in middle-sized cities. Furthermore, even in large cities, the cynicism reported may be more of a culturally expected response—traditionally almost everybody damns the politics of large cities—than of an actual abandonment of faith in democracy. The person who says "both candidates were no good" or "voting was a waste of time" may also give strong support for political action through interest groups, such as his union, trade association, neighborhood improvement association, or church. Elections may leave him unmoved, but he may see the interaction of groups in lobbying rather than elections as the key to policy making. An elaborate study of New York City politics found that "anyone can fight city hall," that most groups do, and that many are very successful.[13]

Most people who stay away from the polls do so deliberately and by their own choice. They are not interested, and they feel that voting in the particular instance will avail them nothing. Except where cynicism is pervasive, the important question is not whether people *do* vote but rather whether they *may* vote if they so choose. Studies made of why people do not vote show that, outside of illness or a broken fan belt on the way to the voting booth, most people stay

12 Levin, *op. cit.,* p. 28.
13 Wallace S. Sayre and Herbert Kaufman, *Governing New York City,* Russell Sage Foundation, New York, 1960. Alienation studies to date do not show whether or not the alienated regard all possible roads to political influence as equally blockaded.

home because of lack of interest. To most people, choice of candidates is of marginal interest. When something they consider to be truly important comes up, they will vote. Americans are more interested in voting against candidates than for them.[14] They become excited about elections when they are determined to register a protest. The ballot box is the safety valve of democracy.

Political Participation. Not only do a large number of Americans not vote in elections, and particularly state and local elections, but another huge bloc of citizens does nothing politically except to vote. In the 1952 presidential contest, 27 percent of the eligible voters said that they talked politics and tried to persuade others to vote for their candidates, and 11 percent engaged in some kind of organized party activity. In this category, 3 percent said they did some party work such as stuffing envelopes; 7 percent said they attended political meetings, rallies, picnics, and the like; only 4 percent contributed money or bought fund-raising tickets. Some people, of course, were active in all three types of positive activity; and some did not vote because of ineligibility or for some other reason.[15] In a postelection survey in the same year, 9 percent of the United Automobile Workers' membership claimed (in a sample study) to have been active in the campaign in such things as handing out leaflets, displaying posters, and the like. Another 17 percent said they had talked politics during the campaign, and 73 percent stated that they had done nothing active.[16]

Who Goes to the Polls? Certain generalizations can be hazarded concerning the qualitative makeup of our voting population. We know that, in terms of percentages, more men vote than do women, more whites vote than do blacks (there is some evidence to indicate that blacks in some Northern urban areas vote in higher percentages than do whites in the same economic category),[17] more people who are property-tax payers vote than do those who are not, and more conservatives vote than do liberals. Except for persons who must stay at home because of the infirmities of old age, people vote in larger proportions as they grow older. Almost twice as many vote at the age of fifty-one as vote at twenty-one. This seems to support the general theory that people do not vote because they theoretically ought to or because they feel it is a duty or a great privilege, but rather they vote when they feel that they have a direct stake in the outcome.

There is a direct relationship between size of income and partici-

---

[14] For more data, see Charles R. Adrian and Charles Press, *The American Political Process*, McGraw-Hill Book Company, New York, 2d ed., 1969, chap. 8.
[15] Campbell and others, *op. cit.*, p. 30.
[16] Kornhauser, Sheppard, and Mayer, *When Labor Votes*, chap. 1.
[17] *Ibid.*, pp. 49–50.

pation in elections and between amount of education and participation. In the postwar years, at least, urbanites have voted in greater proportion than have farmers. The white-collar middle-class votes in greater proportion than do nonunion members of the working class.

It is not known whether these state and national voting-population characteristics generally fit municipal voting, too. One study has addressed itself to the question.[18] In a Midwestern state, it found that the above characteristic patterns generally applied. There was one significant modification: The evidence indicated that, in municipal elections, voter turnout tended to be greatest among the groups that were normally most influential in controlling municipal politics. In three cities where Republican-conservative groups dominated, voters of these interests had the highest voter-turnout habits. In one other city, where Democratic-labor groups controlled, the wards dominated by Democratic labor-union members had the superior voting record. Apparently, the prospects for victory encouraged participation—and helped to ensure it.

All of these patterns affect the balance of forces in the political arena. Apathy or a sense of futility within any given category can have the effect of further weakening the particular interest involved. Each group in society, therefore, has a stake in getting its supporters to the polls, for the vote may be a genuine force in affecting the content of public policy.

An alert public is probably a prerequisite to progress in the art of democratic government. But cheerful homilies about the obligations of the citizen will not serve to inspire the individual who believes that the outcome of the election will have no effect upon the conditions of his existence. Far more effective than sermons would be serious campaigns to remove the factors that have tended to create a sense of futility in the nonvoter, in other words, to make public officials more accessible and more representative of a cross section of the public.

BALLOTS, NOMINATIONS, AND ELECTIONS

American cities use both partisan and nonpartisan ballots in their municipal elections. In a few cases, a system called proportional representation is used. The ballot itself may take several forms.

General Parties on the Local Scene. From necessity, the basic strength and organization of a political party is in the local community. Until nonpartisan elections came into use around 1910, municipal election campaigns were invariably conducted by the local party

[18] Oliver P. Williams and Charles R. Adrian, "The Insulation of Local Politics under the Nonpartisan Ballot," *American Political Science Review*, 53:1052–1063, December, 1959.

organizations. In that earlier day, many large cities were dominated by well-organized political machines, particularly of the majority party of the community. The minority party was usually less well organized and often had very little chance for success at the polls. In most cities the ward was, and is today, the basic unit of party organization. It was often subdivided into precincts.

Today few political machines remain, and partisan elections are used in only about 40 percent of American cities. Despite the trend away from partisan municipal elections, some political activists argue that such elections are desirable, at least for large cities, because the strength of state and national parties depends upon effective local organization and because public policy today is executed simultaneously on all levels of government. The functions performed by cities are interdependent parts of the whole process of government. Politics and politicians on the local level do not differ fundamentally from their counterparts on the higher levels. Charles A. Beard once asserted that many local problems can be solved only by cooperation with either the state or the national government or both. Today this is surely true of such functions as public health, welfare, highways, safety, housing, and unemployment. Since political parties serve as a liaison between politicians and since a party approach toward a public problem may include plans that require action at all levels of government, partisanship on the local scene may be desirable.[19]

Opponents of partisanship, on the other hand, argue that running a city is not a matter of skillful politics but rather one of efficient business management. The editors of the *National Civic Review,* for example, argue in the following vein:[20]

> There is, after all, no valid reason for national and state parties to be involved and every reason why they should not.
> It has been amply demonstrated that, to be effective and self-reliant cities must be emancipated from the tyranny of the national and state political parties. Good citizens who agree on vital local issues should not be divided by blind loyalties that serve only to confuse these issues.
> The way to decency and honesty in national as well as local politics is to eliminate parties from the local scene and thus make all voters "independent."

The arguments on both sides are doubtless exaggerated. Many municipal officers elected on a nonpartisan ballot do cooperate successfully with partisan state and national officers. Our general par-

[19] See Charles A. Beard, "Politics and City Government," *National Municipal Review,* 6:201–205, March, 1917.
[20] Editorial, "Revolt of the 'Independents,'" *National Municipal Review* (now *National Civic Review*), 40:564–565, December, 1951.

ties have not proved to be very effective in a liaison role, neither do they stand on definite principles or policies.

Local organizations of the national and state parties, on the other hand, are often quite independent of the higher party structure, especially on local questions. The "blind loyalties" of party exist, without doubt, especially in cities where the remnants of political machines are to be found, but this phenomenon may be exaggerated, too. Devoted members of a political party in national and state elections may well vote quite independently in municipal elections. This is especially true if city and general elections are held at different times.

Certainly, party leaders often try to inject state or national issues into local campaigns. Sometimes they are successful, sometimes not. However, it is a fallacy in logic to say that local campaigns in which candidates run as Republicans or Democrats cannot be conducted on local issues.

Whatever the merits of the conflicting arguments presented, there remains one very serious obstacle to the effective use of national parties for city elections: Most of our cities, instead of having two well-balanced parties where one stands ready at all times to take control away from the other, actually have only one strong party. This is highly undesirable, for our political system is conceived of as an in-party—out-party relationship. Where one party dominates almost to the total exclusion of the other, there is no effective criticism, there is no control of the party in power, and there is no real responsibility to the electorate. The city with a working two-party system is rare. The pattern in New York, where the Democratic party is almost never defeated except by its own dissidents, or in Philadelphia, where the Republicans once controlled the city government for over eighty consecutive years, is a common one. It is this situation, and not some of the more often-cited objections, that forms the greatest weakness of partisanship in municipal affairs.

Wherever partisan elections are used, however, the political party label provides an important cue to a large number of voters. In a great many cases, the voter need not be concerned about positions on issues or other types of information. In elections in which he feels a relatively low stake, he simply decides how to vote according to the party label. In the absence of that label, he is forced to find other cues. These may stem from the personality or perceived life style of the candidate, the recommendations of newspaper editors in whom he has confidence, or suggestions of opinion leaders, such as chamber of commerce secretaries or labor-union stewards.

Two studies have found that party affiliation is more important than class or any other factor in partisan elections and that it remains the best indicator of voting tendencies in nonpartisan elections, although of less importance there than in partisan.[21]

In the South, a somewhat different pattern has been found. In Democratic primary elections, race was a better indication of voting tendency than was party, although for a nonpartisan mayoralty election, these two were about of equal importance. Party seems to be relatively unimportant in Atlanta, because of the importance of coalitions within the Democratic party. Elections in that city tend to be dominated by an alliance among professional political leaders, the civic elite, and the Negro leadership.[22] Perhaps in all cities using a nonpartisan ballot but with political parties that now have, or are perceived as having, potentially competitive party systems, a latent partisanship can be found in the voting patterns.[23]

Nonpartisan Elections: The Prevailing Urban Pattern. Early in the twentieth century, many members of the reform movement began to advocate the use of nonpartisan elections. They argued that city government was a matter of efficient business administration and that state and national politics had nothing in common with local politics.

The nonpartisan ballot is used in over 60 percent of the American cities of over 5,000 population. It is especially popular in council-manager cities, over 85 percent of which use it. A nonpartisan ballot does not, of course, in itself eliminate party activity from local politics, though it certainly appears to encourage such a development. To the extent that partisanship is removed, the goals of the reformers of two or three generations ago are achieved.

Many patterns appear to result from a nonpartisan ballot. The principal ones are the following:[24]

1. A system of elections in which the only candidates who normally have any chance to win are those supported by a major political party organization. In these cities, a short ballot is used, candidates are easily identifiable by party, and the result is not much different from partisan elections. Chicago is an example of this type of "nonpartisan" city; Jersey City was another during the time of the powerful machine of Frank Hague.

2. A system of elections in which slates of candidates are supported by various groups, including political party organiza-

[21] Robert Salisbury and Gordon Black, "Classes and Party in Partisan and Nonpartisan Elections," *American Political Science Review,* 57:584–592, September, 1963; and Oliver P. Williams and Charles R. Adrian, *Four Cities,* University of Pennsylvania Press, Philadelphia, 1963, chap. 4.
[22] M. Kent Jennings and Harmon Zeigler, "Class, Party, and Race in Four Types of Elections," *Journal of Politics,* 28:391–407, May, 1966.
[23] Heinz Eulau, Betty H. Zisk, and Kenneth Prewitt, "Latent Partisanship in Nonpartisan Elections," in M. Kent Jennings and Harmon Zeigler (eds.), *The Electoral Process,* Prentice-Hall, Inc., Englewood Cliffs, N.J., 1966, chap. 10.
[24] Charles R. Adrian, "A Typology for Nonpartisan Elections," *Western Political Quarterly,* 12:449–458, June, 1959, and citations.

tions. Here the voters perceive nonpartisan elections as being a distinctive type, but the political party groups are able to compete against slates of candidates presented by nonparty groups. The politics of Albuquerque, Cincinnati, and Wichita, along with other cities, appear to fit this pattern.[25]

3. A system of elections in which slates of candidates are supported by various interest groups, but political party organizations have little or no part in campaigns. In these cities, candidates may have no party affiliation, or it may be unknown, or the voters may consider it to be irrelevant. This pattern appears to be far more common than the two listed above. Kansas City (since the fall of the Pendergast machine), Dallas, Fort Worth, and many California and Michigan cities appear to fit this category.[26]

4. A system of elections in which neither political parties nor slates of candidates are important. This type appears to be very common, possibly even more so than the third type. It is especially important in small cities, for in these communities what Eugene Lee has called the "politics of acquaintance" is often the decisive factor.[27] Under this system, according to Lee, the typical pattern is "the development of support, organization and funds by the individual candidate himself on an ad hoc basis. Rather than being recruited by a group and assuming its apparatus, the average candidate must build his own campaign from the ground up."

The Effects of Nonpartisanship. In small cities and villages, where government is largely on an informal personal basis, nonpartisanship has worked satisfactorily. In the largest cities, however, nonpartisanship has not aided in producing a satisfactory degree of representative and responsive government. Without a guiding label on the ballot, the large-city voter has difficulty in identifying candidates, especially for council. The most important thing for the candidate is, therefore, not to have a platform but rather to have a name that rings a bell in the voter's mind. Publicity becomes all important, and the election is normally won by those who can control the media of mass communication, the newspapers in particular. This has been largely the pattern, for example, in Dallas, Fort Worth, Los Angeles, San Francisco, San Diego, and Detroit.

In large cities, nonpartisanship makes it difficult for voters to cast a protest vote for members of the council. The discontented will normally vote against the in-party and for the out-party. They cannot

---

[25] See Dorothy I. Cline, *Albuquerque and the City Manager Plan,* The University of New Mexico Press, Albuquerque, N. Mex., 1951; Ralph A. Straetz, *PR Politics in Cincinnati,* New York University Press, New York, 1958; and, for Wichita, Marvin A. Harder, *Nonpartisan Election: A Political Illusion?* Holt, Rinehart and Winston, Inc., New York, 1958.

[26] See Eugene C. Lee, *The Politics of Nonpartisanship: A Study of California City Elections,* University of California Press, Berkeley, Calif., 1960; Williams and Adrian, *Four Cities,* chap. 4.

[27] See Lee, *op. cit.;* and Richard S. Childs, *Civic Victories,* Harper & Row, Publishers, Incorporated, New York, 1952, appendix. C.

do this under nonpartisanship. The incumbent is thus given an advantage in a campaign, for his name is often the best known to the voter.[28]

Some evidence indicates that partisan and nonpartisan politicians are not insulated into two separate compartments. If this was once true, as seems to have been the case,[29] it is probably less so today.[30] In such cities as Minneapolis and Detroit, as well as some cities in California, persons who begin their careers in the nonpartisan arena move into candidature for offices on partisan ballots. In a few cases, the opposite career pattern has appeared. It seems likely that the following generalization is valid: The more visible the office, the greater the options available to the incumbent officeholder as he seeks career advancement, regardless of whether the office is partisan or nonpartisan.

A study of nonpartisan municipal elections in California indicated a notable degree of competition for office and considerable opportunity for dissent and for casting a protest vote. On the other hand, Republicans were found to have a decided advantage in nonpartisan elections in the state, which has a majority of Democratic voters. Councilmanic elections were found to be as competitive as the partisan elections for the state legislature. The two major political parties had little formal relationship to local nonpartisan campaigns, but nonpartisan officeholders were found quite commonly to compete for partisan office, often successfully. Most incumbents and most Republican county chairmen wanted to continue nonpartisan elections, but 60 percent of the Democratic chairmen favored a change to the partisan ballot. In elections, Republicans and conservatives exercised greater influence because of their higher propensity to vote. The larger the city, the more likely the political party organizations were to be formally involved in campaigns; the larger the city, the more influential the role of the local press was considered to be in influencing voter decisions.[31]

Evidence that the type of ballot does not segregate careers in large cities to either a partisan or nonpartisan pattern is found in a study of Milwaukee politics, where the recruitment of candidates for nonpartisan office was not found to be sharply separated from that for partisan office. Nonpartisan officeholders were not found to have

---

[28] See Charles R. Adrian, "Some General Characteristics of Nonpartisan Elections," *American Political Science Review*, 46:766–776, September, 1952. For examples of professional public relations work through the mass media of communication in communities with little political structure, see Irwin Ross, "The Supersalesmen of California Politics," *Harper's Magazine*, July, 1959, pp. 55–61; and more generally, Dan Nimmo, *The Political Persuaders: The Techniques of Modern Election Campaigns*, Prentice-Hall, Inc., Englewood Cliffs, N.J., 1970.
[29] Adrian, "Some General Characteristics of Nonpartisan Elections."
[30] A. Clarke Hagensick, "Influences of Partisanship and Incumbency on a Nonpartisan Elections System," *Western Political Quarterly*, 17:117–124, March, 1964.
[31] Lee, *op. cit.*

any particular incumbency advantage, in comparison with partisan officeholders, when seeking reelection.[32] It is also doubtful if non-partisanship aids conservative policies in large cities, as was once believed.[33] Factors other than formal structure of the electoral system, particularly state government policies and metropolitan population patterns, are probably more important influences upon public policy.[34]

Local Parties: The Exception.[35] Numerous examples of local parties exist in municipal politics, although they have in no way become an integral part of the American political system. Americans in overwhelming numbers have taken the attitude that efforts toward third parties are a waste of time, and this viewpoint probably spills over into local politics. Local parties for the most part consist of small-town parties and reform parties.

Local Parties for Small Towns. Local parties are to be found in many villages and in small and even middle-sized cities where politics is on a personal basis, national parties are not desired, and yet for one reason or another (perhaps local custom, or state laws which do not permit nonpartisanship), a party label must be used. A small Iowa city, for example, may have a municipal contest between members of the People's party and the Citizen's party, or the Liberal party and the Temperance party, or the Progressive party and the Conservative party. These labels are most often nothing more than collective terms for slates of candidates having no organization, platform, or treasury. Politics is on a personal basis, and the label is meaningless.

Reform Parties. Reform parties have been organized from time to time in various cities chiefly for purposes of driving out existing machines or corrupt politicians, or for establishing some of the principles of "efficiency and economy." Most of these parties have been short-lived, and their general failure has encouraged reform groups to organize themselves as *interest groups* rather then political parties, endorsing candidates and policies, but not putting men of their own into the field. This is true today of the New York Citizens' Union, the Chicago Municipal Voters' League, and the Detroit Citizens' League, for example.

---

[32] Hagensick, *op. cit.*
[33] John H. Kessel, "Governmental Structure and Political Environment," *American Political Science Review,* 56:615–620, September, 1962.
[34] Charles E. Gilbert, "Some Aspects of Nonpartisan Elections in Large Cities," *Midwest Journal of Political Science,* 6:345–362, November, 1962.
[35] See J. Leiper Freeman, "Local Party Systems: Theoretical Considerations and a Case Analysis," *American Journal of Sociology,* 64:282–289, November, 1958.

Some of these groups, such as the one in New York, began as local parties but found this impractical for one reason or another (the Citizens' Union was nearly taken over by a Tammany Hall fifth column). They then proceeded to work toward their goals on a bipartisan or nonpartisan basis.

New York City saw a genuine local party created during the Great Depression in the form of the fusion party with Fiorello H. La Guardia as its principal driving force. The organization was made up of Citizens' Unionists, many Republicans (including La Guardia), sundry persons not usually politically active, and antimachine Democrats.

Two other local parties exist in the city of New York. Both of them are statewide parties in form but draw nearly all their support from within the city. The American Labor party was organized in 1936 chiefly by several labor leaders and some Socialists who had broken with their national party. It campaigned against Tammany Hall and proclaimed itself the "true" New Deal party of New York. It reached its greatest power in the city election of 1937, following a practice of endorsing other candidates or running its own, whichever might prove most advantageous in each individual case. The party became infiltrated with Communists, and a long fight ensued for control of the organization, culminating in 1944 with the withdrawal of the bulk of the non-Communists, who then formed the Liberal party. (The Amalgamated Clothing Workers of America did not withdraw until 1948.) Since that time, the Liberals have usually preferred to endorse other candidates (generally Democrats on the state level and Republicans in city contests) rather than run their own, although they do run their own whenever they think it desirable.

The Charter Party. Perhaps the best-known and most successful local party in the United States is the City Charter Committee of Cincinnati, often referred to as the "Charter party." Although the organization does not formally call itself a party and although its name does not appear on the Cincinnati nonpartisan ballot following the names of its candidates, it is thoroughly organized in the general pattern of urban parties, and it functions very definitely as a local party.

Cincinnati had long been controlled by a powerful Republican machine when, in 1924, a reform effort secured the adoption of the council-manager plan and proportional representation. It was in order to safeguard these achievements that the Charter party was formed immediately after the election. Its organization has come to equal the best of political machines of the old type: It not only has complete men's and women's ward and precinct organizations but is actually built upon a broad base of the block worker.

It has publicity, literature, and speakers committees, poll watchers, telephone brigades, and all the other paraphernalia necessary to get out the vote. Perhaps most important of all, it has a permanent and effective organization for financing its efforts. The party differs from traditional machines in that it is interested in good government per se and makes no political promises in return for volunteered efforts. That is, it is not based on patronage, as are other political machines, but relies entirely on unpaid citizens.

From its inception, the Charter party has been opposed in elections by the regular Republican organization. About one-half of the time the Charterites have organized the city council. At other times, either the Republicans have taken control or there has been a 4-4-1 split, with an independent holding the balance of power. This spirited and closely balanced two-party system has forced the regular Republican organization to reform itself (a large number of Charterites are Republicans in state and national elections).

Groups in several smaller cities, especially with council-manager forms of government, have sought to imitate the Cincinnati type of local party with varying degrees of success. Generally they fail to solve the problem of how to establish themselves as a party if no labels are on the ballot, or of maintaining a permanent organization, or both. In many cities, however, reform or business groups put candidates into the field and help finance their campaigns. These groups often have the backing of the local press. They should perhaps be classified as interest groups rather than local parties, although the line between the two is not easy to draw in this case.

Local Parties: An Appraisal. Local parties suffer from serious handicaps that make the Charter party or even the Fusion party rare successes in America. It is often argued that such parties would quickly become mere adjuncts of national parties—the same old parties under different names. This does not necessarily follow and it would be quite possible to maintain these parties as separate entities; however, some very real problems do confront local parties.

In the first place, local parties require constant attention and interest from a large part of the public. This is difficult to secure, and the normal result is that shortly after "the rascals" are thrown out, the party begins to disintegrate. This has happened many times in the United States. A permanent organization with permanent electioneering on the Cincinnati model is imperative for longevity of local parties. Secondly, local parties are difficult to organize in any case. Political party structures are complex and require much coordinated effort. It is virtually impossible to organize a successful local party except under unusual circumstances (a deep economic depression, a particularly corrupt administration), and even then it is not easy. Thirdly, attempts to organize local parties, as such, are likely to be resisted by the informal ruling group of businessmen who put up candidates, finance them, and—in lieu of having an organized party structure—control the media of communication. Lastly, local parties have a great deal of difficulty in securing enough funds for survival. People will not make contributions unless they believe in the cause to begin with and further believe that a particular organization is capable of advancing that cause. The Cincinnati Charter party has been successful because it has been able both to develop an effective money-raising organization and to get the confidence and support of businessmen who have funds that can be tapped. The American Labor and later the Liberal party could survive in New York because they had a firm financial base in labor-union support. A poorly financed party has no chance of survival.

Methods of Nomination. Before there can be an election, the individuals who are going to make the race must first be nominated. There are numerous ways of placing candidates in nomination. The overwhelming majority of nominations on the local (or any other) level made in the United States today are by way of either the partisan or the nonpartisan direct primary election. There are, or have been, however, numerous other techniques, including caucus or convention nomination, sponsorship, and petition.

Early Nomination Devices. The *caucus,* the oldest form of nomination in the United States, consisted originally of an informal meeting to choose candidates deserving of support for the various public offices becoming vacant. In America's early days, the caucus members could print a ballot and distribute it themselves.

With the development of cities, the caucus system degenerated. A more formal method and one that would make known the desires of the common voter, rather than those of the organized few, was demanded. The *convention* method called for nominations at a formal gathering whose membership was chosen by caucus at the precinct level. With the organization of nineteenth-century political machines, both the caucus and the convention tended to be dominated by a few people, with the general public having little real choice in the nomination—and in most cities nomination by the dominant party was tantamount to election.

Reforms in Nomination. Beginning at the turn of the century, the reform movement produced a change in nomination procedure. The *direct primary election* was substituted for the caucus and convention. It is now almost universal in the United States, although a few states do not use it for important state offices and there are cities in such populous states as California, Texas, New Jersey, and Massachusetts that do not use it.

Strictly speaking, a primary election is nothing more than a *non-assembled* caucus. In an earlier day every eligible voter was entitled to take part in the selection of candidates. Later, part of this job had to be turned over to what were theoretically his representatives acting at a *convention.* When the convention proved to be unrepresentative and boss-ridden, the primary election was devised to return nominations "to the people." The plan in large measure transfers control of the nomination machinery from the party to the state, all parties choosing their candidates on the same day under the supervision of public election officials, with ballots standardized and printed at public expense, and with a secret ballot (in contrast with most caucus and convention systems).

The primary election has never been understood by the vast majority of American voters. They are annoyed by the fantastically long "bedsheet" ballot with which they are confronted; they resent the fact that they must usually reveal their party preference in order to vote; and even when the open primary is used, they become incensed when they discover that splitting the ticket is not permitted.

Types of Primaries. Primary elections are of two types, nonpartisan and partisan. The latter is subdivided into two classes, open and closed. The *nonpartisan* primary is actually an elimination contest. Names appear on the ballot without party designation. The first election, popularly and sometimes legally called a primary, serves to eliminate all candidates except twice the number to be elected. Hence, if seven file for the office of mayor, only two will survive the primary—the two with the highest number of votes. If seven councilmen are to be elected, the fourteen highest at the primary are nominated. In some cases, such as in many California cities and in elections for the Chicago council, if any candidate receives a majority of the vote cast in the primary he is declared elected, and the taxpayer is saved the cost of placing him on the final ballot.

In nonpartisan as well as partisan primaries, one gets on the ballot in the first place in one of three ways: by a simple formal declaration, by signature petition (in either of these two, a small filing fee to defray part of the expense of putting the name on the ballot may be charged), or by filing a forfeitable deposit.

The *partisan* primary may be open or closed. An open primary is open to any eligible voter, regardless of which party may be his own, or whether he is a party member or a confirmed independent. He need not demonstrate or declare anything other than that he is a qualified voter in order to receive a ballot. A closed primary, on the other hand, is closed to everyone except members of the political party concerned.

Other Nomination Devices. Some cities in a number of states make use of nomination by *petition* directly onto the final ballot. This method saves the expense of a primary election and usually has satisfactory results in small cities. But when the plan was used in Boston, the mayor was often a plurality rather than a majority choice, for there were nearly always more than two major candidates. (A *plurality* is more votes than any other candidate receives. A *majority* is at least one vote more than one-half of the number cast.) Boss James Michael Curley, as the best-known mayoralty candidate, sometimes found this plan of considerable help to him.

The *Model City Charter* of the National Municipal League recommends a plan, especially in connection with proportional representation, called the *sponsor system*. It has been used in some California cities for several years. It is similar to the British system of nomination, for it requires a petition signed by ten persons, who are listed as "sponsors" of the candidate, and the filing of a sum of money, to be returned under certain conditions.

EXPERIMENTS IN DIRECT DEMOCRACY

The Initiative and Referendum. With the decline in the prestige of governing bodies in the last half of the nineteenth century came also a decline in citizen faith in representative democracy. As a consequence, reformers proposed what were then considered radical solutions. They renovated and reorganized some old American institutions, introduced some new ones, and hopefully presented us with techniques for direct democracy as a check upon excesses and incompetence. The *initiative* permits a legally defined number of voters to propose changes in the city charter or ordinances which are then accepted or rejected by the voters at the polls. This device permits legislation to be effected with no recourse at all to the legislative body. The *referendum* permits the voters to accept or reject at the polls council-proposed changes in the city charter or ordinances. The referendum differs from the initiative in that it *follows* favorable action by the legislative body, whereas such an institutional device as the initiative takes place independently of the legislative body.

The Procedure. An initiated proposal is normally drafted by the attorneys for the particular interest group seeking the legislation. Petitions to put the proposal on the ballot are then circulated by volunteers or by persons hired for the purpose, often at the price of a certain amount per signature. The quantity of signatures required may be a specific numerical total or be those of a certain percentage of voters (registered, or voting for a certain office at the last general election, or some other formula). Where such a percentage is used, it is generally from 5 to 10 percent, but may be higher. In most instances, the proposal is adopted if a majority of those voting on the proposal vote in its favor, although in some cases a majority of those voting *in the election* is required (this means that if a voter ignores the proposal he is in effect voting "no"), or some special formula may be used. It is often provided that an initiated ordinance may not be amended or repealed by the city council, at least within a certain prescribed time limit.

The initiative and referendum (I. and R.), particularly the latter, have ancient origins in America and elsewhere. Antecedents are to be found in the direct democracy of ancient Greece, the ancient tribal governments of Germany, the right to petition the king in medieval England, the town meeting of colonial New England, and the direct democracy of Switzerland.[36] As early as 1825, the Maryland legislature provided for a referendum on the question of establishing a public school system. It later became very common to hold referendums on liquor questions, charter amendments, public utility franchises, bond issues, and other matters. California, Iowa, and Nebraska in the late nineteenth century authorized municipal use of the initiative and referendum. The San Francisco home rule charter of 1898 was the first such document to provide for them. From then the movement spread rapidly, and it is today widely authorized for municipal governments.

Around the beginning of the century, when many cities adopted the initiative and referendum, proponents made greatly exaggerated claims of their merits. Opponents were equally vociferous, viewing with alarm the potentiality for hamstringing the governmental process by their use. The results have not borne out the claims of either side.

Arguments concerning I. and R. Proponents of direct democracy argued that corrupt and low-quality city councils made it necessary for people to have a check upon the government. Reformers also

---

[36] See William Munro (ed.), *The Initiative, Referendum, and Recall*, The Macmillan Company, New York, 1913, chap. 1. Also Ralph M. Goldman, "The Advisory Referendum in America," *Public Opinion Quarterly*, 14:303–315, Summer, 1950.

took note of the trend toward a concentration of authority in government and a breakdown of the traditional check-and-balance system. The initiative and referendum could serve to replace some of these disappearing checks. It was argued that the use of these devices strengthened popular control over city government by giving the people "a gun behind the door" which could serve as a means of requiring greater alertness, honesty, and responsiveness on the part of council members.

It was believed that I. and R. would protect the people from political tricks and thefts from the public treasury. Some argued that it would encourage voters to become better informed on issues, since they would have to vote on so many of them directly and since they could now feel that they had a real chance to get things done in local affairs.

Opponents of the system argued that it confused legislative responsibility, lengthened an already overly long ballot, created a bad psychological effect upon the city council, expected more than was reasonable from an uninformed and uninterested electorate, would promote radicalism and a disrespect for property rights, was opposed to the best principles of Americanism (since the Constitution is based upon *representative,* and not *direct,* democracy), and would allow well-organized interest groups representing a minority of the population to exercise an inordinate advantage.[37]

I. and R.: An Appraisal. The debate over the use of I. and R. has subsided in recent years, though the use of these devices is, if anything, increasing. Perhaps it is necessary here to make only two points, without discussing the merits of the arguments briefly outlined above.

First, the I. and R. seem to carry the implicit assumption that the individual voter is always informed and rational in his choices. Actually, of course, this assumption is false. Furthermore, democracy as we know it does not require such an assumption. In an ordinary election, the voter is merely asked whether or not he is relatively satisfied with things as they are. According to the state of his satisfactions, he votes for those in power or he casts a protest vote. His reasons for his vote are his own, and they need not be rational, logical, or informed. He is not asked to rule but merely to choose those who are to rule. But the I. and R. ask more than this of the voter. They ask him to help rule himself and to make policy decisions on questions that are often complex, technical, and minutely detailed.

[37] Extensive arguments on the pros and cons are presented in Munro, chaps. 1–11.

It is not uncommon, for example, for the voter to be asked a question such as the following:[38]

General Retirement System Amendment

Do you favor an amendment to Title IX, Chapter VI, General Retirement System, of the Charter of the City of Detroit, changing membership service pension from $\frac{1}{120}$ of average final compensation to $\frac{1}{100}$ average final compensation times years of membership service; to increase maximum city pension from $1,800 per annum to $2,400 per annum; to provide for optional benefit to widow or dependent husband for member who continues in service after becoming eligible to retire and to provide for increase of employees' annuity contributions from 5% on $3,600 to 5% on $7,200 or under per annum?

Yes □
No □

Where the law permits or requires complex questions to be submitted to the general public for direct action, the results are sometimes humorous—or would be if government were not such a serious business. In the November, 1952, election, the voters of Waldwick, New Jersey (1950 population: 3,963), on the edge of the New York metropolitan area, voted to establish a full-time police force; but on another question, refused to appropriate the additional $10,000 a year to finance the project; and on a third question, voted to retain the existing part-time system. And all this at the same election.

Second, opponents of the I. and R. are wont to overlook the fact that the American political structure is pluralistic and not neatly integrated, and that the American political process is typically based upon the interaction of pressure groups. American cities, for the most part, do not have responsible political party structures, and few cities have a two-party system of any kind regularly competing for voter support. Furthermore, it is unlikely that this pattern will be changed much in the foreseeable future. Since this system may result in city councils that are not representative of a cross section of the population, the I. and R. may well be used as a check, "a gun behind the door."[39]

The typical citizen probably favors the retention of the initiative and referendum, viewing them as safety measures, but he does not pay a great deal of attention to the typical issue. In Chicago, between 1924 and 1935, 85 of the 114 bond-issue referendums attracted less than one-half of the registered voters. This was true even though

[38] Proposed Amendment E to the Detroit City Charter, election of Nov. 6, 1951. Incidentally, the proposal passed. City employees urged a favorable vote. Probably most voters did not know that they were raising city expenses by one-half million dollars a year.
[39] In this connection, see Joseph La Palombara and Charles B. Hagan, "Direct Legislation: An Appraisal and a Suggestion," *American Political Science Review*, 45:400–421, June, 1951.

some of the proposed issues elicited campaigns involving a great deal of conflict.[40] A series of bond-issue referendums in DeKalb County, Georgia, which is suburban Atlanta, produced a turnout of only 24.2 percent in 1961. Higher-status individuals in all parts of the county were more likely to vote on the I. and R. questions than were lower-status individuals.[41] The greatest support for bond issues came from high-income persons. Support for the issues, which in general were designed to provide more of life's amenities of the type that are usually supplied by municipal governments, was highest among suburban voters. Least support came from persons in the outer fringe. Perhaps this was in part a reflection of the perceived needs for the various services. Support for the bonds was greatest among persons in the forty-to-sixty-year-old category.

A study of referendums in Michigan in the 1950s showed that voter interest and support for proposals that had city-council support varied directly with socioeconomic status. Some evidence indicated that support for referendums tended to vary with the level of confidence that various groups of voters had in their city government.[42]

A study of defeated school-bond issues in two communities indicated that persons with a strong sense of political alienation (powerlessness) tended to cast negative votes. To them, the referendum apparently served not as a device for indicating how the community could be improved, or even for casting a class-oriented protest, but rather as a generalized protest against personal feelings of helplessness in the face of political forces bigger than they could comprehend or hope to be able to influence.[43] The 1,512 bond and tax referendums held in the United States between 1948 and 1959 indicated that a high turnout of voters generally signals defeat for a proposal.[44]

The Recall. The third member of the triumvirate that was to produce popular control of city government was the *recall*. This is a device whereby any elective officer may be removed from office by a popular vote prior to the expiration of his term. Although it is often mentioned in connection with the initiative and referendum, the recall may exist independently of them. It was brought into extensive use by the same people, and for largely the same reasons. They argued

[40] Harold F. Gosnell, *Machine Politics: Chicago Model*, The University of Chicago Press, Chicago, 1937, p. 134.
[41] Alvin Boskoff and Harmon Zeigler, *Voting Patterns in a Local Election*, J. P. Lippincott Company, Philadelphia, 1964, chap. 6.
[42] Oliver P. Williams and Charles R. Adrian, *Four Cities*, University of Pennsylvania Press, Philadelphia, 1963, chap. 5.
[43] John E. Horton and Wayne E. Thompson, "Powerlessness and Political Negativism: A Study of Defeated Referendums," *American Journal of Sociology*, 67:485–493, March, 1962.
[44] Richard F. Carter and William G. Savard, *The Influence of Voter Turnout on School Bond and Tax Elections*, U.S. Department of Health, Education, and Welfare, 1961.

that a faithless or incompetent public servant should not be inflicted upon the people for the duration of his term—that he should be removed as soon as his shortcomings were discovered. Again, Jacksonians who were not too happy with the increasing popularity of the four-year term, as against the traditional two years, found it easier to accept the longer term if "continuous responsibility" were maintained through the availability of the recall. The mechanism was probably first provided for in the Los Angeles home rule charter of 1903; unlike its two sisters, it has no direct precedents in American political practices.

The Procedure. In order to recall an official, a petition must be circulated. Since a large number of signatures are usually required—such as 15 to 25 or even as high as 51 percent of the vote cast for the office of mayor in the last election—an organized group with a good deal of motivation and a sizable treasury is usually required. After enough signatures are certified by the city clerk or other appropriate election officer, an election becomes obligatory. There are several variants of the recall ballot, and its form may itself serve to either aid or discourage the prospects for removal of the official.

Arguments Pro and Con. The principal argument for the recall is that it provides for continuous responsibility (especially important with the four-year term), so that citizens need not wait in exasperation and frustration until the term comes to an end. It is similarly argued that, with a sword constantly hanging over the head of the public official, he will feel a need to remain alert at all times.

Opponents of the recall point to its costliness: A *special* election is imperative for its use, since it would be unfair to conduct such an election in connection with other questions (although this is sometimes done). A second objection to the recall is that it does not attempt to *prove charges* against an officeholder but merely to persuade the electorate, by whatever means, to remove the incumbent. A third objection is that the recall is unnecessary. In all states, improper conduct by public officials is grounds for removal by other judicial, councilmanic, or sometimes gubernatorial action.[45]

A final objection to the recall centers in the assertion that it serves as a tool for well-organized interest groups and for political recrimination. Similarly, it is said that the threat of the recall is a constant and perfectly legal means for intimidation of public officials who must therefore slavishly follow public whims and sentimentality. A strong leader with a positive program may find that

[45] See chap. 9.

some interest group will stand in his path threatening him with a recall action if he seeks to carry out his plans.

There is a trend away from the recall, and it has never been widely used. Few new adoptions of it have taken place since about 1920. The question of the use of the recall is no longer a very burning one, but it does seem as if the experiment has been of little success.

The Public Hearing. A few words should be said about another important American device for involving the citizen in decision making, the public hearing. This institution is unusual in Europe but is well established in American tradition, which calls for the general public to be consulted, or at least informed, about every significant decision affecting public policy. Public hearings generally involve a rather informal procedure at which every citizen present is allowed to speak if he cares to do so. They are commonly used prior to the making of decisions concerning such matters as the zoning of land, the location of taverns, the moving of highways, the changing of public utilities rates, the exempting of certain property from the tax rolls (as in the granting of a permit for a cemetery), the location of a new school, and for dozens of other purposes.

Political neophytes find the hearing procedure puzzling, because at a typical meeting nearly all persons expressing themselves are opposed to the proposal which is the subject of the hearing. The official or public body conducting the hearing does not, of course, take a vote at the time and dispose of the issue on that basis. Instead, the hearing is used as a safety-valve device for allowing disapproving persons to vent their feelings. These people thus gain a feeling of having had their "day in court," and they may succeed in having the proposed policy modified somewhat so as to meet, at least partially, some of their objections. The hearing also allows the responsible officials to judge in advance of decisions the political climate in which they will find themselves. They may also learn something that will suggest to them the language in which to couch the announcement of a decision so as to minimize the number and intensity of unfavorable responses.

PROPORTIONAL AND PREFERENTIAL VOTING SYSTEMS

The Hare System of Proportional Representation.[46] One of the schemes advocated by members of the reform movement was the Hare system of proportional representation by single transferable

[46] See George H. Hallet, Jr., *Proportional Representation: The Key to Democracy*, 2d ed., National Municipal League, New York, 1940.

vote. P.R. reflected the untiring efforts of reformers to reduce the power of political machines and constituted a definite improvement over other attempts to remedy faults in both the old ward system and the newer at-large system of councilmanic elections. The ward system encouraged parochialism in politics, and election at large could give 100 percent control of the council to whatever group might receive a plurality in the voting.

Some cities experimented with the St. Louis practice of nominating by wards and electing at large; many others elected part of the council at large and part of it by wards. Some (including New York, Boston, and the present Philadelphia charter) tried *limited* voting, by which each elector was required to vote for less than the total number of councilmen to be elected. This gave the minority representation, as a rule, but not necessarily in exact proportion to the vote.

The Hare system, named for an English schoolteacher, Thomas Hare, is designed to give representation upon a multimembered body in direct proportion to the numerical strength of the various interest groups in the community. Its object is to give each voter only one vote for the council (or such multimembered bodies as school, park, and library boards, if elective) but to make every effort to see that the vote is eventually used to help someone get into office.

P.R. has had little use in the United States, although several Massachusetts cities have used it, as did the city of New York between 1936 and 1947. Any chance it may have had for gaining popularity in this country seems to have died with its repeal in 1957 in Cincinnati, the city that had used it the longest. Opposition by the dominant political party in both New York and Cincinnati eventually proved fatal to the plan.[47]

---

[47] See Belle Zeller and Hugh A. Bone, "The Repeal of P.R. in New York City: Ten Years in Retrospect," *American Political Science Review,* 42:1127–1148, December, 1948; and Straetz, *op. cit.*

SELECTED
READINGS

Adrian, Charles R.: "Some General Characteristics of Nonpartisan Elections," *American Political Science Review,* 46:766–776, September, 1952.

———: "A Typology for Nonpartisan Elections," *Western Political Quarterly,* 12:449–458, June, 1959.

Alford, Robert R., and Eugene C. Lee: "Voting Turnout in American Cities," *American Political Science Review,* 62:796–813, September, 1968. (Pioneer comparative study. Turnout is higher in cities with cleavages.)

Berelson, Bernard R., and others: *Voting,* The University of Chicago Press, Chicago, 1954. (An important landmark in the development of voter behavior theory.)

Boskoff, Alvin, and Harmon Zeigler: *Voting Patterns in a Local Election,* J. B. Lippincott Company, Philadelphia, 1964. (An analysis of voting on ten bond-issue referendums in DeKalb County, Georgia.)

Brown, Robert E.: *Middle-class Democracy and the Revolution in Massachusetts,* Cornell University Press, Ithaca, N.Y., 1955. (A study of voter eligibility in colonial times. Shows that most men were eligible.)

Campbell, Angus, and others: *The American Voter,* John Wiley & Sons, Inc., New York, 1960. (A theory of voter behavior based on the empirical work of the Survey Research Center.)

——— and others: *The Voter Decides,* Harper & Row, Publishers, Incorporated, New York, 1954.

Freeman, J. Leiper: "Local Party Systems: Theoretical Considerations and a Case Analysis," *American Journal of Sociology,* vol. 64, November, 1958.

Gove, Samuel K.: *The Illinois Municipal Electoral Process,* Institute of Government and Public Affairs, University of Illinois, Urbana, 1964.

Harder, Marvin A.: *Nonpartisan Election: A Political Illusion?* Holt, Rinehart and Winston, Inc., New York, 1958. (A case study in Wichita, Kans.)

Hoan, Daniel W.: *City Government: The Record of the Milwaukee Experiment,* Harcourt, Brace & World, Inc., New York, 1936. (The story of a famous mayor.)

Kornhauser, Arthur, H. L. Sheppard, and A. J. Mayer: *When Labor Votes,* University Books, Inc., New York, 1956. (Voting behavior and political attitudes of auto workers.)

La Palombara, Joseph, and Charles B. Hagan: "Direct Legislation: An Appraisal and a Suggestion," *American Political Science Review,* 45:400–421, June, 1951.

Lazarfeld, Paul F., and others: *The People's Choice,* Columbia University Press, New York, 1948. (One of the first voter behavior studies—by social psychologists.)

Lee, Eugene C.: *The Politics of Nonpartisanship: A Study of California City Elections,* University of California Press, Berkeley, Calif., 1960.

Levin, Murray B.: *The Alienated Voter: Politics in Boston,* Holt, Rinehart and Winston, Inc., New York, 1960.

Merriam, Charles E., and Harold F. Gosnell: *Non-voting,* The University of Chicago Press, Chicago, 1924. (A pioneer study, using Chicago in the early 1920s.)

Munro, William B. (ed.): *The Initiative, Referendum, and Recall,* The Macmillan Company, New York, 1913. (Good study, written during reform era.)

National Municipal League: *Citizen Organization for Political Activity: The Cincinnati Plan,* 3d ed., National Municipal League, New York, 1949. (Local parties and proportional representation—the latter now abandoned.)

Pollock, James K.: *Voting Behavior: A Case Study,* The University of Michigan Press, Ann Arbor, Mich., 1939. (An early study.)

Porter, Kirk H.: *A History of Suffrage in the United States,* The University of Chicago Press, Chicago, 1918. (The principal historical source, but see also Brown, above.)

Reichley, James: *The Art of Government: Reform and Organization Politics in Philadelphia,* The Fund for the Republic, New York, 1958.

Rosenberg, Morris: "Some Determinants of Voter Apathy," *Public Opinion Quarterly,* 18:349–366, Winter, 1954–1955.

Sharp, Harold: "Migration and Voting Behavior in a Metropolitan County," *Public Opinion Quarterly,* vol. 19, Summer, 1955.

Straetz, Ralph A.: *PR Politics in Cincinnati,* New York University Press, New York, 1958.

Watson, Richard A.: *The Politics of Urban Change,* Community Studies, Inc., Kansas City, Mo., 1963.

Williams, Oliver P., and Charles R. Adrian: *Four Cities,* University of Pennsylvania Press, Philadelphia, 1963. (Chapter 4 deals with voting behavior in four middle-sized Michigan cities.)

Zeller, Belle, and Hugh A. Bone: "The Repeal of P.R. in New York City: Ten Years in Retrospect," *American Political Science Review,* 42:1127–1148, December, 1948.

Zimmerman, Joseph F.: "Electoral Reform Needed to End Political Alienation," *National Civic Review,* 60:6ff., January, 1971. (Changes in voting systems can improve minority-group representation.)

C THE LAW

CHAPTER
6 THE LAW
OF
MUNICIPALITIES

Americans have a penchant for discussing problems of public policy in terms of constitutional law rather than in terms of public policy. This is particularly true in municipal affairs, for the legal position of the city is one of lowest priority: "The city is a political subdivision of the state, created as a convenient agency for the exercise of such of the governmental powers of the state as may be intrusted to it."[1]

May a city perform whatever functions a substantial proportion of its residents wants to have performed? Not at all. It may perform only those that the state legislature or the state courts allow it.

THE CITY AS A CORPORATION

The Problem of Sufficient Authority: A Case Study. Let us suppose that the city council wishes to eliminate a group of billboards that surround a city park. The council members believe that the billboards are destroying the natural beauty of the park and that people use the park in order to get away from the prosaic, hurried, commercialized world of everyday. The council has had numerous complaints about the billboards, and a majority of the members promised in their

---

[1] *Trenton v. New Jersey,* 262 U.S. 182 (1923). This is the standard rule, and its substance may be found repeated in dozens of cases.

campaigns for election to vote them out of existence. Is this sufficient justification for council action? Certainly not.

Before any action can be taken effectively, these questions, and perhaps many more, might have to be answered: Does the city charter authorize regulation of billboards? And because the legal mind is razor-sharp and hence capable of splitting hairs, the further question, perhaps: Does the city charter authorize regulation of billboards *on the periphery of public parks?* If the city charter does authorize regulation, is there a contravening general act of the legislature? Is such regulation, in any case, *reasonable?* Would it somehow violate the state or Federal constitution? Would this particular regulation constitute, according to the common law, an *abuse of discretion* by the council? And is the proposed ordinance for a *public purpose?* Before World War I, regulation of billboards was considered by the courts an invasion of the rights of private property.[2] Then the courts began to allow regulation on the basis of the police power.[3]

In order for a city ordinance regulating billboards to be valid, it must be shown that such regulation is necessary to the safety and welfare of the people. The city must show that a rickety billboard might topple over on an unsuspecting pedestrian, or that a billboard might well be used as a place of ambush by a rapist, or that a billboard might serve to collect flammable newspapers and leaves.

It was not until 1935 that a high court was willing to allow regulation of billboards on a simple basis of aesthetics in the public interest. "Grandeur and beauty of scenery," the Supreme Judicial Court of Massachusetts said, "contribute highly important factors to the public welfare." This concept, although gaining in recognition, has not become the generally accepted rule.[4] Note the skepticism of an Illinois judge: "Authorities in general agree to the essentials of a public health program, while the public view as to what is necessary for aesthetic progress greatly varies. Certain legislatures might consider that it was more important to cultivate a taste for jazz than for Beethoven, for posters than for Rembrandt, and for limericks than for Keats. Successive city councils might never agree as to what the public needs from an aesthetic standpoint, and this fact makes the aesthetic standard impractical as a standard for use restriction upon property."[5] The judge said, in effect, that he can determine better

[2] *Massachusetts v. Boston Advertising Company*, 188 Mass. 348 (1905); *New York ex rel. Wineburgh v. Murphy*, 195 N.Y. 126 (1909); and other cases. See also Illinois Legislative Council, *Regulation of Billboards*, State of Illinois, Springfield, Ill., 1953, pp. 17–20.

[3] The *police power* is usually defined as the power of the state to "protect the health, safety, and morals" of society. See *St. Louis Gunning Advertising Company v. St. Louis*, 235 Mo. 99 (1911) and nearly all subsequent cases where billboard regulation was upheld.

[4] *General Outdoor Advertising Company v. Massachusetts Department of Public Works*, 193 N.E. 799 (1935). A more recent supporting case is *Berman v. Parker*, 348 U.S. 26 (1954).

[5] *Forbes v. Hubbard*, 180 N.E. 767 (1932). In accord with this more common opinion, see *Youngstown v. Kahn Brothers Building Company*, 148 N.E. 842 (1925); and *Wondrak v. Kelley*, 195 N.E. 65 (1935).

than can the council the point at which the public interest becomes more important than the private interest.

If all the many questions that may be raised can be answered in a satisfactory manner, the city may, perhaps after paying expensive court costs, proceed with its drive to eliminate the offensive bill-boards. Such are the limitations of authority under which city government must operate.

The Nature of a Corporation. The city, in lawyers' language, is a municipal corporation. A corporation, in turn, is an artificial *person* created by the state. In this sense, the city is something of a cross between the national or state governments on the one hand and the private corporation on the other. It differs from both, however. In theory, both the United States and the states are *sovereign,* or at least share sovereignty. A sovereign body is one possessing supreme temporal power, a state that owes allegiance to no one. Actually, of course, neither the United States nor any of the states possesses full and true sovereignty. The plenary powers of government are divided in a federal system in such a manner that the ancient concept becomes somewhat obscured. However, cities, villages, and other municipal corporations possess no sovereignty at all. They are children of the state, created usually by the action of the state legislature, and even in those states most dedicated to the principle of home rule, the *state* courts remain the final arbiters of what are local concerns.

The municipality, like any other corporation, derives its powers from the state, and those powers granted to it are expressed in a *charter.* A charter is the fundamental law of a corporation which establishes (1) the structure or form of government, (2) the powers that may be exercised by it, and (3) the general manner in which the powers granted may be exercised. The charter is almost never a single document, but includes all state laws and judicial opinions that affect the structure, powers, or manner of exercising the powers of the corporation.

The city, in some respects, has a legal position not unlike that of a private corporation. In fact, it has been only in the last two centuries or so that a definite distinction has developed. The two are still similar in that each has an existence independent of the members of the corporation, may own property, may make contracts, may exist, normally, in perpetuity, and may sue and be sued. They possess very important differences, too. A private corporation is created entirely by the *voluntary* request of a group of people who wish to form a corporation. They know the corporation law in advance and hence know the conditions under which they will operate. Furthermore, once the corporation charter is granted, it becomes a *contract* which cannot be altered or taken away (except under the rarest circumstances involving an overriding "public interest").[6] A public corporation, on the other hand, may be created with or without the consent of its membership (the persons living in the area), the terms of its charter may be quite different from what the people of the community desire, and, even more important, the charter is *not* a contract and is hence subject to constant, involuntary, and sometimes arbitrary changes. It can even be taken away without advance notice, unless the state constitution specifically prohibits this.

There are two other important differences between public and private corporations. A public corporation can act only in the legally described *public* interest and for a public purpose. A private corporation must always have the public interest in mind (one could not long exist, for example, if it were organized for the purpose of robbing banks), but it may also have private interests (such as profit making for the individual owners). The two also differ in the amount of control the state exercises over them. A private corporation can carry on any activities it wishes, so long as it does not violate some law; a public corporation can do only those things that it is authorized to do. A corporation producing cigarettes, for example, could take on a sideline of producing, say plowshares, without seeking an amendment to its charter or any other kind of permission from the state. (It could not, however, put in a sideline of marijuana cigarettes, since this would not be in the public interest and could be curbed by the state under its police powers.) A municipal, or public, corporation, on the other hand, could not decide to enter into such a sideline as, say, municipal parking lots or a municipal theater or to adopt a new form of taxation without having first the specific authority to do so.

The Elements of a Corporation. What are the elements necessary in order to have a municipal corporation? Stated by McQuillin in the language of the law, they are:[7]

> 1. Incorporation as such pursuant to the constitution of the state or to a statute.
> 2. A charter.
> 3. A population and prescribed area within which the local civil government and corporate functions are exercised. However, the inhabitants of the municipality are not a separate legal entity and do not themselves constitute the municipality, and the common council or other governing body of the municipal officers does not constitute the corporation.

---

[6] The contract could be altered or taken away, of course, if provision for this existed in the contract itself.
[7] Reprinted from Eugene McQuillin, *The Law of Municipal Corporations*, 3d ed., vol. 1, sec. 2.07, published by Callaghan and Company, 6141 North Cicero Avenue, Chicago, Illinois, 60646.

4. Consent of the inhabitants of the territory to the creation of the corporation, with certain exceptions [actually, the legislature in most states may act without consulting the local residents].

5. A corporate name.

6. The right of local self-government, although in most states this is held to be not an inherent right.[8] Unless otherwise provided by statute, a test as to whether an organization is a municipal corporation, using the term in its strict sense, is whether it has the power of local government as distinguished from merely possessing powers which are merely executive and administrative in their character. The characteristic feature of a municipal corporation beyond all others is the power and right of local self-government.

The Corporation and the Quasi Corporation. In the above passage, McQuillin suggests that there may be local units of government that are not in the strict sense municipal corporations. He is referring to a legal distinction that is made between corporations and quasi corporations. The former include cities, villages, and the relatively few *incorporated* (under a separate written charter) counties and school districts. The latter include most of the counties, townships, unincorporated New England towns, and the so-called "special districts" such as sewage-disposal, airport, drainage, mosquito-abatement, fire, and irrigation districts.[9]

So far as the lay citizen is concerned, the principal distinction between genuine corporations and quasi corporations is to be found in the fact that quasi corporations serve only as administrative agents of the state, but the true municipal corporation serves a dual purpose. It not only acts as a local agent for the state but also performs certain local functions exclusively in the interests of the people living within the corporate boundaries of the city.

In theory, the city acts as an agent of the state whenever it performs a function in which the state as a whole has a certain interest; for example, when it enforces the law, or maintains public health standards, or collects taxes. On the other hand, the city may perform some tasks purely for the comfort and convenience of the local inhabitants, in theory at least. This classification includes such things as the operation of a water-supply or public transportation system. Counties and school districts, in contrast, perform only such functions of statewide interest as the maintenance of records, the prosecution of crimes, the maintenance of roads, and the education of children.

Since the city acts in a dual capacity, it is said that the city per-

---

[8] This is an example of the cautious legal mind. In *no* state is the concept of local self-government as an inherent right legally acceptable. See above, chap. 3.
[9] The special districts are discussed in chap. 11.

forms two types of functions, *governmental* (as an agent of the state) and *proprietary* (as an agent of the local inhabitants and for their comfort and convenience). This distinction is less important for lay-men than it is for lawyers. As will be seen later, the line of demarca-tion is in any event difficult to draw, is an artificial legalism, and has probably created more problems than it has solved. Property owned for carrying on governmental functions is in theory held for the state, which may dispose of it without consulting the city and without pay-ment to it. On the other hand, property owned by the city for carrying on its proprietary functions cannot ordinarily be taken by the state without compensation, on the theory that constitutional guarantees of property rights extend to property held by the city in its propri-etary capacity.[10] The same distinction is followed in the law of munic-ipal-tort liability.[11]

Powers of the Corporation. The subordinate legal status of cities makes it necessary that the question of whether or not a particular city has the power to perform a particular function in a particular way be decided by the courts. Because the city is merely a creature of the state while the state itself is a sovereign body, the courts have established a rule of a narrow construction of municipal powers and a broad construction of state powers. To put it another way, the courts say that, if in doubt, the city does *not* have the power to do something it wishes to do. The authority that is almost invariably cited by courts in support of this interpretation is *Dillon's rule.* John F. Dillon, a renowned Iowa judge and author, summarized the legal position of cities in the following words.[12]

> It is a general and undisputed proposition of law that a *munic-ipal corporation possesses and can exercise the following powers, and no others:* First, those granted in *express words;* second, those *necessarily or fairly implied* in or *incident* to the powers expressly granted; third, those essential to the accomplishment of the declared objects and purposes of the corporation—not simply convenient, but indispensable. Any fair, reasonable, substantial doubt concerning the existence of power is resolved by the courts against the corporation, and the power is denied.

It is this rule that explains why a city might have to spend weeks of time and thousands of dollars in actions before the state courts

---

[10] See McQuillin, *op. cit.,* vol. II, sec. 4.132. The United States Supreme Court makes no such dis-tinction so far as the United States Constitution is concerned. *Trenton v. New Jersey,* 262 U.S. 182 (1923).
[11] See below, pp. 179–181.
[12] John F. Dillon, *Commentaries on the Law of Municipal Corporations,* 5th ed., Little, Brown and Company, Boston, 1911.

seeking to justify its decision to finance a municipal parking lot from the parking-meter fund rather than from the general-revenue fund, or seeking to find some theoretical justification for an FEPC or a smoke-abatement ordinance. That the community should demand them and that they should be adopted according to democratic procedures is not enough.

Dillon's rule allows the courts a good deal of leeway in determining what a city may or may not do. What are necessarily or fairly implied powers? What powers are essential to "the accomplishment of the declared objects and purposes" of the city? Only the judges know. They apply the principle of *stare decisis*—the rule of law in one case is the basis for the decision in later cases—but much is left to their discretion. It may be implied, for example, that a city may offer a reward for the arrest and conviction of someone who violates an ordinance (an act by the municipal governing body which, in theory, merely applies state law to local situations) but not for the violator of a state law, even for the murderer of the city's chief of police.[13] An implied power may vary greatly from one state to another. For example, it *cannot* be implied from anything in the Cleveland charter that the city has the right to spend its money in order to send councilmen to the state capital as lobbyists,[14] but it *can* be implied from the Minneapolis charter that aldermen may be sent to attend meetings of the Rivers and Harbors Congress in Washington.[15]

Creation and Dissolution of the Corporation. Cities and villages are normally created upon the receipt of a charter. The charter may be granted in any one of several different ways.[16] It is also possible, however, for a municipality to be created in other ways. Most people in a city might believe that the community is incorporated and act accordingly over a long period of time, only to discover later—perhaps years later—that somehow a mistake was made when it was "incorporated" and that the precise requirements of the law were not met. In such a case, it would be unreasonable to try to undo all the presumed legal acts that the city had committed up to that time. The courts, therefore, provided that the legislature has in the meantime treated the supposed city as if it were indeed a city, will say that the area is a municipal corporation *de facto* (in fact), even thought not *de jure* (in law).[17]

Some years ago, the Minnesota Supreme Court discovered that

[13] Compare *Choice v. Dallas*, 210 S.W. 753 (1919), and *Madry v. Scotland Neck*, 199 S.E. 618 (1938).
[14] *Cleveland v. Artl*, 23 N.E.2d 525 (1939).
[15] *Tousley v. Leach*, 230 N.W. 788 (1930).
[16] See above, pp. 165–174.
[17] *Tulare Irrigation District v. Shepard*, 185 U.S. 1 (1901).

when the state constitution granted a city the power to "frame a charter for its own government," it meant that it could do so only once and that subsequent changes would have to be in the form of amendments and not in a completely new charter.[18] This bit of divination had the immediate effect of changing every home rule city not using an amended form of its original charter from a *de jure* to a *de facto* corporation. The people living in the affected cities were not seriously shaken by the development; in fact, they were hardly aware of any difference.[19]

Some cities and villages flourish, and others become "ghost towns." Deserted shacks stand in places that once represented cities and villages in the mining areas of the Mountain and Pacific states, in the timbering regions of Minnesota, Wisconsin, and New England, and in the hill country of North Carolina and Tennessee. Crossroads trading centers are decaying in many places throughout the nation— victims of the automobile, the telephone, and the migratory movement toward the large cities. It sometimes happens, therefore, that an incorporated municipality loses its original need for a charter. The question arises as to when a municipality ceases to be a corporation.

In actual practice, when a community becomes so depopulated as no longer to need a municipal government, it usually simply stops electing officers, collecting taxes, and functioning as a municipality. In legal theory, however, the corporation does not cease to exist merely because it is not functioning. It has simply gone into hibernation, from which it can reawaken at any time by resuming its activities. Permanent destruction of the creature that was created by the state can be accomplished only under laws established by the state. **Charters: General and Special Act.** The concept of the city as a corporation dates back to Roman times, and noblemen granted charters of special privileges to unincorporated cities of Europe as early as the eleventh century, but the modern practice of incorporating urban communities and prescribing their powers did not appear in England until the fourteenth century.[20] Often these charters merely legalized the informal situations that already existed. In any case, the Crown (or an important lord or colonial governor) began to grant special charters wherein the specific city to be incorporated was named and its powers enumerated. This plan became the standard practice in England, on the continent of Europe, and in the British colonies of North America.

[18] *Leighton v. Abell,* 31 N.W.2d 646 (1948). This highly technical decision destroyed the results of months of effort by the Minneapolis Charter Commission.
[19] Municipalities may also be legally created by implication or prescription. See McQuillin, *op. cit.,* vol. II, sec. 7.09.
[20] William B. Munro, *Municipal Government and Administration,* The Macmillan Company, New York, 1923, chap. 9.

It was not until the French Revolution that the *general charter* came into use. As one of the reforms of 1789, the French established a general municipal code to apply to all communes, giving them equal status and powers. From that time on, the use of the general charter became standard in European democracies, although the pattern was somewhat modified in the United Kingdom, where the general laws were often supplemented by special laws and administrative orders granting special powers to particular municipalities.

The Special Act Charter. The special charter plan, inherited from the mother country, was standard practice in America from colonial times and remained so until well past the middle of the nineteenth century. In 1851, Ohio, and a few months later, Indiana, outlawed special legislation, including special act charters of incorporation.[21] The following century produced a series of attempts to eliminate or modify the use of the special act charter. The major objection to it was to be found in the tendency of legislators to substitute their preferences for those of a locally elected city council. In theory, the special act was useful: It provided a tailor-made charter to fit the special circumstances of the particular city. In practice, however, the legislature often permitted local governments little discretion concerning local affairs. Urban dwellers, therefore, sought to find ways of retaining or recapturing local control.

Where special legislation was not completely outlawed, an attempt was made after about 1870 to allow it only after formal notice had been given that the legislature was considering changes in the fundamental law of a city and after an open hearing at which interested persons and groups could testify. This plan was modeled on the British plan. It is in use in several states but has met with considerable success only in Massachusetts. Legislators will usually not cooperate with approaches that have the effect of restricting their powers, as this plan does.

In a few states, special legislation was permitted only if the proposed legislation received local approval. The New York constitution of 1894, for example, allowed special legislation if the proposal, after passage in the general assembly, was approved by the mayor in a first-class city (New York, Rochester, and Buffalo) or by the mayor and council in other cities. The bill would then go to the governor for his consideration in the usual manner. If disapproved either locally or by the governor, it could be repassed by the legislature and become law nonetheless. The New York plan appears to have given considerable protection to localities, although quite a few bills

---

[21] State legislative control over cities, and attempts to curb these controls, are discussed in chap. 3 above.

continued to be passed despite local disapproval.[22] The adoption of home rule in 1923 made the plan obsolete.

An amendment to the Illinois constitution in 1904 sought to give Chicago some degree of local self-rule. It provided for a referendum on all special legislation applying to Chicago. The provision had the effect of protecting Chicago voters from what they did not want, but it established no method by which the city could obtain what it did want.[23] As a result, the provision has had little use, and the Chicago charter is seldom amended.

Some states permitted special acts only if no general act could "be made to apply" to the situation. This rule contained a loophole that could be discovered by even the dullest legislator. Since the courts are normally inclined to resolve doubts in favor of the action of the legislature, a pretense could almost always be found to argue that a given situation could not be met by general legislation.

Special legislation is not used only to prevent local policy making. In Iowa, when special act charters were used, "the people of the local community not only had in many instances a considerable share in formulating their charters in accordance with local needs, but they also had in effect authority to amend their charters. Special charter cities had little difficulty in securing amendments from the legislature. . . . While such charters and their amendments were subject to legislative control, the records do not show the existence of a meddlesome attitude on the part of the General Assembly."[24] But the picture was, and is, different in other states, and it has aroused considerable urban resentment.

Despite its unpopularity in urban communities, special legislation is still used, especially in New England and the South, and particularly in Alabama, Florida, Maryland, North Carolina, Tennessee, and Georgia. In Maryland, for example, 70 percent of the bills passed by the 1951 legislature were local in character. About one-half of the states are constitutionally authorized to grant special charters or special acts, and a number of the states still employ this system either exclusively or predominantly. In more than one-half of the states, special act charters are still in existence, but no new ones are being created, either as a matter of policy or as a result of subsequent constitutional prohibition. About twelve states provide, at least in some instances, for a local referendum on new special act charters. This practice dates from the nineteenth century.

[22] Howard L. McBain, *The Law and the Practice of Municipal Home Rule,* Columbia University Press, New York, 1916, gives a detailed account.
[23] As had been pointed out in Munro, *op. cit.,* pp. 180–181.
[24] George F. Robeson, *The Government of Special Charter Cities in Iowa,* Iowa State Historical Society, Iowa City, Iowa, 1923, p. 178.

The General Act Charter. The general act charter, designed to provide for uniform powers, privileges, and structures for every city in the state, has not met with much success, except where it has been modified by home rule or local option. Because American towns vary from hamlets to empires of millions of people, it is unrealistic to expect that every city government should be exactly like every other in powers and structure. The failure of general acts to allow for an expansion of local autonomy is, however, more importantly attributable to the fact that legislators have been largely unwilling to relinquish traditional areas of authority over local government. They have sought loopholes of evasion and have met with considerable success.

Constitutionally required use of general legislation has been circumvented by three techniques, principally: by the passage of laws that purport to be general but are not in fact; by the establishment of special districts; and by prostituting the classification device. If special legislation is prohibited, the question arises: What *is* special legislation? The answer, of course, comes from the courts. Following the general rule of broad construction of state legislative powers, the courts have hesitated to rule against the legislature. Most of the state high courts have therefore been willing to allow as "general" any legislation that on the surface appears to be general, or any legislation that may potentially apply to another city, even though at the moment it affects only one. In one case,[25] the Ohio legislature, despite a constitutional prohibition against special legislation, passed an act applying to "any city having within its limits an avenue more than 100 feet wide known as Lincoln Avenue." Is this special legislation? Not at all. Practically any city could qualify if it chose to build such a street. If, however, the legislators had added "on January 1, 1900," or some such prohibitive qualification, the supreme court would almost have been forced to void it. In point of fact, however, it has been easy to achieve special legislation without judicial proscription.

Another method of avoiding the ban on special legislation has been by establishing special districts: for parks and recreation, sewage disposal, police, and the like. This has been possible because the prohibition on special legislation applied only against "municipal corporations" or "cities."

Some state constitutions, while outlawing special legislation, recognized that, say, the city of New York and the village of Au Sable Forks in the northern lakes country of the state could not be treated adequately with the same legislation, and therefore permitted the

---

[25] Munro, *op. cit.,* p. 178.

classification of cities. In some states the constitution established the classifications, in others it authorized the legislature to do so, and in a third group of states, where the constitution was silent, the courts permitted the legislature to classify, holding this to be general legislation. Whatever the source of authority for classification, the identical treatment of all cities, large and small, was generally recognized as being impractical. General acts did not allow for unique problems.

In some states, for example in Wisconsin, classification legislation has been used sparingly and for its intended purposes. In other states, however, legislators have sought to use the classification device as a disguise for special legislation. Sometimes the courts have insisted that classifications be reasonable, but in most cases they have been tolerant when the legislators have resorted to subterfuges. True, the courts have on occasion prohibited some types of classifications, especially those using a *geographical*, rather than a *population*, basis, but the lawmakers usually have had their way. Classification has made it particularly easy to pass special legislation for the largest cities.

In Pennsylvania, each of the three largest cities were once placed in separate classes, and in Ohio the *eleven* largest cities at one time each had its own class. [After classification had been reduced to an absurdity in Ohio, the Supreme Court outlawed *all* classification in *Ohio ex rel. Knisely v. Jones,* 64 N.E. 424 (1902). The legislature then unsuccessfully attempted to treat all cases alike. The problem was resolved in 1912 with the introduction into the state of municipal home rule.] Although some classification is necessary because the problems of large cities are not the same as those of small cities, state legislatures under the guise of classification have deprived the larger cities in many states of much of their power of local self-government.

General Act Charters: Cafeteria Style. In those states without home rule or special act charters, it has been necessary to devise some way of meeting the particular needs of individual cities. Variations in needs occur in connection with both powers and forms of government. A large city might want the strong-mayor form, a middle-sized city the council-manager, and a village the traditional weak-mayor. In order to meet these variants, some states have adopted *optional charter laws.* Most states make use of this device, with about one-third using it as the principal source of city charters.

Under this plan, upon petition of a prescribed number of voters, or by resolution of the council, the council or the voters of a city may decide which *form* of government they wish to adopt. They are limited in choice, of course, to the type of options the legislature provides. A state may offer two or three basic charters; or five, as in Massachusetts; or as many as fourteen, as in New Jersey. The people of the city may go through the cafeteria line, picking from among the state's offerings. They may take only those things offered, however, and without variations or alterations. There can be no special orders to the kitchen. This plan is convenient for the state, and it offers some local choices as to type of government, although the powers that the city is authorized are normally much less variable. The plan is gaining in popularity in the United States. Of course, the legislature still determines the structure of government for each city, and *all* amendments to charters must still be obtained from the state, but the local population can determine whether it prefers to abandon the weak-mayor form, for example, or perhaps whether it wants the council-manager form with or without ward elections for council. A generous optional charter plan, such as that of New Jersey, may, to local residents, be a satisfactory method of bestowing charters.

Appraisal. Efforts to prevent or reduce legislative domination over local government have been made through such devices as the constitutional control of classification of cities and the use of the optional charter plan. These efforts have met with limited success. The legislature remains paramount, and its members have found it relatively easy to legislate for specific cities whenever they have desired to do so.

But in seeking to grant independence to cities, advocates of general legislation tended to minimize the fact that cities do have unique requirements that must be met by specific legislation. As a matter of fact, no state today has a single general act to cover the powers, functions, and structure of all its cities.

Although legal restrictions on legislative control were circumvented by imaginative legislators, often with the cooperation of the courts, and while legislative participation is still common in several states, notably in the South, the legislatures of an increasing number of states have, as a matter of public policy, given the people of cities considerable autonomy in local affairs. In some states, home rule has provided for some local autonomy. This is especially true in California, Michigan, and Wisconsin, as well as perhaps Minnesota and Texas. Optional laws in many states enable cities to modify their forms of government as to details, and sometimes such laws establish permissive, as distinguished from mandatory, legislation which each locality may avail itself of as it sees fit. This is especially true in Wisconsin, Washington, and Nevada.

Some types of state control and supervision have been helpful to cities and not preemptive of local policy making. In many cases, city officials, instead of chafing under the existing degree of state controls, approve of this control or are unconcerned with it. Cities will always be subject to much legislative control. Nearly every function performed by cities affects the people of the state as a whole. In a day of large economic units and rapid means of transportation and communication, it is impossible for the cities to isolate themselves. Furthermore, there is no natural cleavage between state and local interests and functions. Because one tends to grow out of the other gradually, the state and its cities are under pressure to work together.

Charters: Municipal Home Rule. As towns were founded in colonial Rhode Island, "the local communities . . . organized and managed their own local affairs and services. Each town retained its own individuality and functioned to a great degree without reference to any higher authority, except for those few laws which were commonly accepted by all communities."[26] It was not until after the Revolutionary War that the general assembly of Rhode Island, together with the legislatures of other states, began to enforce claims of sovereign and plenary powers over matters of local concern. In the new United States, the earlier idea that local communities should be left alone as much as possible all but disappeared. Municipal home rule charters represent a somewhat romantic attempt to return to an earlier situation that is often pictured as ideal. The home rule movement was another device that won the support of early-twentieth-century reformers in their drive to free the local community from the state legislature.

Municipal home rule, which is an indigenous Americanism, involves the power of municipal corporations to frame, adopt, and amend a charter for their government and to exercise all powers of local self-government, subject to the constitution and general laws of the state. Home rule may be provided for in the state constitution or by enabling acts of the state legislature. It may be available to all cities and villages (e.g., Oregon and Wisconsin), or only those of over a certain population (e.g., California and Colorado), or to a very limited number of cities (e.g., eleven in Washington, one in Pennsylvania). It may be a self-executing provision of the state constitution (e.g., Arizona and Nebraska), or it may require legislation before a city can adopt a charter (e.g., Texas and Wisconsin). It may be used by many municipalities in the state (e.g., in Oregon and Michigan), or by relatively few of them (e.g., in Ohio, Missouri, and West Virginia).

[26] Robert J. M. O'Hare, "Cities Rush Home Rule Gate," *National Municipal Review* (now *National Civic Review*), 42:73–77, February, 1953.

Home rule provides an important difference in the procedure for securing charters and subsequent amendments to them. Under the older system of special and general act charters, a charter is secured through the process of lobbying before the legislature, and every amendment to the charter requires the sending of city officials and other interested persons to the state capital to bargain with legislators. Under home rule, this is not necessary: The amendment is proposed (usually) by the council and is voted upon by the eligible voters. Under general act charters of either the classification or optional charter type, a city that lobbies for an amendment may find itself in the peculiar position of being opposed by another city in the same class or using the same option. This never happens under home rule.

Framing a Charter. The procedural rules for writing a new charter or making major revisions in an old one vary, of course, from one state to another. In states having self-executing constitutional home rule, the procedures are outlined in the constitution itself. About one-half of them do not do this, however, but simply authorize the legislature to make the rules. The constitution of Wisconsin, for example, provides that "the method . . . shall be prescribed by the legislature." All states operating under legislative home rule, of course, use procedures established by the legislature.

The common procedure is for the voters of the city to elect a charter commission. In Minnesota, the commission is appointed by the local district judge; in Oregon, the city council acts as the charter commission, or a charter may be presented through the procedure of the initiative. The commission is usually given a certain length of time in which to draft a charter for submission to the voters, who must then approve (usually by a simple majority vote). It may sometimes be necessary to elect a second or third commission if the first cannot agree upon a charter or if its proposed charter is defeated at the polls. Sometimes state approval is required in addition to that of the voters.

Once a home rule charter is adopted, it may be amended from time to time. In some states the charter commission is a permanent body that can propose amendments at any time (e.g., Minnesota and West Virginia), but the most common system is to have the proposals for amendment come from the city council or through the use of the initiative. Ratification is normally by popular vote.

Because of the practical effects of Dillon's rule, city charters must be lengthy, complex, and technical in some sections. (The index to the Los Angeles charter alone contains more words than does the United States Constitution.) The result is that in many home rule cities the voters are frequently called upon to consider amendments to the charter. Many proposed amendments are of minor importance; others are highly technical. The voter is often either apathetic, confused, or both. In order to overcome this handicap to the effective operation of home rule, the New York constitution allows a city council to draft and adopt all charter amendments of a minor character without submitting them to a popular vote. If, however, organized opposition to the action of the council appears, a referendum can force a public vote; for certain types of amendments involving important questions of public policy, the conventional type of referendum is always required. A similar rule applies in Wisconsin, while Oregon and West Virginia (for third-class cities) allow charter amendment without popular vote under certain conditions. These methods reduce the length of the already crowded ballot and remove some of the technical amendments from decision by the voters.

The Origin and Spread of Home Rule. Like many American political institutions, including the United States Constitution itself, municipal home rule had its origins in the expedient actions of practical politicians. The first state to establish a version of it was Iowa, which did so under an 1851 act of the legislature. After operating since territorial days under the special act charter system, the legislature in that year established a single method of charter adoption for newly incorporated communities or for towns desiring to become cities. If the inhabitants decided to incorporate, the law provided that an election would be held to choose persons to prepare a charter. The legislature provided the general limits of authority that could be granted by the charter, but these were broad. The charter, once written, was submitted to the voters for approval or disapproval.[27]

This unique and liberal law was not given a full opportunity to show its merit and hence was not actually the beginning of the home rule movement. Few uses seem to have been made of it. Most of Iowa's municipalities had already been established by earlier special charters. In 1858 the law was repealed, for the new Iowa constitution adopted the preceding year followed the contemporary fashion and required the use of a general incorporation act. However, the new law allowed the already existing city charters to be amended locally, and the four remaining cities to which this applies still exercise this privilege.[28]

The Missouri constitutional convention of 1875 furnished the

[27] State of Iowa, *Code of 1851,* chap. 42. For even earlier antecedents for home rule, especially in New York, see Howard L. McBain, *American City Progress and the Law,* Columbia University Press, New York, 1918, pp. 22–29.
[28] Robeson, *op. cit.,* pp. 178–180.

stage for the first provision for *constitutional* home rule. The people and political leaders of St. Louis had long been dissatisfied with legislative oversight of the city government and the need to secure the approval of the legislature for any changes in the city charter. The St. Louis delegation, therefore, came to the convention with a set of proposals for the government of the city, including one for what is now known as home rule. This plan was included in the constitution and was adopted by the voters of the state, although home rule was restricted to St. Louis at that time. The reform period that followed helped to spread the idea of home rule throughout much of the nation.

The Practical Meaning of Home Rule. Some reformers have incorrectly assumed that municipal home rule results in the granting of greater powers to cities, with more independence from the state legislature. The granting of home rule makes for changes in several aspects of the local political scene, but does it grant more power or greater independence to cities? The questions cannot be answered categorically. A 1938 study suggested that home rule had been "helpful but not of great importance in enlarging the zone of municipal activity."[29] Home rule apparently gives cities their greatest freedom in choosing the form of government they are to employ and in exercising routine housekeeping functions (civil service rules, the fixing of salaries, the establishment of pension systems, etc.). In these areas, non-home rule cities must nearly always accept or secure enabling legislation from the state. Home rule cities may *possibly* be freer on matters that are legally *local* in interest (the establishment of parks, the control of building regulations), but "their freedom is not measurably greater in matters of education, general police control and utility rates and services (except in Colorado)."[30] On financial matters, in which the state can always claim an interest, home rule cities have virtually no advantage over special and general act charter cities, except in California.

In many states, home rule has helped to give municipalities greater powers of discretion in making routine decisions. Cities without home rule often must go to the legislature in order to get authorization to perform some minor function or to exercise some power that most laymen would consider to be obviously a local responsibility. For example, a North Carolina town had to have the legislature pass an act in order that the council might declare it a misdemeanor to use roller skates on the public sidewalks. A Maryland city had to get

[29] George C. S. Benson, "Sources of Municipal Powers," *Municipal Year Book, 1938,* International City Management Association, Chicago, 1938, pp. 149–165.
[30] *State-Local Relations,* Council of State Governments, Chicago, 1946, pp. 164–166.

special permission to increase the salary of a stenographer by $300 a year. A Nevada city had to get legislative permission in order to purchase a rotary pump for the fire department. An Iowa town discovered that it lacked power to purchase uniforms for the members of its police force.[31] Home rule is not a guarantee against such municipal impotence, but it has been helpful in overcoming it.

Although home rule cities often, in fact, enjoy greater powers than do non-home rule cities, most of them are potentially subject to state control over their affairs. In most home rule states, the legislature enjoys concurrent or superior power to the city government in matters of local concern. And the legislature is, of course, supreme in those areas that the judges consider to be of state, rather than of local, concern. In most states, general acts of the legislature, or what purport to be general acts, take precedence over ordinances or charter provisions. Under these circumstances, the question of whether municipal home rule will promote greater local discretion, and the extent to which it will do so, is a question not of law but of public policy determined by the legislature, at whose sufferance home rule exists. To be sure, the enactment of a constitutional amendment providing for home rule places an implied moral obligation upon the legislature to carry out the spirit of its provisions, and this moral pressure appears to have had an effect upon the legislatures of several states.

A somewhat different, more autonomous kind of home rule exists in California, Colorado, Ohio, Oklahoma, and perhaps Arizona and Nebraska. In these states, a distinction is made either by the courts or the constitution between matters of local and of state concern. The legislature has less power over localities, and general laws do not supersede local ordinances or charter provisions, although the state may preempt a field in California.

In some of these states, the constitution attempts to define some municipal powers, but it cannot define them all, nor can it attempt detailed definitions of powers so as to explain where they end and statewide interests begin. Because this is so, this type tends to transfer control from the state legislature to the state courts. (Ohio offers the clearest example.) The courts, in most cases, strongly tend to resolve doubts in favor of the state. A leading authority has pointed out that "after all, it seems clear that the determination of the actual extent of power to be exercised is wholly a question of policy and not at all a question of law."[32] The task, under the theory of American government, belongs to the legislature.

31 Examples from among those cited in *Home Rule in Nevada*, Legislative Counsel Bureau, Carson City, Nev., 1952.
32 McBain, *American City Progress and the Law*, p. 7.

Home Rule: An Appraisal. Home rule allows charters to be tailor-made to suit the preferences of the particular community and permits them to be more flexible than the types provided by the legislature in allowing for changing exigencies and in taking advantage of new developments in administrative techniques. Home rule probably makes it easier to experiment with charter provisions, since the amendments are locally proposed and adopted.

Perhaps the greatest effect of home rule lies in its psychological value. To those interested in local government, it may give the impression of granting more independence to the city than is the actual case. This gives encouragement and incentive to those who would be active in local government and thus gives the reformer the feeling that if he fails, he has only himself to blame. The psychological effect upon legislators is also significant. Most legislators have been willing to accept the mandate of the voters when a home rule provision is written into a consitution and to permit home rule to operate even where legal authority to commit sabotage lies with the legislature. This is not always the case, but it often is. In home rule states, bills which would deal with local matters are sometimes opposed by legislators who wonder if they would not "interfere with the rights of local self-government" or "violate the principle of home rule." Home rule is hence more often an *attitude* toward local government than it is a legal injunction against legislative action.

THE CITY AND STATE

The state has been most unwilling to allow its child, the city, to grow up. A theory of perpetual infancy was adopted by nineteenth-century legislatures in their attitudes toward their offspring. Efforts at achieving independence for municipalities through the legal device of constitutional limitations were largely unsuccessful. Cities in most states did achieve more independence and less legislative supervision of their affairs after the first decade or so of the twentieth century, but the change seems to have been produced principally by a changing climate of opinion toward cities that accompanied the urbanization of the nation, together with a slight increase of public trust in the politician, both state and local.

Legislative oversight of local government declined in the twentieth century for another reason: Government became too complicated to be sufficiently understood by amateur legislators meeting for a few weeks annually or biannually as an interlude away from their principal occupations. City government became professionalized and technical; its complex details came to be understandable only to the professional, full-time technician. Flexibility, which legislatures did not possess, was needed. So was continuous, rather than spo-radic, oversight. The twentieth century represented, therefore, a period during which state legislators were somewhat reluctantly, but inexorably, forced to transfer increasing amounts of local govern-ment supervision to the professional bureaucracies of the admin-istrative branch of state government.

In addition to state legislative and administrative oversight of cities, the judicial branch also acts in a supervisory capacity. Some facets of this control require development.

State Judicial Oversight of Cities. Standing behind every city official, looking over his shoulder, is a judge. He is the individual who settles all disputes between the city and the state, a taxpayer and the city, one local government and another. He is the umpire. Although he makes a determination only when asked to do so, and then upon the basis of laws and ordinances made by other people, he is himself a lawmaker, for the judge decides ultimately what the law *means* and hence what the city can and cannot do.

Because the city is not a sovereign body, its standing at law is approximately the same as the standing of a private corporation, except when it is acting in the name of the sovereign (the state). Because of this legal position and because it enjoys only those powers granted to it under the principle of Dillon's rule, the city is constantly faced with the task of proving in court that it has the power to do what it seeks to do.

The Taxpayer's Action. The court actions in which the municipality constantly finds itself embroiled may in some cases be brought by a state official, but most of them are brought by a taxpayer resident in the city, or by a corporation that is a taxpayer, for a corporation is an artificial person at law.

In Anglo-Saxon common law, "the King is the fountainhead of all power," and therefore "the King can do no wrong" and "the King cannot be sued without his own consent." This principle was trans-ferred to the American republic, where the word "people" was substituted for "King" in the first quotation, but "state" was used in the last two. The United States Supreme Court has held that status as a taxpayer does not give one sufficient interest in the matter to test the legality of an act of Congress in a judicial action,[33] and this rule also applies in most of the states relative to legislative acts. The same protection does not extend to municipalities, however, for they are normally subject under the common law to taxpayers' suits even when there has been no statutory grant of the right.

[33] *Massachusetts v. Mellon,* 262 U.S. 447 (1923).

Taxpayers' suits may be brought for three purposes: (1) to enjoin acts of the municipality that are unauthorized, unlawful, or *ultra vires;*[34] (2) to compel unfaithful officers, or even third persons, to repay into the treasury sums illegally paid out; and (3) to protect the interests of the municipality where its officers wrongfully refuse or neglect to perform their duties. This third type may involve legal actions by the taxpayer in the name of the city to protect municipal powers and rights that the officers of the city fail to protect.

In theory, taxpayer actions are analogous to the actions a stockholder may bring against the officials of a private corporation (who are legally acting as his agents). The purpose is to stop acts that are allegedly illegal or to stop or remedy situations that give evidence of fraud, corruption, or other wrongdoing. The taxpayer suit has sometimes prevented the granting of fraudulent contracts, the issuing of improvident bonds, or the granting of illegal franchises.

The taxpayer action is often used as a weapon by interests that disagree with proposed municipal policies. Theoretically, an action cannot be brought simply because the taxpayer dislikes the judgment or doubts the wisdom of the city officials, or because their politics might damage the profits of his business. In practice, however, these are often the real reasons behind suits. Almost any public policy that deviates even slightly from traditional municipal behavior will result in action in which the policy is claimed to be *ultra vires.* The individual or corporation in such a case may be seeking to protect his own economic interests or to impose his own personal ideology upon local policy making. The courts are often the last resort of the obstructionist, and state court judges have often lent a sympathetic ear. City-government proposals have often been delayed by expensive, time-consuming legal actions.

A parking-lot owner may have a right to bring action to prevent a city from entering the parking-lot business on the ground that it is *ultra vires* to use money from the general-revenue fund (rather than the parking-meter fund) for this purpose. A home builder may be permitted legal action to stop a public housing project on the ground that such a project is not for a public purpose. A television-station owner may be permitted legal action to prevent the city from operating a municipal television station on the ground that the city charter permits only a radio station. In such cases, the interests opposing the action are able to use the machinery of the law to support their positions, for the burden of proof is on the city government.

[34] *Ultra vires* actions are actions legally beyond the power of the municipal corporation or its officers.

Taxpayer actions cause so much delay and are so nearly inevitable —that many cities, especially the larger ones, commonly arrange for a "friendly suit" to be instigated in order to clear away the legal cobwebs before launching into a new program or attempting to issue bonds under an untried procedure. Such actions not only save time and avoid the wasting of money in preparations that might otherwise later have to be abandoned, but they sometimes lead to the discovery of possible legal alternatives even when the original proposal does not survive the legal process. Middle-sized and small cities tend to allow the large municipalities to break legal ground; they are often slower in moving into a new area of activity, and by the time they do so, the court rulings may already have been made.

THE CITY AND THE CITIZEN

Because cities are corporations and not sovereignties, they are responsible for contract violations and torts. Almost every culture, even the most primitive, distinguishes between a *tort,* or wrong against an individual, and a *crime,* a wrong against society. A tort is a violation of a personal right established and protected by law. A violation of a contract is the violation of a personal right established by mutual agreement and protected by law. For purposes of this text, a tort is an injury to a person that is neither a crime nor a violation of a contract. Cities have much the same legal position as do private corporations. The basic rules of municipal liability are established in the common law, but they are subject, as is any part of the common law, to statutory modifications in the individual states.

Municipal-contract Liability. Cities enter into countless contracts with individuals and corporations. In general, they are answerable for these contracts in the same manner as are private corporations. Even when there is no question of good faith involved in the carrying out of a contract, many other problems may arise—problems of inter- pretation of the contract, of determining when its conditions have been completed, of making settlement when performance of the conditions of the contract becomes impossible. Cities may therefore find themselves in court in the normal course of carrying out their activities.

The principal problem that faces the courts in the interpretation of contracts to which the city is a party is that of determining the conditions under which a contract is valid. In general, a valid con- tract is one that the city is authorized to make, that is made by the proper officer according to law, and that has been adopted according to proper procedures. (For example, the law may require that certain contracts be let only after advertising for bids, and then only to the lowest responsible bidder.) An *ultra vires* contract is normally invalid, but state courts sometimes order monetary settlements where the city has benefited from the contract. Similarly, a contract made by the wrong officer, or without following proper procedures, may sometimes, but not always, be validated, and the other party to the contract may have to assume any loss. Court practices vary from one state to another.[35]

Municipal-tort Liability. It will be recalled that the city was earlier described as performing two different types of functions: those which it does involuntarily as an agent of the state, and those done at local option as a service to the immediate community. In performing the former type of activity, the city becomes a veritable department of the state government and, as such, becomes cloaked in the state's mantle of sovereignty. It is said to be performing a *governmental* (or public) function. In performing services of comfort and convenience to the immediate community, however, the city acts very much as if it were simply a private corporation doing the same job. It is said to be performing a *proprietary* (or corporate, or sometimes private) function.

Clearly a theoretical line could well be drawn between those functions where the city directly represents the sovereign, and hence cannot be sued without its own consent, as is the rule with the sovereign power; and where the city acts as an ordinary corporation, and hence could reasonably be expected to assume the same responsibilities as other corporations. The difficulty with such a legal fiction arises when an attempt is made to classify the multitudinous activities of a modern city. The theory requires a perfect bifurcation, with every function being either governmental or proprietary, and with no messy edges or leftover pieces. The functions themselves, however, are not very cooperative when a classification is attempted.

Is the parks and recreation function, for example, carried on only for the comfort and convenience of the community, or is it part of the sovereign's responsibility to protect the health, safety, and welfare of the inhabitants of the state? How about airports, hospitals, or garbage disposal? The answers to these questions are not easy to find. Furthermore, the law of municipal-tort liability is not the same in any two states of the union.

The classification of functions is done in the various states either by legislative statute or, in its absence, by the judges. The legislature is free to overrule the judges and can, if it chooses, make functions that are the most clearly governmental in character subject to tort

---

[35] Details of municipal-contract liability are developed by McQuillin, *op. cit.*, vol. X, secs. 29.01–29.04.

action. The whole law of tort liability is based upon the judge-made common law, however, and most legislatures have been content to allow the judges to work their way through the problem on their own.

The courts almost invariably place certain functions in the governmental category, for which the city may not be sued. These include police, fire, education, libraries, traffic signals (they act in lieu of policemen), and public health. Functions that are nearly always held to be proprietary include city-owned public utilities, such as water, public transportation, gas, and electricity. Many functions vary considerably from state to state in their classification: parks and recreation (which tend to be governmental), hospitals (likewise), airports (which tend to be proprietary), street lighting, street cleaning, garbage collection and disposal, and the construction and maintenance of sewers.

Certain functions are generally recognized as being essentially governmental, but for which the municipalities must nonetheless maintain responsibility for torts. These are functions dealing with the *public ways*. Historically, the state has expected the municipal corporation to be responsible for torts committed in the maintenance (but usually not in the construction) of streets, sidewalks, bridges, culverts, and the like. The citizen has a right to expect that a bridge will not collapse under him or that he will not walk into an open manhole in the sidewalk. Even in these cases, however, doubts are resolved against the individual. It is always held, for example, that the city must be given a reasonable time in which to correct a fault or post a warning. (In the absence of statutes to the contrary, quasi corporations such as school districts, counties, and townships are not responsible for *any* torts. The theoretical reasoning holds that all of the functions of a quasi corporation are performed involuntarily as an agent of the state.)

The Rule on Discretion. Regardless of whether a function is claimed to be governmental or proprietary, most courts will ask another question before deciding whether tort liability exists. That question deals with whether the action in litigation involved a *discretionary* or a *ministerial* act. That is to say, is damage claimed because the city decided to do or not to do something, or is it claimed because of the manner in which city officials or employees carried out established policy? Discretionary acts involve the making of public policy decisions, and they are *not* subject to tort action. Ministerial acts involve the carrying out of established policy, and they are normally the only type of acts that will allow for a legal action. For example, if the city council decides not to extend a water main or not to build a bridge across a stream, or if a police officer (acting in good faith and upon probable cause) decides to arrest a person who subsequently proves to be innocent of any crime, there could be no maintainable action, since these all involve decision making. On the other hand, once a bridge is built, the public has a right to expect the ministerial function of maintaining it to be carried out, and once the city decides to operate a bus line, the public has a right to expect that individuals will not be injured while riding on the buses.

The Rule of Respondeat Superior. According to the common law, the master is responsible for the actions of his servant, providing that those actions may reasonably be said to follow from the orders given to the servant. This is the rule of *respondeat superior.* In municipal-tort liability, it means that the city must answer for the action of its officers and employees, providing that the city is suable for the particular function involved and that the officer or employee was acting in general compliance with the requirements of his job.

If a city official or employee does something not called for in the performance of his duty, his actions are *ultra vires,* and the city bears no responsibility for them. Since an individual is responsible for his own actions where there is no master-servant relationship to protect him, this means that the citizen who is wronged may sometimes be able to sue the *individual* city official or employee when he cannot sue the city itself. This may sometimes protect the injured person when he is wronged in the course of the city's performing a governmental function. But the individual, it must be remembered, is not responsible when the city cannot be sued—unless his actions are *ultra vires.* If a city policeman arrests an innocent man against whom he holds a grudge, or if a fire-truck driver operates his vehicle in a grossly negligent manner, the individual who is harmed may be able to collect from the officer or employee as an individual. The chances are excellent, however, that even if he gets a court judgment, the city employee will not earn enough from his job to pay for such damages.

Recapitulation. A tort is an injury to a person that is neither a crime nor a violation of a contract. Cities and villages are responsible for torts committed by their officers and employees (generally speaking) when the tort was committed in the performance of a ministerial act, by an employee who was not acting in an *ultra vires* fashion, in connection with the public ways, or in connection with a municipal function of a proprietary character, and not one of a government character. In most states, if any one of these conditions is not met, the city is not responsible in tort action.[36]

---

[36] The basic material on municipal-tort liability is to be found in the treatises by McQuillin and Dillon.

Closing Comment. The question of whether the municipality is or is not liable in tort action is controlled by state legislatures, which can overrule court decisions when they choose to do so. Legislatures do not act on the basis of equity or logic but rather, as with other legislation, on the basis of the balance of the pressures upon the membership. City attorneys, mayors, and managers, who must be concerned about their budgets, generally oppose expanding the city's responsibility. Lawyers who specialize in tort cases, persons who want to try making easy money through spurious suits, persons who have been injured on or by city property, logicians, and others would like to see municipal liability expanded. In contrast, some persons who are especially concerned about governmental expenditure levels would prefer that the municipality be made as immune as is the state.

The balance of interests seems to be such that the status quo is maintained, by and large. In most cities, it remains less costly to the individual to be struck by a water-department truck than by a police-department patrol car.

199

SELECTED
READINGS

Council of State Governments: *State-Local Relations,* Council of State Governments, Chicago, 1946.

David, Leon T.: *The Tort Liability of Public Officers,* Public Administration Service, Chicago, 1940.

Dillon, John F.: *Commentaries on the Law of Municipal Corporations,* 5th ed., Little, Brown and Company, Boston, 1911. (A classic study of local government law.)

Drury, James W.: *Home Rule in Kansas,* Governmental Research Center, University of Kansas, Lawrence, Kans., 1965. (A case study of adoption of constitutional home rule in 1960.)

Fordham, Jefferson B.: *Local Government Law: Text, Cases and Other Materials,* Foundation Press, Brooklyn, N.Y., 1949.

Journal of Urban Law. (A quarterly, first published in 1966.)

McBain, Howard L.: *American City Progress and the Law,* Columbia University Press, New York, 1918. (A reform-era analysis of legal factors.)

——— : *The Law and Practice of Municipal Home Rule,* Columbia University Press, New York, 1916. (Classic legal analysis.)

McGoldrick, J. D.: *Law and Practice of Municipal Home Rule, 1916–1930,* Columbia University Press, New York, 1933.

McQuillin, Eugene: *The Law of Municipal Corporations,* 3d ed., Callaghan and Company, Chicago, 1949.

Model City Charter, 6th ed., National Municipal League, New York, 1964. (Incorporates structural features favored by contemporary reformers.)

"Municipal Home Rule in Iowa," *Iowa Law Review,* 49; 826–862, Spring, 1964. (An example of legislative home rule.)

Rhyne, Charles S.: *Municipal Law,* National Institute of Municipal Law Officers, Washington, 1957.

Stauber, Richard L.: *New Cities in America,* Governmental Research Center, University of Kansas, Lawrence, Kans., 1965. (A study of municipal incorporations during the decade of the 1950s.)

Williams, J. D.: *The Defeat of Home Rule in Salt Lake City,* Eagleton Institute Case 2, McGraw-Hill Book Company, New York, 1960. (A case study of a 1957 referendum campaign.)

D   THE
STRUCTURE

CHAPTER
7 FORMS
OF
GOVERNMENT

A Minneapolis alderman once told one of us that forms of government have nothing at all to do with the effectiveness or honesty of government. He felt that Minneapolis, which has a nineteenth-century form, operates under a government as good as could be had under any of the newer forms which are so often advocated by supporters of reform. The viewpoint was scarcely new with him, however; similar expressions have come from Alexander Pope, Edmund Burke, and Lincoln Steffens.

It is true that Americans have been rather obsessed in recent decades with the idea of a relationship between structure and effectiveness of government. Many advocates of reform have been guilty of overstatement in this direction. Much literature may be found urging the commission or council-manager plan, for example, on the ground that these plans follow the organization form of the business world, the corporation. The implication is that the success of the one should ensure the success of the other.

The truth of the matter, it would seem, is that structural arrangements do have an effect upon the pattern of government, but they neither guarantee nor prevent the type of government a particular group of citizens might want. The forms of government are important because they affect the pattern of influence of various groups upon policy making. The specific structure in any given case helps to establish behavior patterns and attitudes toward power and the exercise of power that definitely affect the process whereby decisions are made.

A study of St. Louis government found that structure "plays an important role in determining the scope and intensity of political conflict in the community."[1] The mayor of that city is the dominant policy-making figure and, as such, groups interested in policy seek to influence his election and to secure access to him. Business leaders look to him for the development of programs affecting the location of industry, tax rates, adequate city services, and "the social climate of the community necessary to attract technical personnel for their businesses." If the mayor were not as effective a policy leader as he is, these groups might be disadvantaged.

Another set of interests—those of low-income people, of the small merchants and businessmen, and of the Negro minority—seek to have their positions protected by the elective "county" officers (St. Louis is a city-county) and by the ward aldermen. These groups are interested, not in broad policy, but in such things as patronage jobs and individual favors of all kinds, such as the location of stop signs, parking regulations, help in getting an apartment in a public housing unit, and the other traditional types of political assistance to individuals. If the county officers were subject to the same rules as city officers—as could happen by elimination of the formal structural distinction—most of the patronage would disappear. If the councilmen were elected at large, they would have far less interest in doing favors for individuals than is the case under a ward system. In 1968, county voters adopted a new "streamlined" charter, and these changes in structure will have a political impact as yet unclear.

In another study of four Midwestern cities with about 50,000 population,[2] structural differences also seemed to be significantly related to the pattern of politics in the cities. The nonpartisan ballot, for example, appeared to weaken the potential influence of national parties in municipal elections. The level of education of councilmen was lower and the degree to which ethnic groups were represented was higher in cities using the ward system, as compared with those using at-large elections. The absence of a primary election in one city appeared to favor organized groups, or groups that had achieved a high degree of consensus on goals, as compared with independent candidates. The ward system militated against an aggressive annexation policy such as existed in the at-large cities. Why? Because alder-

[1] See Robert H. Salisbury, "St. Louis Politics: Relationships among Interests, Parties, and Governmental Structure," *Western Political Quarterly,* 13:498–506, June, 1960.
[2] Oliver P. Williams and Charles R. Adrian, *Four Cities,* University of Pennsylvania Press, Philadelphia, 1963.

men feared that annexed territory might be added to their particular wards, thus upsetting the balance of forces that had, in the past, permitted them to secure election.

In 1954, Indiana mayors, acting through the state municipal league, succeeded in killing a proposed home rule amendment to the state constitution. They feared that its passage might result in a spate of adoptions of the council-manager plan, which was not permitted in that state under existing law. The unwanted plan represented a threat to the mayors, both in terms of political power and of compensation. In Indiana, St. Louis, and the four middle-sized cities, formal structure of government *did* make a difference in the making of policy and in determining which individuals and groups would be most influential in the process of making decisions.

Yet, one can overstate the impact of structure. For example, while boss systems most frequently have existed in weak-mayor and strong-mayor cities, the commission system of Jersey City came under the boss control of Hague and that of Memphis under Crump, and the city manager system of Kansas City succumbed to Boss Pendergast. Also while the nonpartisan system generally has weakened national parties in local politics, the Chicago Democratic and Republican organizations continue effectively to control the outcome of its nonpartisan councilmen races. Structural reorganization is perhaps a necessary but not a sufficient condition for achieving political reform. The second, third, and other variables relate to characteristics of the citizens being governed.

The Basic Forms. There are three basic forms of city government in the United States: the mayor-council, commission, and council-manager plans. To this must be added the New England town meeting and its accommodation to modern urban conditions, the representative town meeting. There are many variations of these plans, and especially of the mayor-council plan. A 1968 tabulation of cities over 5,000 population shows 50.6 percent have the mayor-council plan, 43.0 percent the council-manager plan, and 6.4 percent the commission system.[3]

A word of caution should be given at the outset in examining forms of government: There are probably no two cities in the United States that have *exactly* the same structure of government. Very few fit the theoretical ideal of the general plan they follow. Nearly every charter commission or state legislature, in considering structure, finds it politically expedient to add its own improvisations on the given theme. For example, the strong-mayor–council system calls for the

---

[3] *Municipal Year Book, 1968*, International City Management Association, Chicago, 1968, pp. 52–63.

appointment of department heads by the mayor, yet many such cities have elective clerks and treasurers.

The mayor of New York has many administrative powers, a characteristic of stong-mayor cities, but the chief fiscal officer of the city reports to the board of estimate, rather than the mayor. Detroit clearly has a strong-mayor government, yet its organization chart is cluttered with a series of *advisory* boards and commissions that are vestiges of the old weak-mayor *administrative* boards and commissions.

The manager plan calls for the manager to appoint all department heads, yet in most cities with this form some administrative officers are either elective or selected by the council. The variations are quite endless, and the structural descriptions that follow must be thought of as models which city charters tend to imitate. The difference between the weak- and strong-mayor systems, in particular, is a relative one. The models of each are at opposite ends of a continuum, and the various mayor-council cities must be thought as of being located somewhere along the continuum—rarely, if ever, at one of the extremities.

CITIES WITH A SEPARATION OF POWERS

The general historical context in which the structures of American city government developed has already been discussed. During nearly all of the nineteenth century, American cities were operated under the weak-mayor–council (or weak-mayor) system. Near the end of that century, what is now called the strong-mayor system gradually evolved. In recent years, a third principal derivative of the plan, a result of efforts to strengthen administratively the strong-mayor system in large cities, has evolved. For purposes of this text, it will be called the strong-mayor–council plan with chief administrative officer (or strong mayor with CAO). This plan will be described later.

Taken collectively, the various types of mayor-council cities make up over one-half of all cities of the nation under any form of government.[4] Most smaller cities use this form, too, except in New England, where the town-meeting form is common. All but five of America's twenty-seven largest cities (over 500,000 population) use the mayor-council plan, usually of a strong-mayor type. Nearly two-thirds of the small cities of 5,000 to 10,000 people have the mayor-council form, usually of a weak-mayor type.

[4] *Municipal Year Book, 1970,* International City Management Association, Chicago, 1970, pp. 76, 535.

207

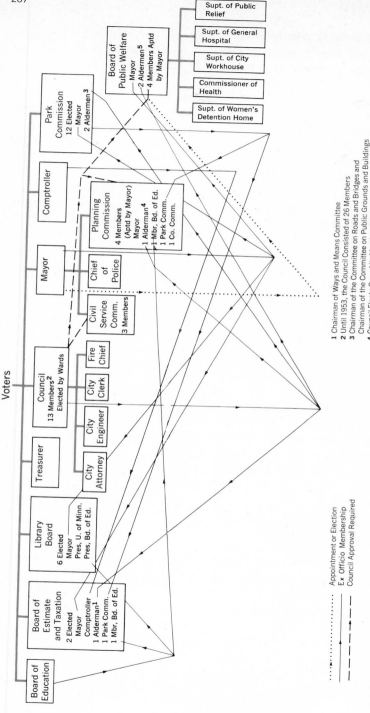

Figure 7-1. An actual weak-mayor–council city: Minneapolis, Minnesota. Note: There are many other appointive and ex officio boards and commissions which are not shown. Departmental subdivisions are also not shown.

1 Chairman of Ways and Means Committee
2 Until 1953, the Council Consisted of 26 Members
3 Chairman of the Committee on Roads and Bridges and Chairman of the Committee on Public Grounds and Buildings
4 Council Elects One of its Membership
5 Council Elects Two of its Membership

· · · · · · · · · Appointment or Election
———————— Ex Officio Membership
– – – – – – – Council Approval Required

The Weak-mayor–Council Plan. In the early decades of the nineteenth century, America's budding cities borrowed from rural government certain essential concepts. Today we call it the weak-mayor–council plan.

Characteristics. The weak-mayor plan is a product of Jacksonian democracy. It reflects the spirit of the frontier, with a skepticism both of politicians and of government itself. It grew out of a time when the functions of city government were few, when the need for a single executive was not recognized, and when people were afraid to give powers to a single executive. Implicit in the weak-mayor plan are the beliefs that if a politician has few powers and many checks upon him, he can do relatively little damage, and that if one politician becomes corrupt, he will not necessarily corrupt the whole city government.

The council is both a legislative and an executive organization under the weak-mayor plan. In small cities today, the council is small —five or seven members—but in bigger cities it is usually a fairly large body of perhaps eleven to fifty members. At one time councils were as large as 200. Members are (except in small cities) ordinarily elected by wards on a partisan ballot. In the past, many councils, copying the state and Federal systems, were bicameral (they had two houses). With the abandonment of the second house by Waterville, Maine in 1968, only Everett, Massachusetts retains the bicameral arrangement.

In addition to making policy, the council appoints several administrative officers, such as the city engineer and the city attorney. Councilmen (sometimes called aldermen if they represent wards) may serve on several ex officio boards and commissions.[5] A committee of the council usually prepares the budget and may even appoint the controller, who administers the expenditure of the budget.[6]

The mayor is not "weak" because he lacks policy-making power— he normally has a veto, can recommend legislation, and may even preside over the council. He is "weak" because he lacks administrative power. There is, in fact, no single individual charged with the responsibility of seeing to it that the laws and ordinances are properly carried out or that the city administration proceeds in accord with an overall plan. The mayor has very restricted appointive powers; even when he is allowed to make appointments, he may not be able to remove those he places in office, so that he is deprived of any real control over them or responsibility for them.

---

[5] Ex officio boards and commissions have a membership of persons who hold office by right of holding another office. For example, the airports commission might be made up of the mayor, the clerk, the treasurer, and two aldermen.
[6] See chap. 13 on fiscal administration.

Ordinarily several of the principal city offices are filled by direct election—the long ballot is a characteristic of the weak-mayor plan. Other offices, in addition to those filled by election and the council, may be of the ex officio type. Even the governor or some other state official may make some appointments, such as that of the police chief. Without a chief executive, the weak-mayor system is likely to be one in which the various departments are independent of one another and without coordinated effort.

The weak-mayor system requires the voters of the municipality to choose members of sundry boards plus such administrators as, perhaps, the clerk, treasurer, assessor, controller, and attorney. Two candidates for the park board might well offer differing platforms of policy (one might want a new park on the west side, while the other might prefer a new swimming pool on the east side), but will the voter have the time and inclination to look past the mayoralty contest as far as the councilmanic contests, much less to that for the park board?

In electing a clerk, treasurer, or assessor, the voter is even more sorely beset. Most of the voters will not know which candidate is best qualified to be the assessor, and they will not even know what functions are exercised by the clerk, treasurer, or, especially, the controller. In most cities, the clerk is a glorified file clerk, keeping the records of the city, while the treasurer is a bookkeeper, maintaining the financial records of the city. Both officers are important, but they are ministerial rather than policy making. Theirs are normally routine jobs of an office-manager type that could well be performed by either appointive or merit-system personnel. The voter, unacquainted with criteria usable in selecting persons to serve in offices such as these, is likely, in a large city, to vote for the person whose name is best known to him—usually the incumbent—regardless of the candidate's qualifications. In small cities, the voter is likely to support a candidate on the basis of sympathy. A qualified person may be passed over in favor of his opponent who is a veteran, or a handicapped person, or one with a large family who needs the pay, but who is not qualified.

The number of elective offices in American cities, even under the weak-mayor plan, has been declining for many decades. In 1936, 70 percent of the cities of over 5,000 population elected one or more administrative officers other than the mayor. By 1966, this figure had dropped to 48 percent. In 1936, 240 cities elected their police chiefs. Despite a great increase in the number of cities since then, only 125 elected the chief in 1966.[7]

---

[7] See the current issue of the *Municipal Year Book*, International City Management Association, Chicago.

TABLE 7-1. Municipal Elective Offices In Cities
over 5,000, Exclusive of the Mayor and Council

Title of Office	Percent of Cities Electing*	Number of Cities Electing
Treasurer	29	883
Clerk	24	713
Assessor	13	384
Auditor	10	304
Attorney	8	235
Controller	4	114
Police chief	4	125
Public works director	1	45
None of the above elective	52	1,554

*There were 158 cities not reporting and not included
in the above. The list includes *all* forms of government.
Percentages for mayor-council cities alone would be
higher.
Source: Municipal Year Book, 1966, International City
Management Association, Chicago, 1966, p. 97.

Appraisal. The arguments for the weak-mayor plan are based upon
the precepts of Jacksonianism. Many of these ideas are still popular
with a large number of American people. For example, Americans
may not know which officers are elected and which are appointed,
but they are likely to insist that those who are elected should continue to be elected. They may not know what tasks are performed
by a particular officer or what the criteria are for choosing an officer
for the post, but they want him elected.[8] The weak-mayor system
encourages this frontier type of concept.

The weak-mayor plan was a product of a different world from that
which Americans occupy today. It was never intended to serve large,
impersonal urban communities. The plan does not encourage modern
methods of housekeeping—budgeting, personnel, purchasing, and
the like. In fact, with its resort to performance by amateurs acting
without coordinated leadership, it fosters the use of the spoils plan.
For example, the city engineer (in charge of maintenance of public
ways) may well be appointed by the council in a weak-mayor city.
If this is the case, the ward aldermen on the council may personally
direct the activities of the engineer's office within each of their wards
and will probably have considerable control over selection of the
employees of the office. Street maintenance becomes not a matter
of professional judgment and performance but one of doing repairs

[8] Donald S. Hecock, "Too Many Elective Officials?" *National Municipal Review* (now *National Civic
Review*), 41: 449–454, October, 1952, offers a case study of this phenomenon on the state level.

where they will be of the most help in the next election. The mending of political fences rather than of public ways becomes the first order or business.

Most of the great nineteenth-century machines operated under this plan, for it encourages the boss by its very clumsiness and lack of coordination. Under this plan, the voter can scarcely determine, after the most conscientious effort, who is responsible for what, or even what functions are being performed by whom. With no clear-cut locus of answerability to the voter, the boss has a real advantage. The weak-mayor plan is the most easily corrupted and bossed because of the confusing pattern of organization.

Probably the greatest criticism levied against the weak-mayor plan concerns its lack of provision for administrative leadership. The mayor, with very limited appointing powers and even more limited removal powers, is not a true chief executive. There is no officer to coordinate the various activities of the city. The mayor may not even make up the budget, which would serve at least to give an overall picture of the needs of the city and of someone's rank-ordering of the relative importance of proposed expenditures of departments. Suppose, for example, that the city is short of funds (and all cities are short of funds). In a form of city government in which one person is legally responsible for all administration, it would be possible for this person to determine that the parks and recreation department should spend less for the coming year so that more streets could be repaired. He might be opposed by interest groups, but his decisions would carry great weight. Under the weak-mayor plan, however, the park board is a law unto itself, not answerable to either the mayor or the council, especially if it has its own tax levy and hence funds independent of the council, as might well be the case. Each department is likely to move in its own direction with no one empowered to coordinate. The effect of all these independent agencies is to make city government into a series of many little governments rather than one. There is one city government for parks, another for libraries, another for airports, another for sewage disposal, and so on.

Despite the great amount of criticism that has been levied against the weak-mayor plan, modifications of it remain the most common form of municipal government in the United States today. This is so in large part because the traditional form of village government throughout the United States is that of the weak mayor. Of course, the form of government is less important in the smaller municipality because government is more personal, performs fewer functions, and has less elaborate machinery. It has therefore been less important for smaller cities to experiment with newer forms of government, and there has been less agitation for them to do so.

While the weak-mayor system is characteristically found in small cities and villages, quite a few cities of considerable size still have relatively weak mayors, especially in the South. Atlanta (1970 population: 498,973) is the largest city in the United States with what is clearly a weak-mayor system. Outside of the South, large cities using the plan include Minneapolis and Providence. Chicago, with its huge council of fifty members elected by wards, retains many of the characteristics of the weak-mayor system, as does Los Angeles, where administrative boards and commissions are extensively used.

In Chicago, government is coordinated through the political party. The last effective large-city machine in the nation controls nearly all aldermanic seats and about 35,000 patronage jobs. In Los Angeles, with nonpartisanship and a strong merit system, the seventeen departments are largely independent under autonomous boards, and they play the mayor off against the councilmen. As a result, one newspaper reporter has noted, "We have Custer's Last Stand almost every week, with the mayor and the council taking turns playing Indian."[9] The system includes so many veto loci that policy development has become almost impossible in a city with a multitude of rapidly changing problems.

Rather extreme examples of the weak-mayor system may still be found in many places. Stevens Point, Wisconsin (1970 population: about 23,479), is an example. The voters select directly the mayor, controller, clerk, treasurer, assessor, city engineer, health officer, street superintendent, park superintendent, city attorney, and ward aldermen, in addition to school officials. The pattern is even more complicated, for control of the police and fire departments is vested in a commission separate from the council.

The structure of the weak-mayor–council plan is not regarded as being satisfactory for modern government. It is clumsy, uncoordinated, and has, for a long time, been declining in use for all but the smallest cities.

The Strong-mayor–Council Plan. The development of a strong-mayor system of government in the last two decades of the nineteenth century was a gradual one. The new plan differed only in degree from that of the weak mayor. It was not conceived of as a distinctly new form of government, nor was it one. Actually, the weak-mayor form resembled the structure of most state governments of that day and this. The strong-mayor system, on the other hand, was modeled on the national government, with its integrated administrative structure under the control of the President.

[9]Quoted in Iola O. Hessler, *Twenty-nine Ways to Govern a City: A Comparative Analysis of the Governments of 29 of the Largest Cities in the United States,* Hamilton County Research Foundation, Cincinnati, 1966, p. 10.

Few, if any, cities meet exactly all the conditions of the theoretical model of the strong-mayor system as it is described below. Most mayor-council cities represent a compromise between the very weak- and the very strong-mayor plan. The typical one is difficult to classify.

Characteristics. In the strong-mayor–council city, administrative responsibility is concentrated in the hands of the mayor, and policy making is a joint function of the mayor and the council. (The strong-mayor plan is sometimes called the "federal" plan, because it follows roughly the plan of the Federal government, but this term is confusing and will not be used in this text.) The plan calls for a short ballot with the mayor as the only elected administrative officer. He appoints and dismisses department heads, often without councilmanic approval. The mayor thus becomes the officer responsible for the carrying out of established policy and for coordinating the efforts of the various departments. The mayor also prepares the annual budget and controls its administration once it is adopted by the council. This allows the whole financial picture and the claims of the various departments to be compared in financial policy making, in contrast to the piecemeal methods by which these things are approached under the weak-mayor plan.

The mayor's legal position allows him to exert strong political leadership. Not only does he have the veto power and the right to recommend legislative policy to the council, as is the case under the weak-mayor system, but his wide control over administration gives him great power, which can be used in many ways as a weapon to overcome opposition, and furnishes a vantage point from which to recommend policy. Furthermore, his strong administrative position encourages the newspapers to give him credit or blame for events that take place within city government. The resultant publicity makes the public keenly aware of his activities and of his recommendations to the council. As in the case of the President of the United States, when a strong mayor speaks, he receives far more attention than does even the most experienced or most respected member of the legislative branch. The fact that the mayor presents a comprehensive budget to the council for consideration also adds to his dominant political position, for by this very act public attention is focused on the mayor and the burden of proof for any changes in the budget is placed upon the council.

The council plays a highly subordinate role in a strong-mayor city. It does not, as in the weak-mayor city, share in the performance of administrative duties. Its functions are limited to the exercise of legislative policy making, and even this role must be shared with the mayor. If there is an aggressive member of the council, this body may

214

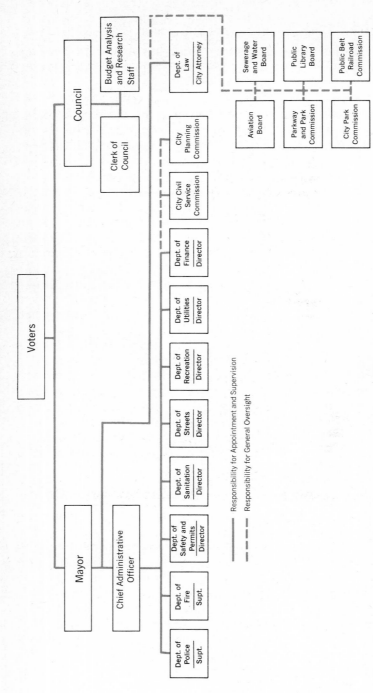

Figure 7-2. An actual strong-mayor–council city with chief administrative officer: New Orleans, Louisiana. Note: Not all agencies are shown. *Source:* Adapted from *Annual Report of the Mayor*, City of New Orleans, La., 1953.

seek to make policy for itself. But it is more likely that the mayor's recommendations, backed as they are by the greater public attention focused on him, by his constant oversight of the city administration, and by his veto power, will be dutifully enacted by the council, per-haps after insignificant changes or after a symbolic show of independ-ence. The average citizen is not likely to have much knowledge of council activities in a strong-mayor city. In a large city he is unlikely even to know the names of more than one or two of the councilmen, especially if the council is elected at large, as is often the case.

Because the council is exclusively a policy-making body for the city as a whole, it is likely to be small (typically seven or nine members) and elected at large on either a partisan or a nonpartisan ballot. Unless the city is very large, members serve on a part-time basis, since they have no administrative duties to perform and are not ex-pected, as they are in the weak-mayor system, to be errand boys for residents of their wards. When council members serve only part time, the effect is to give the mayor even greater powers, since he has the advantage of spending the whole of his day studying the needs of the city. This may tend to place the council in an even more subordinate position. It will certainly put its members at a disad-vantage in obtaining and evaluating information from the various departments and will place an even greater burden of proof upon the council when it disagrees with the proposed policies of the mayor. Terms of office for both mayor and council are likely to be four years in length. This is the result of the reform-movement attitude that public officials should be given time enough in office to prove them-selves.

In addition to performing part of the legislative functions, the council is also entrusted with the important task of serving as critic. This is a function of all legislative bodies, of course, but it becomes unusually important where vast administrative power is vested in one official. The council is usually given full power to conduct investi-gations into any department or any phase of administration. In addi-tion, an officer, usually called the auditor and responsible to the council, checks upon the way in which the administrative branch of the city has spent the moneys appropriated by the council.[10]

Appraisal. Because of its provision for vigorous political leader-ship, the strong-mayor plan is especially desirable in large cities, where the complexities of government require someone to give firm leadership and direction. No other form of government in use in

[10] See chap. 13 on fiscal administration.

American cities makes an equal provision for leadership. Nearly all the nation's largest cities have some version of the strong-mayor plan. In smaller cities, where the functions performed are fewer and simpler and where government is more personal, the need for this type of leadership is somewhat less.

The strong-mayor plan, in comparison with the weak-mayor–council plan, permits use of the executive budget and merit-system personnel administration, overall executive planning, coordination of administrative activities, and greater public visibility for decision makers.

It has some problems, too. Perhaps the major one is that it expects too much of the mayor. In addition to serving as ceremonial head of the city, he is supposed to be both an adroit politician and an expert administrator. This combination is not easy to find. The able politician is likely to be either inexperienced with administration or bored by it, or both. The person whose training and interest are in administration, or some specialized phase of it, is very possibly a colorless campaigner or one who finds politics personally distasteful. Although the popular view that all politicians are extroverts and all public bureaucrats are introverts is not correct, it is true that skill in campaigning and administrative leadership are not often combined in the same person. The strong-mayor system expects that they will be.

Another problem in the strong-mayor system is that of getting persons with the required qualifications to run for office. A person who can do all the things expected of a strong mayor is usually highly successful in business and industry and is ordinarily unwilling to give up a position which pays a high salary and in which he has reasonable security to conduct a political campaign for a position which carries far less salary and no security.

In selecting a mayor, many voters would no doubt like to consider the qualifications of each candidate as a capable administrator, but they are necessarily unable to do so. Judging whether or not a person is a good administrator is very difficult—more difficult than judging whether a person is technically qualified as an engineer or a physician. The candidates themselves are not of much help to the voter; the one who makes the greatest claims of administrative ability may be the one least qualified.

It has sometimes been said that the strong-mayor plan is undesirable because it "mixes politics with administration," but this is not a valid argument. As a matter of fact, this could be offered as an argument *for* the plan. The mayor is able to place administrative problems in their political context—where they must eventually be placed in a democracy. He can compromise between these two inseparable aspects of government.

Because it is based upon that American favorite, the separation of powers, in combination with its obverse, the checks-and-balances system, the possibility of a deadlock between the mayor and the council on the formulation of policy is always present. On the national level, where the same system exists, most students are aware of serious deadlocks that have taken place—during the last two years of Wilson's administration, the last two of Hoover's, almost the whole of Truman's after 1946, and much of the Nixon term. It is perhaps less common on the local level than on the national, however, because the strong mayor usually dominates the political scene and is in a position to keep the council subordinate to him. The threat is, however, inherent in the system.

The Strong-mayor–Council Plan with Chief Administrative Officer. The chief executive in a strong-mayor city may well recognize his own shortcomings as an administrator and attempt to do something about it. The most common method of buttressing his position is to appoint an able, professionally experienced administrator to the position of chief fiscal officer, usually called the controller. He may act as something of a deputy mayor and attend to many details of administration.

The typical political–mayor is not always willing to choose professional deputies, however. In order to provide some legal incentive for him to do so, a recent trend has been toward establishing by charter or ordinance an official known by various titles and here called a chief administrative officer (CAO). His powers vary considerably from one city to another, and sometimes he can scarcely be differentiated from the chief budget or fiscal officer, but according to the theory of the position, he should be appointed by the mayor and serve at his pleasure. That is to say, the mayor may dismiss the CAO without having to show cause or gain the council's permission for his action.

The Chief Administrative Officer should perform such functions as the supervision of heads of various departments, preparation of the budget (or supervision over the budget director), and personnel direction. It is his task to correlate the various departments in the important routines of day-to-day administration, to give technical and professional advice to the mayor, and hence to free the mayor for his other two major jobs of serving as ceremonial head of the city (greeting the governor, laying cornerstones, and crowning the latest beauty queen) and of proposing and launching broad overall policy.

The origins of the CAO are somewhat obscure, for the position grew out of the garden-variety mayor-council plans, but the city and county of San Francisco appointed one in 1931 who must have been one of the earliest.[11] Many CAOs have been appointed in California in the postwar years, but these all appear to be *managers* with reduced administrative authority. These so-called CAOs are appointed by the council, as is a manager, rather than by the mayor. In California, only San Francisco has a CAO in the sense defined in this book, and even in that city he heads a group of city offices dealing only with public works. He does not make up the budget or coordinate city departments.[12]

Some authorities believe the CAO plan should be classified as a variation of the manager plan, rather than of the mayor-council plan; it combines some of the characteristics of each. Its classification is probably not too important. It is listed here in this book because it is a plan that continues the use of the separation-of-powers theory and places formal responsibility for administration in the hands of the mayor, rather than with the council as is the case with the manager plan. In states where cities have broad home rule powers, many of the characteristics of the council-manager plan can be incorporated under the strong-mayor form. As a result, there is no rigid dividing line between the two forms.

The Current Trend. Large-city interest in the strong-mayor plan with CAO has been increasing since the end of World War II. The Philadelphia charter of 1951 provides for a CAO, as does the 1952 model of the New Orleans charter. Both are home rule cities. The New Orleans charter, for example, calls for a council of seven, five elected by districts and two elected at large, for four-year terms. The mayor has the usual powers in policy making and, in addition, appoints a CAO, who serves at his pleasure. The CAO, with the approval of the mayor, appoints the heads of departments, except for those whose positions are filled according to state law. The CAO, of course, has supervisory and coordinative powers over the departments whose heads he appoints.[13]

A CAO established by ordinance has served in Louisville under two mayors. St. Cloud, Minnesota, adopted the CAO plan in its 1952 charter. A director of administrative services, with some of the powers of a CAO, has been established in Boston. A 1951 charter

[11] John C. Bollens, *Appointed Executive Local Government: The California Experience,* University of California Press, Berkeley, Calif., 1952, pp. 12–14; John M. Selig, "The San Francisco Idea," *National Municipal Review* (now *National Civic Review*), 46:290–295, June, 1957. See Lent D. Upson, "A Proposal for an Administrative Assistant to the Mayor," reported in *The American City,* 44:93, June, 1931; or, more generally, Wallace S. Sayre, "The General Manager Idea for Large Cities," *Public Administration Review,* 14:253–257, Autumn, 1954; and, for an argument that the council-manager plan may be more appropriate, even for large cities, John E. Bebout, "Management for Large Cities," *ibid.,* 15:188–195, Summer, 1955.
[12] See Bollens, *op. cit.,* pp. 9–11, 119–123; and Selig, *op. cit.*
[13] See *National Municipal Review* (now *National Civic Review*), 41:250, May, 1952; 41:570, December, 1952.

amendment provides for an administrative officer for Los Angeles. He is appointed by the mayor with majority confirmation by the council and is removable by the same process or by a two-thirds vote in the council. This officer is probably not a CAO, since Los Angeles is basically a weak-mayor city, and the administrative officer is principally the mayor's budget officer. In that city, the council has numerous administrative duties, and a score of departments are controlled by five-man commissions appointed by the mayor with the check of councilmanic approval and with a limited removal power. The city attorney and controller are elected officials.

The 1950 Faulkner Act in New Jersey provides for optional charters which may be adopted in the various cities after a local charter commission decides to present one of the options to the voters for approval. It makes the strong-mayor plan with CAO one of the options.

Adoption in New York. In 1953, two study groups recommended the CAO plan for use in the city of New York. After a three-year study which cost $2,200,000, the Mayor's Commission on Management Survey in its final report recommended against a general overhaul of the city's organizational structure and suggested the creation of a new office, that of a CAO to be called a "director of administration." It was also suggested that a "management cabinet," to consist of seven ex officio members, be appointed to aid the mayor. The director of administration would perform supervisory and coordinative functions over most of the city's departments and agencies. The deputy mayor would be assigned nearly all the ceremonial duties of the city.

Immediately after his election as mayor of the city in November, 1953, Robert F. Wagner, Jr., announced that he would appoint a CAO to the new post of "city administrator." For this task he selected a widely known student and practitioner of public administration, Luther H. Gulick.

Although the administrator had to engage in a fight for survival against jealous older city agencies, he and his office have "become the most fully realized assets of the mayor's office. They have become the mayor's most active problem-solvers, especially in matters requiring interdepartmental agreements or departmental reorganization."[14]

Appraisal. The strong-mayor plan with chief administrative officer seeks to free the mayor for policy making and give the city a professionally competent man to head administration. This new variation

14 Wallace S. Sayre and Herbert Kaufman, *Governing New York City*, Russell Sage Foundation, New York, 1960, pp. 665–666.

on the old theme would appear to be especially acceptable in large cities, and these are the ones that, in fact, seem most interested in the development. The use of the strong-mayor plan with this modification would, however, leave that system still with at least one major potential defect: the continuing threat of a legislative-executive deadlock. It would appear, too, that there would be a great potential for jealous rivalry between the mayor and the CAO, or for an uncooperative mayor to appropriate for himself the powers and functions of the appointive CAO.

CITIES WITHOUT A SEPARATION OF POWERS

The Commission Plan. A hurricane in September, 1900, almost completely destroyed the city of Galveston, Texas, and in doing so, created the conditions under which the commission plan was produced. Actually, as Richard S. Childs has pointed out, the commission structure was not planned; it was the result of an accident.[15] During the period of rebuilding Galveston, the legislature suspended local self-government in the city and substituted a temporary government of five local businessmen, the Galveston *commission*—hence the name for the system. The commission, working with great zeal under extraordinary conditions, accomplished much more at less cost than had its almost bankrupt predecessor. A new charter in 1903 tried to retain the system that had been working well and provided for a continuation of the commission, with three of its members appointed by the governor and two to be elected within the city. The courts held this unconstitutional, since an emergency no longer existed and, in ordinary circumstances, a city has a right to elect its councilmen. The legislature then made all five commissioners elective.

The success of the commission plan in Galveston soon attracted wide attention. Other Texas cities adopted the plan, and it quickly became popular in many parts of the nation. A Des Moines attorney, visiting Galveston, was impressed with the new "businessman's government" and proceeded to persuade the Iowa legislature to permit his city to adopt the plan. The legislature added other reform devices to the new charter—nonpartisan elections, and the initiative, referendum, and recall. It then became the "Des Moines plan."

The commission plan was adopted in Houston in 1905 and in Des Moines in 1907; by 1910, it had spread to some 108 cities. In 1917,

[15] Richard S. Childs, *Civic Victories*, Harper & Row, Publishers, Incorporated, New York, 1952, pp. 134–136. Earlier precedents for the commission idea are cited in Ernst B. Schulz, *American City Government*, The Stackpole Company, Pittsburgh, 1949, pp. 319–321.

at least 500 cities were using the plan. Then a reversal took place. The number of commission-governed cities began to diminish. Municipal reformers lost interest in the commission plan and began to advocate the council-manager plan as the true embodiment of a business form of organization. There have been almost no new adoptions since the 1930s, and the total number of commission cities has declined each year since World War I.

Characteristics. The commission plan's outstanding feature is the dual role of the commissioners. Each of them serves individually as the head of one of the city's administrative departments, while collectively they serve as the policy-making council for the city. This plan, unlike the various mayor-council structures, provides for no separation of powers. The commission performs both legislative and executive functions.

The commission is always small, usually consisting of five members, as did the original Galveston model. Some cities, especially small ones, have only three members, and quite a number have seven. The mayor, in the theoretical model, has no powers beyond those of the other commissioners, except that he performs the ceremonial duties for the city and presides over the council. He has no veto power. In most cities the office of mayor is specifically named on the ballot and is hence filled by popular vote. In some cities, however, the council chooses one of its own members to serve; and in a few places, the person who receives the highest number of votes among all the candidates becomes mayor.

Because the plan is a product of the reform movement, the commissioners are usually elected on a nonpartisan ticket. This is the case in about three-quarters of the municipalities. The commissioners are usually expected to serve as full-time public servants, even in fairly small cities; and in the original plan it was hoped that they would possess business or engineering experience and not be "mere politicians." They are nearly always elected at large, and four-year terms are the most common.

The ballot is short. According to the original plan, only the commissioners are elected. Often staggered terms are used, so that only two or three members of a five-member commission are elected at one time.

Appraisal. The commission plan was a radical departure from the prevailing weak-mayor systems of the turn of the century. It concentrated power in the hands of a few men, so that the decision makers became more visible to the voters. It greatly shortened the ballot from that which existed under the weak-mayor, or even most strong-mayor, systems. This gave the average voter a chance to know something about the candidates. Furthermore, only commissioners were chosen. Voters were not asked to select persons to fill routine offices (such as clerk or treasurer) or offices requiring technical skills (such as controller or assessor). Since the separation-of-powers doctrine was not used, there was no problem of the deadlock between the legislative and executive branches that is always a threat in a mayor-council city.

The commission plan had, however, too many disadvantages to make it workable. It was supposed to provide for a city policy-making body on which businessmen on leave from their ordinary pursuits would be willing to serve. Sometimes this was the case—for a few years. Actually, as a regular practice, it was not possible to select commissioners from among high-status businessmen, or such persons from any walk of life, for they were unwilling to give up their own businesses and run for an office that paid a low salary.

Responsibility to the public was not definitely fixed; it was divided among the several commissioners. The plan did not eliminate amateur administrators as department heads. In this respect it was not much different from the weak-mayor plan. A local citizen might well be able to help make basic policy for the police department or for public ways, but he would be able to serve capably as *administrative* head of either department only as the result of political accident.

The commission was often too small to provide for the function of *criticism*. It is essential in a democracy that the actions of public officials be constantly subjected to critical evaluation. Although the mayor-council system might lead to deadlocks, it at least provided a mechanism for criticism. This was not true of the commission plan. With no separation of powers, only the commission members were left to criticize one another. In theory they could do so, but in a small group, people seeing one another day after day put their relation-

TABLE 7-2. Largest Commission Cities in the United States 1968

City	1965 Population (est.)	Size of Council	No. at Large	Type of Election*	Term, Years	Salary, 1965
Portland, Ore.	380,000	5	5	NP-s	4	12,800
St. Paul	208,000	7	7	NP	2	12,000
Tulsa	280,000	4	4	P	2	11,925

*Under "Type of election," "NP" refers to nonpartisan elections; "P" to partisan; and "-s" following means that commission terms are staggered so that all do not expire at once. "Salary" refers to that of commission members.
Source: Municipal Year Book, International City Management Association, Chicago, 1966, pp. 99–100 and 1968, pp. 64–131.

ships on a personal basis. As politicians, they are certain to desire to avoid criticism. The commission very often, therefore, became a fraternity of tolerance.

Instead of watching one another, the commissioners would agree to mutual accommodation: "If you stay out of my department, I will stay out of yours." Criticism came to an end. No minority party watched the majority. No "backbenchers" eagerly awaited the chance to replace a member of the cabinet, as they do in the parliamentary system of government. There was no mayor with policy message and veto ready. The mutual hands-off policy went even further. In many cities it meant that several different city governments existed, each operating independently of the others, but with an occasional five-power conference being held to satisfy the demands of the charter.

Two further serious weaknesses affected the commission plan, both of them dealing with a lack of leadership. The plan did not provide for a chief executive. The strong-mayor and manager forms provide for administrative integration with a top official ultimately answerable for all administrative operations. No such person existed in the formal structure of the commission plan. And jealousy of the independence of one's department was likely to keep it from existing in practice. The top of the administrative pyramid was sawed off. Each department moved in its own administrative direction with no coordination at the top. This might be true to a degree even exceeding that found in the weak-mayor system.

No provision was made for top-policy leadership either, except fortuitously. The commissioners were equals and were likely to guard their equality zealously. There was no top policy maker, as under the strong-mayor system. An individual commissioner might by personality, experience, or skill at political organization come to dominate the council, but this was not common.

The plan attracted a great deal of attention for a brief period, but it was quickly outmoded by the invention of the manager plan and the development of a modern strong mayor. The inherent weaknesses of the commission plan then rapidly become manifest.

Present Status. Many commission-governed cities remain in the United States today (190 in 1968), although all the many Canadian cities that once used it have abandoned it. The total number of cities under the plan has been on the decline since about 1917, and the drop has been especially sharp since 1946. Even so, about 8 percent of the cities with a population of more than 5,000 still use it, the largest city in 1967 being Memphis.

Abandonments, especially in larger cities, were frequent after 1945. The "Des Moines plan" was abandoned in Des Moines in 1949 in favor of the council-manager form. San Antonio, after thirty-seven years as a commission city, switched to the manager plan in 1951. The Hoboken, New Jersey, charter commission denounced the commission plan in that city as having been "a complete failure," and the city changed in 1952 to the strong-mayor plan with CAO. So did New Orleans. Inadequacy of policy leadership is felt most in the largest cities. Medium-sized and small cities, however, are also abandoning the commission plan.

Outmoded structures of government live beyond the time when they are needed, as do all human institutions which suffer the rigidity of formal organization. There is no future for the commission structure of government. Those commission cities that remain do so as a result of apathy or inertia.

The Council-Manager Plan. The origin of the idea for the council-manager plan is not known with certainty. It seems that one of the first instances in which it was urged was in an editorial in the August, 1899, issue of *California Municipalities*. Haven A. Mason, editor of the magazine, urged that there should be "a distinct profession of municipal managers." He listed desirable qualifications, saying that a manager should know something about engineering, street construction, sewers, building construction, water and lighting systems, personnel, accounting, municipal law, fire protection, and library management. "Every city that receives or expends $50,000 annually," he said, "ought to have a salaried business manager." He even went so far as to say that "when we require adepts to run our cities, our universities will establish a department to specially fit our young men to enter the new profession of conducting municipal business."[16]

The claim for having the first council-manager city is sometimes disputed between Staunton, Virginia, and Sumter, South Carolina. In 1908, Staunton, with a weak mayor and a bicameral council, sought a different form of city government. Getting a new charter from the legislature would not have been easy. It was decided, therefore, to hire a "general manager" for the city on the basis of an ordinance. He was to be a full-time employee in charge of administration, was to be hired by the council, and could be dismissed by it at any time.

While the Staunton experiment did not produce a neat organization chart and was not based upon a systematic theory, it may be said to have become a manager-plan city in that year. Richard S. Childs, a businessman, who was at that time secretary of the National Short Ballot Organization and who later was to become president of the National Municipal League, took a leading part in the develop-

---

[16] The editorial is reprinted in Bollens, *op. cit.*, appendix III.

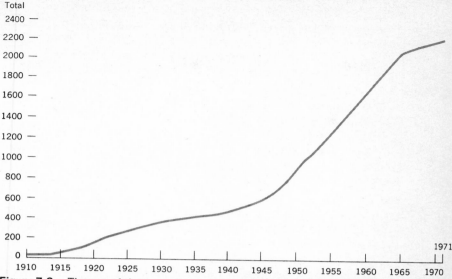

Figure 7-3. The use of the council-manager plan in American municipal corporations as of February 1, 1971. *Source: The City Manager Directory,* International City Management Association, Chicago, 1971, p. 2.

ment and popularizing of the plan. In 1911, he drew up a proposed city charter which was endorsed by the Board of Trade (chamber of commerce) of Lockport, New York. As it happened, the state general assembly refused to permit the city to use this model manager charter, but the charter attracted a good bit of attention and was adopted by Sumter, South Carolina, in the following year.

The manager-plan idea spread with great speed. During 1913, several small cities and towns adopted the Childs charter. At the same time, the Dayton Chamber of Commerce appointed a committee to study the need for a new charter in that city, for the state of Ohio had just granted to its municipalities the power of home rule. The committee, which was headed by John M. Patterson, president of the National Cash Register Company, came to favor the manager plan. While the group was pursuing its efforts, the Miami River, which passes through the city, overflowed its banks in spring flood. The ineptitude of the existing city government in meeting the problems that followed gave unanticipated support to the efforts of the charter-study committee. The voters adopted the proposed new charter in August. It went into effect on January 1, 1914, and the new council hired the city engineer of Cincinnati as manager, thus setting a precedent for the type of person who is still often preferred for the position.

The Dayton episode, partly because it occurred in a large city, partly because of the personal publicity efforts of Patterson, and partly because of the extraordinary drama connected with it, gave a tremendous boost to the council-manager plan. By 1915, there were 49 manager cities. Five years later, there were 158. The number has increased uninterruptedly ever since. On January 1, 1970, there were 2289 manager cities and other local governments in the United States and Canada. Fifty percent of the cities between 10,000 and 500,000 population had managers.

The manager plan has enjoyed a rapid expansion in the period following World War II. Its growth has closely paralleled that of suburbia. It seems to be especially suited to the politics of consensus and the acceptance of professionalism that we find there.[17]

Characteristics. [18] The outstanding identifying marks of the council-manager-plan model are a council of laymen responsible for policy making and a professional administration under a chief administrator responsible to the council. The theoretical structure rivals that of the British parliamentary system in its simplicity.

The council is small, five to nine members, and is commonly elected at large, on a nonpartisan ballot, often for four-year staggered terms. It is responsible to the public for all policy making and ultimately for the overall character of administration. Under the model charter,[19] members of the council are the only officers who are popularly elected. The intended purpose of the short ballot is to concentrate responsibility upon these people and to ask the voters to fill only important policy-making positions in which they can reasonably be expected to take an interest.

There is no separation of powers, nor are there checks and balances. The mayor or president of the city or village normally performs only ceremonial functions and presides over the council. He has no administrative powers, except in the case of an emergency, and no veto. In almost one-half of the manager cities over 5,000 population (48 percent in 1966), the council chooses the mayor from among its own membership. In most other cities, he is directly elected; a few give the post to the person with the most votes in the councilmanic race.

The administration of the city is integrated under the control of a professional manager, who is hired by the council. In the model

[17] See Robert C. Wood, *Suburbia: Its People and Their Politics,* Houghton Mifflin Company, Boston, 1959, pp. 183–186.
[18] The National Municipal League, New York, has issued several pamphlets and books in popular form. See especially *Forms of Municipal Government* (rev., 1958), and Richard Childs, *The First 50 Years of the Council Manager Plan of Municipal Government* (1969).
[19] See the *Model City Charter,* 6th ed., 1964, of the National Municipal League, New York. The manager plan has been endorsed by the League since 1916.

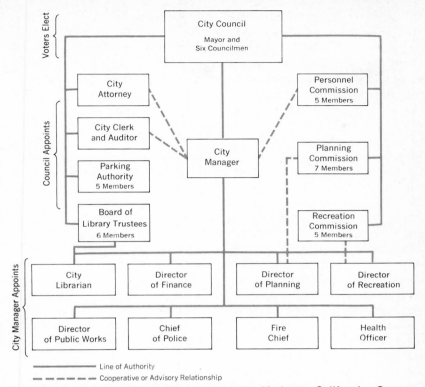

Figure 7-4. An actual council-manager city: Modesto, California. *Source:* Adapted from *A Report of Progress,* City of Modesto, Calif., 1952.

plan, he serves for no definite term of office but rather at the pleasure of a majority of the council. He is not subject to recall by the voters, for they did not hire him and, furthermore, ultimate responsibility for municipal government belongs to the council. No manager may serve effectively if he does not enjoy the confidence of a majority of the council, and therefore the credit or blame for what he does rests with the council.

The manager is a professional person, and he is expected to hire professionally competent technicians to operate the various departments of the city. The lower administrative positions, roughly those below the department heads, are also filled with persons who are technically competent. They are usually chosen by civil service merit examination.

Appraisal. Municipal reformers have tended to accord to this plan inordinate praise, often attributing to it miraculous powers to bring about efficient and economical city administration, regardless of the traditions of city government, the kind of personnel which it employs, and whether the public understands and supports the basic principles of the plan. These exaggerated claims for the plan, as well as some of the specious arguments used against it, should be discounted by the sophisticated student of municipal affairs.

The council-manager plan calls for lay citizens, commonly political amateurs, to serve on the council and make public policy as representatives of the community. No professional politicians are expected to make a living from the positions, for the councilmanic jobs normally pay only a nominal salary or only a per meeting allowance. The execution of policy, as approved by the council, is in the hands of a professional staff of administrators headed by the manager. All administrators and technicians are supposed to be especially qualified for their jobs. The chief administrator can be selected by the council, not from among local politicians of one party, as would be the case if it were a patronage appointment, but rather from among trained persons anywhere in the nation. The choice is limited only by what the council believes it should offer as salary.

But while the manager plan emphasizes professional administration, it does not turn the city over to the whims of an independent bureaucracy. The manager and his subordinates are answerable to the council. They normally attend council sessions, where they are expected to answer questions, report on progress of various projects, and explain any of their actions that involve matters in which the council is interested. And there are none of the legislative-executive conflicts that arise from time to time in the mayor-council city, since, as in the parliamentary system, those who carry out policy serve at the pleasure of the legislative branch.

In contrast to the commission plan, however, criticism is provided for. Administrative spoils are not distributed among the council members, and hence there is less need for collusion against criticism. The legislative branch remains free to oversee the operation of administration, and the people who appropriate the funds are not the people who spend them. The council votes the funds and then checks upon the manager and his staff, both through its own supervision and through the receipt of auditors' reports.

Although the manager plan is a simple mechanism, it is not always understood by the general public. An important factor contributing to this is the carry-over to the present day of many elements of Jacksonian ideology. For example, the plan is sometimes challenged as "dictatorial" or "un-American" because the chief administrator is not elected. To be sure, this fact violates a basic precept of Jacksonianism. But the argument is invalid, since responsibility for administration is clearly established. The manager plan also requires acceptance of the professional administrator. One study has found that where values of professionalism were in conflict with local value patterns, the plan was not accepted.[20]

Some people argue that the manager plan is too expensive for small cities because the position of manager must command enough pay to attract competent personnel, or they say that the manager would not have enough work to keep him busy in a small city. These arguments would seem invalid for most small places, however, for the plan is in operation in a large number of municipalities of under 5,000 population.[21]

There are more serious objections to the plan, however. The number of cities needing managers and professional department heads has increased rapidly in the last generation, and a shortage of able managers has been a chronic problem. The numerous positions in private business for administrators and engineers has also helped to reduce the number of persons available to cities. Some cities have tried the plan, only to complain that the manager was incompetent.

Managers are sometimes criticized on another ground. In the past many of them were engineers who had no education in the social sciences. As such, some of them tended to view issues of public policy as a series of engineering or budgeting problems rather than as matters of economics and sociology.

Some advocates of the manager plan have made the erroneous assumption that a sharp distinction can be made between politics and administration. No such line exists. One shades off into the other. Their idea is that the manager is a nonelective employee who should not make policy but should concern himself only with the details of administration. Actually, it is almost a necessity for the lay, part-time council to look to the professional, full-time manager for recommendations concerning policy. If harmonious relations exist and the manager and the council are competent, the council will ordinarily not act on any policy matter without first getting the recommendations and a statement of the pertinent facts from the manager.[22] On some types of highly controversial issues, a manager, if he is prudent, will avoid taking a stand, but apart from these, it is his job to make recommendations and, in fact, to initiate policy recommenda-

[20] Garth N. Jones, "Integration of Political Ethos and Local Government Systems," *Human Organization*, 23:210–223, Fall, 1964.
[21] The pattern of managership in these cities is described in W. C. Busby, "The Small Council-Manager City," *Public Management*, 35:154–156, July, 1953.
[22] See Charles R. Adrian, "Leadership and Decision-making in Manager Cities: A Study of Three Communities," *Public Administration Review*, 18:208–213, Summer, 1958; Karl A. Bosworth, "The Manager *Is* a Politician," *ibid.*, pp. 216–222; Charles A. Harrell and D. G. Weiford, "The City Manager and the Policy Process," *ibid.*, 19:101–107, Spring, 1959, and B. James Kweder, *The Roles of Manager, Mayor, and Councilmen in Policy Making: A Study of Twenty-one North Carolina Cities*, Institute of Government, The University of North Carolina, Chapel Hill, 1965.

tions. He is nearly always in a better position to interpret policy demands than is the council. If the council accepts the recommendations of the manager with regularity, it does not necessarily mean that it is a rubber stamp; it may mean that the council has hired a competent manager and that his recommendations accord nicely with the consensus of values in the community.

Among managers themselves two ideologies (perhaps it is more a matter of two personality types) express the proper relationship of the manager to the council. Some managers center their attention on administrative operations and routine matters, avoiding taking a stand on any issue; others center their attention on policy matters and the development of the city. In some instances—Berkeley and East Cleveland at one time were examples—a well-entrenched manager, long in office, may completely dominate a council. He may not only make it into a rubber stamp but may even have considerable influence in determining who is elected to the council.

Though the manager may tend to dominate the council in some cases, the policy-making arm may also tend to invade the area theoretically reserved for professional administrators. If the manager is weak, or if several members of the council do not accept the spirit of the manager plan, a good deal of "political" interference in administration may result. Councilmen may bypass the manager and deal directly with members of departments or seek to influence administrative decisions on the basis of short-range constituency considerations rather than professional standards and values. Hostile councilmen may even appoint a local politician to the post of manager. In cases such as these, the manager plan cannot operate according to the model plan.

It is not uncommon to find, especially where a modified manager plan leaves some administrative powers with the mayor, a disrupting power struggle between the mayor and the manager. One study has found manager tenure to be shorter where mayors were independently elected and where managers lacked political ties in the community.[23] This may also happen in cities where the mayor does not understand or accept his role under the manager plan. If the public does not understand the principles of the plan, it is likely to support the mayor in such a fight, for the title of his office implies to many people that he ought to be the chief administrator. In some cities, certain officials, such as the city attorney, the city engineer, or the police chief, may be appointed by the mayor rather than by the manager. In such cases, there may in effect be two managers, one ama-

[23] Gladys M. Kammerer and others, *City Managers in Politics*, University of Florida Press, Gainesville, Fla., 1962.

TABLE 7-3.   Votes and Popular Action on Council-manager Government 1955–1965 Inclusive*

Population Class	Number of Cities in Class		Popular Action on Proposals to Change			
			To Adopt		To Abandon	
	Total	Council-manager	Yes	No	No	Yes
Over 500,000	21	4 (19%)	0†	0	0	0
250,000–500,000	30	12 (40%)	0	0	3	0
100,000–250,000	80	39 (48%)	2	2	8	0
50,000–100,000	192	96 (50%)	7	12	13	2
25,000–50,000	406	211 (52%)	24	25	27	13
10,000–25,000	1,033	447 (43%)	86	68	40	10
2,500–10,000	3,065	695 (23%)	191	109	57	31
Totals	4,827	1,504 (31%)	310	216	145	56

*Population classes based upon 1960 census.
† Dade County, Fla., adopted the county-manager plan in 1957, but this table does not include counties unless they provide general municipal services in the area.
Source: Edwin O. Stene, *The City Manager: Professional Training and Tenure,* Governmental Research Center, University of Kansas, Lawrence, Kans., 1966.

teur and the other professional. It may follow that the council members are eventually forced to "choose up sides" if either the mayor or the manager launches into a policy of aggrandizement. The result is usually a dead, or at least badly wounded, manager plan.

Perhaps the greatest potential weakness in the plan is to be found in connection with the problem of policy leadership. No adequate provision for it is made in the model plan. The council is a body of equals. One of the members may emerge as a leader in policy making, but if this is so, it is the result of accident. More likely, the council will flounder about or turn to the manager. Managers have become such effective policy leaders that the plan appears to be working well even in large cities with their complex patterns of interests and conflicting ideologies. In 1970, managers were in office in six cities of over 400,000 population. The plan appeared to be working satisfactorily in all of them, and no movements for abandonment were underway.[24]

Some evidence indicates that the operation of the manager plan in a style somewhat approximating that of the model is dependent upon the existence of a fairly high degree of consensus in the community. When a city's politics produces a lineup of two fairly well-balanced groups, each of which, when it comes to power, dismisses

[24] Hessler, *op. cit.,* chap. 5 and *Municipal Year Book, 1968–1969–1970, op. cit.*

the manager hired by the opposition and finds one loyal to itself—as sometimes happens—the plan is in difficulties. Similarly, it apparently does not operate effectively in communities where the function of city government is viewed by a large number of citizens as that of an arbiter,[25] for this implies the need for a strong elective leader.[26]

The lack of a chief policy maker causes another problem. In large cities, especially, it is difficult for the general public to know much about the various candidates for the council or about the voting records of incumbents. The problem is especially great when the council is elected at large on a nonpartisan ballot, as is often the case. It is therefore not necessarily true that concentration of responsibility in the council will result in informed voting. In cities small enough for candidates to be known by reputation, this is not likely to be as serious a problem, if indeed it is a problem at all.

Actual Results.[27] The adoption of the council-manager plan has led to increased prestige for the council and in greater control by it over municipal affairs. Managers have generally been appointed by the council without regard to political activity, and tenure for the manager has, in most cases, not been interrupted by considerations other than administrative competence. Most managers have provided administration based upon professional values and standards and have brought far more coordination to the activities of their governments than had existed before. They have furthered long-range policy planning, and have encouraged the employment of specialists for advice on technical problems, have emphasized the merit principle in personnel administration, and have increased the interest of employees in their jobs. Managers have promoted coordinated, executive budgeting methods and have provided more financial information and better financial management than was afforded under the older forms of government.

The adoption of the council-manager form has not reduced the size of the total budget in most cities, but it has increased the public's confidence in municipal government, it has sometimes reduced *unit* costs by eliminating graft and waste and by utilizing personnel and methods of greater efficiency. There is some evidence that any competent manager, regardless of the size of the city, can save his own salary many times over each year and that the plan has therefore been an economical one, even for small cities.

---

[25] See above, p. 86.
[26] See Williams and Adrian, *op. cit.*
[27] This section is based upon the findings reported in Harold A. Stone, Don K. Price, and Katherine H. Stone, *City Manager Government in the United States*, Public Administration Service, Chicago, 1940, which is a report on a three-year survey of fifty cities.

TABLE 7-4. Largest Council-manager Cities—1970

City	1970 Population	Date in Effect	Size of Council	No. at Large	Type of Election*	Term	Other Elective Officers
Dallas	836,121	1931	9	9	NP	2	None
San Antonio	650,188	1952	9	9	NP	2	None
San Diego	675,788	1932	8	0	NP-s	4	Attorney
Kansas City	530,000	1926	13	6	NP	4	None
Phoenix	580,275	1914	7	7	NP	2	None
Cincinnati	495,000	1926	9	9	NP	2	None
Oklahoma City	380,000	1927	8	0	NP-s	4	None
Oakland	378,000	1931	9	9	NP-s	4	Auditor Controller
Long Beach	368,000	1921	9	9	NP	3	Auditor Attorney
Fort Worth	360,000	1925	9	9	NP	2	None

*"NP" refers to nonpartisan; "-s" means that council terms are staggered so that all do not expire at once.
Source: Municipal Year Book, 1970, International City Management Association, Chicago, 1970, Table XV.

The council-manager plan, then, suffers from some weaknesses, as do all human institutions. It has, however, so satisfied the bulk of the voters in cities using it that, once adopted, abandonments are rare.

Prevalence of Manager Governments. Studies of adoptions of the council-manager plan find an affinity between it and higher-income and more homogeneous communities. A study of seventy-four suburbs of more than 2,500 population found the plan to exist most frequently in suburbs with high housing values. However, after these suburbs adopted it, it also spread gradually to suburbs of lower housing values.[28] A second study of 300 suburbs in the nation's twenty-five most urbanized areas found council-manager government to be more frequent where (1) a greater number of heads-of-households worked fifty to fifty-two weeks a year; (2) heads-of-households held white-collar jobs; (3) more women in the household held outside jobs; (4) median family incomes and education levels were high; (5) new homes were being built; and (6) most homes were for single families and were occupied by owners.[29] A third study found council-manager government to be most frequently adopted in middle-sized cities

[28] Edgar L. Sherbenou, "Class, Participation, and the Council Manager Plan," *Public Administration Review*, 21:131–135, Summer, 1961.
[29] Leo F. Schnore and Robert R. Alford, "Forms of Government and Socio-economic Characteristics of Suburbs," *Administrative Science Quarterly*, 8:1–17, June, 1963.

(25,000–250,000), in cities with native-born populations, cities with a primary economic activity concentrating on personal service, retail or finance, cities that were growing rapidly, and cities in one-party states.[30]

Proponents and Opponents: The Politics of Reform. The council-manager plan is often launched and supported by good-government and business groups, chambers of commerce, property owners' associations, taxpayers' associations, civic associations, citizens' action groups, women's clubs, and, very often, newspapers. Opposition to proposals for adoption frequently comes from organized labor, politicians in office (especially mayors who stand to lose both power and prestige in their offices by the employment of a manager), and political parties. Political leaders often dislike the manager plan because it offers little in the way of patronage and because it is often coupled with nonpartisan elections.

In many cities, the two leading contenders in campaigns over manager charters have been the local chamber of commerce and local organized labor. The impression that the plan is antithetical to the best interests of organized labor is held by many, though not all, labor leaders in various parts of the country.

In contrast, the plan has been accepted with enthusiasm by business groups, for many reasons. It was the Board of Trade of Lockport that first endorsed the Childs plan, and the chamber of commerce in Dayton was responsible for the first large-city adoption. The plan is often lauded as a "businesslike government" in imitation of the corporate form of private business.

The upper-middle-class suburbs which are the homes of metropolitan businessmen are characteristically administered by a manager. Many managers are engineers, and some are trained in schools of business administration. This means that they received much of their education in the more conservative colleges of our universities. They are likely to be personally conservative in political views. They are business-oriented in their social values. Many of. them have had experience in private business before becoming managers; others may hope to move into good positions in private business after serving for a number of years in city government.

Labor leaders fear that the council-manager plan requires them to take an all-or-nothing plunge into local politics. The risk in this is especially great if elections are at large. Under such circumstances, labor leaders are faced with getting a majority on the council in a city-

[30] John H. Kessel, "Government Structure and Political Environment: A Statistical Note about American Cities," *American Political Science Review*, 56:615–620, September, 1962.

wide contest. Failing this, the entire administration of the city may fall into opposition, or (at least from their viewpoint) undependable and unpredictable hands. In most core cities, the AFL-CIO works closely with the Democratic party which is likely to dominate partisan elections. The council-manager plan advocates nearly always favor nonpartisan elections, however, and this is a device that usually favors conservatives and weakens the effectiveness of a labor-Democratic coalition.

Other reasons exist for labor's skepticism about the plan, too. Business leaders and chamber of commerce managers may be concerned with large issues of policy, but the typical workingman thinks of the machinery of government as something to be used for personal favors, to help him in an emergency. For his purposes, the ward aldermanic system is more effective than are the at-large elections which are the rule under the manager plan. Furthermore, at-large elections tend to select councilmen from middle-class ranks, men who often have had little experience with the problems of low-income persons or the members of unions. Not only may they be unfamiliar with the concerns of these people, but they may be overtly hostile to unionism, especially if they are small businessmen. In cities where labor leaders have been active in municipal politics, workingmen are especially likely to be dissatisfied with the manager plan.[31]

In contrast to the general pattern, some unions have taken the lead in urging the manager plan. Furthermore, it would appear that labor usually supports the plan once it is well established in a city.

The manager plan enjoys labor support in Cincinnati, Kansas City, and Toledo. The AFL-CIO takes no national stand on forms of local government; it allows local organizations to decide positions in local campaigns for themselves. In 1950, union leaders in eighty cities where the plan had been in effect for twenty years or longer overwhelmingly approved of the plan. In only three of the cities was definite opposition expressed.[32] Labor is being somewhat reassured concerning the motives of those who favor the manager plan. It is likely, however, that the device will remain especially the favorite of chambers of commerce and middle-class good-government groups.

More recently the Kerner Commission (National Advisory Commission on Civil Disorders) in its 1969 report stated that council-manager city governments played a significant if unintentional role in the eruption of racial disorders during 1967 by discouraging black ghetto participation in city government. Using the Commission's data, a

[31] See Kenneth E. Beasley, *Attitudes of Labor toward City Government*, Governmental Research Center, University of Kansas, Lawrence, Kans., 1954.
[32] See the pamphlet *Labor Unions and the Council-Manager Plan* (1950), issued by the National Municipal League, New York, and designed to be read by workingmen.

study by Professor Delbert Taebel showed a lower incidence of racial disorders for council-manager cities in every one of the commonly used seven population groups, except for cities in the 10,000–25,000 category where all three riots occurring in 1967 in that size of city occurred in council-manager cities.[33]

OTHER FORMS OF GOVERNMENT

The New England Town. The direct democracy of the town meeting characterized local government in New England until the urbanization of that area began to force the acceptance of modifications. In some urban areas, the town-government feature has been abandoned, while in others it has been made into a representative form.

The town makes no distinction between rural and urban places. As an area becomes more and more urbanized, it continues under the town system, sharing the same government with the neighboring rural area. The town is governed by a meeting of all the qualified voters, who choose officers and make basic policy. There is an annual meeting, traditionally in March, with as many other meetings as may be necessary. After making basic policy, the people choose a board of selectmen, usually three but in some places as many as nine, and a fairly large number of other officers. The selectmen and elective officers are then entrusted with carrying out the basic policies established by community action.

The urbanization of many towns has been accompanied by a sharp decrease in attendance at town meetings and a consequent decline in the effectiveness of this form of government. In many areas of New England, therefore, a *representative* town meeting plan has been developed. Under this plan, the voters choose a large number of citizens, perhaps a hundred or more, to attend the meeting, represent them, and vote. Any citizen can attend and take part in debates, but he no longer has a direct vote. This plan is used in such large urban places as Brookline, Massachusetts (1960 population: 54,044).

Town government, outside of the meeting feature, resembles the weak-mayor or, more particularly, the American village form, except that there is no mayor at all, only a president of the council, and no one has a veto power. More and more commonly, the selectmen choose a manager and assign routine administration to him. This is particularly the case in Maine and Vermont and is to be found in all New England states.

The New England legislatures have long been under pressure

[33] Delbert A. Taebel, "Managers and Riots," *National Civic Review*, 57:554–555, September, 1968.

to alter the traditional town government in order to help meet contemporary needs. They have created new offices and commissions such as those of aviation commissioner, planning boards, civil service commissions, library trustees, and finance committees, the last in order to help provide for better planning in budget making so that this document is not pieced together in haphazard fashion at the public meeting. (Titles vary by states and even towns, of course.)

Closing Statement. Structures of government are tools. They make a difference as to how a community is governed and as to which groups and interests in the community are most influential. Local cultural circumstances help determine the type of structure that is wanted by politically dominant groups and the type of government that will be produced under any chosen form. Structure is significant, but it is only one of the factors that make up the particular characteristics of politics and community decision making in a city.

SELECTED
READINGS

Abbott, Frank C.: "The Cambridge City Manager," in Harold Stein (ed.), *Public Administration and Policy Development,* Harcourt, Brace & World, Inc., New York, 1952, pp. 573–620. (A case study of a manager involved in controversy.)

Arnold, David S.: *Council-Manager Abandonment Referendums,* International City Management Association, Chicago, 1964. (Evaluates ninety-seven referendums held in ninety cities.)

Banfield, Edward C.: *Big City Politics,* Random House, Inc., New York, 1965. (Describes the politics of several strong-mayor—council cities.)

Beasley, Kenneth E.: *Attitudes of Labor toward City Government,* Governmental Research Center, University of Kansas, Lawrence, Kans., 1954. (Examines attitudes of labor-union leaders toward the council-manager plan.)

Bollens, John C., and John C. Ries: *The City Manager Profession, Myths and Realities,* Public Administration Service, Chicago, 1969.

Booth, David A. (comp.): *Council-Manager Government, 1940–1964: An Annotated Bibliography,* International City Management Association, Chicago, 1965.

Bradford, E. S.: *Commission Government in American Cities,* The Macmillan Company, New York, 1911. (A study during the heyday of the commission plan.)

Bromage, Arthur W.: *Councilmen at Work,* George Wahr Publishing Company, Ann Arbor, Mich., 1954. (Bromage, a councilman-political scientist concludes that the weak-mayor plan can be made to work in a middle-sized city, but only at the cost of large investments of time and resources by amateur councilmen.)

————: *Urban Policy Making: The Council-Manager Partnership,* Public Administration Service, Chicago, 1971.

Brominz, Beverly C.: *North Kingdom Selects Two Town Managers,* Bureau of Governmental Research, University of Rhode Island, Kingston, R. I., 1962. (A case study of controversy over the manager plan.)

Carrell, Jeptha: *The Role of the City Manager,* Community Studies, Inc., Kansas City, Mo., 1962. (A study of council-manager conflict in Kansas City.)

Childs, Richard S.: *The First 50 Years of the Council-Manager Plan of Municipal Government,* National Municipal League, New York, 1965. (Statement by founder of the council-manager plan.)

Cline, Dorothy I.: *Albuquerque and the City Manager Plan,* The University of New Mexico Press, Albuquerque, N. Mex., 1951. (Compares reform and grass-roots values.)

East, John Porter: *Council-Manager Government: The Political Thought of Its Founder, Richard S. Childs,* The University of North Carolina Press, Chapel Hill, N.C., 1965. (A study of the ideas of the founder of the council-manager plan and of the way those views are now evaluated.)

Humes, Samuel, and Eileen Martin: *The Structure of Local Governments Throughout the World,* Martinus, The Hague, 1961.

Kammerer, Gladys M., and others: *City Managers in Politics,* University of Florida Press, Gainesville, Fla., 1962. (A study of manager tenure in Florida.)

Mills, Werner E., and Harry R. Davis: *Small City Government,* Random House, Inc., New York, 1962. [Includes a study of a small city with a low-tax (caretaker) ideology and the council-manager structure.]

Nolting, Orin F.: *Progress and Impact of the Council-Manager Plan,* Public Administration Service, Chicago, 1969. (The history of the second 25 years of the International City Managers' Association by its former executive director. In 1969, the organization's name was changed to the International City Management Association to encourage membership by persons in general management positions with various titles.)

Presthus, Robert V.: *Men at the Top,* Oxford University Press, Fair Lawn, N.J., 1964. (Officeholders were found to rival businessmen in importance in small weak-mayor–council cities.)

Robson, William A.: *Great Cities of the World, Their Governments, Politics and Planning,* George Allen and Unwin, London, 2d ed., 1957.

Smith, Lincoln: "The Manager System and Collectivism," *American Journal of Economics and Sociology*, 24:21–39, January, 1965. (The council-manager plan is seen as having the effect of promoting municipal ownership of utilities and other enterprises.)

Stene, Edwin O.: *The City Manager: Professional Training and Tenure*, Governmental Research Center, University of Kansas Press, Lawrence, Kans., 1966.

Stene, E. O., and G. K. Floro: *Abandonments of the Manager Plan: A Study of Four Small Cities*, University of Kansas Press, Lawrence, Kans., 1953.

Stinchcombe, Jean L.: *Reform and Reaction: City Politics in Toledo*, Wadsworth, Belmont, Calif., 1968.

Stone, Harold A., Don K. Price, and Katherine H. Stone: *City Manager Government in the United States*, Public Administration Service, Chicago, 1940.

Wilson, James Q.: "Manager under Fire," in Richard T. Frost (ed.), *Cases in State and Local Government*, Prentice-Hall, Inc., Englewood Cliffs, N.J., 1961. (A case study.)

Zimmerman, Joseph F.: *The Massachusetts Town Meeting: A Tenacious Institution*, Graduate School of Public Affairs, State University of New York, Albany, 1967.

CHAPTER
8 EXECUTIVE OFFICERS

The mayor of today's American small town is commonly a moderately successful small businessman, long active in local politics and civic affairs and well liked by his neighbors. In the large city of an earlier day, the mayor was often corrupt and incompetent—although there were outstanding exceptions. Today, our large cities seem to be producing an increasingly large number of capable chief executives. Still, many contemporary mayors are amiable mediocrities, lacking in ability and imagination and under obligation to a few interest groups that put them in office.

Cleveland, with a strong mayor elected on a partisan basis, has been an exceptional city so far as chief executives are concerned. It has not only had able reformers but has sent several men on to positions in state and national government. Tom L. Johnson (1901), a prominent businessman, became famous for fighting the "special interests." His campaigns were carried on by his successor, Newton D. Baker (1909), who was chosen a few years later to be President Wilson's Secretary of War. In 1935, Harold H. Burton was elected mayor of Cleveland. After being reelected for two more terms, he was elected to the United States Senate and later was appointed to the United States Supreme Court. Although he was not outstanding in these positions, his record is an indication that the mayor's office can be used as a step toward higher-status positions. Burton was succeeded as mayor in 1941 by Frank J. Lausche, a man of little administrative ability but with much political skill and ambition.

He was reelected in 1943, receiving almost three-quarters of the votes cast. Later, he became Governor of Ohio and then United States Senator. In 1953, Lausche appointed his successor, Thomas A. Burke, to fill a vacancy in the United States Senate. Burke's successor, Anthony J. Celebrezze, became Secretary of Health, Education, and Welfare in 1962. In 1968, Carl B. Stokes, the first black mayor of a large city, took office and immediately assumed an important role in the national politics of the Democratic party. But the Cleveland system of consistent promotion to higher office is not typical.

The problem of securing able men as mayors of large cities is complicated because men who seek these offices are likely to have to place themselves under obligation to interest groups with specific political goals. This is so because someone must furnish the money for the expensive large-city campaign.

The need for forceful, imaginative leadership from the mayor has been emphasized in large cities as a result of concern about potential deterioration of property and economic obsolescence resulting from the flight of people, business, and industry to the suburbs.[1]

The strong mayor—the policy leader of today's large city—has great powers and many sanctions which he can apply in order to clear the path for the things he wants to do. But he is also hemmed in by restrictions—he works in a glass house, a prisoner to a considerable extent of the civil servants who serve him and of the rival boards and commissions that each have reserved some city policy making for themselves. The house is heavily mortgaged to the state and the fence around it is a barricade manned by earnest defenders of suburban independence.

POWERS OF THE MAYOR

The powers exercised by the mayor vary widely throughout the United States. The person called the mayor in a commission or council-manager city normally has few powers other than those of presiding over the council and performing the ceremonial role for the city. The mayor in a mayor-council city may have a great many powers, or he may be merely one of many virtually coordinate members of the city administration, as is the case in a weak-mayor city.

Legislative Powers. No difference necessarily exists between weak and strong mayors so far as their legislative powers are concerned. In virtually all instances, the mayor has the right to submit messages

[1] See Seymour Freedgood, "New Strength in City Hall," in Editors of Fortune, *The Exploding Metropolis,* Anchor Books, Doubleday & Company, Inc., Garden City, N.Y., 1958, pp. 63–64.

to the council and hence to recommend policy. These messages carry with them the prestige and the publicity potential of the mayor's office and must be considered by the council in light of this. Some mayors have the right to attend council sessions and to introduce measures. In those municipalities that have remained closest to English precedents, the mayor is actually a member of the council and presides over it. This is true in a common form of village government and is also the case in nearly all commission and council-manager cities.

Most mayors in mayor-council cities have a veto power. This is, of course, a substantial supporting weapon when the mayor recommends policy. The greatest power of the veto in the hands of a mayor, as of a president, is measured by its threatened use rather than by the number of times it is actually invoked. A veto may be overridden either by a simple majority or by some extraordinary vote such as two-thirds or three-fourths. In a few cities, notably Boston, a veto is absolute.

In strong-mayor cities, it is not uncommon to find a mayor so powerful that the council does not attempt to make policy independently of him. Under such circumstances, he need rarely use the veto. The use to which the veto is put will depend, of course, on local custom, prevailing circumstances, and the personal ideology and political strategy of the incumbent mayor.

In some cities the mayor has the power of casting a vote in case of a tie, even though he may not be a member of the council. If he presides over the council, he is quite certain to have this power. When the mayor is a member of the council, he, of course, has a vote.

Powers over Administration. The characteristic differences between the weak and strong mayors of America are to be found in their powers over administration. The strong mayor, unlike the weak

TABLE 8-1. Veto Power of Mayors in Cities over 5,000 Population

Form of Government	Percent of Mayors Who May		
	Veto All Measures	Veto Selected Items	Not Veto Anything
Mayor-council	35.1	33.9	31.0
Commission	11.3	3.5	85.2
Council-manager	6.7	9.4	83.9
Town meeting			
Representative town meeting	0.0	0.0	100.0
All cities over 5,000	20.8	20.1	58.1

Source: Municipal Year Book, 1968, International City Management Association, Chicago, 1968, p. 57.

mayor, is given powers to make him the chief administrative officer. He has supervisory and coordinative powers over the activities of the various departments and is in charge of the preparation and administration of the budget. In a few cities he has so much power in budget preparation that the council is empowered to do no more than decrease or strike out items in the budget. The controller, who supervises expenditures by the operational departments, is normally an appointee of the chief executive in a strong-mayor city. At the opposite extreme, the budget is sometimes prepared by a committee of the council well out of the hands of the mayor, and the controller may be an elective official or a council appointee. When the mayor has control over the preparation and expenditure of the budget, he has great powers which he can use to reach into agencies that might otherwise be totally independent. For example, he can use this power to influence policies within agencies otherwise controlled by an elective board (e.g., parks in many cities) or by the bureaucracy (e.g., public health).

Despite the vast legal powers they often possess, the mayors of large cities:[2]

> frequently must mediate between the claims of contending groups, no one of which is dominant in the community. In such instances their role as decision-makers assumes greater importance. Holding the balance of power, they occupy a strategic position of influence which they can exploit to further their total program and objectives. The mayors of large cities, particularly, enjoy such opportunities. It would be grossly misleading, however, to assume that men who have reputations as strong mayors, such as Daley in Chicago, Lee in New Haven or Tucker in St. Louis, rule by fiat or by arbitrary exercise of their official prerogatives.

Robert Dahl made a similar observation relative to New Haven. He found that the mayor "was not the peak of a pyramid but rather at the center of intersecting circles. He rarely commanded. He negotiated, cajoled, exhorted, beguiled, charmed, pressed, appealed, reasoned, promised, insisted, demanded, even threatened, but he most needed support from other leaders who simply could not be commanded. Because the mayor could not command, he had to bargain."[3]

Law Enforcement. Most city charters impose upon the mayor the executive function of seeing to it that laws and ordinances are enforced and that peace and order are maintained. Actual power

[2] John C. Bollens and Henry J. Schmandt, *The Metropolis,* Harper & Row, Publishers, Incorporated, New York, 1965, p. 208.
[3] Robert A. Dahl, *Who Governs?* Yale University Press, New Haven, Conn., 1961, p. 204.

TABLE 8-2. Voting Power of Mayors in Cities over 5,000 Population, by Form of Government*

Form of Government	Percent of Mayors Who May Vote	
	On All Issues	In Case of Tie Only
Mayor-council	16.3	58.7
Commission	92.0	7.1
Council-manager	54.1	41.3
All cities over 5,000	31.7	50.7

*Statistics include only mayors directly elected by the people.
Source: *Municipal Year Book, 1968,* International City Management Association, Chicago, 1968, p. 56.

to do this is not always granted. It is traditional, however, to give the mayor control over the police department. Even when he has no other exclusive power of appointment, he is usually given the right to hire and dismiss the police chief or commissioner. Sometimes, however, the mayor is given the responsibility for enforcement of laws and ordinances but is deprived of any control over the law-enforcement agency. St. Louis and Kansas City have police heads appointed by the state. A few cities elect the police chief; in some he is chosen by the council; and in others, by a semi-independent police board.

Appointments. For effective control over administration and to coordinate its activities, the mayor must have the powers both of appointment and of removal. Weak-mayor cities are likely to have several elective administrative officers and others selected by the council. In a strong-mayor city, these officers are appointed by the mayor. In some cities, such as New York and Detroit, his powers extend to virtually all of the department heads in the administrative branch and he need not consult the council or anyone else in making appointments. He is in full charge of administration. He may appoint the heads of the major subdivisions within the departments, or this power may go to the department heads. In actual practice, it does not make much difference which method is used, for a serious conflict between mayor and department head over any matter would mean the resignation or dismissal of the recalcitrant department head.

In many cities, the mayor must have the approval of the council in making appointments. This is the more common pattern and is in keeping with the system of checks and balances upon which the mayor-council plan is based. It is in accord with American traditions, but it confuses responsibility for administration; the public cannot directly fix the blame, since several persons have a hand in each appointment. In addition, it provides a gratuitous system of patronage to council members. The mayor must, in practice, consult the council before making appointments, and as in the case of the President in relation to the United States Senate, many or perhaps most of the appointments become patronage items for council members. Councilmen are not elected in order to make appointments, of course, and placating their patronage demands is not likely to provide an effective system for procuring able administrators in city government. The mayor, clearly answerable for administration, will more probably select persons of ability. He is likely to combine patronage and competence considerations in making choices; councilmen will probably consider only patronage. There is no pressure upon them to do otherwise.

Removals. In the strong-mayor city, the chief executive can remove any member of his administration in whom he has lost confidence. In New York and Detroit, the mayor can remove almost all his appointees at pleasure, even those who are nominally appointed for a specific term of years.

Because of the frontiersman's distrust of government, however, it is more common to find restraints on the removal power. Unlike the President of the United States, who commonly must have the approval of the Senate in order to make appointments but may remove all except members of the independent regulatory establishments at pleasure, the mayor often must have councilmanic approval for both appointments and removals. This pattern is found, for example, in Los Angeles. It is subject to the same criticism as is approval for appointment. The mayor cannot control the acts of those nominally subordinate to him where this system exists.

It is also common to restrict the mayor's removal power by providing that he may make removals only "for cause." This means, usually, removal only after notice and hearing, and the action of the mayor is in such cases normally subject to review by the courts. The mayor's status is lowered if appointees may defy him or if he is forced into a court fight over a dismissal. If a mayor loses such a fight, morale problems are especially likely to be serious. In practice, however, the notice-and-hearing requirement may not seriously impair the removal power of the mayor, although it does discourage him from making hasty decisions.

In many cities, department heads are civil service employees. Despite this, the mayor usually has the right to choose his department heads and to remove them if he thinks they are not doing a good job. In the event of the removal of a department head who has civil service tenure, the employee is reduced in status and given other assignments but is not dismissed from the service.

Ceremonial Functions. In every city, beauty queens must be crowned, conventions greeted, presidents introduced, parks dedicated, cornerstones laid, baseball seasons opened, parades led, and charity drives launched. The mayor is expected to do all these things. In fact, it is partly because he must do them that the office of mayor is retained under the commission and council-manager forms. He is the symbol for the whole city.

Probably the typical mayor enjoys the attention that is his on these occasions. He is surely aware of the free publicity. In smaller cities, this duty of the mayor is not time-consuming, as it is in larger cities. In the very largest cities, the ceremonial function becomes a real burden, taking up valuable time that could be spent upon the pressing problems of administration or policy making. It is partly for this reason that a deputy mayor is appointed in New York.

Whatever the size of the municipality, Americans are always likely to "try to get the mayor to be there" whenever a committee plans some function, modest or mammoth. If the mayor is interested in his political future, he will try to be on hand.

Duties as a Lobbyist. Because cities are largely at the mercy of the state legislatures, city officials necessarily follow closely the course of proposed legislation affecting them. The cities are collectively protected in most states by the lobbying activities of the state league of municipalities, just as their interests on the national level are looked after by the American League of Cities and the United States Conference of Mayors. Large cities may have paid lobbyists at the state capital and in Washington.

At times, when legislation of particular importance to a certain city or group of cities is being considered, their mayors may be called to the state capital by the secretary of the league of municipalities so they may use the prestige of their offices in an attempt to protect the interests of their cities. Political skill is especially important at such times.

Judicial Powers. In early America, the mayor exercised minor *judicial* powers as well as having a seat in the *legislative* body and serving as chief *executive.* For example, a provision of the 1851 special act charter of Davenport, Iowa, provided that the mayor "shall by virtue of his office be a justice of the peace, and as such shall be a conservator of the peace."

Some cities still have a "mayor's court," and legally the mayor of New York is such a judge, but in practice the use of this power is disappearing. Also, because the mayor is in a position analogous to that of the governor and the President, he may have power to grant pardons for violations of city ordinances (but not of state or national law). The exercise of this power is today comparatively rare.

THE OFFICE OF MAYOR

Selection of the Mayor. The way in which the mayor is chosen varies a good deal according to the form of government. In all but a few mayor-council cities, he is elected directly by the voters. He is chosen in this fashion in about 78 percent of the commission-plan cities but in only one-half of the council-manager cities.[4] In such large municipalities as Kansas City, Dallas, and San Diego, however, he is elected directly.

The public is accustomed to electing the mayor and probably feels more comfortable with a charter that gives it that privilege. The popular election of the mayor tends to elevate him in public prestige and to provide him with high status, which he finds useful if he seeks to be a legislative leader.

A study comparing recruitment patterns for mayors of Nashville, New Haven, and Chicago concluded that, reflecting national trends, the mayor's office was increasingly held by those with a good deal of formal education and by professional politicians rather than amateurs. The office was, however, found relatively unattractive by local social and economic elites and regarded as less prestigeful than state or national office.[5]

The mayor may also be selected by the council. This is the method used in slightly less than half of the council-manager cities and in many commission cities. But it is used in only 3 percent of the mayor-council cities of over 5,000 population. These appear to be chiefly in places in which the government has evolved from the village or township structure.

In a few cities, the man who receives the highest number of votes for council becomes mayor. This is uncommon but can be found, for example, in Hartford and Kalamazoo, both manager cities, and in a very few commission cities. A few mayor-council cities also make the person with the highest number of votes for council the mayor. This is true, however, only where the structure has grown from the old village type of government, based upon English traditions and without a clear separation of powers.

[4] Data on the methods of selection of mayors are available in the current issue of the *Municipal Year Book*, International City Management Association, Chicago, 1968, p. 55.
[5] Mayer N. Zald and Thomas A. Anderson, "Secular Trends and Historical Contingencies in the Recruitment of Mayors," *Urban Affairs Quarterly*, 3:53–68, June 1968.

TABLE 8-3. Method of Selection of Mayors in Cities over 5,000 Population, by Form of Government

Form of Government	Percent Directly Elected	Percent Selected by Council	Highest Number Votes in Council Election
Mayor-council	97	3	0.1
Commission	78	21	1
Council-manager	50	49	1
All cities over 5,000	75	24	1

Source: *Municipal Year Book, 1968,* International City Management Association, Chicago, 1968, p. 55.

Salary. The pay of the mayor varies according to both the size of the city and the structure of its government. In general, the salary varies directly with the size of the city, as might be expected. Small cities are likely to pay only a token salary, something less than $1,000 a year. New York, at the opposite extreme, pays $45,000.

In a commission-plan city, the mayor usually receives the same pay as the other commissioners, or a few hundred dollars additional. There are some exceptions where he may receive quite an appreciable amount more. In manager cities, the same general rule applies.

It is not uncommon for the mayor to be paid less than some of his subordinates. The city engineer, the health officer, the attorney, and especially the superintendent of schools are likely to be paid more than he is, except in the very largest cities.

The average length of service of a mayor is approximately four years, and in running for and accepting the office he takes a grave risk of damaging his personal reputation. Clearly, persons with administrative and leadership ability can make more money, with a longer professional life, in private endeavor. Yet few arguments presented to the voters are greeted more coldly than those suggesting a higher salary for the mayor.

Term of Office. The Jacksonians insisted upon terms of not over two years, for they believed in keeping government "close to the people." The traditional term of office in New England was one year—from one town meeting until the next.

The term of office of the American mayor today depends to some extent upon the type of city-government structure in the particular city. The two-year term was still dominant in mayor-council cities in 1971, especially in those of the weak-mayor type and in cities under 5,000 population. Most council-manager cities had two-year terms,

TABLE 8-4. Term of Office of Mayor in Cities over 5,000 Population

Form of Government	Percent of Reporting Cities				
	One Year	Two Years	Three Years	Four Years	Five Years
Mayor-council	3	54	1	42	0
Commission	4	19	6	67	3
Council-manager*	21	53	2	24	0
All cities over 5,000	10	51	2	37	0

*The large number of one- and two-year terms for mayor in council-manager cities is partly a result of town-meeting communities adopting this form while retaining the New England traditional short term of office for elective officials. In other cases, the short terms stem from the practice of rotating the essentially honorary office among the councilmen.
Source: Municipal Year Book, 1966, International City Management Association, Chicago, 1966, p. 92.

too. Commission-governed cities, on the other hand, were likely to have four-year terms.

Terms of less than four years allow the mayor little time to establish a record or to devote to his job. With a two-year term, he begins his campaign for reelection almost as soon as the results of his first campaign are in. Some cities cling to the cynical rule prohibiting the mayor from succeeding himself. During the palmy days of the Republican machine in Philadelphia (until 1951), the charter of that city had such a rule. However, it did not appear to weaken the machine in the least.

Removals. The mayor who is incompetent, callous, or unrepresentative, of the wants of the dominant public may be removed by allowing his term to expire or by securing his defeat at the next election. There are times, however, when the public may wish to terminate the authority of a chief executive before his regular term expires. This is particularly true when he is thought to be guilty of what the lawyers call non-, mis-, or malfeasance in office. That is to say, if he fails to perform his duties, or does them in an unlawful manner, or does illegal things under the mantle of office. There are several remedies at law in such cases.

First of all, there is the *recall.* As has already been noted, it is unlikely, under this device, that the case will be decided on its merits.[6] But several other (and incidentally older) remedies are available.

In most cities, the mayor may be removed by action of the council —an ancient common-law power. Most charters require a vote of

[6] See above, pp. 165–167.

something more than a simple majority to effect a removal, however. It is also possible for the mayor to be removed by a court order for certain causes as prescribed by law. In Michigan, New York, North Dakota, and Ohio, the mayor may be removed by the governor. All three of these removal techniques are "for cause" only. The courts have regularly held this to mean that there must be a presentation of specific charges, due notice to the official whose removal is sought, and a hearing, usually public. It also means that the official may appeal to the courts if he feels that the procedural safeguards to which he is entitled have not been followed.

Vacancies. If a mayor dies, resigns, or is removed from office, the law or charter provides for his immediate replacement. It is quite important that there always be someone to serve as mayor. Since the mayor leaves the city from time to time for a vacation, a conference, or a convention, it is also necessary for someone to act in his temporary absence.

The succession may pass to the presiding officer of the council or to some administrative officer, most commonly the controller. In some cities, if the office is vacated, the council is allowed to choose the new mayor, not necessarily from its own membership. If the next election is some time off, say more than six months or a year, the law may provide for an acting mayor and a special election to choose a person to serve out the term.

Legal Qualifications. Virtually every city has charter provisions requiring the mayor to be a United States citizen, to be of a certain minimum age, and to have lived in the city for a certain minimum number of years. It might be required, for example, that the mayor must be at least thirty years old and have been a city resident for three years. These rules are probably largely in imitation of the requirements in the United States Constitution for the presidency. They are of little practical meaning—even the citizenship requirement—for no alien could be elected to a mayoralty position in any American city today.

THE CITY MANAGER

The city manager is a man of importance in most cities where his office exists. He is also a man of great power. But the power he possesses is, in most cases, used in a different manner and toward different ends than that of the old-fashioned machine leader.

Qualifications of the Manager. It is a basic part of the theory of council-manager government that the entire administration of the city be professionalized. Managers are supposed to be trained to use the tools of administration and, especially in smaller cities, to possess a technical skill, such as engineering, as well. The manager needs to be a diplomat, for his job is dependent upon his ability to get along with the council. He is supposed to be a politician of a special sort, too, for his job calls upon him to give advice on matters of public policy without becoming ensnared in the political process when these problems become campaign issues. Are managers actually able to do all these things? What sort of people are they?

In the mid-1960s, the typical manager was in his early forties, had a college degree in one of the social sciences, earned just over $11,000 a year, and served in a city of under 10,000 located within a metropolitan area.[7] In the years after World War II, the manager plan had become most popular in small, suburban communities, but only in a statistical sense. It had also been growing in popularity in middle-sized and large cities.

In the early days of the plan, managers were most often engineers, and in smaller cities this profession is still preferred, the manager also serving as the city engineer. The trend in medium- and larger-sized cities is away from hiring engineers and persons trained in business administration as managers. More and more universities are offering special training in public administration designed to prepare students for the city-manager profession. After graduation, these trainees advance through the administrative hierarchy of city governments until they become managers, many of them later moving on to larger cities with higher pay and greater prestige. This training provides the future manager with more of a background in the social and economic character of the city than was formerly the case.

Only 7 percent of the managers appointed in 1965 came from nongovernmental jobs; 60 percent had been employed in other manager cities—as the manager, as his administrative assistant, or as an intern. Managers are thus receiving better on-the-job training today. In 1939, only 23 percent of those hired came from administrative positions in other cities.

The profession of manager appears to carry enough salary and prestige to make it a sufficiently worthwhile occupation for many to spend a lifetime in it. In 1964, only 6.4 percent of the managers left the field, a number which included those who died and retired.[8] **Selection and Tenure of the Manager.** Perhaps the most important task faced by a council is the selection of the manager. How does the council go about doing this? Councilmen, encountering the problem relatively seldom, may not know how to approach it. They may know

[7] David S. Arnold, "A Profile of City Managers," *Public Management*, 46:56–60, March, 1964.
[8] See the *Municipal Year Book, 1966,* International City Management Association, 1966, p. 508.

that there are qualified persons about the country who might be interested in the position, but they may not know their names or how to go about finding them. The International City Management Association has published a helpful pamphlet for cities, *The Selection of a City Manager* (revised, 1965). On request, the Chicago headquarters of the Association often assists cities in securing qualified applicants and publishes notices of available openings. Similar assistance may also be secured from the state leagues of cities and departments of political science in nearby universities.

The council may consider one of the city's department heads for promotion to manager. Leading managers whose names and reputations are known to the councilmen will probably be asked to offer names of possible candidates. From such a list the council can then proceed to invite interested persons to apply. (Some unsolicited applications will be received.) The council may next reduce further the size of the list and then invite those still being considered to appear, if possible for personal interviews, before finally choosing the person to whom the job is to be offered. The process is thus similar to the selection of other *professional* staff members in government. The procedures described here are favored by the managers' professional organization, for they tend to discourage the selection of a nonprofessional.

The manager is normally selected by the council by majority vote and is dismissable by the council at any time by the same method. For the plan to work according to the model, it is essential that the council be allowed to remove the manager at any time and for any reason that the council majority thinks sufficient. Otherwise, the

TABLE 8-5.   Comparison of City-manager Appointments

Background of Appointees	Ten-year Period 1940–1949 Incl. Percent	For 1958 Percent	For 1965 Percent
Governmental:			
Manager promotions from other cities	18	33	33
Former managers accepting appointments	11	8	12
Administrative assistants and assistant managers	4	19	15
Other public administrative positions	40	26	31
Nongovernmental positions	15	12	7
Appointments from outside city	58	78	66

Source: Municipal Year Book, 1966, International City Management Association, Chicago, 1966, p. 521.

administration of the city becomes autonomous and irresponsible, uncontrolled by the machinery of democracy. Since ultimate responsibility for all that takes place in city government rests with the council, this body is assigned the job of overseeing the manager's activities.

In some cities, a practice has developed whereby each new council majority chooses its own manager, but this is not the general rule. The manager is supposed to be a professional administrator. If this is how he is perceived by councilmen, there is no reason why he should not be continued in his job despite transient council majorities. It is significant to note that the average tenure of a manager in a city today is about seven years and that it would be longer except for the shortage of managers, which has encouraged their promotion to higher-paying jobs.

In Florida, a study found that the tenure of managers was highest in cities where politics was low keyed, with little competition for office and few policy conflicts. In cities with high conflict levels, the manager often came to be identified with a particular faction, as a result of his position as a community leader. If the faction with which he had been identified lost, he might find himself out of a job. In such cities, councilmen also tended to protect themselves by seeking to have major policies identified with the manager rather than with themselves. The manager, therefore, was sometimes the victim of scapegoating if the policies proved unpopular.[9]

Tenure varies considerably from one community to another. In the Florida cities studied, average tenure was only slightly more than three years,[10] about one-half that in Illinois.[11] Most commonly, terminations are given to managers in their first two years on a job, to those with relatively less experience and education,[12] and to managers in cities with declining or slowly growing populations.[13]

A few charters permit the removal of the manager through the use of the recall. This is not in keeping with the model, because it allows the council to shirk its responsibility for the manager and because it almost of necessity embroils the manager in campaigning: He becomes something of an appointive mayor instead of a manager and must ride the political waves to prevent his own removal. Political, rather than professional, motivations become, of necessity, paramount to him.

---

[9] Gladys M. Kammerer and John M. DeGrove, *Florida City Managers: Profile and Tenure,* Public Administration Clearing Service, University of Florida, Gainesville, Fla., 1961, pp. 34–35.
[10] *Ibid.*
[11] Charles A. Willis and Thomas Page, "Tenure and Turnover in Illinois Managers," *Illinois Government,* 12:3, October, 1961.
[12] Edwin O. Stene, "Short-term Managers," *Public Management,* 43:146–152, July, 1961.
[13] Edwin O. Stene, *The City Manager: Professional Training and Tenure,* Governmental Research Center, University of Kansas, Lawrence, Kans., 1966, p. 34.

The Jacksonian influence dies slowly in American politics, and it is still to be found affecting the hand that writes the council-manager charter. The extraordinary majority, such as two-thirds or three-fourths of the council, sometimes appears in the rules governing the removal of the manager. Charters also may permit dismissal only "for cause." Such a rule has the effect of putting final discretion in the hands of the courts rather than the council. Some charters require advance notice of one or more months to the manager if he is to be removed. This creates lameduck managers and a stalemated government.

The model calls for the council to have full power over hiring and dismissing the manager. No argument for limiting the powers of the council can circumvent the fact that the manager plan can work effectively only if a majority of the councilmen have confidence in the manager.

Place of Residence. Most council-manager charters logically provide that the manager need not be a resident of the city at the time of his appointment, for the council is looking, not for a deserving local politician, but for a professionally competent administrator. At one time, it was quite common to hire a person from outside the city. Until 1929, about one-half of the managers hired were non-residents. With the coming of the Great Depression there was a reversal of this trend, and in 1933, only 17 percent of those appointed came from outside the city. This was probably the result of two considerations: (1) a desire of local politicians to keep scarce jobs "at home" and (2) the possibility of hiring local persons at a lower salary.

During and after World War II, high employment, combined with a rapid expansion in the number of manager cities, resulted in a definite shortage of qualified managers. Cities turned to other cities in order to get chief administrators. The number of appointments from outside the city accordingly rose to all-time highs. In 1965, two-thirds of new managers hired were from outside the city. These figures probably also reflect a growing emphasis upon securing trained and experienced persons, persons who may not be available locally. Furthermore, the percentage of nonresidents hired as the first manager of a city adopting this form has always been high, and the rate of new adoptions has been unusually high in recent years.

Salaries. Obviously, if managership is to become a real profession with persons willing to make a lifetime career of it, the pay opportunities must be sufficient to attract able persons. The data indicate that managership affords fairly good salaries.

TABLE 8-6. Salaries of City Managers, 1969

Cities of a Population Range	Mean	Lowest	Median	High
500,000 plus	33,349	27,482	32,500	40,764
250,000–500,000	33,210	25,000	33,282	41,195
100,000–250,000	26,954	20,000	25,769	36,888
50,000–100,000	23,466	13,200	23,000	36,780
25,000–50,000	19,912	10,000	19,635	34,000
10,000–25,000	16,159	7,150	15,900	35,000

Source: *Municipal Year Book, 1970,* International City Management Association, Chicago, 1970, pp. 187–210.

Some opposition to the manager plan has been generated because salaries are thought to be *too* high. Public opinion in this country is often not sophisticated on this matter and may sometimes oppose the payment of salaries necessary to attract the talent wanted. This tendency is one of the common causes of disillusionment in the manager plan. In the postwar period of high employment and inflation plus a shortage of trained managers, many of those hired were incompetent. A city may not expect to find a manager capable of doing a satisfactory job unless sufficient salary is offered.

The Duties of the Manager. While charters vary widely and none conform in all details to the provisions of the *Model City Charter* of the National Municipal League, a manager, in the model and often in practice, has all or most of the following responsibilities:

1.   Overseeing enforcement of all laws and ordinances
2.   Controlling all departments, with power to appoint, supervise, and remove department heads and bureau chiefs
3.   Making recommendations to the council on such matters as he thinks desirable
4.   Keeping the council advised of the financial condition of the city and concerning future needs and trends
5.   Preparing and submitting to the council the annual budget
6.   Preparing and submitting to the council reports and memoranda such as are requested
7.   Keeping the council, and indirectly the public, informed concerning the operations of all aspects of the city government
8.   Performing such other duties as the council may legally assign to him

In a sentence, the manager has full responsibility to the council for the conduct of the administration of the city.

The Manager and the Council. When a city adopts the manager plan, the function of the council undergoes a considerable change, even if the city has previously operated under the strong-mayor form. The study by Stone, Price, and Stone[14] found that the council was relieved of most of its tasks of hiring department heads and subordinate employees. In all but a few cities, the mayor and council were relieved of the duties of supervising the employees. Because of provisions of charters and state laws, however, councils were not relieved of the great mass of minor details that have historically been handled by that body. Even though the volume of work performed by the council could not be reduced, "the point of view and the approach of the council to municipal policy was different."[15] The difference resulted from reliance upon the manager for many things that could not be furnished in the same fashion by the mayor or a council committee.

Members of the council may disagree with the manager concerning the characteristics of the managerial role. In cities that have not long had the manager plan, this disagreement may be serious, with most of the council to one degree or another rejecting the manager's concept of his job.[16] In Colorado cities where the plan had been operating for a number of years, relatively few councilmen were found to dissent from the manager's definition of his role. But in another study, of all council-manager cities in the San Francisco Bay area, conflicting images of the manager's role seemed to be deep-seated and permanent in character.[17] (See Table 8–7.) Even so, the actual amount of strife generated over conflicts in role perception historically seems to have been very limited.

In most cities, the manager presents significant matters to the council for consideration. Since they are not initiated by councilmen, these men are normally free to consider such items on their merits, having no vested interest in them. New business coming before the council is normally first referred to the manager for a report at a future meeting. The manager, in making his report, is in a position to consider the effect of possible forms of action upon all departments of the city.

Most managers prefer to make their reports in writing. Of course, they are also quizzed orally by councilmen concerning various aspects and implications of the report at council meetings. Most man-

[14] Harold A. Stone, Don K. Price, and Katherine H. Stone, *City Manager Government in the United States,* Public Administration Service, Chicago, 1940, chap. 8.
[15] *Ibid.,* p. 174.
[16] John C. Buechner, *Differences in Role Perception in Colorado Council-Manager Cities,* Bureau of Governmental Research, University of Colorado, Boulder, Colo., 1965.
[17] Ronald O. Loveridge, *The City Manager in Legislative Politics,* Bobbs-Merrill Company, Indianapolis, 1971.

TABLE 8-7.   Conflicting Images of the Manager's Role

	Percentages			
	Agree	Tend to Agree	Tend to Disagree	Disagree
A city manager should assume leadership in shaping municipal policies				
Manager responses (n = 57)	39	49	7	5
Councilmen responses (n = 296)	16	26	19	39
A city manager should act as an administrator and leave policy matters to the council				
Manager responses (n = 58)	7	15	57	21
Councilmen responses (n = 298)	69	19	11	1

Source: Derived from Ronald O. Loveridge, *The City Manager in Legislative Politics,* Bobbs-Merrill Company, Indianapolis, 1971.

agers also make recommendations for action in connection with a report.[18] Some managers present only one recommended line of action, the one they consider the professionally sound solution. Other managers present two or more possible approaches, thus affording the council opportunity to choose. The council may not always choose as the manager would prefer, but the latter knows that the council may be the best judge of what is most acceptable under prevailing local conditions.

Although the manager plays a public role of "the expert" who is available only to answer questions and to administer, in practice, he or his subordinates are the principal sources of policy innovation in cities today. Ideas, if the manager or his staff do not think of them in the first place, are likely, in most cities, to come from interest groups, rather than from council members. Once an idea is placed upon the community agenda, the manager becomes a major leader in securing its adoption, although he is usually discreet concerning his own views until the council has given formal approval.

[18] See Clarence E. Ridley, *The Role of the City Manager in Policy Formulation,* International City Management Association, Chicago, 1958; Charles R. Adrian, "Leadership and Decision-making in Manager Cities: A Study of Three Communities," *Public Administration Review,* 18:208–213, Summer, 1958; B. James Kweder, *The Roles of Manager, Mayor and Councilmen in Policy Making: A Study of Twenty-one North Carolina Cities,* Institute of Government, The University of North Carolina, Chapel Hill, 1965.

The Manager and Elections. The manager performs many functions of community leadership similar to those performed by councilmen or the mayor. He is often active in service clubs, charitable organizations, churches, and the like.[19] He may make public speeches in which he seeks to explain a new policy which has been approved by the council (and which he may have originated). He may speak on the positive side of a proposed referendum on a bond issue (as frequently does the school superintendent who holds a parallel position with the school board), but he is prudent not to do so if the question involves partisan or factional issues.

One study of the council-manager form in Illinois has concluded:[20]

> While the initial choice of a manager to serve at the pleasure of the council may not be a political question, the question of his retention becomes political in the sense that each councilman is likely to be answerable to some organized segments of his constituency on his attitude toward the manager. Thus, much of what a city manager does has a continually measured political impact. His prominence in the city administration necessarily focuses some attention on him which is subtracted from the elective political body to which he is answerable.

Neither in the model nor in practice, however, does a manager engage in direct political activities. He does not appeal to the voters over the heads of the councilmen, or campaign against councilmen who have frequently opposed his policy recommendations, or support candidates or policies for personal or factional reasons. He can fulfill his almost inevitable role as a policy leader without himself becoming a political issue, by making sure that his recommendations are always "controlled by his expert knowledge and professional interest, never by selfish considerations or political friendships."[21]

The manager who does not observe this rule will eventually lose his job, and his reputation—and hence his employability elsewhere—will likely suffer. Sometimes a manager does offer assistance to one faction in a campaign, as the Cincinnati manager did in 1953, but under those circumstances he ceases to be a professional manager, becomes a politician, and will keep his post only so long as his faction has a majority on the council.

The Manager and Public Relations. Unlike the government of any other type of city, the city with a manager has a nonelective person serving in the position upon which chief public interest and attention

[19] Stone, Price, and Stone, *op. cit.*, pp. 243–244.
[20] Willis and Page, *op. cit.*, p. 3.
[21] Stone, Price, and Stone, *op. cit.*, p. 244.

TABLE 8-8.   Manner of Selection of Department Heads in Florida Council-manager Cities

Selection Method	Number of Cities	Percentage
All appointed by manager, with virtually automatic council approval	58	76.3
Some appointed by the manager with virtually automatic approval; council appoints the rest	14	18.4
Check with council on who it wants; if at all qualified, manager appoints their choice	2	2.6
Council majority faction dictates appointments	1	1.3
Not reported	1	1.3
Total	76	99.9

Source: Gladys M. Kammerer and John M. DeGrove, *Florida City Managers: Profile and Tenure,* Public Administration Clearing Service, University of Florida, Gainesville, Fla., 1961, table 17.

is focused. Whether he likes it or not, to the manager falls the greatest responsibility for "selling" the manager plan, for making citizens satisfied with their government, and, often, for popularizing policies which the council has decided to undertake. The manager and his assistants meet the public daily, and the nature of these contacts has a great deal to do with the popularity of the manager, of the councilmen by whose leave he holds his job, and of city government itself.

All managers are necessarily aware of the importance of public relations, but they are not all equally adept in handling them. The Stone, Price, and Stone study found that some managers "had the knack of speaking and acting in a way that won confidence and brought about harmonious relations; others, no matter how hard they tried, never seemed to say in the right way what they wanted to say or to do in the right way what they wanted to do. How the manager spoke, acted, and conducted himself was often more important than what he said or accomplished."[22]

Some managers, like other chief executives, have assumed that the services of the city speak for themselves and have paid little attention to municipal reports to the public, have disliked making speeches, and have sought to avoid newspaper publicity. Most of them have recognized, however, the importance of informing the

[22] *Ibid.,* p. 159.

TABLE 8-9.   Approaches to Policy Recommendations by Florida Managers

Method of Presentation	Number of Managers	Percentage
Present alternatives with supporting facts, manager's choice	52	68.4
Present only manager's choice with supporting facts to avoid confusing council	8	10.5
Combination of the above	6	7.9
Present major alternatives with facts, no specific manager recommendation	4	5.3
Present manager's solution with little or no supporting facts	1	1.3
Other	5	6.6
Total	76	100.0

Source: Gladys M. Kammerer and John M. DeGrove, *Florida City Managers: Profile and Tenure,* Public Administration Clearing Service, University of Florida, Gainesville, Fla., 1961, table 11.

public about the functions performed by city government and the manner in which they are performed.

The Manager as a Professional. The International City Management Association (ICMA) is the professional organization to which most managers belong. The Association seeks to encourage high standards. It has a code of ethics and a committee on professional conduct. There would probably be legal complications if a city attempted to require formally that the manager be a member of the ICMA, but such a rule seems unnecessary, since the council is always answerable to the voters for the manager and since it might be considered improper for a private organization to determine qualifications for a public position. State licenses are less necessary than in, say, law or medicine, since managers do not practice directly before a relatively helpless and uninformed public, but rather before a council with complete power over the professional life of the manager.

The Stone, Price, and Stone study found that:[23]

> Perhaps the strongest support for the position the city managers took in regarding themselves as professional men lay in their attitude and in their conduct. Many city managers thought

[23] *Ibid.,* pp. 67–68. By permission of the Public Administration Service. On managers as professionals, see also two articles by George K. Floro: "Continuity in City-manager Careers," *American Journal of Sociology,* 61:240–246, November, 1955; and "Types of City Managers," *Public Management,* 36:221–225, October, 1954.

of themselves as professional executives devoting themselves to a job which required technical skill and a high sense of moral obligation. Many felt that they were selected as managers because they possessed special qualifications for the position and that political and private connections played no part in their appointment. With a large majority of managers, the job was the thing. Because city managers generally lived up to the ideals which they had set for themselves through the International City Managers' Association, they were quite widely recognized as professional men.

LESSER EXECUTIVE OFFICERS

Most cities elect at least one administrative officer in addition to the mayor. Some elect as many as five others. For the most part, such officers are likely to be the clerk (or recorder), the city attorney (or corporation counsel), and various fiscal officers. In addition, certain department heads who are nearly always appointed are important persons in the policy-making process. Of these, the treasurer, controller, auditor, and assessor are discussed in Chapter 13. The police chief, still sometimes elected, is discussed in Chapter 14, the city engineer in Chapter 16, and the planner in Chapter 17. The duties of two other officers will be mentioned here.[24]

The clerk is, in form, only the records keeper of the city. He also usually serves as secretary to the council and keeps the formal minutes of its meetings. In practice, however, the clerk may become much more than an office manager. Indeed, he may become a virtual city manager in small communities. One reason for this is that he often serves a long time in the job. The public prefers to keep the position elective, but it also regards the clerk as being essentially noncontroversial in character. Thus, in municipalities of all sizes, the clerk is likely to be a person of modest ability who makes the job a career. Because he gradually comes to know more about the minutiae of government perhaps than any one else, he is relied upon for background details. From this responsibility, it is often a short step to giving advice when asked and then to initiating suggestions. Because the consequences of any action this advice may generate will be attributed to others—the councilmen, the mayor, or the manager— the clerk goes on his bland way toward retirement, calmly riding above the storms of controversy that confront his colleagues.

---

[24] Special districts also sometimes have elective officers, or they may have elective governing boards which appoint professional managers as chief administrators. For the example of the school superintendent in this role, see Thomas H. Eliot, "Toward an Understanding of Public School Politics," *American Political Science Review*, 53:1032–1951, December, 1959.

One study has indicated that, in cities of under 10,000 population, a clerk has a great deal to do with policy formulation—that he does do, in a great many cases, the things suggested here. The study also indicated that certain factors reduced the importance of the clerk in a policy-making role, however. A part-time clerk was generally less effective than one who was constantly on duty. Women clerks were not usually effective as policy leaders. And clerks in council-manager cities were more likely to be restricted to ministerial (routine) duties than was the case in other cities.[25]

Cities today are not likely to elect the city attorney. He remains, however, an important policy-making officer, as he was a few generations ago when the voters expected to be allowed to select him directly. In larger cities, in strong-mayor, and in council-manager cities, the attorney is usually selected by the chief administrative officer and reports directly to him. In such cases, the attorney is influential as a policy maker, but he is subject to general oversight and direction by his chief, and this gives him a fairly definite policy framework within which to work. In other cities, and particularly in small communities, the council may select the attorney and rely heavily on his advice since he has a near monopoly on the legal skills that are essential for effective municipal management.[26] The attorney and the clerk are the two most likely policy leaders in places of under, say, 10,000 people.

Regardless of size of community, the city attorney is important for other reasons: (1) Dillon's rule makes both councilmen and administrators dependent upon him for opinions as to what the city is legally authorized to do. Because he must be consulted constantly in this regard, he has great opportunities for becoming a general policy advisor. (2) To a considerable extent, he decides upon enforcement levels, though he may not be permitted to do so unilaterally, especially if he is not elected directly. The attorney has much to say about which laws are to be enforced and how sternly they are to be enforced. He does not have the great power of the elective state's attorney in this connection as a rule, but he may be able to make great changes in the original intent of city ordinances and state laws in the way in which he administers them.

The lesser executive officers of the city, whether elected or appointed, are important to citizens because, despite their low visibility

[25] Walter D. De Vries, "The Role of the Fourth Class Michigan City Clerk in Municipal Decision-making," Unpublished master's thesis, Michigan State University, East Lansing, Mich., 1955.
[26] For a case study of an upstate New York village, see A. J. Vidich and Joseph Bensman, *Small Town in Mass Society*, Princeton University Press, Princeton, N.J., 1958, pp. 127–129. For the clerk in the town surrounding the village, pp. 144–146.

level, they significantly affect policy making. Though the citizen may not know it, when the headlines proclaim "Mayor Zilch Announces New Bonding Program" or "Councilman Announces Tax-free Parking Scheme," the men given the credit are only acting out their roles in the play. The playwright probably will not even be mentioned in the news story. His is merely one of those "unimportant routine" offices of the city.

SELECTED
READINGS

Baida, Robert H.: "The City Attorney: What's Ahead?" *Public Management,* 53:4–8, August, 1971.

Blackwood, George: "Boston Politics and Boston Politicians," in Murray B. Levin, *The Alienated Voter: Politics in Boston,* Holt, Rinehart and Winston, Inc., New York, 1960. (Recent Boston mayors.)

Booth, David A. (comp.): *Council-Manager Government, 1940–1964: An Annotated Bibliography,* International City Management Association, Chicago, 1965.

Bromage, Arthur W.: *Urban Policy Making: The Council-Manager Partnership,* Public Administration Service, Chicago, 1970.

Hadden, Jeffrey K., Louis H. Masotti, and Victor Thiessen: "The Making of the Negro Mayors, 1967" *Trans-action,* January–February, 1967, pp. 21–30.

Hamburger, Philip: "The Mayor," *The New Yorker,* Jan. 26 and Feb. 2, 1957. (A profile of Robert F. Wagner, Jr. of New York.)

Hentoff, Nat: "The Mayor," *The New Yorker,* Oct. 7, 1967, and May 3, 1969. (Profiles of Mayor John Lindsay.)

Hoan, Daniel W.: *City Government: The Record of the Milwaukee Experiment,* Harcourt, Brace & World, Inc., New York, 1936. (The experiences of a famous mayor.)

Hollis, Melvin G.: *Reform in Detroit,* Oxford University Press, New York, 1969. (A history of the turn-of-the-century businessman-reformer, Mayor Hazen S. Pingree.)

International City Management Association: *A Suggested Code of Ethics,* International City Management Association, Chicago, 1962. (A code suggested for all municipal officials and employees.)

266 THE URBAN POLITICAL PROCESS

Johnson, Tom L.: *My Story,* B. W. Huebsch, Inc., New York, 1911. (Autobiography of a famous mayor of Cleveland.)

Kammerer, Gladys M., and others: *The Urban Political Community: Profiles in Town Politics,* Houghton Mifflin Company, Boston, 1963. (Case studies of council-manager politics in Florida.)

Kinnard, William N., Jr.: *Appointed by the Mayor,* rev. ed., The Bobbs-Merrill Company, Inc., Indianapolis, ICP no. 63, 1961. (The study of a "weak" mayor on appointments in a small Eastern city.)

Loveridge, Ronald O.: *City Managers in Legislative Politics,* The Bobbs-Merrill Company, Inc., Indianapolis, 1971. (Finds that managers perceive the councilmanic role differently from the way councilmen do—and vice versa.)

Lowi, Theodore J.: *At the Pleasure of the Mayor,* The Free Press of Glencoe, New York, 1964. (A study of the recruitment, performance, and powers of New York political and career bureaucrats.)

Maier, Henry W.: *Challenge to the Cities,* Random House, Inc., New York, 1966. (Argues that only the mayor can provide the leadership needed in the contemporary city. By a Milwaukee mayor.)

Mulrooney, Keith F. (ed.): "Symposium on the American City Manager," *Public Administration Review,* 31:6–46, January–February, 1971. (The strengths and weaknesses of the manager relative to contemporary urban social issues.)

"New York City: Is it Governable?" *Newsweek,* May 31, 1965. (An article cataloging some of the great numbers of fantastically difficult problems the mayor of New York must cope with as a policy leader.)

Reichley, James: *The Art of Government: Reform and Organization Politics in Philadelphia,* The Fund for the Republic, New York, 1959.

Ridley, Clarence E.: *The Role of the City Manager in Policy Formulation,* International City Management Association, Chicago, 1948.

Rowat, Donald C.: *The Ombudsman: Citizen's Defender,* University of Toronto Press, Toronto, 1965. (Description of existing and proposed complaint officers and arguments pro and con concerning the post.)

Ruchelman, Leonard (ed.): *Big City Mayors: The Crisis in Urban Politics,* Indiana University Press, Bloomington, 1970. (Collection of essays by political commentators, including mayors, on problems in such cities as New York, Chicago, Boston, Cleveland, and Los Angeles.)

Sherwood, Frank P.: *A City Manager Tries to Fire His Police Chief,* The Bobbs-Merrill Company, Inc., Indianapolis, ICP no. 76, 1963. (Conflict in a Southern California city. A conflict between managerial and police values.)

Stene, Edwin O.: *The City Manager: Professional Training and Tenure,* Governmental Research Center, University of Kansas, Lawrence, Kans., 1966.

Stillman, Richard J., II: *The Modern City Manager: A 1971 Profile,* International City Management Association, Washington, 1971.

Talbot, Allan R.: *The Mayor's Game, Richard Lee of New Haven and the Politics of Change,* Praeger, New York, 1967.

Wendt, Lloyd, and Herman Kogan: *Big Bill of Chicago,* The Bobbs-Merrill Company, Inc., Indianapolis, 1953. (The story of Mayor William H. Thompson.)

Whitlock, Brand: *Forty Years of It,* Appleton-Century-Crofts, Inc., New York, 1925. (By a reform mayor of Toledo, Ohio.)

CHAPTER 9 THE CITY COUNCIL

The historic functions of legislative bodies in Western civilization have been those of communication, debate, criticism, investigation, and modification. In recent centuries, the popular assemblies have also been accorded the task of declaring and thus legitimatizing the law—a function once performed by the courts.[1]

City councils, as local legislatures, have generally performed the historic role of assemblies. Under colonial frontier influence, however, American councils became somewhat more positive instruments of policy leadership. The weak-mayor–council arrangement of frontier days placed the council in center stage and Americans became accustomed to thinking of the councilmen as community leaders and as policy innovators. With the rise of the strong-mayor and council-manager plans, however, the council retreated to its traditional, essentially passive and symbolic functions—debate, criticism, investigation, and the formal declaration of the rules through resolutions and ordinances.

Reformers of several decades ago distrusted councilmen, or the role of the ward alderman, at any rate. Aldermen, by and large, were interested in the daily, short-range considerations of neighborhood constituents, in favors to beset individuals, and in jobs—but not in

[1] See Charles R. Adrian and Charles Press, *The American Political Process*, McGraw-Hill Book Company, New York, 2d ed., 1969, chap. 13.

overall policy development or in middle-class morality. Those who wrote the modern charters of cities, therefore, concentrated power in the chief executive—the mayor or manager—where they could expect policy leadership without the beclouding influences of errand running, of patronage considerations before program content, or of neighborhood concerns before community-wide interests. As a result, the council's role is now less that of leadership and innovation than it was a century ago.

The pattern of councilmanic functions varies with the forms of city government, however. The duties of councilmen vary from the situation in weak-mayor cities, where each alderman, in addition to sharing in policy-making duties, serves very often as a ward foreman supervising administrative functions, to the council-manager city, where he usually has only policy-making duties. The type of person who serves on the council also varies considerably from place to place, but the differences are based upon the size of the city as well as the forms of government.

LEADERSHIP AND CONFLICT

Varying Functions of the Council. In cities in which councilmen are elected by wards, the popular assembly of the community is most likely to perform the function it did during the nineteenth century. In one study of a city of about 50,000 population, the ward aldermen controlled patronage in their wards, carefully divided up the allocation of money for street repair, and were generally much more concerned with caring for the special wants of constituents than they were with overall policy development. In a city largely untouched by reform, the councilmen from all except the middle-class wards had not finished high school. They were neither very articulate nor capable of conducting public deliberations in an effective fashion. As a result, they sought protection from outside criticism through collective action. The majority faction (made up of aldermen from the working-class wards) spoke, to a considerable extent, as a single voice. There were no outstanding policy leaders on the council. The minority could not even exploit the weaknesses of the dominant faction.[2]

Three other cities with strong managers, on the other hand, had councils consisting of men with considerable education and business or professional experience. The members were elected at large and generally did not want to be bothered with errand running for con-

---

[2] Oliver P. Williams and Charles R. Adrian, *Four Cities*, University of Pennsylvania Press, Philadelphia, 1963, chap. 11. For aldermanic politics in Chicago, see Martin Meyerson and E. C. Banfield, *Politics, Planning and the Public Interest*, The Free Press of Glencoe, New York, 1957.

stituents—in one city it was customary practice to refuse to do so under all conditions. In these cities, members "did not emerge as either general policy innovators or as general policy leaders. The individual councilman, rather, was likely to assume leadership in connection with a specific issue or function of government. He developed pet interests or came to know one area of municipal activity especially well and concentrated upon that."[3]

A larger study—of eighty-eight council-manager cities—found that "while the number of policies initiated by councilmen in any one city is not large, they usually are on issues of considerable importance." Also it was found that:[4]

> Although the prestige of the council has not diminished in council-manager cities, the character of council action has changed as the city manager and others in the administrative organization make more of the recommendations for council consideration. The council naturally depends on the manager and his staff to study the problems and recommend solutions.

Of 206 proposals introduced in the city council of Los Angeles, a weak-mayor city, in a single month of 1959, only 10 percent were initiated by the mayor or councilmen; about 40 percent were developed by members of the city's bureaucratic experts; the remaining one-half came from individuals or various interest groups.[5] The mayor or members of the council often served as leaders in guiding proposals toward adoption. Bureaucrats were of great influence because of their near-monopoly of the technical competence needed to evaluate proposals in terms of their applicability to the local administrative process and to local existing conditions.

Conflict and Consensus. In general, the larger the city, the less likely there is to be consensus. Conflict becomes a part of daily public life in the large city, and public policies that are hammered out are likely to represent uneasy compromises, not supported by a stable majority of either citizens or councilmen. In these cities, conflict among the citizens is normally reflected by conflict on the council—and this in turn leads to factionalism on the governing board.

Of fifty-one Los Angeles County cities in one study, 36 percent (eighteen cities) reported the existence of factions on the council. In addition, many other cities had councils which divided occasionally

---

[3] Charles R. Adrian, "Leadership and Decision-making in Manager Cities: A Study of Three Communities," *Public Administration Review*, 18:211, Summer, 1958.
[4] Clarence E. Ridley, *The Role of the City Manager in Policy Formulation*, International City Management Association, Chicago, 1958, pp. 17, 52.
[5] Harry W. Reynolds, Jr., "The Career Public Service and Statute Lawmaking," *Western Political Quarterly*, 18:621–639, September, 1965.

over a basic issue of policy. The councils split most often over zoning matters, but it was policies concerning personnel and capital improvements that were most likely to create enduring splits.[6]

Factions may be organized, or they may be made up of the majority group, which was elected through endorsement of some recruiting organization, against the unorganized minority. They may exist primarily along liberal-conservative lines, as in the Minneapolis council for a long time, or they may divide according to neighborhood versus more general interests, or city boosters versus low-tax advocates, or on some other basis. The dominant faction may have a strong majority or, because city councils are usually small, a majority of one. In the latter case, of course, any tendency of majority-faction members to defect on certain issues is crucial, for such a defection reverses the majority and minority situations. In one study—of a Massachusetts city of 50,000—such defections were most likely to occur when a councilman was faced with supporting the particular demands—for improved water supply, sidewalks, or for street repairs—of his own constituents. The sanctions of his colleagues as a group were powerful, but not as powerful as the sounds coming from those who would, at the next election, support him—or turn him out.[7]

In contrast to the large and middle-sized cities are the small towns. In populous communities, those who disagree are expected to say so, even at the final vote on a measure, if necessary. But the picture is quite different in the village where a consensus of values reduces political disagreements to a discussion of jots and where society may expect councilmen to agree unanimously:[8]

> Within the formally constituted governing agency of the village, the village board, politics is conducted on the principle of unanimity of decision. In two years of observation of village board meetings in Springdale, all decisions brought to a vote were passed unanimously. The dissent, disagreement and factionalism which exist in the community are not expressed at board meetings. Through a process of consultation prior to an official meeting and by extended discussion involving the entire group during the meeting itself, a point is reached when it seems reasonable to assume that everyone will go along with the proposed action. Only then, as a final parry, will someone suggest that a motion be made to propose the action. After a short period of silence

[6] Robert J. Huckshorn and C. E. Young, "A Study of Voting Splits on City Councils in Los Angeles County," *Western Political Quarterly* 13:479–497, June, 1960.
[7] J. Leiper Freeman, "A Case Study of the Legislative Process in Municipal Government," in John C. Wahlke and Heinz Eulau, *Legislative Behavior*, The Free Press of Glencoe, New York, 1959, pp. 228–237.
[8] A. J. Vidich and Joseph Bensman, *Small Town in Mass Society*, Princeton University Press, Princeton, N.J., 1958, p. 110.

which provides a last opportunity for further discussion prior to the motion, the motion is made. Whereupon it is assumed that the motion is passed, or, if brought to a vote, as occasionally happens, it passes unanimously.

THE PEOPLE WHO SIT ON COUNCILS

Council Types. Councilmen have many impressions of their own role. Some of them are frankly concerned with representing a particular interest, perhaps blacks or realtors. Others want to create a "city beautiful." Still others regard themselves as caretakers, guardians of the taxpayers' pocketbooks. Most commonly—according to one study—councilmen hold one of two self-perceptions:[9]

> Some drew an analogy between the functions of the councilman and the member of the corporation board of directors. Others viewed themselves as a vehicle through which the wishes of the public could be translated into public action.
> The first view implies that the public interest is both ascertainable and indivisible. The good of the city, like the good of the corporation, must be stated in all-encompassing terms. This requires the councilman to view himself not as a delegate, but as a person possessing a mandate to use his own judgment in solving the problems presented to him. This judgment is shaped not only by his personal values, but by the exchange of views on the council. Thus the councilman is a participant in dialogue which "serves the interests of all the people."
> The second view asserts instead that the job of the legislator is to do what the people, both individually and collectively, want. The councilman is a public servant who should entertain the requests and grievances of citizens and attempt to accommodate their desires, if it is possible within the framework of the law. The public interest is articulated by the adjustment of individual claims expressed through the representatives. Each councilman is an advocate of what he believes to be his constituents' desires.

The City Hall Club. Because councils are generally small—the national average size is six members—the councilman is not merely the impersonal spokesman for his conscience or his constituency. He is also a member of a small group. The council is a club which tends to band together against the outsiders. It also has certain rules concerning what a member can say about another member without being ostracized. The intimate knowledge that members gain of one another's idiosyncrasies modifies their behavior.

As one study has noted:[10]

[9] Williams and Adrian, *op. cit.*, chap. 11.
[10] Freeman, *op. cit.*, p. 231.

> Once elected to the council, the legislator became part of an organization in which members had different roles to play and the different degrees of prestige, participation, and authority he enjoyed depended in considerable measure upon the committee posts assigned him. As in most other legislative bodies in the United States, the criterion of seniority was a traditional basis . . . for determining committee assignments.

The Members. In the vast majority of American cities, the typical council member is a local businessman, well respected in the community, active in civic organizations, and often a college graduate. He runs for the council because of the prestige and power the position affords.[11] He may consider the fact that the prominence of the position will help his business, but often he is merely acting out of sense of community responsibility. He is not likely to be among the top businessmen in his earnings and standing, but generally he is prosperous. He is usually above average in intelligence, but it is not necessary for the council to consist of a group of intellectual giants or the leading men of the community.

Most councilmen do not expect to move on to other political offices and do not consider themselves "politicians." The great majority of them are, by self-perception, strictly amateurs. Two-thirds of the councilmen in a Kansas study had never held any other position in government or in their political party. They were in overwhelming agreement that what they most disliked about the job was the public relations (campaigning) aspect.[12] In the San Francisco Bay area, 71 percent of the councilmen had no political ambitions beyond their present position, and 62 percent of them said they would give up their council seats rather than make great personal sacrifices if their regular jobs demanded that they do so.[13]

The councilmen of Los Angeles County in 1957 were, on the average, forty-nine years old; they ranged from twenty-five to seventy-six. Only 18 of 283 (6.7 percent) were women. In an area of rapid population movement, 39 percent had served two years or less. Communities with greater population stability probably have much less turnover.[14]

---

[11] For a discussion of why councilmen run in nonpartisan Toledo, see Jean L. Stinchcombe, *Reform and Reaction, City Politics in Toledo,* Wadsworth, Belmont, Calif., 1968, pp. 79–83.
[12] R. L. Stauber and Mary Kline, "A Profile of City Commissioners in Kansas," *Your Government,* Apr. 15, 1965. Similar findings were reported for a three-member Southern city, in Robert T. Daland, *Dixie City: A Portrait of Political Leadership,* Bureau of Public Administration, University of Alabama, University, Ala., 1956; and in John C. Buechner, *Differences in Role Perceptions in Colorado Council-Manager Cities,* Bureau of Governmental Research, University of Colorado, Boulder, Colo., 1965, pp. 23–29.
[13] Kenneth Prewitt, "Career Patterns of Local Elected Officials," a paper read at the annual meeting of the American Political Science Association, Chicago, September, 1964. See also Kenneth Prewitt and William Nowlin, "Political Ambitions and the Behavior of Incumbent Politicians," *Western Political Quarterly,* 22:298–308, June, 1969.
[14] Huckshorn and Young, *op. cit.*

Outside of the very largest cities, the pay for councilmanic positions is very nominal, and the job is thought of as being a community service. An exception to this is to be found in commission-governed cities, where the council (commission) is supposed to be made up, not simply of representative citizens of the community, but specifically of persons with executive or engineering experience. Relatively low salaries, however, have tended to attract ordinary office seekers instead. Topeka, for example, once had a commission made up of a barber, a house mover, and a cub reporter—hardly logical occupations for training in public administration.

In general, the smaller the city, the more likely it will be that council members are from among the top elite of the community. As cities increase in size, the social status of councilmen, in general, tends to decrease. In the largest cities, the councilmen may well devote full time to work at the city hall and may have run for the office partly because of the salary involved. Although venal and corrupt councilmen were once commonly found in these large cities, they are now a rarity. The greatest sin of the councilmen of the metropolis today is likely to be their allegiance to particular interest groups—a real estate board, a labor union, a group of builders, liquor dealers, downtown merchants. They are likely to view their function as that of protecting these particular groups, although they invariably claim to act "for all the people."[15]

The difference between the council in a middle-sized and a large city can be demonstrated by contrasting Davenport with Detroit.

Davenport, Iowa (1970 population: 98,469), might be called a not untypical middle-sized Middle Western city. It has a mayor-council form of government tending toward the weak category. Councilmen receive a $900 annual salary. In 1953, fifteen candidates ran for the eight positions on the council. Among these were four insurance salesmen and three real estate dealers or agents. There was one retired minister and one career woman. The remaining candidates were small businessmen or white-collar workers, including a barber, a bookkeeper, a filling-station operator, a baker, a retired grocer, and a tax consultant. It is likely that in a middle-sized city with the council-manager plan and at-large elections, the candidates would have been drawn more from professional and executive categories.

[15] The old-time ward alderman was a little mayor in his own bailiwick and was sometimes, for example in Chicago, quite independent of the party organization. For brief sketches of colorful Chicago aldermen such as "Bathhouse" John Coughlin, "Hinky Dink Mike" Kenna, and "Foxy Ed" Cullerton, see Charles E. Merriam, *Chicago: A More Intimate View of Urban Politics*, The Macmillan Company, New York, 1929, pp. 223–225. Lloyd Wendt and Herman Kogan, *Lords of the Levee*, The Bobbs-Merrill Company, Inc., Indianapolis, 1943, is the biography of Coughlin and Kenna, who ran the "levee"—Chicago's First Ward. A more recent ward alderman, Mathias J. ("Paddy") Bauler, is portrayed in A. J. Liebling, *Chicago: The Second City*, Alfred A. Knopf, Inc., New York, 1952, pp. 116–125.

Detroit (1970 population: 1,492,914) has a strong-mayor–council form of government. The council is elected at large and members receive a salary of $17,500 a year. In 1954, the council consisted of four persons who could best be called professional politicians, three lawyers, an automobile saleswoman, and a retired baseball player. Because a council position is ostensibly a full-time job and because long tenure is typical, it is not easy to distinguish clearly between professional and amateur politicians in its membership.

Minority Groups. In small cities, minority-group representation is not likely to be a major problem. In larger cities, the number of minority-group representatives on the city council tends to vary according to whether or not the council is elected at large. Where the council is fairly large and elected by wards, the ethnic groups that include political-activity patterns as part of their sub-culture tend to dominate; but in the case of a small council elected at large, the groups that are usually perceived of as "minorities" tend to be excluded.

Other factors are involved, too. Where political parties play a prominent part in local elections, minority-group representation is likely to be greater, since parties have historically sought the support of these groups in large cities. In cities with nonpartisan elections and a political process dominated by the business community, minority groups are usually quite badly underrepresented on city councils. The only exception to this seems to be in the case of the Irish, an ethnic group that has made political participation part of its way of life. Other minority groups appear to be too poorly organized or too little interested in local politics to be effective, or at least proportionately effective, in the larger cities.

No Negro or Jew was elected to the Los Angeles council between the time of the adoption of the present charter (1925) and 1953. Only one person of Italian descent had served, and Protestants had dominated the council in a city in which a majority of the inhabitants were, and still are, Catholic. The same pattern existed in Detroit between 1919 and 1953. In the latter city, the large Polish ethnic group has also been greatly underrepresented, though in the 1960s several blacks were elected.

Negroes, lacking a cultural tradition of political participation and hence often poorly organized politically, have not yet learned to use their ever increasing political strength effectively in most cities. Oscar Stanton DePriest (1871–1951) was the first black to serve on the Chicago city council, beginning in 1915. Because that city elects its councilmen by wards, the "Black Belt" is assured of some representation.[16] Negroes are always represented on the New York coun-

---

[16] On Negro councilmen in Chicago, see Martin Meyerson and Edward C. Banfield, *Politics, Planning and the Public Interest,* The Free Press of Glencoe, New York, 1957.

TABLE 9-1. Black Representation on City Councils, Selected Non-southern Cities, March, 1965

City	Total Council Seats	No. at Large	Seats Held by Negroes	Percent Seats Held by Negroes	Negroes as Percent of Population (1960)
Detroit	9	9	0	0.0	28.9
Cleveland	33	0	10	30.0	28.6
St. Louis	29	1	6	20.7	28.6
Philadelphia	17	7	2	11.8	26.4
Chicago	50	0	7	14.0	22.9
Cincinnati	9	9	1	11.1	21.6
New York	35	10	2	5.7	14.0
Los Angeles	15	0	3	20.0	13.5
Boston	9	9	0	0.0	9.1

Source: Adapted from James Q. Wilson, "The Negro in American Politics," in John P. Davis (ed.), The American Negro Reference Book, Prentice-Hall, Inc., Englewood Cliffs, N.J., 1966; from data in Edward C. Banfield and James Q. Wilson, City Politics, Harvard University Press, Cambridge, Mass. Copyright 1963 by the President and Fellows of Harvard College and the Massachusetts Institute of Technology.

cil today. As the Negro migration from the Southern sharecropper farm to the Northern city continues, more and more Negro representation has been appearing on councils.

In the South, the increasing enfranchisement of the Negro since about 1944 has taken place largely in the cities, with the result that the political influence of Negroes is beginning to be felt there, too. Blacks have long been influential in San Antonio politics in the Southwest. In 1947, a Negro alderman was elected in one ward of Winston-Salem, defeating a white opponent. The nine-member at-large council that was elected in Richmond in 1948, after that city first adopted the manager plan, included a Negro as one of its members.[17] Negroes are today commonly elected to large-city councils even in the South.[18] However, when elections are held at large or mostly at large, blacks are seriously underrepresented. Under a ward system, they have representation closely proportionate to population. (See Table 9-1.)
Women on the Council. Although in a definite minority, it is quite common to find women serving on school boards throughout the nation. They also often serve on park boards, library boards, and other special-purpose bodies. Their numbers on councils have been smaller, however, although some cities have a tradition of always having at least one woman on the city council. Peoria and Los An-

[17] Maurice R. Davie, Negroes in American Society, McGraw-Hill Book Company, New York, 1949, pp. 274–282.
[18] Edward C. Banfield, Big City Politics, Random House, Inc., New York, 1965.

geles did not elect a woman to the council until 1953. In Milwaukee, the first woman was elected in 1956. Portland, Oregon, elected a woman mayor-commissioner in 1948, but this is rare in so large a city. The occasional "skirt slates" that appear in small-city clean-up campaigns are reported in the newspapers throughout the land for the very reason that they are so unusual. Although the pattern is changing, American men and women both still tend to think of politics as being male territory.

College Students on the Council. With the adoption of the constitutional amendment lowering the voting age to eighteen, students began to be active in the local politics of college communities. In East Lansing, Michigan, no student survived the 1971 primary election, partly because of lack of organization so soon after the amendment went into effect and partly because it was held in August. In Madison, Wisconsin, students have served on the city council for a number of years, while in Berkeley, California, some students, in coalition with nonstudent radicals and "street people," came within one seat of controlling the council in 1971. The outlook is for increased student participation with some state leaders countering with residency requirements which would encourage students to vote in their parents' communities. Such laws may not survive a court challenge. If students take a majority of seats on a council, they will come under close scrutiny by legislators, who hold complete control over the powers of municipalities.

Qualifications. As in the case of the mayor, the city charter commonly provides for certain minimum qualifications in age, residence, and citizenship. Other requirements may include required residence in the ward from which elected or disqualification of persons holding contracts with the city.

Most observers believe that the quality of councilmen has improved in the last fifty years. There are no measurements for this, of course, and the degree to which it may be attributed to an improvement in the forms of government, to a decrease in the size of the council, to a change from ward to at-large elections and from partisan to nonpartisan elections, or to other causes is not known.

THE STRUCTURE OF THE COUNCIL

Salary. In the British tradition, councilmanic salaries are deliberately fixed at a low rate in most small and medium-sized cities to discourage candidates who are interested in the salary and to make the job one in which the prestige and honor of it are the decisive elements.

For this reason, membership on school and park boards and some others, including city councils, carries no salary at all in many communities.

In cities of more than about 50,000, the task of being a councilman requires a good deal of time, even under the manager plan, and those who serve are required to make a considerable sacrifice. High salaries for councilmen in these cities often attract candidates who would make a profession of officeholding. Median salaries in 1968 for cities over 500,000 were $8,250 for mayor-council and $3,900 in council-manager cities.

Salaries tend to be highest in commission-plan cities, for here the councilmen are also being paid as administrative heads of departments. Council-manager cities tend to have the lowest salaries, since under this form the council is a part-time body even in large cities and is restricted to legislative functions alone. In 1965, for example, the councilmen in Austin (a city of almost 250,000 people) and Hartford received no pay at all; in Paterson, New Jersey, they were paid $750 a year. There are some exceptions in manager cities: Niagara Falls, New York, for example, paid $3,000 a year, and Medford, Massachusetts, $4,000, which is more than was paid in Denver, a city of over 500,000, and a mayor-council city.[19]

Term of Office. Councilmanic terms range from one year to six years. One-year terms are found in cities with the town-meeting form. The six-year term is found mostly in a few commission cities, but a very few manager cities also use it.

In recent years, the four-year term has become the most common in American cities. In general, the larger the city, the more likely it is to have a four-year term. In about 35 percent of the cities, the terms of all councilmen expire at the same time. The larger the city, the more likely this is to be true. Overlapping, or staggered, terms are most likely to be found in council-manager cities, where the emphasis has traditionally been upon imitating the business corporation and in playing down the "errand boy" aspects of city government. Some argue that staggered terms provide desirable continuity in a council, but this is achieved in any case by the American practice of giving long tenure in office to councilmen.

In 20 percent of the cities of over 25,000 population, councilmanic elections are held simultaneously with school or other local elections; in 14 percent, with state or national elections; and in 66 percent, independently. Seventy-one percent of the nonpartisan, but

[19] Councilmanic salaries are reported in the current issue of the *Municipal Year Book*, International City Management Association, Chicago. Population estimates are for 1965, published in the 1966 edition.

TABLE 9-2. Terms of Office, Members of Council, in Municipalities of over 5,000 (in percent)

Type of City Government	Two Years	Four Years	Overlapping Terms
Mayor-council	46	44	55
Commission	16	64	40
Council-manager	33	57	82
Town meeting	33	7	
Representative town meeting	33	0	

Source: Municipal Year Book, International City Management Association, Chicago, 1966, p. 96 and 1968, p. 62.

only fifty-one percent of the partisan, cities hold independent elections.[20]

Size of Council. Councils range in size from two members in several cities to Chicago's fifty. In the case of the former, the mayor practically becomes a councilman, for he must break any tie. In an earlier day, councils sometimes ranged in size to above 200 members. Something of a dilemma is encountered in trying to determine the most effective size for a council. A large council is cumbersome and tends to obscure the legislative process by working through committees. A small council is sometimes said to lack representativeness and raises some questions concerning the function of criticism. A small council becomes involved in personal relationships that make it difficult for members to criticize other members freely. Some reformers have held, however, that the small council has not been proved bad, while the large one has. In any case, the trend in recent years has been toward smaller councils.

Very roughly speaking, the size of the council increases as the size of the city increases. A more important variable, however, is to be found in the type of structural form. In commission cities, the size of the commission tends to remain the same regardless of the size of the city. The commission is made up of five members in a preponderant number of cases. Council-manager cities tend to increase from five to nine members as the size of the city increases, but there are many exceptions to this. In the case of mayor-council cities, it is not possible to find very much of a relationship between size of city and size of council.

Unicameralism. At the turn of the century, about one-third of the cities of over 25,000 population had bicameral (two-house) councils. The figure had once been higher, but never included one-half of the

[20] Eugene C. Lee, "City Elections: A Statistical Profile," *Municipal Year Book, 1963*, International City Managers' Association, Chicago, 1963, pp. 74–84.

TABLE 9-3.   Size of Council

Population of City	Mayor-council Range*	Mayor-council Median	Commission Range*	Commission Median	Council-manager Range*	Council-manager Median
Over 500,000	7–50	13				
250,000–500,000	4–41	9			5–9	8
100,000–250,000	5–40	9	3–13	5	5–12	7
All over 5,000	3–50	7	2–13	5	2–42	5

*"Range" refers to the largest and smallest number of council members within each class.
Source: *Municipal Year Book, 1966,* International City Management Association, Chicago, 1966, p. 94.

cities. From the days of the reform movement of that period until the present, the number of these imitations of Congress and the state legislatures has diminished. No logical basis can be found for a two-house municipal council, and only one community still is known to use it (Everett, Massachusetts).

The city of New York has a council elected by wards and a board of estimate with an ex officio membership. The board consists of the mayor, the controller, the president of the council, and the president of each of the five boroughs. However, a system of weighting the votes of each of these elective officers gives control to the first three. The board had the power to make up the New York budget before 1933. Since that time, the board has the budgets of the city submitted to it first. It holds hearings and may alter the budgets in any way it sees fit. After it has passed them, they are sent to the council, which has powers only to reduce or delete. The council "has no important power in adopting local laws which the Board does not share on equal terms; the Board is, in effect, the upper chamber in a bicameral city legislature."[21]

Election by Wards. There is a strong tendency today to elect members of the council at large, except in cities of over 500,000.[22] Well over one-half of the cities of more than 5,000 population now elect at large, and a much greater percentage of the smaller cities do so. Again, the pattern that prevails depends to a large extent upon the structural form. Nearly all commission cities, for example, elect their members at large, since each member of the commission is a department head and almost necessarily is chosen by all the voters. The towns of New England almost always elect at large, since most of

[21] Wallace S. Sayre and Herbert Kaufman, *Governing New York City,* Russell Sage Foundation, New York, 1960, p. 627.
[22] See, however, George E. Berkley, "Flaws in At-Large Voting," *National Civic Review,* 55:370–373, May, 1966.

these places are quite small and all of them grew out of a rural tradition. The manager plan strongly leans toward election at large. Weak-mayor cities tend to use a ward system, which they have inherited from the nineteenth century. A few cities nominate by wards and elect at large in an attempt to secure better geographical distribution without complete parochialism on the council.

Cities that elect by wards face apportionment problems. Once the United States Supreme Court had decided, in the *Reynolds* case, that state legislatures must be apportioned as strictly as possible according to population and that when legislatures determine the boundaries of Congressional districts, they must make certain that these districts are, "as nearly as practical," equal in size, it was generally believed that the Court would also soon require local governing bodies, including city councils, to follow the same general rule and this did prove to be the case. A number of cities promptly proceeded to amend their charters to comply with the Supreme Court position; others were brought into state and Federal courts in cases urging that city charters and state statutes not providing for substantially equal representation be declared unconstitutional. But most of the municipalities in the United States are not directly affected by this problem, for they elect their councilmen at large.

The great size of cities such as New York and Chicago seems to suggest the use of ward representation. It is argued that election by wards provides a short ballot and gives representation on the council to the various ethnic, racial, and economic areas of the city. On the other hand, aldermen selected from small wards tend to become local errand boys. They are unable safely to consider the needs of

TABLE 9-4. Method of Electing Members of Council in All Municipalities of over 5,000 (in percent)

Type of City Government	Elected at Large	Elected by Wards	Elected by Combination*
Mayor-council	44	32	21
Commission	85	12	80
Council-manager	70	20	8
Town meeting	88	6	2
Representative town meeting	78	17	4
All over 500,000	35	20	23
All over 5,000	59	25	14

*"Elected by combination" refers to the election of some councilmen by wards and others at large within the same city.
Source: *Municipal Year Book, 1968,* International City Management Association, Chicago, 1968, p. 59.

the whole city lest they be told by their constituents that they were sent to the city hall to protect the interests of their own ward. Attempts at "statesmanship" only produce candidates who say, "If Torkelson can't look after this ward and its interests, I can." Furthermore, city populations are constantly shifting—in general toward the periphery. This means that a ward system, especially one written into the charter, eventually becomes gerrymandered. The slums and the periphery become underrepresented, at least temporarily, to the profit of the intermediate areas.

Minority groups sometimes make strong arguments for ward election on the ground that this is the only way for them to get a voice on the council. Black groups have felt especially strongly about this though as their populations approach 50 percent of the city, they see more advantages in at-large elections. In the past, in many cities, it has not been difficult for white politicians to gerrymander ward boundaries to keep Negroes off the council. Los Angeles and Detroit each have large Negro populations. Detroit elects all at large. Until the mid-1950s, neither city elected a Negro to the council.

Election at large lengthens the ballot, forces the establishment of a council so small that it may not be representative in a large city, and gives the election to the candidates who can find financial backers able to pay the expense of a city-wide campaign. Because large and medium-sized cities encounter a dilemma in seeking to choose between ward and at-large elections, compromises are common. Houston elects three members at large and five by wards. Buffalo chooses nine councilmen by wards for two-year terms and six at large for four-year staggered terms. Nearly one-fourth of the mayor-council cities use some sort of combination of the two devices.

Type of Ballot. Almost two-thirds of the city councils in the United States in places of over 5,000 population are elected on a ballot without party designation. The nonpartisan ballot is found most commonly in manager cities, since both nonpartisanship and the manager plan grew out of the reform movement. Because the representative town meeting is a recent development in New England, it, too, is usually nonpartisan. The commission plan, also a product of the early reform-movement years, is predominantly nonpartisan, but to a lesser extent. Its popularity declined before it received the full impact of the nonpartisan movement.

This leaves only the mayor-council city and the traditional New England town as the centers of partisan municipal activity, but even here only one-half or less have partisan ballots. City and town governments that have not been reconstructed tend to retain the partisan ballot, and some cities are required by state law to use it.

Large cities might be said to tend to use the partisan ballot for

TABLE 9-5.   Type of Ballot, Members of Council, in All
Municipalities of over 5,000 (in percent)

Type of City Government	Partisan	Nonpartisan
Mayor-council	51	49
Commission	31	69
Council-manager	18	82
Town meeting	44	56
Representative town meeting	39	61
All over 5,000	35	65

Source: Municipal Year Book, 1968, International City Management Association, Chicago, 1968, p. 58.

the council, but such a statement would have to be made with caution. Two cities of over 1 million people, Los Angeles and Detroit,
use nonpartisan ballots. Chicago has nonpartisan elections, but this
is true only in a formal sense. All offices other than those of the
aldermen are on a partisan ballot. All the aldermen are elected in
single-member wards. This makes it so easy for the parties to give
direct support to an aldermanic candidate and to have this support
made known to the voters that Chicago does not fit into the pattern
of most cities with a nonpartisan ballot.[23]

ORGANIZATION AND PROCEDURE

The Presiding Officer. The mayor may preside over the council, or
a member of the council may serve as its presiding officer. In the
latter case, he may be selected either by direct popular vote, by the
council members from among their own membership, or by making
the person who receives the highest number of votes for council the
president. When the president is elected separately for that specific office, as is the case in several cities, including the city of New
York, he is sometimes not formally a member of the council and often
cannot vote except in case of a tie. The function of the presiding
officer is in keeping with the usual powers and duties assigned to
this officer in American legislative bodies. The council may also
select other officers, including a secretary or clerk, although the
city clerk usually serves in this capacity.
Committees. Because city governments tend to imitate those of the
state and nation, the use of committees for the preliminary work on
ordinances was customary in the nineteenth century. Even today
almost all city councils make some use of committees. Reformers

[23] The effect of nonpartisanship upon the political process is discussed in chap. 5.

have generally frowned on this device, since it obscures the nature of the work of the council, confuses responsibility to the public, and allows a majority of a committee (a minority of the council) frequently to determine policy by minority rule. Standing committees also tend to take over administrative functions and for this reason are opposed by advocates of the reform-movement principles.

Standing committees are generally used in mayor-council governments, particularly of the weak-mayor type, but they are less common in council-manager governments. In manager cities, the council as a whole looks to the manager to do the preliminary work on ordinances, making committees less necessary. Because such committees tend to become involved with routine administration, they are especially disapproved of by experts on the manager form. Special committees are frequently utilized, however.

In those cities making extensive use of committees, the system works largely in the same manner as does the committee system of Congress or the state legislatures: The council as a whole becomes chiefly a ratifying body for the actions of the committees. Even if the council has authority to override a committee recommendation or relieve the committee of further consideration of a bill, these things are not likely to happen, since each councilman—like each Congressman—will tacitly agree to allow other councilmen to be supreme in their committee areas if they will extend the same privilege to him.[24]

Some cities with small councils make frequent use of the committee of the whole, which is not a committee at all but simply a convenient method for considering legislation in an informal atmosphere. Other cities hold an informal executive "conference session" before each meeting. If the city has a manager, he will probably attend. These sessions may be used to decide in advance the manner in which each item on the agenda will be disposed of. The formal session then becomes a hollow ritual, having given way to an informal, extralegal committee. This device is criticized as creating a "hidden government." Secret council sessions are an issue in many cities from time to time, and Akron banned secret meetings of all city boards and commissions in 1954, indicating that the problem is not confined to the council alone.

Meetings. The frequency of council meetings depends upon the size of the city, local custom, and the complexity of current issues in the community. In cities with part-time lay councils, meetings are

[24] A description of a large, machine-controlled council working through committees is given in Merriam, *op. cit.* See also Arthur W. Bromage, *Councilmen at Work*, George Wahr Publishing Co., Ann Arbor, 1954.

likely to be at night. In small towns the meetings may be only once a month. In the largest cities the councilmen will probably meet almost daily in committee or committee-of-the-whole sessions, with one formal meeting each week, perhaps at night, in order to allow interested citizens to attend.

POWERS OF THE COUNCIL

The functions, and hence powers, of the council are basically the same in mayor-council and council-manager cities. In places operating under the commission plan, the council is also the multiple-executive administrative body. For purposes of this section, this special function of the commission will be ignored.

Determination of Public Policy. The most important task of the council, of course, is to pass ordinances and resolutions formally establishing public policy for the community. The council passes on public improvements and exercises such portions of the state police power to regulate and control the health, safety, and morals of the community as it is authorized to do. City plans are passed upon by the council, as well as modifications of the land-use control ordinances. The council makes policy for the municipally owned utilities and exercises control over those that are privately owned to the extent allowed by state law. A study of ninety cities in the San Francisco Bay region emphasizes the importance of the councilmen's own perceptions, orientations, and images of the future when faced with similar problems.[25]

Taxation and Appropriation. While the current trend is toward executive preparation of the budget, the council must still vote the funds. Changes in the city tax structure are also made by the council, subject to the rules of the charter. The council also buys and sells city property. In most cities, the council has the power to pass upon all contracts, or at least upon the large ones. This is really an administrative function, but the power traditionally belongs to the council. Its action of approval or disapproval is a symbolic act on behalf of the citizenry.

Supervision of Administration. In a manager city, the administration is directly answerable to the council through the manager. In other forms of government, the council has an obligation to check upon the activities of the administration. It does this by receiving auditor's reports, by appointing investigating committees, by requiring testimony or reports from department heads and others, and by reviewing

[25] Heinz Eulau and Robert Eyestone, "Policy Maps of City Councils and Policy Outcomes: A Developmental Analysis," *American Political Science Review*, 57:124–143, March, 1968.

the activities of the various departments at budget hearings. Depending on the provisions of the charter, the council may be able to shuffle functions and bureaus to suit itself and to establish many rules of procedure of the departments.

In weak-mayor cities of the past and present, and especially where aldermen represent wards, the council has carried its oversight of administration to great extremes. Each committee of the council may engage in constant and detailed oversight of the department heads, creating problems of morale and confusion as to who is boss. Each alderman may tend to supervise functions operating within his own ward, concerning himself with details essentially administrative in character.[26]

Other Powers. The council in many cities serves as the city board of equalization or review, hearing appeals from taxpayers on their property assessments. The council often has the power to pass on the appointments of the mayor, and in many cities it makes a goodly number of appointments of its own. In addition, it has the power to remove the mayor and other officials under certain conditions. Many other minor functions are assigned to the council. Their nature varies considerably from one city to another.

PRACTICAL PROBLEMS FACING THE COUNCILMAN

Certain problems confront the councilman in any city of any size: metropolis, suburb, county seat, or small town. M. Nelson McGeary, a political scientist, while serving as president of the State College, Pennsylvania, Borough Council, made most of the observations summarized in the following section.

Difficulties in Determining Public Opinion. The councilman always has difficulty in determining the prevailing views of the public. This is the case in cities of all sizes, not just in the large ones. McGeary, for example, found that it was very true in his modest-sized borough of about 9,500. A few people are always vociferous. The great majority are silent most of the time. Because this is so, a councilman quickly learns (or should quickly learn) that he cannot determine public opinion simply by counting the pros and cons expressed by office visitors or in letters to him or to the editor. (Letters to the editor in the local newspaper may have been written by the editor himself.) The councilman also soon learns that he will hear from his constituents more quickly if they disapprove of one of his acts than if they approve.

[26] Arthur W. Bromage, "Mayors, Councilmen, and Citizens," *Governmental Affairs Bulletin,* Bureau of Governmental Research, University of Colorado, Boulder, Colo., June, 1966.

McGeary found that even when a person expresses himself, he may not state his true opinion. He writes of one case in which a man wrote a lengthy letter to the local newspaper on some current issue. When the councilman said he was glad to know where the citizen stood, the letter writer astounded everyone by explaining that his comments in the newspaper did not express his "real feelings."[27]

Although the importance of interest groups in the political process is generally well accepted by political scientists and by members of state legislatures and Congress, organized interest groups appear to be much less active and influential at the municipal level. They are not important in some cities even as a communications apparatus. Interviews with 112 councilmen from twenty-two cities in the San Francisco Bay area revealed that:[28]

> Most councilmen do not view interest group activities as indispensable to the political system. About three-quarters of our respondents are either neutral or negative toward such groups. They do not encourage group approaches, and they do not turn to such groups for help. It appears that the "group struggle" in local political systems (at least in these twenty-two cities) takes place largely in a one-way street upon which relatively little traffic is noticed or invited by those who dwell at the upper end.

Difficulties in Adjusting to Criticism. A citizen is accustomed to the elaborate ritual of criticism by circumlocution found in everyday life. If he is elected to the local council, he finds that his actions now become subjected to a different, more open, more straightforward, and more vigorous criticism. Some of it is informed and responsible. Some of it is uninformed and irresponsible. The councilman must learn to hide his feelings and to accept these comments without undue sensitivity. But he must not become so immune as to ignore the warning flags of changing public opinion, at least not if he wants to be reelected.

Difficulties in Learning to Trust Expert Advisers. The councilman is usually a lay citizen serving only part time at his job. Even in fairly small cities, and especially in large ones, he must learn to trust the advice given by specialists and to rely upon this in making public policy decisions. If the shade-tree expert says that extensive trimming will help preserve the trees, the councilman must overcome his preference for trimming the budget and instead vote the money

[27] M. Nelson McGeary, "The Councilman Learns His Job," *National Municipal Review* (now *National Civic Review*), 43:284–287, June, 1954.
[28] Betty H. Zisk, Heinz Eulau, and Kenneth Prewitt, "City Councilmen and the Group Struggle," *Journal of Politics*, 27:618–646, August, 1965. Quotation from p. 644.

for the trees—if any is available. Of course, the councilman cannot simply accept the advice of experts, enact it into an ordinance, and go home. It is not that simple. McGeary points to difficulties that the councilman must face when (1) the experts present, as they often do, original estimates of the costs of large projects that are unrealistically low; and (2) the experts disagree among themselves as to the best solution to a problem. Many a councilman has voted for a sewage-disposal plant only to discover later that it cost 50 percent more than the original estimates. Not only may disagreeing experts keep councilmen awake nights, but so may differences between prevailing grass-roots opinion and expert opinion, for these often differ. No councilman can simply accept the word of a civil engineer as to how and where to build a sewage-treatment plant or what its capacity should be. As the neophyte councilman will quickly learn, dozens of butchers, bakers, and housewives consider themselves lay experts on all types of engineering and other technologically complex problems.

Difficulties of Informing the Public. The councilman must let the people know what he is doing and why he is doing it. Communication with a preoccupied and often apathetic public is difficult.

Difficulties in Making the Right Decision at the Right Time. An inexperienced or impetuous councilman is sometimes guilty of making a decision too rapidly for it to represent informed behavior. All the arguments pro and con may not appear in the first few discussions of an issue. Facts that arise later may make the councilman who has already committed himself look ridiculous. Of course, the man who will not make up his mind, or who always follows the lead of someone else, is of limited value, but "a councilman seems to command respect, and may save himself considerable embarrassment if he takes a definite position only after the facts are in."[29]

Concluding Statement. McGeary has summarized his experiences by saying that "serving on the council is a headache. But democracy is based on the supposition that some citizens will be willing to endure headaches. Actually the travail is not unbearable. And sometimes, for brief periods, it is forgotten—believe it or not—in the knowledge that some little service is being offered."[30]

[29] McGeary, *op. cit.*, p. 287.
[30] *Ibid.*

SELECTED READINGS

Barber, James D.: *Power in Committees,* Rand McNally & Company, Chicago, 1966. (Examines the Connecticut town boards of finance and their decision-making procedures in a laboratory setting.)

Bromage, Arthur W.: *Councilmen at Work,* George Wahr Publishing Company, Ann Arbor, Mich., 1954. (By a political scientist who served on a council.)

Downes, Bryan T.: "Issue Conflict, Factionalism, and Consensus in Suburban City Councils," *Urban Affairs Quarterly,* 4:477–497, June, 1969.

Eulau, Heinz, and Robert Eyestone: "Policy Maps of City Councils and Policy Outcomes: A Developmental Analysis" *American Political Science Review,* 57:124–143, March, 1968.

Freeman, J. Leiper: "A Case Study of the Legislative Process in Municipal Government," in John C. Wahlke and Heinz Eulau, *Legislative Behavior,* The Free Press of Glencoe, New York, 1959. (A middle-sized Massachusetts city.)

Huckshorn, Robert J., and C. E. Young: "A Study of Voting Splits on City Councils in Los Angeles County," *Western Political Quarterly,* 13:479–497, June, 1960. (A study of councilmanic factions and coalitions.)

Sayre, Wallace S., and Herbert Kaufman: *Governing New York City,* Russell Sage Foundation, New York, 1960. (Contains information and bibliography on New York City Council.)

Stinchcombe, Jean L.: *Reform and Reaction—City Politics in Toledo,* Wadsworth, Belmont, Calif., 1968.

Vidich, A. J., and Joseph Bensman: *Small Town in Mass Society,* Princeton University Press, Princeton, N.J., 1958. (The council of an upstate New York village.)

Wendt, Lloyd, and Herman Kogan: *Lords of the Levee,* The Bobbs-Merrill Company, Inc., Indianapolis, 1943. (Concerning the aldermen from Chicago's first ward, the "levee.")

Williams, Oliver P., and Charles R. Adrian: *Four Cities,* University of Pennsylvania Press, Philadelphia, 1963, chap. 11. (Social backgrounds of councilmen in four middle-sized cities.)

Zisk, Betty H., Heinz Eulau, and Kenneth Prewitt: "City Councilmen and the Group Struggle," *Journal of Politics,* 27:618–646, August, 1965. (Part of a study of councilmen in the San Francisco Bay area.)

E THE
RELATIONSHIPS
AMONG
GOVERNMENTS

CHAPTER
10 DECISIONS
FOR
METROPOLITAN
AREAS

Nowhere in the United States today does the sociological and economic metropolitan area coincide with a single governmental unit that includes the entire area. Many of the problems that result from this have been mentioned in Chapter 1. There is a great deal of inertia, not to mention much overt opposition, to the reorganization of urban government. Why is a change advocated by students of "metropology"? Victor Jones, a leading authority, has put it this way:[1]

A metropolitan government is desirable (1) when coordination of a function over the whole area is essential to effective service or control in any part of the area; (2) when it is desired to apply the ability to pay theory of taxation to the area as a whole, instead of allowing each part to support its own activities at whatever level its own economic base will allow; (3) when services can be supplied more efficiently through large-scale operations; and (4) when it is necessary in order to assure citizens a voice in decisions that affect them at their places of work and recreation as well as at their places of residence.

[1]Victor Jones,"Local Government Organization in Metropolitan Areas," in Coleman Woodbury (ed.), *The Future of Cities and Urban Redevelopment,* The University of Chicago Press, Chicago, 1953, part IV, p. 508. Quotation by permission.

Numerous proposals have been made over the years in seeking solutions for metropolitan government. There is no current trend toward the adoption of a particular governmental arrangement, nor has anyone been able to devise a plan that would be both practical and successful. Some isolated exceptions are to be found, however, some makeshift and temporary devices have been put to use in various places, and the past efforts are worth studying, in any case, if only that the reasons for their lack of success may be seen.

PROPOSALS FOR METROPOLITAN-AREA GOVERNMENT

Annexation. Superficially, the most obvious method of keeping the sociological and legal cities identical would seem to be for the core city to annex fringe areas as they become urbanized. Formerly this method was widely used to expand the city's legal boundaries to keep pace with the actual urban growth, but it has become increasingly unsatisfactory, because noncity residents are no longer concentrated along city boundaries but are widely dispersed. Although annexations have increased in both number and importance in the last generation for all sizes of cities, they seldom succeed in equating the political with the sociological city. Milwaukee, as a not untypical example, has annexed a good deal of territory over the years, but it does not have metropolitan-wide government. The reason for this is that the laws in nearly all states provide that outlying areas may be annexed only after a referendum has been held and the annexation is approved by the voters of the outlying area as well as those of the core city. Only in a few states, notably in Texas and Virginia, is the core city relatively free to expand its boundaries as the surrounding area becomes urbanized.

Annexation is usually unpopular in the fringe areas. This is a reflection both of local pride and of the persistent belief that taxes will be higher within the core city, as well as of various other values of suburbanites discussed in Chapter 2.[2] After 1890, few large annexations took place in the United States until after World War II, when there were several, especially in Texas. Most recent annexations have been of only a few acres. However, in the decade of the 1950s, more than 6 million persons were annexed to core cities and the amount of annexation activity appears to have increased in the

[2] Charles Press, "Attitudes toward Annexation in a Small City Area," *Western Political Quarterly,* 16:271–278, June, 1963; and Charles Press, "Efficiency and Economy Arguments for Metropolitan Reorganization," *Public Opinion Quarterly,* 28:584–594, Winter, 1964.

TABLE 10-1. Municipal Annexations

Year	All Cities over 5,000 Population	All Cities over 10,000 Population
1945	25	22
1950	60	48
1955	125	106
1960	183	139
1965	141	120

Note: Includes only annexations of one-half square mile or more.
Source: Municipal Year Book, 1966, International City Management Association, Chicago, 1966, p. 60.

1960s. In 1962, 20 percent of the cities of 5,000 population or more annexed some territory.[3]

Easily the most important factors encouraging fringe areas to want to become annexed are sewerage and water-supply services and high schools. All other services furnished by cities are of far less interest. Sewerage—and especially sewage-disposal—facilities are very expensive and inefficient if used only by small units of government. An adequate source of water supply is often a serious problem, too. Building a high school is also expensive; but in some states, school districts can consolidate without political annexation of the outlying area to the city.

A 1952 study indicated that officials in cities annexing territory felt, in more than four-fifths of the cases, that the new areas in the years immediately ahead would not pay as much in taxes as the city would spend on them. About the same proportion believed, however, that in the long run the areas would pay for themselves.[4]

Most state laws on annexation are unsuitable as a means for securing a single metropolitan government. The requirement of obtaining permission from all areas concerned, combined with the fact that suburban dwellers are likely to take a short view, heavily overlaid with concerns about access, representativeness, and the maintenance of life styles (all carefully cultivated by fringe-area officeholders protecting their own jobs) help make this approach a slow-moving one. It is significant that the large annexations usually take

[3] Thomas R. Dye, "Urban Political Integration," Midwest Journal of Political Science, 8:430–446, November, 1964.
[4] John C. Bollens, "Metropolitan and Fringe Area Developments in 1952," Municipal Year Book, 1953, International City Management Association, Chicago, 1953, pp. 33–48.

place where state laws do not require the direct approval of fringe dwellers.

One study has found, however, that the permissiveness of annexation laws is not a particularly important consideration in determining success in annexation. Neither is the size of the urbanized area; that is, it is only slightly easier to secure annexations to small central cities than it is to large ones. Since the end of World War II, several factors have been associated with successful annexation. One of these was the form of government of the core city. Council-manager cities were more successful in annexation than were other types of cities. Another important factor was related to the socioeconomic character of the core city. Those with a large number of persons of the middle class were generally more successful, probably because of the greater compatibility of life styles between suburbanites and core-city dwellers. Newer cities were also more likely to be able to annex territories than were older ones, for the latter seemed to have well-established political styles and traditions creating an inertia that was not easily overcome. This study concluded that "Annexation is a likely integrative device in younger urbanized areas and those in which social differentials between city and suburb have not crystallized. . . . On the other hand, in older urbanized areas and in urbanized areas where the suburbs have become socially differentiated from the central city, integrative demands will have to be met through devices other than annexation."[5]

Texas, California, and Virginia lead in annexations in the postwar period. Texas and Missouri allow annexation of unincorporated territory by amendment of home rule charters without a popular vote. Texas also permits annexation simply by an ordinance of the core city, if the home rule charter so provides.[6] This was the technique used in San Antonio in 1952.

Virginia has an unusual annexation procedure whose origins are hidden in colonial obscurity. In that state, whenever a fringe area begins to urbanize, the core city seeks control over the outlying land through a judicial proceeding before a three-judge court. The city is permitted to present the rational case for annexation, and the court is obligated to decide the question on the basis of its interpretation of the interests of the entire community—not on the basis of pecuniary interests of the suburban or city taxpayers. Under these circumstances, the city usually wins its case. Limited possibilities

[5] Dye, *op. cit.*
[6] Stuart A. MacCorkle, *Municipal Annexation in Texas,* Institute of Public Affairs, University of Texas, Austin, Tex., 1965.

for judicial annexation of suburban areas by core cities also exist in five other states.[7]

Jones, while viewing the Virginia method as more productive than that in nearly all other states, has suggested that annexation questions might best be handled by a state administrative body on the order of the postwar Local Government Boundary Commission in England.[8] It is not easy for a court to settle annexation questions on facts alone or to separate facts from values and interests. These distinctions need not be made by an administrative body, which could also more easily reflect changes in public policy, could initiate action rather than wait for cases to come before it, and could settle problems on bases other than those proposed by the parties at issue.

A definite if slow trend away from the referendum as a necessary part of the annexation procedure has been noted in recent years. In 1959, the Minnesota legislature established a Municipal Commission. It was given authority to hear petitions for incorporation, detachment, and annexation of land within the state. On the basis of certain criteria, the commission was authorized to decide, after hearing, on questions of proposed incorporation of villages or cities within the three most populous counties of the state. In the other counties of the state, the county governing board was authorized to decide the same questions, using the same criteria. A similar law, also designed to provide more rational and systematic procedure for incorporation and annexation, was adopted in Wisconsin that same year and in New Mexico in 1965.

In 1963, the California legislature provided for a Local Agencies Formation and Annexation Commission for each county. The purpose of this legislation was not only to require some kind of systematic study of proposals to create additional special districts in the state (at the time, California had 1,962) but also to provide a more rational approach to incorporation and annexation. The commission consists of two county officers, appointed by the board of supervisors, and two city councilmen, appointed by all the mayors of the county meeting as a selection committee. These four persons choose a fifth member. On the basis of criteria prescribed in the statute, they decide whether or not to permit the creation of a new special district, the incorporation of a new city, or the annexation of territory to an existing city or special district. It seems unlikely that annexation to the core city will be the approach used in the foreseeable future for

[7] Victor Jones gives details, *op. cit.*, part IV, pp. 564–566. The Virginia plan is evaluated in Chester W. Bain, *Annexation in Virginia: The Use of Judicial Process for Readjusting City-County Boundaries*, University Press of Virginia, Charlottesville, Va., 1966.
[8] *Ibid.*, pp. 568–572.

achieving metropolitan-wide government, however. The new patterns for annexation and incorporation are designed to provide more rational local government boundaries, not to make metropolitan-area governments easier to secure.[9]

Special Districts. If annexation becomes impossible, the next approach that might suggest itself would be to take those functions in which a particularly evident need for metropolitan-wide administration is seen and create one or more special districts to administer them. Hence, covering all or part of a metropolitan area, there might be park, sewerage, water, parking, airport, planning, or other districts.

"Special districts," one observer has noted, "are the least known and least understood units of government in the United States. Yet, paradoxically, there are some 27,000 more special-district governments in the nation than all other units of governments combined."[10]

A special district is an organized unit of government, having substantial autonomy from other governments, its own taxing and—usually—its own bonding authority.[11] In particular, since it has its own fiscal authority and a governing body, it exists as a separate unit of government performing some public service. Districts exist for such varied purposes as recreation, sewage disposal, airports, planning, parking, and mosquito abatement. They may have boundaries coterminous with other units of government, such as cities or counties, or they may overlap other units. They exist in both rural and urban areas and are to be found in every state in the Union, though 60 percent of the national total are located in nine states: California, Illinois, Kansas, Missouri, Nebraska, New York, Oregon, Texas, and Washington.

Growth of Special Districts. The general trend of special districts has been one of an increase in numbers since the end of World War II. This is true even though the most common form of special district, the school district, *decreased* by 53 percent between 1942 and 1957. This countertrend was the result of special factors, however, and nonschool special districts increased by 74 percent over the same period. By 1967, there were seven times as many nonschool special districts as there were counties. The total of such special districts exceeded the total of municipalities in the nation. These same districts had twice as much debt as counties and one-half as much as the state governments. Despite all the vast amount of school construction that has taken place in the postwar years, special districts

[9] See Kenneth G. Bueche, *Incorporation Laws: One Aspect of the Urban Problem,* Bureau of Governmental Research, University of Colorado, Boulder, Colo., 1963.
[10] W. G. Thrombley, "Texas Special Districts," *Public Affairs Comment,* 4:1, March, 1958.
[11] U.S. Bureau of the Census, *Governments in the United States,* 1957, p. 9.

other than for schools have debts nearly the size of those for schools —a reflection of the fact that the functions generally assigned to special districts are of a high-cost, capital-outlay type.

Most nonschool special districts are in rural areas, particularly those for fire protection, soil conservation, and drainage, which together make up about one-half the total districts. But quite a few are in urban areas, especially fringe areas, as are many cemetery districts and most housing authorities. These five types taken together make up about two-thirds of the number of special districts.

Ad hoc districts may be governed by a body appointed by the state; one appointed by officials from the local governments overlaid by the district, with members being either appointed especially for the position or in ex officio capacities; one appointed by a judge; or, sometimes, one elected by the voters of the area. The variety is almost endless, but since the last possibility is not the usual one, special-purpose districts ordinarily do not come within the direct oversight of the voting public.

Reasons for Postwar Trend. The need for an area-wide approach to problems exists in rural areas (as in the case of drains that cross township and county lines) and in urban areas. Problems requiring such an approach have especially increased as urban populations have increased. Other solutions failing or seeming to be politically impossible, the special district has been turned to. It has been very popular in many rapidly urbanizing states and has, as in California, served as a substitute for incorporation or for a fringe government of less area than the county.

Often districts are the only means by which essential services can be supplied in a metropolitan area. The pattern of use for the special district is a strange one, however, seeming to depend upon local customs and perhaps upon the accident of the gradual accumulation of rigid constitutional and statutory restrictions controlling general governments and discouraging the use of the existing units for newer services. For example, one might expect special districts to be used especially in states not having townships, but six of the ten states with the most special districts also have townships in all or part of the state. Special districts are very popular in the West, where they are especially used for the procurement, distribution, and allocation of scarce water supplies. But they are found in every part of the land.

In both rural and metropolitan areas, the number or complexity of arrangements of governmental units does not appear to be based on observable need. The number in 1967 varied from 19 in Hawaii to 6,453 in Illinois. Thirty-one percent of all governmental units were located in but five states (ten percent of the total number): Illinois,

TABLE 10-2.   Units of Government, 1952–1967

Governments	1952	1967	Percent Change
United States	1	1	
States	48	50	4.2
Counties	3,052	3,049	− 0.1
Municipalities	16,807	18,048	7.4
Townships and towns	17,202	17,105	− 0.6
School districts	67,355	21,782	− 67.7
Special districts	12,340	21,264	73.3

Source: U.S. Bureau of the Census, *1967 Census of Governments.*

Kansas, Minnesota, Nebraska, and Pennsylvania. Of the nonschool special districts, 40 percent were located in five states: California, Illinois, New York, Pennsylvania, and Washington. All of these were among the most urbanized states in the Union, yet the highly urbanized states of Connecticut, Massachusetts, Michigan, and Ohio had relatively few such districts.[12]

There are several reasons for the trend toward special districts. Citizens learn that their state or other states authorize districts to perform certain services. The approach usually has strong appeal. Citizens do not resist it as they do attempts at governmental consolidation, since they expect that it will be less expensive and that it will preserve the independence of their local government. Interest groups that may want services performed by government (amateur pilots wanting an airport, physicians wanting a hospital), together with the professional administrators of particular functions, characteristically want their special problems handled in a special way by a special organization.[13] School administrators have long ago convinced the American public that they should be independent of the rest of local government, and the school district is both the most common and the best-known special district. Others have followed the lead of the educators and the interest groups supporting them. The special district has also had great appeal to the wistful who would take their pet governmental function "out of politics."

Pros and Cons of Districts. The advantages of special districts are said to be several. Special districts make possible the provision of governmental services when and where they are most needed and limit the financial burden to residents most directly benefited, while at the same time they skip lightly over the myriad local-government boundaries which otherwise stand in the way of making these serv-

[12] U.S. Bureau of the Census, *1962 Census of Governments.*
[13] As Victor Jones has pointed out, *op. cit.*, pp. 527–528.

ices available. Other units of government frequently cannot or will not supply these services. Consolidating local units is often politically unfeasible. By leaving the political status quo undisturbed, the social need is met with a minimum of resistance; political loyalties are not disturbed; jobs are not threatened; property-tax payers need have little fear of being assessed for someone else's benefit. Usually, the debts and costs of special districts do not count in determining debt and tax limits of regular local governments, and the bonds of such districts are sometimes more easily marketed than are those of other local governments.

Disadvantages of special districts, it is argued, include the fact that the behind-the-scenes way in which they generally operate helps to make them especially profitable for lawyers, engineers, bankers, bonding houses, and salesmen of equipment, services, and real estate. They are often designed to meet short-range needs and not only do not consider more permanent approaches but, by taking the urgency out of the situation for at least a considerable portion of a community, serve to forestall efforts toward long-range, rational governmental organization.[14]

Special districts have often done very good jobs in construction and engineering and sometimes in management. They do not necessarily eliminate political patronage, however, do not guarantee professional administration of functions, and do not remove from the arena of politics governmental functions that involve issues of policy. Special districts often result in increased costs of local government because of duplication of personnel, inefficient utilization of equipment, and inability to save through centralized purchasing and other centralized housekeeping activities. They do not balance the various needs for services of a community, do not recognize the interdependence of various functions, and are not usually provided with a method for coordinating their activities and budgets with those of the other governments in the area in which they exist. If the governing board is elective, the ballot is made longer and voters are asked to fill offices in which they have little interest or competence to choose. If the governing board is indirectly chosen, as is usually the case, there is no real responsibility to the public for the function performed. Victor Jones has concluded:[15]

> A corporate form of metropolitan government in which the selection of the authority or district commission members is once or more removed from the electoral controls may give us efficient and effective government but it cannot give us good government.

---

[14] *Ibid.*
[15] Jones, *op. cit.*, pp. 585–586. By permission of the University of Chicago Press.

It is not necessary, nor is it desirable, for all policy-making officials to be directly elected by popular vote. They should, however, be subject to the budgetary control of popularly elected
legislators and their policies should be subject to debate and
discussion.

Of course, any legislative body, whether it have jurisdiction
over the matter or not, may debate anything it wishes. The object,
however, is not futile and irresponsible talk. Our uneasiness
should not be allayed by saying that the ordinary municipal governments are frequently corrupt, irresponsible, ineffective, and
inefficient. Our job is to make them responsible and efficient.
This cannot be done by slicing off the most important functions
of local government and handing them over to one or several
autonomous bodies.

Multipurpose Special Districts. Most *ad hoc* districts serve a single
purpose, such as the Sanitary District of Chicago, which handles
sewerage for over 95 percent of Cook County's population,[16] the
Metropolitan Airports Commission of Minneapolis—St. Paul, and the
Metropolitan Water District of Southern California, which brings
water some 300 miles from the Colorado River to serve many communities in the Los Angeles area. There are some multipurpose
districts in use and some states authorize them where they do not
exist. Perhaps the best known is the Port of New York Authority,
which handles many aspects of water, highway, and air transportation. It is, however, a joint agent of the states of New York and New
Jersey rather than a unit of local government.

Some observers of local government have supported the use of
single-purpose special districts partly on the assumption that they
will lead to general-purpose districts for metropolitan government.
Such expansion has usually not occurred, however. It has not happened in the Boston, Chicago, Los Angeles, Minneapolis, and Detroit
areas. Jones illustrates this failure by pointing to the history of the
Massachusetts Metropolitan District Commission. This district is
controlled by a commission appointed by the Governor of Massachusetts and is not in any way directly responsible to the local community. It was created in 1919 by the consolidation of three districts
which furnished sewerage, water, and park services. In 1923, regional planning was added to its functions (but this has since been transferred to the state), and in 1952 refuse disposal was added. In 1929,
however, a separate Boston Metropolitan District was created for
rapid transit, and in 1947 a Metropolitan Transit Authority was es-

[16]Unifunctional districts normally carry on incidental functions. The Chicago district produces
electric power and fertilizer, and its channels are used for navigation. Illinois Legislative Council,
Chicago Sanitary District, State of Illinois, Springfield, Ill., 1953, pp. 22–27; Ward Walker, *The
Story of the Metropolitan Sanitary District of Greater Chicago,* Metropolitan Sanitary District,
Chicago, 1956.

tablished to take over the previously privately operated elevated railway system.[17] There appears to be no trend toward making super-governments out of the special districts.

City-county Consolidation. Until recent years, reformers have felt that consolidating the city with the metropolitan county was a desirability second only to annexation and a truer and more permanent solution than the use of the special district. This plan (there are dozens of possible variations of it) calls for an integration of the functions of the core city with the county. The county retains a partial identity, and incorporated municipalities remain independent for local purposes. City and county police, attorneys, clerks, treasurers, and health, welfare, and other departments can be combined to save the core-city taxpayer from paying for county services that he does not use and that in any event duplicate those he is already paying the city to do.

Around twenty attempts at city-county consolidation have been made in the twentieth century. Only four have succeeded. (All permitted municipalities to retain autonomy for certain "local" purposes, so that the plans could also be viewed as metropolitan "federations.") These involved the combination of Baton Rouge with East Baton Rouge Parish (*parish* is the Louisiana term for *county*) in 1947; that of Miami with Dade County, Florida, in 1957; the Nashville-Davidson County, Tennessee, consolidation of 1962; and that of Indianapolis and Marion County in 1970.

All such attempts have been difficult politically and complex legally. Often they require statewide approval on a constitutional amendment referendum, or legislative approval, or a majority vote on referendum in the core city and in the portions of the county outside. Thus, the Davidson County proposal had to "run the gamut of a dress rehearsal in 1958, a reprise that involved the two local legislative bodies, the state legislature, an advisory vote by the electorate, and the drafting of a new proposal, a bitter campaign, and the adoption of the charter at the polls," and still was faced with judicial challenges in the lower courts and the state supreme court.[18]

In Baton Rouge, one of the chronic obstacles to approval was overcome by setting up three taxing districts so that taxes were paid at one rate in urban areas, at another in rural portions of the parish where fewer services were provided or needed, and at a third, the lowest, in some industrial areas where no services were provided. Representation, another difficult knot to untie before consolidation can be consummated, was solved by adding to persons elected from

[17] Jones, *op. cit.*, pp. 582–583.

[18] David A. Booth, *Metropolitics: The Nashville Consolidation,* Institute for Community Development, Michigan State University, East Lansing, Mich., 1963, p. 88.

the portions of the parish outside of Baton Rouge to the city council whenever that body sits as the parish council.

Three attempts, beginning in 1945, were made to consolidate the city and county in the Miami area in one way or another, but all failed. A fourth effort succeeded. A Metropolitan Miami Municipal Board was created in 1953 by the Miami City Council in cooperation with suburban municipalities which joined in after several months of negotiations. Many of the suburbs apparently were fearful of being excluded from a general metropolitan plan. A number of pressures had brought on the consolidation. They included especially those from the local daily newspapers and businessmen interested in efficiency and economy. Their activities were given indirect support by the long history of governments in the area with reputations for ineffectiveness and corruption.

The newly established board drafted a plan for a metropolitan government, with the help of the Public Administration Service of Chicago, which was strongly influenced by traditional efficiency and economy values. After the board had made its recommendations, it discussed them with the Dade County delegation to the Florida legislature in 1955. During the next year, the legislature approved the holding of a referendum on the proposal and created a Metropolitan Charter Board. In November, 1956, an amendment to the constitution was approved, and the following May, the Metro Charter was adopted. It was highly controversial from the beginning. Most municipal officials and employees in the area saw it as a threat; some suburban citizens were concerned lest they would lose access to decision makers; but residents of areas with high assessed valuations saw the plan as a device for spreading their taxes over a larger area. About a dozen efforts were made in the years following adoption to force abandonment of the plan.

The board to govern the metropolitan area was made up of five members nominated from each of the county commission districts but elected at large, one nominated and elected from each of the five districts, and one member from each city of 60,000 population or more. The county manager was to be appointed by the governing board and removable by it. Provision was made for a rather orthodox council-manager plan. The major problems in Dade County have centered around the question of the allocation of authority over various functions of government. Most of the major functions have been assigned to the metropolitan government, but with local units having some powers over what have been identified as local aspects, and with the metropolitan government setting minimum standards of performance. In cases where local units do not meet the minimum standards, the metropolitan government is authorized to assume responsibility for that function.

Metropolitan Davidson County has a mayor plus a metropolitan council consisting of thirty-five members elected by districts and five elected at large. A number of traditional county offices remain popularly elective, but boards and heads of agencies that perform essentially municipal functions are appointed by the mayor, subject to council approval. The metropolitan government can perform all functions authorized by Tennessee law for either cities or counties.[19] It is divided into urban-services and general-services districts to avoid the problem of taxing property owners for services they do not yet receive or, perhaps, even need.

Adoption of plans for metropolitan government is often dependent upon the attitudes of persons with a middle-class ideology. Support in the Nashville area came principally from persons who had a relatively high level of knowledge concerning political issues in the metropolitan area and was correlated directly with level of education. Persons who were dissatisfied with existing municipal services (especially sewers and sewage disposal) were also more likely to be in favor of metropolitan government, as were those who did not anticipate that metropolitan government might be associated with higher taxes.[20]

Not only is city-county consolidation difficult politically, but it does not guarantee that the city-county will have sufficient powers to meet all metropolitan problems, and it causes even greater political difficulties if the metropolitan area expands beyond the county limits. Despite the successful development in the Baton Rouge area, this approach to metropolitan government is not likely to bear fruit in many areas of the nation.

City-county Separation. Core-city dwellers, watching the county snowplows at work in the unincorporated reaches of suburbia and remembering that the core city bears most of the cost of county government while securing few services from it, are likely to be intrigued with the idea of separating the city from the rest of the county. This plan is not far different from the preceding one, except that instead of integrating the offices and leaving the county boundaries as they are, separation would create a city-county of the core city and create a new county of the outlying areas.

San Francisco, Baltimore, St. Louis, Denver, and all cities of over 10,000 in Virginia are separate city-counties and have been for a long time. Except in Virginia, there have been no separations in nearly half a century. The plan encounters much the same problems as does city-county consolidation and is no more practical politically.

[19] Beverly Briley, "The Davidson County Story," *The County Officer*, September, 1962, pp. 406–407.

[20] Bret W. Hawkins, "Public Opinion and Metropolitan Reorganization in Nashville," *Journal of Politics*, 28:408–418, May, 1966.

Outlying sections of the county desire to control the county government, as they would under separation, but they also wish to retain the benefits of county services paid for mostly by core-city taxpayers. Furthermore, this is not really an approach to metropolitan government at all, since it traps the city within its own walls (except in Virginia) and, instead of treating metropolitan problems on an area-wide basis, it serves as a kind of parochialism, with the core city retreating to its own enclosure.

Metropolitan Federation. Strong arguments, based upon efficiency, economy, and equity call for functions of government to be integrated throughout the metropolitan area. At the same time, many citizens prefer keeping government as close to the people as possible and find a psychological value in retaining the community spirit of the smaller suburb as against the impersonality of the core city. Because of the dilemma thus created, some specialists have suggested that a federal plan of government be applied to the metropolitan area with two tiers of government: one area-wide to perform functions fitting into that classification, and another for the local community to handle functions of a more parochial interest. It is sometimes suggested, for example, that such things as sewage disposal, water supply, police protection, and planning should be area-wide, while perhaps garbage collection and local street maintenance would be appropriate for the lower-tier government. This plan has been used in London, England, and Toronto, Ontario. Perhaps half a dozen American communities have considered it, but all such proposals have been defeated.

The Municipality of Metropolitan Toronto. The first example of the federal plan of urban government on the North American continent was established by unilateral action of the Ontario Legislature in 1953. Without a referendum vote in the areas affected, but after extensive public hearings, the Legislature created a federal plan with a metropolitan government over the thirteen municipalities of the Toronto area. In addition, the area was disconnected from the county which had had control over it and county functions were assigned to the metropolitan government.

The action established a supergovernment six times the area of Toronto proper. The metropolitan council of twenty-five consists of the twelve suburban mayors of the cities, or reeves (supervisors) of the townships, plus twelve representatives from Toronto proper. The chairman is appointed by the provincial government. The Toronto members are the mayor, two of the four elective members of the board of control, and one of the two aldermen from each of the nine city wards.

The assignment of powers to the metropolitan government and to local units is somewhat arbitrary. The metropolis controls assessments, water supply and distribution, sewerage and sewage treatment, main highways, public transportation, administration of justice, some welfare functions, land-use planning, and supervision of local zoning. It also has concurrent powers with the local municipalities on public housing and redevelopment and parks and recreation. Other powers are left to the local units, including some that are often thought of as being metropolitan-wide in scope: fire protection, libraries, public health, building codes, and direct public relief. No provision is made in the enabling act for a later redistribution of functions. In 1967, the municipalities were reduced in number from thirteen to six and the council membership increased from twenty-four to thirty-three. Twelve seats were given to Toronto. Toronto officials were displeased, but suburbanites favored the proposal, which permitted them to continue to control when they vote as a bloc.

The Municipality of Metropolitan Toronto represents a major step toward an integrated approach to metropolitan government. There are some apparent weaknesses in the model established at Toronto, however. The dual responsibility of the metropolitan council to the voters is confusing. All but two of the council members must be elected annually, an approach that does not seem likely to encourage long-range planning. Furthermore, the representation is inequitable when measured by a population standard.

The Municipality, as it has been established, does not include all of the metropolitan area. Some duplication of personnel and equipment still exists because the metropolitan government and the municipalities have concurrent jurisdiction over most functions of government.

Whether American metropolitan areas will follow the lines established by the Ontario Legislature seems unlikely, for American state legislatures are not likely to use direct and drastic action.

The County as a Metropolitan Unit. Because about two-thirds of the standard metropolitan areas are located in single counties, it is sometimes suggested that the already-existing county governments might be used as a basis for forming supergovernments. There are, however, several disadvantages to such an approach. In the first place, the county may be a poor profile of the metropolitan area. The core city may be tucked off in a corner of a county that is otherwise rural, or the metropolitan area may extend over several counties. Second, in most states, there are many legal obstacles to the county acting as a municipality. Third, the traditional structure of county government, under either the supervisor or commissioner system, is unsatisfactory for urban government, especially because of the absence of a chief executive officer.

A very few urban counties have been given powers and governmental structures that enable them to act as supergovernments.[21] One example is Los Angeles County, which has a chief administrative officer and furnishes many urban services to unincorporated areas as well as, by contract, to incorporated municipalities. Of the thirty-one cities incorporated in Los Angeles County between 1955 and 1965, twenty-nine contracted with the county to provide all their services. Westchester County in New York has, in effect, the strong-mayor plan of government with an elective chief executive. Several counties have the council-manager form.

Because of the various factors militating against the use of the county as an "upper-tier" unit of government, the trend has been toward functional consolidation. Either a single function at a time is turned over to the county, or *ad hoc* arrangements are made for a function to be operated jointly by the county and the core city. This trend in metropolitan areas is perhaps supported by the fact that many officials of large cities, unlike their counterparts in smaller communities, find acceptable such transfers of power.[22]

An increasing number of city-county hospitals are being established. City-county health units are becoming more common, as are joint traffic commissions. Many core cities combine with the county to build a city-county building, or to operate library, animal shelter, and police technical services. Planning, zoning, parks, welfare, and correction are among the other functions being turned over to counties or being jointly administered with counties.

The movement toward a greater use of the county has, however, been slow and piecemeal.

Extraterritorial Jurisdiction. Under certain conditions, a city may own and control land outside of its own boundaries. It may do this either under its governmental powers, if state law permits, or it may own land in the same manner as a private corporation, in which case its powers are limited to those of the ordinary property owner.

About thirty states authorize some municipal control over the subdivision of land outside of the city limits.[23] The areas of jurisdiction vary from 1 to 5 miles. This type of control sometimes enables the core city to require the building up of land within the city before further plots are offered for sale on the periphery. Usually, however,

---

[21] See Jones, *op. cit.*, p. 597–601.
[22] Edward W. Weidner, *Intergovernmental Relations as Seen by Public Officials*, The University of Minnesota Press, Minneapolis, 1960, pp. 110–113.
[23] Russell W. Maddox, Jr., *Extraterritorial Powers of Municipalities in the United States*, The College Press, Corvallis, Oregon, 1955.

it helps to prevent the uncontrolled growth of surburban slums by requiring suitable standards for new subdivisions. Many heavily urban states, including Massachusetts, Michigan, Missouri, New Jersey, and New York, have no such control.

Extraterritorial powers are sometimes given a city for such functions as controlling roadhouses; securing a water supply; abatement of nuisances; providing for parks (this need is often ignored until the city is built up and no land within the city limits is left); building stone quarries, airports, or hospitals for contagious cases; and many other activities. Many California cities have summer camps and recreational centers in the mountains and elsewhere outside their corporate limits.

The suburbs often resent extraterritorial powers of the core city. Airports may be unpopular in one's neighborhood; yet they are necessary, and the core city rarely has space for them. A careless suburb cannot expect to be left alone if it allows a health menace to exist along the boundary between itself and the core city. If the core city constructs a park in the suburbs, there will be resentment over the city folk coming in droves into the area each Sunday. Yet the suburbanites swarm into the core city each workday. Somehow, the suburbanite is not likely to feel that the one counterbalances the other. Clearly, the dispute over extraterritorial powers is a reflection of uncoordinated independent municipalities in the metropolitan area.

Voluntary Cooperation. The lack of an overall government in the metropolitan area can be compensated for, to a degree, through the use of informal or contractual agreements between one or more cities in the area. Agreements may be made by one suburb with other suburbs, or by a suburb with the core city. These may be formally established but may also be quite informal.

It is becoming increasingly common for such intergovernmental arrangements to be made for the disposal of sewage, garbage, and rubbish; to share police radio networks; or to have the core-city police radio supply the suburban departments. Formal agreements or informal understandings concerning emergency standby assistance in the case of unusual police or fire problems are also common. A large number of core cities sell water to the suburbs on a contractual basis, either directly to the suburbanite, or to the suburb itself at a master meter. Many cities have understandings of an informal type concerning traffic-flow patterns, including such necessities as the establishment of one-way streets through two or more communities. Thousands of other cooperative arrangements have been worked out in various parts of the nation.

Voluntary agreements are edged with a coloration of the haphaz-

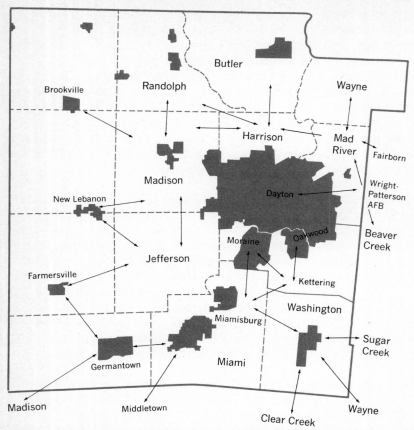

Figure 10-1. Mutual-aid contracts for fire protection, Montgomery County local governments, 1958. Americans are seeking to meet the problems of multiunit urban areas with their traditional empiricism. Here is one of dozens of examples of functional cooperation in the Dayton, Ohio, area. *Source:* John C. Bollens and others, Metropolitan Community Studies, Inc., Dayton, Ohio, 1959, fig. 20.

ard. They represent an unsystematic approach, but they ease some of the strains encountered in furnishing services to urbanites.

Councils of Governments. In the 1960s, a major trend toward intergovernmental cooperation was taken in the form of councils of governments in metropolitan areas. Ninety-one such agencies existed in 1969. Examples included the Association of Bay Area Governments (ABAG), established in the San Francisco area in 1961 as part of an effort to prevent metropolitan problems from being assumed by the state government. In concept, it is a confederation, with favorable decisions depending upon a concurrent majority of both city and county representatives. The general assembly meets at least twice a year, with the presidency alternating between city and county representatives, and with representation based upon membership rather than population of the various governmental units in the area.

A council of governments (COG) is usually formed as a result of activities by local officials or existing organizations that believe there is a need for an overall organization. Or it may come about from an outside stimulus, usually one leading to a fear of state- or national-government control of decisions. Councils of governments usually seek to improve communications within local units, prevent domination by a single governmental unit, and improve overall planning for the future in the metropolitan area.[24]

Metropolitics. A vast literature has been accumulated on metropolitan areas and the difficulties of supplying urban services to them. Well over 100 surveys have been conducted. Yet, despite the reams of paper devoted to the subject, most of the proposed solutions had been based upon a priori reasoning rather than empirical data; few studies have been made concerning the climate of opinion existing in metropolitan areas or of the limits of tolerance within which proposed approaches might be feasible; little work has been done concerning the levels of awareness which metropolitan residents have of their community and its problems; no rank order of values has been worked out; few studies have been made as to why integration proposals fail.

Perspectives on the Metropolis. Interpretations of metropolitan-area politics depend in part upon one's perspective of the metropolitan area. Several perspectives have been, or might be, used in interpreting this aspect of American politics:

1. The traditional, reform-movement emphasis was upon a search for *solutions,* with an emphasis upon efficiency and economy goals rather than upon problems of securing access and representation. The emphasis was on structural reform, with the implicit assumption that, given metropolitan-wide formal institutions, metropolitan areas would be well governed. These reformers generally assumed that other citizens in the area were as well informed as they, or at least adequately well informed to react favorably to their arguments. Because they themselves had no problems of access and representation—being overwhelmingly upper middle class—they failed to observe this central problem.[25]

2. The metropolitan area may be viewed as a problem in diplomacy. That is, decision making in the metropolitan area may

---

[24] Urban Data Service, *Councils of Governments: Trends and Issues,* International City Management Association, Washington, 1969.
[25] See Paul Studenski, *Government of Metropolitan Areas,* National Municipal League, New York, 1930.

be seen as resembling that of the diplomatic community more than that of the political. When it is, relative size of communities, although a factor, is not so important as that of securing unanimity in decisions, as is required for agreement in diplomatic negotiations. Viewing the area as a diplomatic problem also permits us to analyze it in terms of alliances of various groups. These alliances are not always so simple as one of the core city against the suburbs. They may involve groups of suburbs against other groups, or alliances may be formed on the basis of particular functions, rather than for all purposes of negotiation.[26]

3. The metropolitan area may be viewed as a market for services. In this sense, it can be analyzed in economic terms.[27] In large metropolitan areas, many, or at least several, suppliers of services may exist. For example, the core city, plus the county government, plus some of the larger suburbs may all compete for customers among suburbs for the distribution of water, or for sewage disposal, or for some other function. Cooperative arrangements involving buying from the lowest bidder are possible where both the purveyor and the consumer of services feel that they gain through the transaction—the fundamental requirement for an exchange in economic theory. The concept of the market also applies to the fact that residents of the area appear to choose their place of residence in terms of the amenities they desire and can afford.

4. The dozens, sometimes hundreds, of governmental units in a metropolitan area make it especially appropriate to view the metropolitan area as a part of the system of cooperative federalism. Shared decision making involves not only the traditional three levels of government, but a great amount of interlocal cooperation. To the extent that this is the case, the emphasis in cooperative federalism upon shared values and goals by professional administrators in various areas of government is especially appropriate. If the theory of cooperative federalism is reasonably satisfactory as an explanation of how decisions are made relative to American domestic policy today, the implication is that metropolitan areas will be able to operate satisfactorily (though certainly not ideally) through the use of negotiation and shared decision making and financing.[28]

5. The metropolitan area may be viewed as a complex of local governments which, if combined into a single unit, would no longer be a local government, but which through county and state governments might be able to provide those services that strictly local governments cannot provide by themselves. Although one-third of the metropolitan areas cover more than one county—and these are generally the largest such areas—the other two-thirds may increasingly find the county a useful unit of metropolitan

[26] Matthew Holden, Jr., "The Governance of the Metropolis as a Problem in Diplomacy," *Journal of Politics,* 26:627–647, August, 1964.
[27] Vincent Ostrom and others, "The Organization of Government in Metropolitan Areas," *American Political Science Review,* 55:831–842, December, 1961; Thomas R. Dye, "Metropolitan Integration by Bargaining among Sub-areas," *American Behavioral Scientist,* 5:11, May, 1962.
[28] See citations for chap. 1.

government. In these areas, as well as in those that cover more than a single county, the state is likely to provide metropolitan-wide services in future years. Reapportionment is especially likely to encourage the use of the state as an instrument for meeting metropolitan problems. In such fields as air and water pollution, highway systems, health services, welfare services, urban renewal, and area-wide planning, the state is particularly likely to be able to serve as a metropolitan unit of government.[29]

6.   The metropolitan area can also be viewed as a set of competing and sometimes conflicting ideologies. Perhaps this view has been least investigated, but we may in the future find research relative to it important in developing public policy in metropolitan areas, where some residents are committed to the urban industrial liberalism of organized labor, others are representative of the middle-class-oriented ideology of the organization man typically found in the suburbs, and a small but sometimes politically important minority remains committed to the small-town ideology of the nineteenth century.[30]

The Failure of Integration. The value patterns of those who support plans for metropolitan supergovernments are not dominant in the community, and the leaders of integration movements characteristically do not give adequate consideration to other values. The result is that proposals for reorganization of metropolitan governments are rarely implemented.

Upper-income business and professional people tend to favor metropolitan government for a number of reasons. Some are concerned lest, as a result of the middle-class exodus to the suburbs, the political control of the core city be lost to low-income groups with little education. Some believe that governmental consolidation will reduce costs through economies of scale. Low-income groups tend to oppose metropolitan government for a number of reasons. Negroes fear that such a government will weaken their political power, since Negroes are concentrated in the core city of the metropolitan area. Labor leaders sometimes oppose consolidation because business leaders favor it, and they assume it must therefore be to the advantage of the business leaders. Labor leaders or working-class people sometimes also oppose metropolitan plans because they include proposals for a short ballot and professional leadership. That is, they fear a loss of access and representation. Some low-income persons fear that metropolitan government would be more expensive to them, that it would result in more rapid tax increases than would

[29] Charles R. Adrian, "Public Attitudes and Metropolitan Decision Making," in Russell W. Maddox, Jr. (ed.), *Issues in State and Local Government,* D. Van Nostrand Company, Inc., Princeton, N.J., 1965, pp. 311–321.
[30] Charles R. Adrian and Charles Press, *The American Political Process,* McGraw-Hill Book Company, New York, 2d ed., 1969, chap. 7.

otherwise be the case. The question of whether or not to have metro-politan government is not, therefore, simply a question of efficiency and economy, as the reformers of a generation ago believed, but is a political question closely related to costs and to perceived abilities to influence policy making.[31]

Suburban officeholders and the entrenched bureaucracy of the area will almost always oppose metropolitan government, and reformers seldom pay enough attention to their values and interests or show any imagination in compromising with them. They fail to recognize that *representativeness* of government and *access* to the decision makers are likely to be more important considerations for the typical citizen than are questions of efficiency and economy. Rarely does a metropolitan-area study even mention these two psychologically important factors, to say nothing of adequately providing for them.

Negro voters, in particular, have been suspicious of proposals for metropolitan-wide government. In Cleveland, on ten issues submitted to referendum between 1933 and 1959, the level of support for metropolitan government steadily declined, but it declined much more rapidly among Negro voters than it did among whites. The percentage of positive vote among Negroes declined from 79 percent in 1933 to 29 percent in 1959, while the vote in predominantly white wards declined from 69 percent to 46 percent.[32]

Reformers tend to forget that the symbols—efficiency, a bigger and better Zilchville, and the like—that they respond to with enthusiasm ring no bells for *hoi polloi.* It is the latter, of course, which dominates the decision when a proposal is put to a popular referendum. The ordinary citizen is characteristically apathetic. If water flows from the tap and the toilet flushes today, he is not likely to ask whether it will do so tomorrow.

Yet, votes against metropolitan government are not necessarily votes in favor of the status quo. They may be votes in favor of gradual or incremental change rather than revolutionary change.[33]

Communicating a concept of future needs on a realistic basis is seldom done by groups organized to support metropolitan governmental reorganization. Furthermore, the reformers tend to put their arguments on a theoretical plane, discussing efficiency ("We have sixteen different fire departments in the metropolitan area!") without translating it into concrete terms as it affects the ordinary citizen.

[31] See Richard A. Watson and John H. Romani, "Metropolitan Government for Metropolitan Cleveland," *Midwest Journal of Political Science,* 5:365–390, November, 1961.
[32] *Ibid.,* table 2.
[33] Robert Warren, "Political Form and Metropolitan Reform," *Public Administration Review,* 24: 180–187, September, 1964.

Examples are often not made meaningful. It makes little impression on the suburbanite to be told that his police force is amateurish and inferior if, in practice, his community has little crime and the state police take care of the arterial highway traffic.

Concluding Statement. Each structural plan so far tried for the government of metropolitan areas in most cases either is basically unacceptable to groups politically powerful enough to block adoption or has proved to be ineffective as a method for dealing with perceived problems. Any proposal that does not meet the requirement of responsiveness to the general public must be dismissed—as it will be by the electorate—as lacking accord with our basic concepts of democratic theory.

Referring back to the Aristotelian mode of analysis, Norton Long has noted that "the search for metropolitan government is the search for a potential metropolitan governing class, the institutions through which it can function and a set of ideal goals which it can embody and which will render its leadership legitimate in the eyes of the people."[34] Here we find the reasons for slow progress in metropolitan-area government. The institutions for such government have not evolved because there is no consensus on goals and no acceptable governing group. The proposals put forth by self-appointed community leaders diverge so widely from the wants of a great portion of the citizenry that these volunteers for a leadership class are not accepted as legitimate spokesmen. Their offerings are rejected when the voters are polled, and no trend toward consensus on the three Aristotelian components can be discerned.

[34] Norton E. Long, "Recent Theories and Problems of Local Government," in Carl J. Friedrich and Seymour E. Harris (eds.), *Public Policy,* Graduate School of Public Administration, Harvard University, Cambridge, Mass., 1958, pp. 285–295. Quote is from p. 295. Reprinted in Norton E. Long, *The Polity,* Rand McNally & Company, Chicago, 1962.

316

**SELECTED
READINGS**

Adrian, Charles R.: "Metropology: Folklore and Field Research," *Public Administration Review,* 21:148–157, Summer, 1961. (A criticism of conventional metropolitan-area studies.)

Bain, Chester W.: *Annexation in Virginia: The Use of Judicial Process for Readjusting City-County Boundaries,* University Press of Virginia, Charlottesville, Va., 1966. (The oldest nonreferendum system.)

Banfield, Edward C., and Morton Grodzins: *Government and Housing in Metropolitan Areas,* McGraw-Hill Book Company, New York, 1958.

Banovetz, James M.: "Metropolitan Subsidies: An Appraisal," *Public Administration Review,* 25:297–301, December, 1965. (The amount of subsidy between core city and suburb is not consequential, but metropolitan consolidation would increase subsidies somewhat to the advantage of suburbs.)

Bollens, John C.: *Special District Governments in the United States,* University of California Press, Berkeley, Calif., 1957.

——— : *The States and the Metropolitan Problem,* Public Administration Service, Chicago, 1956.

——— and Henry J. Schmandt: *The Metropolis,* Harper & Row, Publishers, Incorporated, New York, 2d ed., 1969. (A summary of studies on metropolitan politics, ecology, and economics. Includes a fine bibliography.)

Booth, David A.: *Metropolitics: The Nashville Consolidation,* Institute for Community Development, Michigan State University, East Lansing, Mich., 1963.

Bromage, Arthur W.: *Political Representation in Metropolitan Agencies,* Institute of Public Administration, University of Michigan, Ann Arbor, Mich., 1962. (Examines the problems of representation apportionment for metropolitan governments.)

Chute, Charlton F.: "The Honolulu Metropolitan Area: A Challenge to Traditional Thinking," *Public Administration Review,* 18:36–47, Winter, 1958. (Honolulu offers a neglected example of a consolidated metropolitan area—it is a city-county with the natural boundaries of the island of Oahu.)

"COGs—Governing for the 21st Century": *Public Management,* 51: entire issue, January, 1969. (A generally sympathetic evaluation of councils of government.)

Donaldson, Scott: *The Suburban Myth,* Columbia University Press, New York, 1969. (Reviews the literature and concludes that suburbia "has been grossly and unfairly maligned.")

Duncan, Beverly, and Stanley Lieberson: *Metropolis and Region in Transition,* Sage Publications, Inc., Beverly Hills, Calif., 1970. (The evolution of some major urban centers.)

Dye, Thomas R., and others: "Differentiation and Cooperation in a Metropolitan Area," *Midwest Journal of Political Science,* 7:145–155, May, 1963. (Social and economic differences among communities are a factor discouraging metropolitan government.)

Freeman, Linton C., and others: *Metropolitan Decision-making,* University College, Syracuse University, Syracuse, N.Y., 1962.

Friesma, H. Paul: "The Metropolis and the Maze of Local Government," *Urban Affairs Quarterly,* 2:68–90, December, 1966. (A criticism of the assumptions made in recent metropolitan research.)

Greer, Scott: *Metropolitics: A Study of Political Culture,* John Wiley & Sons, Inc., New York, 1963. (The politics of reform in Cleveland, Miami, and St. Louis.)

Grumm, John G.: *Metropolitan Area Government: The Toronto Experience,* Governmental Research Center, University of Kansas, Lawrence, Kans., 1959.

Gutman, Robert, and David Popenoe (eds.): "Urban Studies," *American Behavioral Scientist,* 6: entire issue, February, 1963. (Useful bibliography.)

Hanson, Royce: *Metropolitan Councils of Governments,* U.S. Government Printing Office, 1966. (A report on the experiences of eight councils.)

Havard, William C., and Floyd C. Corty: *Rural-Urban Consolidation: The Merger of Governments in the Baton Rouge Area,* Louisiana State University Press, Baton Rouge, La., 1964.

Hawkins, Brett W.: *Nashville Metro: The Politics of City-County Consolidation,* Vanderbilt University Press, Nashville, Tenn., 1966. (Study of the Nashville-Davidson County consolidation of 1962, which Hawkins sees as stemming from unique local political conditions.)

Hawley, Amos H., and Basil G. Zimmer: *The Metropolitan Community,* Sage Publications, Inc., Beverly Hills, Calif., 1969. (Explores attitudes of citizens and officials of both core cities and suburbs.)

Hayes, Forbes B.: *Community Leadership,* Columbia University Press, New York, 1965. (A study of one of the oldest private metropolitan-area research organizations, the New York Regional Plan Association.)

Hill, R. Steven, and W. P. Maxam: "UNIGOV: The First Year," *National Civic Review,* 60:310–314, June, 1971.

Jones, Victor: "Local Government Organization in Metropolitan Areas," in Coleman Woodbury (ed.), *The Future of Cities and Urban Redevelopment,* The University of Chicago Press, Chicago, 1953. (The best historical study of metropolitan organization.)

Larson, Christian L., and others: *Growth and Government in Sacramento,* Indiana University Press, Bloomington, Ind., 1965.

MacCorkle, Stuart A.: *Municipal Annexation in Texas,* Institute of Public Affairs, University of Texas, Austin, Tex., 1965. (Story of a state with liberal annexation laws.)

Martin, Roscoe C.: *Metropolis in Transition,* Housing and Home Finance Agency, Washington, 1963. (A study of efforts to achieve metropolitan-wide government. Has good bibliography.)

Metropolitan Area Problems. (A bimonthly publication of the Graduate School of Public Affairs, State University of New York, Albany, N.Y., supplying news and a digest of research reports relative to metropolitan affairs. Unfortunately, publication was suspended in 1971.)

Metropolitan Communities: A Bibliography with Special Emphasis Upon Government and Politics, Public Administration Service, Chicago, 4 vols., 1956–1969.

Mowitz, Robert J., and Deil S. Wright: *Profile of a Metropolis,* Wayne State University Press, Detroit, Mich., 1962. (A study of several metropolitan decisions in the Detroit area.)

Norton, James A.: "Referenda Voting in a Metropolitan Area," *Western Political Quarterly,* 16:195–212, March, 1963. (Attitudes in the Cleveland area.)

Press, Charles: "The Cities within a Great City," *Centennial Review,*

7:113–130, Winter, 1963. (Metropolitan federation should start within the core city itself.)

Reining, Henry, Jr. (ed.): "Governing Megacentropolis," *Public Administration Review*, 30:473–520, September–October, 1970. (Six articles on problems of governing the metropolis.)

Sacks, Seymour, and others: *Metropolitan Cleveland: A Fiscal Profile*, Metropolitan Services Commission, Cleveland, 1958.

Schmandt, Henry J.: *The Municipal Incorporation Trend*, Bureau of Government, University of Wisconsin, Madison, Wis., 1961. (Reviews developments during the decade of the 1950s.)

—— and William H. Standing: *The Milwaukee Metropolitan Study Commission*, Indiana University Press, Bloomington, Ind., 1965.

——, Paul G. Steinbicker, and George D. Wendel: *Metropolitan Reform in St. Louis: A Case Study*, Holt, Rinehart and Winston, Inc., New York, 1961.

Schnore, Leo F.: "Municipal Annexations and the Growth of Metropolitan Suburbs," *American Journal of Sociology*, 67:406–417, January, 1962. (A comparison of suburban and core-city growth rates.)

Senate Subcommittee on Intergovernmental Relations, United States, *Metropolitan America: A Selected Bibliography*, 1964.

Simon, Herbert: *Fiscal Aspects of Metropolitan Consolidation*, Bureau of Public Administration, University of California, Berkeley, Calif., 1943. (A classic study, still valuable. Shows that with metropolitan-wide government, consolidation would result in higher taxes if services were made uniform.)

Smallwood, Frank: *Metro Toronto: A Decade Later*, Bureau of Municipal Research, Toronto, 1963.

Smith, Robert G.: *Public Authorities, Special Districts and Local Government*, National Association of Counties Research Foundation, Washington, 1964. (A study covering five states.)

Sofen, Edward: *The Miami Metropolitan Experiment*, Indiana University Press, Bloomington, Ind., 1963.

Steiner, Gilbert Y.: *Metropolitan Government and the Real World: The Case of Chicago*, Center for Research in Urban Government, Loyola University, Chicago, 1966. (A sharply critical evaluation of a metropolitan-government proposal for Chicago.)

U.S. Advisory Commission on Intergovernmental Relations: *Metropolitan America: Challenge to Federalism*, 1966. (Recommendations for metropolitan-area policies.)

U.S. Advisory Commission on Intergovernmental Relations: *Reports*, continuing from 1960.

Whyte, W. H., Jr., and others: *The Exploding Metropolis*, Doubleday & Company, Inc., Garden City, N.Y., 1958.

Wilbern, York: *The Withering Away of the City,* University of Alabama Press, University, Ala., 1964.

Williams, Oliver P., and others: *Suburban Differences and Metropolitan Policies,* University of Pennsylvania Press, Philadelphia, 1965.

Wood, Robert C.: *1400 Governments,* Harvard University Press, Cambridge, Mass., 1961. (The New York metropolitan area.)

———: *Suburbia: Its People and Their Politics,* Houghton Mifflin Company, Boston, 1959.

CHAPTER
11 CITIES IN THE FEDERAL SYSTEM

The city in the metropolitan area must learn to live with its incorporated and unincorporated neighbors, and all municipalities must cooperate regularly with special districts, school districts, and the county. In addition they must make satisfactory adjustments with both state and national governments.

The state government, as a parent, has a special relationship with the city. It has sought to oversee many of the activities of cities through its administrative agencies. The national government, which has no control over cities as such, has nonetheless forged countless connecting links between its own administrative structure and that of the cities. In 1966, a cabinet post of Secretary of Housing and Urban Development was created, partly in order to centralize to some degree in a single agency Federal contacts with urban governments.

STATE ADMINISTRATIVE RELATIONS WITH CITIES

State Administrative Oversight of Cities. The administrative branch of state government follows the typical frontier pattern of decentralization. Because of the influence of this philosophy, departments of local government, such as the Ministry of the Interior in France or the Ministry of Local Government in Great Britain, are not to be found in the United States. Administrative contacts between the city and the state are characteristically on a *functional* basis. That is, members of the state department of education oversee the activities of the local school district; the state department of health watches the activities of the local department of health; and so on. Perhaps six American states have made some move toward centralized supervision.[1]

Areas of Supervision. What local government functions are subject to state oversight today? Most of them, might be a brief answer. In particular, the state is especially watchful of municipal activities that involve (1) the expenditure of state grants-in-aid (e.g., in education, the building of expressways within cities); (2) those areas of national grants-in-aid which are administered through the states, but under conditions requiring state supervision of the expenditures (e.g., the building of airports in some states); and (3) those activities in which the state as a whole has a particular interest (e.g., the spread of communicable diseases, law enforcement, finances). The principal areas of control are those of education, finance, health, highways, and welfare, but to these must be added airports, fire prevention, libraries, housing, personnel, planning, police administration, and even control of municipally owned public utilities, among others.[2]

Techniques of Supervision. From all that has been said in this book and elsewhere about the tendency for the state to become involved in policies affecting local areas, it might be assumed that the above-mentioned activities are controlled by heavy-handed bureaucrats from the state capital, armed with court decrees and administrative orders. Although these devices do play a part, it has been the practice of most of the state agencies to try persuasion, education, and other noncoercive techniques wherever possible. The big stick is brought into play principally whenever the state overseers find evidence of incompetence, irresponsibility, or corruption.

State agencies exercising supervision usually start by requiring *reports* from local communities. This serves the purpose of warning the state when and where trouble spots begin to appear, and it tends to channel local activity, since the reporting official, knowing that he will be judged by his professional peers, will want to "look good." The state agency can furnish *advice and information.* This is especially important for the smaller communities, where amateurs may

[1] See above, pp. 291–294.
[2] Control over some of these functions will be discussed further in chaps. 16–19.

be floundering about seeking to do an adequate job with little experience or where overworked professionals may not have time to keep up with the latest techniques in their fields. The relationship between the state and the large-city technical specialist may sometimes become strained when the city functionary believes he is professionally more competent than is his nominal supervisor on the state level. Is the manager of a large-city airport able to get along without advice from the state airports commissioner? He is likely to think so. It is by no means unheard of for an extended feud to color relationships between the department of a large city and the corresponding agency of the state. Usually, however, relations are friendly and cooperative. The smaller cities and villages have technicians who are likely to recognize the genuine need for advice and to seek it. To simplify requests for such help, Tennessee and Maryland have established a clearinghouse for information—a Municipal Technical Advisory Service—in connection with the state university, and some other states have municipal research bureaus which may or may not be connected with a state school.

One step beyond advice is *technical aid.* State agencies, with (perhaps) a relatively larger budget and with more specialized equipment and personnel, are particularly in a position to aid the local amateur or semiprofessional. How effective can the chief of police in a village of 1,500 people be against the professional criminal? And how much experience or scientific equipment can be put to use in the rare event of a murder in his town? What would his colleague, the water commissioner, know about the technical problems of drilling a new deep well for the town? And how much does the overworked local general practitioner know about public health, even though he may bear the title of health officer? How much special equipment are the citizens of the town willing to afford when it is needed? State agencies in these and in dozens of other circumstances and activities stand ready to offer technical information, advice, and equipment.

Other approaches failing, the state may also make use of its *coercive power.* Among other things, its agencies can *grant or withhold permits* for certain things (e.g., to dump raw sewage into a stream under prescribed conditions); or *issue orders* (e.g., to build a sewage-treatment plant); or *issue rules and regulations* which are technically called ordinances (e.g., to prescribe the technical standards for water-supply purification); or *withhold grants-in-aid* if standards prescribed by state, or sometimes Federal, law are not complied with; or *review decisions* of local agencies (e.g., the power of the state tax-equalization board to review the determination of local boards and perhaps to order reassessment in extreme situations); or require *prior permission* from a state agency (e.g., the power of some state health departments to pass on the qualifications of local health-officer nominees); or *appoint certain local officials or remove them* (e.g., the local police chief). It is even possible in most states, as a last resort, to apply *substitute administration.* That is to say, in extreme cases the state may suspend local self-government altogether for some or all functions and allow state officials to govern instead. This is particularly true in the fields of finance, public health, and education.[3]

Organization for Supervision. The increasing tendency in recent years to turn supervisory functions over to the administrative rather than to the legislative branch of state government has probably changed the pattern of state-local relationships to a considerable degree. Local professional technicians feel more at ease and have less of a feeling that they will be exploited when they deal with state professionals rather than with the politicians of the state legislature.[4] A smoother, more confident relationship is the result. The community is likely to gain, too, for the *motivation* of the professional administrator is different from that of the politician, and this is likely to have an important effect upon the eventual solution of local problems. The professional administrator has his reputation at stake in everything he does, and his success is measured in terms of acceptance of his work by his professional peers, not only within the state, but also within the professional organizations to which he belongs. The politician has his job at stake in everything he does, and his success is measured in terms of the number of votes he can get in comparison with those of his opponents. The administrator is hence interested in doing the best possible job in accord with prevailing professional standards and techniques. The politician will meet the same problem with the thought in mind: What approach will produce the most votes? If he wishes to stay in office he has little choice but to appeal to popular opinion. The administrator's approach will likely result in an effective solution; the politician's will only accidentally produce the same result.

The Balance between State and Local Government. What has been happening to the relative balance between the states and their subdivisions? The picture is quite clear: The states have expanded their role in society at a greater rate than have local governments.

[3] This section borrows from Dale Pontius, *State Supervision of Local Government: Its Development in Massachusetts,* Public Affairs Press, Washington, 1942; and *Report of the Committee on State-Local Relations,* Council of State Governments, Chicago, 1946, part 2.
[4] Edward W. Weidner, *Intergovernmental Relations as Seen by Public Officials,* The University of Minnesota Press, Minneapolis, 1960. But such relationships may not be smooth if the local community is dominated by Jacksonian values. See Paul N. Ylvisaker, *Intergovernmental Relations at the Grass Roots,* The University of Minnesota Press, Minneapolis, 1956.

Local governments have come to depend more and more upon the states for financial assistance, and the states have generally seemed to prefer to give this assistance through grants-in-aid or shared taxes rather than through expanding the tax base of local government. Furthermore, certain functions that were once principally the responsibility of some local unit of government have been or are being transferred to the states or are now shared by state and local governments. Thus, the states are financing (with the Federal government) most of the cost of public welfare, once exclusively a local function. Furthermore, increasing highway mileage is being turned over to the states from counties and cities, and the states are rapidly expanding their contributions to primary and secondary education, once financed entirely out of local property taxes paid to the local school district.

State expenditures totaled only 12 percent of all state-local expenditures in 1902, but by 1967 they equaled just over 55 percent; state revenues in 1902 represented 17 percent of total state-local revenues, but this figure had climbed to over 57 percent in 1967.[5]

All these figures indicate an increasing financial superiority on the part of states in relation to their local subdivisions. They show that we can expect an increasing amount of lobbying by local government officials before state legislatures and that state governments will become more and more the political battleground for the resolution of many financial problems relative to local services.

Functional Relationships, the Typical Pattern. Because city-state relations have experienced a gradual unplanned growth on a piecemeal, function-by-function basis and because there have been few systematic overhauls of municipal government in this country of the type that have taken place in England, city-state relations are for the most part uncoordinated and subject to duplications and omissions.

New Jersey, with a Division of Local Government in the state Department of Finance and Taxation, has gone the furthest toward an integrated bureau to direct state contacts with local governments. The New Jersey division has the duty of investigating on a continuous basis the programs of local government and hence has information available for the legislature that does not exist in most states. The principal action of the division has been in the fiscal area. It has power to regulate local methods of budgeting and financial procedure. It makes certain that localities provide enough funds to service their debts and can even require local levies to reduce deficits. It supervises regular audits of the cities. Annual fiscal

---

[5] U.S. Bureau of the Census, *1967 Census of Governments.*

TABLE 11-1. State Offices of Local Affairs

	New York	Pennsylvania	Rhode Island	Alaska	Tennessee	Washington	California
Name of Agency	Office of Local Government	Department of Community Affairs	Division of Local and Metropolitan Government	Local Affairs Agency	Office of Local Government	Local Affairs Division	Intergovernmental Council on Urban Growth
Year Established Where Located	1959 Executive Department	1965 Independent Administrative Department	1961 Department of Administration	1959 Office of Governor	1963 Office of Comptroller of Treasury	1963 Department of Commerce and Economic Development	1965 Governor's Office
Functions:							
Municipal management	X	X	X	X	X	X	
Finance	X	X	X	X		X	
Engineering aspects	X			X		X	
Boundary considerations				X		X	
Legal aid	X			X			
Research, statistics, information	X	X	X	X	X		X
Personnel	X	X	X	X		X	
Local planning	X	X		X		X	X
Regional planning and intermunicipal cooperation	X	X		X	X	X	X
Coordination with statewide planning		X				X	X
Proposed programs and legislation	X	X		X	X	X	X
Assists Governor in coordinating State activities affecting localities	X	X	X	X	X		X

Source: Advisory Commission on Intergovernmental Relations, January, 1966. Adapted from "Toward More Effective Government: A Proposed Department of Community Affairs," final report to Gov. Richard J. Hughes, Trenton, N.J., 1963, p. 13.

reports must be made by the cities on state-prepared forms. The Local Government Board, which sets policies for the division, may even take over control of a municipality if it falls into an "unsound financial condition," as defined by law.

Although the board has been active primarily in the field of finance, it has become a general overseer of local government to a degree. It has made investigations into conservation, public health, education, housing, planning, and metropolitan consolidation.[6]

Indiana has centralized fiscal control under the state Board of Tax Commissioners, but this agency does not act as a local government office otherwise. It has the power to review local budgets and reduce appropriations, tax levies, and bond issues. It may prohibit the issuance of bonds. The commission has a wide range of discretion under the law.

Alaska has a Department of Local Affairs. Without resorting to the use of an integrated agency for the supervision of local government, other states control some aspects of local finance. A Local Government Commission in North Carolina has wide powers in controlling local bond issues, and Iowa and New Mexico exercise more direct fiscal supervision than does the typical state.

An Office for Local Government was established in New York in 1959. The purpose of the office was to assist the governor by providing advice relative to policy affecting local governments, to act as spokesman for local governments with regard to state programs, and to provide a service to municipalities through consultation and information.[7]

Beginning in about 1957, and coincident with the rising demand for a Federal urban affairs department, state agencies for local government began to be created. These newer agencies have a great variety of powers and are organized in various ways. Quite a number are legislative agencies, designed to assist the legislature in the development of local-government legislation. Some are concerned primarily with finance. Hence, California in 1959 established a local allocation division and office of planning in the Department of Finance. This agency was oriented toward the approach earlier adopted in New Jersey. In Minnesota, the Municipal Commission, established that same year, is concerned fundamentally with the question of determining local-government boundaries in metropolitan areas in a rational and systematic manner. Some are designed principally to provide technical information and assistance to local governments and may be connected with a state university. Thus,

[6] Report of the Committee on State-Local Relations, pp. 37–38, 48–50.
[7] Office for Local Government, State of New York, Albany, N.Y., 1964.

in 1959, Maryland established a Municipal Technical Advisory Service as a part of the University of Maryland. This agency was modeled on one by the same name established a decade earlier in Tennessee. Today, much interest centers around the establishment of state planning commissions and state agencies to provide area-wide services, particularly in metropolitan areas.

Some states prescribe uniform systems of accounts for municipalities. Most states have some degree of state jurisdiction over auditing of municipal accounts. Nearly one-half of the states require municipalities to submit financial reports periodically. Many states provide budget forms for municipalities, and the state form is compulsory in many states. Nearly one-half of the states supervise municipal debt to one degree or another, often passing upon the legality of an issue before it is sold. A few states actually inquire into the "necessity" and wisdom of municipal bond issues. North Carolina and sometimes Virginia handle the sale of bonds to private investors on behalf of municipalities.[8] In most cases, however, these state activities are carried on in the time-honored decentralized manner.

A Comment on State Supervision. Two basic issues concern the relationship of the state to local administration. One is that of the use of a single state agency over local affairs versus the use of functional relationships;[9] the other centers in the question of the desirable degree of state coercive supervision over cities, whatever the method of organization. It is not likely that an integrated department of municipal affairs will soon be acceptable in American politics. Plans such as those in New Jersey, North Carolina, and Indiana appear to be reasonably successful, but they do not fit into the general trend. The overall supervision of local government by a single central department, as in France, results in a high degree of central control, not only over techniques, but over programs and policies. One of the strengths of municipal government in this country is believed to lie in the initiative and autonomy exercised by local officials, in contrast to the French municipal officer, who must get approval for even small decisions from the prefect who represents the Minister of the Interior. Overall supervision leads to uniformity, which in turn may destroy the opportunity for experimentation. It is likely that in most states, improved administrative methods have more often originated in the city hall than in the state capitol. And because of the generally slow rate of professionalization

[8]T. E. McMillan, Jr., *State Supervision of Municipal Finance,* Institute of Public Affairs, University of Texas, Austin, Tex., 1953, provides details. See also, Leonard E. Goodall, *State Regulation of Local Indebtedness,* Bureau of Government Research, Arizona State University, Tempe, 1964.
[9]See *Report of the Committee on State-Local Relations;* and Joseph E. McLean, "Threat to Responsible Rule," *National Municipal Review,* 40:411–417, September, 1951.

of state bureaucracies, state services to municipalities often tend to be mediocre in quality. Furthermore, state agencies sometimes have little interest in rendering services to local governments.

In general, technical assistance and advice, rather than supervision and control, is the ideal sought in this country by both state and local officials. Although state supervision and control are sometimes used, state dictation to local officials has been unusual, and state officials have applied sanctions only very reluctantly. In most cases, political expediency dictates this practice even when it is not called for by good administrative procedure, as it usually is. Local officials are powerful and well organized for political action and lobbying. The state agency that seeks to apply pressure thoughtlessly may find its appropriation reduced for enforcement purposes for the next year. The advancement of standards and techniques is being achieved, in any case, more through voluntary associations of local officials and professional technicians in the same field than through central tutelage of local officers.

NATIONAL ADMINISTRATIVE RELATIONS WITH CITIES

National Government Advice and Assistance to Cities. More than 100 Federal government agencies supply more than 500 services to cities in the United States. These include items as varied as the well-known cooperation between local police officers and the FBI and the thousands of technical pamphlets on every subject from adequate specifications for firemen's gas masks to techniques for estimating land values.[10]

The U.S. Civil Service Commission furnishes local personnel agencies with information on examination techniques and will furnish testing materials. The Bureau of Standards makes technical information available to cities concerning commodity specifications, a valuable service, since not many cities can operate adequate testing bureaus. The bureau will make performance tests on all kinds of material and equipment at cost. It also provides cities with model building, fire, plumbing, elevator, and other codes.

The Bureau of Mines gives technical advice on air-pollution problems. The Civil Aeronautics Administration tells city officials about the uses to which they might put airplanes or furnishes them with a model airport-zoning ordinance and may even give them a surplus Federal airport. The General Services Administration sells surplus Federal buildings to cities at "50 percent off."

---

[10] See R. H. Blundred and D. W. Hanks, *Federal Services to Cities and Towns,* American Municipal Association, Chicago, 1950, from which the following illustrations are drawn. Some of them may have since been discontinued, others added.

The U.S. Public Health Service furnishes a host of things: advice on sanitation problems; technical assistance; grants for planning and loans for constructing sewage-treatment plants to overcome water pollution; advice on organizing and staffing a municipal health department; and cash grants through the state for research on heart disease.

FBI agents not only arrest law violators who have left the state, but they testify without charge as experts on handwriting, tire treads, hairs and fibers, and shoe prints. The local police can find out from them without charge the marks made by a certain typewriter or the kind of headlight glass used in a 1955 Ford. The FBI academy trains city police officers to serve as instructors in local police academies, while the Bureau of Narcotics instructs uniformed policemen in drug identification and enforcement methods at the bureau's training school.

Many other Federal agencies cooperate with local officials from time to time, giving advice or assistance upon request. Local administrators can go to the Housing and Home Finance Agency for advice on problems of race relations in unsegregated public housing; to the Bureau of Prisons for methods of designing, building, and operating a jail; to the Bureau of Public Roads for help in making a parking survey; to the Bureau of Ships for help in learning how to fight a harbor fire; to the Fish and Wildlife Service for surplus bison and elk for the local zoo; and to the Curator of the Navy for a list showing the shipping weights and handling charges on obsolete warships for the city park. These are only a few of the total number of services available.

Federal Approval of Municipal Activities. The city, in its proprietary capacity, often acts as an ordinary corporation, and when it does so, it must get Federal approval wherever such approval would be necessary in the case of a private corporation. When Federal grants-in-aid are involved, the city must often get approval from the appropriate Federal agency for governmental functions, too. For example, if a city operates a radio station, it must get a Federal Communications Commission license; if it builds a freeway with the aid of Federal funds, it must have the proposed route approved by the Federal Bureau of Public Roads; if it builds a bridge, it must have the plans approved by the Corps of Engineers. Municipal administrators thus have frequent and varied contacts with Federal agencies.

Federal Grants-in-aid to Cities. Beginning in the early 1930s, the national government began a policy of extending aid through loans and subsidies to municipalities, either directly or through redistribution of grants made to the states. The beginning of Federal-city direct relations came with the Emergency Relief and Construction Act of

1932 in the closing days of the Hoover administration. The act permitted the newly created Reconstruction Finance Corporation (a Federal agency) to make loans to municipalities in order to finance self-liquidating projects. The act was notable in that it not only established the first Federal-city fiscal relationship but also provided the beginnings of *conditional* grants to municipalities by establishing certain standards of labor that must prevail in any project receiving a grant. The act was not a success, for it in effect required interest rates higher than the cities would accept and the conditions of repayment were overly stringent. But it was a beginning.

The New Deal provided for a host of Federal-city financial arrangements. It began by tiding over the nearly bankrupt cities and states by making grants to the states to care for the unemployed under the Federal Emergency Relief Act of 1933. The Federal government later began to deal directly with the cities through projects financed by the Civil Works Administration and the Works Progress Administration and sponsored and supervised by municipal and other local governments. It also made grants and loans to municipalities and school districts to construct athletic fields, water standpipes, hospitals, sewerage systems, and other permanent improvements through the Public Works Administration.

The Federal government began to offer grants-in-aid for highways in 1916, but streets within municipal boundaries were specifically excluded from the program. In the early days of the automobile, the problem was to build hard-surfaced highways between cities. Once these were built, the problem of bringing the streams of traffic from the city limits into the downtown area was confronted. Funds became available for municipalities, beginning in 1932, and the Federal Aid Highway Act of 1944 specifically provided that one-fourth of the aid funds were to be used for the extension of\ U.S. highways within cities.[11] All this money, however, was channeled through the state highway departments.

Legislation during the Great Depression and also under the War Mobilization and Reconversion Act of 1944 permitted cities to receive Federal aid for planning public works, such as city halls, and water and sewerage systems. In the field of low-rent housing, the United States Housing Act of 1937 authorized the making of contracts with municipal, county, or state housing authorities to supply most of the money on long-term credit for building housing projects. The act also authorized Federal contributions to these authorities as a subsidy to keep rents low. Where these authorities are county

---

[11] R. A. Gomez, *Intergovernmental Relations in Highways,* The University of Minnesota Press, Minneapolis, 1950, chaps. 1, 4, and 9.

or municipal organizations, the Federal Public Housing Authority has dealt directly with the local government unless state law prohibits it.

President Roosevelt's recommendation for a postwar Federal aid program to cities for several activities was lost in the conservative trend in politics after 1945. Most of the existing aids were continued, however, and the Federal Airport Act of 1946 provided for Federal grants to cities (directly if state law allowed) to buy sites and build airports.

The Small Business Administration, established in 1953 to replace the RFC, was authorized, among other things, to continue the RFC practice of making loans to municipalities in the event of emergencies and disaster. The Federal government also provided, in the postwar era, matching funds for hospital construction by states and municipalities. Some housing subsidies were continued. Aid for the control of communicable and venereal diseases was made available to cities via the states. Federal aid was offered for civil defense. Special aid was also provided for communities suddenly overwhelmed by an influx of new people into an area of importance to the national defense program. Another law permitted Federal surplus properties to be made available to states for distribution to municipalities in the event of major disasters, such as floods or tornadoes.

More recently, two programs have intensified Federal contact with urban areas. The Department of Housing and Urban Development has supervision over more than 100 programs aimed at improving the urban physical environment. Its first secretary, Robert C. Weaver, announced that metropolitan-wide planning would be a principal aim.[12] Grant programs would be related to this goal. Such programs include "substantive grant and loan programs deal-[ing] with urban mass transportation facilities and equipment; public works and facilities; open space acquisition and development; urban beautification; neighborhood facilities; urban renewal; sewer and water facilities; all types of housing; and relocation."[13] These programs were supplemented by a program of demonstration cities, inaugurated in 1967, which seeks to rehabilitate large areas of existing cities and particularly to serve as examples to other cities.

Also of importance in its potential impact on city life are the programs of the Department of Transportation, established in 1967. One of its major interests will necessarily be urban mass transportation and its relation to motor-vehicle transport.

The agencies concerned with the social problems of large cities

[12] Robert C. Weaver, "Creative Federalism and Metropolitan Development," *Metropolitan Viewpoint,* Graduate School of Public Affairs, State University of New York, Albany, N.Y., 1966.
[13] *Ibid.,* p. 2.

have been more controversial than those working on urban beauty and transportation.[14] The Office of Economic Opportunity was established in 1964 as a unit of the Executive Office of the President. Its program has been to fight poverty. One of its most ambitious programs was Project Head Start, begun in 1965 in 2,500 urban and rural communities. The program was to prepare children for schooling and included educational stimulation, medical checkups and treatment, and an attack on dietary problems. About one-half of the antipoverty funds were dedicated to a community-action program designed to help the poor help themselves. It included literary courses for adults, birth-control clinics, legal aid, and the Head Start project. A domestic peace corps named VISTA (Volunteers in Service to America) was also established to aid economically depressed areas.

The list of Federal supervisory controls is almost endless. However, it would be wrong to conclude that the Federal government makes all the rules in American society. The areas of Federal control are relatively few, and it is not politically expedient for Congress or Federal administrators to seek to impose many effective policy controls upon the states or their subdivisions. In fact, many—perhaps most—administrators do not even want to have coercive powers of this kind.[15] But where they exist, Federal controls are often absolutely necessary. State and local radio stations, for example, could not operate effectively without being coordinated with commercial stations. Other rules are not viewed with alarm by state and local administrators because their sense of professional standards agrees with the sense of professional standards of the Federal employees with whom they deal. They therefore see themselves as being involved in a cooperative venture to apply professional standards and do not feel coerced. This was the finding, for example, of the Michigan "Little Hoover" Commission study in 1950. Furthermore, despite the impression sometimes created, Federal administrators usually try to be reasonable in administering the law and seek to work out problems jointly rather than by fiat. Still, in the event of an unresolved difference between a Federal agency and the state or local government with which it is dealing, the Federal requirements must be met if the state or local government wishes to qualify for Federal aid.

Federal-city Relations and Urban Problems. The trend, established in the 1930s, toward closer and more direct Federal-city relations and increased financial aid to cities seems destined to continue and

[14] See Seymour Z. Mann, *Chicago's War on Poverty,* Center for Research in Urban Government, Loyola University, Chicago, May, 1966; and Norton E. Long, "Urban Poverty and Public Policy," *Business and Government Review,* University of Missouri, July–August, 1964, pp. 31–38.
[15] Weidner, *op. cit.,* chap. 4.

eventually to expand. This is so for several reasons: (1) Federal agencies have a great potential for assisting cities because they have both specialized personnel and equipment which the cities need but cannot afford, or are unwilling to afford, and often cannot get from the state; (2) legislatures have often closed their eyes to the financial problems of the cities, while the national government has met the call, at least to a degree—and if the national government has helped a few times when the states have failed, it is likely to be asked for help again; (3) the present level of taxes and the nature of the tax structure leave both the municipalities and the states in a position that will put them in financial distress in the event of even a moderate depression, and it is therefore likely that, in "bad times," cities will ask for increased Federal government assistance.

The principal continuing issues are two: (1) Is it proper or desirable for the national government to deal directly with the cities, by-passing the parent state government? (2) What can or should the national government do to improve the financial condition of cities? Concerning the former, what damage is done by direct dealing? Does the state perform a function other than to provide another desk with an "in" and "out" box? Does direct relationship encourage greater Federal control of cities? Might Washington one day seize the state's children and adopt them forcibly? If the cities refuse Federal aid, or the states refuse to permit them Federal aid (as has happened in some cases involving urban planning, housing, and airports aid), how long must the cities wait before the states provide what their leaders consider to be adequate substitute legislation?

Concerning the financial needs of cities and Federal government power, there are several questions. Since Federal instrumentalities are not taxable by the states, are present Federal payments in lieu of taxes to cities equitable? Is the Federal subsidy to cities in the form of tax exemption for income from municipal bonds a rational basis for aid? If not, what should be substituted? What tax areas should the national government stay out of and leave to the cities? What kind of grants-in-aid and what size should the national government provide for cities beyond those already provided for? How much of the fiddler's bill is the national government willing to pay while still allowing the city governments to call the tune? Shortly after President Eisenhower took office he named a Commission of Intergovernmental Relations to make a study of national-state-local interrelationships. It discussed these questions.[16] But Congress and the state legislatures will have to make policy. As a step toward an insti-

[16]United States Commission on Intergovernmental Relations, *A Report to the President,* 1955.

tutionalized approach to cooperation, Congress in 1959 established an Advisory Commission on Intergovernmental Relations.

In the 1970s, the critical question was one of whether the national government would or should move away from specific grants-in-aid with strings attached and make greater use of block grants. Such a shift would be politically feasible only if such grants were to go to the states rather than directly to cities. President Nixon proposed block grants in a 1971 message to Congress and many local officials favored the idea, but opponents argued that the states would give most of the money to smaller communities and to suburbs rather than to allow it to be spent in the deteriorated, problem-ridden centers of the core cities. The debate over Federal block grants with few if any strings attached promised to become a long and bitter controversy, especially after Congressman Wilbur Mills, chairman of the Committee on Ways and Means, announced his opposition, arguing that much of the money so granted would be wasted by state and local governments and that the Federal government should have some control over the use of funds for which it was responsible.

A Closing Note. Increasingly, the major functions of government can be performed only through the joint activity and cooperation of national, state, and local governments. It is not a question of which level is to carry on these functions but rather of how all three may effectively aid and participate. This is true in education, highways, health, welfare, housing, airports, law enforcement, and other functions. The future will see more, rather than less, cooperation among the three levels of government in the United States.

SELECTED READINGS

Anderson, William, and Edward W. Weidner (eds.): *Research in Intergovernmental Relations,* The University of Minnesota Press, Minneapolis, 1950–1960. (A series of monographs reporting on relationships in Minnesota.)

Cleaveland, Frederic N.: "Congress and Urban Problems: Legislating for Urban Areas," *Journal of Politics,* 28:289–307, May, 1966. (A preliminary report of a Brookings Institution study of Congressional response to urban problems.)

Connery, Robert H., and Richard H. Leach: *The Federal Government and Metropolitan Areas,* Harvard University Press, Cambridge, Mass., 1960. (Discusses the important issues involved in Federal-local relations.)

Council of State Governments: *Report of the Committee on State-Local Relations,* Council of State Governments, Chicago, 1946.

Elazar, Daniel J.: *American Federalism: A View from the States,* Thomas Y. Crowell Company, New York, 1966.

Goodall, Leonard E.: *State Regulation of Local Indebtedness in the United States,* Bureau of Government Research, Arizona State University, Tempe, 1964.

Grant, Daniel R.: "Federal-Municipal Relationships and Metropolitan Integration," *Public Administration Review,* vol. 14, Autumn, 1954.

Graves, W. Brooke: *Intergovernmental Relations in the United States,* Legislative Reference Service, Library of Congress, 1956. (An important source book.)

Gulick, Luther H.: *The Metropolitan Problem and American Ideas,* Alfred A. Knopf, Inc., New York, 1966. (A proposal concerning Federal-local relationships in light of American ideology.)

Hein, Clarence J.: *State Administrative Supervision of Local Government Functions in Kansas,* Governmental Research Center, University of Kansas, Lawrence, Kans., 1955.

Kaplan, Marshall, and others: *The Model Cities Program,* Praeger Publishers, New York, 1970. (A study of the first year of this federally funded program in three cities.)

Kaufman, Herbert: *Gotham in the Air Age,* The Bobbs-Merrill Company, Inc., Indianapolis, CPAC, Case no. 10, 1952. (The decision to transfer New York City aviation facilities to the Port of New York Authority.)

McMillan, T. E., Jr.: *State Supervision of Municipal Finance,* Institute of Public Affairs, University of Texas, Austin, Tex., 1953.

Marando, Vincent L.: "Inter-local Cooperation in a Metropolitan Area," *Urban Affairs Quarterly,* 4:185–200, December, 1968. (Intergovernmental cooperation discourages search for more comprehensive approaches.)

Martin, Roscoe C.: *The Cities and the Federal System,* Atherton Press, New York, 1965. (Argues for a cooperative approach to urban problems by all levels of government.)

National Institute of Municipal Law Officers: *Federal-City Relations,* National Institute of Municipal Law Officers, Washington, 1953.

Oakland Task Force: *Federal Decision-making and Impact in Urban Areas,* Praeger Publishers, New York, 1970. (Study in Oakland, Calif.; shows that Federal programs lose much of their effectiveness because of procedural and coordination problems.)

Schroth, Thomas N., and others: *Congress and the Nation,* 1945–1964, Congressional Quarterly Service, Washington, 1965, chaps. 4 and 10. (Excellent summary of Federal-local relationships in the last generation. See also 1969 supplement.)

Segal, Morley, and A. Lee Fritschler: "Emerging Patterns of Intergovernmental Relations," *Municipal Year Book,* International City Management Association, Washington, 1970.

United States Commission on Intergovernmental Relations: *A Report to the President,* 1955.

Virginia's Answers to Congressional Questions on State and Federal Authority, Virginia Commission on Constitutional Government, Richmond, 1963. (The states' rights, or competitive, view of federalism.)

F THE
ROUTINE
AND
THE
MONEY

CHAPTER
12 ADMINISTRATION

Administration is a part of the political process. The term generally applies to that process of government involved in the application of general policies to specific cases. One specialist in the field, after much effort, has produced the following summary of what administration is:[1]

> *Administration* is cooperative human action with a high degree of rationality. . . .
> The distinguishing characteristics of an administrative system, seen in the customary perspective of administrative students, are best subsumed under two concepts, organization and management, thought of as analogous to anatomy and physiology in a biological system. *Organization* is the structure of authoritative and habitual personal interrelations in an administrative system. *Management* is action intended to achieve rational cooperation in an administrative system.

DEVELOPMENTS IN ADMINISTRATION

The Growth of Administration. To have an understanding of the great size and influence of modern public management, it is necessary to compare the functions of local government today with those of, say, two generations ago. Local units spent 1,960 million dollars in 1913, most of it for schools. In 1962, they spent 44,000 million dollars.

---

[1] Dwight Waldo, *The Study of Public Administration,* Random House, Inc., New York, 1955, pp. 11–12. By permission of the publisher, Random House, Inc., New York. Copyright 1955.

Even allowing for the declining value of the dollar, expenditures increased nearly sixfold in two generations.

In 1913, local governments provided much of the education of the day through the one-room school, offering minimal programs taught by poorly trained and largely inexperienced teachers who received low pay. Roads, another major expenditure program today, were largely cared for by the local unit two generations ago. They were often unsurfaced and required little care in the preautomobile age. Most states had little to do with highways before the beginnings of the good-roads movement and the adoption of the first Federal-aid Highway Act. The mentally ill received no rehabilitative treatment in those days. They were given custodial care in ramshackle asylums run by untrained persons who received patronage appointments from the city, county, or state. Some patients were housed in the local jail. Welfare was a local function provided reluctantly and at the bare subsistence level; the states kept out of the field except for some institutional care. In general, state government was distant and had few direct contacts with the ordinary citizen. Local government was more active and spent more—about 6.6 times as much as state government—but it was a thin shadow of its present-day self as a supplier of services to the citizen. The growth in the activities of state governments has been the more spectacular, but both the state and local governments have become vitally important social institutions affecting the lives of each citizen each day. There were more than 5.61 million local employees in 1964. These people perform functions vastly more complicated and technical than those handled by the public bureaucracy of their grandparents' day.

The Historical Trend. Some of the developments in administrative organization have been noted earlier in this book.[2] We have seen that the legislatures at first dominated government at both the state and local levels. As legislative bodies and city councils declined in prestige and importance during the nineteenth century, they were replaced both by the direct democracy of the initiative and referendum and by a large number of elective administrative officials. Both of these trends contributed to the development of the long ballot.

As the number of governmental functions increased, so did the number of governmental agencies. Each new function tended to be established in a separate agency, usually in order to give it protection against the competing fiscal demands of the older, better-established functions. The interest groups which secured the adoption of new programs and policies generally preferred this

[2] See chaps. 2 and 7. This account borrows from York Willbern, "Administration in State Governments," in The American Assembly, *The Forty-eight States: Their Tasks as Policy Makers and Administrators,* Graduate School of Business, Columbia University, New York, 1955, chap. 5.

arrangement. The more populous cities were once highly departmentalized, though reorganizations resulting from the adoption of the strong-mayor, council-manager, or commission forms have generally decreased the number of separate municipal agencies.[3] The rising number of agencies resulted after a while in a problem of accountability. It became highly difficult for the chief executive, the councilman, or the citizen to know what was being done in the agencies or who was responsible for their activities.

Administrative Developments. The municipal-reorganization movement began in the 1890s and, to a degree, even earlier. It was concerned with both the eradication of corruption and the stopping of administrative sprawl. Administrative reorganization of states, counties, and other nonschool local units followed along at a much slower pace.

The Assumptions of the Reform Movement. Nearly all the reform efforts at the state and local levels have concentrated upon making administrative changes that have been based upon the following assumptions:[4]

1. Authority and responsibility should be concentrated in the chief executive officer by placing the heads of agencies under his authority and subject to his appointment, removal, and control. This was perhaps the most basic assumption and proved to be the most difficult to achieve. Groups wishing to dominate the governmental administration of their interests have feared, probably with justification, that executive unity would increase the executive's power at the expense of their own. In cities, the dominant groups were more unified than at the county or state levels, and they wanted what they considered businesslike efficiency. As a result, strong mayors and city managers generally were given wide (but rarely complete) administrative powers, but governors were not; and counties remained without a chief executive of any kind.

2. Related functions should be integrated into single departments, and the number of departments should be few enough to permit the executive to require direct accountability from the department head. Reformers complained that there were often many agencies performing functions in the same general field with little coordination, effective planning, or responsibility.

3. Boards and commissions might properly be used for advisory, but not for administrative, purposes. Boards sometimes serve as quasi-legislative or quasi-judicial bodies; that is, they act much as

---

[3] See chap. 7.
[4] Arthur E. Buck, *The Reorganization of State Governments in the United States*, Columbia University Press, New York, 1938, gives a complete statement of the orthodox view.

legislative or judicial bodies. This type of activity arose, for example, in the case of public service commissions which had to establish rates for public utilities, and were considered acceptable. In weak-mayor cities, these boards were and still are common devices for administration.

4. Budget control should be centralized under the direction of the chief executive with auditing under the legislative body. Some characteristics of the executive budget are discussed in Chapter 15. This administrative device has had widespread acceptance in principle and has had perhaps the greatest effect of any single development upon executive control over agencies. Budget staffs, in the larger cities at least, have become the general-management arm of the chief executive, not only reviewing the budget estimates of the agencies, but also aiding in coordinating their activities. Budget offices have become important agencies for administrative supervision, though they generally have only a limited amount of control over expenditures by the departments. They apportion funds over the fiscal year and exercise certain minor controls, but they are not usually in a legal or political position to claim sweeping jurisdiction over detailed expenditures. The check-and-balance tradition has been maintained through the establishment of an independent audit—independent, that is, of the executive branch.

5. The staff services of administration should be coordinated, usually through central agencies, to serve all the operating departments. This principle has received more acceptance than the others. The reason is to be found in the fact that the centralizing of house-keeping functions has been thought to be a means of saving money without the loss of policy influence by the interest groups watching over the individual agency. As a result there has been a strong trend toward the central purchasing of materials and supplies (large-volume buying brings lower prices); the operation of central warehouses, records archives, motor pools, and mailing and telephone services; and the central maintenance of buildings and grounds. Personnel recruitment has also been centralized to a considerable degree.

6. An executive cabinet should be established as a device for the coordination of governmental agencies. Cabinet members should be appointed by the chief executive, rather than elected, so that he might hold them responsible for their acts.

Forces for Separatism. Many forces are at work to discourage reorganization. Some of these include the following:

1. Agencies prefer a maximum of autonomy. A department head feels that he will lose status if his agency becomes merely one of many bureaus in a larger department. He is likely to argue, often from conviction, that his agency is unique both as to function and as to the process by which it performs its service. He may claim, with interest-group representatives shouting "Amen" in the background, that the integration of his agency with another will result in a lower level of service to its clientele groups.

2.   There is a strong tradition of separate responsibility to the electorate for many functions of government. Generally, the public prefers to elect an officer who has traditionally been elected, even when the functions of the officer are obscure. Many voters believe that direct election is more democratic than appointment by the chief executive. Political leaders like to have several elective offices on the ballot, since this enables them to develop a slate with widespread racial, ethnic, or geographic appeal.

3.   The clean-up campaigns that follow scandals often result in recommendations that encourage separatism. The usual suggestion is that the tainted function should be separated from the rest of government, given autonomous status, and "taken out of politics."

4.   Clientele and interest groups normally prefer to have the function of their special concern separated from the rest of government. This preference also encourages the use of separate or "dedicated" funds. Pilots prefer a separate airport commission to a vast parks and recreation agency or public works agency involved in a dozen different activities. Their interest groups can more easily dominate policy under the former structure, but the department head or the chief executive is more likely to do so under the latter. Citizens are often in favor of the principle of "improved administration" but opposed to specific proposals that would alter the existing pattern of operation of governmental functions in which they have interests.

5.   Professional groups prefer separate organization for the functions that they regard as being a part of their profession. These groups have "organized bodies of knowledge, generally available only to members; group standards of training and performance; codes of ethical conduct; and, particularly, close group ties and associations."[5] Under these circumstances, they believe that their goals, procedures, and knowledge can best be organized to benefit their clientele groups if their function is not commingled with others. Librarians do not want libraries to be administered by the school board; penologists do not want the local jail administered by the same agency that handles social welfare.

6.   The strings attached to Federal grants-in-aid encourage a link

[5] Willbern, op. cit., p. 116.

between Federal and state and local administrators of functions, but they discourage the association of various state and local programs into a single agency. In some cases, Federal-grant conditions require the establishment of earmarked or dedicated funds, which in turn encourages separate organization.

7. Citizens and legislators often believe that certain special programs should be placed "above politics" and hence in a separate agency. This has been true of fair-employment-practices activities, liquor control, and education, among others.

8. Legislators are reluctant to give greater power to the chief executive. They are jealous of his glamour, political power, and policy-leadership potential. Urban chief executives have been less subjected than governors to this kind of suspicion, partly because councilmen in cities where the reform movement has been influential, many of them busy businessmen, do not want to be involved in the details of administration, and partly because of the widespread use of the council-manager plan, which keeps the manager always potentially subject to control by the council, since he is not an independent agent with a direct popular mandate.

9. Americans have generally been suspicious of strong administrative leaders and have been more concerned with specific functions than with the abstract principle of efficient, well-coordinated government in general. Many people believe that mayors are not usually elected on the basis of issues and that turning full administrative power over to them is as uncomfortable as signing a blank check. Managers have always been viewed with suspicion because of their great power, though this feeling is, in most cities, confined to a minority of voters.

Separatism of agencies remains the rule in state and county government because of the diversity of interests and forces involved in the political arena. In cities, the dominant groups have generally preferred integration and, with some qualifications, have been able to achieve it through the strong-mayor and council-manager plans. Groups for separatism have seldom been strong enough to prevail.

The Arguments for Integration. Persons supporting reorganization movements have used two principal arguments to support their cause: (1) Integration will produce coordinated governmental activities; and (2) responsibility to the public will be increased. It is sometimes held that there is really not much to coordinate in government. How much coordination, it is asked, is needed between those who work in the department of streets and those who work in the department of public health? The concept of coordination, it is held, goes beyond this, however. It involves more than the bringing about of cooperation between, say, the psychiatric social workers in the public welfare department and the psychiatric social workers in the juvenile section of the probate court. Coordination also makes possible the economies of joint housekeeping activities and of the balancing off, in the executive budget, of the relative priorities of various functions of government. The chief executive is the only feasible person available to perform the role of coordinator.

The argument on responsibility is based upon the assumption that there should be but a single legitimate source of authority, the chief executive, and that his lieutenants should receive their authority from him. If this is the case, authority and accountability are equal to one another. Authority cannot be exercised, in the words of the Hoover Commission, unless there is a "clear line of command from the top to the bottom and a return line of responsibility and accountability from the bottom to the top."[6]

Government, its services, and its many clientele groups are all too complicated for a simple, single line of responsibility, of course. Most of those who would reorganize government recognize this, but they argue that "a general responsibility to the general public interest may be better achieved through the main line of political responsibility . . . than through the limited, specific, hidden responsibilities involved in some of the other relationships." Government, it is held, becomes more visible, and hence more subject to public scrutiny, if there is a single chief executive to be held accountable.

The Middle Ground. Once again, things are never completely black or completely white in politics. Total integration is probably never possible, and not even the most enthusiastic reorganizer could argue that separatism is the equivalent of anarchy. As York Willbern has said:[7]

> Separatism and integration are not opposites without middle ground. Neither is ever absolute. Even with an agency that appears completely independent, the [chief executive] may have much influence simply because he has produced a majority of the popular votes, has influence with the legislature, and has public prestige and constitutional responsibilities. And even in an agency over which the [chief executive] appears to have complete control, the influence of a special clientele, of the group connections and thought habits of employees, of interested [councilmen], and of intergovernmental relationships all will be of incalculable importance. Agencies will be grouped all along the spectrum from nearly complete independence to nearly complete subordination to central political control.

[6] Quoted in Willbern, *op. cit.*, p. 120.
[7] *Ibid.*, p. 121. Willbern was discussing state government, but the comment applies equally to municipalities.

The precise details of agency organization differ according to such things as historical accident, the wants and needs of the clientele of a particular agency, the desires of interest groups, and the personal idiosyncrasies of transient administrators, chief executives, and legislators. Because differing points of view are often held by various interested parties, questions as to whether an agency will be headed by a board or by a single administrator, the manner in which board appointments, if any, are to be made, who is to be represented on the board, the internal structure of the agency, and other such considerations are a matter not so much of deliberate planning as of negotiation among the interested parties.[8] The politics of the organization of an agency, in other words, follows the same pattern as that by which the policies of the agency are determined.

ADMINISTRATION AND CULTURE

Administration cannot be wholly scientific or neutral. It must be related to the values of the culture in which it exists. The manner in which a social-welfare, police, or educational system is administered will depend upon cultural values of the contemporary society. There is no "one best way" to care for people on welfare, for example. The level of assistance they get, whether the needs of children or of old people are emphasized, the amount of outside income that is permitted by overlooking the precise requirements of the law, the amount of training which social workers are expected to have, the philosophy of social workers toward society, government, and, in particular, toward those at the lower end of the social scale—all these things will be conditioned by the culture in which the program exists.
The Administrative Process. Administration is a part of the political process, not an activity fundamentally different from it. The determination of policy in the legislative body will at the same time inevitably involve questions of the means of carrying out policy. Similarly, the execution of policy always involves modification of the policy and its selective application to actual circumstances as they arise.

It should not be assumed that the degree of specialization of equipment, training of personnel, or types of organizational structure employed in a governmental unit are irrelevant. They are important variables in determining the level and cost of services, no doubt, but the kinds of equipment used, the training expected of personnel, the organizational structure, and the level of service itself that

[8] On this point, see Robert A. Dahl and Charles E. Lindblom, *Politics, Economics and Welfare*, Harper & Row, Publishers, Incorporated, New York, 1953.

exists in connection with a given governmental function are a result of a balancing off of public attitudes, the values of those who are involved in the decision making within the legislature, the city council, and the administrative organization, and the expectations and goals of interested pressure groups. It will probably never be possible to eliminate these political considerations and to replace them with objective criteria as to how an agency should be organized and operated.

Efficiency as a Point of View. There is no one best way to administer a program or a governmental unit. This is so because the best way to one individual may be the worst way to another. It is a matter of a point of view. For example, a management consultant might be asked to inspect a city health department and make recommendations as to its proper administrative structure and processes. Because, in private business, he is expected to look for ways of reducing costs and strengthening the hand of management, he may see a "one best way" to organize the agency. But his recommendations, if adopted, might not only upset established lines of communication and operation—thus threatening to damage the *esprit de corps* of the agency—they might also threaten to weaken the influence that an important interest group (in this case, the state or local medical society) might have over the agency. This threat would certainly result in damage-control operations on the part of the interest group. It would take its case to the council or the legislature.

Who would be right in this case—the management consultant or the medical society? Who can say? If the medical society refuses to cooperate with the agency, its whole program may founder. The medical society might claim that the proposal would discourage young men from going into the medical profession. The society might be right or it might be wrong in making the claim. It might be sincere in advancing the claim, or it might simply be seeking to retain its traditional monopolistic control over medical practice and programs. Suppose that it is right and does really mean what it says. Are the few dollars that the management consultant would save for the reorganized agency—assuming that he is right in saying that his proposal would save money—worth more to society than the social cost of a decreased supply of medical manpower?

There might well be other potential effects of the proposal by the management consultant, too. For dozens of reasons that cannot be examined in detail here, the proposal, if adopted, might have the ultimate effect of reducing the scope or effectiveness of the end program of the agency, the actual services it provides for society and its members, individually and collectively. Thus, what is said to be saving money may really be a downgrading of the program, either as an intended or as an unanticipated result. The latter may come about because of changes in training requirements or pay levels or prospects for advancement or other factors involving recruiting potential and employee morale.

This example should not be taken to mean that the concept of efficiency is meaningless or that a review of administrative structure and practice could not result in improvements. To use an exaggerated illustration, it might be found that a health department is using physicians in laboratory work that could readily be done by technicians. It is doubtful if many undesirable results would follow a reclassification of such positions. Yet one could not say this for certain without an extensive examination of the whole environment in which the circumstance is found.

ORGANIZATION

Municipal-government agencies may be organized in a great variety of ways. Some of them are headed by an elective officer. Some have a single administrator appointed by, and responsible to, the chief executive. In other cases, the administrator may be chosen by the chief executive but may be removable only by a complicated process involving perhaps the civil service commission or the courts. In a fourth category are the agencies headed by boards or commissions. (The two terms mean the same.) Board members are usually appointed for long, staggered terms, and the chief executive may find members to be irremovable for practical purposes. When a board controls, an agency may be administered in a variety of ways. The chairman of the board may also serve as the chief administrator of the agency; the board may choose an executive secretary or a director, with its own powers reserved in law or practice to board policy making; the commission may be advisory only, with the chief executive appointing the administrative head; but the most common arrangement has been for the board to divide up its work among its members, each exercising considerable autonomy. Each of these structures of the boards is likely to produce a different pattern of administration.

The Administrative Code of the City. The administrative organization of cities in the past was established in state law. Changes could be made only by the legislature. Functions assigned to a particular department could not be changed to another department by order of the mayor or council, no matter how much of an improvement in municipal services might result from the proposed change. This is still the case in some states. Even in home rule cities, administrative structure can often be changed only by the local charter-amending procedures.

Modern charters, however, do not attempt to establish a rigid departmental structure but rather authorize the council to adopt an *administrative code* for the city establishing a plan of organization. The council is then able to rearrange departments, bureaus, and lesser agencies as changing requirements dictate. This practice is not yet the rule, however. Often city officials must go to the state legislature with a request for authority to transfer garbage collection, for example, from the public health department to the public works department. Even in home rule cities, the public is often expected to decide by referendum such things as whether there should be a separate department of traffic engineering or whether central purchasing should be consolidated with the controller's office. Some specialists believe that many decisions on administrative organization might well be left to the chief executive himself, without even councilmanic action being required.

A complete administrative code or manual is useful in all except perhaps small cities not only to describe basic structure, but for another reason: It explains the responsibilities and authority of the various departments and their principal officers. The need for this is illustrated in an example cited in the Stone, Price, and Stone study.[9] Some years ago in Austin, Texas:

> There was a complete lack of agreement between the manager and several department heads about the responsibilities of each. The manager assumed, and it was clear in his own mind, that one department was composed of the water, the electric, and the sewage divisions, but the superintendent of one of these divisions had no such idea. He reported directly to the manager instead of to the supposed head of the department, whom he did not recognize as his superior. The manager and the division head never got together to reach a common understanding. Similarly, the health officer in Austin had the notion that he should report directly to the council, which appointed him, rather than to the manager. On the other hand, the manager believed that it was his job to supervise the health officer. No written record of the council's desire was available to the manager and the health officer for guidance.

Clearly such a situation does not aid in the development of effective organization. But confusion as to administrative responsibility is quite a common thing in cities, and Stone, Price, and Stone found that many managers did not seem to know what an administrative code was or how it operated. They found that, in one city, officials paid no attention to the code and "most of them were unaware of

[9] Harold A. Stone, Don K. Price, and Katherine H. Stone, *City Manager Government in the United States,* Public Administration Service, Chicago, 1940, p. 84. By permission of the Public Administration Service.

its existence."[10] As municipal management becomes more professionalized, however, the flexible and complete administrative code becomes more important.

The Choice of Organization: A Problem. It is not only difficult to determine the best organizational structure, it is equally a problem to determine the allocation of functions within agencies or the best place to assign new functions. For example, in the 1970s, many local officials became interested in the establishment of programs dealing with the problems of the poor. These programs cut across traditional department lines, since they deal with housing, welfare, health, employment, and many other things. How should the program be established in order to minimize conflict with existing programs and organizational patterns? What organizational pattern would best fit the needs of the aged and be most acceptable to their interest groups? The answer is not easy to find, but there is a strong tendency to establish new programs as separate organizations. This usually best suits the interests involved and seems to give the new program its best chance for survival.

Single Agency Head. As compared with other types of organization, in that where an individual serves as head of an agency and is appointed by the chief executive, the agency programs are likely to be more diversified, more related to the overall balance of needs in the annual budget, less able to avoid cuts during an economy drive, more involved in the decisions that are important to the political future of the mayor or councilmen, less dominated by one interest group, and more easily shaken out of bureaucratic lethargy by a chief executive who is necessarily concerned with public reactions to governmental programs.

Independent Head. When the head of an agency is independent of the chief executive because he is elected to office, because he cannot easily be removed, or because he is a civil servant, the agency is likely to develop a strong in-group sense against the rest of the government, professional standards are likely to be the criteria used as an important measuring stick in making decisions, and bureaucratic inertia, if it becomes very great, cannot easily be overcome because of the difficulty of exerting pressure from outside. The agency becomes largely insulated from ordinary controls, although it will usually have to seek to maintain good relations with the legislative body unless it can find some means of obtaining an independent budget. Agencies with independent heads often include parks, police,

[10] *Ibid.*, p. 85.

social-welfare, or public health departments, although other examples also exist.

Boards and Commissions. The use of boards and commissions became widespread after the Civil War. This marked a transition from control of departments by council committees to control by the chief executive—a transition more nearly completed in cities than in state or local units of government. It also reflected a desire to take government "out of politics." Boards were either bipartisan or, later, nonpartisan in structure, members were usually appointed for long and overlapping terms, and their removal from office was normally extremely difficult.

Librarians, educators, and other professional people strongly favor independent boards over their departments. Powerful and vociferous pressure groups often wish to take functions under their wings and protect them as infants that should not be exposed to the rigorous and competitive circumstances of the ordinary governmental agency. An attempt to make the agency autonomous almost always exists in the case of functions involving special-interest groups or special-clientele groups. Other instances of this sort of thing may be found in connection with the functions of public health, public transportation, airports, parks and recreation, art galleries, and museums.

Boards and commissions seem quite inappropriate for the direct administration of any agency, and the tendency to organize in this fashion is declining. On the other hand, a board chairman, if he possesses administrative skill, can sometimes serve adequately as the agency head. It is not uncommon in agencies which have boards as policy-making bodies for most of the policies ultimately adopted to be generated within the bureaucracy of the agency and to be "sold" to the commission by the administrative head. In some cases, as in public health, the board views its principal job as being that of preserving orthodoxy and preventing the administrative head, who may be a layman, from doing something the profession would not approve of.

Many boards and commissions are established by law in such a way as to require interest-group representation upon them. In other cases, it is a firmly established custom for certain groups to be included in the membership. The idea of group representation seems antithetical to the traditional American skepticism about "the interests" and "special privilege," but it is very much in harmony with the concept of a pluralistic society that is a basic part of our culture and one which is accepted by most Americans.[11]

[11] See Alfred de Grazia, *Public and Republic,* Alfred A. Knopf, Inc., New York, 1951.

An Evaluation of Boards. Millions of man-hours are probably spent in the United States each year by unpaid citizens serving on advisory and policy-controlling boards at the state and local levels of government. What do they accomplish? These were the findings of a study in Pennsylvania:[12]

1. Boards "study complex problems to which the elected body cannot devote enough time."
2. They insulate the legislative body and executive from certain types of political pressures. Since the members are (usually) nonelective, they can more easily do things that are thought necessary and desirable but which, in the short run at least, might be politically unpopular.
3. They do not "take politics out of important areas" of government.
4. The effectiveness of the boards depends upon the quality of the members "and not upon the advisory commission device itself."
5. They provide, especially at the local level, a great amount of staff work which, if paid for, would be very expensive. They, in other words, serve to socialize some of the cost of government.
6. Members perceive their jobs rather narrowly, tending to avoid performing a function about which they are in doubt. That is, they do not engage in "empire building."
7. Members often feel that they are not consulted frequently enough, that their advice is too freely ignored, and that they are not informed of the disposition made of their recommendations.
8. For things requiring decisive action and, outside of the work done by boards of adjustment, civil service commissions, and planning commissions, the professional administrative staff of a department works more "efficiently" than can boards.
9. "Citizens boards and commissions can still offer effective and useful aid to officials and the community."

The larger a city is, the more likely it is to use boards and commissions.[13] This is probably also generally true of other local units. In weak-mayor cities, they are especially likely to have formal policy-making powers that exceed mere advisory status.

The reason for the existence of advisory boards in the structure of the more populous units of government stems from the old problem of citizens having less opportunity to know their officials personally when population density is high. There is, at the same time, less opportunity to participate directly in policy making. The citizens group serves in lieu of the direct consultation between officeholder and constituent that is typical in the small suburb or the rural town-

[12] *Horizons*, 5:1, April, 1958.
[13] R. B. Richert, "How Michigan Cities Make Use of Lay Citizens in Government," *Michigan Municipal Review*, 26:33ff., February, 1953.

ship. It provides a measuring stick by which public reactions to programs can be gotten and a more gentle stick it is than the one that may otherwise rap the politician's knuckles at the next election. A cross section of ideas and of opinion can be furnished to those whose political life depends upon a proper assessment of community attitudes.

Boards and commissions are extremely useful to the chief executive, whether he is an elective mayor or appointed manager. For one thing, boards allow groups that are interested in a function to give positive advice to the administration through their appointed members. They might otherwise carp from the sidelines or complain at public hearings. For another, the use of boards involves a number of citizens in such a manner as to give them a stake in the success of an administration. This is a device that helps develop support for other programs of the chief executive in addition to the one in which the citizen is active as a member of a board. It also provides a built-in shock absorber so that the chief executive is protected from the full force of criticism against policy in a particular field. The chief executive can point out that, after all, "it was developed by the citizens on the committee," even though it may really have been a product of the fertile minds of the municipal bureaucracy and the advisory commission may merely have given its stamp of approval. And, of course, unpaid boards provide a socially acceptable form of patronage which adds to the number of persons who become obligated to defend the administration—a situation useful to the mayor if he becomes a candidate for reelection, or to the manager if he should run into difficulties with his council.

THE CHIEF EXECUTIVE

The chief executive is important in the administrative process, not alone because he may have the power to hire and fire department heads, but also because he is the coordinator of a variety of different programs and interests, the principal architect of policy, and the liaison between the agencies that provide services and the clientele groups that receive them. His role is so crucial that a portion of Chapter 8 is devoted to it.

The Chief Executive's Personal Staff. In addition to major advisers, such as the budget officer, the city attorney (if appointed by the chief executive), and the planning director, and such advisory commissions as may exist, the chief executive usually, except in small cities, chooses a staff of personal advisers and assistants. These may include an administrative assistant or two, or sometimes, especially in manager cities, an intern trainee just graduated from a university training program. In larger cities, the chief executive may have a personal, confidential secretary and a number of stenographers and office assistants.

The staff of the chief executive has the task of helping him keep abreast of the functions for which he is responsible. Needless to say, these persons must have his complete confidence, for they are often more closely associated with his success or failure in office than are his department heads.

THE DEPARTMENT HEAD

Beneath the chief executive but above middle management and the clerical and minor employees is the principal administrator—the agency head or head of a large division. He plays a vital role in policy formulation because he is likely to know his particular governmental activity better than the chief executive and the councilmen do. If he does not, he has easy access to those who do. He advises the chief executive, who wants ideas on a program; he testifies before the legislative body or its committees, telling them what he wants them to know and often demonstrating great skill at withholding information unfavorable to his point of view.

The Agency Head as a Symbol. The agency head, like the chief executive and members of the legislative body, spends a great deal of time in symbolic activities. While matters requiring his decision pile up on his desk, he trudges from one meeting to another, often spending an afternoon in the mayor's or manager's office, or in an interdepartmental meeting, or as an ex officio member of some board, or at a convention of a professional group with which his agency has important relations, making a comment here and there or perhaps a platitudinous speech of welcome. In this way his activities follow much the same pattern as do those of principal executives in large corporations.

From a rational or "efficiency" point of view, this activity may seem enormously wasteful. Yet it is most important, for at the top level, the administrator (often he has worked his way up and knows the tasks of the lesser positions within his agency) leaves to trusted aides much of the actual work that goes out over his signature. He spends most of his own time in molding the agency members into an effective working unit; reassuring them of their importance by expressing their values in public speeches and by awarding a pin to the clerk-steno who has just completed thirty years of service; and in seeking to maintain smooth relationships between the agency and its clientele groups, its interest-group support, the chief executive, the council, the state legislature, and potential friends and enemies of all kinds.

His principal job is to understand and to communicate to others the values, loyalties, and goals of his organization.

In the process of seeking to placate their various publics, the personnel in the various departments often come into conflict with one another. They compete over budgetary matters and in seeking status in the community. Some department heads feud publicly with other department heads—with resultant damage to all government, since the citizen is likely to believe the worst that each official says about other officials.

Because the status and even the survival of a government agency may depend upon the way it is perceived by the public, large local agencies maintain their own public relations staffs. Often these may not be large—the council will generally see to that—but they are important.

ADMINISTRATION AND THE PUBLIC

Public Relations in City Government. Much of the activity of everyday administration goes along with little or no notice taken of it by the average citizen. His knowledge of the services that are available to him, or of the nature of bureaucrats or of the administrative process, is likely to be very skimpy indeed. But the average citizen does not automatically come by an understanding of these things. He must be told what his government is doing, and why.

It has already been noted that the political process involves not just one monolithic "public" but a series of publics, each demanding satisfactions. Citizens are rarely unanimous in their attitudes toward public matters. If they were, government officials would have few problems in public relations. Given the nature of the political process as involving the interaction of conflicting groups, public relations must normally be directed toward one or more of the interested groups in the community. Groups may be interested in municipal government because of their physical location within the community, their businesses, their tax bills, their income, their (high or low) status positions within the community, or for other reasons. Each individual belongs to several publics and can become displeased with city government in connection with any one of them. He can also be informed about the activities of his city by being reached as a member of any one of these publics.

Municipal departments often have peculiar publics of their own, and each of them must therefore be conscious of the importance of public relations. Departments dealing with particular professional or clientele groups are especially likely to have uniquely identifiable publics. The welfare department, for example, must please (1) welfare recipients; (2) the high-status members of the community who take an interest in welfare as an avocation; (3) taxpayers who pay the bills; (4) editors, who may want to take the occasional welfare cheat and make a headline case out of him; (5) grocers and other businessmen who have welfare recipients as customers; (6) professional social workers, who may want the department to be established as an autonomous agency; (7) ordinary citizens, who are likely to believe that people on public relief are lazy, shiftless, and of a category akin to the criminal. The manager of the local airport must cope with publics that include passengers, pilots, airline officials, and people who live near airports or proposed airports; the health department must reach an understanding with the medical profession, with the Parent-Teachers Association and other pressure groups interested in the schools, with social reformers who want expanded public health services; and so on.

Gauging Public Attitudes. The public official who would keep his publics informed through an active public relations program must first of all be acquainted with the attitudes existing in the community. This is no easy task to accomplish.

How can the public official go about gauging attitudes? He may employ one of the so-called public opinion polling organizations or alternatively establish a polling unit within, say, the city complaint department. But public opinion polling is quite a technical task and therefore requires specially trained personnel. It is also too expensive for most cities to finance. It is time-consuming, and the information is therefore often not available when it is needed. Perhaps most difficult of all, poll results that are unfavorable serve as ammunition for opponents of the administration, and this discourages their use.

The official is therefore likely to turn to older methods of measurement, most of which are of doubtful reliability. All persons in the political arena, for example, engage in *informal polling* by noting the views expressed by visitors and letter writers. But these views may be highly unrepresentative and are of uncertain value at all times. *Advisory bodies* are often used as a means of measuring the attitudes and the intensity of attitudes of the important pressure group interested in a particular activity. *Letters, petitions,* and *resolutions* from groups are expressions of group attitudes and are useful as such. Usually they express protests rather than offer positive suggestions such as advisory bodies often make. *Elections,* of course, may serve as a final public opinion poll by which to measure important controversies. Municipal election campaigns, in the usual theoretical model, should be conducted primarily over important policy issues, but this is not often the case. Candidates usually prefer to deal in glittering generalities and indulge in name calling and other propaganda techniques rather than to take a stand on specific issues which may lose votes, and the citizen has not usually strongly objected to this practice.

Contacts with Citizens. Every public official has an obligation to inform the public of what government is doing, what it has done, and what it plans to do. Groundwork for future plans must be especially well laid if a city is to approach its problems on the basis of long-range planning. Many voters want to know what services are available from each agency of government, what it is costing, and why it is costing what it is. On the other hand, most Americans would say that no official has a moral right to use taxpayer money in a public relations program that is simply a defense of incumbent officeholders, although this is sometimes done.

Public employees who daily meet the ordinary citizen in the course of their work are probably the most important persons in helping to determine whether a public relations program is to be successful. Many public works employees are in a position to make city government either popular or unpopular. Refuse collectors, for example, meet the public daily. If they are efficient in their work and courteous in receiving complaints or informing citizens of ordinance violations, they can create much good will. So can public works foremen in replying to "sidewalk superintendents" who want to know what is being done, why, and what the cost will be.

Policemen are perhaps the most important public relations men the city government has. Their uniform makes them conspicuous. Policemen are indoctrinated in the rules of courtesy and taught while in recruit training to be living city directories, for their responses to requests for information become in effect measurements of the efficiency of the force so far as the typical citizen is concerned. And, of course, one police officer seen in uniform in a bar or caught in some wrongdoing does untold harm. He may represent a tiny fraction of 1 percent of the force, but he can do more damage than can be repaired by a dozen elaborate annual reports.

Firemen have some special advantages in public relations. Fire fighting is dramatic and a public relations activity in itself. Firemen also gain good will by rescuing rat terriers from culverts and young boys from trees, and by making and repairing toys in their spare time for distribution to needy children at Christmas time. On the other hand, they must overcome the popular notion that firemen chop down doors, smash windows, and spill chemicals on the living-room rug with malicious glee. Fire fighting is a good example of the value in public relations of dramatic activities. Americans are quite generous in permitting the purchase of expensive fire equipment, although they are not very much interested in fire prevention, which would make the equipment less necessary. Lectures on fire prevention are normally not dramatic.

Departments vary a good deal in the nature of their public relations problems. Some of them must work hard to satisfy their clientele, but they do not often attract general public attention (e.g., recreation); some of them are vital but work largely in a manner that seldom attracts general public notice (e.g., public health); some perform functions that are generally approved of, but are potential public relations dynamite (e.g., urban renewal); some of them are constantly under public surveillance (especially police and public works). All of them have a good deal to do with the status position of public employees in the community and the general repute of local government.

The Complaint Officer. As American cities have developed, the citizenry has grown more distant from its officialdom in terms of access, and the professional bureaucracy has become both more powerful and the more common point of contact between the citizen and his government, demands for some sort of complaint machinery have increased. In the early 1950s, a number of large cities established bureaus designed to hear out the citizen who felt aggrieved and to remedy any situation considered to be unfair or contrary to law. These offices were most commonly established as a part of the office of mayor, for the chief executive has traditionally had a special responsibility to protect the citizen from miscarriages of justice. The mayor, like the medieval king, has seen his job as one of providing for a proceeding in equity.

More recently, interest has centered on the establishment of an officer who would be independent, not only of the chief executive, but also of the bureaucracy and the council, one who would represent the ordinary citizen who feels not merely aggrieved but also helpless in the face of the organized power of government. This officer, whose task is similar to the public defender in relation to judicial matters and the inspector general in the military, is an American adaptation of the *ombudsman,* an officer found in Scandinavia and some other countries. The Swedish constitution of 1809 established the office of *Justitieombudsman,* a position that still exists. Literally, it means officer of justice or, perhaps by implication, of equity. It has spread to many other countries and seeks to cope with the problem of the feeling of helplessness found in ordinary citizens as they confront the impersonal, formalized procedures of bureaucratic government.[14]

[14] Walter Gellhorn, *When Americans Complain,* Harvard University Press, Cambridge, Mass., 1966; and, by the same author and publisher, *Ombudsmen and Others* (1966), which describes grievance machinery in other nations.

City Officials and the Newspapers. Nothing is more important to the reputation that city government enjoys in the community than the relationship city officials have with the local newspapers. These publications, reflecting the varied views of their editors and publishers, take many different attitudes toward local governments. Many of them are responsible in their criticism. Others believe that criticism of any sort is good for circulation building. Some of them encourage the continued existence of popular superstitions, prejudices, and misconceptions concerning the nature of government. Some of them are ably edited; others are headed by men who run the newspaper as a profitable business, but who have no discernible social, economic, or administrative concerns.

The department head may find the reporter or editor informed, responsible, and intelligent, in which case their relationship is likely to be happy and easy. On the other hand, he may consider the reporter or editor to be uninformed or stupid. But, whether responsible or not, the newspaperman controls the most important medium of communication in the city. Newspapers are normally of special influence in the formulation of *local* attitudes, as distinguished from attitudes on national or international matters.

Of course, the problem may be that the newspapers are represented by able men seeking to keep the public informed, but the councilman or department head has developed a confused notion of what the press is entitled to know. Arthur W. Bromage has pointed out to public officials that:[15]

> The only attitude appropriate to press and radio relations is one of open frankness. When a newspaper or radio representative calls, there is no use pretending that you don't know something which you actually know. If you do not wish to be quoted, you can always say so. One must keep constantly in mind that public office is not private business. The press and radio operate to convey news, and you are a source of local news.

Public Reports. Outside of direct contacts between public officials and employees and the citizen, and information distributed through the press, local governments inform their publics in a variety of ways: through the use of annual reports, leaflets, radio and television programs, movies, "open house" days, and talks before clubs and groups. Cities have long been required to issue some sort of annual statement of finances for public consumption. Out of this background, some cities have come to issue general annual municipal reports

---

[15] Arthur W. Bromage, *On the City Council,* George Wahr Publishing Company, Ann Arbor, Mich., 1950, p. 73. This section has borrowed from E. D. Woolpert, *Municipal Public Relations,* Public Administration Service, Chicago, 1940.

aimed at the citizens of the community. Often these are in traditional form—dull, formal, and understandable only to persons having some knowledge of accounting. Other cities have produced clever abbreviated annual reports, with dramatic graphs, pictures, cartoons, and other eye-catching devices that still manage to convey a great deal of information.

An increasing number of cities have adopted the practice of preparing leaflets in lieu of the more expensive report. Radio and television are used by some communities. A few have brought these media into the council chamber, but most meetings are so routine in nature that it is doubtful if they appeal to many listeners and viewers, except on very special occasions. A handful of cities have produced movies to be shown to various groups about town, and other techniques have been resorted to, both by mayors anxious to defend their actions prior to an election, and by managers who want continued public support for their budget requests.

In a day of intensely competitive commercial advertising, city governments have difficulty in competing. The public has been conditioned to expect representatives of all institutions to come to the individual and explain in a clear, firm voice and simple style the wares they have to sell. Many city administrations scarcely try; those that do, find the task a challenging one.

PERSONNEL SYSTEMS

Issues of policy abound in the area of municipal employee-employer relations. Many of these are submitted from time to time directly to the voters of the city. Some of them become campaign issues. All of them relate to the effectiveness of city government.

Should public employees be allowed to join regular trade unions? Should they be allowed to join any kind of union at all? Should public employees have a right to strike? What sort of job security should they have? Are public employees' salaries adequate, or are they too high? These are some of the questions that the citizen may be expected to know something about.

MODERN PERSONNEL PRACTICES

It seems likely that most urban citizens do not realize the degree of professionalization that has taken place in the municipal civil service in recent decades. Over 2 million people are employed in local government service in the United States (not counting school employees). Most of them are employed by municipalities, and most of them are performing specialized jobs that require training of one degree or another. While the number of Federal employees has had a general downward trend since 1945, municipalities continue to expand their services, the total number of employees, and the total size of the payroll.

A great many people still believe, as they believed in the mid-1930s, according to a survey, and as Andrew Jackson believed well over a century ago, that government jobs are so "simple that men of intelligence may readily qualify themselves for their performance."[16] Of course, a moment's reflection leads to the conclusion that this is no longer the case. Government now performs a great many, rather than a few, functions. In the last century or so, the performance of most of man's activities has become specialized and mechanized. Governmental activities are no exception. Since the turn of the century, government employment has become increasingly specialized and increasingly performed by professionally trained personnel with professional attitudes toward their work.

The public, although it still has reservations about the worth of employment by government, seems to be giving ground in recognition of the changing role of government in our society. The prestige value of public jobs has increased markedly since before the Great Depression, and this is especially true among working-class, lesser-educated persons, that is, among the persons most benefiting from the availability of governmental services and from the increased security that they provide.[17]

Civil Service and the Merit System. The term *civil service* refers to civilian employees of government. In practice it is often used interchangeably with *merit system.* The latter properly refers to a method of choosing government employees on the basis of examinations demonstrating the technical or professional competence of the applicant. The beginnings of a municipal service based upon the merit principle appeared in 1884, but, as in the case of the states, the principle did not become widely accepted until the 1930s. The national government, through its insistence upon professional competence of administrators for some programs receiving Federal grants-in-aid, prodded many cities and states along in this direction.

The Civil Service Commission. The acts establishing civil service merit systems in 1883 (Federal) and 1884 (New York and Massachusetts) established a semi-independent civil service commission and began a pattern that is still typical in cities as well as higher

---

[16] See Commission of Inquiry on Public Service Personnel, *Better Government Personnel,* McGraw-Hill Book Company, New York, 1935; and Andrew Jackson's first message to Congress (1829).
[17] See Morris Janowitz and Deil Wright, "The Prestige of Public Employment: 1929 and 1954," *Public Administration Review,* 16:15–21, Winter, 1954.

units of government. It is common to have a three-member civil service commission appointed (usually by the mayor) for overlapping terms, not more than two of the members being of the same political party. An executive secretary is normally hired to handle the actual administration of its activities.

The commission makes rules respecting examinations, classifies positions, conducts examinations, and keeps a list of eligible appointees.[18] It establishes uniform wages, hours, and conditions of labor (so that two clerks doing about the same job, but in different departments, will receive the same pay). It makes rules on transfers and promotions. It may, especially in large cities, conduct training programs. It certifies the payrolls so as to discourage payroll padding. It may have other functions, too.

The Personnel Director. In recent years, students of public administration have often criticized the use of the civil service commission to head personnel recruitment. It is argued that the commission competes with the mayor or manager for control over city employees. The resultant conflict is considered harmful to administration and to morale. It is argued further that personnel control is inherently a function of management and hence should be handled as a part of the chief executive's office—as it is in patronage systems.

The commission system was preferred in the early days of civil service reform because the administrative branch of government was corrupt and was opposed to the merit principle. Today, however, a chief executive who wants to run a smooth, effective administration desires competent personnel. He dare not resort to spoilsmanship; if he tried to do so, he would in any case be detected immediately.

A trend exists, therefore, toward the establishment of a personnel department under a single head, the personnel director who is responsible to the mayor or manager. Personnel then becomes an executive function and responsibility. (Many cities use an *advisory* civil service commission or have the commission make policy, but with all administration of policy left to the personnel director.) This form of organization has been used most often in manager cities, where it began. It is more easily accepted in such cities because the manager is himself a professional careerist.[19]

The old-fashioned, independent civil service commission, usually consisting of three members selected on a bipartisan or nonpartisan basis, has been much criticized. It has encouraged hostility between the personnel agency and the chief executive. Its very existence has implied that the chief executive was standing by, ready to return

---

[18] See Thomas H. Reed, *Municipal Management,* McGraw-Hill Book Company, New York, 1941, chap. 12.
[19] See Reed, *op. cit.,* pp. 253–256; and the *Model City Charter* of the National Municipal League.

city employment to a patronage status at the first opportunity. Sometimes the commissions have actually been less anxious than the chief executive to establish a true merit principle of employment. Some commissions have sought to administer their policies themselves but have been lacking in the technical qualifications that a personnel director would possess. Others, as independent agencies, have been unable to get funds in order to hire a technical staff capable of preparing and administering valid and reliable examinations—and neither the council nor the chief executive has had much incentive to go to bat for the independent commission at budget hearings.

Today many specialists believe that personnel administration needs to be a part of management, as it invariably is in private enterprise. Under the leadership of a director whose professional interest is in the improvement of personnel and the methods of selecting personnel, the chief executive is given one of his most effective tools for a successful administrative record.

The Merit System and the Culture. Many artificial safeguards have been established in the past in attempts to require use of the merit system. These have included the independent commission, elaborate rules concerning tenure and dismissal, detailed examinations, complex position-classification systems, and the like. All are inadequate protection, and many devices exist for evasion of the merit principle if that is the officeholder's desire. Yet, the professional career approach to personnel administration does work in many communities because it has become a part of the political-cultural pattern. And in England, where there are no formal safeguards at all against making every appointment a political one, the system works very well indeed. The voters would not allow it to be otherwise.

The spirit, rather than the letter, of the merit system is the important thing. Many small and middle-sized municipalities cannot afford to employ professional personnel directors and staffs. The mayor, manager, clerk, or some other official may act as personnel officer. Yet in many cities that have no organized merit system, there are no spoils, and existing policy is to get the best available man for the job. The personnel methods used in any city, incidentally, are not likely to be more modern in character than are those used in private enterprise in that community, and the major personnel problem in municipal government today is likely to be not spoils but low pay, particularly in smaller communities.

Position Classification. In the establishment of a merit system of civil service, the various jobs of the municipality are categorized. Position classification consists of determining the duties and responsibilities of each individual job, whether occupied or vacant, and the assignment of that position to a class together with other positions of similar or related duties and responsibilities. Thus positions may be classified, for example, as junior clerk-typist, senior budget analyst, patrolman, chauffeur, or personnel director. Once the duties of each position have been described, the number and type of classes must be determined, classes given a descriptive title, and positions assigned to classes. This last activity may create a good deal of controversy. Because it is part of a supervisor's duty to look after the welfare of his subordinates, a bureau chief may well engage in a controversy with the personnel agency over whether his best stenographer fits the job description of intermediate stenographer or senior stenographer.

Although a position-classification plan may be greeted as "bureaucratic red tape" by the general public and municipal employees alike, it performs many useful functions. Classification raises employee morale by standardizing job titles. It permits the use of a uniform pay plan so that persons doing approximately the same work receive the same pay. If salaries are standardized, classification permits the use of a system of periodic pay raises. These may be based on the employee's increased value and faithful service over a period of time or on his receiving additional training. Often, however, they are based almost purely on the length of employment. Since the opportunities for promotion are necessarily limited, it is important to the morale of employees that they may be advanced in pay up to a maximum limit while continuing to perform the same type of duties. Classification allows for the transfer of employees among departments on the basis of their job descriptions. It simplifies recruitment, since a single standard examination may be given for a class, even though many positions in that class are to be filled.

The Requirement of Local Residence. Except for teachers and city managers, a common rule established by state law, the city charter, or the civil service commission requires that a city employee be a resident of the city—and often for a specified length of time, such as one year, before employment. This rule is an anomaly in a contemporary personnel system. It is based upon a spoils rather than a merit concept. It is a vestige of Jacksonian thinking that government jobs should be reserved for hometown persons. A merit system assumes that employees are chosen for demonstrated competence. If that is the true criterion, it matters not where the person may live or how long he has lived there. A residence requirement sometimes works a hardship upon the city administration by requiring the employment of a mediocre person when a superior one may live a few miles away outside the city limits. This problem may be especially acute in metropolitan areas with their numerous independent suburbs. Out of necessity, cities are increasingly waiving residence requirements in recruiting persons for positions demanding technical and administrative training and experience.

The Method of Dismissal. Much controversy may appear from time to time in local newspapers over the discharge of a particular municipal employee. The public's attitude concerning these widely publicized dismissals is often one of ambivalence. Nearly everyone today works for someone else—has a supervisory superior. Through the process of identification, therefore, the individual is likely to have an initial reaction of sympathy for someone who is dismissed from his job. ("After all, the same thing might have happened to me!") But on the other hand, the lay citizen is likely to complain that—according to hearsay—no one is ever dismissed from a government job, that an incompetent may be transferred, or retired, or given nothing to do, but that he is never dismissed. Some will insist that the law does not permit dismissal once the status of civil service tenure is given.

This ambivalence has its counterpart among public administrators in the conflict over the "open back door" versus the "closed back door" methods of dismissal from the service. Should a supervisor have the authority to discharge an unwanted employee summarily? Or should he have to serve a notice and accord a hearing before removal, and then discharge the employee only for "cause" as described in the law? And should the decision be left to the department head, or should it be made by the civil service commission?

In the early days of merit practice, it was believed that department heads—political appointees—would dismiss employees of the "wrong" political faith if there were no safeguards, and so the back door was often closed. This was essentially a negative view of administration, of course. Today the emphasis is upon executive responsibility. This means that department heads must be given wide latitude of discretionary power in running their departments so that they may show they can produce worthwhile results. If they fail, or if they abuse the responsibility, they must be prepared to answer for it.

Yet many city charters provide that civil service employees may be discharged only for cause and give the employee the right to appeal the decision to the independent civil service commission, which may order his reinstatement. The results have not been an aid to effective administration, as a rule. Independent civil service commissions often order the employee reinstated if a majority believes that dismissal is too severe a penalty for the charges made against him. Sometimes the employee engages a skillful attorney to represent him at the hearings before the commission, and his attorney succeeds in turning the hearings into a trial of the head of the department, instead of an appraisal of the charges against the employee. After such an experience, the department head may decide that it is better to put up with employees who are incompetent, lazy, and even insubordinate, rather than to go through the ordeal required to discharge them.

On the other hand, municipal civil service employees expect to be accorded reasonable protection against arbitrary dismissal or discharge for political reasons. This can be provided in one of several ways. The personnel director is sometimes given, as one of his duties, the investigation of any cases involving suspension or discharge of employees, which will have a restraining influence on arbitrary actions by department heads. Similarly, in cities where the personnel board is advisory rather than administrative, it may be authorized to investigate dismissals and to make recommendations to the manager or the mayor, who exercises final decision. This arrangement provides safeguards against abuse, without the problems that might result if an independent review were to be undertaken by a civil service commission with power to reinstate the employee.

THE PUBLIC ATTITUDE

Community Status and Municipal Employment. The Jacksonian frontiersman taught us to be skeptical of those who would "feed at the public trough." The lesson was taught so well that Americans often still accept uncritically the notion that public employees are loafers, far less efficient than those in private employment. Some citizens believe that the nature of public employment itself makes people lazy and inefficient.

While students and practitioners of municipal government are in virtually universal agreement that this viewpoint is false, it is difficult to present conclusive evidence to that effect because there is no certain basis for comparing public and private employment. In the field of private endeavor, the test of profit exists. Cities, however, operate few services that are expected to be revenue-producing. Even when they do—such as in public transportation—the service is often one in which profit opportunities are too doubtful for most businessmen to be interested. The effectiveness of most city services—its recreation, welfare, highways, fire fighting, and other functions—can be given only a subjective evaluation. Where one person may think the city recreation program, for example, is inefficient and a waste of the taxpayers' money, another may think it excellent. No clear standard of measurement exists, and the recreation program certainly cannot be compared in efficiency with the method by which some local manufacturer makes motorboats.

Analogies with Private Business. The tendency in the United States is to deify "business efficiency." In the light of the rapid development of industrialization and the commensurate rise in the standard of living that have taken place in this country since the Civil War, it is understandable that the businessman and his methods should be greatly admired. But we should guard against exaggeration.

It is well to remember that a great deal of business is conducted today by large corporations and that these corporations are operated for the most part by self-perpetuating bureaucracies. These bureaucracies enjoy the same advantages and suffer the same disadvantages, for the most part, as do public bureaucracies.

Like their sisters in the city hall, clerk-typists in private industry will start putting on their coats fifteen minutes before quitting time if the supervisor permits it. The public employee has no monopoly on morning and afternoon coffee breaks. Today, stenographers would quit if a private company tried to stop this type of "loafing." Magazines are not read during working hours in the street commissioner's office alone. Minor forms of bribery—tickets to next Saturday's football game, a turkey at Christmas—are not limited to councilmanic recipients; they are standard operating procedure in business. Bureaucratic maneuvering for advantage and struggles for power exist in the city hall, in the corporation offices, and wherever else bureaucracies exist.

Obscure, ritualistic, and technical language—gobbledygook—exists in business and in government. Red tape—a necessary means of maintaining and identifying responsibility in a large, impersonal organization—exists in big business as well as big government. The mimeograph machine, the typewriter, and the ream of paper are everywhere today. Almost everyone, when he thinks about it, recalls incidents of excessive delays and excessive filling out of forms in connection with a business matter involving a private company, especially a large company.

Private endeavor may be more efficient than public endeavor. We do not know. We do know that they have much in common. We do know that each is dependent upon professional, technical specialists in a day of mechanization and specialization.

MUNICIPAL EMPLOYMENT AND ORGANIZED LABOR

At least some employees in all the largest cities in the United States are members of labor unions. The smaller the city, the less likely the employees are to be organized. The AFL-CIO has two unions for municipal employees, the American Federation of State, County and Municipal Employees (AFSCME) and the International Association of Fire Fighters (IAFF). In addition, many city employees, such as truck drivers, belong to their own craft unions, just as do persons in private industry plying the same trade. The United Public Workers of America (UPWA) is an independent union. Many local unions are unaffiliated. Some of them are "company unions," which are illegal under the National Labor Relations Act, but the provisions of that act do not apply to municipal corporations.

PAY SCALES AND POLITICS

Salaries in Public Employment. The total monthly payroll for municipal employees in March, 1967, was over $700 million. This equalled roughly 45 percent of municipal budgets. Obviously wage and salary levels are major factors in determining government costs.

The lesser-skilled and unskilled employees in large cities receive pay that tends to run somewhat above the average for comparable private employment. In smaller cities, pay is likely to be no better or less than private employment, although there is considerable variation. The higher pay in larger cities probably reflects in part the generally higher cost of living in those areas. It also reflects to some extent the trend toward the organization of public employees into trade unions and employee associations for collective bargaining and the greater power of organized labor in large-city politics generally. Whether trade unions exist or not, however, the sheer numbers of governmental employees, their families, relatives, and friends are enough to exert considerable pressure upon councils to provide pay scales at a high level.

If salaries at the lower levels tend to be fairly good, pay for top government technicians and administrators is usually below the average paid similar employees in private industry. No labor union looks after the salary needs of the city attorney or the chief engineer at the city power station. Furthermore, persons in positions like these have, because of fewer numbers, far less political influence in getting pay increases.

When the rank-and-file workers in the mass transit or public works departments of a city ask for a raise, councilmen will consider the possible repercussions in the next election if they are refused.

No such fears need sway the councilmen when it is suggested that $7,000 is an inadequate salary for the city attorney in a city of 150,000 people. Quite to the contrary, the Jacksonian tradition lends public support in opposition to an increase. Since the average citizen is making less than the present salary of the attorney, psychologically he is unsympathetic to arguments for an increase. Councilmen and other legislators can make friends by refusing a raise to chief administrators and technicians. In the years after World War II, however, there has been a trend toward paying salaries at the higher levels that are equal to those on private payrolls. Only the very top positions have not been included in this trend.

Concluding Statement. Americans expect more and more services from city government. As a result, the public employee has become a technical specialist, skilled in his task. In order to obtain such persons for the public service, the elaborate art of modern personnel administration and management has been applied to our cities. The day has passed when city employment could quite harmlessly serve as a reward for faithful political effort.

To those who work for the city, their positions are not far different from similar positions in private employment. As a result, the same problems of labor-management relations arise in the city hall and in the offices of the business corporation.

The labor union is a basic institution in American life today, and public employees usually desire to share in its benefits. The principle of unionism does not conflict with that of the merit system. This is true even of the union shop under which employees might be *required* to join a union after employment. The union sometimes is, in fact, the only collective method of settling employee-employer disputes.

There may be some areas of union interest that conflict with the merit system. A strict emphasis upon seniority, often a union goal, is not in harmony with the principle. The closed shop is not permitted in public employment, since it would require one to be a union member *before* employment, and this would enable the union to supplant the personnel director or commission. In general, however, city governments have learned to live with labor unions. Although the two will have occasional conflicts, they can also work together toward the common goals of a better personnel system and a more satisfied group of employees.

SELECTED READINGS

Altshuler, Alan: *The Ancker Hospital Site Controversy,* The Bobbs-Merrill Company, Inc., Indianapolis, ICP no. 82, 1964. (Problems involved in contradictory technical information reflecting different professional values—in this case medical administrators and urban planners.)

Automated Data Processing in Municipal Government: Public Administration Service, Chicago, 1966.

Earle, Chester B., and Valerie A. Earle: *The Promotion of Lem Merrill,* University of Alabama Press, University, Ala., 1953. (A case study in which a councilman sought to secure the promotion of a city employee to a department headship.)

Joiner, Charles A.: *Organizational Analysis: Political, Sociological, and Administrative Processes of Local Government,* Institute for Community Development, Michigan State University, East Lansing, 1964. (The application of organization theory to local political systems.)

Municipal Manpower Commission: *Governmental Manpower for Tomorrow's Cities,* McGraw-Hill Book Company, New York, 1962. (A study of future personnel needs of municipal bureaucracies.)

Nigro, Felix A. (ed.): "Collective Negotiations in the Public Service," *Public Administration Review,* 18:111–138, March–April, 1968. (A symposium on the function of labor unions in urban government.)

Stanley, David T.: *Professional Personnel for the City of New York,* The Brookings Institution, Washington, 1963. (An examination of existing conditions and problems, with recommendations.)

CHAPTER
13 REVENUES
AND
EXPENDITURES

Municipal expenditures have expanded enormously in the last three generations. In the period following World War II, they have increased with almost every fiscal year.

Where Does the Money Go? In a period of rising costs and increasing urban populations, the demands for local government services have been regularly increasing. At the same time, however, revenue sources have remained relatively unchanged. The result is that local-government debt continues each year to reach all-time highs.

A sharp expansion of services and of their costs cannot be met without a considerable amount of effort. Part of the cost has been offset by a great increase in the standard of living and consequent ability to pay. But the development has also helped to incite a desperate search for new revenue sources. The property tax remains the most important local tax, but local governments have sought to broaden their tax bases, looking to sales, excise, and income taxes.

Why Taxes? The typical citizen probably has little understanding of the relationships that exist between government revenues and expenditures. The traditional practice of politicians is one of promising to perform more services in a better fashion and at lower cost than can or will the opposition. This behavior has probably helped preserve the citizen's habit of making no association between service levels and costs. Each person, of course, has some knowledge about taxes. Every homeowner understands his property tax, at least he is able to determine how much he must pay, and he is likely to know whether it is more or less than the preceding year. The sales tax is known to most people because of the general practice of adding it to the marked price of goods in making a sale. The income tax cannot escape the attention of the employed person in any jurisdiction which levies it, especially since most states do not use the withholding system but require payment in one or two installments—each of which produces anguish on the part of the citizen. (Cities levying a payroll tax do use the withholding method.) Yet the economic merits of particular taxes are unknown to the typical citizen. He knows little more about the services that his taxes buy (except that he may associate the property tax with schools), and he certainly does not attempt to find his way through a wonderland of double taxation, grants-in-aid, shared taxes, dedicated funds, joint financing, and service charges.

It is easy for the citizen to agree with the politician or commentator who tells him that taxes are too high, since he has no criterion against which to measure them. He balks from time to time when major tax increases are submitted to him on referendum, and his reluctance to pay taxes which he does not associate with services has encouraged the extensive use in America of dedicated funds, so that a new or increased tax is pledged to a specific purpose. This helps the citizen understand why it is being asked for and helps persuade him to vote for it. Thus, an additional cent on the gasoline tax is pledged for road building; extra millage on the property tax may be exclusively for a library; most of the state sales tax may be pledged for grants to aid school operations. The use of dedicated funds has long been denounced by specialists in financial administration because of the rigidity it produces in the system. It leaves less room for the executive or legislative branches to make adjustments for changing demands. But the practice undoubtedly makes new taxes or service charges more palatable to the typical citizen.

EXPENDITURE PATTERNS

New functions of government have been added, and there have been some basic changes in the pattern of municipal expenditures over the years since the beginning of the century. Among them are these:[1]

1. New functions of government have appeared and have begun to challenge the old functions for importance. Some that might be

[1] See U.S. Bureau of the Census, Historical Statistics on State and Local Government Finances, 1955.

mentioned include urban redevelopment, public housing, smoke abatement, airports, and parking lots.

2. Old functions have been greatly expanded and changed in concept. This applies to recreation, highways, health, and welfare programs.

3. State and national governments have assumed an increasing share of the cost of local government. Intergovernmental payments increased at an average rate of 21 percent a year during the decade ending in 1968. The states have enormously expanded the number, and increased the quality, of their direct services to the public in the present century.[2]

4. The states have gradually been becoming more and more collection agencies for local governments. In the late 1960s, about two-thirds of state-government education expenditures were actually in the form of payments to local governments. The same disposition was made of about 20 percent of state highway fund expenditures and over 40 percent of state welfare expenditures. Shared taxes and grants-in-aid were also important parts of other state budget items. This pattern represents, in part, the result of legislative recognition of the need for additional revenues at the local level combined with an unwillingness to delegate adequate taxing powers to local governments. So the states collect the money and then disburse it to their local governments.

5. Local expenditures have represented an increasingly large proportion of society's earnings, as measured by the gross national product (GNP). This increase has not been enormous, but it has been significant. In the 1920s, expenditures ran around 6 percent of the GNP; by 1962, they had increased to 8 percent.

6. Increases in municipal expenditures in the last generation (since about 1945) have been greater than in any previous generation, although they have not been as great as some critics have argued. In terms of personal income, local expenditures were about 50 percent higher in the mid-1960s than they had been in 1910. In Iowa, a study concluded, the "modest but significant increases can probably be attributed most directly to the improvements in the quality and extent of services provided."[3] Probably, this is generally true.

Reasonable Expenditure Levels. The question often arises: What are reasonable expenditure levels for state and local governments? The citizen is bombarded with propaganda, much of it conflicting in na-

[2] *Municipal Year Book, 1970,* International City Management Association, Washington, 1970, p. 226.
[3] Deil S. Wright, "A Half-century of Trends in Municipal Expenditures," *Municipal Finance,* 37:1–8, February, 1965.

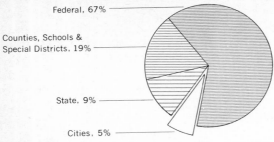

Figure 13-1. Your government dollar. *Source:* California Taxpayers' Association.

ture, which tells him of the unfinished business of government in providing highways, health programs, recreation for increasing leisure time, and so forth, but also of increasing debt burdens, of the need for increased taxes if current service levels are to be maintained, and of "all-encroaching government." The citizen wonders whether a new or increased tax is fair or whether he is being taken advantage of.

The question the citizen raises cannot easily be answered. Essentially, expenditure levels are culturally determined. In the 1920s, Americans would not permit elaborate welfare or unemployment-compensation programs, to say nothing of public housing or limited-access highways. But since the Great Depression, they have come to expect government to provide a measure of security that is not otherwise available in an interdependent society, and they trust government further and are now willing to allow it to experiment with new programs where needs are felt to exist.

The relative ease with which money can be raised is also important in determining expenditure levels. Congress agrees more readily than a state legislature to add a new grant-in-aid program because it is relatively easy for Congress to raise the additional funds. A city or state that cannot increase services without also raising taxes or adding new taxes will be very slow to do so and will demand impressive proof before acting.

The size of expenditures in any given community tends to vary, not surprisingly, with personal income levels and according to socio-economic status characteristics, which tend to measure the same thing. The average age of community residents is a factor, however. Younger people expect more from governmental programs, perhaps in part because a younger community population tends to correlate with larger public school enrollments. Expenditures also tend to be somewhat higher in communities where the population is growing rapidly and there is an above-average rate of family formation. Rapid growth usually also requires the establishment of new municipal services and the expansion of those that already exist. Such a pattern is particularly common in new communities on the fringes of metropolitan areas.[4]

Some people—individuals or groups who want government expenditures kept to a lower portion of gross national product than do most of the people—try to keep governments from making maximum use of their taxing and spending powers. They seek to restrict spending, not so much through counterpressures upon governing bodies (though that is an important technique for them), as through the adoption of restrictive constitutional and charter provisions. Once nestled in this protective armor, restrictions cannot usually be dislodged except by an extraordinary-majority vote or a complicated procedure or both. The fact that most state constitutions have such restrictions built into them, commonly by an accumulation of amendments, makes the conservative an opponent of constitutional revision. Thus, the Citizens Public Expenditure Survey of New York opposed a 1957 proposal for a constitutional convention in that state, pointing out that "had the convention proposition been approved . . . there would have been many pressures upon the delegates to enlarge government functions and open the door to increased spending on both state and local levels."[5]

REVENUE FOR PRESENT-DAY CITIES

All taxes are ultimately derived from either of two sources: total wealth or annual income. Taxes are theoretically based upon some criterion of *ability to pay,* although the criteria used in various periods of history have not been the same, and a tax created in one period and logical and equitable at that time may live on into another time when its justification becomes less apparent. In some instances, payments to the government are based upon a *benefit theory* rather than on ability to pay, but such payments are more in the nature of service charges than taxes. The benefit theory is applied, for example, in cases of special assessments for streets, sidewalks, street lighting, and similar improvements. It is also applied in determining water and light charges and, to a degree, in motor-vehicle license fees.

---

[4] Louis H. Masotti and Don R. Bowen, "Communities and Budgets: The Sociology of Municipal Expenditures," *Urban Affairs Quarterly,* 1:39–58, December, 1965. Similar findings are reported in Walter Isard and Robert Coughlin, *Municipal Costs and Revenues Resulting from Community Growth,* Chandler-Davis Publishing Co., Wellesley, Mass., 1957; Stanley Scott and E. L. Feder, *Factors Associated with Variations in Municipal Expenditure Levels,* Institute of Public Administration, University of California, Berkeley, Calif., 1957; and Robert C. Wood, *1400 Governments,* Harvard University Press, Cambridge, Mass., 1961.
[5] *New York State Taxpayer,* 18:1, November, 1957.

TABLE 13-1. Estimated per Capita Direct General Expenditures of Local Governments in Central Cities and Outside of Central Cities, 12 Largest Metropolitan Areas,* 1957 (Dollars)

Central City	Total Direct General Expenditure		Education		Highways		Welfare		Police and Fire Protection		All Other	
	Central City	Outside C.C.	Central City	Outside C.C.	Central City	Outside C.C.	Central City	Outside C.C.	Central City	Outside C.C.	Central City	Outside C.C.
New York	257	212†	63	106†	18	16†	28	9†	28	19†	120	62†
Newark	242	212†	74	106†	7	16†	12	9†	38	19†	111	62†
Jersey City	235	212†	49	106†	7	16†	11	9†	35	19†	133	62†
Chicago	200	145‡	48	82‡	35	14‡	8	4‡	24	10‡	85	35‡
Los Angeles	261	202	95	93	16	11	29	26	30	14	91	58
Long Beach	325§	202	115	93	25	11	32	26	29	14	124§	58
Philadelphia	165	138	49	72	12	23	4	5	23	8	77	30
Detroit	201	200	62	114	16	19	9	3	25	12	89	52
San Francisco	220	230	62	112	11	15	33	23	35	15	79	65
Oakland	232	230	73	112	16	15	30	23	27	15	86	65
Baltimore	199	149	59	71	19	20	18	3	31	10	72	45
Cleveland	183	189	50	85	19	22	12	12	24	15	78	55
Minneapolis	182	194	59	97	16	17	22	15	16	6	69	59
St. Paul	189	194	51	97	19	17	22	15	19	6	78	59
St. Louis	147	125	45	71	10	15	1	3	23	10	68	26
Boston	272	182	48	70	12	17	41	22	37	21	134	52
Pittsburgh	188	132	41	66	13	13	5	3	24	8	105	42

* Metropolitan areas are those defined as of the 1950 Census of Population, rather than "standard metropolitan areas."
† Includes Paterson-Clifton-Passaic.
‡ Includes Gary-Hammond-East Chicago.
§ Excludes payment to the state of California in settlement of oil land litigation, a total of $138 million.
Source: Derived from U.S. Department of Commerce, Bureau of the Census, Local Government Finances in Standard Metropolitan Areas, 1957 Census of Governments, vol. III, no. 6, 1959, tables 3 and 4; expenditures of counties containing the central city were apportioned according to the ratio of central city to county population, based on 1957 estimates of county population and 1950 to 1960 straight-line interpolation for the central cities; minor amounts of special district expenditures were not apportioned to the central cities. From Harvey E. Brazer, Some Fiscal Implications of Metropolitanism, The Brookings Institution, Washington, 1962, table 2.

State Limits on Taxing and Spending. Cities have only those powers of taxation which are granted to them by the state. The only exceptions to this rule are to be found in a few home rule states, notably California and Wisconsin, where court interpretations of the constitutional home rule clause have given cities a general grant of powers to levy taxes. (Even in Wisconsin, a general act limiting municipal taxing powers in particular areas at the discretion of the legislature is valid.) States, either through the constitution or through statutes, will normally place limitations upon the taxing power of cities. The law usually states a maximum tax rate in terms of so many dollars per capita or allows an increase of only a certain small percentage over the previous year's rate or permits the city to levy a tax on only a certain percentage of the assessed value of the taxable property within the city. The last restriction is by far the most common. States also often impose conditions and regulations on the administration of municipal finances.[6]

Cities are limited in other ways, too. As a result of the famous case of *McCulloch v. Maryland* (1819), Federal properties within the city are not taxable. The state may exempt many other categories, such as private educational and religious properties. Beginning in the days of the Great Depression, a large number of states have adopted "homestead exemption" laws, which exclude part or even all the value of owner-occupied homes from the general property tax.

Limitations on Subjects of Taxation. The subjects that may be taxed by the municipality are often strictly controlled by the state. Nearly all the states determine which taxes cities may levy, for what period of time they may be levied, and under what conditions. A city that finds its property tax consistently inadequate may not, for example, decide to levy a payroll or a sales tax. The state must first authorize such a levy on a new subject.

Only a few states have been willing to permit cities to choose from a wide variety of tax sources by adopting broad enabling acts. California and Wisconsin cities have wide taxing powers as a result of judicial interpretation of constitutional home rule clauses. Pennsylvania and New York have given their cities broad taxing powers through legislation.

Limitations on Borrowing Power. In addition to limitations upon taxation, the state normally also seeks to protect the public credit by limiting the *borrowing* powers of cities. Such a limitation may be

[6]Control over spending is described in T. E. McMillan, Jr., *State Supervision of Municipal Finance*, Institute of Public Affairs, University of Texas, Austin, Tex., 1953; and Leonard E. Goodall, *State Regulation of Local Indebtedness in the United States*, Bureau of Governmental Research, Arizona State University, Tempe, Ariz., 1964.

written into the city charter or into state law or the constitution. The limit is usually expressed in terms of a percentage of the assessed value of the taxable property within the city, but it may also be a specific number of dollars, or the debt may be limited to a figure equal to the annual tax revenue of the city.[7]

These debt limits may be unrealistic and bear no necessary relationship to the wants of the city. The artificial limitations are, therefore, sometimes circumvented. Many techniques have been devised for doing this. For example, bonds issued for certain purposes, especially public utilities, may not be included under the limitation if they may theoretically be retired through revenue from the proposed project. Bonds to build a stadium, an auditorium, or a toll bridge might be paid out of revenues, and hence the courts or the legislature will sometimes exempt them from the limitation. In some states, the voters (in a few states, the property-tax payers) of a city may vote to raise the debt limit.

If either the debt or the tax limit is expressed in terms of a percentage of the assessed evaluation, the city can nearly always—and frequently does—resort to raising the assessed value of property in order to raise both the debt and tax limits. Before the Great Depression, when many states depended heavily upon the general property tax, a serious inequity resulted when large cities, encountering increasing costs, assessed property at or above full value in order to circumvent debt and tax limits. Suburbs, country towns, and rural areas might at the same time be at one-third or one-fourth of market value. Obviously, this meant that the city, with a higher evaluation criterion, would pay a much larger proportionate share of the state tax. Few state governments today utilize the general property tax as a source of revenue, most of them leaving the field for local taxation. Large cities, however, still pay a disproportionate share of the *county* property tax wherever proper equalization of local assessing unit evaluations is not made. This is also sometimes a problem when rural and urban areas are combined in a school district.

Limitations on Use of Dedicated Funds. The income of cities, instead of being channeled into the general fund to be used as the council sees fit, is sometimes diverted into a series of special funds, each dedicated to a particular use. This may be required by either the city charter or state law. It is common, for example, to provide that the city's portion of a state-shared gasoline tax is to be placed in a special fund for highway use only. Or 1 mill of the property-tax levy may go to the library fund, for library use only.

[7] McMillan, *op. cit.*, appendix E.

Some sinking funds represent money that has been set aside to pay off bonds that will become due in the future. Others are not really funds at all, merely appropriations from the general fund, but titled "funds" in the auditor's reports.

The General Property Tax. It was stated earlier that all taxes must ultimately come from either income or total wealth. A tax must produce adequate revenue, but a long-range tax policy is often discussed in terms of equity, too. *Equity* is usually thought of as meaning *ability to pay.* In colonial America, ability to pay could best be measured in terms of property, or total wealth. Today, when most people receive a regular pay check (unlike the situation in the predominantly agricultural colonies), income is generally considered to be a better criterion.

The income tax takes into consideration the fact that not all property is equally a basis for taxes. A home, most Americans would agree, is less suitable for taxation than is a factory. A factory that is losing money is less a subject for taxation than one that is making a profit (although it might be expected to pay some taxes). The property tax makes them pay equally, the income tax does not. Saxophones, to an amateur musician, are as much a consumer good as are rutabagas, yet the former are (theoretically) taxable in many states as property. The income tax, in a complicated modern world, can be much more equitably administered and is less subject to evasion than is the property tax.

In colonial America, the property tax was a fairly good measure of ability to pay. There was then a much closer relationship between property owned and income received than is the case today. Despite the fact, however, that the property tax has been bitterly attacked in more recent years as being unsuitable for a modern world, and especially for urban society, it remains by far the most important source of revenue for local government. It furnished about 75 percent of all city *tax* revenues in 1967.

The great authority on the property tax, E. R. A. Seligman, once suggested that there is nothing the matter with the general property tax except that it is wrong in theory and does not work in practice. What are the objections to the tax?

It has already been suggested that the property tax is no longer a good measurement of ability to pay. Today, when large incomes are sometimes possible from relatively small investments, it seems inappropriate for the city to derive a major portion of its income from a tax upon homes, many of which are owned by relatively low-income persons.

Over a fifty-year period, property taxes have risen somewhat, even allowing for the changing value of the dollar. At no time in the present century have these taxes tended to decline relative to the ability to pay.[8]

The general property tax has often been poorly administered. A large proportion of property today is intangible: stocks, bonds, mortgages, and the like. These are easily hidden from the assessor. So are much jewelry and other small tangible valuables. Depreciation allowances on automobiles, furniture, and other properties far in excess of what is reasonable by market conditions are claimed by taxpayers—and are frequently allowed by assessors.

The arbitrariness of property assessment and the failure to relate it to market value is indicated in a study once conducted by the Oregon state tax commission. It found that assessments in one county ranged from 6.5 percent to 187.5 percent of the commission's figures on residential properties. Such extremes are no longer typical, however.

Assessors are sometimes elected to office, even though theirs is a job requiring technical competence. Others are appointed on the basis of political considerations other than those of competence. Most assessors are honest, but many are not trained for their jobs. In the largest cities, trends toward professionalization have encouraged the development of a trained staff. Assessment in large cities is usually technically superior to the type of job done in small places.

Some attempts have been made to modify the general property tax in recent years. The withdrawal of the state from the scene has reduced or eliminated the old evils of competitive underassessment to reduce the burden of the state tax. Some states have classified property, taxing some of it at lower rates. Others have exempted intangibles or provided for the taxation of some of them at a low rate. An increasing number of them have virtually or completely exempted personal, as distinguished from real, property. The general property tax is not so inequitable or so poorly administered as it once was, but it is still not a uniformly applied tax. Furthermore, it remains an important factor in the development and maintenance of urban slums. This is so because improvements on property are subject to increased taxation. Many slum owners find no difficulty in charging high rents and maintaining full occupancy no matter how dilapidated the property. They, therefore, regard improvements as uneconomic. This system stands in contrast to the English, where the "rates" are levied upon the fair net income value of the property.

[8] Deil S. Wright and Robert W. Marker, "A Half-century of Local Finances," National Tax Journal, 3:274–291, September, 1964.

Why Is the Property Tax Retained? If there are so many objections to the general property tax, why does it remain as the core of financial support of the local government? For one thing, inertia itself helps to preserve the tax. It would seem that taxpayers generally do not support improved property tax assessments. In Wisconsin, for example, voters have repeatedly turned down referendum proposals to place assessors on a professional basis and have rejected the efforts of governing bodies to provide a reassessment of all property within some municipalities. Hence, inertia works against either elimination or modification of the tax and its administration.

A second reason is to be found in the venerable argument that any old tax is a good tax and any new tax is a bad tax. The argument, to the extent that it is accurate, is based upon the fact that society has accommodated itself to the old tax. Property values are adjusted to the property tax. When a person buys a home, he considers the annual tax levy as a maintenance cost, and its relative size is a factor in determining the price he is willing to pay.

A third reason is that the subjects of local-government taxation must necessarily be things that will "stay put"—and most real property (if not personal property) is not easily moved out of the city the day the assessor comes around. Sales taxes on the local level tend to drive shoppers and buyers out of the city. Taxes upon income tend to cause political complications if levied upon nonresidents and if not, tend to drive people into the suburbs. On the other hand, the real property tax does not stay perfectly put, either. High property taxes tend to drive homeowners, businesses, and industry outside the municipal limits and thus undermine the tax base.

A fourth reason for retaining the tax is that it produces a very high yield, except in severe depressions. It probably meets the test of *adequacy* better than does any other tax with the exception of the retail sales tax, which is collected a bit at a time and often upon the necessities of life.

Lastly, the general property tax is retained because cities need money and no one has suggested a substitute satisfactory enough to replace the yield of the tax.

The Search for Municipal Tax Variety. In looking for likely subjects of local taxation, it is necessary to consider whether or not a subject will stay in one place long enough to be taxed there and whether or not the field has already been completely preempted by the national or state government. These considerations are in addition, of course, to the requirements for a tax system seen by Adam Smith—certainty, equity, economy, and convenience.

A study of Iowa municipal taxation over a fifty-year period con-

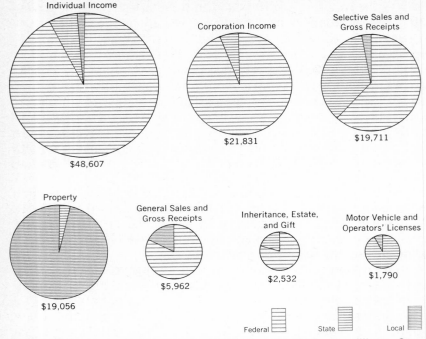

Figure 13-2. The national tax pie. 1962 tax collections, in millions. *Source:* U.S. Advisory Commission on Intergovernmental Relations, *Tax Overlapping in the United States,* 1964, p. 14.

cluded that established programs tended to be financed by property taxes and new programs by other means. But there was doubt as to whether the property tax could continue to finance established programs.[9]

The *sales tax* became popular during the Great Depression because it yielded well even in such times. It became the backbone of many state tax systems and has had limited use as a secondary tax for city governments. In 1914, St. Louis adopted a sales tax on all sales made by merchants and manufacturers. Kansas City levied a gross receipts tax in 1934. The city of New York adopted it in 1934 as a "temporary" expedient. As is the fate of most "temporary" taxes, it has become a permanent fixture in that city, varying over time from 1 to 3 percent. New Orleans, Denver, and other cities have adopted sales taxes. It has become especially popular in postwar California, where most cities have adopted such a tax ranging up to 1 percent, but with most of them at 0.5 percent. The yield from

[9] Deil S. Wright, "A Half-century of Trends in Municipal Property Taxes: 1910–1960," *Municipal Finance,* 37:149–155, 1965.

municipal sales taxes increased by 125 percent during the decade of the 1950s. In California cities and in most others, the regressive tendency of the tax has been ameliorated to a degree by exempting foods and other necessities. (A regressive tax is one the burden of which is lessened as ability to pay increases. A sales tax on necessities is considered regressive, since low-income people spend a larger percentage of their income on necessities than do high-income people.)

The *income tax* supplanted the tariff as the principal source of revenue for the Federal government during World War I and has become increasingly important since that time. In recent years, many states have turned to this tax. Cities have, therefore, found the field largely preempted. Philadelphia, however, adopted an income tax in 1939 which has come to produce about one-fourth of the city's revenue. Many municipalities in Pennsylvania and Ohio, as well as St. Louis, Louisville, and other cities levy an income tax. The use of the municipal income tax expanded by 200 percent during the decade preceding 1960. Most city income taxes might more accurately be called "payroll taxes," for they normally do not permit any deductions, but are simply a certain percentage of the total amount of money earned by individuals, and sometimes corporations, within a city. The payroll tax has the great advantage to the core city of forcing suburbanites to help bear the cost of maintaining the city in which they earn their living and whose facilities they use daily. It is in effect regressive, however, if it allows no deductions or exemptions.[10] In many cities, moreover, the tax applies only to earned income and not income from stocks, bonds, and rents.

Organized labor has tended to oppose the payroll tax because of its regressivity. In 1954, for example, a Cincinnati councilman who was also a CIO official resigned from the Charter party after that organization helped adopt a payroll tax in the city.[11]

Cities secure some revenue from *business taxes.* These may be primarily levies to pay the cost of supervising a business directly affecting the public health, but some of them are higher levies and are designed to produce revenue beyond the cost of inspections. A city may, for example, levy a modest tax in the form of restaurant licenses, most of which must be spent upon health inspections of eating places. But other taxes may be levied upon businesses for which there exist no regulatory activities under the police power.

Public utilities often, and other businesses sometimes, are taxed upon gross earnings. One version of this tax, called an "occupational

[10] See Robert A. Sigafoos, *The Municipal Income Tax: Its History and Problems,* Public Administration Service, Chicago, 1954.
[11] *The New York Times,* Feb. 28, 1954.

TABLE 13-2. Summary of City Finances

Item	Amount (In Millions)		
	1967–1968	1962	1954
Total revenue	$26,521	$16,794	$9,584
General revenue, total	21,276	13,127	7,327
Taxes, total	11,291	7,934	4,796
Property	7,769	5,807	3,585
Sales and gross receipts	1,837	1,303	659
Other	1,686	824	552
Intergovernmental revenue	5,971	2,674	1,336
Charges and miscellaneous	4,014	2,519	1,195
Current charges	2,418	1,511	668
Other	1,596	1,008	527
Utility revenue	4,361	3,136	1,955
Liquor stores revenue	121	77	56
Insurance trust revenue	763	454	246
Total expenditure	27,007	17,329	9,906
Expenditure by character and object:			
Direct expenditure	26,676	17,136	9,809
Current operation	18,021	11,273	6,361
Capital outlay	5,664	4,127	2,417
Construction	4,307	3,228	2,020
Land and existing structures	795	554	183
Equipment	562	345	215
Assistance and subsidies	966	408	370
Interest on debt	1,202	804	389
Insurance benefits and repayments	822	524	272
Intergovernmental expenditure	332	193	97
Exhibit: expenditure for personal services	11,596	7,676	4,463
Expenditure by function:			
General expenditure	21,563	13,475	7,500
Police protection	2,261	1,475	816
Fire protection	1,400	988	588
Highways	2,142	1,701	1,023
Sanitation	2,051	1,501	911
Sewerage	1,188	875	(NA)
Other	863	626	(NA)
Public welfare	1,739	710	448
Education	3,405	1,952	1,093
Libraries	341	211	120
Health and hospitals	1,541	890	547
Parks and recreation	1,003	640	370
Housing and urban renewal	948	642	269
Water transport and terminals	84	77	37
Airports	276	193	69
Financial administration	361	248	417

Item	Amount (In Millions)		
	1967–1968	1962	1954
General control	$ 592	$ 401	
General public buildings	350	206	$ 120
Interest on general debt	817	512	232
Other and unallocable	2,252	1,059	442
Utility expenditure	4,520	3,265	2,087
Liquor stores expenditure	102	65	47
Insurance-trust expenditure	822	524	272

(NA) means data not available.
Source: Municipal Year Book, 1970, International City Management Association, Chicago, 1970, pp. 226–227.

tax" (usually upon gross earned income, but excluding unearned income), is becoming widely used, especially in the South and West. Because it is difficult to determine the value of inventory and other personal property for tax purposes, experts in public finance sometimes advocate the use of such a tax on business in lieu of the personal property tax. It is often used in addition to other taxes, however.

Some cities levy a local cigarette tax. Some resort and vacation cities, such as New York and Atlantic City, tax hotel-room occupancy. Mount Clemens, Michigan, another resort center, levies a tax upon every mineral bath taken within the city limits. Some tax admissions to public events. Tourists and transients are favorite objects of taxation: They cannot vote in local elections.

In a search for taxes other than on general property, cities have often followed the practice of using any subject that will yield well and will not be moved away. Equity is a secondary consideration, and taxes are added piecemeal rather than combined into a system. Paul E. Malone has said that "local financial practices are becoming more a process of scrounging than of revenue administration."[12]

Nontax Revenues. Cities receive some money annually from fines and fees. The fines are paid for violating city ordinances and state laws. The fees are charges for certain services, such as issuing marriage licenses or transferring titles of real estate.

Rather than pay for many services from general taxes, an increasing number of municipalities are levying service charges. These have traditionally been used for water supply. They are now levied in the

[12] *Wall Street Journal,* Nov. 10, 1953 (Chicago ed.).

form of charges on sewerage, garbage collection, street lighting and cleaning, snow removal, weed cutting, and others. Various formulas are used in determining these charges, but in general they are based upon the concept of payment according to benefits received.

Often service charges are levied as a means of avoiding a raise in the general tax rate. It is a means of making the tax level appear to be lower than it actually is. This can be done effectively, for example, if the sewerage charge is a flat rate or a percentage of the water bill and is added to the periodic water bill. On the other hand, service charges may serve as a means of promoting equity in local taxation. Sewerage charges, for example, may be used as a method of reaching tax-exempt property, of which there is a good deal in some cities, so that the cost of this service does not fall upon the rest of the public. Such charges are also useful where some industries contribute disproportionate amounts of sewerage to the system while others contribute nothing, and where cities are close to their tax limit (service charges are not usually counted as taxes for limitation purposes).

Some cities make a small profit from the operation of utilities. This is seldom an important source of revenue. Few transportation systems meet operating expenses today. Water departments and other utilities generally charge only enough to meet costs and to permit a reasonable allowance for depreciation and potential expansion. Sometimes, however, a surplus will be turned in to the city treasury.

Some villages and cities own and operate municipal liquor stores. These may be package stores or ordinary liquor-by-the-drink bars. Where these have been permitted by state law, they have often proved immensely profitable. Needless to say, powerful groups oppose enabling legislation for such stores.

Grants-in-aid. Grants-in-aid are payments made by voluntary appropriation from one level of government to a lower level of government. The amount of a grant is generally independent of the yield from any particular tax or other source of income.

Specific grants are normally made with conditions attached. These conditions may require, for example, the matching of funds, the use of technically trained personnel in administering them, the maintenance of technical standards of equipment and material, or the use of the money only for certain very specific purposes.

Three principal objections are usually levied against the use of grants-in-aid.[13] First, it is said that they may stimulate extravagant expenditures because the locality is spending funds which are not an

[13] Robert S. Ford, "State and Local Finance," *The Annals of the American Academy of Political and Social Science,* 266:15–23, November, 1949.

immediate and obvious burden upon local taxpayers. It is said that if local officials spend money that they need not solicit from the voters, they may feel no need to spend it wisely or on necessities. Second, grants are considered a threat to local self-government and local responsibility. Since the state or national government ordinarily provides the funds only if conditions are met, they may come to supplant local government in the making of policies in these areas. Last, grants are held, potentially at least, to lead toward disproportionate expenditures in favor of those functions receiving grants. In other words, regardless of the merits or need of the various functions performed, some will always have a plentiful budgetary appropriation because of the grants, while others, perhaps more needy and deserving (by local value standards), may be skimped. Grants for venereal-disease and tuberculosis control may promote these services nicely while other functions of the health department shrivel for lack of funds. Although these objections arise virtually every time grant-in-aid problems are discussed, there appears to be little empirical study to support their validity. They may well be proper objections, but further research is needed on the matter of the effects of grants-in-aid.

Shared Taxes. A shared tax is one imposed by one unit of government but shared with other governments according to a formula. The amount sent to each receiving unit is sometimes intended to be representative of the portion of the tax produced within the area of that unit, but shared taxes may be distributed on any basis the collector chooses. Unlike the grant-in-aid, a shared tax delivers no fixed amount; rather, receipts are entirely dependent upon the yield of the tax.[14]

Shared taxes have become increasingly popular in recent decades, and they seem to be preferred by local officials to either grants-in-aid or an enlargement of the taxing powers of local governments. Part of the reason for this is to be found in the fact that fewer strings are normally attached to shared taxes than to grants. Shared taxes also bring less criticism from local citizens than does the enactment of additional local taxes.

Taxes most often shared by the state with local units of government include those on motor fuel, motor vehicles, liquor sales, and income. Shared taxes are sometimes defended as being less in the nature of charity than the grant-in-aid, for although they are state-imposed and state-collected, they are levied upon local wealth and hence are not a largess. Because they are viewed as a local tax with

14 J. R. McKinley, *Local Revenue Problems and Trends,* Bureau of Public Administration, University of California, Berkeley, Calif., 1949.

the state acting as a collecting agent, local units are usually more free in using the revenue as they see fit than they are in the case of grants.

Many criticisms are made of shared taxes, however. New York State commissions, in 1936 and again in 1946, discouraged the use of them.[15] These study groups pointed out that shared taxes cannot be adjusted to local needs. Some areas with little need receive more from such taxes than they can spend, while others receive much less than their greater needs require. Grants-in-aid are better adjustable to need. Shared taxes, further, do not help to stabilize local revenues. They yield well in prosperous times but tend to be withdrawn by the state during depressions, when local need for funds is most critical. Last, the manner in which shared taxes are used is less subject to control than are grants. From an ideological viewpoint, this may be argued as either an advantage or a disadvantage. But from the viewpoint of imposing standards, the state cannot be as effective through shared taxes as it can be through grants. Whatever the argument, a long look into the future will no doubt reveal the shared tax still with us.

Postwar Trends. Intergovernmental financial payments exist between the Federal government and the states; to a much smaller extent, between the Federal government and local units; between the states and their political subdivisions; and even between units of local governments. The amounts spent for each of these has been increasing in recent years, and the principal way in which most local governments have diversified their revenue sources and relieved the pressure on the property tax has been through the receipt of grants and shared taxes.[16]

In the postwar years, municipal expenditures, taken collectively, have increased so rapidly that the intergovernmental-payments portion of total revenues has changed but modestly. In 1948, local governments received about 26 percent of their revenues from the states. Twenty years later, the figure was 32 percent. In 1942, 35 percent of state general revenue was passed along to local governments. A quarter of a century later, the figure was only 37. Just over 1 percent of local revenues came directly from the Federal government in 1948, only 3 percent after twenty more years of new Federal grants-in-aid.

Patterns vary greatly from state to state on policies for intergovernmental payments. A very low percentage of total state expendi-

[15] Report of the New York Commission on State Aid to Municipal Subdivisions, State of New York, Albany, N.Y., 1936; Report of the New York State Commission on Municipal Revenues, State of New York, Albany, N.Y., 1946.
[16] See Rowland Egger, "Nature over Art: No More Local Finance," American Political Science Review, 47:461–477, June, 1955; U.S. Bureau of the Census, Historical Statistics on State and Local Government Finances, 1955; 1967 Census of Governments, 1969.

tures are for local-government aid in New England (except for Massachusetts), Montana, and South Dakota; a high but declining percentage in Wisconsin and Colorado. In 1956, over one-half of the state appropriations in Wisconsin went for local aid.[17] But a decade later, the figure was down to 41.4 percent. Aid seems to be a function more of the balances among existing local pressures than of anything else. The national pattern does not appear to show a high correlation with any factors, whether one considers geography (except for the New England situation), rural-urban balances, or ranking by personal income as a measure of relative wealth. New York, an urban Eastern state, had an elaborate and generous program of state payments to local units in 1956. Pennsylvania, also an urban Eastern state, ranked forty-second in percentage of state budget devoted to payments to local units. Pennsylvania's state aid for public health amounted to 1 cent per capita, New York's to $1.00.[18]

Most state payments to local governments are in the areas of education, welfare, and highways. Collectively, these make up about 85 percent of the total, though practice varies by states. Payments are also made for public safety, health, hospitals, nonhighway transportation, housing, urban redevelopment, and natural resources, among others, and some are lump-sum, or block, grants for no prescribed purpose. Intergovernmental payments are important parts of the revenues of all local units of government, and they seem destined to continue.

The Future Pattern. A conclusion on municipal taxation might hold that the general property tax will remain the backbone of the system. Several possible supplementary taxes have been considered, but none of them can replace the tax that has held the center of the stage for so long.[19]

Special Assessments. Special assessments have become relatively less important since the Great Depression than they were before that time, but they are still used to a considerable extent, especially in rapidly expanding suburbs with their gross lack of services and conveniences. Special assessments are extra levies upon specific pieces of property designed to defray the costs of services or conveniences of particular value to that property.

By far the most common use of special assessments is to pay all or part of the cost of new street paving, installation of water lines, construction of off-street parking areas, and street lighting. In the last

---

[17] U.S. Bureau of the Census, *State Government Finances in 1956,* Table 17; *1967 Census of Governments,* vol. 4, Table 48.
[18] *Ibid.*
[19] See Frederick L. Bird, *The General Property Tax: Findings of the 1957 Census of Governments,* Public Administration Service, Chicago, 1960.

case, special assessments are most commonly levied only for orna-
mental lighting and not for the ordinary type. In smaller suburbs,
however, and especially in unincorporated places, special-assessment districts may be created for all street lighting. Some cities
defray part of the cost of developing new parks and playgrounds by
special assessment.

The theory behind the special assessment is that certain neighborhood improvements installed by the city are of greater value to the
nearby property owners than they are to the citizenry at large. On
the other hand, they are not of *exclusive* interest to the nearby property owners, and the citizenry at large profit, as does perhaps the
city government itself. Because of special benefit, special charges
are levied. Yet it is difficult to determine a formula.

Obviously, you benefit greatly if the street in front of your home
is paved. You might be expected to pay for this benefit and not enjoy
this advantage at the expense of the general taxpayers of the city.
Should you pay *all* the cost, however? The neighbor on the next street
now finds your street a handy shortcut when he wants to reach the
arterial highway. Should he pay, too? How about the Torkelsons, who
are your best friends? They live miles away, but they use the street
almost every day. And how about Cousin Alfreda, who comes to visit
once a year? Or the department store that delivers parcels on the
street? Obviously, the cost cannot be apportioned directly and precisely in relation to benefit. (Special assessments are sometimes
used for arterial streets and highways, but traffic on these streets
may actually depreciate the value of homes along them.)

The problem is even greater in connection with the construction
of boulevards, parks, and playgrounds. A widened, beautified boule-
vard may generate increased traffic, noise, and dirt. Cities do not
often try to determine the economic benefits or costs from such
improvements. They may assess owners other than those whose
property is immediately abutting, but the formula is likely to be
rather arbitrary.

In trying to determine actual benefit, cities generally use a rule
of thumb, assessing part of the cost to the local property owner, and
having the general taxpayers of the city pay the rest. Where the city
shares the cost, there seems to be no predictable basis for the percentage of the cost that it will accept. Some cities pay 25 percent of
the cost; others pay 50, 80, or almost any other percentage one might
name.

There is also no general agreement as to when the special assessment should be used. Cleveland, Ohio, and Alhambra, California,
use it very extensively, for example. But Cranston, Rhode Island,

uses it only for water lines; Albuquerque, only for new street paving; and Fall River, Massachusetts, only for sidewalks.[20]

In newly developed urban areas, the older residents are likely to feel that special assessments should be used for nearly all capital improvements and that approximately 100 percent of the cost of improvements should be paid by the benefited property owner. Older residents often contend that they have already met all the costs of their own improvements and they do not think they should be required to help pay for those of the newcomers. This type of controversy is likely to be a part of the fringe-area problem.

Four principal methods of payment for special assessments are used. One is to demand advance payments from property owners. This requires them to be prosperous or to borrow the money from a private source. The use of this method is not uncommon. Secondly, the city may make temporary loans from a revolving fund. The property owners must repay these within a relatively short length of time. Thirdly, a few cities still issue property liens to the contractor who did the work, with the contractor then selling the liens to a local bank at a discount. These liens must usually be paid off in a time period of less than a year. They are lucrative for the bank but are not very satisfactory for the property owner. Lastly, and most commonly, cities issue special-assessment bonds in order to get cash to pay the contractor. The bonds, with interest charged on the unpaid portion, must then be paid off over a period of time, usually several years. This is simply another application of that popular institution, the installment plan. In Chicago, bonds must be paid in five years; in New York, in fifteen. At one time these bonds were commonly nothing but liens against property and hence could be sold to investors only if they bore a rather high rate of interest. Today, about two-thirds of the cities over 10,000 pledge the full faith and credit of the city as a guarantee that the bonds will be paid. This serves to safeguard the money of the investor and the good standing of the public credit and to make special improvements available to more property owners by reducing their interest costs.

Pay Cash or Issue Bonds? A debate that arises in every city from time to time centers in the alternatives of paying for capital improvements by issuing bonds or by increasing taxes and paying cash. The principles of borrowing on the municipal level are far different from those on the national level. The national government itself is the principal institution for the establishment of credit-creating institutions, chiefly the banks. If the national government borrows from

---

[20] *The Municipal Year Book* annually reports extensive data on special assessments.

banks, it is borrowing credit made possible largely by its own rules. Furthermore, the internally held national debt is not passed on to other generations. The credit of the United States is psychologically intertwined with nearly all that is held worthwhile by most Americans. Its borrowing power is limited only by the faith the American people have in their government, and that faith is enormous.

Municipalities enjoy none of these advantages of the national government when it comes to borrowing. Cities cannot create credit. Municipal debt can be, and is, passed on to future generations. When it is paid off, it is not a matter of taxing Americans to pay other Americans, as is the case with the national government. The debt of Nashville is held in many parts of the nation. If it is paid off in later years, Nashvillians must pay increased taxes, the proceeds of which are then distributed throughout the nation to bondholders. The result is a lower standard of living for the people of Nashville. The public faith in any given city is also immensely less than the public faith in the United States. Municipal borrowing power is accordingly greatly limited. Except for the nontax feature, municipal bonds are treated with no more respect on the open market than are the bonds of private corporations.

When should a city borrow money? Almost everyone is agreed that it should never be in a position of having to borrow to meet current operating expenses. In the past this has happened, either because a depression has dried up the revenue sources and the city was desperate, or because local officials desired to keep taxes low as a vote-gathering technique for the next election. Borrowing to pay for permanent improvements is another matter, at least if the bonds are to be paid off before the improvement becomes obsolescent or dilapidated. Borrowing to cover a period greater than the life of the improvement is never *economically* sound, although city councilmen find that it is often *politically* sound to postpone payment as long as possible. Cities sometimes borrow in anticipation of receipts that are scheduled to come in later in the fiscal year. They also borrow sometimes in the face of unanticipated emergencies.

Some people have argued that municipal-bond rates are so low that cities cannot afford *not* to borrow; others argue that cities should not borrow at all and should use a pay-as-you-go approach. It is sometimes said that cities should always pay cash because in this way they avoid the decades of interest payments that are often involved in borrowing, payments that may total several times the original cost of the improvement. There is also no chance of default or of bankruptcy if the city pays cash. And the city is less likely to be extravagant and buy more than its taxpayers are willing to afford.

Operating a city on a strict cash basis is impossible so long as the general property tax is the basic form of revenue. A cash basis means that the expenditures of the city will vary greatly from year to year, for one does not build a municipal auditorium, a new sewer system, or an expressway every year. If expenditures vary, the tax levy will also vary, and this creates problems in the property tax. This tax tends to become capitalized, affecting the value of the property directly. A varying tax would add a great element of uncertainty to the real estate market. People also prefer to know in advance what to expect in the way of taxes.

Some municipalities attempt to reduce the need for borrowing by the use of reserve funds which may be built up in anticipation of expenditures on capital improvements. Through the use of this device, tax rates can be kept stable and yet interest need not be paid on money used for many improvements. If the municipal government can determine the normal amount of annual capital outlay, the tax rate can be set high enough to provide funds for this purpose. Often, however, cities do not plan this well, or the money on hand is used for other than capital-development purposes. Political pressures often prevent the stockpiling of funds. Bonds, then, appear to be necessary or at least the most practical approach, politically, in many communities.[21]

Characteristics of Municipal Bonds. Traditionally, municipal bonds were paid off by the establishment of a *sinking fund* which would, in theory, provide sufficient funds to retire the bonds when they came due. Most of the bonds of this type would be issued so that all of them would fall due at the same time. The sinking-fund method has proved to be seriously defective in several respects, particularly because: (1) The council often failed to make adequate appropriations to the fund, which must be built up regularly and systematically, or the fund was otherwise tampered with for "political" reasons; and (2) the sinking fund could come to disaster in depression times if its investments failed.

More recently, most cities have tended to favor the use of *serial bonds.* These bonds mature gradually, a certain percentage of them each year. The council, instead of appropriating money into a sinking fund, appropriates the amount for the direct retirement of part of the debt. This is the same plan that is so popular in bank loans to private individuals today: Part of the principal is paid back each month, simplifying the planning for retiring the debt.

[21] See Carl H. Chatters and A. M. Hillhouse, *Local Government Debt Administration,* Prentice-Hall, Inc., Englewood Cliffs, N.J., 1939.

Another development is the inclusion of a call provision in municipal bonds. This is a feature, long included in many private bond issues, whereby the bonds can be paid off at any time prior to the date of maturity, at the option of the debtor. Of course, exercising such a privilege must be offset by paying a premium—a higher price —for the bonds than would otherwise be necessary. The call provision is nevertheless likely to be profitable for a sharp drop in interest rates, or a suddenly increased income of the city might make it desirable to pay off debts ahead of maturity dates.

Types of Municipal Bonds. In addition to the special-assessment bonds already mentioned above, cities commonly issue three types of bonds: general-obligation, mortgage, and revenue. General-obligation bonds are secured through a pledge that the full faith and credit of the local unit of government is available to pay them off. The community thus agrees to levy whatever tax is necessary in order to pay the interest and eventually to retire the bonds. Unless constitutional tax limits threaten to make this pledge meaningless, general-obligation bonds normally bear a relatively low rate of interest.

Mortgage bonds are normally used in connection with the purchase or construction of utilities, and they offer a mortgage on the utility as security. This type of bond has usually required a higher rate of interest than bonds of general obligation and as a result has been less popular. Sometimes mortgage bonds also involve a pledge of full faith and credit.

Revenue bonds have become increasingly popular in the years since the Great Depression. These bonds are secured by a pledge of the revenue from some self-liquidating project. Toll bridges, tunnels, and electric-light and water-supply systems may be financed in this way. Municipalities must agree to set rates high enough to pay the debt charges. Sometimes the bondholders are also given a mortgage on the utilities. Revenue bonds have several advantages for the municipality. These bonds are often not counted as part of the debt where a statutory or constitutional limitation exists. The ease with which their provisions can be enforced has made them very attractive to bond buyers.

Bond Prices and National-government Policies. The monetary policies of the national government are a major factor in determining the interest rates that must be paid by cities on their bonds. This is not the only factor: The credit standing of the city, the amount of existing debt, state restrictions upon taxing powers of the city, and other items are included in credit ratings. But when the United

States Treasury and Federal Reserve System follow an easy-credit policy, state and local governments are encouraged to borrow; possibly they are encouraged beyond what they may later consider to have been prudent. When the Federal government follows a hard-credit policy, state and local governments will find it more expensive to borrow money in order to make improvements they believe to be needed. In a time of expanding school-age populations, for example, it may be necessary to build schools regardless of the current cost of borrowing money. Federal policies are tied to political philosophies or to the business cycle; they do not consider current state and local needs and may work hardships on these units of government.

A second national-government money policy of importance to state and local governments is that of exempting the income from their bonds from taxation by the national government. A series of nineteenth-century Supreme Court decisions established the principle of intergovernmental tax immunity, according to which one government cannot tax the instrumentalities of another. This principle was, in effect, set aside by the Supreme Court around 1940, but Congress has not taxed the yield of state and local bonds because of opposition from those units of governments, from bond houses, and from holders of the bonds.

The advantage of tax exemption to the city is clear. With no taxes to be paid on interest income, the city can sell the bonds at a lower rate of interest and thus, in effect, receive a subsidy from the national government. Municipal bonds are purchased in large part by persons of high income who are seeking to avoid being placed in a still higher income tax bracket. The exemption feature thus, in effect, subsidizes individuals who least need subsidization. It is possible that this results in a greater loss in Federal revenue than the amount that it saves the cities.

Some students of taxation have urged that municipal bonds be made taxable by the Federal government and that the cities receive a Federal grant-in-aid to replace their lost interest-rate advantage. There are many complications involved in such a proposal, however, and municipal finance officers undoubtedly prefer to keep the present system rather than to experiment with something new and unknown.[22]

Municipal Tax Exemption for Industries. For a long time some of the states have authorized, sometimes even required, cities to exempt from property taxation for a certain number of years the manufac-

---

[22] See Lyle C. Fitch, *Taxing Municipal Bond Income*, University of California Press, Berkeley, Calif., 1950.

turing establishments of new industries in the city. The aim, obviously, is to attract industry to a city and thus provide greater wealth for the community. In some cases, tax exemption of a negative sort has been granted, too: An industry will threaten to leave the city and the state unless it is granted special tax consideration.

Beginning in 1936, the state of Mississippi went one step further with its "Balance Agriculture with Industry" program. It authorized cities to borrow money and to spend that money to buy or build industrial plants which would, in turn, be rented at a low rate to newly arrived industries. The bonds were to be retired from the rentals. Since 1951, a number of other states have adopted similar laws. These programs, like ordinary tax exemption, have been used particularly in the South in attempts to attract manufacturing. The textile industry has been most often enticed by them.

How effective has tax exemption been in attracting wealth-producing industries to a community? Studies offer some evidence to show that industries consider other factors as more important in determining sites, especially the availability of ample nonunion labor, and that cities offering special inducements gain little by such activity. In contrast, the risk is considerable, for the local tax base is undermined, and this produces serious problems in the event of a depression. When bonds have to be issued in order to build factories, a depression will find the community saddled with both the bonds and a "white elephant" factory. The Investment Bankers Association of the United States has condemned the practice for these reasons.

Tax exemptions are inequitable, too, for they are unfair to those businesses and private homeowners that do not receive exemptions. They are demoralizing to those who pay taxes faithfully. Tax exemptions assume that all in the community gain enough to warrant charging the cost to all the other taxpayers. Such is not necessarily the case, however. The system is also likely to attract unstable, fly-by-night industries that are the least likely to permanently strengthen the tax base.

Most students of taxation and of business economics condemn tax exemption or the use of public credit to attract industry. If economic conditions are favorable, if the city is well run, and if local groups such as the chamber of commerce are active, these authorities argue, there is no need to resort to inequitable and unsafe subsidies.[23]

---

[23] The contrary argument is given in W. E. Barksdale, "Mississippi's BAWI Program," *State Government,* 25:151–152, July, 1952.

The Politics of Industrial Recruitment. In previous generations, local government was not concerned with providing jobs in private industry for its citizens. The great business tycoons of those days possessed the image of the job giver. John D. Rockefeller, Henry Ford, and others like them were honored, in part, because they were seen as creators of work. As business became less personal and the heads of giant firms less dominating of total society, this image became blurred. Today, the role of the job giver is shared by many, but particularly by the secretary-manager of the local chamber of commerce and by the mayor or manager of the city. Effort to attract new industry is seen as a duty of the chief executive, and sometimes of the council members, too. This activity is in part ritual—it fits nicely into the image of the city as an instrument of economic growth—but it is in part in dead earnest. With American industry constantly expanding and decentralizing, many opportunities exist for cities to ensnare new plants. These differ according to the specific location of the community, of course, and the efforts made by the chief executive and the chamber of commerce representative tend to be canceled out by the almost identical efforts being made in the next town down the road, but local civic leaders are likely to feel that the effort must be made—if for no other reason than to try to keep up with the Jonesvilles.

As with other public policy matters, interests both favor and oppose city-government activity in industrial recruitment efforts. Generally speaking, local merchants and public utilities executives favor expanding the local work force because to do so offers them potentially more customers. The same interest exists for the local editor. The city manager can expect his pay to vary somewhat with the size of city, so in-migration of people or annexation of new territory may be profitable to him personally.

There are opponents of expansion, too. Marginal homeowners may fear that a policy of wooing new firms will mean generous tax allowances or the extension of municipally owned utilities to new locations at less than full cost. The person who can barely afford to own his home, and especially the retired person on relatively fixed income, is likely to see no benefit to him in the coming of another plant. He may see it as a threatened increase in the water bill and property tax. Industry already existing in the community may also oppose boosterism unless the firms that might be attracted could also become customers. If they could not, however, they are likely to be seen as competitors for the existing labor force. This means that new industry might bring pressure for higher wages. Or, especially if it is a national firm, it may bring into town a strong, active trade union. The union may represent a threat to the local balance of political as well as economic forces. Citizens, even some who may benefit financially from an increase in the local retail market size, sometimes oppose industrial expansion if it threatens to bring into the community new racial or ethnic groups or to alter substantially the existing ethnic balance.

The specific policies that a city may pursue as part of a program of boosterism vary with local conditions. Typical activities include the rezoning of land for industrial use, the extension of sewer and water lines to factory sites, efforts at annexation designed to bring potential industrial areas into the city, and a tax policy favorable to vacant land zoned industrial and to new plants. There may be a variety of other activities, too, such as a general program of beautification and of subtle or open advertising of the city as a "center of culture" and a nice place to live. (Wives of branch managers are said to sometimes have considerable influence over the precise location of plants. They are likely to reject grim, undistinguished, "uncultured" communities.)

FINANCIAL ADMINISTRATION

To most of the public, the city treasurer seems to be a very important person indeed, while the controller is an obscure bureaucrat who might do almost anything—or nothing. The auditor performs functions but hazily conceived of, but there is no doubt as to the duties of the tax collector. It is well, at this point, to examine the functions of the top fiscal administrators.

The Council. The city council formalizes basic financial policy for the city. It determines the tax rate, adopts the budget, and demands an accounting of the funds subsequently spent by the city. The budget is so much thought of as an administration document today that it is easy to overlook the fact that the council always must perform the final symbolic act of ratification on behalf of the people.

The Chief Administrator. The mayor or manager (in commission cities, the finance commissioner) acts as the chief fiscal officer of the city. Not only is he responsible for administration, but he often takes the lead in determining policies both of raising and of spending money.

The Treasurer. The office held by this person is one of the oldest in local government. As a traditional office, it was one that Jacksonians insisted upon making elective. Yet, the treasurer is really a glorified bookkeeper. He receives moneys according to law, the amounts of which have been determined by others. He is custodian of the city funds, although these are normally actually deposited in local banks. He must be able to account for each cent received. He pays out moneys only on orders from the controller. In none of these acts does he exercise any discretion, and he is not often called upon to advise the mayor or council on fiscal policies since, as an elected official, he is independent of them. His is a ministerial office, yet one-third of the cities still do elect him.

The Tax Collector. At one time, especially in New England, an officer of this title commonly existed. Today tax collection is merely one of the jobs of the treasurer in nearly all cities. In a few places, the job is retained as a separate one from that of the treasurer, who keeps and disburses the funds.

The Controller. The controller, or comptroller (pronounced "controller" in either case), or equivalent person, is an obscure officer to the general public, but he is the chief fiscal assistant to the mayor or manager. He is thus the person who performs the functions that the public often attributes to the treasurer. In about one hundred cities, the controller is elected, but in over 96 percent of the cities in which the office exists he is appointed.

The budget is often assembled, in the name of the mayor or manager and under his direction, by the controller or the budget officer in the controller's office. After the budget is assembled, it is reviewed and revised by the mayor or manager, and is then submitted to the council, which usually may alter it in any way it sees fit. After the council has adopted the budget for the ensuing year, the controller assumes the task of administering it. He must see to it that no department spends more than is authorized, that no department spends all its appropriation in the first quarter and is then without funds for the rest of the year, that all expenditures are legally authorized in every way, and that the departments have permission to spend *before* they proceed to make purchases. He must sign every payment voucher, and normally the treasurer can pay no claim against the city without the approval of the controller. He also serves constantly as the chief adviser to the mayor or manager on financial and frequently on other matters. In some cities he serves as deputy mayor.

In small cities, and often in larger ones, the functions of the controller are performed wholly or in part by the council itself. Many a council session is devoted principally to the approval of routine bills. In some cases, state law requires the council to perform this ministerial function.

The Assessor. The assessor (or board of assessors) is responsible for the valuation of property to serve as a basis for determining the general property tax. He is sometimes located within the department of finance, but often he has a separate office. And not all municipalities serve as assessing units. It was once common to elect the assessor, and about 13 percent of the municipalities in the country still do so, even though the job requires technical training.

Assessment, in theory, does not involve policy making but only the application of state and local rules to the evaluation of property. In practice, however, assessors are often important policy makers. They may have considerable latitude in deciding on the relative percentage of market value that they will assess homes as against businesses, or in rating the worth of one subdivision against another in terms of site value, or in granting favoritism to certain individuals or groups.

The assessor's office, once it has prepared the tax rolls after assessment, may send out tax bills, although this is more commonly the job of the treasurer and many tax jurisdictions do not send a bill to the taxpayer at all—it saves money not to do so. The assessor may also handle condemnation proceedings.

Boards of Tax Appeal. Because of the potential imcompetence, carelessness, or arbitrariness of the assessor, machinery for appeal and review of assessments exists in every taxing jurisdiction. The board of tax appeal (it has many different names) may be a special body, or it may be the city council. In either case, its work is difficult and its members are not likely to gain many friends through the decisions that are made. The board is ordinarily subjected to great pressures from the large taxpayers of the community, and individual householders who bring in appeals are likely to present their cases in highly emotional fashion.

Beyond the local board, in theory, lie appeals to higher authority, sometimes to a county board, usually to the state tax commission, and always to the courts. But these procedures are costly, time-consuming, and, unless the local assessor is vastly incompetent, usually unavailing. Only the largest taxpayers are likely to have enough influence and find the stakes large enough to expend the effort that is required.

The Purchasing Agent. Finance departments today often contain a division of purchasing. Through it most of the city's needs for supplies, materials, and equipment are procured so that savings of large-scale purchasing may be achieved.

The Department of Finance. In some cities, all the above officers are grouped together into a department of finance headed by a director. Authorities on financial administration believe that this is a desirable organization, since it provides for direction and coordination of these several financial activities. Council-manager cities, especially smaller ones, are likely to have an integrated department of this type. But in many cities each of the finance officers is independent and may be popularly elected.

The Auditor. The auditor is the agent for the *legislative* branch of government. His job is to check upon the executive branch to determine if expenditures it has made were according to appropriation and were otherwise legal. In a few cities, the auditor also makes recommendations to the council concerning the effectiveness of operation of the administrative agencies. Because the job is an old one, one auditor in ten is still elected, even though the position requires a knowledge of accounting. The auditor sometimes performs some of the functions described in this chapter as those of the controller.

Where the auditor is not elected, he may be chosen by the council, he may be sent to the city periodically from the state auditor's office, or the council may hire a private accounting firm to do a periodic audit. Large cities are likely to have their own auditing officers, smaller cities to use private firms or be subjected to a check by the state office, or both.

The important characteristic of the auditor is that he is independent of the chief executive officer. If this were not the case, the executive would simply be checking on himself. The independent auditor, however, is likely to be free to investigate and report as he sees fit. And he usually has a professional interest in doing so.

FINANCIAL PLANNING

The Executive Budget. During the enterprising years of municipal reform, "efficiency" and "economy" pressures were so great that many city councils lost part of their traditional power of control over the purse. This permitted the establishment of all or part of the executive-budget system which divided up the financial process so that the chief executive makes a recommendation for revenues and expenditures in the form of a systematic, comprehensive statement of income and outgo. The council then adopts this budget, nearly always with some, and perhaps with many, modifications. The executive next oversees the expenditure of the appropriations by the various departments, requiring them to spend at a rate that will not exhaust their appropriations prematurely and will keep expenditures within the requirements of the law. Finally, the council, through its auditors, checks to ascertain whether or not its instructions have been carried out and whether or not appropriate provisions of the state law have been followed by the executive. The power of the chief executive, through his budget officer, is potentially very great, both in preparing the budget itself—the document is, of course, a major policy statement, explaining how he would spend moneys—and in controlling its expenditure after the council votes the funds. The budget officer is, therefore, one of the chief executive's top aides today. He and his budget examiners serve to advise both the executive and the councilmen, reviewing appropriations requests and preparing evidence in support of policy positions. He often controls the conditions under which appropriations may be spent.

The trend toward centralized administration, the increasing number of functions of government, and the increasing complexity of those functions have contributed to the rapid rise in the use of the executive budget in the United States since the turn of the century. As a result of the change, responsibility—except in cities of the weak-mayor and commission types—for the innovation of taxation and appropriation proposals is placed in the hands of the executive, but with the council continuing to perform its ancient functions of criticism, review, modification, and, sometimes, rejection.

Until recent years, every budget dealt with all the minutiae that are needed to operate an office or function of government. Often the budget consisted of "line items" specifying the exact amount to be spent on a particular aspect of a function, and the funds were commonly not transferable from one line in the budget to another, even within the same department. The emphasis was upon the things to be acquired—paper clips, snow shovels, wheelbarrows—rather than upon the services to be rendered. This was necessary when public funds had to be guarded at all times against ingenious attempts at fraud. It encouraged, however, the citizen's habit of dissociating taxes from services provided. Many specialists in the field of fiscal administration have long urged that the budget should propose appropriations on a lump-sum basis. Under this plan, each agency or major subdivision would receive a single sum of money which the responsible administrator would then spend as he thought best—within generally established policies of the chief executive and the legislative body. Flexibility to meet unexpected emergencies and changes in service demands would result.

Since the original Hoover Commission reports in the late 1940s, a trend has been established toward a "performance" budget. This is a method of classifying expenditures so that each agency receives a lump sum for the operation of each of its different activities: so much for snow removal, so much for purchase of new park land, so much for public welfare programs. Although the method has its weaknesses, it is designed to help make clear to both legislators and the public what funds are being used for; it makes it easier to compare past performances with future requests; and it may encourage agencies to do a better job of thinking through their needs in making requests. The budget is designed to reduce the tendency under the older budget method (appropriation by objects) to stockpile materials and accelerate the purchase of services in order to exhaust appropriations. Legislators are sometimes cool toward the performance-budget idea, feeling that it has the effect of transferring still more fiscal power to the chief executive and the bureaucracy. The most rapid adoption of the performance budget has come in council-manager cities. It is used for all or part of the budget in other cities, some as large as Los Angeles.

The Budget as Policy. The budgeting function "is a specialized way of looking at problems in decision-making."[24] It is something of a negative view in the sense that after the agencies and interest groups have made known their positions, the budget examiners, and ultimately the chief executive, must balance off the various interests against one another and against a plausible estimate of income, often reducing requests. Budget making is also positive in the sense that a public budget is a basic statement of program and policy by the chief executive. He explains in it how he would evaluate the various demands upon the public funds, gives reasons for taking the stand that he does on the more controversial aspects of the program, and necessarily must stand willing to defend the explicit and implicit policies proposed in the budget. Many governments require agencies to estimate capital-outlay needs for several years—perhaps five years—in advance, thus making this part of the budget a long-range planning instrument, since capital needs cannot be considered apart from program needs. The budget, in this way, becomes to each agency a means for promoting both fiscal and program planning.

Contemporary budget practices have given state and local chief executives:[25]

> . . . an opportunity to take the initiative in the most encompassing set of policy decisions that a legislative session makes. Budget decisions are in detail decisions to continue, discontinue, extend, or diminish existing programs and to initiate new programs at a particular scale. They are also decisions about proposed and other construction and capital outlay. Budget decisions are, on a more general level, decisions on tax rates and tax policy and on the general scale of [governmental] activity. How much money agencies "need" depends upon the premises entertained by the estimator, and the estimates can vary substantially.

[24] Paul Appleby, "The Role of the Budget Division," *Public Administration Review*, 17:156–158, Summer, 1957.
[25] Karl A. Bosworth, "Lawmaking in State Governments," in The American Assembly, *The Forty-eight States: Their Tasks as Policy Makers and Administrators*, Graduate School of Business, Columbia University, New York, 1955, p. 106.

Nevertheless, these opportunities are not always taken. A study of the budget process in three Illinois cities concluded that in two cities officials do little more than to continue activities already established. However, in the third city, "budget preparation provides an occasion to challenge all current activities, to search out and identify new problems, and to suggest changes in activities to meet a re-defined set of priorities. A commitment to rationalism, furthermore, guarantees that the search for new problems and new alternatives will continue."[26]

The Parts of a Budget. A budget usually begins with a message from the chief executive which may say simply, in effect, "Here is the budget for the next fiscal year," or it may explain proposed new expenditures, tell why tax changes are requested, and otherwise explain policy positions. A brief summary of the budget for the benefit of citizens and reporters usually follows. Next comes the detailed breakdown. It may start with a statement of anticipated revenues from all taxes and other sources. This will be followed by the expenditures section, often broken down by funds: the general fund, plus a small or large number of others, such as a streets and highway fund, sometimes even a municipal-bond fund. A capital-outlay budget for new streets, buildings, and other structures will usually be presented separately from the operations budget, and the same may be true of utilities budgets, such as that of a municipal water-supply system. Provision must also often be made for governmental debt service. The budget may conclude with a statement concerning new taxes needed or the property-tax levy necessary to bring the budget into balance.

Preparing the Budget. In municipalities operating under the executive-budget plan, the document is prepared by a budget officer or controller under the chief executive. In a few cases, the budget is prepared by an independent, elected controller or an ex officio board. In weak-mayor cities, a council committee often prepares the budgets.

The process begins with the collection of estimates for the following year's needs prepared by the various agencies. In all but small cities, these are gone over by budget analysts who look for padding, inaccuracies, and inconsistencies. There may be conferences between the agencies and members of the budget division when differences arise. Such differences are likely to result from differing premises. The chief executive's own philosophy, and perhaps his evaluation of his own political strategy requirements, will affect his

[26]Thomas J. Anton, "Budgeting in Three Illinois Cities," *Papers of the Institute of Governmental Affairs*, University of Illinois, Urbana, Ill., 1964, p. 24.

own view of how "needs" should be interpreted in each agency. The agency will, however, probably use different criteria in arriving at "needs." It may base these on professional concepts of standards, or upon the pet interests of the agency head, or on the pressures it feels most from its clientele groups, or upon other considerations.

When detailed estimates of the needs of each department for the coming year are available, they are set out in parallel columns with statements of the estimated expenditures for the same items in the current year and the actual expenditures for those items in the fiscal year just completed. The budget officer next goes over the document in detail with the chief executive so that proposed changes in policy may be incorporated in the estimates.

The completely assembled budget is then ready to be sent to the council. Enclosed with it may also be the political future of the mayor, the career prospects of the young city manager, the hopes of the chief executive's critics for new ammunition in their fight, and the welfare of all the publics that reside within the boundaries of the city.

Enacting the Budget. The council has the responsibility for adopting the budget, nearly always with some, more commonly with many, modifications. It will usually hold budget hearings, either before the full body or before the tax and appropriations committees, the chairmen of which are normally senior legislators of great power. These hearings do not often give the councilmen information they do not already have, but they serve to allow groups and individuals to vent their annoyances, bitterness, or frustrations. They are an important part of the democratic process. A budget hearing is more likely to be attended by representatives of interest groups, however, than by a representative cross section of the general public. Some department heads may lobby at this time to get a bigger share of the pie than was given to them in the budget division. If the chief executive is weak administratively, this may be done quite openly. If he is strong, however, it must be done more subtly, for a dissident department head may risk his job by going over the head of the executive. Interest groups will at this time try to get favorable hearings, and those that find the legislative climate more receptive than was the executive may succeed in getting an increase in the department budgets in which they are interested. Other groups will have to fight to retain the level of funds recommended in the executive budget as legislators strive to reestablish a balance between income and outgo. Public employees may take the opportunity to try to improve their working conditions and pay, and the newspapers may use the occasion to view with alarm the ever increasing cost of government.

Usually the council is free to add, reduce, delete, or modify any part of the budget, although in some cases it may only reduce items or leave them unchanged and cannot introduce new items. In mayor-council cities, the chief executive usually has the power of the item veto and thus a final chance to preserve the integrity of his budget. **Administering the Budget.** In cities with the executive budget, the head of each department must submit a work program to the chief executive (or often, in practice, to the controller) before the beginning of a new fiscal year. This program will show how much of the total appropriation for that department is desired in each month or quarter of the coming fiscal year. This is known as the "allotment system." After approval, the allotments are turned over to the accounting division of the controller's office, which will then refuse to allow any money to be spent by that department unless it is authorized by the appropriations ordinance or statute and falls within the time provided in the allotment schedule. In cases where budget administration is less well organized, no allotment system may exist, and the auditor may be the only one to check for the legality of expenditure. In small cities, the governing body may itself exercise the control function by passing directly on individual bills presented for payment.

After the moneys have been spent, the auditor checks to ascertain the legality of all expenditures and reports his findings to the council and sometimes also to the state auditor. Even as the money is being spent throughout the year, however, the budget officer is surveying the scene for possible alterations in the next budget, for the governmental process is an unending one.

SELECTED
READINGS

Buehler, Alfred G.: "Problems Presented by Proliferation of Municipal Nonproperty Taxes," *Municipal Finance*, 34:106–111, February, 1962. (Shows that nonproperty taxes can raise considerable revenue, but that these offer more a palliative than a cure for local revenue problems.)

Burkhead, Jesse: *Government Budgeting*, John Wiley & Sons, Inc., New York, 1956. (A basic source, by an economist.)

———: *Public School Finance: Economics and Politics*, Syracuse University Press, Syracuse, N.Y., 1964.

Business Week, Dec. 16, 1961. (Offers a complete summary of tax benefits offered as inducements for industrial location.)

Crecine, John P. (ed.): *Financing the Metropolis*, Sage Publications, Inc., Beverly Hills, Calif., 1971. (Emphasizes the interaction between public and private sectors.)

Financing Government in New York City, Graduate School of Public Administration, New York University, New York, 1966. (Report to a study commission.)

Goodall, Leonard E.: *State Regulation of Local Indebtedness in the United States*, Bureau of Government Research, Arizona State University, Tempe, 1964.

Hillhouse, A. M.: *Municipal Bonds: A Century of Experience*, Municipal Finance Officers' Association, Chicago, 1936.

——— and Muriel Magelsson: *Where Cities Get Their Money*, Municipal Finance Officers' Association, Chicago, 1946. (Not current, but still useful.)

International City Managers' Association: *Municipal Finance Administration,* 6th ed., International City Management Association, Chicago, 1962

Isard, Walter, and Robert Coughlin: *Municipal Costs and Revenues Resulting from Community Growth,* Chandler-Davis Publishing Co., Wellesley, Mass., 1957.

Martin, Roscoe C.: *The Cities and the Federal System,* Atherton Press, New York, 1965.

Moak, Lennox L.: *Administration of Local Government Debt,* Municipal Finance Officers' Association, Chicago, 1970.

Mosher, Frederick C., and Orville F. Poland: *The Costs of American Governments,* Dodd, Mead & Company, Inc., New York, 1964. (An especially valuable collection of data and analysis of revenue, spending, and indebtedness.)

Peabody, Robert L.: *Seattle Seeks a Tax,* The Bobbs-Merrill Company, Inc., Indianapolis, ICP no. 49, 1959.

Schroth, Thomas N., and others: *Congress and the Nation, 1945–1964,* Congressional Quarterly Service, Washington, 1965, chap. 10. See also 1969 supplement.

Scott, Stanley, and E. L. Feder: *Factors Associated with Variations in Municipal Expenditure Levels,* Institute of Public Administration, University of California, Berkeley, Calif., 1957.

Sigafoos, Robert A.: *The Municipal Income Tax: Its History and Problems,* Public Administration Service, Chicago, 1954.

Tax Foundation, Inc.: *Factors Affecting Industrial Location: A Bibliography,* Tax Foundation, Inc., New York, 1956.

——— : *The Financial Challenge to the States,* Tax Foundation, Inc., New York, 1958.

——— : *Research Bibliography: Financing Municipal Government,* Tax Foundation, Inc., New York, 1960.

U.S. Advisory Commission on Intergovernmental Relations: *State Constitutional and Statutory Restrictions on Local Government Debt,* 1961.

——— : *State Constitutional and Statutory Restrictions on Local Taxing Powers,* 1962.

——— : *Tax Overlapping in the United States,* 1964.

——— : *The Commuter and the Municipal Income Tax,* 1970.

U.S. Bureau of the Census: *Historical Statistics on State and Local Government Finances,* 1955.

——— : *Local Government Finances in Selected Standard Metropolitan Statistical Areas,* 1966.

Vernon, Raymond: "The Economies and Finances of the Large Metropolis," *Daedalus,* 90:31–47, Winter, 1961. (The revenue problems of core cities and suburbs.)

Winter, William O.: *The Special Assessment Today,* Institute of Public Administration, University of Michigan, Ann Arbor, Mich., 1952. (Standard reference. Since it was written, use of this approach has continued to spread.)

———— and R. W. Rickey: *The Special Assessment in Illinois,* Public Affairs Research Bureau, Southern Illinois University, Carbondale, Ill., 1959.

Wright, Deil S.: *Trends and Variations in Local Finances, The Case of Iowa Counties,* Institute of Public Affairs, the University of Iowa, Iowa City, Iowa, 1965.

PART
2 THE POLITICS OF URBAN FUNCTIONS AND SERVICES

In the remaining chapters, we will look at policy outputs and issues surrounding policy making in given areas of urban governmental activity. Earlier chapters described the political environment and the machinery that makes the political process operate. What is said in them will be more enduring than what follows, for the agenda of city government is transitory, subject to extreme and often unexpected changes, and the issues of one year (no matter how vigorously debated) may seem very stale the next. Here, however, were some of the agenda items and on-going policies of the early 1970s.

A THE
POLITICS
OF LAW
AND
JUSTICE

CHAPTER
14 PUBLIC SAFETY

A great many of the functions of municipal government are related to the safety of the public. In this chapter, fire protection, smoke abatement, traffic engineering, civil defense, and, in particular, police functions will be discussed. Except in a relatively few cities, these functions are not grouped together into a single department. Their methods of operation and their technical requirements are so different that most cities assign police and fire to separate departments.

A PUBLIC ATTITUDE OF LAISSEZ FAIRE

An Old Story. In 1951, American televiewers were fascinated by the unsystematic but overwhelming collection of evidence concerning organized crime activities in the United States gathered by the staff of a Senate committee and presented, largely through the interrogation of witnesses, to the public. The Special Committee to Investigate Organized Crime in Interstate Commerce, headed first by Senator Estes Kefauver of Tennessee and later by Senator Herbert O'Conor of Maryland, amazed even cynical Americans. It frightened some local officials, if no professional gamblers. It made Senator Kefauver a hero to many Americans and made him a formidable presidential candidate at the 1952 Democratic National Convention. The investigation did considerable damage to the already shaky reputation of local-government officials and reinforced many misconceptions of long standing concerning public officials.[1] But whether any permanent diminution in the activities of organized criminals resulted is doubtful. With the exception of a few communities, the ordinary citizen did not rise up in wrath at the reports. The problem of a policy toward the social functions performed traditionally by organized crime is yet to be met, or even faced frankly. Certainly it was not much considered in the Kefauver reports.

The situations uncovered by the Kefauver committee are not new or different: They are a restatement of long-existing practices. In fact, they may be viewed as one aspect of old-time machine politics that has not been eradicated.

The professional criminal is sometimes strictly predatory—the bank robber and the pickpocket, for example—but those who are organized into crime syndicates are normally providers of services to the general public. These services differ from those of the butcher, physician, or insurance salesman chiefly in that they are illegal and are usually considered immoral or detrimental to health. It was concerning these services that the Kefauver committee made the flat statement that "these operations could not continue without the protection of police and without the connivance of local authorities."[2]

What Makes Crime Possible? Part of the difficulty in suppressing crime stems from an ambivalent attitude. We have inherited certain puritanical values which condemn gambling and purely pleasurable activity. On the other hand, we live in a culture that is dynamic, complex, impersonal, and materialistic. Our whole economic and cultural pattern is based upon competition and "getting ahead."[3] Gambling and crime against property, therefore, are partly a result of a *hope for gain,* a desperate need to succeed.

In our competitive society, it is often difficult to distinguish the criminal from the noncriminal. Many business activities verge on the classification of racketeering; certainly they often violate the moral values of many individuals. "Anything's fair in business if you can get away with it." If so, how does one distinguish legitimate and illegitimate businesses? Many Americans believe that you cannot do so. Americans have never strongly believed that *all* laws should be obeyed.[4] A multimillionaire once told a Senate committee that it was

---

[1] The Kefauver hearings and reports include some twenty-five volumes. See *Hearings before the Special Committee to Investigate Organized Crime in Interstate Commerce,* 1951. There were also three *Interim Reports* and a *Final Report* of the Special Committee, 1951, cited hereafter as Kefauver committee, *Third Interim Report,* etc.

[2] Kefauver committee, *Second Interim Report,* p. 3.

[3] Donald R. Taft, *Criminology,* 3d ed., The Macmillan Company, New York, 1956, chap. 15. On crime as a ladder of social mobility, see Daniel Bell, *The End of Ideology,* The Free Press of Glencoe, New York, 1960, chaps. 7–8.

[4] Taft, *op. cit.,* p. 236.

morally right for an individual to avoid paying all taxes that he could possibly shirk. "Everyone has his racket." So why condemn gamblers, prostitutes, narcotics peddlers, or bootleggers?

An additional complication arises as a result of the fact that we are a heterogeneous population consisting of many sub-cultures, each with a variant set of values. There is no general agreement as to what is right or wrong. So the individual follows his own value pattern. He does not agree with the views of his neighbor, but he tolerates them.

The *Uniform Crime Reports* of the Federal Bureau of Investigation year after year indicate that, of all crimes, murder is the one most likely to be solved. This is partly because solution is aided by a strong and obvious motive which is usually present whenever this crime is committed. But it is also partly because the public *wants* murderers to be apprehended. The punishment for the crime is likely to be severe, because what the public *says* is its attitude toward murder agrees with what the public actually *does* hold as its attitude toward murder. Social mores and criminal law do not always agree so nicely.

Prostitution and the sale or use of narcotics are everywhere illegal. Gambling, with certain exceptions, is illegal in all states except Nevada. (Lotteries and some other types of gambling are legal in a number of states.) Yet in every large city, and in a great many medium- and small-sized cities, one may find gamblers, prostitutes, and narcotics and other drug peddlers engaging in their occupations. There is a large demand for these services, and hence some people will supply them in spite of almost all hazards. Unlike murder, gambling is not identically viewed by the citizen in his public and his private opinions. For the sake of social appearances, the individual is likely to condemn it publicly regardless of his real views. The same thing is true, in lessening degrees, of prostitution and narcotics peddling, particularly in respect to marijuana.

Laws in serious conflict with the mores of society are unenforceable. A large segment of the public does not want the laws on gambling rigidly enforced. An even larger segment is indifferent to the question of how they are enforced. Many people do not gamble, but they do not object if their neighbors do.[5] Likewise, some cultural groups in our society accept the existence of the prostitute as an ordinary part of life. And a large number of persons who would themselves never enter what was once called a "house of ill fame" are not incensed at the thought that such places exist in their city. A 1958 study of the American Social Hygiene Association found that prostitution was commonplace in thirty-eight out of one hundred and

[5] Virgil W. Peterson, "Obstacles to Enforcement of Gambling Laws," The Annals of the American *Academy of Political and Social Science*, 269:9–20, May, 1950, holds that "self-interest, personal conveniences, and expediency" are the principal motivating factors in law evasion and in the public attitude toward law enforcement. But this does not fully explain the tolerance of nonparticipants for some types of law evasion and intolerance for others.

twenty-five communities studied. In the other eighty-seven, it was at an "irreducible minimum."[6]

A growing number of persons are slaves of narcotics. Their use produces many physical, psychological, and social problems. The cravings of the addict are powerful and the demand for the product is so inelastic that this risky business remains alive if for no other reason than that it is greatly profitable.

Psychological Factors. In our society, gambling, either in the casino or in taking a chance on not being caught in illegal activity, often serves to fill important psychological needs. To some, it is an escape from a troublesome, unsuccessful world. To others, it is, like liquor, and drugs, a crutch, and hence something highly necessary, or it is simply enjoyment, excitement, and the vicarious conquering of worlds that will not lend themselves readily to conquering outside the gambling casino. Millions of Americans—psychopaths and normal people—spend greater or lesser amounts of time gambling.

The psychological factors behind such other illegal occupations as prostitution and narcotic-drug sales are complex and beyond the scope of this text. It must be borne in mind that psychological factors are stimulated and conditioned by their sociological environment. There is, for example, almost certainly no inherent desire or need to gamble. But there is a need for security, and this psychological desire may be directed toward gambling as a possible means of fulfillment.

Legal Factors. Americans, especially of the middle classes, have a rather naïve faith in law and punishment as solutions for social problems.[7] As a result, the superficial action of making an occupation illegal is mistaken for a move toward the abolition of the occupation. Psychological and sociological phenomena cannot be legislated away, for their causes are complex and deep-seated. Since demand is not eliminated by making the occupation illegal, such action merely has the effect of creating racketeering and gangsterism as well as an increased disrespect for the law.

The Pattern of Corruption. It should not be assumed, because a certain number of houses of prostitution are known to exist in the city, or because rumors have it that there are some narcotics peddlers about, or because the numbers racket is still in business, that the officer on the beat is being bribed or that the city administration is necessarily corrupt. It is true that none of these things could take

---

[6] *Social Hygiene News*, 34:1, February, 1959.
[7] Taft, *op. cit.*, p. 235.

place without knowledge of the city administration and police offi-cials. That does not always mean that they *want* or *like* it that way.

In a large city, almost inevitably at least some prostitution exists. The administration may want to eliminate all of it, but it will find this to be an impossibility, practically speaking. The administration may decide upon a compromise with the strict letter of the law, permitting prostitution within narrowly defined areas of the city and with the stipulation that it not attract unfavorable publicity. A policy such as this does not necessarily indicate corruption, and the administrators who establish it would defend it as "practical."

Although quite a few city administrations may cooperate with gambling and some with prostitution, few will make an alliance with purveyors of narcotics. Even if they should want to, state and Federal law-enforcement officers are particularly alert and active in seeking out these persons. Yet most cities are quite certain to have dope peddlers. There is no simple formula for destroying the elaborate and extensive narcotics rings that are organized to carry on this profit-able business.

Gambling. Gambling, an ancient type of human activity, is very widespread and it takes many forms: the policy racket or numbers game; the bookmakers who take bets on horse races, athletic events, and even the outcome of presidential elections; the casinos with a great variety of card and dice games, the slot machines, which add mechanical ingenuity to the pattern, and others.

The police can never escape knowing of the existence of gambling, but they may not be able to eliminate it even when they wish to do so. Sometimes, of course, they have no such wish. The attitude of a city administration toward gambling can be determined to some degree simply by observing the type of gambling that is tolerated. The policy racket, for example, probably could not be completely eliminated in large cities. Convictions are difficult, the evidence is easily hidden, and the operators are highly mobile. On the other hand, gaudy ca-sinos in the Monte Carlo tradition or heavy, bulky slot machines cannot be operated except with the passive cooperation of the police.

Gambling is big business in many American cities. Rough esti-mates by Kefauver staff workers found that nationwide illegal off-track betting on horse racing totaled from 3 to 5 *billion* dollars annu-ally. This was in addition to some 2 billion dollars legally bet each year at the racetracks. It was estimated that the net profit on 3 billion dollars to illegal bookmakers would be not less than 600 million dollars each year. All these figures have expanded since the early 1950s.

Similarly, "In Chicago some $10,000,000 is spent annually on policy playing alone; no other business in the Negro community is so large or so influential. As elsewhere in Negro communities, the policy racket in Harlem is the most widespread form of lawbreaking."[8]

The Kefauver committee concluded that at least 20 billion dollars changed hands each year in organized illegal gambling of all kinds. No estimate was attempted as to the amount of this that was paid in protection money, except to state that it must amount to millions of dollars annually.[9]

Police Graft. Where illegal occupations take place with the permission of the police, graft may be collected at either the top or the bottom of the hierarchy. The patrolman may receive petty bribes. If payments are at the top, however, the money is not likely to be passed along downward. But in that event, the effect upon the morale of the ordinary patrolmen cannot be anything but unhappy. A policeman under these circumstances will meet with nothing but futility and frustration. He will find that, even if he is not personally bribed, there is no point in his attempting to enforce laws that it is not the policy of the department to have enforced. He will not secure convictions—or promotions for himself—if he does. He may become cynical and resort to picking up graft on his own. The knowledge of rookie officers that the top administration does not respect the law leads to low morale that will reflect itself in poor law enforcement in all fields, not in just the "protected" areas.

The Kefauver investigations demonstrated some of the methods of graft payments to top police administrators and to members of the city administration.[10] The hearings and the summaries of conditions in various cities in the reports show that traditional techniques are still being used:[11]

> In some cases, the protection is obtained by the payment of bribes to public officials, often on a regular basis pursuant to a carefully conceived system. In other cases, the racketeering elements make substantial contributions to political campaigns of officials who can be relied upon to tolerate their activities. Sometimes these contributors will support a whole slate of officers in more than one political party, giving racketeers virtual control of the governing body.

The interests of those who favor lax enforcement may be power-

[8] Maurice R. Davie, *Negroes in American Society,* McGraw-Hill Book Company, New York, 1949, p. 254.
[9] Kefauver committee, *Second Interim Report,* pp. 13–14.
[10] A history of the relationship of crime and politics in Chicago is given in Virgil W. Peterson, *Barbarians in Our Midst,* Little, Brown and Company, Boston, 1952.
[11] Kefauver committee, *Final Report,* p. 5.

ful and highly effective. The city council of Camden, New Jersey, stripped the mayor of control over the police department and took away other powers in 1960, after he tried to eradicate organized gambling in the city. The mayor had been elected a year earlier on a reform platform, ousting an incumbent who had held office nearly a quarter of a century.

The Vice-squad Pattern. Where a city government or only the top police leadership of a city has been corrupted by organized crime, it is necessary to find a method of making certain that promised protection is actually afforded. A police commissioner and his chief lieutenants will not wish to share their payments with ordinary policemen, yet the rank and file of the departments are sworn to enforce the law. To circumvent the ordinary policeman—who may, after all, be an honest individual who took his job thinking that it was the task of policemen to enforce laws—police heads commonly resort to what the Kefauver investigators called the "vice-squad pattern":[12]

> This device is used in many cities where the rackets thrive. The political department bosses set up a vice squad composed of a chosen few directly accountable to them. They instruct the remaining law enforcement officers to stay away from gambling and vice and to channel any complaints to the vice squad for action or, in most cases, inaction. By this device a small clique frequently controls the collection of the protection pay-off.

The person who observes the existence of corruption in some particular city should not assume that the cop on the beat is lining his pockets with illegal payments or that he is callously unconcerned with the law. His hands are tied.[13]

Crime and the Culture. Gambling, prostitution, and predatory crimes against property, as well as (in a modified way) crimes against the person, are a product of the culture. Our own values, goals, and behavior patterns to a large extent determine the extent of their existence. Certain kinds of overt behavior can be punished by the judicial system, but the behavior itself cannot be legislated away. Organized criminal gangs as a means toward recognition, wealth, and power; gambling by the respectable businessman; embezzlement as means toward quick cash; even the sex-crime rate—none of these will deviate from their present statistical trends unless society's values

[12] Kefauver committee, *Third Interim Report*, pp. 95–96. Most police departments have vice squads. It should not be inferred that the existence of such a group implies corruption.
[13] It is sometimes argued that gambling, if not prostitution, could be better controlled if it were legalized. For arguments, see Kefauver committee, *Final Report; The Annals of the American Academy of Political Science*, the entire issue titled, "Gambling," vol. 269, May, 1950; and David D. Allen, *The Nature of Gambling*, Coward-McCann, Inc., New York, 1952.

and life patterns change. They are, whether the individual may want them or not, part of our way of life, and they are the daily bread and butter of the policeman and the judge.

POLICE PROTECTION

Although vice and organized crime are not the major police problems of today, they are among the most difficult to combat. In the typical city, these occupations exist in spite of the efforts of the police department, if they exist at all. Most departments, it should be understood, enforce the law to the extent that they are permitted by public opinion as reflected in the political process. Two of the major problems in connection with police work in recent years have been the continuing increase in the crime rate in postwar America and the increasing cost of police protection.

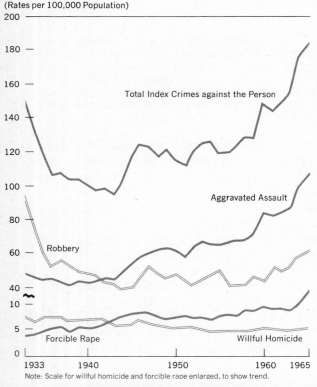

Figure 14-1. Index crime trends, 1933–1965. Reported crimes against the person. *Source:* The President's Commission on Law Enforcement and Administration of Justice, *The Challenge of Crime in a Free Society,* 1967.

The insecurities of continued international tensions have added a new psychological factor to the many other reasons for a high American crime rate. The number of serious crimes committed in the United States, according to the *Uniform Crime Reports* of the FBI, increases every year almost without exception.[14]

The Crime Rate. The crime rate increased at four times the rate of the population in the years 1950 to 1958, and the conviction rate declined. Significant increases have taken place in all types of crimes, except murder and manslaughter, the rates of which have remained near their prewar levels. One reason for this, perhaps, is that the odds are in favor of the robber, auto thief, or burglar each time he commits a crime (unless he resorts to violence). The police catch relatively few thieves—only in about three cases in ten is anyone even charged with the offense. The public does not tolerate a similar lack of success where a person loses his life.

The American crime rate is several times as high as that of any European nation; yet, as in the case of the fire department, the police are the best equipped in the world. A well-known police chief once said: "Despite the technology that has been acquired through no small effort and expense, the police service today fulfills its task with no greater success than it did a quarter- or half-century ago."[15]

Americans tend to be careless of property losses resulting from robbery just as they tend to be careless of fire losses. The poor record of American police is, therefore, partly a result of public apathy. Furthermore, "the individual police officer operates with a remarkable lack of public support, cooperation or trust."[16] The police are sometimes partly hampered by efforts to "save" tax money. American police forces are small by comparison with European forces.

The Omnibus Crime Control and Safe Streets Act. In 1968, Congress passed the first legislation giving the Federal government a substantial role in local law enforcement efforts. Planning grants and funds for training programs, equipment, and research are funneled through the states to urban areas. One aspect is to increase professionalization of local departments. A second is to encourage coordination among local units. A major emphasis was placed on techniques for controlling riots and combating organized crime. Among the features of the act is an increase in FBI training activities.

---

[14] See Taft, *op. cit.*, or one of the other textbooks in that field. For a view that crime is not increasing, that the contrary impression is a result of newspaper exploitation and statistical anomalies, see Bell, *op. cit.*, chap. 8. See also "Has Crime Passed Its Peak: City-by-City Report," *U.S. News and World Report*, Jan. 18, 1971, pp. 13–19. This discusses the drop in crime rate in twenty-three major U.S. cities and examines the question of whether it is a lasting or temporary change. Major factors claimed for the decrease were increased public support of police efforts, professionalization, quicker trials, sterner courts, new techniques, and improved funding and staffing of police.
[15] William H. Parker, "The Police Challenge in Our Great Cities," *The Annals of the American Academy of Political and Social Science*, 291:5–13, January, 1954.
[16] *Ibid.*, p. 5.

Funding still falls short of what experts desire and emphasis is on dealing with crime rather than its prevention, but as in other areas following the introduction of Federal funds and standards, the result will in time be a more professionalized program.[17]

Police Organization. Police and fire departments, by tradition, are organized along quasi-military lines. The head of the police department is commonly a professional policeman called the chief. (Terminology for various ranks is not standardized. The most common titles will be used in this section.) In some cities, especially in the largest cities, the highest-ranking uniformed officer may be subordinate to a lay department head, called the commissioner, director, or in a few cities, the chief. The lay department head usually does not perform details of departmental administration. His job is to serve as liaison officer between the force and the chief executive. At one time a council committee administered the police department, and in the last half of the nineteenth century, it was common for the department to be operated by a semiautonomous board. This is still the case in about seventy cities but is increasingly giving way to control of the department by the chief executive.

When the head of the department is a professional policeman, he usually serves the chief executive at his pleasure. Under this arrangement, if the appointing chief executive or his successor wishes to appoint a new chief, the incumbent is not dismissed from the service but is dropped back to a lower position in the departmental hierarchy.

Under the chief, and depending largely upon the size of the city, are numerous supervisory officers arranged in a hierarchy. They are traditionally given military titles. Under the chief, there may be assistant chiefs, then majors or inspectors (especially if the city is large enough to have precinct or district stations), captains, lieutenants, and sergeants. The patrolmen make up the broad base of the pyramid. Detectives may outrank patrolmen, or they may merely be patrolmen with a special job-position classification.

The force is organized according to the nature of the tasks performed (e.g., patrol and traffic divisions). Larger cities are divided into geographical districts, or precincts, especially for administering the patrol force. In some cities, some of the specialized divisions may also be decentralized so that they operate out of the district stations. Since police work, particularly that of the patrol division, is continuous, the force is also divided into platoons, or shifts.[18]

[17] For a criticism of the act's strengths and shortcomings, see Charles B. Saunders, Jr., *Upgrading the American Police: Education and Training for Better Law Enforcement*, Brookings Institution, Washington, 1970, especially pp. 152–172.
[18] On police organization, see O. W. Wilson, *Police Administration*, 2d ed., McGraw-Hill Book Company, New York, 1963.

Recruitment. American policemen, although improving in ability, are generally considered by authorities to be of inferior quality when compared with European policemen. A part of the cause of this may be traced to low salary schedules. Because policemen are usually prohibited from holding a second job, low pay is probably a particularly important inhibition against recruitment.

The earliest salaried policemen in America were political appointees. Gradually applicants came to be subjected to physical, mental, and moral examinations or scrutiny. In many cities of all sizes, the recruitment and disciplining of police are under the control of the municipal personnel agency. Police administrators in general disapprove of this practice and desire independent control over personnel. (Police administrators, like members of other professions, desire autonomy for their function of government. Because of the unique nature of their task, they often succeed in securing independence from central municipal staff services in budgeting, personnel, purchasing, and maintenance, and from traffic engineering.)

The Jail. The city jail is usually administered by the police department. The local prison is likely to be primarily of the congregate type of design with a large bullpen to house most prisoners. There may be a few cells to segregate notoriously tough prisoners and the violently insane. Jails are seldom constructed to meet the multifunctional demands placed upon them. They house a great variety of persons: major offenders awaiting trial; habitual misdemeanants, many of them psychopaths; elderly degenerates; youthful minor offenders; traffic violators; drunks locked up for a single night; vagrants; material witnesses; and others.[19]

At least 1 million persons spend some time in jail each year. It is doubtful if many profit from the experience. The general public has never regarded jails as being of much importance and does not approve of the expenditure of large amounts of money "to make things comfortable for crooks and drunks." Police administrators of jails, in the great majority of cases, are concerned with custody, and little effort is made in most cities to identify the personal problems which helped cause incarceration. Even less effort goes toward rehabilitation or preventive activities.

Many professional students of police administration believe that the image of the policeman would be better if the police could be freed from responsibility for the custodial function of operating the jail. An independent custodial agency or one under the control of the prosecutor who is responsible for preparing criminal cases would serve to eliminate some of the suspicions as to what happens to an

[19] U.S. Bureau of Prisons, *Handbook of Correctional Institution Design and Construction,* 1949, p. 168.

individual while in the hands of the police and awaiting trial. Much of the criticism of the police has concentrated upon the treatment of an accused immediately after he is taken into custody and upon the conditions existing in the jail while he is awaiting trial. Although many police executives would prefer to be free of responsibility for this portion of the criminal-justice process, apathy, lack of understanding of the process, and fear of increased costs make such a separation of responsibilities difficult to achieve.

Public Relations. The police have enormous problems in seeking public acceptance of their policies. It is almost impossible to satisfy all the public that the police are doing their jobs effectively and properly. Because the police symbolize power, authority, and the status quo, they are viewed with fear and suspicion by some persons. New Left radicals tend to see police as the enemy, rather than the protector, of society and consider them unthinking defenders of the status quo and of middle-class morality. The police are often accused of ignoring the fact that various minority groups have other value systems which they view as being equally deserving of acceptance and protection. Liberals often seem to suspect the police of having no commitment to the principles of civil rights and liberties and of viewing these as nothing more than obstacles to effective law enforcement.

Members of minority groups are often thought to be hostile toward the police and some militant reformers among them certainly are. They often charge the police with "brutality," and without doubt some police are sometimes discourteous, thoughtless, and even insulting in dealing with people who, they fear, see them only as enemies. Yet, a study in 1966 indicated that Negroes living in urban ghettos are more concerned about securing police protection than they are about problems of police brutality. They are deeply concerned about crime and the problems of narcotics addiction. The study concluded that: "Police brutality, as such, was not a volunteered problem of concern for the people of Harlem."[20] The same was true in the Watts area of Los Angeles. The first 300 complaints to the New York Civilian Review Board came principally from middle-class rather than slum areas of the city. When the board was established, it was expected that the large bulk of complaints would be from Negroes and Puerto Ricans concerning brutality. Actually fewer than one-half of the complaints came from these minority groups, and most seem to have dealt with unnecessary use of force against, or discourtesy to, middle-class persons. These are persons who are more likely to protect themselves from what they regard

[20] John F. Kraft, *Attitudes of Negroes in Various Cities,* John F. Kraft, Inc., New York, 1966. A report prepared for the American Broadcasting Company.

as abuse, of course, while slum dwellers may be afraid to complain, or regard it as useless.[21]

Complaints, especially from liberal reformers, concerning alleged discourteous and brutal behavior by police have led to demands for establishing review boards consisting wholly or in part of civilians unconnected with the police department. Such a board is designed to hear complaints from citizens. It usually is not proposed that the board should have disciplinary powers, but only that it make recommendations to the chief of police. Policemen, from patrol to command positions, oppose civilian review boards, generally arguing that while they may help correct some injustices, they do more harm than good by undermining morale and reduce efficiency by inhibiting the policeman in the exercise of his duties. The New York Patrolmen's Benevolent Association, for example, succeeded in having a referendum vote to abolish such a board established in that city in mid-1966. Voters overwhelmingly agreed with the association in the November, 1966, election.

Police argue that complaints should go to command officers and, if necessary, to police trial boards, which have long existed in large- and medium-sized departments. Critics reply, however, that police, like members of all professions, tend to cover up for the errors made by colleagues and that such trial boards are effective only when a policeman has violated the informal expectations of the police fraternity, such as by endangering the life of a fellow officer through carelessness or by threatening to bring bad publicity to the department.

The police hear thunder from both ends of the political continuum. They are also subject to attack from right-wing extremists. In this case for exactly the opposite reasons used by the New Left—they are accused of not using enough force, of giving in to alleged liberal pressures to "coddle" criminals, of not meeting violence with violence. The John Birch Society has used the slogan, "Support Your Local Police," an appeal that gives the police an additional cross to bear, since it causes liberals and left-wing radicals to wonder about the desirability of their doing so. Rightist groups have attempted to infiltrate some police departments, and some police executives have been forced to decide whether John Birch Society members should be allowed to serve on the force. Publicity relative to such problems makes public relations an extremely sensitive problem.

Additional problems for police come from the fact that their activities are a ready source for news stories. The police are always

[21] *The New York Times*, Oct. 21, 1966.

"in a vulnerable position in regard to the press; since they deal with human beings, it is easy for the press to criticize almost every police act and be assured of sympathetic support at least from those citizens who have been subjected to some police control,"[22] and, usually, from many others as well. It is generally easier for a reporter to portray the accused in a sympathetic light than it is to show a policeman as a hero (unless he has happened to rescue a wounded dog from a sinking boat) or to show that police help to maintain order in an always potentially violent society.

The police themselves contribute to the low esteem in which they are held. Every year some serious police scandal occurs in a major city. Similar scandals also occur in small towns and small cities. Although the vast bulk of our police forces are undoubtedly men of honor who want to do good jobs, the ones who get the headlines establish the public image. High-ranking police officers sometimes make serious tactical blunders, too.

The police often try to build up a favorable image of themselves among grammar school children, hoping thus to develop an attitude that will carry over into adult life. Unfortunately for the police, much of this image is undone when the children become adolescents and begin to drive automobiles. Every college student knows that the police watch younger drivers especially carefully and that they are less likely to be given the benefit of the doubt in marginal cases. It is also likely that the police, on the average, are less courteous to young drivers than they are to older ones. The police have a reason for their suspicion of young drivers, of course. These represent, by all odds, the least competent drivers on the road, as a group, and the ones most likely to cause accidents and to have serious injuries in the event of accidents. (Insurance company rates reflect the same findings.) But whatever the cause of the attitude, it is damaging to the image of the police officer and probably has its effect upon the citizen in later life.

FIRE PROTECTION

Color, Drama—and Carelessness. American cities have the finest fire equipment in the world, but they also have the greatest annual fire losses. Such losses in the United States exceed 1,000 million dollars annually—most of it in cities. Americans are not economy-conscious. Europeans, endowed with fewer of nature's gifts, must be conservationists. Americans, for example, are seldom prosecuted for contributory negligence in cases of fires. Losses, it is felt, are

---

[22] Wilson, *op. cit.,* p. 203.

somehow "paid by the insurance company." Insurance rates are not associated with fire rates. (In nearly all American states, fire-insurance rates are determined by the quality of *fire-defense equipment* in each community, with no consideration given to actual *fire-loss* experience.)

The politics of fire prevention is colored by the low priority it is given by the general public. Firemen sometimes regard assignment to the prevention bureau as exile resulting from presumed incompetence or disciplinary considerations. The head of the bureau may be an experienced fireman who was injured in line of duty; that is, the office may be treated as a sinecure rather than as a grave responsibility for an especially trained person. Members of the bureau may expect to be pressured to approve various materials and building arrangements. Few departments have adequate test facilities and must depend on reports of Federal agencies or the state fire marshal. They usually end up banning only the most obviously unacceptable materials or designs, for they may lack needed information on hazards and, in any case, are likely to find it difficult and unpleasant to order someone to clean up trash or make expensive repairs. In some cases, persons are assigned to the bureau on a rotating basis, which is likely to mean that about the time they begin to gain some special skills, they are reassigned to fire fighting. But this recruiting pattern is sometimes made necessary because the typical fireman does not want assignment permanently to prevention work.

The core cities of urban areas typically have modern, professional fire departments. The larger the city, the more specialized the equipment is likely to be. Suburbs and small cities, on the other hand, often depend upon amateur departments. Some small residential communities make it a practice to hire a few full-time members who man the station and equipment, with volunteer amateurs on call to follow along at each fire alarm. Other municipalities, especially suburbs, are following the practice of training men as both police and firemen.[23]

It is a peculiar phenomenon of American life, best left to the explanation of psychologists, perhaps, that citizens will be apathetic in responding to calls for volunteers for blood donations, civil defense, or even the manning of a charity booth at a church bazaar, but will establish waiting lists to join a volunteer fire department. In fact, volunteer companies were such powerful interest groups in New York and Philadelphia that they were able to prevent the installation of professional systems in those cities until 1865

[23] See C. S. James, "The Integration of Fire and Police Services," *Public Management*, 36:26–29, February, 1954.

and 1870, respectively, even though the first paid department had been inaugurated in Boston as early as 1837. This urge to assist is useful to the city government but is also a nuisance at times.

Fire Prevention. Fire departments have a responsibility for preventing fires as they do for fire fighting. Europeans have long placed heavy emphasis upon fire-prevention procedures, but the idea has received serious attention in the United States only since the 1920s. In their prevention activities, fire departments depend heavily upon routine inspections performed by the men of neighborhood fire stations. They seek to correct common hazards (e.g., accumulated rubbish, dirty chimneys, defective heating equipment). Periodically, technical surveys by engineers are made in some cities to suggest major improvements in the use and construction of buildings.

Fire prevention also involves the granting of permits, licenses, and certificates of approval (e.g., for the design of fire escapes, the use of dry-cleaning materials, the licensing of motion-picture operators, and the installation of oil burners). It is the responsibility of the city council (and in some cases of the state legislature) to provide adequate fire-prevention codes. The department also investigates the causes of fires and seeks to give publicity to fire statistics.

Departmental Organization. Fire-department organization generally parallels that of the police department. At least fifty cities still have a lay fire commissioner in charge, although in others, departments are headed by professional chiefs chosen from the departments or, in a few instances, from fire departments in other cities. Fire or safety boards still appoint the chief in quite a few cities, and in nearly one hundred weak-mayor cities the council makes the appointment. Normally, however, the appointment is made by the chief executive. In all but small cities, district stations are established with a company under the command of a lieutenant or captain. In very large cities, several companies in a section of the city may be organized into a battalion or district. In suburbs and small cities the volunteer firemen usually learn a good deal about the government of the community (political gossip is one of the staples around the firehouse) and often become important figures in local election campaigns. They may be active because the mayor has chosen them with an eye to developing a low-voltage political device, or because they have stakes in the decisions of the council (allowances for clothing, a new pumper), or simply because they are a well-knit group that enjoys politics as a game and have time on their hands in which to play it.

Training. Stemming from the traditions of volunteer days, fire departments did not have trained personnel until recent decades. The result of lack of training was, of course, unnecessary property damage and unnecessary fire losses. Today large cities have facilities for training their own recruits in the use of the highly complicated equipment that is now common. About two-thirds of the states provide for statewide training courses, which are available to all cities and villages in the training of their personnel. Training programs involve not only physical conditioning but also instruction in the use of equipment, chemicals, and explosives, in fire-fighting techniques, in ventilation, and in making fire-prevention inspections.

OTHER PUBLIC SAFETY FUNCTIONS

Cities also have responsibility for overseeing the use of devices to determine weights and measures, for smoke abatement, prevention of water pollution, noise abatement,[24] civil defense, traffic engineering, and the licensing of persons engaged in various activities which are viewed as having a special relationship to the public health or safety. In recent years, emphasis on ecological problems has resulted in more serious attention being paid to water and air pollution by industry. Licensing is always a potential area of corruption, for some permits, such as those to operate a taxi fleet or to sell liquor, may be worth much more than the amount paid for them to the city because they are in scarce supply. In some cities, upon approval, these licenses can be transferred from one person or firm to another and can be, in effect, sold for a large profit. Even when licenses are easily secured, they may still be of economic importance to the recipient, for he cannot continue in his trade or profession if the license is suspended or revoked for any reason.[25]

[24] Kevin Lynch, "The City as Environment," *Scientific American*, 213:209–214, September, 1965.
[25] Jack M. Siegel, *Chicago's Power to License and Regulate*, Center for Research in Urban Government, Loyola University, Chicago, 1965.

SELECTED READINGS

Brandstatter, A. F., and Louis A. Radelet: *Police and Community Relations: A Sourcebook,* The Macmillan Company, New York, 1968.

Chevigny, Paul: *Police Power, Police Abuse in New York City,* Vintage Books, New York, 1969.

Curran, H. H.: *Magistrates' Courts,* Charles Scribner's Sons, New York, 1942.

Farmer, David J.: *Civil Disorder Control,* Public Administration Service, Chicago, 1971. (A suggested planning program.)

Hahn, Harlan (ed.): *American Behavioral Scientist,* complete issue titled "Police and Society," 13: May–August, 1970.

Illinois Association for Criminal Justice: *Illinois Crime Survey,* Chicago, 1929. (A famous study, conducted during the Capone era.)

Municipal Fire Administration, 7th ed., International City Management Association, Chicago, 1967. (Describes professional values, standards, procedures, and goals.)

Municipal Police Administration, 5th ed., International City Management Association, Chicago, 1961. (Describes professional values, standards, procedures, and goals.)

The Police Yearbook, 1970, International Association of Chiefs of Police, Washington, 1970.

President's Commission on Law Enforcement and Administration of Justice: *The Challenge of Crime in a Free Society,* 1967. (A major study of crime, criminal procedures, courts, and corrections.)

————: *Task Force Report: The Police,* 1967. Also published commercially as *Violent Crime: The Challenge to our Cities,* George Braziller, New York, 1969, with an introduction by Daniel P. Moynihan.

Public Management: complete issue, "What Now for Fire Service?" November, 1970.

Saunders, Charles B., Jr.: *Upgrading the American Police: Education and Training for Better Law Enforcement,* Brookings Institution, Washington, 1970.

Trump, J. K., Morton Kroll, and J. R. Donoghue: *Metropolitan Los Angeles: A Study in Integration, VI. Fire Protection,* The Haynes Foundation, Los Angeles, 1952.

United States Senate: *Hearings before the Special Committee to Investigate Organized Crime in Interstate Commerce,* 1951. (Reports of a famous Senate investigation by the Kefauver committee.)

Virtue, Maxine B.: *Survey of Metropolitan Courts, Detroit Area,* The University of Michigan Press, Ann Arbor, Mich., 1950.

Werner, M. R.: "Dr. Parkhurst's Crusade," *The New Yorker,* Nov. 19 and Nov. 26, 1955. (The story of crime investigation by the Lexow committee of the New York Senate.)

Wilson, James Q. (ed.): *City Politics and Public Policy,* John Wiley, New York, 1968. (See especially Part IV, the study of comparative traffic law enforcement by John A. Gardiner, and the study of two cities, one with professionalized police force and one not, and the handling by police of juvenile cases by James Q. Wilson.)

————: *Varieties of Police Behavior: The Management of Law and Order in Eight Communities,* Harvard University Press, Cambridge, Mass., 1968. (Analysis of police systems in Albany, Newburgh, Oakland, Syracuse, Amsterdam, Brighton, Highland Park, and Nassau County. Police styles are characterized as the watchman, legalistic, or service types.)

Wilson, O. W.: *Police Administration,* 2d ed., McGraw-Hill Book Company, New York, 1963.

CHAPTER
15 CIVIL RIGHTS AND LIBERTIES

"City air is free air," shouted the residents of the growing towns of the Middle Ages. The expression symbolized that city dwellers had to some degree escaped the confinement of the feudal social system. Such freedom in the beginning had an economic base. But the freedom of the merchant also led to social freedom of other kinds. The city beckoned to all who were restless in the shelter of a closed social system. This included the criminal and the ne'er-do-well, the adventurer and artist, as well as the incipient rugged individualist.[1]

Critics of the city to this day have bemoaned its relaxation of neighborhood social controls. The sociologist Louis Wirth noted that the essence of urban life is its impersonality and lack of gemeinschaft.[2] The problem of the city has been one of maintaining a degree of order while preserving such freedom.[3]

Particularly because of the weakness of social controls and the

---

[1] See especially Henri Pirenne, *Medieval Cities,* Anchor Books, Doubleday & Company, Inc., Garden City, N.Y.; published originally in 1925 by the Princeton University Press.
[2] Louis Wirth, "Urbanism as a Way of Life," reprinted in Paul K. Hatt and Albert J. Reiss, Jr. (eds.), *Cities and Society,* rev. ed., The Free Press of Glencoe, New York, 1957, pp. 46–63.
[3] Jane Jacobs, *The Death and Life of Great American Cities,* Random House, Inc., New York, 1961. See especially part 1. She argues that while the prying eye and gossip of the village cannot be transplanted to the big city, something like it is needed to make city streets safe for strangers.

impersonality of large cities, public regulations by government define a great many more of the actions permitted citizens in cities than can be done in rural areas. Under urban conditions, regulations by government may paradoxically result in more freedom for the general citizen than unlimited freedom would. Traffic lights provide an example. Without public regulation, freedom to drive 60 miles an hour on a freeway into the downtown area would be of little value, since few would dare move this rapidly through crowded anarchic traffic. The zoning law, the milk-inspection system, the warnings against littering the sidewalk—all testify to the greater degree of government control in the city, and all in their way are designed to make city life more livable. Thus, in the city, regulation by government becomes the substitute for the gossip and social pressure of the village.

Yet there are limits to the government's right to control the citizen for reasons of health, safety, or morals. In our constitutional system, the citizen has rights and liberties which neither government nor the community can abridge. The requirement of striking the balance between citizen liberties and the need for order in an urban society is the theme that ties this chapter together.[4]

GOVERNMENT CONTROL IN URBAN AREAS

In this section, we shall review the major agencies concerned with the enforcement of law in cities. These are the agencies most intimately involved with a citizen's civil liberties.

The Police. America's police are primarily agencies of urban governments. The laws they enforce in cities are frequently written by state bodies and even sometimes by the United States Congress, but the enforcement mechanism is largely under local control. The city police force is a major instrument for urban social control.

Urban police forces since the beginning of the century have progressed toward greater professionalization. On-the-job training and the latest application of scientific techniques to crime control have become commonplace. Recruitment is no longer a hit-and-miss process but in many areas is designed to screen out undesirable applicants. Job security and professional advancement on merit are built into many police systems.[5]

---

[4] H. Frank Way, *Liberty in the Balance: Current Issues in Civil Liberties*, 2d ed., McGraw-Hill Book Company, New York, 1967; Alan P. Grimes, *Equality in America: Religion, Race, and the Urban Majority*, Oxford University Press, Fair Lawn, N.J., 1964. Also reports of the American Civil Liberties Union, which each year detail major events concerning the tension between liberty and order in America.

[5] For a history of this development, see Samuel G. Chapman (ed.), *The Police Heritage in England and America*, Institute for Community Development, Michigan State University, East Lansing, Mich., 1962. See also the discussion by William H. Parker, late chief of police of Los Angeles, in Donald McDonald (ed.), *The Police*, Center for the Study of Democratic Institutions, Santa Barbara, California, 1962.

What then is the effect of police professionalization upon the civil liberties of the urban citizen? On the one hand, it has meant a reduction in the cruder violations of citizen privileges and rights. The professional policeman is less likely than the amateur to browbeat citizens when he pulls them over to the curb for speeding. He is less likely to be a bully or an ignorant incompetent in the manner of the Keystone Kops. Rather, he is likely to attempt to emulate the deadpan, courteous neutrality of Sgt. Joe Friday of the *Dragnet* television series. The sociologist Joseph Lohman, who, for a period, also functioned as sheriff of Cook County (Chicago), described the significance of this sense of professionalism in a tense racial situation. Some years ago, the city of Washington, D.C., decided to desegregate its swimming pools. The police of the city were asked to enforce this regulation, though it was clear that many policemen were out of sympathy with it. Lohman suggested that in instructing the police it be emphasized to them that their private opinions on the matter were their own business. They were encouraged to think as they pleased. However, as policemen, their actions should conform to professional standards of police practice. They were being asked to play the *role* of a professional. He notes that the desegregation was accomplished efficiently and promptly, without incident.[6] Professionalism thus discourages the invasions of civil liberties resulting from personal prejudices of the law-enforcement officer.

Professionalism may also have its repressive impact upon a citizen's civil liberties. The professionalized policeman can become very skillful in the use of modern technical equipment, such as the devices designed to tap phones or eavesdrop on conversations; the polygraph, or lie detector; devices including stomach-pump mechanisms, to test the amount of alcohol or narcotics that a person has consumed; or fingerprint files and other data records used to compile extensive dossiers on citizens. All these have been attacked by one or another group of civil libertarians as unwarranted invasions of a citizen's privacy. Professionalism has also had the same effect on police as on other administrators: It has narrowed an individual's conception of the goals to be pursued. Typically, the professional specialist tends to disregard many elements of a situation while concentrating on his specialty. Thus, a highway traffic engineer is likely to think primarily in terms of moving traffic as rapidly as possible without giving much thought to those who may feel themselves affected adversely by the manner in which highways are designed and the places they are located. In the same way, a professional policeman is likely to define his goal as prevention of crime and be less concerned about the occasional invasion of privacy that may help

[6] H. Warren Dunham (ed.), *The City at Midcentury*, Wayne State University Press, Detroit, Mich., 1957.

him more readily accomplish this end. The goal becomes more important than the means. The niceties of civil liberties are particularly likely to be disregarded when the policeman is dealing with persons he feels to be almost certainly guilty. One of the leaders of the movement for professionalization, William H. Parker, long-time chief of the Los Angeles police force, summed up his experience as a policeman this way: "I look back over almost 35 years of dealing with the worst that humanity has to offer. I meet the failures of humanity daily, and I meet them in the worst possible context. It is hard to keep an objective viewpoint."[7]

No matter how professional the police become, however, they are never completely removed from the political arena. The mayor generally has considerable direct and indirect influence over their actions. In many cities, including some with the council-manager system, the mayor has the power to appoint the chief of police. In larger cities, he commonly appoints the police commissioner. Citizens tend to interpret this power as giving him influence over how the law will be enforced and which areas of crime prevention will be emphasized. Bars in cities catering to conventioneers are interested in some leniency in enforcing laws against such visitors. In Minneapolis, since the 1934 teamster strike, labor has sought to control the mayoralty post in order to assure a neutral or friendly police chief. Civil rights groups in a recent Detroit election and in Chicago have indicated that they hold mayors responsible for the way the law is enforced by police against black citizens. In Detroit, about a year before the election, the police in investigating two murders detained some 1,500 blacks who were then later released without charges. The mayor was blamed for this action and was defeated in the subsequent election by a relatively unknown candidate.[8]

The police, thus, because of professionalization and also because of the political significance of their job, have become increasingly public relations conscious. They cannot enforce laws without being aware of criticism by those who feel their civil liberties are infringed upon. At the same time, they cannot expect to be effective if they strive only for popularity.

A public opinion survey of the citizens of Los Angeles was conducted some years ago by a captain of the Los Angeles Police Department and Training Division, G. Douglas Gourley.[9] He found that 20

---

[7] McDonald, *op. cit.*, p. 25.
[8] Edward C. Banfield, *Big City Politics,* Random House, Inc., New York, p. 58.
[9] G. Douglas Gourley, *Public Relations and the Police,* Charles C Thomas, Publisher, Springfield, Ill., 1953. A study following the Watts riot in 1966 showed a sharp shift of opinion against the Los Angeles police in the intervening period. Of the blacks, 54 percent disagreed with the statement "you can generally trust the police" as compared to only 6 percent of the whites. David O. Sears, "Black Attitudes Toward the Political System in the Aftermath of the Watts-Insurrection," *Midwest Journal of Political Science,* 13:515–544, November, 1969.

percent of his black sample considered the Los Angeles police department "definitely below standard," as compared to 14 percent of the Mexican-American community and 8 percent of the white community. Those naming it "one of the very best police departments in the country" were 14 percent of the blacks, 23 percent of the Mexican-Americans, and 30 percent of the whites. These opinions have intensified and criticism has been expressed more openly and vehemently since the study was made.

Other Regulatory Bodies. Even though the police are the major agents of governmental control within cities, a number of other public bodies also exercise some influence over citizen actions. They include zoning boards, building inspection, fire-prevention bureaus, urban renewal boards, and others, but most of these depend upon the police for the enforcement of their regulations. Thus, they will not be dealt with separately here. Their role will be noted in later chapters dealing with policy areas.

The Courts. The courts in smaller cities often exercise jurisdiction only over minor offenses, particularly traffic violations. Their powers thus are not much greater than the justice of the peace courts in rural areas. In such cities, the significant courts are those established by the state on a county or district basis. Generally, however, in larger cities, the municipal courts are given added jurisdiction and sometimes special names to indicate their greater powers. Municipal courts of this type are in some states equivalent to the state courts established at the county level. But in other states, municipal courts have somewhat different jurisdictions. Municipal judges are generally paid on a salary basis, and in the larger cities their salaries may be higher than those of the state supreme court justices. Local judges are often elected on a nonpartisan ballot and serve for relatively long terms.

In the past, local courts were clearly under the control of urban political organizations. Today such influence still exists, but the courts, like the police, have undergone greater and greater professionalization. In most states, municipal courts have been closely meshed into the total state court system, unlike justice of the peace courts, which tend still to have greater independence and lack of professionalization. Such a system is headed by the state supreme court and may perhaps have an additional appellate level of courts, with county courts and municipal courts in the larger cities carrying most of the judicial load as courts of original jurisdiction. The municipal courts in smaller cities and the justice of peace courts remain for minor violations.

The City Attorney. The city attorney is a less important political official than his counterpart at the county, state, or Federal level. He is

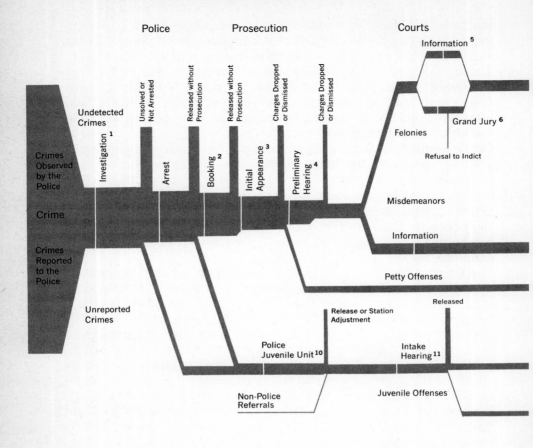

1 May continue until trial.

2 Administrative record of arrest. First step at which temporary release on bail may be available.

3 Before magistrate, commissioner, or justice of peace. Formal notice of charge, advice of rights. Bail set. Summary trials for petty offenses usually conducted here without further processing.

4 Preliminary testing of evidence against defendant. Charge may be reduced. No separate preliminary hearing for misdemeanors in some systems.

5 Charge filed by prosecutor on basis of information submitted by police or citizens. Alternative to grand jury indictment; often used in felonies, almost always in misdemeanors.

6 Reviews whether Government evidence sufficient to justify trial. Some States have no grand jury system; others seldom use it.

Figure 15-1. A general view of the criminal justice system. *Source:* The President's Commission on Law Enforcement and Administration of Justice, *The Challenge of Crime in a Free Society,* 1967.

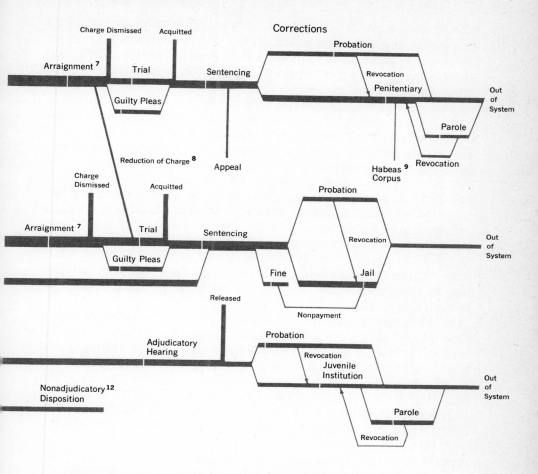

Corrections

Charge Dismissed   Acquitted

Probation

Arraignment [7]   Trial   Sentencing   Revocation
                                                    Penitentiary   Out of System

Guilty Pleas   Parole

Reduction of Charge [8]   Appeal   Habeas [9] Corpus   Revocation

Charge Dismissed   Acquitted   Probation

Arraignment [7]   Trial   Sentencing   Revocation   Out of System

Guilty Pleas   Fine   Jail

Released   Nonpayment

Probation

Adjudicatory Hearing   Revocation   Juvenile Institution   Out of System

Nonadjudicatory [12] Disposition   Parole

Revocation

7 Appearance for plea; defendant elects trial by judge or jury (if available); counsel for indigent usually appointed here in felonies. Often not at all in other cases.

8 Charge may be reduced at any time prior to trial in return for plea of guilty or for other reasons.

9 Challenge on constitutional grounds to legality of detention. May be sought at any point in process.

10 Police often hold informal hearings, dismiss, or adjust many cases without further processing.

11 Probation officer decides desirability of further court action.

12 Welfare agency, social services, counseling, medical care, etc., for cases where adjudicatory handling not needed.

almost always appointed rather than elected, with his primary duty being that of giving legal advice to the city government and representing it in court. Less frequently is he involved in the prosecution of violators, though this aspect of his position is growing in importance. Cases against civil rights demonstrators, for example, in some cities have led to prosecutions by the city attorney. Nevertheless, the district or state's attorney, an official of the state who is generally elected by county voters, more frequently is the local prosecutor of importance because state law is generally involved in the important cases. Crusading district attorneys, like Thomas E. Dewey in the 1930s and 1940s, have worked closely with local grand juries exposing crime within cities, but such action by city attorneys is much rarer. Allied with the district attorney's office is the sheriff. In most urban areas, an informal agreement exists between city and county law-enforcement officials for the sheriff to be the chief law-enforcement officer outside the city limits and the city police to be the chief law-enforcement agency in each municipality. The sheriff's office frequently provides jail facilities for serious offenders, though in larger cities such facilities also exist.[10]

State Influence on Urban Law Enforcement. The legislature, with the consent of the governor, prescribes the powers of city governing bodies. It can also legislate relative to certain cities in the state and will expect the local police agencies to enforce such regulations. Thus, Sunday closing laws and blue laws may be resisted by urban populations, but must be enforced formally by the local police.

Theodore Roosevelt in his autobiography reports such a conflict. While police commissioner of New York City, he elected to enforce the state Sunday closing law on saloons. The uproar was great. He reports ruefully: "All kinds of ways of evading the law were tried, and some of them were successful. The statute, for instance, permitted any man to take liquor with meals. After two or three months, a magistrate was found who decided judicially that 17 beers and 1 pretzel made a meal—after which decision joy again became unconfined in at least some of the saloons and the yellow press gleefully announced my 'tyranny' had been curbed."[11]

Other state influences are much less important or continuous in their effect than the lawmaking function. From time to time, an attorney general may take action to correct what he regards as crime within urban areas and may even conduct prosecutions. The state police force usually limits itself to enforcement of crimes outside of cities, but there is a growing tendency for such forces to investi-

---

[10] For a discussion of the overlapping of county and city functions, see John Bollens, *Metropolitan Challenge,* Metropolitan Community Studies, Inc., Dayton, Ohio, 1959, pp. 119–124.
[11] *Theodore Roosevelt: An Autobiography,* Charles Scribner's Sons, New York, 1913, p. 192.

gate serious crimes in the smaller urban areas. In a number of states, the governor has the power to remove local urban officials for cause; and as commander of the state militia, he may or may not order it into urban areas when rioting or another emergency occurs. Generally however, the governor waits for a request for such aid from the mayor.

Federal Influence on Urban Law Enforcement. The impact of the Federal government on law enforcement in cities has been mainly on procedural matters. The FBI, of course, investigates Federal crimes that occur within city limits; and other Federal agencies, such as the treasury agents, may do the same. But more important in its impact has been a series of decisions by the United States Supreme Court defining the powers of local law-enforcement officers. Using the Bill of Rights of the United States Constitution, the Supreme Court has set aside convictions in a number of criminal cases because procedures were found to be improper. In a series of cases in 1966, the Supreme Court held that police could not question a suspect until they had first told him that he has a right to remain silent, that whatever he says may be used against him, that he is entitled to have his lawyer with him when being questioned after arrest, and that an attorney would be provided if the accused person could not afford one on his own. Police officials almost unanimously have criticized these decisions, as have some municipal leaders. Mayor Samuel Yorty of Los Angeles, for example, stated that the decisions put handcuffs on the police instead of the criminal. Civil libertarians, however, including lawyers and even some prosecuting attorneys, have praised these decisions as placing desirable restraints on the action of the police, not unlike the restraints placed on prosecutors during a criminal trial.[12]

The Pattern of Local Law Enforcement. To summarize, law enforcement in cities is thus the combined effort of Federal, state and county, as well as municipal, officials. The city police force is the major unit for apprehending offenders. Mayors, and sometimes city councils, have a great deal to say about which laws will be enforced and how well they will be enforced within city limits. The mayor, particularly, is held responsible for police action by many voters. The council, of course, has the power to pass local ordinances, which the police enforce. But significant laws that are enforced within city limits have often been written by state legislators; procedures police follow have been prescribed by the United States Supreme Court; and the courts at trial are frequently controlled by state statute, or are lower state courts established at the county level. Occasionally a governor,

[12] "Rewriting the Rules," *Newsweek*, June 27, 1966, pp. 21–31.

a state's attorney, or state attorney general may influence the process, particularly in the larger cities.

For most citizens, urban law enforcement is their major contact with the nation's law. If it is arbitrary and unjust, this will be their picture of the way their rights are treated.

In most cities, the heterogeneity of power sources within the population prevents a single person or group from having the kind of social or political influence that may be found in a small town with a single prominent family or industry. No responsible observer though, claims the law is equally enforced for all segments of the urban population, though this is the stated goal of justice. However, this goal appears to be implemented to a greater degree by government in large cities than by that in rural areas. One observer writes:[13]

> It may be said that there exist two constituencies behind American politics—one, essentially cosmopolitan and urban-oriented, which seeks to push forward the policy of equality. The other, essentially provincial and rural-oriented, seeks to maintain in religion, race, and politics the superiorities of the past. . . . The urban majority is proving to be a liberating force in American politics, redistributing freedom by equalizing claims of the contestants.

Nevertheless, the problem of law enforcement and civil liberties in the cities, as in all American society, has centered on protecting the rights of those groups having low status. The middle-class resident and taxpayer, whose contact with the police is likely to be in matters involving traffic violations, generally is treated with some deference by both police and courts. This is particularly the case in smaller residential suburbs. However, lower-income groups; strangers; minority-, racial-, or ethnic-group members frequently argue that the niceties of procedure are not as strictly followed in their cases. A student of second- and third-generation Italians on the west side of Boston of today found:[14]

> Most westenders are convinced that the police, the government, the elected officials, and the courts are corrupt and are engaged in a never ending conspiracy to deprive the citizens of what is morally theirs. Although suspicion of government and politics can be found among all social strata, in smaller communities, as well as in the city, the westenders' feelings on this subject are more intense and less open to change. Consequently, they try to have as little to do with government as possible and pass on to the area politician the task of dealing with it on their behalf. By government, westenders mean city government.

[13] Grimes, op. cit., pp. ix and x.
[14] Herbert J. Gans, The Urban Villagers: Group and Class in the Life of Italian-Americans, The Free Press of Glencoe, New York, 1962, p. 163.

This attitude is also prevalent among subsistence-level groups, like Puerto Ricans and blacks. Such groups are also likely to have frequent contacts with police over serious crimes. Because of conflicts in the past, both police and members of such groups are wary of each other. Police department personnel themselves have tended to be recruited from lower-middle-class groups primarily of the white race, and this, too, may affect their attitude toward low-income blacks and Puerto Ricans. The police are inclined to show some deference to the middle-class black and white but are more likely to treat those below them on the social scale with less professional consideration.

The result has been that American civil liberties have generally been defined as the result of actions by groups representing the low-status elements of urban society. Members of civil rights organizations, such as the NAACP, civil libertarians of the American Civil Liberties Union or of religious groups, such as the Jehovah's Witnesses, have brought cases to the United States Supreme Court or to state courts on behalf of such minorities.

The cases such groups have brought before the Supreme Court range over many topics, including the right of citizens to hold parades on Saturday afternoons, to speak in public places, to distribute literature, to use sound trucks, or to conduct sit-ins. In addition, as we have already noted, representatives of such groups have challenged the right of local law-enforcement officials to use electronic devices for obtaining evidence, to use third-degree methods in interrogating suspects, to search on suspicion, or to search homes without warrants. They have challenged a host of other procedures long thought by law-enforcement agents to be within their prerogative, Finally, the same kind of challenges have been made against procedures in the courtroom, including selection of juries and admission of evidence.

PROCEDURAL DUE PROCESS

In 1965, James J. Kilpatrick, chairman of publications for the Virginia Commission on Constitutional Government, complained that "The whole drift of our law these days is toward the absolute prohibition of all ideas that diverge in the slightest form from a Federal standard. The entire field of criminal law, which the Constitution reserved almost exclusively to the states, rapidly is becoming subject to increasing scrutiny by the United States Supreme Court and once the Court scrutinizes, the Court is reluctant not to impose Federal standards upon a state's administration of criminal justice."[15]

---

[15] James J. Kilpatrick, *Nor Cruel and Unusual Punishments Inflicted,* Virginia Commission on Constitutional Government, Richmond, 1965, p. 31.

The Police and Civil Liberties. The task of urban law-enforcement officials is always difficult. Frequently they must make quick decisions, and these decisions may directly affect the civil rights and liberties of citizens. If a policeman lacks zealousness in seeking to enforce the law, he will be criticized. If he is overly zealous, he may not encounter criticism from local newspapers or his professional colleagues, but he may do great damage to the peace, property, and psychological well-being of private citizens.

Due Process and Arrest. Until the nineteenth century, responsibility for bringing violators before the court was essentially that of the individual citizen. The professional police officer did not appear in England until the early nineteenth century, and in the United States until later than that. In the early period, a "citizen's arrest" was common and perhaps the most customary means of apprehending a criminal. As organized professional police forces have developed, participation by the citizen has become less common; indeed, today a citizen's arrest is a dangerous move, in the view of many persons, for they fear the possibilities of lawsuits for false arrest. The tendency of the contemporary American is to argue that he does not "want to become involved." As a result, today in most states, arrest is almost exclusively an activity of persons holding a formal warrant as peace officers.[16]

Under normal circumstances, an arrest cannot be made in the absence of a warrant. A warrant is a command issued by a judge or other magistrate ordering the arrest of the person named in the warrant. An arrest may be legally made without a warrant, however, in emergency situations. These must be defined in statute or by precedent. When an arresting officer acts in the course of carrying out an order provided in a warrant, he is safe from any charge of misfeasance; but if he makes an arrest without a warrant, he is personally responsible for his act and may be sued for false arrest under some circumstances. Even so, illegal arrests in the United States probably exceed by far the legal ones.[17]

The law-enforcement officer does not merely arrest an alleged offender. He is also expected to produce for use in court the articles and documents that may be used in evidence. Because this is his responsibility, he has a right to search the person of an individual arrested and also the premises on which the arrest takes place, if he can reasonably believe that evidence is located there.[18]

In many states it was once customary for the courts to admit evi-

[16] Paul E. Wilson, *Basic Rules of Arrest, Search, and Seizure,* Governmental Research Center, University of Kansas, Lawrence, Kans., 1963.
[17] Marshall Houts, *From Arrest to Release,* Charles C Thomas, Publisher, Springfield, Ill., 1958, p. 24.
[18] Wilson, *op. cit.*

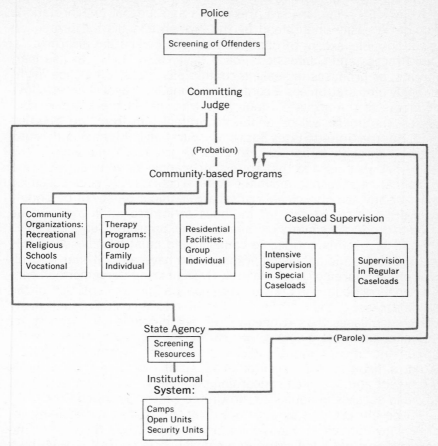

Figure 15-2. Elements of correctional system. *Source:* The President's Commission on Law Enforcement and Administration of Justice, *The Challenge of Crime in a Free Society,* 1967.

dence without inquiring as to the method by which it was obtained. Until 1961, states could determine for themselves whether evidence was admissible. In that year, however, the United States Supreme Court abandoned its laissez-faire attitude and ruled that no evidence could be admitted in state or Federal court proceedings unless it had been lawfully obtained. The practical effect of this decision is to require persons to be acquitted if prosecutors do not follow precisely the requirements of the law.[19]

Search and seizure regulations are complicated and technical. They vary from one state to another. As is characteristic of the com-

[19] *Mapp v. Ohio,* 367 U.S. 643 (1961).

plex law of the modern era, these laws and judicial interpretations cannot be easily understood by the layman and his full protection is not possible, except through the help of a competent attorney.

Due Process and Confession. Police have been known to use fear, threats, or promises in seeking confessions. Thus, the police might strongly hint that unless a confession is made, they will arrest close members of the accused's family, or that unless the accused confesses, the police will be unable to protect him from the awaiting mob. But the United States Supreme Court has held that confessions secured through force, fear, threats, or promises are illegal. The Court has also insisted that state courts apply, in general, the same rules that must be followed in the Federal courts. That is, the accused must be advised of his legal rights; arraignment must not be unduly delayed; and "third degree" methods of interrogation may not be used to produce a confession. Similarly, the Supreme Court has ruled that an accused is entitled to counsel, and must be advised of this right. Despite the criticisms of those who have argued that the rulings of the Supreme Court make the task of law-enforcement officers extremely difficult, the Court reviews only a miniscule portion of the criminal cases of the land. Even if it wanted to, it could not hear many more such cases than it does at the present time. As a result, its influence upon state courts, on matters of the behavior of law-enforcement officers and of judicial proceedings, is small. Indeed, it is not difficult for a prosecutor or judge at the state level, if he is intelligent and informed concerning prior Supreme Court decisions, to avoid successful appeal to the United States Supreme Court.[20]

Police officers and prosecutors complain that it is becoming increasingly difficult to use a voluntary confession on the part of the accused as a basis for securing a conviction in court. In 1964, by a 5-to-4 vote, the United States Supreme Court reversed the conviction of an alleged killer, not because they questioned his guilt, but because the police had refused to let the suspect consult a lawyer until after they had finished questioning him. During the questioning, the suspect made an incriminating statement, and this was a fundamental basis for his conviction in state court. The Supreme Court, however, held that this was not a voluntary confession and could not be admitted in evidence. Justice Arthur J. Goldberg, for the majority, argued that it is the responsibility of the prosecutor to find his own evidence, rather than to rely upon a confession, whether or not it was completely voluntary.[21]

Ample evidence exists to show that a "confession" is not neces-

---

[20] Way, *op. cit.*, chap. V. See, for example, *Collins v. Texas*, 352 S.W.2d 841 (1961).
[21] *Escobedo v. Illinois*, 378 U.S. 478 (1963); further restricted in *Miranda v. Arizona*, 16 L.Ed.2d 7 (1966).

sarily proof that the accused has committed a crime. In the case of a murder committed in New York City in 1964, the police arrested a young Negro and secured a confession from him. Later it was proven that he was innocent of the crime. At the time of the subject's release, a member of the staff of the district attorney said he was "positive" that the police had actually prepared the confession the suspect had signed.

In 1965, former New York Police Commissioner Michael J. Murphy, in a talk before judges of the United States courts, criticized a decision of the United States Supreme Court which extended to the state courts a rule making inadmissible evidence that had been illegally seized. He also complained that "it has been our experience that if suspects are told of their rights, they will not confess."[22]

In response, Yale Camisar, a law professor, said: "Fighting crime is a difficult, frustrating business. When you cannot handle it, the easiest and most politically attractive device is to blame it on the courts. It is a lot more popular than raising taxes to increase the police force."

A Jury of One's Peers. The United States Supreme Court has attempted in many ways to impose upon the states obligations to observe procedural civil rights where the state-government officials have themselves failed to do so. Thus, the Court has ruled that Negroes and minority-ethnic-group members cannot be systematically excluded from jury duty.[23]

This decision has had little practical meaning, however, for many techniques exist for the exclusion of such persons from juries in fact.[24] First, most jury lists include only a token representation of Negroes or unwanted minority-group members. Second, it is common in the South for the defense and prosecuting attorneys to agree not to accept Negro jurors. Third, an attorney has a certain number of peremptory challenges to which he is entitled. Furthermore, Negroes often ask to be excused on the grounds that jury duty would be an economic hardship.[25] More recently, since the adoption of eighteen-year-old voting, attorneys for younger persons on trial have argued that juries should include persons of the age group of the accused.

The jury system itself has often been subject to attack. A study by two law professors, however, suggests it is a reasonable cross section of the total population.[26]

---

[22] United Press-International dispatch, Sept. 10, 1965; the case referred to was *Mapp v. Ohio*, 367 U.S. 643 (1961).
[23] *Hernandez v. Texas*, 347 U.S. 475 (1954); *Eubanks v. Louisiana*, 356 U.S. 584 (1958); *Swain v. Alabama*, 380 U.S. 202 (1965).
[24] Way, *op. cit.*, chap. V.
[25] See, for example, *Avery v. Georgia*, 345 U.S. 559 (1953).
[26] Fletcher Knebel, "How Good Are Our Juries?" *Look Magazine*, Aug. 23, 1966, pp. 75ff.

The Right to Counsel. In 1963 the United States Supreme Court ruled that every state must provide counsel to persons accused of felonies and serious misdemeanors if, in the judgment of the trial judge, the defendant is not able to pay for such advice. The case involved an ex-convict Clarence Gideon, who had been accused of breaking into a poolroom. He asked the judge to appoint a defense attorney, but the judge refused, pointing out that under Florida law the government did not have to pay for legal counsel, except in murder cases. Gideon was sentenced to five years in the state prison, but largely through his own efforts to learn the law and to bring his case directly to the attention of the United States Supreme Court, he was able to secure a retrial at which he was found innocent. His case was responsible for bringing pressure once again upon the states to bring their criminal proceedings up to standards required by the Federal courts.[27]

As a result of this decision, the Florida Supreme Court immediately provided a framework for handling appeals from other persons in state penal institutions. A few months later, the Florida Legislature created the office of "public defender" in each of the state's judicial circuits. He was assigned the task of representing any person accused of a felony who, in the opinion of the judge, was not able to pay the fees of an attorney.

Florida officials accepted the decision of the United States Supreme Court and attempted to comply with its ruling at considerable cost to the state and with many resulting problems. After the decision, "The Florida Division of Corrections had to provide additional notary service, arrange to transport prisoners, recompute sentences, and perform a host of other related tasks for its inmate population. Evidence seems to show that this has been accomplished with more than reasonable dispatch."[28]

At the time of the Gideon decision, fifteen states did not provide a guarantee of the right to counsel for indigent defendants in all felony cases.[29] In those states where a right to counsel did exist, it was common for the judge to name as attorney for the defense an inexperienced newcomer to the bar. Even in the case of more experienced lawyers, they often have found little profit in these kinds of cases and, unless they take a personal interest in the defendant and his position or see some broader purpose in the case, they have a vested interest in getting the case over with rapidly. Of course, many attorneys appointed by the court do a conscientious job. Fur-

[27] *Gideon v. Wainwright,* 372 U.S. 335 (1963). See also Anthony Lewis, *Gideon's Trumpet,* Random House, Inc., New York, 1963.
[28] David G. Temple, "Facing up to Gideon," *National Civic Review,* 54:354ff., July, 1965.
[29] Murray T. Bloom, "Justice for the Poor," *National Civic Review,* 54:131–135, March, 1965.

thermore, in quite a few states, the Legal Aid Society seeks to help indigents, but it is dependent almost entirely on private contributions. In most urban areas, it would probably be accurate to say that the poorer you are, the poorer are your chances for an adequate defense in court. In states where the public defender system works well, however, this pattern is modified somewhat and the low-income person who does not quite qualify as indigent is probably the least well represented.

The Press and Criminal Procedure. A major issue in the field of civil rights and liberties has been that of balancing the right of freedom of the press against the right of an individual to a fair trial. If a newspaper editor is denied information he wants, he is likely to print in 14-point type and boldface that the historic freedom of the press is being invaded and that this constitutes a dangerous threat to democracy. He apparently is likely to make the most noise or use the boldest type when he is denied information that he thinks will help sell newspapers. The responsibility of judges and legislators is, of course, not one of trying to keep newspapers solvent but rather of trying to protect the basic elements of a fair trial. Many judges have emphasized that the American system of jurisprudence calls for trial by court and not by newspaper, but their arguments are frequently rejected by editors.

In 1959, the editor of the Eugene, Oregon, *Register Guard* said, "Whenever a boy is arrested on a major charge, we will print his name if we can get it and, of course, we can get it. I don't think the public would want us to do otherwise."[30] This pious statement misses the point, of course. The question is not what the public would like— much of the public would like as many enticing, dramatic details of a crime as the newspapers are willing to print. The fundamental problem centers around providing the conditions under which an individual can be given a fair trial and those who are accused but innocent can be protected from a lifelong stigma.

Although the press has sometimes abused its powers and privileges, it also performs a highly important function as a critic of those in power. Thomas Jefferson put it this way in a letter to George Washington in 1792: "No government ought to be without censors and, while the press is free, none will." Criticism of the law and those who execute it and the reporting of events is not, according to our traditions, supposed to prejudice the rights of individuals.

Freedom of Expression. One specialist on civil liberties has noted that:[31]

[30] Quoted in "Publicity and Juvenile Courts," Freedom of Information Center, University of Missouri, Columbia, Mo., Publication no. 140, 1965.
[31] Way, *op. cit.*, p. 40. The case is *Roth v. United States*, 354 U.S. 476 (1957).

Prior to 1957 the Supreme Court had never faced the issues of censorship of obscene printed matter. That year, the Court examined the validity of the Federal mail statute which declares obscene printed matter to be nonmailable.

The Court upheld the validity of the statute and declared that obscenity is not within the area of constitutionally protected speech and press. The Court noted that historically the constitutional protection for freedom of the press was not considered to cover every utterance. It reasoned that "all ideas having the slightest redeeming social importance—unorthodox ideas, controversial ideas, and even ideas hateful to the prevailing climate of opinion—have the full protection of the guarantees. . . ." But the Court concluded that obscenity is utterly without redeeming social importance.

Conflict over where freedom of expression ends and pornography begins extended into the 1970s. As the decade opened, President Nixon's Commission on Obscenity issued a report which concluded that pornography seems to have no adverse effects upon adults, even when it seems to appeal only to "prurient interests." The President and a host of public officials at all levels hastened to dissociate themselves from the report, suggesting that they did not believe the public was prepared to accept such materials as innocuous to adults.

The importance of the Roth Case is not the conclusion that obscenity has no constitutional protection; few people would seriously argue for such a position. The importance lies in its attempt to establish a standard for measuring what is and what is not obscene. The Court established the following obscenity standard: whether, for the average person applying contemporary community standards, the dominant theme of the material, taken as a whole, appeals to prurient interests and to nothing else.

The problem of what some civic and religious groups in the community regard as obscene or pornographic sales has been an issue in a number of large cities in recent years. In Minneapolis, a police officer arrested a bookseller for selling a Henry Miller work, on the grounds that the book was obscene. The mayor, a former political science professor, found himself caught between backing his police chief and gaining the support of certain civic and church-group leaders who defended his act or offending civil libertarians, many of whom were his former colleagues on the University of Minnesota faculty.

Censorship boards or procedures in respect to motion pictures are to be found in a number of large cities including Chicago and Detroit. In 1957, in reversing the Chicago Censorship Board, the Supreme Court held that obscenity is not protected by the First

Amendment but that matters related to sex were not in themselves to be interpreted as obscene.[32]

The effect of the language of the Supreme Court decision in the Roth case, according to the literary critic and poet John Ciardi, of the *Saturday Review,* is to allow the movie producer or book publisher to win in every obscenity case if he is willing to spend the money necessary to appeal until he reaches a court level where the censorship decision must be reversed.[33] The problem faced by would-be censors is that it is extremely difficult to show that a particular film or publication is without "any redeeming social importance," a restriction imposed by the Supreme Court. Ciardi's conclusion may have been premature, however, for the Court in 1966 modified the rule to permit consideration of *intent* as well as possible social importance. It held that a work can be condemned if the intention of the publisher is deliberately and primarily to exploit prurient interests.[34]

The Supreme Court has also held that a state or city may not authorize mass seizures of material unless it can be proved that the distributors knew that the materials were regarded as obscene by law. Law-enforcement officials must also specifically describe the allegedly obscene items to be seized.[35] It has also generally held that laws applying to minors are of a different category from those affecting adults. In 1969 in *Stanley v. Georgia,* the court held that statutes regulating obscenity do not reach into the privacy of one's home.[36]

THE SPECIAL PROBLEM OF THE URBAN BLACKS

Simeon Booker has commented that "the Negro ghetto now stands as the last remaining vestige of mass exploitation, poverty, and crime in America." The black, particularly in large cities, has objected to such discrimination on two major counts: (1) It is an assault on his present status as an individual and citizen and (2) its effects cripple his potential for the future. When asked by interviewers how discrimination has affected him personally, one-third of the black sample said it, "prevents my getting a job and wages I want"; another 11 percent noted it "limited my education"; and another 7 percent said, "It created an inferiority complex." Only 13 percent said, "It has not affected me." Answers from a selected leadership sample were almost identical in that 26 percent said it prevented them from

[32] *Times Film Corp. v. Chicago,* 244 F.2d 423 (1957).
[33] John Ciardi, "Manner of Speaking," *Saturday Review,* Mar. 6, 1965, p. 414.
[34] *Ginzberg v. United States,* 16 L.Ed.2d 31 (1966); and *Mishkin v. New York,* 16 L.Ed.2d 560 (1966).
[35] *Smith v. California,* 361 U.P. 147 (1959); and *Marcus v. Search Warrants,* 367 U.S. 7717 (1961).
[36] See a collection of articles on the issue in *The Public Interest,* 22:3–61, Winter, 1971.

getting jobs and wages they wanted and 13 percent that it limited their education. However, three times as many leaders (22 percent) noted that discrimination created an inferiority complex in them.[37]

At the same time, World War II marked the end of the ready acceptance of such second-class citizenship by many American blacks, particularly those in the middle class in Northern urban centers.[38] Some whites also came to have misgivings about the situation. Earlier, other minority groups had rejected such status and been successful in attaining a treatment closer to that of equality, but the task was much more difficult for blacks since open or tacit racial discrimination against them is often supported by the sanction of local government. Yet the problem as defined by many urban blacks is not whether but how reform will be achieved.

Until recently, the attitude in many American white communities has been one of indifference to the problems of social disorganization in the black community. Many a community leader could make the comment that was made in the San Francisco Bay area that if:[39]

> . . . communities had done a more effective job of making room for Negro newcomers during the past two decades, one could be more hopeful about the two decades ahead, a period in which the Negro population will more than double. In looking at developments since 1940, one cannot avoid being struck by the fantastic growth of the Negro population and the rapid development of Negro-white tensions. Equally impressive is the fact that not a single city in the Bay area had or tried to develop plans for easing the movement of Negroes or for directing inescapable conflicts into affirmative civic channels.

The first generation of blacks coming into adolescence after World War II fired black communities in urban areas to a new militancy. The first black sit-in seems to have taken place in the city of Greensboro, North Carolina, in February, 1960. The technique spread rapidly through the South and then to Northern cities so that, since 1963, demonstrations to protest discrimination and segregation in education, employment, transportation, and housing have become commonplace, even for small- and middle-sized urban areas. At first, local officials resisted the black efforts vigorously. The early clashes in such Southern cities as Birmingham, Alabama, where fire hoses and police dogs were used against blacks demonstrating, gained the sympathy of many white citizens for the black cause. But by the

---

[37] William Brink and Louis Harris, *The Negro Revolution in America,* Simon and Schuster, Inc., New York, 1964, p. 190.
[38] See Martin Luther King, *Why We Can't Wait,* New American Library of World Literature, Inc., New York, 1963; and Louis E. Lomax, *The Negro Revolt,* New American Library of World Literature, Inc., 1962. See also, for soul-searching by white businessmen, Eli Ginzberg (ed.), *The Negro Challenge to the Business Community,* McGraw-Hill Book Company, New York, 1964. Paperback.
[39] Wilson Record, *Minority Groups and Intergroup Relations in the San Francisco Bay Area,* Institute of Governmental Studies, University of California, Berkeley, Calif., 1963, p. 48.

453 CIVIL RIGHTS AND LIBERTIES

middle 1960s, riots were common in many Southern cities, including Tallahassee, Atlanta, and New Orleans, and had spread to Northern cities as well. In some cases, the black groups openly fought police just as they had Eugene "Bull" Connor of Birmingham. Some blacks, disillusioned by the white response, turned from integration to separatism and from passive resistance to guerrilla tactics. Predictably, some whites responded in kind.

In any period of intense conflict such as this one, flagrant violations of civil rights will occur but such periods are also periods of change. This has been one in which the definition of acceptable practices in respect to the treatment of blacks has improved overall. And what gains have been made have generally been made in urban areas.

The Urban Black Community. The black ghettos have created severe problems for urban residents. The crime rate for urban blacks is markedly higher than for other groups of the population. The same is true in respect to other indices of social disorganization: illegitimacy, desertions, divorce, and juvenile delinquency.[40]

A number of factors can be cited to account for this state of affairs:

1.   Over 70 percent of America's 21 million blacks live in urban areas, but many have migrated there from the rural South only within the last decade. This means that within the black community, there has always been, in recent years, a sizable block unused to the problems faced in living in a large city. Their behavior has been similar to that of the Southern rural white in urban areas or the turn-of-the-century European immigrant.

2.   Most urban blacks are in a lower-class, depressed segment of the community. The hopelessness of their economic situation in many cases encourages blacks to look for quick ways to move up the social scale. Criminal activity and gambling seem to offer such possibilities. One student of the subject notes that the lower-class black also is often necessarily concerned with welfare goals while the small middle-class black segment is concerned with status goals—that is, the opportunity to move into an unsegregated suburb, to give his children a good education, and so forth. The welfare orientation of the lower-class black identifies him often as a ready seeker of patronage handouts either from a political machine or from social-welfare agencies.[41] A related factor of the low-subsistence status has been

[40] See E. Franklin Frazier, *The Negro Family in the United States,* The University of Chicago Press, Chicago, 1939; St. Clair Drake and Horace B. Cayton, *Black Metropolis,* Harcourt, Brace & World, Inc., New York, 1945; President's Commission on Law Enforcement, *The Challenge of Crime in a Free Society,* 1967.
[41] James Q. Wilson, *Negro Politics: The Search for Leadership,* The Free Press of Glencoe, New York, 1960, chap. 8. See also E. Franklin Frazier, *Black Bourgeoisie: The Rise of a New Middle Class in the United States,* Collier Books, Crowell-Collier Publishing Co., New York, 1957.

the relative absence of the entrepreneur among urban blacks. It was through small-business operations that many of the earlier ethnic groups climbed to middle-class status. Fewer blacks find this outlet possible.[42]

    3.   The black is subject to the special pressures of segregation on the basis of race which handicapped his rise up the social scale in legitimate ways.

    4.   The black family since slavery days has had a history of social disorganization. A one-time Federal official, Daniel Patrick Moynihan, has presented a thesis to explain the special problems of black family life, a thesis strongly criticized by many black activists as having racial overtones. Moynihan has argued that black families lack fathers because of the slave heritage. During the slavery period and since that time, mothers were the dominant members holding together families.[43] The black male, on the other hand, could not find status as head of his own family and so was encouraged to irresponsible action. In criticizing this kind of argument, Robert C. Weaver notes, "Hogarth and Dickens painted a picture of urban misery and poverty, the social disorganization and disease which was greater than anything we have to face today, and in this country from the 1840s on, European immigrants were crowded into our cities and the same frightful toll was taken in the disruption of families and illegitimacy and desertion by husbands, in disease, alcoholism, and madness."[44] We need only read the descriptions of the urban ghettos by Jacob Riis and his contemporaries to discover that some of our problems are not new. They are more shocking and dangerous, however, because they occur and continue at a time when ours is an affluent society.

    The social disorganization in black areas creates special problems in respect to law enforcement. Police often argue that they need special powers in such areas, and black leaders say that such procedures reflect attitudes based on racial discrimination. Black groups particularly object to what police officials call field interrogation and which blacks describe as "stop and frisk" procedures. Following racial incidents in Detroit in 1966, Mayor Jerome Cavanaugh proposed such an ordinance to permit police to search citizens for concealed weapons on the basis of suspicion. Black leaders objected so strenuously that the proposed ordinance was dropped. But such laws

[42] Nathan Glazer and Daniel Patrick Moynihan, *Beyond the Melting Pot,* The M.I.T. Press, Cambridge, Mass., 1963, pp. 29–44.
[43] Daniel Patrick Moynihan, *The Negro Family: The Case for National Action,* Office of Planning and Research, U.S. Department of Labor, 1965.
[44] Robert C. Weaver, *The Urban Complex,* Anchor Books, Doubleday & Company, Inc., Garden City, N.Y., 1966, p. 240.

are in effect in New York State and in Miami, Florida; an Illinois law was, however, vetoed in 1965 by Governor Otto Kerner.[45]

Adding to the problems of mayors of large cities has been the impact of the black vote, particularly with the passage of the several civil rights acts of the early 1960s. Increasingly, blacks are told by their own leaders that not to vote where they can do so readily is to attack black interests. In many Northern cities and in some Southern cities, the black blocs have clearly demonstrated they are the balance of power in local elections. This power will increase further as middle-class whites continue to move to the suburbs.[46] The black vote is already important in some Northern cities such as Springfield, Ohio, Saginaw, Michigan, and Gary, Indiana. In 1967, Cleveland became the first large city to have a black mayor elected by the citizens, Carl Stokes. Previously, the Flint, Michigan city council had elected one of its black members mayor. In 1970, Newark elected a black mayor.

Black councilmen have been elected in recent years in such Southern cities as Richmond, Virginia, Greensboro, North Carolina, and Nashville, Tennessee. A black has been elected to the Atlanta Board of Education.

Civil Liberties and the Urban Black. Today blacks and whites differ significantly on several points and, as one would anticipate, these points mark the lines of most intense conflict. Table 15–1 indicates these disagreements.

The civil rights movement began with attacks on discrimination in semipublic facilities such as buses and dime-store lunch counters. This battle was, for the most part, fought in Southern cities where such discrimination was most common. The same was true in the battle for voting rights. In Northern cities, blacks could register and

[45] American Civil Liberties Union, *Tension, Change and Liberty,* 45th Annual Report, American Civil Liberties Union, New York, 1965, p. 67.
[46] Matthew H. Ahmann (ed.), *The New Negro,* Fides Publishers, Notre Dame, Indiana, 1961, p. 30.

TABLE 15-1.   Where Whites and Blacks Disagree Most (In percent)

	Negroes	Whites' Reaction
Want integrated housing	68	42 oppose
Think demonstrations helpful	73	63 think harmful
Think riots helpful	34	75 think harmful
Think police unfair	33	58 think fair

Source: Newsweek, Aug. 22, 1966. Copyright, Newsweek, Inc., August, 1966.

vote if they wished to. Discrimination was likely to be more subtle, using such tactics as two-year registration laws.

More important for the nation as a whole were the blacks' objections to the effects of discrimination in education. Civil rights leaders argued that in the North such segregation was a fact even though not openly declared a legal policy. It seemed to blacks that such discrimination would close off opportunity for their children, since the schools they attended were not on a par with schools for whites. Charges of discrimination are common in all parts of the country, not just in the South. The school board in the city of New York had a great deal of difficulty in the 1960s, trying to break up actual segregation by transporting students by bus to schools which are not always the closest to their homes. In 1965, heavy pressure was placed upon the superintendent of schools in Chicago to break up *de facto* segregation and the mayor's office was picketed that summer in protest against existing policies. Even in Portland, Oregon, a city with relatively few blacks, the board of education thought it necessary to appoint a large study committee to investigate the charges of *de facto* segregation.

Many blacks have also been concerned about the unfair treatment they believe they receive at the hands of urban police. The defeat of the civilian police review board proposal by New York City voters suggests the stiffening of opposition by whites in urban areas to black demands. Other battles were fought against discrimination on the job, but most significant for the future of the black in both North and South would be the battle over discrimination in housing.[47]

The play *Raisin in the Sun* dramatized the plight of middle-class blacks as they reluctantly chose militancy to achieve decent housing rather than live in the slums of the large city, in this case, Chicago. Up until recently, blacks were unable to receive adequate housing loans from any but black banks. For example, Oscar Handlin, writing in 1959 about New York City, said,[48] "The FHA [Federal Housing Authority] generally refuses to insure loans on a home for a Negro in a predominantly white neighborhood, no matter what collateral is offered." Official policy has changed, though informal sanctions still apply.

It was perhaps housing pressure as much as any other factor that contributed to the racial explosions in Northern cities in 1965 and 1966, and it was seemingly this aspect of the civil rights movement against which the white backlash translated from opinion to overt

[47] For a case study of discrimination in the Grosse Pointe suburbs of Detroit, see Norman C. Thomas, *Rule 9: Politics, Administration and Civil Rights*, Random House, Inc., New York, 1966.
[48] Oscar Handlin, *The Newcomers: Negroes and Puerto Ricans in a Changing Metropolis*, Harvard University Press, Cambridge, Mass., 1959, p. 89.

behavior most vigorously. Many Northerners willing to grant blacks equality in other areas of life were strongly opposed to integration of their neighborhoods. Even a mild open-occupancy ordinance that did little more than affirm state law was defeated in 1966 in East Lansing, Michigan, the home of John Hannah, head of the United States Civil Rights Commission and George Romney, Governor of Michigan. Both, it should be noted, made public statements in support of the ordinance.

In 1968, the National Advisory Commission on Urban Disorders (the Kerner Commission) in its report concluded the major cause for riots was the "racism" of whites that resulted in the destructive environment of the black ghetto. The report states "What white Americans have never fully understood—but the Negro never can forget—is that white society is deeply implicated in the ghetto. White institutions created it, white institutions maintain it, and white society condones it."

A survey of attitudes of Illinois residents following the Kerner Commission Report showed sharp disagreements between whites and blacks on what caused riots and what should be done to prevent further disorder. Of blacks, 69 percent strongly blamed "racism" as opposed to only 28 percent of whites, and 86 percent of blacks strongly recommended special programs for blacks in employment, education, and housing as opposed to 45 percent of whites.[49]

Growing Militancy. In a sample survey of black opinion concerning civil rights in the Boston area in 1964, those in the younger age groups, and especially women, had little knowledge about civil rights issues but often had strong feelings on the subject. This corresponds with the general pattern of American politics in which younger people are relatively uninformed and relatively unlikely to participate in the decision-making process. It was also found that low-income, unschooled men were generally apathetic concerning civil rights questions but at the same time demonstrated strong feelings of hostility toward white men. They were generally cynical concerning the efficacy of political participation. In general, the more education the black had, the more aware and informed he was concerning civil rights matters. By comparing the responses of blacks with those of whites, this study concluded that there was a ". . . widening chasm between the American Negro and the American white with each firmly convinced that his position is soundly grounded in the basic values of our society."[50] In the nation as a whole, blacks expect to

[49] Louis Gold and Philip Meranto, "Public Attitudes on the Kerner Commission Findings: The Case of Illinois," *Illinois Government,* Institute of Government and Public Affairs, Urbana, Illinois, vol. 31, March, 1969.
[50] George D. Blackwood, "Civil Rights and Direct Action in the Urban North," a paper read at the 1964 meetings of the American Political Science Association in Chicago. Also, Thomas F. Pettigrew, *A Profile of the Negro American,* D. Van Nostrand Company, Inc., Princeton, N.J., 1964.

make progress in the coming years. They expect most help to come from private direct-action groups, and they expect less help from local or state governments than from the Federal government.

A study of San Francisco black politicians in 1968 revealed a growing influence of protest leaders over black politicians and particularly the growing mobilization of low-income blacks behind militant protest leaders.[51]

The older established black political-action organizations are the National Association for the Advancement of Colored People (NAACP) and the Urban League. The newer organizations still working within the system for the most part have included the Congress of Racial Equality (CORE), the Southern Christian Leadership Conference, and a number of *ad hoc* groups specific to the locality. None of these organizations has had much appeal to lower-class blacks, and all of them have been financed principally by white citizens. The white reaction to demonstrations and riots in black areas and the militancy of some black leaders since 1966 has significantly reduced such contributions.[52]

Newer black groups have been those emphasizing black separatism, beginning with the Black Muslims and including the Black Panthers, and black militants using tactics of urban guerrilla warfare against the police. While small in size, these groups have had a major impact on all blacks, including especially high school students. Like other movements based on ideology, they have emphasized simple and radical action as solutions to complex issues. So long as this was rhetoric it was sometimes even admired by liberal whites. When it switched to violent action in the style of such heroes as "Che" Guevera, it invited swift and violent retaliatory action, both legal and illegal. The years 1968 to 1970 marked a bloody series of encounters between police and Panthers. But the Panthers also had a positive effect in their contribution to a growing black self reliance, unity, and pride. A Harris poll of 1970 showed that while only 25 percent of blacks agreed with the Panther philosophy, 64 percent said that the Panthers gave them a sense of pride and 80 percent that shooting of Panthers by police made them feel "blacks have to stand together." At the same time 60 percent of whites categorized the Panthers "a serious menace" and 81 percent that Panther deaths were the result of violence begun by the Black Panthers.

Black citizens in urban centers have shown greater willingness to

[51] Richard Young, "The Impact of Protest Leadership on Negro Politicians in San Francisco," *Western Political Quarterly,* 22:94-111, March, 1969.
[52] For a discussion of the types of black leadership, militant or moderate, see Wilson, *op. cit.,* chap. 9; Langston Hughes, *Fight for Freedom: The Story of the NAACP,* Berkley Medallion Book, New York, 1962; and Daniel C. Thompson, *The Negro Leadership Class,* Prentice-Hall, Inc., Englewood Cliffs, N.J., 1963.

try new ways to achieve their goals from 1965 on. The civil rights movement was frequently punctured by violence, including full-fledged riots which raged out of control for hours and days at a time. One such major riot occurred in the Hough area, a black slum of Cleveland. Another occurred in Harlem; a third, in Chicago's Puerto Rican section; but some also occurred in smaller cities, such as Benton Harbor, Michigan. It was clear that riots were most likely to happen in Northern slums, where frustrated lower-class blacks are more willing to resort to violence than are national black leaders (see Table 15-2). Each such occasion is a basis for speculative editorial writing and frenetic activity by public officeholders. In the great riot in South Central Los Angeles in 1965, for example, at least 36 persons were killed; more than 900 were injured; property damage ran to not less than $200 million; and more than 4,000 persons were arrested. After the Los Angeles police and California National Guard units, operating under virtually full combat conditions, finally restored order, the politicians began to play "pin the tail on the donkey." The mayor of Los Angeles, the Governor of California, and the director of the Federal antipoverty program all attempted to explain the factors that caused the riot and to show that the policies they had advocated were policies that would alleviate tension in the area and that they were not themselves to blame. (Mayor Samuel Yorty did not seem to fare so well as the others in the propaganda battle. Among other things, he had made a serious mistake—one that was certain to hurt him in the eyes of persons on all sides of the issue—by leaving the city in the midst of the riot in order to make a political speech in San Francisco.) Pundits of all kinds also immediately sought to explain the causes of the event. Left-wing leaders of the black movement for civil rights reaffirmed their view that occasional violence was necessary in the struggle.

TABLE 15-2. **Willingness to Resort to Violence (In percent)**

Future Action	Non-Southern Low-Income Blacks	Total Black Sample	Black Leaders
Nonviolent	50	63	93
Violent	25	22	4
Not sure	25	15	3

Source: William Brink and Louis Harris, *The Negro Revolution in America*, Simon and Schuster, Inc., New York, 1964, p. 73. Copyright © 1963 by Newsweek, Inc.

Persons committed to nonviolence, such as Martin Luther King, Jr., tried to talk to the people of the area in terms of what was being done and why some patience and certainly nonviolence was a necessary approach, but he made little impact with his sophisticated arguments upon the emotion-ridden people of the area, most of whom had little education, only brief urban-life experience, and few prospects for economic advancement.[53] Persons embracing a middle-class ideology deplored the violence and law violation as well as the social and psychological conditions under which the people of the area have lived. Others, still committed to the small-town ideology, insisted that the participants "must be prosecuted and punished" and that "a society that tolerates such self-indulgence ought not to be surprised when the destructive flame suddenly lashes up."[54]

Violent action of this type can be explained only in terms of the fact that (1) it results from a cumulation of many factors and events, and (2) in any society that is not a complete police state, social order is fundamentally dependent upon the willingness of members of society to abide by the rules. As Table 15-3 indicates, this was clearly not the case with many non-Southern blacks who live in Northern urban centers.

As every policeman who has ever been involved in a riot situation knows, latent aggressive behavior erupts in many people as soon as they recognize that the normal rules, constraints, and sanctions are not being applied. Once a riot begins, the psychological factors governing the mob are evoked and the psychological factors contributing to social control are temporarily set aside. Under such circumstances, a person will do things, including murder, which he would not do under any other circumstances. To hundreds of people, a riot is an opportunity to react aggressively against any persons or groups against whom they feel aggrieved. Thus, the 38-percent figure for non-Southern blacks who would join a riot or who state they are

[53] On the Watts riot, see Jerry Cohen and William S. Murphy, *Burn, Baby, Burn!* E. P. Dutton & Co., Inc., New York, 1966.
[54] *National Review*, Aug. 31, 1965.

TABLE 15-3. How Blacks Feel about Riots (In percent)

	Total Rank and File	Non-South	South	Leadership Group
Would join a riot	15	13	18	1
Would not join a riot	61	62	59	75
Not sure	24	25	23	24

Source: Newsweek, Aug. 22, 1966, p. 22. Copyright, Newsweek, Inc., August, 1966.

not sure they would probably underestimates the numbers who would join such action.

A tendency also exists, as is always the case where conventional wisdom is involved, to find simple explanations for such riots even though the causes are certainly multiple and the behavior pattern is complex. Mayor Samuel Yorty, for example, first blamed the California highway patrol for the riot because of an arrest patrolmen had made. Yet, the arrest was a routine one for alleged drunken driving. The Communists and some non-Communist left-wing groups were his next target. He said that they were responsible for the riot through their insistence that the police had behaved brutally toward blacks of the city. Later he blamed Sargent Shriver, director of the Federal antipoverty program, for being slow in providing funds to the Los Angeles area. Still later, he engaged in a loud political controversy with Governor Edmund G. (Pat) Brown of California over the causes.[55]

The reporting to the public was by no means all ignorant, self-seeking, or simplistic. *Newsweek* reporters, for example, noted, "Yet for all the public finger pointing, there were no short answers as to why the riots happened—or how to keep them from happening again." In the summer of 1967, a number of serious riots took place, culminating in one in Detroit which caused more property damage than any previous riot in American history and the greatest loss of life of any American riot since the Civil War draft riots.

Summary: The Urban Black and Civil Rights. The result of demonstrations, riots, increasing black political militancy, and increasing political power has been tension and conflict between blacks and whites. It has also, however, led to a rethinking of their relationships and particularly of the role played by law-enforcement agencies. Police agencies have often taken the lead in this reassessment. Mayors have also become more sensitive to the opinions of black constituencies. Open-occupancy ordinances have been debated and occasionally adopted and, to some degree, white attitudes have changed. (Table 15–4.)

The battle over housing in urban centers of the North appears to be crucial in deciding the future of black civil rights.

One political scientist, Edward Banfield, argues the position of the black has been steadily improving. He sees the problems as economic rather than racial and thus capable of amelioration.[56] Whether this is correct or not in the long run, in the immediate years ahead more violence between whites and blacks and considerable verbal conflict is likely. In the process, civil liberties will be violated as

[55] *Newsweek,* Aug. 30, 1965.
[56] Edward C. Banfield, *The Unheavenly City,* Little Brown and Company, Boston, 1970.

TABLE 15-4. How White Views of the Black Have Changed (In percent)

	All Whites		Southern Whites	
Whites Would Mind	1963	1966	1963	1966
Sitting next to a black in restaurant	20	16	50	42
Sitting next to a black in movie	24	20	54	46
Using same restroom as black	24	21	56	56
Trying on same clothing black had tried on	36	28	57	54
Sitting next to black on bus			47	44
If teen-age child dated a black	90	88	97	94
If a black family moved next door	51	46	74	69

Source: Newsweek, Aug. 22, 1966. Copyright, Newsweek, Inc., August, 1966.

tempers rise, but overall it is likely that the status of the Northern black will increase and his civil liberties will be honored to a greater degree than in the past.

SELECTED READINGS

Aumann, Francis R.: *The Instrumentalities of Justice,* Ohio State University Press, Columbus, Ohio, 1956.

Booker, Simeon: *Black Man's America,* Prentice-Hall, Inc., Englewood Cliffs, N.J., 1965.

Brooks, Thomas R.: "Necessary Force—or Police Brutality?" *New York Times Magazine,* Dec. 5, 1965, pp. 60ff.

Cohen, Jerry, and William S. Murphy: *Burn, Baby, Burn!* E. P. Dutton & Co., Inc., New York, 1966. (The Watts riot of 1965, reported by on-the-scene reporters of *The Los Angeles Times.*)

Cray, Ed: *The Big Blue Line: Police Power versus Human Rights,* Coward-McCann, Inc., New York, 1966. (A criticism of American police forces, arguing that they suffer from low standards of recruitment and training.)

Curran, H. H.: *Magistrates' Courts,* Charles Scribner's Sons, New York, 1942.

Eley, Lynn, and Thomas W. Casstevens (eds.): *The Politics of Fair-Housing Legislation: State and Local Case Studies,* Chandler, San Francisco, 1968.

Fellman, David: *The Defendant's Rights,* Holt, Rinehart and Winston, Inc., New York, 1958.

Karlen, Delmar: *The Citizen in Court,* Holt, Rinehart and Winston, Inc., New York, 1964.

Muse, Benjamin: *The American Negro Revolution, From Nonviolence to Black Power, 1963–1967,* Indiana University Press, Blooming-ton, 1968.

National Committee against Discrimination in Housing: *The Fair Housing Statutes and Ordinances,* NCADH, New York, 1966. (A survey of legislation, ordinances, and administrative action at state and local levels.)

Pierce, Neal R., J. G. Phillips, and Victoria Velsey (eds.): *Revolution in Civil Rights,* Congressional Quarterly Service, Washington, 1965. (Detailed history and summary of legislation.)

Ploscowe, Morris: "The Inferior Criminal Courts in Action," *The Annals of the American Academy of Political and Social Science,* 287:3–12, May, 1953.

Pound, Roscoe: *Criminal Justice in America,* Holt, Rinehart and Winston, Inc., New York, 1945.

President's Commission on Law Enforcement and Administration of Justice: *The Challenge of Crime in a Free Society,* 1967. (A major study of crime, criminal procedures, courts, and corrections.)

Rosenblum, Victor G.: *Law as a Political Instrument,* Random House, Inc., New York, 1955.

Rossi, Peter H. (ed.): *Ghetto Revolts,* Aldine, Chicago, 1970. *Urban Affairs Quarterly* "Special Issue on the Urban Negro," September, 1968.

Warren, George: *Traffic Courts,* Little, Brown and Company, Boston, 1942.

Westin, Alan F.: *The Miracle Case: The Supreme Court and the Movies,* The Bobbs-Merrill Company, Inc., Indianapolis, ICP no. 64, 1961. (Are films a means of expression protected by the First Amendment? Is sacrilege a basis for censorship?)

Woodward, C. Vann: *The Strange Career of Jim Crow,* 2d ed., Oxford University Press, Fair Lawn, N.J., 1966. In paperback. Original publication, 1955. (A classic study of racial segregation.)

B THE POLITICS OF LAND USE

CHAPTER
16 PUBLIC UTILITIES AND TRANSPORTATION

Public utilities are industries which provide important public services for which the individual user generally pays a portion of the cost. Of them all, public transportation has probably offered the biggest problem to municipal administrators in all except the smallest cities in the period after World War II. In addition to public utilities, this chapter will also examine the general topic of urban transportation.

PUBLIC UTILITIES

Public utilities are not necessarily publicly owned. Many of them are, but the majority are owned and operated by private corporations, and some by individual proprietors. A list of utilities within a municipality includes street railways, buses, telephone, telegraph, electricity, water, and gas services. Other functions that are of the nature of utilities, although not always legally considered to be such, are auditoriums, port facilities, slaughterhouses, airports, and possibly toll bridges, toll roads, sewers, and public markets.

Public utilities, then, are businesses affected with more than a usual amount of public interest and therefore expected by the public to be subjected to more than a normal amount of governmental control. They are usually granted a monopoly within their areas of operation. This is because experience has shown that competition in these areas is impractical and uneconomical. Competitive utilities have existed in the past—a few still do—but generally they have proved to be wasteful of resources and have offered inferior and costly services to the public. A public utility normally has a right to use public property (over which to string electric wires, or to operate buses) and to exercise the state's power of eminent domain. It usually charges for services rendered on a benefits-received basis, and it is subject to the control of some type of public service commission whose legal responsibility it is to protect both the provider and the purchaser of services.

Regulation. In the nineteenth century, utilities were normally operated on the basis of a *franchise* which was granted to local utilities, most commonly, by the city government. A franchise is a license stipulating the conditions under which a utility may operate and the privileges it is to enjoy. The franchise usually stated the quality of service that was expected of the utility and the rates that could be charged. In practice, the utilities were often little inhibited by their franchises. Sometimes they resorted to bribery of public officials, sometimes they won judicial interpretations of ambiguous provisions of the franchise by the use of superior legal talent, and in almost no cases was there a public body that had the legal authority to hold the utility to the terms of its agreement.

One of the major areas of activity of reform forces at the turn of the present century was that of public utility regulation. The method of control that gradually evolved centers around a public service commission (bearing various titles in various states) whose duty it is to determine rates after investigations and hearings and to supervise both the service and the management of the utilities. Most commissions prescribe uniform accounting methods; they often must approve expansion plans and the issuance of new securities; and they may sometimes even be authorized to order such expansions. Commissions are constantly at work overseeing the activities of the utilities, but there is considerable variation in the degree to which they are effective.

Franchises are still granted, but they are no longer so detailed as they were in the days before public service commissions. They are usually limited to a term of years (perhaps twenty-five), rather than made to exist in perpetuity, as was once common. The franchise usually provides for the privileges to be enjoyed by the utility; it may provide for a special tax structure for it; and it prescribes some conditions which must be met by the utility. It leaves most other controls to the public service commissions. In the worst days of nineteenth-century corruption, control over franchises was assumed by the state, where it has remained for the most part.

The major questions in connection with public utilities have historically been three. First, how are utility rates to be determined? Second, should the state or the city control utilities operating in the city? Third, should utilities be privately or publicly owned?

The Determination of Rates. The question of rate determination is one that can easily take up a term in a college course in public utility regulation without a satisfactory answer being arrived at. The problem in practice has evolved around a question that is almost impossible to answer: What is the true value of a large and complex corporation? If rates are so low that the utility does not receive a fair rate of return on its investment, confiscation of private property results, and this is legally prohibited by the due-process clause of the Fifth Amendment. But what is the "investment" or "worth" of a utility? Is it more equitable to calculate the revenue that a rate should produce on the basis of a percentage of the present cost of replacing the capital equipment of the utility, or of the actual total investment made over the years? The formula used may make a great difference in the allowable rates. Should changes in the price index be considered? Should any value be placed on the franchise, "good will," or "going concern"?

In an attempt to answer these questions, public service commissions have made valuation studies; but these often take years and are inconclusive, and by the time they are completed, their results are no longer applicable to existing conditions. Since due process of law is involved, utilities controversies are commonly adjudicated in the courts on appeal from the commissions. In seeking equity, the United States Supreme Court has for years struggled between the "cost of reproduction" and the "actual amount of prudent investment" theories.[1] The most recent decision leans toward actual investment in capital without considering the problem of subsequent influences of inflation or deflation. But there are many questions and problems. Rate determination, despite able research staffs, is still in large part based upon folklore and subjective evaluations, and it is costly.

Should Utilities Be Privately or Publicly Owned? In nineteenth-century America, when the businessman was paid great homage and when business subsequently attracted the lion's share of talent, utilities were commonly privately owned. This was in contrast to the

---

[1] See *Smyth v. Ames*, 169 U.S. 466 (1898), the first landmark case; *Southwestern Bell Telephone Co. v. Missouri*, 262 U.S. 276 (1923); *F.P.C. v. Hope Natural Gas Co.*, 320 U.S. 591 (1944), the ruling case at present.

practice in Europe, where, apart from any argument concerning the merits of socialism, state and municipal ownership of utilities has always been the rule.

Americans in the past did not trust government, and, with business proving on all sides that it could "get things done," it was quite natural for Americans to expect private business to operate utilities. Nevertheless, starting in the nineteenth century, it became customary for some functions to be publicly owned. Water supply, which is closely related to public health and to fire protection, was the earliest to become commonly a public function.

Most utilities are still privately owned, however, and probably most citizens regard this as preferable. This despite the fact that many leaders of the reform movement around the turn of the century advocated municipal ownership of utilities. They argued that private ownership had failed because the utilities acted irresponsibly, with little effective state control, and with a policy of maximizing profits and minimizing service. They therefore urged municipal ownership of various utilities, but especially of urban transportation.

No categorical argument can be made for or against municipal ownership. It has worked well in some places, poorly in others. The local environment is an important consideration. So is the relative effectiveness of the local privately owned utilities. If these are very unsatisfactory, municipal ownership may be less unsatisfactory. There is neither intrinsic good nor evil in public ownership, nor is it part of the ideology of socialism. In typical American fashion, the question of its desirability must be decided on the merits of the individual situation.

The Extent of Municipal Ownership Today. Certain functions are commonly owned by municipalities today. Nearly three-fourths of the cities of over 5,000 own their own water-distribution systems. Nearly all of them own their own sewerage systems, and one-half of them own sewage-treatment plants. Municipal airports and auditoriums are quite common, and large cities often own incinerators.[2]

Electricity is in the large majority of cases in private hands, although many cities own plants and lines for distributing power to street lights and traffic signals. In some parts of the nation, especially in relatively isolated cities, municipal systems exist—over 500 of them. Of America's eighteen largest cities (those over one-half a million), only Cleveland and Los Angeles have city-owned electrical generating and distributing systems for general use. Municipal gas plants are very rare. Of these largest cities, only Philadelphia and Houston produce and distribute gas.

[2] See current editions of *The Municipal Year Book.*

The street railway has all but disappeared in America, and only seven municipal systems remained in 1960. Thirty-three cities of over 5,000 owned bus systems, however, in addition to the Boston transit, which is controlled by a separate unit of government.

All the largest cities own some utilities, except for Boston, which has them operated on a regional basis by the Massachusetts Metropolitan District Commission. One city in eight, however, owns no utilities of any kind, and private ownership is the overwhelming rule even today for most functions.

WATER AND SANITATION

Probably no single governmental domestic policy is of more importance to the future pattern of development of the United States than is that of water. It has been said, without exaggeration, that "you could write the story of man's growth in terms of his epic concerns with water."[3] Man is utterly dependent upon it. It determined where he first settled as he moved into new lands. It dictates the location of most heavy industry. It controls the size to which a city, whether it be New York, Denver, or Los Angeles, may grow. It limits possible land uses. Its quality affects the state of the public health, the size of the municipal budget, and the taste of a highball. Its quantity determines whether bluegrass lawns may be watered in August, a rowboat must be kept in the garage as an escape vehicle from a flash flood, or the economy of a resort area will flourish or wither. In all aspects of water policy, government—national, state, and local—is involved.

Water Needs. Although the population of the United States only doubled between 1900 and 1955, per capita use of water quadrupled. This was a result not only of changing agricultural and industrial uses but also of the laborsaving devices that have been adopted in the contemporary home: the garbage grinder, the automatic washing machine, the dishwasher, and the air-conditioning unit.

Here are some relevant facts:

1. The average American home used at least 165 gallons of water a day for household needs in 1965. It used less than 95 gallons in 1890.

2. Homes with garbage grinders discharge 50 percent more organic matter into sewers than those without them. This adds greatly to the sewage-treatment problem and potentially to water pollution and to the disappearance of favorable conditions for the growth of fish in streams.

[3] Bernard Frank, "The Story of Water as the Story of Man," in Alfred Stefferud (ed.), *Water*, U.S. Government Printing Office, 1955.

3. Industrial uses of water are enormous. Domestic uses of water account for only about 5 percent of the total. The rest is divided about equally between irrigation and industrial uses, the latter of which is growing much faster than the former. It requires about 110 gallons of water to manufacture a pound of rayon, 300 gallons for a gallon of beer, 65,000 gallons for a ton of steel, and 600,000 gallons for a ton of synthetic rubber.[4]

4. Both industrial and domestic effluents produce problems of water pollution that affect the welfare of downstream communities, of fish and game, and of recreation programs. Of approximately 16,000 American communities that have public water systems, only 9,000 have sewer systems, and no more than 6,000 of these are connected to sewage-treatment plants.

5. Increasing urban usage of lands adds to flood hazards and drainage problems, since land largely covered by roofs and concrete has much greater runoff than does other land.

6. The increasing concentration of the population in urban clusters involving a small percentage of the total land area has added greatly to the problems both of obtaining adequate water and of disposing of treated and untreated wastes.

Water Control and Supply Programs. The responsibility for getting the right amount of water of the right quality in the right place at the right time is shared by national, state, and local governments. The nature of the problems involved vary geographically and according to use. In the East, for example, the principal problems center around the distribution and quality of water; in the West, the major concern is with quantity. Some industries may be able to use raw water, whereas others need the highest quality; but much of the need is taken care of by industry itself, and governments need concern themselves only about regulation. Because water resources do not follow state or local boundaries, intergovernmental arrangements and potential problems and conflicts abound. Water supply and the quality of water in streams is now seen as a state and Federal problem and responsibility.

Water Supply. Many municipalities receive their water supply from wells. This is a relatively inexpensive method for small cities and villages, although the water is often very hard and, until one becomes accustomed to it, unpalatable. As core-city suburbs increase in size, their wells tend to become dry, for the table level of the ground water drops. It has been predicted, for example, that all the

---

[4]*State Administration of Water Resources,* Council of State Governments, Chicago, 1957, p. 5; and Stefferud, *op. cit.,* pp. 636–643.

Chicago suburbs using wells will eventually be forced to abandon them and obtain water from the core city.[5]

Few of the larger cities use wells. Memphis uses them. Brooklyn once did, but for many years citizens objected that the water was salty and brackish. This led to abandonment of the privately owned wells in 1947 and the use throughout New York City of water from the Catskill and other reservoirs. In large cities, however, many wells have been sunk by business firms for air-conditioning purposes. In many cities, the table level is sinking rapidly as a result, and strict regulation of these practices has become necessary. Some cities require all water withdrawn for air-conditioning purposes to be returned to the ground. New York has had such a rule since 1933. Business firms are not likely to do this voluntarily, since it adds to the expense of the system.

Most large cities depend for their water supply upon rivers, the damming of small streams, or lakes. The problem of securing a supply of relatively unpolluted water becomes increasingly difficult as urban populations grow and the amount of industrial and human waste dumped into streams increases. Cities along the Great Lakes have until recently been able to get palatable, germ-free water with a minimum of treatment. Some cities, such as Philadelphia, which uses the Delaware River, must use a great amount of filtration and chemical treatment, for their sources are badly polluted.

Cities along the ocean, such as New York and Los Angeles, have not been able to convert sea water inexpensively and have had to bring their supplies hundreds of miles from the mountains. Congress, in 1952, first authorized the Secretary of the Interior to cooperate with the state and local governments in an effort to devise a process for making use of salt and brackish water for home and factory consumption.[6] Some progress is being made, but the principal problems are economic rather than technological. Some growing inland cities have had to resort to desperate measures to ensure a water supply. Denver, for example, gouged a 23-mile tunnel through solid rock to reach water sources on the western slope of the Rocky Mountains.

A political issue related to water supply concerns the fluoridation of water, a practice designed to reduce dental caries. Fluoridation has been especially opposed by right-wing extremists. A study of voting on the question of fluoridating the water of North Hampton, Massachusetts, concluded that the opponents of fluoridation made appeals particularly in terms of the invasion of individual rights, a fear of poisoning, and a waste of public funds. The opponents'

[5] *Chicago Sanitary District,* Illinois Legislative Council, Springfield, Ill., 1953, p. 28.
[6] R. D. Bugher, "Public Works Development in 1952," *Municipal Year Book, 1953,* International City Management Association, Chicago, 1953, p. 345. See Stefferud, *op. cit.,* pp. 109–118.

arguments were found to be easily understood, while the errors in them were often difficult for a layman to comprehend. In addition, the researchers concluded that the opponents of fluoridation were in part making a symbolic protest against a world that seems to be increasingly menacing and were expressing a popular suspicion of science and scientists. The opponents were "predominantly people of the older age groups, people without children under 12, people of the lower-income brackets and middle- or lower-class occupation." Support for fluoridation came mainly from the younger groups and those in professional, managerial, and other white-collar occupations. One of the most striking differences was in education. A large proportion of the anti-fluoridation voters had failed to finish high school.[7] In that election, held in 1953, fluoridation was defeated by a 2-to-1 vote. The fluoridation issue as a symbolic protest may have declined in importance since that time, in part, perhaps, because the obvious evidence is so strongly in favor of fluoridation. For example, a 1965 study by the health department in Baltimore indicated that cavities in the teeth of slum children were one-half as great as they had been in a similar study before the city's water had been fluoridated. In 1967, Los Angeles was the only one of the ten largest cities in the nation not to fluoridate its water.

The fate at the polls of referendums concerning fluoridation probably depends in part upon the prevailing political ideology and the anxiety levels of a considerable portion of the voting population. One study has indicated, however, that the amount and direction of political leadership may be a marginal factor in deciding the issue. It was found that when a mayor or manager took a strong position in favor of fluoridation, the proposal was very likely to pass. Both councilmen and the voters tended to take their cues from these highly visible leaders, or at least a number sufficient for passage did so. When the mayor or manager was negative or noncommittal, the proposal was much more likely to fail. Of course, when the mayor or manager was favorable, he might in many cases simply be reflecting prevailing sentiment, but the study shows that he was more than just a pawn in the process.[8]

Water-supply problems of cities are as old as are cities themselves. In America, searches for more and better water used to follow disastrous fires and terrible epidemics, such as the cholera wave of 1832 that convinced New Yorkers to try the then-daring engineering feat of going 30 miles to the Croton River for safe water.[9]

[7] Bernard Mausner and Judith Mausner, "A Study of the Anti-scientific Attitude," *Scientific American*, 192:35–39, February, 1955.
[8] Robert L. Crain and Donald B. Rosenthal, "Structure and Values in Local Political Systems," *Journal of Politics*, 28:194, February, 1966; and Donald B. Rosenthal and Robert L. Crain, "Executive Leadership and Community Innovation," *Urban Affairs Quarterly*, 1:39–57, March, 1966.
[9] Nathan M. Blake, *Water for the Cities*, Syracuse University Press, Syracuse, N.Y., 1957.

Today, water supply is regarded as vital for the operation of a modern home and for the irrigation of suburban lawns and gardens. But it is also at times a matter of sheer survival, if we judge from the public reaction in New York, which had serious water-supply problems in 1949 and 1950 as a result of inadequate rainfall. At the time, there were:[10]

> ... daily front-page bulletins showing net gains and losses of precious water in city reservoirs; periodic prayers for rain offered at St. Patrick's Cathedral; fantastic solutions suggested by panicky citizens; bathless Fridays; official announcements that beards will be considered municipal "badges of honor"; official New York city rain-makers who drive around in the Catskill reservoir area, their trailers emitting the magical silver iodide smoke to squeeze water out of reluctant clouds; complaints from sufficiently water-supplied suburbs that the city is thus causing unnecessary snow-storms.

Sanitation. Municipal and other local governments bear the primary responsibility for sewage treatment, including septic-tank installation practices, and for provision of means for carrying off rain water through storm drains and holding back floods through the construction (often with the aid of Federal funds) of levees and retaining walls. All these activities cost a good deal of money. Sewerage and sewage-disposal plants are among the most expensive of municipal capital outlays, and great controversies center about the means of financing them and of holding costs to a minimum. Public forums in a city considering a new sewage-disposal plant give one the distinct impression that every taxpayer is also an expert in sanitary engineering. Storm drains, too, are matters of great concern to citizens— though usually only during wet springs. A complex cost-benefit problem is frequently involved. As a result, the citizen in much of the nation feels convinced in April that a new storm-drain system in his neighborhood is necessary at any cost. By August, he has forgotten his earlier view and is now certain that larger water mains or better supply sources are needed so as to make it possible for him to preserve the color of his precious bluegrass during dry spells.

Boston, in 1823, was the first American city to install a system of sanitary sewers. Other cities followed as their populations increased. In those early days, the sewage was commonly dumped into a nearby stream or other body of water. This was in itself a scientific method of disposal. Contrary to a popular impression that the down-river town drank the raw sewage of the one above it, the chemical reaction of the oxygen in the water with the sewage would convert the organic matter into nitrates and other non-disease-bearing by-

[10]Albert Lepawsky, "Water Resources and American Federalism," *American Political Science Review,* 44:639, September, 1950. Used by permission.

products. If a sufficient supply of water was available and cities were not too close together, this approach was reasonably safe.

Today, as a public health precaution, sewage must be treated before disposal. There are several methods of treatment, and they are all normally expensive. Because cities, and often their suburbs, may try to avoid this expense, several states have established water-pollution commissions. These commissions may, if they find that a municipality is endangering the public health or the fish and wildlife of the state, order a municipality to construct a sewage-treatment plant. The state has sometimes had to resort to its coercive power and force cities into safety precautions.

Sewage-treatment plants, like those for water treatment, are least expensive if used to full capacity and if one or a few rather than many of them exist in a metropolitan area.

In 1965, Congress passed a Water Quality Act and augmented this in 1966 with the Clean Waters Restoration Act. These acts established standards for water-pollution control and provided for Federal funds to communities and states participating in the program. The funds were made available for the administration of planning agencies concerned with pollution control throughout a given river basin. The planning agencies are required to show that they can develop an effective, comprehensive water quality control and abatement plan which can meet Federal water quality standards.

Municipal sanitation also involves the disposal of ashes, rubbish, and garbage. These may be collected separately or in various combinations, depending upon the method of disposal. Ashes are becoming less of a municipal task. Industries normally dispose of their own, while few homes or apartments are now heated by coal. Ashes, together with street dirt, make good fill for low places and are commonly disposed of in this fashion. Sometimes they are simply dumped.

Rubbish (nonorganic trash and discards) is also used for fill, or it may be dumped. Sometimes it is incinerated. Garbage (organic waste) may be disposed of by incineration, use of the reduction process, the sanitary fill, feeding to hogs, dumping, grinding at central locations, or grinding in the home. Incineration is expensive but very effective. It is used particularly in larger cities and is becoming increasingly popular. The expensive reduction process, which is used to recover waste fats, has been tried in large cities but is passing from favor. The sanitary-fill method is used quite extensively, especially in small or medium-sized cities.

Feeding to hogs has been popular, since a part of the cost of collection and disposal can thereby be recouped. It is believed, however, that the feeding of raw garbage may be a method of transmitting vesicular exanthema among hogs and cholera and trichinosis to human beings. As a result, many states now require precooking of the garbage. This additional cost is causing municipalities to switch to other disposal methods, especially to incineration.

Garbage is sometimes dumped, either into a pit to be buried or into a body of water. This is usually a temporary measure, although some small places use it as a regular disposal method.

Grinding of garbage has the effect of converting it into sewage. This is a method wherein solving the garbage problem adds to the sewage problem. Grinding at central locations is quite common and works satisfactorily if an adequate sewage-disposal plant exists. The home garbage grinder has become extremely popular in the post-war period, and new homes throughout the nation are commonly built to include them. In some places they are causing problems by overtaxing the sewerage system or the disposal plant. The increased amount of organic matter that is thereby dumped into bodies of water may constitute a threat to fish and wildlife by removing oxygen from the water to a dangerous extent.[11] But the grinders symbolize, to the housewife, another step in America's material progress.

Municipalities do not necessarily collect and dispose of ashes, rubbish, or garbage themselves. In some places, the job is done by a collector holding a contract from the city. In others, the city licenses several collectors. A great many cities do the job themselves, however, through a department of public works. The sewerage system is almost always operated by the city itself, but an important policy question to be settled in connection with this activity is whether storm drains should be connected to the regular sewers or constructed separately. Engineers prefer the latter method.

TRANSPORTATION

The methods by which persons, goods, and materials are moved from one place to another are so important to the effective operation of a city that they have largely come under the control of government in recent generations. The municipality alone cannot provide for, or supervise, all urban needs for highway, rail, water, and air transportation. State governments are also called upon for regulation, financial aid, and other activities. So is the national government, which, in 1966, recognized its responsibilities to a greater extent than ever before by establishing a Department of Transportation, giving it responsibility for coordinated and effective administration of transportation systems and calling for it to cooperate with state

[11]See the comments of William Vogt, *Road to Survival,* William Sloane Associates, New York, 1948, pp. 34–35.

and local governments as well as private transportation companies in seeking effective transportation policies and programs throughout the nation.

Highways. All cities have problems of street paving, cleaning, and lighting, and sidewalk installation. While basic engineering and financing practices have come to be applied to these functions, more perplexing problems have arisen in connection with the building of high-speed, limited-access freeways and with the finding of off-street parking.

Freeways. In large cities, problems and political issues connected with the construction of modern highways include the following: What route should freeways follow? How often should there be an interchange? Freeways are enormously expensive. How should they be paid for? Would a toll road be feasible? Should they be paid for out of a rebate to the city from the state gasoline tax? Out of the general revenue fund? Out of a local tax on each automobile? Freeways damage property values along their immediate routes but enhance the values of property near and at either end of them. One of their main purposes is to shore up sagging property values in the downtown area and to maintain the dollar volume of business in downtown stores. If these establishments benefit particularly from the highway, should they be asked to pay an extra tax to compensate for this advantage?

The Federal Aid Highway Act of 1944 provided that one-fourth of Federal funds for highways should be used for extensions within cities. As a result, many cities are building roads with up to 90 percent of the cost paid from Federal grants-in-aid. Because this is the case, many questions of routing and technical specifications are determined, not by local considerations, but by the Federal Highway Administration. This agency must approve the route and all technical details before Federal funds are made available. In most cases, the cost of building is so great that without these funds freeways would not be built.

Many states are granting funds to cities for building high-speed, limited-access highways, and they have helped in other ways, too, for example, by allowing cities to issue bonds in anticipation of future receipts of state-collected, locally shared gasoline taxes. The cost is roughly 5 million dollars per mile. The estimate by Professor Vickrey of Columbia University is that this comes to 7 cents for every mile every commuter car drives. [12]

The use of Federal and state grants and of revenue from gasoline taxes have been the most popular methods of financing highways.

[12] *Newsweek*, Jan. 18, 1971, p. 46.

Asking the downtown property owner to contribute a larger share has been suggested by some labor-backed candidates for municipal office, but this has not proved popular with the owners or most voters. In several cities, the county has paid part of the cost.

As part of the interstate system, all large cities have developed plans for freeways leading to the central business district and, for those who wish to bypass, belting the city along the periphery. Negotiations among the various units of government involved—core city, suburbs, county, state, and the Federal Highway Administration—are complex, delicate, and time-consuming. The technicians in the state and Federal agencies are likely to dominate these discussions—though the often-dissenting views of community political figures may dominate the pages of the local newspaper—and these men are in many ways changing the face of the nation, for a modification in the arterial traffic pattern is likely to cause a great many changes in land use.[13] Meanwhile, back at the city hall, however, local interests urge the mayor or manager to intercede on their behalf. The engineers wish to maximize traffic flow in and around cities, and they want to prohibit later rule changes (e.g., in access privileges) that will modify the principal use of a road from a traffic to a business artery; real estate operators will try to mold the shape of the new road to fit their speculations and investments; owners of unsalable land will try to convince the decision makers that their property lies directly along what is certainly the ideal route; the chamber of commerce manager will point out the significance of route choice to his campaign to attract new industry for the community; heavily mortgaged homeowners will claim that if the expressway goes within a few blocks of their homes it will ruin the value of the property—though they may want an interchange located just beyond the sound of roaring truck exhausts; merchants along heavily traveled, free-access routes will complain that the siphoning off of the traffic onto a—to them inaccessible—freeway will threaten them with bankruptcy. With an occasional nod to overriding local demands—the kind that are powerful enough to potentially involve the intervention of a legislator or Congressman—the professional engineers go about applying their professional values to the work of serving the most numerous interest of all, the motoring public.

Traffic and Parking. Despite the expressways and a good deal of work in improving other streets, cities are not making progress against traffic congestion. The commonplace rectangular pattern of streets is inefficient for traffic flow; most streets are still expected to provide the impossible—to serve as rapid thoroughfares and as

[13] See above, p. 11.

access routes to places of business; land is too scarce and valuable and wrecking operations too expensive to clear away many existing structures for parking or to widen existing streets; citizens refuse to use public transportation except as a matter of desperation.

It has been estimated that one-third of the buildings in downtown Boston would have to be torn down to provide adequate parking space for the patrons of the remaining structures. The larger the city, the smaller the proportion of residents using their cars to get downtown. But despite this, the larger the city, the more difficult it is to find adequate parking.

Beginning with its use in Oklahoma City in 1935, the parking meter has become an almost universal phenomenon along commercial streets in American cities. The meters are, in effect, yet another tax upon the motorist. They serve as a good source of revenue for cities. This income is used for street maintenance and traffic control in some cities and to construct off-street parking facilities in others. The meters themselves do not solve the parking problem, except perhaps to speed up the shopper and other parker and to discourage all-day parking along business-area streets.

Parking space is, economically speaking, a responsibility of the firm for whom the driver works or the store to which the driver-shopper is headed. Because the business districts were built before the automobile was developed, such provisions have not been made. Most cities now attempt to require all new commercial places to furnish adequate parking spaces off the street, though the practice is not universal.

A problem in many cities in procuring sufficient parking lots from private sources is found in the fact that the business is monopolized in the hands of one or a few large lot owners possessing considerable political power. There are several parking-lot corporations organized on a nationwide basis, each operating in numerous cities.

Airports: Public Subsidy for Transportation. American governments have traditionally subsidized methods of transportation, especially when they are new. We have subsidized facilities for canalboats, railways, automobiles and trucks, ocean transportation, and, after World War I, air travel. Beginning in the 1920s, cities were authorized to construct, and usually to operate, municipal airports. Today almost all the nation's largest cities have city-owned airports. In some cases this is a county function and there are several ad hoc airport authorities to cover the metropolitan areas, while in other cities the airports are leased to private operators. But in most places the city owns and operates the facilities.

So optimistic have people been about the future of air travel that municipal airports are common even in cities of under 10,000 population. The Federal Airport Act of 1946 probably encouraged many cities to construct airports that are not self-supporting and, for a long time into the future, will not be self-supporting. The act made no allowance for aid in operation and maintenance, and these costs have proved to be a great burden for many municipalities.

Public Transportation. Public transportation systems within cities became white elephants after World War II. The development contains some elements of serious maladjustment, for although *most* people have automobiles and could get along entirely without public transportation if necessary, it still remains an absolutely vital utility to a small minority.

Virtually all transit systems in the United States were losing money in the 1970s. This was true of those privately owned as well as those publicly owned. No large-city system was earning the current rate on its investment. There were several reasons for the failure of these utilities to be able to pay their costs. First of all, of course, is the switch to auto transportation. There were 28 million autos in 1946 and about 90 million in 1971. Largely because of this, the number of passengers carried by transit systems fell from 23 billion to 15 billion between 1946 and 1953.[14]

Further factors in reducing the load of transit systems include the suburban movement and television. Suburbanites, too far out to go to work or to shop downtown by public transportation, use commuter trains, or more likely, the auto. The lessening density of population

[14] *Wall Street Journal,* July 20, 1953 (Chicago ed.).

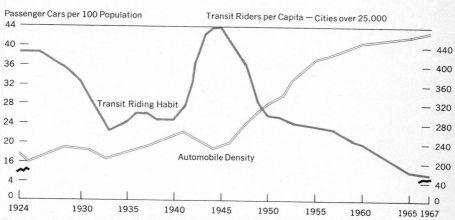

Figure 16-1. Transportation trends, 1924–1967. *Source:* To 1951, adapted from H. S. Simpson, "Mass Transit Can Be Saved," *Public Management,* 35:79, April, 1953. Since 1951, derived from figures in annual editions of *Information Please Almanac,* Dan Golenpaul Associates, New York.

of the core city spells trouble for transit lines. Television has a tendency to reduce entertainment travel, which does further damage. Entertainment travel is important to transit systems which are constantly confronted with the problem of the waste involved when equipment needed for peak-load hours lies idle in the evening.

As long ago as 1940, the number of persons entering the Chicago central business district daily by elevated train, streetcar, or bus amounted to only 47.8 percent of the total number.[15] In 1916, 82.8 percent of persons entering the St. Louis central business district each day came by streetcar. By 1946, only 46.9 percent came by streetcar and bus. Almost an equal number came by private automobile. The decline in public transportation patronage since that time has been great—in most cities it was cut in half, at the least, between 1946 and 1960. National estimates are that 18 million ride mass transportation every day while 50 million drive to work.[16]

The abnormal circumstances of World War II helped stave off the inevitable for a few years for many systems but the shift from the six-day to the five-day work week after 1945 reduced the number of riders considerably. In addition to the decreasing number of riders, postwar inflation brought increasing costs of operation and maintenance. This forced fare increases, which in turn encouraged switching to auto transportation. The transit managers were then forced to reduce service or ask for another fare increase or both. Furthermore, the greater number of autos on the streets made it increasingly difficult to maintain schedules that were fast enough to satisfy the public. All this added to the snowballing effect toward fewer passengers and greater deficits. The problem was not helped by the rise of the bus as a replacement for the streetcar. The bus takes up less room on the street, interferes less with traffic, and costs less to buy and maintain, but it is uncomfortable, vexatiously slow—about one-half as fast as the private auto—and, if diesel fuel is used, a source of unpleasant odors.

Added to the problems were those of obsolescent equipment resulting in uncomfortable and even dangerous conveyances. In New York City, there have been a number of tunnel fires and in 1970 the first fatal accident in 42 years. For the commuting driver, the situation was not much better. Boston, in 1963, had a traffic jam that lasted from 3 P.M. to 9 P.M. one day and on a Los Angeles freeway, 108 cars piled up in one accident. For many commuting drivers, fighting the freeway traffic and then finding a parking space was the day's most tension-filled experience.

---

[15] G. W. Breese, *The Daytime Population of the Central Business District of Chicago*, The University of Chicago Press, Chicago, 1949, pp. 106–109.
[16] Many of the statistics in this section are taken from "The Agony of the Commuter," *Newsweek*, Jan. 18, 1971, pp. 44–49.

Can We Keep Traffic Moving? In an attempt to solve the increasing financial difficulties of transit systems, various desperate measures have been recommended. There are some who urge that subways, monorails, or elevated-train systems be built, but it is unlikely that any but a few cities could, at this time, meet operating expenses out of fares from these, much less pay off any of the original capital investment.

Some laymen have urged that all would be well if cities would sell their systems to private companies, as if that were a panacea. Clearly it is not, for Chicago had to take over its transportation system in 1947 after the private company had gone bankrupt and the system had been administered for years under the eye of a Federal judge. The Boston system lost money first under private and then under public management. In the 1969–1970 fiscal year, city governments had to take over private systems in Baltimore, Minneapolis, St. Paul, Salt Lake City, Santa Cruz, and four other cities, and the Penn Central, which carried 140,000 commuters each day, went bankrupt.

Other laymen, as well as some professional students of public administration, have said that the transit system should be "taken out of politics," an old American antidote. Governor Thomas E. Dewey caused the New York transit system to be separated from the city government in 1953, and it was set up under an authority partly appointed by the Governor. The plan produced numerous cries of interference with local self-government, mostly from the Governor's political opponents.

Federal aid programs are operating in several areas to aid all types of transportation systems and a U.S. Department of Transportation was established in 1967.

In 1969, the first large-scale grant program was passed by Congress. Among its features were purchase of new equipment for existing public transit systems, defraying of some operating costs, and a number of research programs. Some specialists have urged that people stop using their own autos and be persuaded to ride the public transit. This could be done by applying various pressures, such as a special tax on business-district parkers. Few municipal or private managements, however, have made genuine appeals with meaningful promises behind them. As a result, urgings have fallen on deaf ears. For all except those who have no choice in the matter, public transportation is too slow and the fare is too high. Besides, the problem is social as well as economic, and for that reason the solution is not easy. One authority on the subject has explained the shift as follows:[17]

[17] John Bauer, "Municipal Utilities Developments in 1952," *Municipal Year Book,* 1953, International City Management Association, Chicago, 1953, p. 355.

> . . . devolution of transit traffic and earning power has doubtless
> been due in part to gradual shifts in community life. But it has
> been due chiefly to everyone's desire to own an automobile and
> to have the satisfaction of driving to and from work in his own
> or jointly in his neighbor's car. This is not only a matter of
> assumed riding convenience and advantage, but perhaps prin-
> cipally one of inferred prestige.

Public tastes and dominant life styles, reflected in the decisions
of city planners, also contribute to the decline of public transportation. Mass transit is used most in the older cities which have a
relatively high density of population. It is here that disutility of
the automobile is greatest. There might, thus, be something of a
revival in the use of the bus if planners and redevelopers worked
from the principle of concentration rather than deconcentration.
They now have enough techniques in their professional bag of
gimmicks to avoid the creation of slums and to provide for green
spaces despite high-rise buildings. But such planning would defy
the expectations of most Americans, and the fact that it would be
compatible with the preservation of public transportation systems
is not likely to be persuasive to many.

The freeway, the off-street parking lot and garage, and the
prestige factor seem to assure us that transit systems cannot hope
to recapture much of their lost ridership. Should cities abandon
public transportation as a thing of the past? This would work a
great hardship upon enough people to be an unthinkable solution
at this time. Furthermore, there are almost no cities that could
handle either the street traffic or the parking problem if everyone
were to ride by auto.

It seems likely that privately owned companies will have to be
taken over by the cities in the future—perhaps as bankrupts. Municipally owned systems are faced with the need for subsidies in
order to make up the difference between earnings and costs.
Most such systems already enjoy some subsidies. Very often, for
example, they need not pay property taxes. Sometimes the department of public works maintains the space between the tracks
in the few remaining street railway systems, although private
companies normally pay this cost themselves.

But is a subsidy equitable? If the loss is made up from the general-revenue fund, it means that the taxpayer is subsidizing the
bus rider. If municipally owned transit systems are exempted from
the property tax, the same result is obtained. Is this logical? Property-tax payers, for the most part, are not wealthy people.

Is a transit system a convenience to business? If it is, should
some of the deficit be paid by a special tax on business? This plan

is being tried in New York. The New York system receives a total subsidy equal to about 40 percent of its expenses. This comes from business and real estate taxes. In any case, it seems unlikely that many transit systems will be able to break even in the future, given any type of ownership, management, or equipment.

THE ADMINISTRATION OF PUBLIC WORKS

Whenever a city is large enough to be organized on a departmental basis, it will have a department of public works operating under one title or another. The department usually includes many utility and other service functions—for example, divisions in charge of street maintenance, cleaning, and lighting, of bridges, of sewers and sewage disposal, of refuse collection and disposal, and of public property. Traffic engineering is frequently in the department of public works, as are municipally owned utilities, such as electricity, gas supply, public markets, and slaughterhouses, although any of these may be established as independent departments. Public transportation, airports, and water supply are in the great majority of cases, but not always, organized as separate departments.

The Department Head. The general view of professional administrators is that the public works department should be organized with a single department head responsible to the chief executive. The once-common autonomous board has generally been abandoned. This is not true, however, in the case of public transportation and water supply, where the board is still often found, even in strong-mayor and manager cities.

The director of public works (often called the city engineer, especially in smaller cities) is normally an engineer of one kind or another. In small cities, it is expected that the director will possess technical qualities. In large cities, administrative ability is imperative, while engineering ability is less important and may not be a requirement at all.

SELECTED READINGS

"The Agony of the Commuter," *Newsweek*, Jan. 18, 1971, pp. 44–49.

Blake, Nathan M.: *Water for the Cities*, Syracuse University Press, Syracuse, N.Y., 1957.

Danielson, Michael N.: *Federal-Metropolitan Politics and the Commuter Crisis*, Columbia University Press, New York, 1964.

Doig, Jameson W.: *Metropolitan Transportation Politics and the New York Region*, Columbia University Press, New York, 1966. (Advocates a regional policy.)

First National City Bank of New York City: *Public Transportation in the New York Region*, 1970. (An excellent survey of present facilities and policies with detailed facts and figures.)

Horwood, E. M., and R. R. Bayce: *Studies of the Central Business District and Urban Freeway Development*, University of Washington Press, Seattle, Wash., 1959.

Municipal Public Works Administration, 5th ed., International City Management Association, Chicago, 1957.

Ostrom, Vincent: *Water and Politics: A Study of Water Policies and Administration in the Development of Los Angeles*, The Haynes Foundation, Los Angeles, 1953.

Rosenthal, Donald B., and Robert L. Crain: "Executive Leadership and Community Innovation," *Urban Affairs Quarterly*, 1:39–57, March, 1966.

Smerk, George M. (ed.): *Readings in Urban Transportation*, Indiana University Press, Bloomington, 1968.

————: *Urban Transportation, The Federal Role,* Indiana University Press, Bloomington, 1965.

Stefferud, Alfred (ed.): *Water,* U.S. Government Printing Office, 1955. (A U.S. Department of Agriculture yearbook, discussing the problem in its many ramifications.)

CHAPTER
17 LAND
AND
HOUSING
POLICIES

A major responsibility of governments at all levels today, but especially at the community level, is to plan for the use and reuse of both land and housing. In a frontier society, these decisions rested primarily in the hands of private builders and developers and were settled in a rough-and-ready fashion as long as it was expected that low-income, unskilled immigrants and migrants would accept whatever housing was left over, and as long as raw land was readily available.

Planners tend to approach policy making from a different perspective than that of other community decision makers. Instead of making incremental adjustments to the margins of existing policy, they are primarily concerned with the interrelationship of all the parts of the social and physical environment, emphasizing comprehensiveness rather than particularities, and long-run rather than short-run considerations. Thus "The job of the city planner is to propose courses of action, not to execute them. The standards prescribed by elected officials for his guidance are, when they exist at all, usually contradictory or ambivalent. Even the boundaries of his concern resist definition. Although his plans deal directly with only the physical city, their professed object is always to improve the total quality of urban living."[1]

THE SETTING OF GOALS

The Meaning of Planning. Systematic planning in the United States might be said to date from William Penn's 1682 layout of the city of Philadelphia, although most American cities had a chaotic growth until recent decades. In rural areas, planning was even less a community concern until the coming of the automobile and telephone, which made possible the ribbon developments along arterial highways and fringe-area slums just beyond the reach of established land-use controls.

There has always been planning of some kind, of course. In the nineteenth century, informal committees composed of people interested in realty development, or simply in what they considered to be civic improvement, would sometimes present city plans to the council for consideration. Later, committees of the same sort were sometimes appointed by the mayor or council to study and make recommendations on city plans. Like most study groups, once they made a report, their task was finished.

In typical American fashion, land-use decisions were, until recently, made by private businessmen: the realtors, land developers, and bankers in particular. Characteristically, nineteenth-century Americans did not believe that a greater community interest stood above that of the profit motives of these men. Planners were thus concerned with their profit-and-loss statements rather than with making Ackroyd City an attractive community with an imaginative physical design. It would be difficult to exaggerate the effect of their short-range concerns upon the face of urban America. Because bankers decide who gets loans and realtors decide, through their realty boards, who is to be allowed to buy where, their decisions determined, within the limits of cultural values, the face of American cities. They decided the areas in which blacks would live and the quality of housing they would have. They determined when deteriorating areas were to be permitted to switch from single-family dwellings to multifamily apartments and rooming houses. They selected sites for parks (if any), business areas, and factories, and established a basic policy of urban growth through exodus and conversion, so that home construction took place for the higher-income

[1] Alan Altshuler, *The City Planning Process: A Political Analysis,* Cornell University Press, Ithaca, N.Y., 1965, p. 1.

persons only (except in tenements), others taking the vacated property according to their status positions. It was a game of providing according to ability to pay with little concern for the decaying ugliness at the center.

But as American cities began to mature, this pattern changed. Persons in the community began to become concerned with the growing blight around them. Property owners began to fear for the income value of the older sections. The retreating upper middle class began to run into rural and fringe-area slums. Attitudes toward the uninhibited activities of private business began to change.

In 1907, a permanent planning commission as a municipal agency was established at Hartford, Connecticut. It set a pattern that has been followed ever since. Once begun, the movement spread rapidly, and in 1960, over 90 percent of the cities of 10,000 population or larger had official planning commissions. At first, realtors sought to dominate the planning commissions and were often successful in doing so. Gradually, however, a broader representation has been developed, with various community interests, including homeowners, represented, though realtors remain dominant in many communities.

The Planning Commission. The central planning agency is almost always headed by a commission which coordinates the plans of the various municipal departments and carries on planning activities of a community-wide nature. The planning commission usually has five or seven members but may have as many as fifty. It may be entirely ex officio, consisting of designated public officials, or it may be made up of citizens serving without pay, or some combination of these two.

The problems facing planning commissioners are many. They are usually subjected to great pressures from land developers or realtors who may regard them more as peculiar obstacles in their particular business than as guardians of broader community interests. Commissioners may be urged to seek locations for industry in order to strengthen the local tax base, but almost any sites they select will be highly controversial—each citizen wants the industrial zone as far from his home as is physically possible. The commissioners are typically laymen, lacking in any technical knowledge of planning or sometimes even a knowledge as to what planning seeks to do. Yet professional staff is expensive and usually is ill provided for in commission budgets, since this agency lacks a clear-cut constituency to fight for it before the governing board at budget time. It lacks status, too, for although membership on the commission may be sought by high-status citizens, the typical resident is likely to view it as a haven for idle dreamers. The commission often lacks public, political, or administrative support—the last of these because various administrative agencies, like the realtors and bankers, have their own vested interests to which the planning commission is a potential threat. Planners in the agencies dealing with education, streets, housing, recreation, traffic control, industrial development, and others may fear that the commission will not give sufficient attention to the items they consider of top priority. Yet, lay concerns with the effects of possible land uses are becoming intensified, and with this trend, planning commissions are rising in status as well as in power in public policy making.

Planning deals not only with streets, utilities, and the regulation of private property but also with parks, recreation, housing, slum clearance, airports, traffic, parking, public health, and a host of other things. It deals primarily with the problem of converting long-range social goals into public policy. Using prevailing cultural values and professional criteria, it seeks to correct or minimize the effects of past mistakes and to avoid them in future development.

The Professional Staff. Professional planners today enjoy high status, partly as a result of their own efforts to make the public conscious of their relatively new specialty and partly because their skills have become almost indispensable to the suburban leader anxious to mold a community to fit his image of the ideal and to the secretary-manager of the central business district association or chamber of commerce who wants to stop the leaks in his foundering vessel. Training for early planners was concentrated in engineering and landscape architecture (advocates of the "City Beautiful" movement were early supporters of planning). Knowledge from both these professions remains important to the planner today, but increasingly emphasis is upon much broader training, particularly in public administration, economics, and sociology.

In the early days of planning, there was considerable doubt as to whom the commission and its staff should report. Sometimes they reported to the park board or some such secondary body. Usually they reported to the city council, and still do so in many cities, especially those of the weak-mayor type. But the council seldom took the planning commission seriously, often regarding it as a dumping ground for insistent cranks, a place where they could "play with pretty pictures."[2]

When urban planning came to be viewed as a vital municipal function after World War II, the tendency developed to center its activities under the mayor or manager and to make it a staff arm of the administration. This appears to be the dominant pattern today and the planner not only works through the commission, but directly with the chief executive, to whom he has, in many communities, become a major adviser and policy innovator.

[2]Thomas H. Reed, *Municipal Management,* McGraw-Hill Book Company, New York, 1941, p. 305.

Because of this trend, cities that have a resident planning staff have an advantage over cities that hire a planning consultant to visit the community occasionally, or hire the planner from a nearby larger city on an overtime basis, or receive technical assistance from a state agency. (About one-third of the cities over 10,000 population have a full-time planning director.) The resident planner, furthermore, has advantages in seeking to secure public support for the products of his staff. The nonresident consultant has much less opportunity to conduct a sales campaign on behalf of a new part of the overall plan, or a new subdivision, or zoning ordinance.

Planning and Politicians. As Americans have become more concerned about the use of land, so have political leaders. Norton Long has noted:[3]

> Mayor Richard Lee of New Haven has proved to many a prac-tical politician that there is gold in urban renewal and not just Washington gold. Mayor Daley of Chicago finds his planners' pic-tures of Chicago the best sort of election boosters—ones that get published in the press, for free. Housing and urban renewal have made planning attractive politics for some, poison for others. Housing has meant an adventure into sociology, complete with all the headaches of race relations, poverty, and slums. Growing concern with the decay of the central-city core, the location of industry, and the economic viability of the city has forced the planner to become a horseback economist as well as a horseback sociologist. Concern for the problems of highways and transit, sewage, water pollution, the fiscal inequities of government and school districts has forced the planner to become political sci-entist and consider how the fractionated governments of the metropolitan area can be structured to permit planning to take hold.
>
> While the planner may feel most truly at home when he is at his drawing board, he finds his major work as sociologist, econ-omist, and political scientist, or just plain politician. The con-geries of problems which call for planning in their solution run the gamut of the professions. The planner, like the top public administrator, becomes a generalist with a vengeance. As such, his plans are in reality political programs. In the broadest sense they represent political philosophies, ways of implementing dif-fering conceptions of the good life.

The more that the planner deals with things that directly affect the way of life of the citizen and the more funds that are made available to him from national, state, and private sources, the more important his beliefs and proposals become to the practicing politician. The day when councilmen could name upper-middle-class do-gooders to the planning commission and then pay no more attention to that body

[3] Norton E. Long, "Planning and Politics in Urban Development," *Journal of the American Institute of Planners,* 25:167–169, November, 1959.

until vacancies appeared again is a thing of the past in American cities.

The Plan. After a planning commission is established, surveys are made and basic data are gathered. The commission normally relies heavily upon professional help—from the city engineer if there is no planning staff. It is then the job of the commission to interpret the data and to develop plans. Space must be allocated for various types of home building, for commerce, for light and heavy industry, for recreation, and for traffic flow. A master capital-improvements plan may be developed to supplement the land-use recommendations. The plan as it finally emerges will be a compromise between the professional recommendations of the staff and the demands of the various interests which make their views known to the commission and the local governing body.

Planning is a continuous operation, however, since new data and new interpretations of the data must be constantly made by the commission in the light of unanticipated community developments. Master plans suffer from fairly rapid obsolescence. It is true that in 1791 Pierre L'Enfant was asked to draw up a master plan for the new city of Washington and that his foresight was so great that the plan has never needed serious alteration. Brigham Young, too, demonstrated real imagination in laying out Salt Lake City, but even his vision could not anticipate the crowded automobile traffic of today. The magnificent boulevards of his city came about because he wanted to allow room for a Conestoga wagon to make a U turn without backing up.

Most planners must start by accepting the existing situation, a heritage from the past that is not always fully welcome. They must make changes slowly, against inertia and the resistance of vested interests. The planners are rarely men of the vision of a L'Enfant. Even if they were, they would encounter difficulties in long-range planning. A plan in the early nineteenth century founded upon a system of water transportation would have to be seriously altered with the coming of the railroad. Later, the automobile would require even greater changes. And the best plans laid out in 1850 or 1900 could not have made proper arrangements for an airport at a logical and convenient location.

LAND-USE CONTROLS

The master plan drawn up by the commission is not usually enacted into law but serves as a basic guide for the legislative and administrative officials. The governing body may instead formally adopt a map that becomes the official statement of policy. The policies implied in the map or in statements of principle that sometimes accompany it are put into effect through three types of land-use controls: subdivision regulations, zoning, and building-construction codes.

Subdividing. Control over subdividing—the parceling of land into lots—is basic to the implementation of a plan. Subdividing is accomplished by requiring the land developer to present a "plat," that is, a map showing some or all the following: lot sizes and shapes, utilities, topography, soil types, street sizes and patterns, and other relevant data. This plat must be in conformity with established policy and may be subject to review by the planning commission, as well as by health, highway, and other authorities before it is approved. No land can be built upon until a plat is approved, though platting may not be required in commercial, industrial, or rural nonfarm areas. With this control, planners can prevent the development of land without provision for necessary services.

Where subdivision regulations are few or nonexistent, ambitious land developers have subdivided far beyond the foreseeable needs of a community and have talked or pressured the governing body into furnishing utilities to an otherwise vacant subdivision. This, in effect, forces the taxpayers to subsidize speculation in real estate.[4]

Zoning.[5] The control of the height, area, and the use of buildings or lots may be achieved either by zoning or by subdivision deed restrictions. The former is public policy enforceable at law, while the latter are private contractual relationships enforceable in civil action before the courts. Subdivision deed restrictions are often used to protect property values where inadequate or no zoning exists. They are not a substitute for zoning, however, for in order to enforce their provisions, a resident must bring a court action against the violator. This is expensive, time-consuming, perhaps embarrassing, and often thought not worth the bother.

Zoning has now become the standard method of ensuring the efficient use of land and of promulgating many of the provisions of the master plan. The community is normally divided up into residential, commercial, and industrial zones, and perhaps into further subcategories. Zones should not be taken too literally, however, as being belts or areas of the community. A zone may be very small—it may be a narrow strip along a street or railroad track, or it may be a single lot. The location of a single lot or of a few lots of one classification in the midst of a more preferred type—"spot zoning"—may be very profitable to an owner able to sell a lot in an area zoned for single-

---

[4]See Harold W. Lautner, *Subdivision Regulations,* Public Administration Service, Chicago, 1941; Philip H. Cornick, *Premature Subdivision and Its Consequences,* Institute of Public Administration, Columbia University, New York, 1938.
[5]On the legal basis of zoning, see above, pp. 173–175.

family homes to a filling-station or grocery-store operator. But it means a loss in the total value of the community. Because this loss is socialized among many persons who individually have less incentive to exert pressure than does the single profiteer, such practices take place with considerable regularity in some communities, sometimes reducing to an absurdity the concept of zoning.

In addition to restrictions concerning *use* of land, the zoning ordinance will usually restrict the height of buildings in relation to the width of the street, the size of yards, and the use to which the area is put. Residential and commercial zones normally have such restrictions. Further limitations are placed on *area* that is usable for building. In single-family-home areas, the building line may be 20 or 30 feet back of the sidewalk, for example. And apartment buildings are no longer allowed to take up the whole of the lot with little provision for sunlight and air. A building in a residential area is today generally required to come no nearer than a specified distance to the lot line— the distance being determined by the height of the buildings in the neighborhood.

Competent planning and zoning will not in itself guarantee a "city beautiful." This is demonstrated by developments in New York skyscraper construction. Since the war, a large number of moderate-sized skyscrapers—twenty to thirty stories in height—have been built. The financiers of these projects are anxious to make a maximum utilization of Manhattan's expensive land. The architects have therefore been forced to plan them, not with aesthetic considerations paramount, but rather so as to fit the minimum setback requirements of the zoning ordinance. Lewis Mumford has given a fitting title to the resulting "style": wedding-cake modern. (The zoning rules regarding the height of buildings usually require a certain amount of *setback* as the number of stories increases. Thus, a building may use the full ground space for perhaps ten stories, after which there must be 1 foot of setback from the building line for, perhaps, 4 feet of height. This allows air and sunlight to reach the lower floors.)

The Zoning Ordinance. Zoning is intended, of course, to do more than merely protect property values. It is also used to ensure the availability of adequate light, air, and accessibility to all property. It protects the public health and minimizes the number of fire hazards. The zoning ordinance—which is sometimes the only formal and legal promulgation of the efforts of the planning commission— is logically based on the city's overall plans and must, therefore, be adjusted to conform with the almost constant changes in the plans.

The zoning ordinance is sometimes primarily a mosaic of the pressures applied upon the councilmen. Professional planners prefer that it be drawn up by the planning staff and have the endorsement of the planning commission. If this procedure is followed, the ordinance is likely to enjoy some protection from the immediate, short-range demands of effective interests. Unless the zoning ordinance —which usually must be enacted by the council in order to have any legal validity—is coordinated with the work of the planning commission, the latter will lose its principal device for implementing its plans.

Building-construction Codes. A community with a complete set of land-use controls will have one or more building codes. These are usually known as building, plumbing, electrical, heating, and safe-and-sanitary-housing codes. They seek to enforce the subdivision and zoning regulations and the housing standards desired in the community, by requiring permits to build or install equipment. This is coupled with inspections to determine whether or not compliance has taken place or, in the case of safe-and-sanitary-housing ordinances, is being maintained.

The building inspector, or zoning administrator, "can destroy the effectiveness of the [zoning ordinances or building code] by over-looking violations or permitting exceptions to the regulations. The integrity of such officer is, therefore, most essential."[6] Needless to say, he is subjected to great pressures and temptations. The physical appearance, not to say the reputation, of a community may depend upon his competence and incorruptibility. Because of inadequate codes and poor enforcement procedures, FHA regulations have, especially on the outer fringe, often given home buyers more protection than have those of the local government.

PLANNING IN THE URBAN REGION

Planning in the Suburbs. Urban areas have adopted procedures for planning and zoning—long after they were first needed, to be sure. Today, the principal growth in urban areas is on the periphery. And it is here, where planning and zoning are most needed today, that they are most often inadequate or entirely absent.

Suburbs, especially in their earliest years of development, suffer from several things that lead to blight. Premature subdividers are normally little controlled within the core city. In suburbs, and especially in unincorporated areas, they may encounter virtually no restrictions at all. They may be responsible for erratic and inefficient use of land. The outer fringe, which in a few years is to become an

[6] D. H. Webster, *Urban Planning and Municipal Public Policy,* Harper & Row, Publishers, Incorporated, New York, 1958, p. 424.

inner fringe, is characteristically the area where individuals try to build their own homes or purchase jerry-built shacks. With no building code or a very weak one, it may be possible for the person who cannot afford to build or buy a home in the city to construct one in the fringe area. He may be able to afford one that has too little floor space or is of too flimsy construction to meet the core-city building regulations.

In a few years, the outer fringe becomes truly suburban, with a great amount of subdividing and building. But the new homes are now interspersed with dilapidated shacks and nonconforming buildings, according to the belatedly adopted zoning ordinances. In quite a number of metropolitan areas, there is a greater percentage of substandard and dilapidated homes in the suburbs than in the core city.

There are some exceptional situations around the nation, and certainly the new homeowners of suburbia quickly grasp the importance of planning and effective land-use controls in relation to their investment. But the major problem remains—chaotic land usage until the area becomes quite heavily populated and then a belated attempt to prevent the building of any more individual shacks. But by this time, the opportunity for maximum efficiency of land use is probably gone forever.

Efforts at Metropolitan Planning. Because our metropolitan areas are atomized politically while planning must, by its nature, extend continuously across the land, a hiatus exists between the need for planning as seen by professionals and its political practicality. In order to fill this gap, there has been somewhat of a trend toward the development of metropolitan planning commissions or joint city-county commissions. Often these groups are private and unofficial, sometimes they are extralegal, sometimes they are provided for by state enabling acts, but almost always they are advisory only and have no coercive powers. Some of them have their own staffs, but quite a few share the staff of the core-city planning commission. Some have no staffs at all, but are merely operated through occasional meetings.

Planning for utilities, parks and recreation, highways, the location of industry, and many other urban matters might logically be approached on an area or regional, rather than a city, basis. But it has been generally impossible to find a politically expedient method of representing the many communities of the area in a planning organization with any real powers over land use. Although metropolitan-area studies often recommend that planning should be a function of any area-wide government that might be set up, this function is undoubtedly one over which local landowners themselves most want to keep close control.

Though this is the case, at least one planner has noted that "if piecemeal planning is to be the rule, it is evident that the pieces are getting bigger and that a larger variety of factors are being taken into account than ever before."[7] Americans prefer to do their planning on an individual or small-area basis, but they are increasingly viewing the community and the metropolitan area as a medium for some of society's systematic decision making.

The upsurge of metropolitan planning since 1963 can also be directly attributed to Federal grant programs that have emphasized and rewarded such steps. The Demonstration Cities and Metropolitan Development ("Model Cities") Act of 1966 stipulates that all applications for Federal grants and loans for projects such as airports, highways, hospitals, libraries, open-space land projects, sewerage facilities and waste treatment plants, transportation facilities, water development and land conservation projects, water supply and distribution facilities within a metropolitan area must be submitted for review to an area-wide metropolitan planning agency. It is also required that the application be accompanied by the comments of the reviewing agency "concerning the extent to which the project is consistent with comprehensive planning developed or in the process of development for the metropolitan area . . . and the extent to which such project contributes to the fulfillment of such planning." An additional supplementary grant up to 20 percent of project costs depends on the local government showing they will carry out their project "in accord with metropolitan planning."[8]

URBAN HOUSING

Issues that urban citizens must cope with in the future include these, among others: Should slum clearance be integrated with the development of public low-rent housing? Should slum clearance be effected by public or by private effort? If private effort is used, should the municipality grant a subsidy, or purchase land by condemnation for private companies, or otherwise grant assistance? Should low-rent housing be built only on the site of cleared slums, or should some or all of it be built upon vacant land? What policy should be followed in choosing vacant sites, if they are used? If cleared sites are used, where should the displaced families live while new projects are being constructed? Is it desirable or undesirable to clear slums and then build upon the site housing that the persons displaced cannot afford to rent?

[7] Richard L. Meier, "Systems and Principles of Metropolitan Planning," Centennial Review, 3:79–94, Winter, 1959.
[8] Joseph F. Zimmerman, "The Planning Riddle," National Civic Review, 57:189–194, April, 1968.

THE DIRECT APPROACH THROUGH GOVERNMENT

American urban housing conditions have improved along with the rise in the American standard of living in the years since the end of World War II.[9] Owner occupancy was at an all-time high in 1970, and most homes had the basic services and amenities— electricity, radios, television sets, indoor plumbing, refrigerators, automatic washing machines—even among persons of quite modest income. Most of the figures revealed by the census exceed by far comparable statistics in other nations.

Yet many Americans remain ill housed by prevailing standards, and much blight and many dysfunctional buildings characterize our cities.

Some Background. City governments have long had building codes providing for minimum standards for building and for human occupancy. The code (or series of codes, for they are not necessarily unified or administered by a single agency) makes provisions for standards of lighting and ventilation, sanitation, and fire prevention and protection. Historically, these codes have often been subject to pressure demands of manufacturers, builders, real estate people, tenement owners, and building-trades unions. As a result, they have often established minimum standards well below those that the contemporary society would accept as a rock-bottom minimum. Codes sometimes are allowed to become seriously outdated, so that their already meager standards in one era become grotesquely inadequate a few decades later as society's concept of a minimum standard of living changes. Trade unions have frequently used the code as a device to establish make-work rules or to prevent the use of cheaper and faster techniques of home building. Manufacturers have sometimes been able to get codes to require the use of their patented materials, thus creating a monopoly situation. Out-of-date codes have sometimes prevented the introduction of new devices, such as prefabricated homes or dry-wall construction, simply because they are not provided for in a code drawn up decades before these things appeared on the market.

Many cities bring their codes up to date, yet scores of others permit jerry-built housing, or do not allow modern building techniques, or permit the construction of low-rent housing (most likely by the *conversion* of old homes into tenements) that does not meet present standards for human living. On the other hand, in some cases, building codes require materials of a quality far beyond what is reasonably necessary (for example, the use of metal con-

---

[9] See the *1970 Census of Housing* for data.

duits for basement wiring), thus raising the cost of housing. Some communities do not permit the construction of low-rent housing, thus depriving lower-income persons of adequate housing.[10]

The ecological pattern in American cities has been one of allowing the central parts of the city to decay and become low-rent housing while higher-priced housing moves outward along the periphery. Traditional American housing policy has been to let low-income people live in whatever is left over. In the days before the automobile, some exceptions to this were made, since factories were located near the downtown area and workers were dependent upon public transportation or their own legs. In cities such as New York and Chicago, therefore, tenement buildings (multistoried apartments with minimal conveniences) were constructed specifically to provide housing for these people and to provide lucrative investments for absentee owners. In cities that have done most of their growing since World War I, however, few such buildings exist, and the poor live in converted and subdivided homes and apartments abandoned by the fleeing middle class.

A conservative writer has said, "In some respects, a 'slum' is like a used car lot. A 'slum area' offers a supply of second-hand housing of the kind which satisfies a need until such time as a person can afford and wants a better home." He argues further that "if people really want houses, let new ones be built or bought by those most able and anxious to build or buy."[11]

Public Housing. This approach to housing lasted until the Great Depression. At that time, the New Deal sought to encourage a revival of the home-building industry, which had ground to a complete stop, and at the same time to clear away some of the nation's worst slums. (Note that this was a characteristically New Deal effort in that it attempted to do two things simultaneously: to help business recover from the Depression and to effect social reforms.) In 1933, Federal offers of conditional loans for private housing projects were unsuccessful because, with only a few exceptions, private companies did not meet the established standards. Some states also attempted to encourage low-rent private housing, but almost all these efforts were essentially unsuccessful. It was, and still is, more profitable, or at least a safer investment, to build homes for higher-income families.

Public housing had long been constructed abroad, but prior to 1933 it was generally regarded as unconstitutional in this country.

[10] Banfield and Grodzins, *op. cit.*
[11] The laissez-faire argument against subsidized housing is presented in a pamphlet by Paul L. Poirot, *Public Housing,* Foundation for Economic Education, New York, 1954, from which this quotation is taken.

The need for low-cost housing was especially great during the Depression, however, and the national government next turned its attention to public housing. Some fifty projects in thirty-six cities were federally constructed and administered by the Public Works Administration (PWA). It was not, however, until the United States Housing Authority (now the Federal Public Housing Authority of the Housing and Home Finance Agency) was created under the Federal Housing Act of 1937 that public housing could become a new national policy.

The act was bitterly opposed, however, as have been all subsequent acts and propositions calling for public housing. Opposition has come partly from realtors, bankers, and others who profit from the private housing industry. Others have said that public housing is wrong in theory: that housing, within the concepts of our prevailing economic system, belongs properly in the realm of private and not public endeavor. A third type of opposition has come from those persons who fear that public housing projects would in one way or another damage existing property values. Finally opposition has come against the architectural high-rise form which critics argue results in impersonal semi-tenements that encourage alienation and crime.[12]

The Federal Housing Act of 1937. The act of 1937 provided for quasi-public corporations known as "housing authorities" to be established wherever state laws permitted. The authorities were made up of appointed officials serving without pay, in most cities. The authorities drew up the plans for Federal approval, received the loan, and constructed and operated the projects. The city had to agree to eliminate unsafe and unsanitary dwelling units equal in number to the new units to be constructed. State and local governments had to contract to furnish municipal services either free or for a small payment in lieu of taxes by the national government. This generally meant that public housing would be subsidized, not only in the process of building, but afterward, too, and by both the national and local governments.

The status of the housing authority as a separate corporation had the effect of relieving the municipality of responsibility for its debts and could be used to avoid state constitutional debt limits. The local housing units, once constructed, remained to a large degree under Federal control, since questions of rent levels and eligibility to reside in the project were decided by its agency. Per-

---

[12] See especially Editors of *Fortune, The Exploding Metropolis,* Anchor Books, Doubleday & Co., Inc., Garden City, New York, 1958.

sons whose incomes came to exceed the established maximum were required to leave the projects.

Federal Housing Policy. Since 1945, running warfare has been conducted between interest groups representing, or acting on behalf of, low-income urbanites on the one hand and the interest groups of real estate on the other. The battle has been fought in Washington, in the state capitals, and in the city halls.

It was not even possible to get a new housing act through Congress until 1949, despite the powerful support given public housing by three leaders of the liberal Democrats, the Southern Democrats, and the Republicans, in the Wagner-Ellender-Taft Bill. The Federal Housing Act of 1949 reaffirmed the principle that providing for housing was basically a private business matter, and it did not change the fundamentals of the 1937 act. It made adjustments, however, in order to recognize inflation and the changing concepts of a minimum standard of human living.

In 1965, the amendments to the act eliminated the requirement of 20 percent local contribution as a requirement, permitted local authorities to lease units from private owners, and in the turnkey program permitted a local authority to purchase units from private builders after construction or rehabilitation has been completed.

Public housing has never functioned as the planners intended, largely because it acquired a reputation for housing only the most marginal, sub-working-class persons, largely welfare recipients. Thus, the Pruitt-Igoe project in St. Louis was completed in 1956 at a cost of $36 million. It was designed to house some 12,000 persons. But working-class persons moved out as soon as possible. By 1971, only 3,000 remained. Only 16 of the 43 buildings were still in use. The others had been totally vandalized. A study committee has recommended demolition of the whole project.

About 1 percent of all Americans live in public housing units. Opposition to public housing has always been strong. On the state level, attempts were made to require a local referendum before a public housing project could be begun. Five legislatures defeated such proposals in 1952, while Virginia passed one. On the local level, proposals are also placed before the voters from time to time to require referendums before launching into public housing.

The 1949 Detroit and 1953 Los Angeles municipal election campaigns turned largely on the question of public housing policy. Los Angeles, Toledo, Indianapolis, Helena, and other municipalities attempted in 1952 to cancel their cooperation agreements on public housing with the Federal government. They were generally blocked in the courts until Congress, by a 1953 law, prohibited new public housing units, even if under contract or construction, if the governing body of a municipality or a public referendum rejects the proposal. If some Federal money has already been spent in such cases, the municipality must make a "settlement" with the Public Housing Administration. Since 1956, public housing has been relatively noncontroversial, with little support in Congress for much expansion in the modest program.

Municipally administered public housing projects appear to be a permanent fixture as a local function of government. They will probably not expand beyond the small responsibility for total housing they now have, however, for the organized opposition to them is strong. Housing of a kind that would be efficient for rental to low-income people does not fit the American dream. As a result of this, even those who would benefit often oppose it. The problem of gaining neighborhood acceptance of such projects continues to be a serious one.

THE INDIRECT APPROACH THROUGH GOVERNMENT AID

Private Redevelopment with Public Assistance. A few efforts were made by state and local governments during the 1930s to encourage private endeavor to clear slums and build new homes. Tax exemptions were most commonly offered, but they were inadequate as inducements. The State of New York worked out a plan for redevelopment corporations in 1941, but World War II interfered with putting it into effect. A few cities, notably Pittsburgh, completed outstanding renewal programs with local financing. Most communities were not able to do this.

The Federal Housing Act of 1949, among other things, offered aid to communities for slum clearance and urban redevelopment. Grants could be made to local units to acquire, clear, and prepare blighted areas for the construction of new dwellings. The cleared land could then either be used for public housing projects or be resold to private builders for redevelopment.

Some slums were cleared away as a result of the 1949 act, but only ten projects were completed in the ten years that followed its adoption, and only fifty-one by 1964. New slums developed at a faster rate than existing ones were cleared. The Housing Acts of 1954 and others since therefore have emphasized urban renewal. This orientation has been reenforced by the concern felt by local businessmen and realtors over the downward trend in land values in the older parts of cities.

Under the urban-renewal provisions, communities, private business, and the Federal government were to cooperate to prevent the spread of urban blight to new areas, to rehabilitate and conserve areas that could still be restored at reasonable cost, and to clear and redevelop areas that could not be saved. The community was required to prepare an urban-renewal plan, to adopt adequate land-use controls, and to have a comprehensive physical plan for the whole community.

Federal aids are available to assist in the "main phases of project clearance, redevelopment or rehabilitation, rehousing of displaced families, and in community planning and other special operations."[13] Grants and loans cannot be used for the construction or rehabilitation of structures, but the FHA mortgage-insurance program was expanded to include such activities.

The 1954 and subsequent laws sought to overcome some of the earlier problems—of relocating displaced persons, of inducing private business to take part in renewal, of poor planning. But the amount of urban renewal that actually took place after passage of the acts was relatively modest for several reasons: (1) Persons in areas to be renewed objected to relocation, fearing that adequate housing would not be available to them or would be too costly; (2) slum owners feared loss of income and of valuable property if renewal plans went forward; (3) some conservatives, even though they owned deteriorating urban property, regarded government-assisted renewal as an aspect of radicalism and thus undesirable; (4) some property owners feared a rise in taxes or used the renewal referendum as a means of protesting against property-tax rates. In 1966, in the Model Cities Act (the Demonstration Cities and Metropolitan Development Act), the Federal government encouraged concentrated effort in select neighborhoods over a five-year period. Private and public efforts were to be coordinated with the efforts of local residents to bring about planned "showcase neighborhoods" utilizing resources from Federal, state, local, and private agencies. By 1960, the total grants reached 150. A Federal task force recommended continuing the program but not expanding it beyond these cities, arguing that the solution of ghetto area problems depended in part in allowing greater access by ghetto residents to other areas, including particularly those in the urban fringe area.

Urban Renewal: An Evaluation. Although urban renewal often becomes a matter of bitter political controversy, pitting not only liberals against conservatives, but radicals against reactionaries,

[13] U.S. Housing and Home Finance Agency, *Urban Renewal: What It Is,* 1956.

and persons living within the area to be renewed against reformers, it has also taken place under conditions in which the activity has been largely obscured from public view. The Newark Housing Authority, for example, was dominated by professionals, who were the innovators and executors. Popular participation was highly limited and the visibility of the projects to the general public was usually low. This obscurity may have been necessary to the success of the program and was so viewed by some of the professionals.[14]

Although Congress in its 1965 amendments to the Housing Act made a famous provision for "maximum feasible participation" by the residents of slum areas and had even earlier called for consultative and informative meetings to be held in the areas directly affected, such proposed participation in many cases produced only apathy and in others served as a catalyst to bring together left and right extremists in wild conflict. One political scientist, observing the process, has commented: "Far from being indispensable, citizen participation, in many cases, may prove detrimental to the program's progress. Slum clearance in Newark, and probably in most other cities, generates more hostile than favorable responses at the grass roots level. It is easier to organize site residents than to organize those who will ultimately benefit from new middle-income housing."[15]

Urban renewal, like all other aspects of city planning, is hindered both by traditional political styles and past ideologies concerning property and land use and by our lack of information concerning the social effects of the programs of the past generation. Thus:[16]

> The urban renewal program lacks the powers necessary to fulfill its radical aims. It also lacks the precedence that could create legitimacy for those aims. It is hemmed in by laws which support the individual's choice of residence and land use which leave building to the marketplace in real estate, which leave action to the local public agency. But its most important limits are, simply, the limits of our knowledge. We have never before faced a wealthy, rapidly changing urban complex, with a determination to mold it into a form suitable to our desires. We do not know enough about the forces producing the metropolis and we know less of the stratagems that would allow us to control its growth.
>
> The present program operates with little real knowledge of the housing market. What *are* the effects of demolition of given kinds of housing, in certain areas, within given metropolitan housing markets? What are the effects of rehabilitation, of new

[14] Harold Kaplan, *Urban Renewal Politics*, Columbia University Press, New York, 1963.
[15] *Ibid.*, p. 164.
[16] Scott Greer, *Urban Renewal and American Cities*, The Bobbs-Merrill Company, Inc., Indianapolis, 1965, pp. 185–186.

building? And, in redevelopment at the urban core, what are the basic demands for new space and structure? How elastic is the demand, in terms of where that structure is located? What are the alternative supplies? And from this the related questions: What is the total cost and what the total benefit, of such re-development in this center of this metropolis? Most [local public authorities] do not even know the costs and benefits in dollars, much less in the other social values adduced so freely. What are the costs and benefits of centrally sited univer-sities and cultural centers, shopping centers and government centers? How are the costs and benefits distributed—by the governmental jurisdiction, by income class and ethnic class?

Municipal Action against Blighting. It is likely that many deterio-rated neighborhoods could be rehabilitated and others that are declining could be saved without rebuilding. This could be done by requiring landlords (largely absentees) to repair their properties and raise conditions to a minimum standard. An ordinance provid-ing that the city would do the job if the owner failed to do so after adequate notice, with the cost being assessed against the property, would be greatly effective in retarding deterioration.

Political pressure by owners to prevent the adoption or enforce-ment of such ordinances has been strong. The same is true of occupation density, and "safe-and-sanitary-condition" ordinances. They exist commonly enough but are difficult to enforce. For one thing, the slum owner can frequently defy the inspector: "Go ahead, board up the place! See what happens!" What happens, of course, is that the slum dwellers are more concerned about being put out on the street, or forced into more expensive housing, or having to leave a comfortable, well-known neighborhood than they are about unsafe, unsanitary, and illegal conditions which exist. The owner knows this is the case. It is often his most powerful weapon. Owner and renter pressures are both applied against enforcement. Even so, in an increasing number of cities, the various ordinances dealing with the safety, sanitation, and physical appearance of buildings are being effectively enforced, at least to a greater degree than was once the case.

Closing Note. Despite a considerable amount of housing construc-tion in the years following 1946, America seems not to be keeping pace with the increase in population. The problems posed by this became still more complicated as the rate of new family formations increased in the 1960s—the marriage rate increased a generation after the sharp increase in the birthrate beginning in the war year 1942. Because the birthrate remained high until the late 1960s, new family formations increased. The result will be a continuing increase in demand for housing at least for the next decade.

Housing and urban-renewal programs demonstrate the interdependence of governments under a system of cooperative federalism. Municipalities acting alone cannot possibly provide an adequate housing policy for the nation. The resources and sanctions of state and national governments will also need to be invoked, and they will all have to be coordinated effectively if we are not to give in to unparalleled pressures for a decline in housing standards. As Banfield and Grodzins have noted: "Great urban problems are also great national problems; and the full pooling of resources . . . is necessary for their solution."[17]

---

[17] Banfield and Grodzins, *op. cit.*, p. 154.

SELECTED
READINGS

Abrams, Charles: "The Uses of Land in Cities," *Scientific American,* 213:150–160, September, 1965. (Argues that taxing policy is the most effective method of land-use regulation.)

Adrian, Charles R.: "Metropology and the Planner," *Planning 1962,* American Society of Planning Officials, Chicago, 1962. (Discusses the psychological role of the regional planner as the conscience of the community and distinguishes this task from the self-image planners have of themselves as creators of a well-ordered community.)

Altshuler, Alan A.: *The City Planning Process: A Political Analysis,* Cornell University Press, Ithaca, N.Y., 1965.

—— : *A Land-use Plan for St. Paul,* The Bobbs-Merrill Company, Inc., Indianapolis, ICP no. 90, 1965. (Study of values, interests, and processes of preparing a plan.)

—— : *Locating the Intercity Freeway,* The Bobbs-Merrill Company, Inc., Indianapolis, ICP no. 88, 1965. (The conflicting values and interests of highway engineers, city planners, and businessmen.)

Anderson, Martin: *The Federal Bulldozer: A Critical Analysis of Urban Renewal,* The M.I.T. Press, Cambridge, Mass., 1964. (A harsh, exaggerated criticism. Worthwhile as an application of the ideology of industrial individualism to a contemporary urban program.)

Babcock, Richard: *The Zoning Game: Municipal Practices and Policies,* The University of Wisconsin Press, Madison, Wis., 1966. (Zoning laws and practices in the United States and other countries.)

Blackman, Allan: "Environment and Behavior," *American Behavioral Scientist,* 10:entire issue, September, 1966. (A number of articles on the city and urban planning.)

Branch, Melville C.: *Comprehensive Urban Planning,* Sage Publications, Inc., Beverly Hills, Calif., 1970. (An annotated bibliography.)

Chapin, F. Stuart, Jr.: *Urban Land Use Planning,* 2d ed., Harper & Row, Publishers, Incorporated, New York, 1965.

"The Crisis in Water," *Saturday Review,* Oct. 23, 1965. (Entire section devoted to water sources and pollution problems.)

Davies, J. Clarence, III: *Neighborhood Groups and Urban Renewal,* Columbia University Press, New York, 1966. (The neighborhoods to be renewed and those surrounding them are often centers of opposition to renewal plans.)

Ducey, John McMullen: *Who Killed the Urban Renewal Bond Issue?* Center for Research in Urban Government, Loyola University, Chicago, 1966. (A study of urban-renewal opposition in Chicago.)

Editors of *Fortune: The Exploding Metropolis,* Anchor Books, Doubleday & Company, Inc., Garden City, N.Y., 1958. (Essays on large urban problems.)

Fisher, R. M.: *Twenty Years of Public Housing,* Harper & Row, Publishers, Incorporated, New York, 1959.

Green, Arnold W.: *Recreation, Leisure, and Politics,* McGraw-Hill Book Company, New York, 1964. (By a sociologist.)

Greer, Scott: *Urban Renewal and American Cities,* The Bobbs-Merrill Company, Inc., Indianapolis, 1965. (A review and evaluation in sociopolitical terms.)

Jacobs, Jane: *The Death and Life of Great American Cities,* Random House, Inc., New York, 1961. (A vigorous criticism of the housing and life-style preferences of the middle class and of urban planners.)

Kaplan, Harold: *Urban Renewal Politics,* Columbia University Press, New York, 1963. (Urban-renewal policy making in Newark is dominated by the professionals.)

Kaplan, Marshall, and others: *The Model Cities Program: A History and Analysis of the Planning Process in Three Cities, Atlanta, Georgia; Seattle, Washington; and Dayton, Ohio;* U.S. Department of Housing and Urban Development, Washington, 1969.

Keeley, John B.: *Moses on the Green,* The Bobbs-Merrill Company, Inc., Indianapolis, ICP no. 45, 1959. (Study of proposal to convert part of Central Park into a parking lot for a privately owned restaurant.)

Makielski, Stanislaw J., Jr.: *The Politics of Zoning,* Columbia University Press, New York, 1966. (A study of New York City.)

Mumford, Lewis: *The City in History,* Harcourt, Brace & World, Inc., New York, 1961. (Reviews the place of the city in human society through 5,000 years. Highly opinionated.)

Nelson, R. L., and F. T. Aschman: *Real Estate and City Planning,* Urban Land Institute, Washington, 1957. (The professional realtors' point of view.)

Rabinowitz, Francine: *City Politics and Planning,* Atherton Press, New York, 1969. (Discussion of planners' role in cities with differing types of power diffusion.)

Ranney, David C.: *Planning and Politics in the Metropolis,* Charles Merrill Publishing Co., Columbus, Ohio, 1969.

Reps, John W.: *The Making of Urban America: A History of City Planning in the United States,* Princeton University Press, Princeton, N.J., 1964.

Rossi, Peter H., and Robert A. Dentler: *The Politics of Urban Renewal,* The Free Press of Glencoe, New York, 1961.

Schroth, Thomas N., and others: *Congress and the Nation, 1945–1964,* Congressional Quarterly Service, Washington, 1965, chaps. 4, 6, and 7.

Seeley, John R.: "The Slum: Its Nature, Use, and Users," *Journal of the American Institute of Planners,* 25:7–14, February, 1959.

Stein, Clarence S.: *Toward New Towns for America,* rev. ed., Reinhold Publishing Corporation, New York, 1957.

Sternlieb, George: *The Tenement Landlord,* Graduate School of Business Administration, Rutgers University, New Brunswick, N.J., 1966. (Study based on 566 interviews with tenement owners; includes examination of effects of tax policies on ownership.)

Taper, Bernard: "A Lover of Cities," *The New Yorker,* Feb. 4 and 11, 1967. (A profile of Charles Abrams, a noted planner and specialist on urban housing.)

Thomas, Norman C.: *Rule 9: Politics, Administration and Civil Rights,* Random House, Inc., New York, 1966. (A case history of a suburban realty code designed to discriminate against minority ethnic and racial groups.)

Thursz, Daniel: *Where Are They Now?* Health and Welfare Council of the Capital Area, Washington, 1966. (A study of the impact of relocation upon residents of a section of Washington, including where they moved to and the effects of such moves.)

Toll, Seymour I.: *Zoned American,* Grossman Publishers, New York, 1969. (History and role of zoning in the growth of cities.)

U.S. Advisory Commission on Intergovernmental Relations: *Building Codes: A Program for Intergovernmental Reform,* A-28, U.S. Government Printing Office, 1966.

————— : *Intergovernmental Responsibilities for Water Supply and Sewage Disposal in Metropolitan Areas* (1962).

Watson, Richard A.: *The Politics of Urban Change,* Community Studies, Inc., Kansas City, Mo., 1963. (A study of the effect upon local politics of locating middle-income, high-rise apartments in a low-income neighborhood of Kansas City.)

Wheaton, W. L. C., and others: *Urban Housing,* The Free Press of Glencoe, New York, 1966. (Thorough study of housing. Contributors include social scientists.)

Wilson, James Q.: "Planning and Politics: Citizen Participation in Urban Renewal," *Journal of the American Institute of Planners,* 29:210–236, November, 1963.

Woodbury, Coleman: *The Future of Cities and Urban Redevelopment,* The University of Chicago Press, Chicago, 1953. (A major study conducted at the time the subject was first becoming a matter of general public concern.)

C THE
POLITICS
OF SOCIAL
SERVICES

CHAPTER
18 PUBLIC
EDUCATION

In 1961, a sample of citizens in thirty-four metropolitan areas was asked: "How would you vote in a community-bond-issue election to build a new public hospital, a new sewage-disposal plant, a new school building?" The favorable vote for the new school was 80 percent, for the new hospital 70 percent, and for a new sewage plant 68 percent. The citizens were then asked: "If you thought the community could afford only one, which would you rank first in importance?" The division of responses was 57 percent for the new school, 33 percent for the new hospital, and 10 percent for the new sewage-disposal plant. Citizens were then asked to rank five local services in terms of effectiveness: police, fire, health, and welfare services, along with education. Schools were ranked first. A sample of community leaders representing groups like the League of Women Voters and the chamber of commerce agreed with citizens in ranking education first and in favoring a new school over a new hospital or sewage plant. The author of the study concluded: "The findings . . . corroborate a fundamental tenet of the public school credo, for education *is* accepted as *the basic function* of local government by the people, by well educated and reasonably skilled observers as well as by the common citizen."[1]

Robert C. Wood, looking at suburbia where education is perhaps

---

[1] Roscoe Martin, *Government and the Suburban School,* Syracuse University Press, Syracuse, N.Y., 1962, pp. 80–81.

even more enshrined than in the central city, has written: "No real debate can take place about the comparative needs of schools and other functions for no one can seriously argue that the building of a new fire station should be made possible by cutting into the school budget."[2]

Such is the exalted status of education at the local level of government in a nation where nine out of ten students attend *public* schools. Yet despite this significance, and perhaps because of it, little has been written by political scientists about the political aspects of this most important of governmental services. As Thomas Eliot noted, except for national defense, the running of the public schools is the most extensive and expensive governmental activity in this nation. Yet, he pointed out, political scientists have ignored education's political aspects and professional educators have denied that they exist. "The taboo has worked both ways, almost as if by tacit agreement: If politics has been anathema to educators, the governing of the public schools has seemed inconsequential to political scientists."[3] Eliot's review article perhaps signaled a renewed interest in the subject by political scientists. Like all other choices made by governments, the content and style of educational services is a political choice and a most important one for our society.

THE INDEPENDENCE OF EDUCATION

The special status of education has been buttressed by what amounts almost to a credo of public education in the United States. That credo holds that public education must be treated as nonpolitical and controlled locally. It should be organized separately from all other services at the local level (though this separateness is not preserved at the state level, where it is a part of state government, or at the national level, where it is part of a cabinet department with health and welfare). In addition, its relations with the public should be "nonpartisan." Let us first observe the organization of educational services at the local level, their relation to the state, and the significance of such independence for the rest of local government. Then we will examine the ways that school officials participate in democratic decision making. The latter is designated by political scientists as an aspect of public school politics but in the educational literature is referred to more euphemistically as "community relations."

School Organization. Each state has a state department of education headed by a chief state school officer. The heads of state depart-

2 Robert C. Wood, *Suburbia: Its People and Their Politics,* Houghton Mifflin Company, Boston, 1958, p. 191.
3 Thomas H. Eliot, "Toward an Understanding of Public School Politics," *American Political Science Review,* 53:1032–1051, December, 1959.

ments of education have been elective, particularly in the South, Midwest, and West. Under pressure from professional educators, however, there is a growing trend to appointment either by the governor or by members of the state boards of education. Increasingly, such agencies are becoming dominated by the values of the professional educators who man them.

Most states operate their schools through numerous local school districts. In the past, these often had the same geographic boundaries as cities, villages, or townships, but such is not necessarily the case today. States, through financial aid and legislative pressure (requiring each school district to have a high school, for example), have encouraged consolidation of districts. The number of local districts has dropped from 127,422 in 1932 to 34,678 in 1962, and 26,983 by 1967: a reduction of 80 percent. Thus the central city in a metropolitan area is likely to have a school district that includes the whole of that city. But it may also, particularly in smaller metropolitan areas, include parts of the suburban fringe area. In suburban areas, the school-district boundaries frequently do not follow city boundaries but may include in one district large parts of the unincorporated area and even several suburban cities. The pattern depends on local inclination, state law, and historical accident. Quite commonly, the independent local school district does not have the same boundaries as do the cities or other local governments where they exist.

Because most states operate their schools through small districts, many of which have limited resources, intermediate school units also often exist. These units, operating between the state and local district levels, include counties, parts of counties, and various other groupings of districts.

At both the state and intermediate levels, the principal responsibility has been not the operation of schools or control of school policy but the furnishing of consultative, advisory, and statistical services. There has been, however, a trend toward the exercise of regulatory and inspection functions by these levels of administration.[4] The state department has also often been given a veto power over proposed school consolidations and, in some states, has control over the approval of textbooks, school bonding, or plans for school buildings and equipment purchases.

Legally, school districts are merely "creatures of the state" to be structured as state authorities desire. Politically, however, these local districts have significant power. Because of the strong tradition of local control of education in the United States, occasionally

[4] See U.S. Office of Education, *Statistics of State School Systems*, 1956.

conflicts between local school districts and the state board of education can be quite sharp. Frank J. Munger describes an incident that
occurred when a state agency denied financial aid for school construction in two districts that refused to consolidate:[5]

> An explosion followed in which residents of the districts
> charged officials of the State Education Department with "decep-
> tion," "distortion," "dictatorship," and "contempt for the people."
> The charges were taken up by the two state legislators from the
> area . . . [who] appealed to the Governor to investigate the mat-
> ter, enclosed 49 pages of letters protesting the action, and noted:
> "Frankly, it is our opinion that if all the residents of the Jordan-
> Elbridge School District voted on the question, Have you con-
> fidence in the State Education Department? the majority would
> answer no." Governor Rockefeller's answer was courteous but
> noncommittal. He promised to urge the Education Department
> to review the manner in which it handled the merger, but indi-
> cated he had no jurisdiction over the matter. He noted that the
> department was following its master plan. . . . Whether intended
> or not, the Governor's reply contained the implication that the
> State Education Department would have more to say on the sub-
> ject. It also indicated his support of the department's centrali-
> zation policy.

The operation of schools remains, however, in nearly all states,
the major responsibility of local school-district officials. These districts are nearly always a special district of government, independent
of the general unit of local government in the area. Even in New
England, where the usual pattern is for the schools to be operated
by a school committee under town government, the practice has
developed for these committees to act autonomously. Their budgets
are often, in fact, not subject to review by the town government.

Local School-district Autonomy. A critic of school-district independence notes that the problems that result from such independence,
although a constant source of low-level irritation, have "not yet
affected a group sufficiently large or influential to warrant an attempt
to redress."[6] Roscoe C. Martin sees such independence as splintering
the ability of local government to secure the citizen's attention,
financial help, and other means of support. Instead of having a
single decision-making center that allocates resources on the basis
of their overall program planning, one has competing centers of
local government. Such criticisms are the same generally offered in
respect to other special districts. To them may be added the tendency of such special districts to come under greater control of their

[5] Roscoe C. Martin and Frank J. Munger (eds.), *Decisions in Syracuse,* Indiana University Press,
Bloomington, Ind., 1961, p. 169.
[6] Martin, *op. cit.,* pp. 66–89.

administrators with less responsiveness to citizens.[7] Perhaps, however, the most important drawback, for its practical effect, is the financial independence the present arrangements permit school districts. Given their greater measure of public support, school districts can more readily raise money through bond issues and from state and Federal aid sources. In some cases, such funds will be raised at the expense of other services of local government, since they will be unable to make the direct emotional appeals for citizen support that Save-Our-Schools (S.O.S.) programs do.

The arguments for local autonomy of course relate to the desire to keep education free of partisan politics. At present, education is perhaps at the pinnacle of isolation from other units of local government, though the picture has changed somewhat in respect to state agencies. With increased state and Federal aid and regulations, there may be a tendency to strengthen the school districts' ties to other local units of government, particularly those at the county level.

Local School-district Organization. The organization within the local school district is generally decided upon by the citizens of that district from among the choices permitted by state law. In general, the internal organization is very similar to that of the council-manager system of government. In place of a council, a school board usually of five to seven members serves, holding three- or four-year terms. Board members in 85 percent of the nation's school districts are elected, almost always on a nonpartisan ballot. They then appoint a school superintendent who serves at their pleasure, that is, one who may be dismissed if he loses the confidence of the board majority. The superintendent is generally a professionally oriented administrator without previous local ties, who plans to follow a career in school administration and may, in the course of time, move on to other positions in another city or state. He almost always has an advanced academic degree.

Variations from this scheme occur most usually in the nation's largest cities. Here school board members are more frequently appointed; in fact, in the nation's four largest school systems, this is the case. In addition, terms are often longer. The system is often similar to the Missouri plan of judicial appointment: A "citizens' committee" proposes a list of nominees from which the mayor appoints a board member. The choice is confirmed at an election. The reasons for variations from the usual practice are probably two. First, campaigns in large districts are a wearisome and costly business, particularly in nonpartisan elections. Daniel L. Schlafly, former

[7]This argument is also presented by Martin, *op. cit.,* who cites as his source for this tendency Edward W. Weidner, *Intergovernmental Relations as Seen by Public Officials,* The University of Minnesota Press, Minneapolis, 1960.

reform member and president of the St. Louis board, comments: "I could name fifty outstanding men and women who have turned me down simply because they don't want to get involved in the campaigning. We've taken some second-rate people because of this."[8] Secondly, in the larger cities such campaigns often get involved in partisan politics, perhaps because the party is a major means of gaining votes in a large constituency for a race in which relatively few voters may be interested.

According to the professionals' ideal model, the local school board is responsible for policy making while professional administrators and teachers carry out its decisions. Thus, the professional aspect of the educational system is presumably insulated from political questions. In fact, just as we have found to be the case in respect to managers in the council-manager system, the role of the school superintendent in the ideal model is not always a description of reality. The line between a professional matter to be handled by educational experts and one involving policy is difficult to draw. Only within communities having a homogeneous value system is there likely to be an absence of political tensions in the carrying out of education functions. Where disagreements exist within the community over the proper educational policies to be followed, the school superintendent is almost inevitably drawn into the political battle to champion his professional views. Indeed:[9]

> The public school superintendency, especially in the seething big cities, is hardly a position immune to pressure by special interest groups. [Some superintendents must spend] long hours in session with spokesmen of violently conflicting views on education and integration. Nobody challenges the superintendent's solemn duty to have sound educational practices uppermost in his mind and, in the course of such sessions, to be determined not to agree to anything that would jeopardize such practices. But it is absurd to suggest that these sessions are not political bargaining to evolve the most workable consensus, satisfying the greatest number without doing violence to anyone's educational rights.

The School Board: A Profile. In 1927, George S. Counts interviewed a national sample of 6,390 school board members and found that 76 percent were business and professional men and 3 percent were of the working class. Thus, over three-quarters of school board members were recruited from groups that made up about 15 percent of the national population.[10] Twenty-five years later, W. W. Charters,

[8] Peter Binzen, "How to Pick a School Board," *Saturday Review*, Apr. 17, 1965.
[9] Fred M. Hechinger, "Who Runs Our Big City Schools?" *Saturday Review*, Apr. 17, 1965, pp. 70ff.
[10] George S. Counts, *The Social Composition of Boards of Education*, University of Chicago Supplementary Educational Monographs, no. 53, 1927, p. 58.

Jr., reviewed sixty-one other studies, including two replications of Counts's national survey, and concluded that none departed in any significant way from the above findings.[11] As one would anticipate, the income, age, place of residence, and education of school board members was above average. Contrary to what one might expect, however, the number of women members was considerably less than their 50-percent-plus portion of the total population or their presumed special interest in education would justify. A more recent national study of school boards found 51 percent without any women members and another 30 percent with only one woman.[12]

In a number of large cities where a variation of the appointment-election system is followed, a practice has developed of balancing the board among prominent religious and racial groupings. Thus in San Francisco, by informal agreement, the mayor appoints three Protestants, two Catholics, and two Jews. Two of these must be women and one a member of a labor union. Since 1961, it appears that one must also be a Negro. When a school board member retires, newsmen can quickly draw up a profile of the religious and racial characteristics that the new nominee will possess. Only once in forty-two years have the voters rejected a nominee.[13] A similar practice has been followed in New York where each of the major religious groupings is awarded three members.

The Making of Educational Policy: School Boards and Superintendents. The degree to which school boards reflect the social, economic, and religious characteristics of their constituency no doubt has some relation to their general acceptance by the constituency. Minority groups having self-awareness usually desire such representation. Thus, civil rights groups in both New York and Chicago have from time to time argued for an election system to replace the appointment systems followed there. It is also probable that some of the antagonism found in low-income right-wing movements is inspired by an alienation from what they consider "the establishment," as represented by the typical school board member.[14] In such cases, a more broadly representative board, achieved either by appointment or by some form of local-area election, would perhaps lead to greater acceptance of board policy by minority groups.

A broader question is one of whether in fact the overrepresentation of businessmen affects the content of the educational program. One study, by Roy W. Caughran, of Illinois school board members,

[11] W. W. Charters, Jr., "Social Class Analysis and the Control of Public Education," *Harvard Educational Review,* Fall, 1953, p. 270.
[12] Alpheus L. White, *Local School Boards: Organization and Practices,* U.S. Office of Education, Washington, 1962.
[13] Binzen, *op. cit.,* p. 72.
[14] For a description of several such incidents and an analytical discussion of their causes, see James S. Coleman, *Community Conflict,* The Free Press of Glencoe, New York, 1957.

found they were not opposed to experimentation in the curriculum, thought the three R's taught as well now as they ever had been, and were divided over the need for loyalty oaths for teachers. His major conclusion was that there was no significant correlation between social backgrounds and attitudes on important educational issues.[15] However, Claude E. Arnett found the high-status members of boards considerably more liberal than those with lower-middle-class backgrounds.[16] A contrary view is given by an education professor and administrator, Floyd Reeves, who argues: "There are certain very important things in our social, economic and political life that we hardly touch upon in our public schools—such things as the organization of labor unions and consumer cooperatives."[17] From research in other areas, it seems likely that the better-educated upper-income board member is more liberal than his lower-income counterpart on civil liberties and civil rights issues but more conservative in economic matters.[18]

Thus the background of school board members will probably have some effect on the two major decisions they are asked to make. The first is the choice of a school superintendent, including the choice of whether the present incumbent be replaced. This selection affects the tone of the whole system and, more practically, affects all other appointments, since the superintendent will expect to have influence over the choice of subordinates. An upper-income board can probably be expected to support professionalism and follow the advice of the professional educator on the content of the school curriculum. This support could be anticipated to a greater degree than might be the case among lower-income and less-educated groups when the schools are attacked by critics of the extreme right or left because of curriculum content.

The second major area of decision making controlled by school boards respects finances, particularly matters of whether to construct new buildings, ask for increased millage from the voters, or issue bonds. On such questions an upper-income board may be more conservative than the typical school administrator would desire.

Even in these two major areas, however, one should not underestimate the influence of school superintendents on basic policy making. Most frequently, it is the superintendent who is the source

[15] Roy W. Caughran, "The School Board Member Today," *American School Board Journal,* November, 1956, pp. 39–40; December, 1956, pp. 25–26.
[16] Claude E. Arnett, *Social Beliefs and Attitudes of School Board Members,* Emporia Gazette Press, Emporia, Kans., 1932.
[17] Broadcast of University of Chicago Roundtable, "What Should We Teach Our Youth Now?" quoted in William H. Form and Delbert C. Miller, *Industry, Labor and Community,* Harper & Row, Publishers, Incorporated, New York, 1960, pp. 250–251.
[18] See especially Samuel A. Stouffer, *Communism, Conformity, and Civil Liberties,* Doubleday & Company, Inc., Garden City, N.Y., 1955; and Seymour Martin Lipset, *Political Man,* Doubleday & Company, Inc., Garden City, N.Y., 1959.

of policy innovation, whether in curriculum or in financial matters. Like the minister of a church, he is expected to lead rather than be only a servant following the expressed wishes of the board. In the most important matters, boards of course reserve the right to veto and, in rare instances, may even dismiss a superintendent who has lost their confidence. But in day-to-day decision making, the situation is likely to be similar to that existing between councils and mayors. The superintendent as executive is expected to propose a program which he then must justify to his board.[19]

The Making of Educational Policy: Citizens. Evidence from a number of sources suggests that the interest of the average citizen in schools only comes to the fore on financial matters or on those questions that sporadically pique his interest because of their dramatic or scandalous nature. Attendance at school board meetings rarely includes more than the members themselves. Voter turnout at school board elections is generally low, usually even lower than in municipal elections. The opinions of local community leaders would ". . . put the school tax rate in first place, school building and expansion programs second, bond issues to support such programs third and the school budget fourth. Teachers' salaries ranked fifth. . . . The respondents indicated no particular interest in curriculum, textbooks, subversive activities, personalities, athletics, race relations, and independence of the schools."[20] Half of those replying did not know how long their school superintendent had served, well over one-half could not name the president of their school board, and two-thirds did not vote in the last school election. However, 71 percent had voted in the last bond-issue election, although 26 percent did not know how the election had turned out. Seventy-seven percent said they had never attended a school board meeting and less than three percent said they attended often. Well over half did not belong to the Parent-Teachers Association or to other similar groups. Another study made for the U.S. Office of Education by the Stanford University Institute for Communication Research found that roughly one-half the voters "show no evidence of any participation in school affairs and no interest in such participation." The study reported that only about a third took an active part in school affairs and their knowledge about the school program was "only slight."[21]

Similarly in Detroit, in at least one recent election, the city had difficulty recruiting a full slate of candidates, while a group in St.

---

[19] For a description of this process, but one critical of its desirability, see Arthur J. Vidich and Joseph Bensman, *Small Town in Mass Society,* Princeton University Press, Princeton, N.J., 1958, chap. 7.

[20] Martin, *op. cit.,* pp. 53–55.

[21] Richard F. Carter, *Voters and Their Schools,* School of Education, Institute for Communication Research, Stanford University, Palo Alto, Calif., 1960, pp. 7 and 16.

Louis was so sure of general lack of information by voters that they kept a forty-five-hour vigil so that their candidates would be first in line for filing. High position on the ballot, they calculated, was worth 4.5 percent of the vote since many voters only voted for the top names.[22]

Thus it appears that for most voters the information gathering and participation costs are too great to justify a great deal of involvement in educational matters. Those with children regularly show greater concern, but even in their case, involvement is low. Only when a sizable amount of funds are to be spent or when an issue is presented dramatically do voters become much interested in the operation of their school system.

A number of scholars noting that a professional administrative elite largely controls school policy, have argued for a decentralization of school districts, especially in large cities as a method of reducing citizen participation costs. Marilyn Gittell states:[23]

> In large city educational systems . . . professionalism combined with the cumulative development of a highly bureaucratic structure have reinforced the depersonalization process. The result is an insulated system in which decision-makers and decision-making are closed off from a wide group of potential participants. Generally a central headquarters staff maintains a tight hold on power, rationalizing its role in the shibboleths of professional competence . . . the political system is obligated to construct favorable arrangements for [citizen] involvement.

The Making of Educational Policy: Interest Groups. Interest groups involved in other local activities are only partially involved in the shaping of educational policy. What attracts them, however, is the large share of the local tax dollar that is spent on schools. Thus, at one time or another, almost every local organized group is somehow affected by educational policy. In addition, a number of groups are specifically organized around the educational function.

A second major area of interest by local citizen groups has been school integration. Following the initial attempts to integrate local schools where resident patterns permitted such a policy, came the realization that only with busing could even token integration be achieved in many schools. The issue became so heated that even Presidents and Presidential candidates took a stand in respect to it and some Congressmen considered tying Federal aid to a requirement that a busing policy be followed.

In the larger cities, the specifically educational interest groups

[22] Binzen, op. cit.
[23] Marilyn Gittell, "Saving City Schools," National Civic Review, 57:21–26, January, 1968. See also Gittell's other works listed in the end-of-chapter bibliography.

may often be divided along liberal and conservative lines and sometimes along religious lines. They may be organized as *ad hoc* groups to aid in a bond-issue campaign, or they may be permanent groups such as the Parent-Teacher Association. Because the latter is a group whose membership is made up of parents, teachers, and school administrators, it serves as a communications medium through which professional educators' views are disseminated throughout the community and criticisms of educational policies are countered. Teachers, administrators, and even school board members also have their permanent organizations, including the local branch of the National Education Association, the American Federation of Teachers (AFL–CIO), and specialized groups such as the teachers of social studies, mathematics, or English. The latter groups are more active on the state level than in the locality, though their state activities may have important impact for the locality. Increasingly, however, teachers' groups have threatened, and sometimes carried out, local strikes for higher wages. Other groups at the local level may be branches of national groups dedicated to a broad program of agitation. Important among these in recent years have been numerous self-styled anti-Communist groups that attempt to ferret out what they consider radicalism in the curriculum. The American Legion and, less frequently, the Veterans of Foreign Wars have sometimes assumed this role, as have local branches of right-wing groups, such as the John Birch Society or Let Freedom Ring.[24]

Opponents of expanding school budgets are forced to disguise their opposition by phrasing their arguments in terms of socially accepted values. In general, those who have sought to serve as "depressants" have included business groups with a low-tax ideology, those who want to emphasize local control at the expense of state financial aid, politicians who are cautious in adopting new approaches in the face of conflicting public attitudes, and frequently naïve educators themselves. The Roman Catholic Church is powerful in New England because it has numerous and often highly dedicated members. Yet,[25]

There is no evidence whatsoever to suggest that the Roman Catholic Church has been a depressant upon state aid to the public education. Neither is there any evidence to suggest that the Church hierarchy has taken leadership in the struggle for additional state aid, although there is substantial evidence that individual Catholic laymen have provided strong, if intermittent, leadership for the achievement of breakthroughs at the state

[24] For descriptions of activities of this sort inspired by the radical right see Coleman, *op. cit.*, and David Hulburd, *This Happened in Pasadena,* The Macmillan Company, New York, 1951.
[25] Stephen K. Bailey, Richard T. Frost, Paul E. Marsh, and Robert C. Wood, *Schoolmen and Politics,* Syracuse University Press, Syracuse, N.Y., 1962, chap. 3. Quotation from p. 46.

level in granting additional financial assistance to local school districts.

The last part of this statement may be principally a result of the fact that a very large percentage of New England politicians are Roman Catholics. In a number of states, aid to financially distressed parochial schools has become a major issue. In Michigan, a constitutional amendment prohibiting parochial aid in any form was adopted in 1970 despite opposition by both candidates for governor and a well financed publicity campaign.

One study found that persons who give least support to bond issues in suburban areas are those living in the least densely populated areas, those over fifty years of age, with twelve years or less of education, working in a blue-collar job, and with no children in the public schools.[26] A study of a rural township in the process of becoming urbanized showed retired farmers as being most opposed to increasing school costs.[27] With the onset of a recession, opposition to such spending rises sharply.

In a study of those groups which superintendents considered as "blocks to good education" in their cities, the most frequently named were the regularly organized groups or officeholders in the community such as city officials, businessmen, and taxpayer organizations. Older residents and individuals with grudges were not important and they stood in contrast to members of the Parent-Teacher Association, local officials, and businessmen. Housewives and members of "service" clubs were ranked next.[28] The overlapping of supporters and blockers suggests that more than community position tends to account for the classification scheme. Rather it appears that, given a politics as placid as that involving the public schools most of the time, persons holding any position in the community power structure are particularly well situated to hurt or aid the schools materially because of general public indifference. A similar kind of conclusion was reached in a study of education's relation to the community power structure in two small communities.[29]

Another important power group, particularly at the high school level, is the students themselves, or rather that part encouraged by parents or administrators themselves to make demands for greater freedom. In ghetto and integrated schools, black students have demanded greater official attention to their problems.

Because state legislation has an important effect on local school-

[26]Gary W. King, Walter E. Freeman, and Christopher Sower, *Conflict over Schools,* Institute for Community Development, Michigan State University, East Lansing, Mich., 1963.
[27]Charles Press and Clarence J. Hein, *Farmers and Urban Expansion: A Study of Michigan Township,* U.S. Department of Agriculture, 1962.
[28]Neal Gross, *Who Runs Our Schools?* John Wiley & Sons, Inc., New York, 1958, pp. 20–43.
[29]Ralph B. Kimbrough, *Political Power and Educational Decision-making,* Rand McNally & Company, Chicago, 1964.

district policy making, the groups at that level also require attention. Educational groups at the state level are interested in such things as state aid to school districts, curriculum and teacher certification requirements, minimum salaries for teachers, school-district reorganization laws, and the rules concerning school bus transportation (e.g., the conditions under which parochial students may be transported, if at all, or the distance a student must ride in order for the local district to get state financial aid for his transportation cost).

The administrators, faculties, and alumni of state-controlled colleges and universities are also important lobbies before state legislatures. It is necessary for state schools to compete for funds against the other possible uses for which they might be appropriated and to convince legislators to provide educational services at the level the schools' administrators regard as desirable.

Educational interest groups in recent years have campaigned for more state school aid and for guaranteed payments under aid formulas to replace dependence upon the yield of a particular tax. They have, however, also sought to secure dedicated funds from high-yielding taxes. They oppose taxpayers' groups which want constitutional limitations upon spending or tax levies and which question the existence of a "school crisis."

In states where the legislature has voted funds for school operations only, leaving the financing of new plant and equipment to the local district, pressure has been exerted, with increasing success, for aid for school construction. The difficulty that the less-prosperous districts have in marketing their small bond issues and the high costs of marketing them have led to demands for some kind of plan whereby the state can buy local bonds or market them, using the superior borrowing power of the state government to reduce costs.

SCHOOL POLITICS AND ISSUES

A number of issues are common to almost every type of school. We shall discuss these next. Others, important for the overall health of society, are particularly prevalent only in certain districts. These, too, we shall discuss here.

Before beginning, we need to make some distinctions among school districts since the issues vary on this basis. We shall follow the classification scheme devised by James B. Conant, former president of Harvard University, in his series of studies of American schools.[30] He identified, first, the comprehensive school, which is

[30] James B. Conant, *The American High School Today,* McGraw-Hill Book Company, New York, 1959; *The Child, the Parent, and the State,* Harvard University Press, Cambridge, Mass., 1959; *Education in the Junior High School Years,* Educational Testing Service, Princeton, N.J., 1960; *Slums and Suburbs: A Commentary on Schools in the Metropolitan Area,* McGraw-Hill Book Company, New York, 1961.

a self-contained unit in a small- or medium-sized city. Enough students are supplied by the rural hinterland or from the city itself to permit a well-rounded program. Other types he distinguished were schools in the large metropolis, including especially those in urban slums, and those in the suburbs. Some writers have made subdivisions of these classes, noting that suburbs vary from blue-collar to high-income, high-status areas. For our purposes, however, Conant's categories will suffice.

School Finance. Almost every issue in its final stages resolves itself into a question of financial support. Huge amounts of money are spent annually on education at the elementary and secondary levels. In the nation at large, in the early 1960s, approximately $18 billion, or something like 2.5 percent of the gross national product, was being spent annually from public moneys for school buildings, equipment, and operations. Additional billions were spent for books, ballet slippers, gym shoes, PTA suppers, clarinets, and other purchases by parents on behalf of the education of their children. It is hardly surprising that a great deal of politics in any community centers around the schools—these institutions spend great amounts of money, and in many small towns, the consolidated school is the largest single purchaser of the goods and services provided by local merchants.

In the early days of public education, the cost was paid for in part by donations and endowments by the wealthy, but mostly through general-property-tax levies. In recent years, school boards have been approving, albeit with compunction, budgets of enormous size. School costs are a heavy burden to citizens, especially in newer "bedroom" suburbs. But in our child-centered society, these large budgets are approved by most people, though certainly there are loud, and sometimes effective, dissenters. Even in larger cities, the school remains today a community focus, as it has always been. As such, it serves to symbolize the relative status of communities, just as the size and grandeur of the local church or cathedral did in medieval Europe. In the search for higher prestige, citizens approve expenditures for elaborate swimming pools, fancy band uniforms, and well-equipped football stadiums and basketball gymnasiums. The cost is high, but the psychological satisfaction felt by the people of Vertigo Heights when they know that they have a high school swimming pool, while the people of Sequoia Grove do not, is important to them. And, of course, so is the belief that one's children are being given as much in the way of a total education as can be afforded.

The high cost of the present pattern of education has strained the property tax, and other funds have been sought, especially since the end of World War II. The principal source of these has come through the expansion of state aid for school operation. The importance of the use of conditional state aid for putting pressure upon local areas to consolidate is reflected in the fact that state aid is highest in states that have reduced their number of districts most in the years since 1950 and is lowest in those with the least change.

All states, however, provide some direct grants for school operations. An important issue before state legislatures has concerned the details of the school-aid formula, particularly the degree to which state aid should depend upon local ability to pay as against the use of a simple head count. The poorer districts lobby for the former, the wealthier for the latter.

The increasing expense of providing educational facilities at the level expected by contemporary society brought pressure for diversification of the base of support for schools through the use of Federal grants-in-aid. The Federal aid question was debated even more hotly than was the aid question on the state level but, by the mid 1960s, was achieved. The fact that Federal aids to education are not new and have been made for many decades is often overlooked. The future would seem to hold still more state and Federal financing of school programs; there is no other place to turn, unless budgets and programs are cut back, and the public seems unwilling to do that.

The Problem of Large City Finances. In the largest cities, problems of maintaining standards of education have been especially difficult in recent years because of the eroding of the core-city tax base and the exodus of the education-emphasizing middle class to the suburbs. Large cities, for a variety of reasons, including the need to pay higher teacher salaries and demands for greater specialization, have high per-pupil costs. During the 1955–1956 school year, cities of over 100,000 population spent an average of $322 per pupil on education; middle-sized cities spent only $275.[31] More importantly, of the monies spent on new construction, only one out of ten dollars was spent in the central city.

Adding to the expenses of central cities are the problems created by friction between whites and Negroes and the social disorganization typical of slums inhabited by either race. The question of building new facilities in deteriorating neighborhoods is one fiercely debated. Periodically, a newspaper displays pictures of dead rats in school buildings, or obvious fire hazards.

The Suburban School and Finances. Persons who move to the suburbs often are aware only of the promises made by the real estate salesman. Once they have purchased a home and entered their children in school, the complications resulting from the rapid growth of population in a given area come to their attention.

[31] U.S. Office of Education, *Current Expenditures per Pupil in Public School Systems*, 1957.

A school district about 50 miles north of New York City, for example, had 875 students in its public school system in 1951. By 1965, this number had increased to 5,664, an almost sevenfold increase. As a result of the enrollment pressure, it was necessary to begin asking for approval of bond issues for the construction of new buildings. The first two proposals for funds to provide adequate space for school children were defeated, and for four years, grammar school children had to attend split sessions—that is, they could attend only one-half day. Eventually, a bond issue was approved for school construction, but by that time, competent estimates indicated that within another decade the total public school enrollment would nearly double.[32]

As an area on the fringe of a city comes under the eye of land-development companies and gives up its bucolic existence, it is characteristically overrun by children, for those who move into new developments are predominantly young couples. The newcomers find the established governmental structure in the hands of farmers and small-town merchants who have a low-tax attitude. The newcomers demand expanded urban services—beginning with the schools. Generally the first battles between the newcomers and the old-timers center around the questions of issuing bonds to expand the school system and replacing the farm-oriented curriculum with one designed to prepare suburban children for college—for a degree is a cherished goal established by suburban parents for their children. These battles are often furious, but newcomers practically always win through force of numbers and a common purpose.

Because suburbs usually are established with almost no school plant in existence and because the ratio of children to total population in them is high, the financial burden of providing schools of a type the migrants from the core city expect is often very heavy. School-tax rates in Levittown, New York, increased by nearly 500 percent in the ten years following 1945.[33] To have taxes double in less than a decade is common. Because this is so, the puzzled and perhaps angered suburbanite who had thought fringe living was inexpensive is likely to join in the call for state and Federal aid for his schools.

In some cases, the suburban school-district boundaries create gross inequities in the tax base. Such disparities are not always accidental. Robert C. Wood's study of the 1,400 governments in the New York metropolitan area discovered two school districts in the same

[32] Elaine Zimbel, "When a Community Votes 'No,'" Saturday Review, Jan. 16, 1965, pp. 54–55.
[33] Benjamin Fine, "Educational Problems in the Suburbs," in William M. Dobriner (ed.), The Suburban Community, G. P. Putnam's Sons, New York, 1958. See also William M. Dobriner, Class in Suburbia, Prentice-Hall, Inc., Englewood Cliffs, N.J., 1963.

county, one with a tax valuation of $5.5 million, and the other with $33,000, per student.[34]

Such inequities are an additional reason for the growing importance of state and Federal aids. The inability of metropolitan areas to allocate resources roughly according to need has heightened the pressures favoring such outside aid.

An additional measure of the problems of finance in education is the high teacher-dropout rate. Teachers who give up teaching as a career have always been a threat to the standards of American public education. To have two or three teachers in a single year was not uncommon in the rural one-room school. The problem has remained serious throughout the history of public education. Of those who were graduated with teaching certificates in 1956, 30 percent did not enter the teaching profession at all. One-half of those who did were expected to drop out within five years, though some would return again later—especially women, after they had raised a family. Since more than two-thirds of all teachers are women, most of whom do not intend to have a full-time career, the turnover problem appears to be chronic. The result is a highly inefficient utilization of manpower.

An additional problem that will become more apparent as the 1970s progress is related to the declining growth in population. As zero-population growth comes closer to reality, and the falling off of grammar school enrollments in some localities suggests this trend, some school districts will find they have overextended themselves to meet the demands of the one-time baby boom and have now to find ways to pay for facilities too large for present demand.

The Curriculum: An Ideological Battleground. Robert C. Wood, the student of suburbia, defends schoolmen for talking mostly about bricks-and-mortar issues to citizens rather than attempting to promote discussions on curriculum development. He notes that to bring up the question of what should the school teach is to risk opening a Pandora's box—to invite into the community an ideological politics with no holds barred.[35] Such value questions cannot easily be resolved by argument. Rather, as James B. Conant suggests, what schools teach will always to some degree be influenced by the status and ambitions of the families they serve.[36]

One may note this influence in the history of American education. Initially the schools were oriented to the needs of a rural environment. The family was the chief socializer of children, and the schools only provided a smattering of reading, writing, and arithmetic. But

[34] Robert C. Wood, *1400 Governments*, Harvard University Press, Cambridge, Mass., 1961, p. 55.
[35] Wood, *Suburbia*, pp. 192–194.
[36] Conant, *Slums and Suburbs*, pp. 81–82.

the shift to an urban economy separated home and work and reduced the economic value of children. In the process, schools took over from families a major part of the child-educating process. The movement of families to suburbia further increased the importance of the schools, so much so that the authors of *Crestwood Heights* observe that the suburb they studied could aptly be described as having grown up around a school, with its main industry being child socialization.[37]

One writer discerns three distinct ideologies of education resulting from population movement. Each, he argues, reflected the needs of a particular life style in American culture. He identifies these as ideologies of citizenship, though one may broaden their content to include the whole of the curriculum. The first, which he calls the rational-activist ideology, fitted the needs of Protestant, small-town America, and emphasized the values of the small-business entrepreneur and of an autonomous professional class. It stressed rights, duties, and obligations, and the strengthening of "moral character." Its major educational content was the three R's. A second ideology, which he calls the integrative-consensual, grew out of the experiences of the immigrant in large cities. It stressed the reconstruction of society, coupled with a reduction of parochial loyalties to ethnic group, class, or locality. A newer model, which he calls the segmental-organizational, stresses the acquisition of highly technical skills for specialized tasks and the dominance of expertise. It is training for a society with a large-scale bureaucracy.[38]

But not only life experiences of consumers have determined the content of the curriculum. James Conant notes that our school system is often college-oriented to reflect the values of a dominant middle class. This is true even where many students do not plan a college career. For lower-income areas in large cities, he recommends greater emphasis on technical and vocational training.[39] Not all educators or parents greet his suggestion with enthusiasm.

Despite these trends, probably among the most important of the shapers of the educational curriculum is the influence of educators themselves. The colleges of education, influenced by the philosophy of John Dewey and other pragmatists and by the interests of ordinary citizens, have emphasized the desirability of meeting mass needs. On the other hand, persons dedicated to the European tradition of an intellectual elite—they are concentrated in liberal arts colleges— have bemoaned the leveling effects of an ideology designed to make

---

[37] John Seeley, R. A. Sims, and E. W. Loosley, *Crestwood Heights: The Culture of Suburban Life,* Basic Books, Inc., Publishers, New York, 1956, p. 234.
[38] Edgar Litt, "Education and Political Enlightenment in America," *The Annals of the American Academy of Political and Social Science,* 361:32–39, September, 1965.
[39] Conant, *Slums and Suburbs.*

schools fit the average student rather than the excellent student. They especially object to the seeming unwillingness of public schools to give special encouragement to gifted children—the future Ph.D.s, M.D.s, and intellectual leaders. This type of concern became even more sharply verbalized after the Soviet Union launched the first successful earth satellite ahead of the United States in 1957.

Robert M. Hutchins, former president of the University of Chicago, has been among the most telling critics of educators for the lack of intellectual content in the schools and their subservience to community desires for athletic prowess or driver-training instruction. He wrote, "All we can say of American education is that it's a colossal housing project designed to keep young people out of worse places until they can go to work."[40] It is not uncommon to find other comments to the effect that "if the tendency [to be found in contemporary public education] continues, it seems destined to create nothing less than a New Illiteracy."[41]

Also critical of current trends are those who would return the schools to a renewed emphasis on practical subjects and the three R's, and who regard most of modern social science as an adjunct of an international socialist movement. Extreme rightists occasionally express this viewpoint and nostalgically argue for a return to the alleged "character-building" qualities exemplified in the McGuffey readers of two generations ago.

Another sporadic influence on curriculum is that of the various interest groups who wish to see their views treated favorably. In the past, the electric-power industry was particularly active. Today, civil rights groups encourage the writing of textbooks that give blacks a relatively favorable role in American history. Within the community are business and industrial groups who want practical courses (reading, typing, and stenography) taught and who sponsor visits to plants to show students the value of a private-enterprise system.

Except for occasional criticism and pressures, however, in most communities curriculum content is left to professional educators. Only rarely does the citizen show any concern. The choice of what is to be taught results from the interaction of the educator, the community environment, and sometimes extremist critics. One can cite persuasive evidence that, in the process, the educator has not been totally oblivious to the needs of his pupils or to the need for greater intellectual content. In the area of the sciences, education has been much criticized. Yet the criticisms concerning an alleged failure to emphasize these subjects tend to make unfair comparisons of mathe-

[40] Quoted in "Expert on Controversy," The New York Times, Jan. 20, 1967.
[41] Ernest Stabler, "The Intellectual and America Today," AAUP Bulletin, 43:331, June, 1957. See also William H. Whyte, Jr., "The New Illiteracy," Saturday Review, Nov. 21, 1953, pp. 33–35.

matics and science enrollments between pupils attending high school in an earlier time with those of today. A valid comparison would require percentages to be based upon all youths of high school age living in the United States at the times to be compared. Since only 8 percent of all those of high school age were in school in 1900, as against 64 percent in 1950, even a deemphasis of science leaves a greater percentage of those of high school age taking these courses. In foreign languages, twice as many children, in percentage terms, were enrolled in 1950 as in 1900, and five times as many in mathematics and science courses.[42] This does not mean, of course, that we are producing enough scientists. It was estimated in 1958 that the United States had fewer scientists, and was producing fewer scientists, than the Soviet Union. Estimates also indicated that the need for scientists in the future would grow disproportionately to the population or the training rate.

A challenge to administrator control over curriculum comes from teacher's unions. One study of five major cities, concludes that such unions desire more than high salaries for their members. They also wish to share in policy making, including curriculum and instruction, along with personnel policies and school organization.[43]

The American public has received a general impression that so-called progressive education has taken over the schools, although in fact about 60 percent of the courses are still in the academic category and are required. Traditional methods, the progressive educator argues, still dominate our schools and continue to emphasize discipline, obedience, and learning by rote. Persons committed to the tradition of the intellectual elite feel, however, that schools today waste a great amount of time on trivia (courses in manual training, "life adjustment," the family, recreation) and too little on basic courses of language, mathematics, and the sciences. They tend to favor isolating the best students for academic high school work and sending the others to frankly vocational types of schools. Such a plan would approach the standard policies of European countries.[44]

It is difficult to evaluate the criticisms that public education is subjected to. It would seem that our culture calls for a variety of educational programs, serving the interests of both the custodial and

[42] See H. C. Hand, "Black Horses Eat More than White Horses," *AAUP Bulletin*, 43:266–279, June, 1957. This is a criticism of statistics used in "We Are Less Educated than 50 Years Ago," *U.S. News & World Report*, Nov. 30, 1956. Further discussion appears in the *AAUP Bulletin*, 44:476–494, June, 1958.

[43] Alan Rosenthal, "Pedagogues and Power: A Descriptive Survey," *Urban Affairs Quarterly*, 2:64–82, September, 1966.

[44] See the publications, for example, of the Council for Basic Education; or "What Went Wrong with U.S. Schools?" *U.S. News & World Report*, Jan. 24, 1958. In light of contemporary controversies, it may be interesting to read the comments of an aristocrat concerning the inadequacies of a classical education in an industrialized society. See Henry Adams, *The Education of Henry Adams*, Houghton Mifflin Company, Boston, 1907.

educational functions of the schools. There must be both vocational and academic training for teen-agers. Little room exists for the notion of an intellectual elite in America; but, on the other hand, the vast majority of college professors believe that their students are inadequately prepared for collegiate work by most high schools; and many of the ablest students complete high school with little or no challenge to their intellectual capacities.

To compare American public education with that of other lands would also be difficult. One observer has made the following comments:[45]

> The ordinary American of today, the ubiquitous high school product, knows far more about names . . . and what is what in general than the ordinary Englishman of the 19th century, or even the ordinary Englishman of today, who seldom gets past a basic elementary school education. He knows more particularly about psychology, but he does not necessarily think more. He is more sophisticated, but he is less sure of himself.

As a cultural institution meeting a mass social need, public education seems to have done, in general, the job expected of it; as an educational institution seeking to train the best of our young minds, it remains highly controversial.

Nonsegregation as a National Policy. In the period between the Civil War and World War II, the dominant view in the United States was that all persons, regardless of race, should be entitled to public education. But it was also generally believed that educational facilities need not be integrated and made available to all. The "separate but equal" doctrine regarding educational opportunities probably fitted the prevailing social attitudes when it was first announced by the Supreme Court in 1896.[46] Indeed, segregated schools existed throughout much of the nation and as far north as the top tier of states in the 1880s. Southern Indiana and Illinois did not desegregate until after World War II.

Yet, there were many who doubted whether the maintenance of social inferiority through the separation of facilities was in keeping with American values. The Supreme Court and the lower Federal courts continued to hold to the separation doctrine but occasionally held that segregated schools must be kept, in fact, equal to one another. At least as early as 1903, Frank A. Critz, a candidate for gov-

---

[45] Quoted from Geoffrey Moore, "American Novels Mislead Europeans," *Western World,* November, 1957, pp. 24–28. See also Denis W. Brogan, *The American Character,* Alfred A. Knopf, Inc., New York, 1944.
[46] *Plessy v. Ferguson,* 163 U.S. 537 (1896), first applied the doctrine to public transportation. It was later extended to schools as well. See C. E. Williams, "Implementation of the Supreme Court's Decision on Racial Segregation in Public Education," *AAUP Bulletin,* 43:295–305, June, 1957.

ernor of Mississippi, expressed the fear that if black schools were to be closed (as his opponent advocated), the Federal government might require that blacks be admitted to white schools.[47]

In the years after 1953, a civil rights–conscious Supreme Court decided to impose a national policy of integrated public schools. The Court, setting aside precedents almost a century old, held that even if school facilities for both races were in fact equal—as they often were not—the psychological barrier to equality created by segregation was insurmountable and constituted a denial of equal protection of the laws.[48] A great battle had begun.

The Court said that school districts should proceed "with all deliberate speed," and there followed a series of decisions designed to overcome stalling tactics. The decisions threatened some of the principal values in the dominant culture of the states where slavery had once been the central institution of the economy. Educational segregation was there viewed not only as normal—it had always been practiced—but as a means for discouraging racial intermarriage as well as for maintaining a semicaste system. There was, in the South, an enormous increase in the number of organizations dedicated to the maintenance of segregation. Labor unions that gave support to racial equality but were at the same time seeking to recruit membership in the industrializing South found the two goals largely incompatible. But some integration took place fairly promptly, especially in the border states. By 1957, 18 percent of the Southern school districts having both white and black children had begun or completed programs of integration.[49] Elsewhere, resistance was strong. Desegregation ranged, in 1965, from complete formal compliance in Kentucky to only token response in Alabama, Arkansas, Georgia, Louisiana, Mississippi, North Carolina, and South Carolina.[50] At issue was the question of whether the Federal courts could successfully impose upon the nation at large a single ethical concept of equality. The judges seemed to be as determined as were their opponents.

School segregation, in actual practice, is common in both the North and the South. Chicago schools, for example, even in 1970, remained highly segregated, especially at the elementary level. Ninety percent of elementary students in Chicago in 1965 attended either all-white or all-Negro schools.[51] The situation was somewhat different at the

[47] A. D. Kirwan, *Revolt of the Rednecks,* University of Kentucky Press, Lexington, Ky., 1951, p. 151.
[48] *Brown v. Topeka Board of Education,* 347 U.S. 483 (1954).
[49] Southern Education Reporting Service, *With All Deliberate Speed,* Harper & Row, Publishers, Incorporated, New York, 1957. For the effect of inferior education for Negroes upon the social organization of Northern industrial cities, see "The Far-flowing Negro Tide," *Newsweek,* Dec. 23, 1957.
[50] *Southern School News,* June, 1965.
[51] Jack Star, "Chicago's Troubled Schools," *Look Magazine,* May 4, 1965, pp. 59–61.

high school level, but probably because high school attendance districts are much larger than those of elementary schools. In 1965 in Chicago, 82 percent of the high schools were completely segregated. The principal difference between the North and the South was that, in the North, blacks had considerably more political power and their leaders were increasingly in a position to demand equal facilities. Segregation in both the North and South had obviously discriminated against the black pupil. In Chicago as well as in the most segregationist-minded city in the South, black schools were more overcrowded than those of white children; they had the least experienced teachers, the highest rate of dropouts, and the highest truancy rates.

A detailed study of integration of schools in eight Northern cities indicated that, contrary to policy making on other questions, school boards rather than superintendents had more influence on the outcome.[52] In part, the author concluded this was because conflict tended to be over ideological issues rather than detail. He concludes that ideological conflict was more likely to occur because school boards were autonomous and dealt with only a single-issue area. Unlike the mayor, a school board cannot trade off a concession to civil rights groups in one area for a concession to "go slow" groups in another. With the schools, the issue becomes one of all-or-nothing, and conflict often results.

Two issues dominated in the 1970s. One was the drive, by separatist blacks and those who despaired of true integration being achieved, to demand that segregated black schools be upgraded and be manned by black teachers and administrators and have a high degree of local autonomy. The other issue was that of achieving integration, if only token integration, by the busing of students.

Schools in the Slums. James B. Conant, as much as any modern critic, has called the special attention of the nation's educators to the teaching of students in the slums. He argues: "A caste system finds its clearest expression in an educational system."[53] Thus, racial discrimination mixed with poverty has created an environment in which only a few students can be successfully socialized to take on productive roles in the large society. His criticisms, together with more popularized works such as *The Blackboard Jungle* and *Up the Down Staircase,* have called public attention to the plight of large-city schools and inspired such Federal programs as Operation Head Start and private efforts, such as "Sesame Street."

The problems of students who become disillusioned with schools from junior high school on and finally drop out sometime during their

[52] Robert L. Crain, *School Desegregation in the North,* National Opinion Research Center, Chicago, 1966.
[53] Conant, *Slums and Suburbs,* p. 11.

high school years have been especially stressed. Although the number of children remaining in school until completion of the twelfth grade is constantly growing, many still drop out at an earlier time. Most of those who leave school prefer work to further education and do not expect to strive for jobs that would require much formal education. Since the economy needs many such persons, these dropouts may not be serious. Still, in one study, 15 percent of those leaving indicated they did so for financial reasons (other than a desire for spending money); and some of these, at least, it could be presumed, would have been able to make a greater contribution to society by staying in school longer. Dropout rates tend to increase with the size of the city, for in the anonymity of larger cities, there is less social pressure on children to remain in school or on parents to keep children in school. Rarely, however, do children leave school at their parents' suggestion, and there is a high correlation between pre-graduation dropouts and juvenile delinquency. Keeping youngsters in school would, then, appear to be a matter of concern broader than that of the individual and his family.[54]

James B. Conant, after his visits to classrooms in the slum areas of several large cities, reported that almost every kind of problem of social disorganization was faced daily by some of the pupils. Both boys and girls became involved in gang fights; many had seen brutality in their homes. Most commonly they came from homes in which the parents were divorced, where one or both parents were alcoholics, or where the parents faced serious emotional problems. Girls of high school age, when surveyed, reported their greatest problem as avoiding molesters between the sidewalk and their family's apartment upstairs. Another discouraging finding relevant to education was that in some slum schools the students changed almost completely over the course of a year because of dropouts and moving in and out of slum neighborhoods. Thus Conant, like many other educators, concluded that the schools can be only minimally effective under such conditions. They cannot be expected to reform society but must depend on other agencies, both private and governmental, to correct the worst problems. Welfare programs might have an impact if coupled with opportunity to qualify for productive positions in the economy. The solution thus seems related to a circle of frustration in which persons cannot be properly trained for better positions because of their present conditions. Nevertheless, Conant pays tribute to the many teachers and principals in such schools who,

[54] See two publications by the U.S. Office of Education: *Why Do Boys and Girls Drop Out of School?* 1953, and *Retention in High Schools in Large Cities,* 1957.

despite all handicaps, have been able to develop significant educational programs.

A Concluding Comment. The local school in America today is in the process of change. On the one hand, state governments following the advice of educators have encouraged consolidation, and this has resulted in larger and more professional school systems. As the nation becomes more technologically oriented, citizen leaders are also showing increasing concern about the quality of local educational programs and their content. It is likely, though far from certain, that continued emphasis will be given to upgrading the nation's schools with a lessening of local controls. States and even the Federal government can be expected to impose more standards in the future. Among the greatest difficulties still unresolved are those of *de facto* segregation by race and the related problem of the quality of educational training in slum areas. If these problems are to be met, it is likely that the impetus for change must come both from outside the schools and from educators themselves.

SELECTED
READINGS

Berube, Maurice R., and Marilyn Gittell: *Confrontation of Ocean Hill-Brownsville,* Frederick A. Praeger, New York, 1969.

Butts, F. Freeman, and Lawrence A. Cremin: *A History of Education,* Holt, Rinehart and Winston, Inc., New York, 1953.

Conant, James B.: *The Child, the Parent, and the State,* Harvard University Press, Cambridge, Mass., 1959. (From a series of studies of American education by the former president of Harvard University.)

———: *Slums and Suburbs: A Commentary on Schools in the Metropolitan Area,* McGraw-Hill Book Company, New York, 1961.

The Danforth and Ford Foundations: *The School and the Democratic Environment,* Columbia University Press, New York, 1970.

Dunbar, Ernest: "The Plot to Take Over the PTA," *Look Magazine,* Sept. 7, 1965, pp. 27ff. (The actions of the far right in seeking to control the PTA and use it against school boards and administrations.)

Gittell, Marilyn: *Participants and Participation: A Study of School Policy in New York City,* Frederick A. Praeger, New York, 1967.

——— and T. Edward Hollander: *Six Urban School Systems: A Comparative Study of Institutional Response,* Frederick A. Praeger, New York, 1968.

———and Alan Hevesi (eds.): *The Politics of Urban Education,* Frederick A. Praeger, New York, 1969.

Gross, Neal: *Who Runs Our Schools?* John Wiley & Sons, Inc., New York, 1958.

Iannaccone, Laurence: *Politics, Power and Policy: The Governing of Local School Districts,* Charles E. Merrill Publishing Company, Columbus, 1970.

Kimbrough, Ralph B.: *Political Power and Educational Decision-making,* Rand, McNally & Company, Chicago, 1963.

Mathiasen, Carolyn, Victor Block, and Victoria Velsey (eds.): *Federal Role in Education,* Congressional Quarterly Service, Washington, 1965. (Detailed history, and summary of legislation.)

Schroth, Thomas N., and others: *Congress and the Nation, 1945–1964,* Congressional Quarterly Service, Washington, 1965, chap. 8.

Sigel, Roberta S.: *Detroit Experiment: Citizens Plan for a New High School,* The Bobbs-Merrill Company, Inc., Indianapolis, ICP no. 95, 1966.

Southern Education Reporting Service: *With All Deliberate Speed,* Harper & Row, Publishers, Incorporated, New York, 1957.

Thomas, Michael P., Jr.: *Community Governance and the School Board: A Case Study,* Institute of Public Affairs, University of Texas, Austin, 1967. (A Study of the Austin School Board.)

U.S. Office of Education: *Progress of Public Education in the United States of America,* 1964.

————: *Projections of Educational Statistics,* 1964.

Urban Affairs Quarterly: "Urban Education," entire issue, vol. 2, September, 1966.

Usdan, Michael D., and others: *Education and State Politics,* Teachers College Press, Columbia University, New York, 1969. (School politics, especially of finance, in twelve states.)

CHAPTER
19 PUBLIC HEALTH AND WELFARE

Few functions of municipal government affect more urbanites in a greater variety of ways than do those involving health and welfare (which, for purposes of this chapter, includes recreation). Yet these are also usually technical and professional functions which rest on a foundation of stable cultural values. As a result, they provoke relatively little public controversy and tend to be dominated by a professional bureaucracy which administers them according to its own (culturally acceptable) standards.

Yet even though nearly complete consensus often exists, from time to time throughout history, health and welfare have become the subject of intense political controversy. Thus, discovery of the germ theory of disease, coupled with cholera and typhoid epidemics, resulted in sharp public debate and was followed by heavy public outlays and daring engineering projects designed to reach unpolluted water sources. Public welfare based on the harsh seventeenth-century poor law fitted so well into the American myth system that it was not seriously challenged until the Great Depression, when public attitudes quickly changed. Public welfare recipients and others who were potentially members of welfare clientele groups became politically conscious and active. Yet the long period of stable attitudes toward welfare could also block the development of concepts for a contemporary approach, thus delaying the maturation of a new public welfare system. In the 1970s, it was again at issue.

In the times of transition, a governmental function rises to the level of perception and concern of the average citizen. It is then that each of us may help to contribute to the construction of a new concept of the content of that function.

Urban problems were a major concern of the 89th Congress, the Congress that met through 1965 and 1966 and was far more liberal than the typical Congress as a result of the anti-Goldwater balloting in the 1964 presidential election. This Congress provided for a two-year, 1.3 billion-dollar program for so-called "demonstration cities." (Some Congressmen objected to the image created by the name and it was changed to "model" cities.) This program emphasized the rehabilitation of residential areas. The plan was to find between sixty and seventy cities that were willing to meet a set of fourteen criteria and to focus upon a single blighted neighborhood. The goal was to show what could be done by such an approach. If successful, the implication was that additional Federal funds would be made available for similar projects in other parts of the same cities and in other cities.

The 89th Congress also expanded Federal pollution-control programs for both air and water. Congress appropriated 1.6 billion dollars for the antipoverty program, much of it to be spent in cities. But, faced with the cost of the war in Vietnam, it did not provide for full funding of these programs. The 92nd Congress listened without enthusiasm as President Nixon proposed drastic changes in the 1930s-conceived welfare system.

PUBLIC HEALTH

The Nation's Health. Cities, with their high concentration of people in confined areas, are natural targets for communicable diseases. For this reason, local governments have for centuries had responsibilities for the protection of health. The idea that some diseases were in some manner contagious was discovered long ago. Resulting from this knowledge came the practice of having cities require the isolation of afflicted persons. The pesthouse was an early form of isolation. Quarantining of such persons in their houses also became a municipal responsibility. A flag or sign beside the doorway of the homes of those with contagious diseases was the responsibility of the public health officer.

During the Great Plague (bubonic plague) that struck London in 1665 and 1666, for example, the houses of the afflicted were marked with red crosses on the door, "searchers" were sent out to certify the cause of deaths, and municipal authorities sent a man out to kill the dogs of the city, for these creatures were mistakenly blamed for spreading the disease.[1] Cities, now aided by a considerable amount of progress in medical knowledge, still perform similar functions. In recent decades, their tasks have become even greater and their successes in lowering the death rate ever more impressive.

Another development in municipal health activities, and a logical extension of the older practice of isolation, came with the discovery of the techniques of vaccination and inoculation against communicable diseases. A conflict has developed over the question of whether these practices are "treatments" that should be cared for by private physicians or preventive medicine and, as such, a public health function. In the United States, the former view has generally prevailed, except for the vaccination of school children in some cases and the emergency treatment of populations in the event of epidemics.

A third factor in the development of public health departments was the popularity of the filth theory of disease in the middle years of the nineteenth century. This notion led to heavy emphasis upon sanitation, especially the construction of sewers, the collection of garbage, and the abatement of nuisances. During this period public health departments became common and were expanded in size beyond that of a local physician acting on a part-time basis. Although the collection and disposal of sewage and garbage is still a function of the health department in some cities, it has generally been transferred to the public works department. But the health department is still responsible for the health supervision of such activities, and it has been entrusted with an ever increasing number of other functions.

Public Health Administration. The American Public Health Association believes that specialization is so important in a proper health program that its Committee on Local Health Units has recommended the establishment of health units so organized as to contain not less than 50,000 people in each of them.[2] Smaller units not only cannot develop specialization but are likely to be unable to finance a successful program. This means, of course, that the county or a special-purpose district would have to be used as the health unit, except for fair-sized cities. The professional organization also suggests that there should be one public health nurse for each 5,000 people and one sanitarian for each 25,000 people. Few communities in the nation meet these and other standards of the association, however. Cities

---

[1] See Johannes Nohl, *The Black Death,* Ballantine Books, Inc., New York, 1960, chap. 5. "Administrative Precautions."

[2] American Public Health Association, *Local Health Units for the Nation,* The Commonwealth Fund, New York, 1946.

and villages are still the standard units established by state law, although county and city-county departments are increasingly taking over health functions in urban areas and standards are rising. For example, Michigan law provides that any city failing to maintain a full-time health officer comes automatically under the county health department, and that the city and county may, by mutual agreement, share the services of a single health officer to supervise both departments. It is likely, however, that health units will be rapidly consolidated in the future only through the incentive of conditional Federal or state grants-in-aid.

The trend today is toward municipal health departments under a single head responsible to the chief executive. Most municipalities, however, still make use of the traditional board of health. (General municipal health departments first became popular in the heyday of the independent board and commission.) Quite a few cities still have boards but have stripped them of administrative powers, leaving them with but an advisory function. This is, in fact, the structure recommended by the American Public Health Association.

The board of health usually consists of physicians and laymen. In some cities, at least one seat must be given to an engineer. The American Public Health Association and other medical groups favor a heavy representation of physicians on the board. This can perhaps be justified on the basis of the superior interest of these men, but they are also wanted there to "protect" the private medical profession against those who would expand the scope of public health functions.

The health officer in small cities is a local physician, often serving on a part-time basis. In larger cities, a person with professional training in public health and the degree of Doctor of Public Health, as well as that of M.D., is often employed. The specialized professional degree affords training in sanitation, public administration, and other fields, in addition to medical training. In the largest cities, the health officer's time is fully occupied with administration, and technical functions are left to his subordinates.

Public Health Functions. A great many health activities are performed or aided by state health departments and by Federal agencies, especially by the U.S. Public Health Service of the Department of Health, Education and Welfare. But the principal direct health services are performed by local governments. Except in small communities, the health department is normally divided into several specialized divisions.

Communicable-disease Control. The traditional function of the health department deals with communicable-disease control. Despite limited funds, health departments have been so effective in reducing, with the help of private medicine, the incidence of these diseases that they have almost eliminated the need for this function. Almost— but never entirely. The communicable-disease division receives the required reports from physicians and enforces isolation in those cases where it is still required. It must sometimes prod lax physicians into the prompt reporting of diseases.

By keeping watch over water and milk supplies, this division has almost eliminated typhoid fever. At the turn of the present century, there were more than thirty times as many deaths from this disease in the United States as there are today. Yellow fever and malaria, once common in swampy areas frequented by certain types of mosquitoes, have been virtually eliminated in this country by the draining of swamps and the treatment of other standing water. Typhus has been controlled through ratproofing programs and through health education, which has taught the dangers to be found in the body lice that transmit the disease. Smallpox is almost unknown today as a result of educating the public and the occasional use of compulsory vaccination laws. In recent years, trends in communicable-disease control have included (1) development of more effective medical treatment for communicable diseases; (2) realization that there are many more healthy disease carriers than sick ones—hence the abandonment of traditional quarantine practices after about 1945; and (3) the development of immunization techniques for an increased number of diseases.

Tuberculosis, less contagious than most communicable diseases but requiring special equipment and methods, is handled by a separate division of the health department in larger cities. Clinics and special hospitals or hospital sections are needed for its treatment. The prevention of tuberculosis is possible largely through conditions beyond the control of the health department—through better housing and conditions of labor for many urban citizens.

Venereal diseases are also usually treated by a special division of the department. These diseases, like tuberculosis, must be controlled through treatment. Protection against them can be achieved only through health education. The venereal-disease-control section has the major task of persuading people to apply for its help voluntarily and of overcoming the sufferer's wish to keep secret his socially disapproved ailment. Health departments have sought to encourage people to come forward for treatment by making their services available to all, regardless of ability to pay, and by locating treatment clinics as inconspicuously as possible.

Federal grants for venereal-disease control have gone to local units. Some of the "wonder drugs" have been very effective in treatment. However, an unknown, but no doubt very large, number of cases requiring treatment are never brought to the attention of either private practitioners or public health clinics.[3]

Maternal and Child Care. The principal functions of this division are of an educational nature. It offers lectures, pamphlets, publicity releases, and other information services designed to reduce ignorance concerning childbearing among prospective mothers and fathers. The division also gives advice on child care and child rearing. Many cities operate prenatal and postnatal clinics and provide for home visits by public health nurses. The division works closely with hospitals offering free maternity service to the indigent, and it licenses and regulates midwifery in those states where this practice is still permitted.

Sanitation. Many municipal functions related to sanitation are administered outside of the health department. Swamps are drained, water supplied, and sewage disposed of by the public works department or by independent departments, but health aspects are supervised by the health department.

The municipal department shares many inspection duties with state and Federal agencies. Milk must be inspected to guard against watering and against the presence of tuberculosis and typhoid as well as several other types of germs that may be found in raw milk. Local slaughterhouses, if not inspected by representatives of the U.S. Department of Agriculture, are inspected by the local health department. Retail food establishments are inspected and food handlers examined for communicable diseases by the health department, or under its supervision.

In checking the premises of retail food establishments, sanitation-division personnel usually follow the practice of unexpected and irregular inspections. If illegal and unsanitary conditions are found, the usual practice is to issue a warning. In the case of extreme or repeated violations, licenses may be suspended or revoked.

Municipal Hospitals. Municipal hospitals have become common throughout the nation as part of a public health program. There are over 250 city hospitals and over 60 city-county hospitals in the United States. Hospitals in cities under 100,000 are usually managed by semiautonomous boards, while in larger cities they tend to be controlled by the city health departments. In smaller cities, the

[3] *Today's VD Control Program,* The Association of State and Territorial Health Officers, Chicago, 1957.

budget is also usually autonomous, with the council having no power of review, but in larger cities, municipal hospitals as a rule are treated as simply another city agency.

Generally speaking, the smaller the city, the more likely its hospital is to be completely self-supporting, or nearly so. In very few cities of over 50,000 is the municipal hospital even 50 percent self-supporting. The difference is made up from funds appropriated by the city or sometimes the county or state. Municipal hospitals in larger cities exist to a great extent to care for police and indigent cases. The smaller the city, generally speaking, the more likely is the hospital to be a general-service institution. Larger cities are also more likely to operate special hospitals for the treatment of contagious diseases, tuberculosis, poliomyelitis, and mental disorders.

The oldest municipal hospital in the United States, the Philadelphia General, dates from 1732. The largest municipal institution, New York's famed Bellevue, is only four years younger. The city of New York also operates thirteen other hospitals and sanatoria. There are, however, municipal hospitals in cities of all sizes, including about one hundred cities of under 5,000 population.

Public Health Education. This division seeks to increase longevity by teaching citizens the principles of personal hygiene and the need for proper medical care and consultation, and warning them about certain dangers to health. The division may conduct public lectures, issue news releases and public service announcements to press, radio, and television, and furnish lecturers to clubs, school assemblies, and other get-togethers. For example, the division may help the National Cancer Society warn the public of the "seven danger signals of cancer"; in the summer it may issue public service announcements to local radio stations reminding parents of the symptoms of poliomyelitis in children (or themselves); or it may issue news releases to the press warning of the dangers of food poisoning in an unrefrigerated cream puff.

The Staff Services. A staff function of general interest is the collection of vital statistics for the community: records of births, of deaths and their causes, and of communicable diseases. The public health laboratory furnishes analyses of blood, sputum, and other samples in helping physicians diagnose diseases. It also may analyze food suspected of being tainted. As a staff service, public health nurses are furnished to aid the divisions in charge of communicable diseases, tuberculosis, venereal diseases, maternal and child care, public health education, and outpatient care.

Public Health and a Healthy Public. T. H. Reed, city manager, municipal consultant, and professor, writing in his usual style of realism
tinged with satire, has said:[4]

> There is no field of local public administration in which the
> professional staff comes into so many and so varied contacts with
> the public as does that of a department of health. Furthermore,
> it comes into contact not with any special section of the public
> but with representatives of every social and economic group.
> The marvelous development of the technical side of health work
> in the past generation has scarcely, if at all, reduced the im-
> portance of its human side. Health administration cannot, in
> spite of its scientific flavor, be reduced to a series of rigid formu-
> las. It is still a matter of making rich landlords provide suitable
> sanitary conveniences for people who have to be taught not to use
> bathtubs for storing coal. It is as much as ever a question of
> inducing ignorant and wayward men and women to submit to
> restraints and treatments the nature of which they cannot under-
> stand. It furnishes the clearest possible illustration of the dis-
> tinction between the pursuit of professional techniques and the
> application of such techniques to the service of real human
> beings. It is the human relationships involved which separate the
> science of epidemiology from the art of municipal management.

Public Awareness and Attitudes. The public is not well informed
concerning the services performed by public health agencies. Many
private organizations are active in the health field and these are
often confused with governmental organizations. Furthermore, in
one community, 84 percent of the working-class, 51 percent of the
lower-middle-class, and 24 percent of the upper-middle-class samples, could not name one specific activity that was carried on by their
(county) public health agency.[5] This, despite the fact that "there
is no field of local public administration in which the professional
staff comes into so many and so varied contacts with the public as
does that of a department of health."[6] This seeming paradox probably results from the high degree of professionalization in this field
and the stable cultural attitudes that exist toward public health
functions and administrators.

Controversies before municipal governing bodies center around
and are related to several items, especially the following: (1) the
establishment of hospitals for the chronically ill (a group of increasing size in our society, a by-product of lengthening life ex-
pectancy); (2) the development of home-care programs by local
health units through which patients not in need of hospitalization

[4] Thomas H. Reed, *Municipal Management*, McGraw-Hill Book Company, New York, 1941, p. 448.
[5] E. L. Koos, *The Health of Regionville*, Columbia University Press, New York, 1954, pp. 115–116.
[6] Reed, *op. cit.*, p. 448.

or other institutional care may be cared for and followed up in their own homes after hospital release; (3) the public purchase of polio vaccine for children; (4) the development of publicly financed medical-service centers in small towns with too little population to support hospitals or even physicians; (5) expanded services to ghetto residents who cannot afford medical care. All these and some other items being urged as proper areas for public health activity are controversial.

PARKS AND RECREATION

Recreational Administration. Many disputes have arisen over the desirable form of organization in the field of parks and recreation. Although the typical citizen probably thinks of parks and recreation as two aspects of a single function, professionals in the field are not sure. In the past, it was common for the city government to have separate departments for parks and for recreation, but the postwar trend has been away from this. In many cities, the school board also provides an organized summer recreation program.

In the past, parks and recreation departments were commonly set up under autonomous administrative boards, and it was not uncommon for them to have independent sources of income so that they existed practically as separate *ad hoc* units of local government, similar in status to the school boards. Parks and recreation boards were (and still are) very often made up of high-status members of the community. Professional recreation workers have generally tended to favor the independent board because of the support which it gives to the recreation program, particularly when the budget is under consideration. They also argue that such a board offers a continuity of policy not to be found when the head of the department changes at the pleasure of the chief executive.

General administrators in the field of municipal management argue, however, that the parks and recreation function is not unique in its problems of management and that it should be administered as a regular department of the city under the control of the chief executive. They contend that this activity should be financed out of the general fund rather than a separate tax levy, that its budget should be treated like those of other city departments, and that the departments should make use of the municipal staff services for purchasing, personnel, maintenance, and the like. In order to maintain organized community interest in parks and recreation, there is a tendency for a board to be retained as an *advisory* body and hence a watchdog, while at the same time leaving administrative control under the chief executive.

Parks. The inhabitants and public officials of cities have often been slow in providing for the benefits of spacious, beautiful, and useful parks. Parks are of great psychological value, especially to the apartment or slum dweller, to whom they may be the only available substitute for a front lawn or a backyard.

Cities such as New York and Philadelphia were allowed to mature with almost complete disregard of the need for large open spaces, for grass, trees, and shrubs. (Slum dwellers will not use many playgrounds and green spaces that are beyond short walking distance. Open spaces such as Central Park are of limited value to low-income persons.) Even cities that expanded at a much later date, such as Detroit, failed to plan for parks. Today a belated attempt is being made in all large cities to provide small recreational playgrounds and indoor gymnasiums and swimming pools. In most cities it is now too late to provide areas for large parks that might have been set aside twenty-five, fifty, or more years ago. As a result, quite a few cities (or *ad hoc* park districts) have constructed parks and beaches outside of the urban areas. This practice began in 1893 in the Boston region. Outlying parks and "reservations" must sometimes be located two hours' travel or more from the heart of the city. Where this is so, it at the least causes inconvenience and traffic hazards on weekends. To those in the lower-income groups who have no automobiles, but who most need the facilities, these areas may be quite inaccessible.

Some municipalities have sought to require provisions for a reasonable amount of park and playground area at the time of, or in advance of, subdividing. The courts have not been particularly cooperative, however, and several types of such laws and ordinances have been declared unconstitutional. Of course, some cities have planned their parks carefully, fitting them into the long-range scheme of things and not waiting for a park to be located through the accident of a donated piece of land. Quite a few American cities have fine park systems. Minneapolis's is particularly beautiful. Chicago, Boston, and other cities rate near the top, too.

A large city often makes a zoo out of one of its parks. Zoos are sometimes operated by a board and department separate from the parks department. They are expensive to maintain but are immensely popular with children and adults alike. Zoos such as those in Chicago, Philadelphia, St. Louis, San Diego, and Washington are among the finest in the world. All municipal institutions seem to have their opponents. Some people, for example, consider zoos to be either a waste of the taxpayers' money or a cruelty to the confined wild animals. But most people love animals and like to observe them, provided that they are given adequate and expert care and attention.

Places to Read and Learn. The first library supported by taxes was established in Peterborough, New Hampshire, in 1833. Sometimes libraries are privately endowed and privately operated but are indirectly agencies of the city because they receive an annual appropriation either from the council or from a special property-tax levy. This type of library, especially common in New England and the South, is controlled by a self-perpetuating board of trustees. Other libraries are entirely public, controlled either by the school district or by the city government. They usually have autonomous control through a library board, but a few cities have a single librarian reporting directly to the chief executive.

Three problems, in particular, have vexed librarians in recent years. In the first place, the decentralizing tendency of cities means, in many places, that the main public library is often isolated in the center of the city from which the population is receding. This poses the threat that fewer people will use the libraries. The answer seems to be in a greater use of branch libraries and bookmobiles in outlying residential areas. Such a movement has been under way for years but is now being accelerated. Connected with the problem also is the question of allowing suburbanites to use the core-city library, for which they do not pay taxes. Some cities allow free use of the library to anyone who is *employed* in the city regardless of where he may live. This is another form of subsidizing the suburbs. County libraries and *ad hoc* library districts are arising to supply the suburbs in many places.

A second problem lies in the threat posed by the coming of television. Have people stopped reading, thus making the library obsolete, or a luxury maintained only for scholars? Studies indicate that people do read less, in fact, shortly after purchasing a television set, but after the novelty wears off, they return to their old habits.[7] There has been a decrease in library use in recent years, but television is probably only one of several causes.

A third area of controversy centers around the threatened censorship of reading materials in libraries. In times of tension, unrest, confusion, and doubt, people seek security through unity and conformity. Alien ideas become enemies to be fought along with the human enemies. In the period since the beginning of the cold war, and particularly during the period of McCarthyism (1950–1954), some citizens confused the study of communism with allegiance to it. In 1952, for example, the *Boston Post* conducted a campaign to have all materials concerned with communism removed from the

[7] S. Janice Kee, "Public Libraries Developments in 1952," *Municipal Year Book, 1953,* International City Management Association, Chicago, 1953, p. 484.

public library. The effort was not successful in Boston, but in some smaller cities book burnings took place.

Potential attacks upon our libraries—the storehouses of the accumulated knowledge of mankind—are always with us. It does not take a threat as serious as that of communism to serve as the springboard of an assault. Headline seekers can create their own excuses. For example, in 1927, William Hale ("Big Bill") Thompson, Chicago's colorful demagogic mayor, appointed a friend, Sport Herrmann, to the task of ridding the Chicago Public Library of books containing "pro-British propaganda and un-American statements." Herrmann explained his intended method: "I'm gonna burn every book in that there library that's pro-British! . . . The library's supported by public taxes and if this thing of undermining Americanism isn't stopped, the country'll go to pieces, that's all! . . . There must be thousands of propaganda books in the library system. I'll hunt them out and when I find them I'll burn them on the lake shore."[8]

But our culture contains conflicting values. Some of them gave support to Herrmann, but the courts, which sometimes represent the long-range conscience and stable values of society, stood in his way. The threat of legal action stopped him.

Museums and Art Galleries. There are far fewer museums and art galleries in the United States than there are libraries. Most large cities operate them, however. They are usually autonomously controlled in the same fashion as are libraries, and they enjoy the protection of the "patrons of the arts" in the political process. These patrons are often well-to-do and influential persons.

PUBLIC WELFARE

The ancient power of the state to protect the "welfare" of the people is not limited to public assistance programs. The problems of caring for the unemployed and those injured in industrial accidents, and of providing old-age and survivors' insurance, are largely beyond the scope of municipal administration. But many other welfare functions are handled by local governments. These may include the care of the poor, including children whose parents cannot or will not support them, and old people who can neither work nor support themselves from their savings. Delinquents, disabled persons, and the mentally handicapped are also taken care of by welfare agencies

[8] Quoted in Lloyd Wendt and Herman Kogan, *Big Bill of Chicago*, The Bobbs-Merrill Company, Inc., Indianapolis, 1953, pp. 288–289.

in some cities and states, as is the entire recreation program sometimes.

The Development of Welfare Programs. The responsibility for public assistance aid rests with the state, but it has been delegated to local units of government ever since the Elizabethan Poor Law of 1601, the principles of which were adopted in colonial America. The basic approach to the care of the poor taken in the days of the first Elizabeth in England remained unchanged in the American states until its archaism became obvious in the Great Depression. In the years since the Federal government set up its so-called categorical grants-in-aid program in the Social Security Act of 1935, however, there has been a shift of emphasis from the city or township as the administrative unit to the county or to the state itself.

There were some activities by the states designed to modify the ancient poor law even before the Great Depression. In the 1880s, for example, some Eastern private child-welfare agencies would gather up whole trainloads of large-city waifs and bring them to the Midwest to be delivered to farmers who waited at railroad stations. The theory apparently was that any Midwest farmer who offered a child a home would provide a better place than could be found in a large city. The potential abuses of this method of child placement were so great that, in the mid-1880s, Midwestern states enacted legislation bringing child placement under state control.

The needs of the elderly, as distinguished from those of the employable, became obvious as the special problems of urban living made impossible the old system of their being taken into the large farm homes of relatives. Even before the Great Depression, a number of states, including Montana, Kentucky, Wisconsin, and Nevada, had adopted some form of old-age assistance. But generally programs for the aged were adopted after the passage of the Social Security Act in 1935.

The Federal government furnishes grants-in-aid to the states to help in caring for certain categories of persons: old-age assistance, aid to the blind, aid to dependent children, and (since 1950) aid to the permanently and totally disabled. In 1956, Congress expanded these categorical aids by providing a program for hospital care for anyone eligible under the four programs. Some of the states administer these programs through field officers, but in most states they are administered by the counties or other local governments under state aid and supervision.

In some states, although the above categorical aids are administered by the county, general direct relief is left to the cities. The administration of these "welfare cases" is a major task taken alone.

City public welfare agencies are often entrusted, in addition, with responsibility for the licensing of private child-care agencies, the provision of foster care for children unable to live in their own homes, adoption services, work with children's courts, provision for medical and dental care for the needy, and the supervising of private charities.

Persons Dependent upon Public Aid. The idea that some persons might not be capable of caring for their own basic economic needs was long essentially alien to the American tradition of self-sufficiency. Those who went on relief were often characterized as lazy and shiftless. Although this idea has by no means been laid to rest in American folklore, the Great Depression made it clear that, on some occasions at least, the best efforts of a willing worker to find a job were unavailing. As a reaction to the earlier tendency to despise the destitute, some idealists came to describe the marginal members of the working force in glowing terms, ennobling them as martyrs, somewhat as the romantic Rousseau had considered the "noble savage."

In fact, welfare clients are a motley group made up of persons suffering from an extended period of bad luck; lazy persons, alcoholics; psychologically unstable personalities; mentally retarded persons not requiring institutionalization; persons who married young, have several children, but still have low seniority on their factory jobs and are thus often laid off; and many other types. The misfortunes that can bring a family onto public relief are many— exhaustion of unemployment-compensation benefits, successive years of crop failure on the farm, serious and prolonged illness on the part of the breadwinner, and dozens of others.

The attitude of social workers toward their clients is affected by both practical problems and social values. There are, in fact, two general philosophies toward people in need. One holds in essence that all men are rational beings who should be allowed to make decisions for themselves and that social service should provide emergency assistance only if it is wanted; the other is paternalistic in nature, with the caseworker often making decisions for the individual on behalf of society and with the welfare administrator deciding whether or not the client should receive a particular service.[9]

Welfare Administration. The department of welfare is ordinarily a separate agency of city government, although not all welfare functions are placed in such a department. This is another function of

[9] Alan Keith-Lucas, "The Political Theory Implicit in Social Casework Theory," *American Political Science Review*, 47:1076–1091, December, 1953; and, by the same author, *Decisions about People in Need*, The University of North Carolina Press, Chapel Hill, N.C., 1957.

government that has often been supervised by an administrative board, and weak-mayor cities, especially small cities, still treat it as an autonomous function. In large cities, it is normally organized under a single head, although quite a few cities retain an advisory welfare board. Professional social caseworkers and the influential persons of the community who frequently interest themselves in social work as an avocation tend to favor autonomy. Social workers point out that the welfare budget is very large and that the temptation for elective officials to use these funds in order to help win votes is great. This type of reasoning was implicit in the requirement of the Social Security Act, written by professional social workers, that merit systems of personnel administration be established in each state that wished to qualify for Federal aid. Conflicts of interest between politicians and professionals sometimes result.

Late in the nineteenth century, persons interested in social welfare began to organize private charities on an increasing scale, and these institutions came to dominate the relief scene from that time until after World War I. It was through them that the casework system was developed, resulting in the administrative techniques still employed. These charities became so accepted that they were frequently subsidized by local governments, and they began to attract university-trained social workers. During the Great Depression, basic responsibility was shifted to government. Today, private social-service agencies carry only a part of the total load, but they remain important in a great many areas, particularly in activities for the young and old. Their professionally administered fund-raising campaigns are an annual feature of every community. The moneys collected are used to support the Boy Scouts, the YMCA, the Catholic Youth Organization; to provide care for polio and muscular dystrophy victims; to maintain nursing homes for the aged; to assist persons in need who cannot qualify for a public welfare program; to help in the rehabilitation of alcoholics; to care for unwed mothers; and for dozens of other purposes.

Under the contemporary casework system, a social worker is assigned to interview each person asking for assistance. He or she determines whether the individual is eligible for help on the basis of his residence, ability and willingness of the family to work, and reason for lack of self-support. Pending investigation of the facts gathered, temporary relief may be ordered. If investigation substantiates the facts gathered at the initial interview (called the "intake"), the budget to be granted is determined on the basis of established standard allowances. Since the purpose of the casework method is to provide individual attention, social workers follow up each relief case to ascertain whether there has been any change in eligibility status, to give advice, to try to bolster morale, and to help the family regain its self-support.

Despite many changes in the administration of governmental services in recent years, public relief, by its very nature, must be administered by some unit of local government. Any substantial unemployment in the future will find local relief agencies that have, for the most part, become professionalized, modernized, and prepared to fulfill their role.

HUMAN RELATIONS COMMISSIONS

". . . Because of Race, Color, or Creed." In an attempt to bring social democracy abreast of political democracy, a movement after World War II has sought to secure the establishment of laws providing for employment without regard to race, color, or creed, and for equal opportunities in housing.

Identifiable minority groups have, in recent years, demanded equal rights. Their own potential political power as organized minorities has been reenforced by a rising American conscience, a conscience that was pricked by both Nazi and Communist propaganda. Ethnic and racial groups, in addition, have become more verbally and politically skilled as time has passed, and they tend to be concentrated in core cities where their political influence makes office seekers eager to support fair employment practices as well as intergroup-relations bodies.

A large number of cities of over 200,000 population—and many smaller places, if they have substantial self-conscious minorities—have adopted charter amendments or ordinances providing for fair employment and equal opportunities for all citizens. This is true of most of the largest cities of the nation outside the South.

The rules so established seek to prevent discrimination in employment because of the race, religion, color, or national origin of the employee. They apply to cases of private employment in business and industry, to labor-union membership, and to discriminatory practices toward employees in governmental agencies.

Discrimination in employment is not uncommon. Even city personnel agencies have permitted discrimination in the hiring of municipal employees, though their rules may formally forbid it. In some instances, personnel agencies have actually abetted such discrimination.

Most "human relations" groups have avoided coercion or punishment in their attempts to eliminate discrimination. In fact, most municipal commissions have only advisory and noncoercive powers, although some of them have power to bring court actions against offenders, which may result in both restraining orders and criminal punishments. Most human relations agencies, however, depend upon education, conferences, persuasion, social pressure, and the threat of unfavorable publicity to produce compliance.

There is some question as to whether the municipality has adequate jurisdiction to provide for equal opportunities. The problem is at least statewide in nature.

Conservatives in general oppose such legislation, not because they are bigoted, but because they believe such legislation represents another area of governmental interference in private enterprise. They believe it does more harm to freedom than it does good and are likely to argue that progress comes through education, not laws.

Some cities which lack equal-opportunity ordinances have established interracial or intergroup negotiating committees to help improve relations between persons of different ethnic, racial, or religious group membership. They have no coercive powers, but they are sometimes objected to by improvement associations who fear that real equality would threaten property values.

560

SELECTED
READINGS

Altshuler, Alan: *The Ancker Hospital Site Controversy,* The Bobbs-Merrill Company, Inc., Indianapolis, ICP no. 82, 1964. (Problems involved in contradictory technical information reflecting different professional values—in this case, medical administrators and urban planners.)

American Public Health Association: *Local Health Units for the Nation,* The Commonwealth Fund, New York, 1946.

Barron, M. L.: *The Juvenile in Delinquent Society,* Alfred A. Knopf, Inc., New York, 1955.

Butler, G. D.: *Introduction to Community Recreation,* 4th ed., McGraw-Hill Book Company, New York, 1967.

Commission on Community Health Services: *Health Is a Community Affair,* Harvard University Press, Cambridge, Mass., 1966. (Emphasizes intergovernmental aspects of these services and the interaction of public and private aspects.)

Daland, Robert T.: *Government and Health: The Alabama Experience,* Bureau of Public Administration, University of Alabama, University, Ala., 1955.

de Grazia, Alfred (ed.): *Grass Roots Private Welfare,* New York University Press, New York, 1958.

Epstein, Abraham: *Insecurity: A Challenge to America,* Random House, Inc., New York, 1938.

Garceau, Oliver: *The Public Library in the Political Process,* Columbia University Press, New York, 1949.

Hanlon, J. J.: *Principles of Public Health Administration,* 4th ed., The C. V. Mosby Company, St. Louis, 1964.

Heckscher, August: *The City and the Arts,* Institute of Local Government, University of Pittsburgh, Pittsburgh, Pa., 1964. (Municipal government and support of the institutions of fine arts.)

Herman, Harold, and Mary E. McKay: *Community Health Services,* International City Management Association, Washington, 1968.

Keith-Lucas, Alan: *Decisions about People in Need,* The University of North Carolina Press, Chapel Hill, N.C., 1957. (The unarticulated value assumptions in social casework.)

"The Legislative History of Public Housing Traced through 25 Years," *Journal of Housing,* 19:431–445, October, 1962. (History of the Housing Act of 1937 and its amendments.)

Levitan, Sar A.: *Programs in Aid of the Poor,* Upjohn Institute, Kalamazoo, Mich., 1965.

Lubove, Roy: *The Professional Altruist: The Emergence of Social Work as a Career, 1880–1930,* Harvard University Press, Cambridge, Mass., 1965.

MacDonald, Dwight: "Our Invisible Poor," *The New Yorker,* Jan. 19, 1963, pp. 82–132. (A review of books on poverty.)

Meyer, Harold D., and Charles K. Brightbill: *Recreation Administration,* 3d ed., Prentice-Hall, Inc., Englewood Cliffs, N.J., 1964.

National Health Assembly: *America's Health,* Harper & Row, Publishers, Incorporated, New York, 1949.

Paul, B. J. (ed.): *Health, Culture and Community,* Russell Sage Foundation, New York, 1955.

Perkings, Ellen J.: *State and Local Financing of Public Assistance,* U.S. Department of Health, Education and Welfare, Bureau of Public Assistance, 1956.

Poverty and Deprivation in the United States: The Plight of Two-fifths of a Nation, Conference on Economic Progress, Washington, 1962.

Raup, Ruth: *Intergovernmental Relations in Public Welfare,* The University of Minnesota Press, Minneapolis, 1952.

Robinson, Marianna, and Corinne Silverman: *The Reorganization of Philadelphia General Hospital,* University of Alabama Press, University, Ala., 1959. (A case study in professional and administrative pressures.)

Rose, Ernestine: *The Public Library in American Life,* Columbia University Press, New York, 1954.

Schmidt, Frances, and Harold N. Weiner (eds.): *Public Relations in Health and Welfare,* National Public Relations Council of Health and Welfare Services, Inc., New York, 1966.

Sills, David L.: *The Volunteers,* The Free Press of Glencoe, New York, 1958. (A study of the National Foundation and private health and welfare activities.)

Steiner, Gilbert Y.: *Social Insecurity: The Politics of Welfare,* Rand McNally & Company, Chicago, 1966. (A major study, using the analytical tools of political science.)

EPILOGUE
GOVERNING URBAN AMERICA TOMORROW

City governments are likely to continue to play an important part in decisions about services to urban people. The tasks of municipalities in the future, as in the past, will be to perform those functions that are demanded by influential groups—within the limits of revenues that can be raised through the political process. In determining types and levels of services and how to pay for them, government will, as always, have to strike a balance.

The American culture is a product created by people interacting upon one another. It is an independent variable which must be accepted as a basis for understanding present and future American government. Projections seem to show that the future holds "more of the same," with increasing pressures of the same sort that have existed for many years. Citizens in the future will be called upon to meet the problems of living together in vast numbers, problems that seemingly will become more complicated rather than simpler as time passes. If the political process as well as trends in government services are understood, these future challenges will become more understandable, and workable policies perhaps somewhat easier to discover.[1]

[1] On trends, see Charles R. Adrian and Charles Press, *The American Political Process*, 2d ed., McGraw-Hill Book Company, New York, 1969, final chapter.

SUGGESTED
READINGS

PERIODICALS

The following are important periodicals, but they do not necessarily exhaust the field. The periodicals of state municipal leagues provide much detail. For a list of these publications, see the *Municipal Year Book,* International City Management Association, Chicago, published annually.

American City. Monthly. Much detail on administrative developments and less attention to politics and reform action than is found in the *National Civic Review.* Many pictures and a great deal of advertising of the most recent municipal equipment.

American Journal of Public Health. Monthly. American Public Health Association.

American Municipal News. Monthly. Current municipal developments and practices.

City. Bimonthly. National Urban Coalition.

Journal of Housing. Monthly. National Association of Housing Officials. Housing and redevelopment news.

Municipal Finance. Quarterly. Municipal Finance Officers' Association. Also publishes a biweekly *News Letter.*

National Civic Review. Monthly. Formerly the *National Municipal Review.* Perhaps the best source of news of a general nature. Emphasizes political action, especially of the reform type.

National Tax Journal. Quarterly. National Tax Association. Features information on municipal taxation.

Newsletter. Monthly. American Society of Planning Officials.

New York Times. Daily. Reports important political and administrative developments throughout the country if of general interest.

Police Chief. Quarterly. International Association of Chiefs of Police.
Public Employee. Monthly. The American Federation of State, County, and Municipal Employees. The labor viewpoint, especially on personnel practices.
Public Management. Monthly. International City Management Association. A major source of news on administration.
Public Personnel Review. Quarterly. Public Personnel Association. Includes developments in municipal personnel administration.
Public Utilities Fortnightly. Management and technical problems of utilities operation.
Public Welfare. Quarterly. American Public Welfare Association.
Recreation. Monthly. National Recreation Association.
Urban Affairs Quarterly. Sponsored by the City University of New York.
Urban Reporter. Twice monthly. Urban Research Corporation.
Urban Research News. Biweekly. Sage Publications, Inc.

SUGGESTED READINGS

FOR SPECIFIC LOCALITIES

Albuquerque

Cline, Dorothy I., and T. Phillip Wolf: "Albuquerque: The End of a Reform Era," in Leonard E. Goodall (ed.), *Urban Politics in the Southwest,* Institute of Public Administration, Arizona State University, Tempe, Ariz., 1967.

Atlanta

Banfield, Edward C.: *Big City Politics,* Random House, Inc., New York, 1965, chap. 1, "Atlanta: Strange Bedfellows."

Hunter, Floyd: *Community Power Structure,* University of North Carolina Press, Chapel Hill, N.C., 1953.

Jennings, M. Kent: *Community Influentials: The Elites of Atlanta,* The Macmillan Company, New York, 1964.

Austin

Olson, David M.: "Austin: The Capital City," in Leonard E. Goodall (ed.), *Urban Politics in the Southwest,* Institute of Public Administration, Arizona State University, Tempe, Ariz., 1967.

Baltimore

Lukas, J. A.: "Boss Pollack: He Can't Be There but He Is," *Reporter,* 27:35–36, July 19, 1962.

Martin, Harold H.: "The Case of the Bouncing Mayor," *The Saturday Evening Post,* Sept. 24, 1955, pp. 19ff. (Story of Mayor Thomas D'Alesandro.)

Baton Rouge

Havard, William C., and Floyd Corty: *Rural-Urban Consolidation: The Merger of Governments in the Baton Rouge Area,* Louisiana State University Press, Baton Rouge, La., 1964.

Boston

Banfield, Edward C.: *Big City Politics,* Random House, Inc., New York, 1965, chap. 2, "Boston: The New Hurrah."

Blackwood, George: "Boston Politics and Boston Politicians," in Murray B. Levin, *The Alienated Voter: Politics in Boston,* Holt, Rinehart and Winston, Inc., New York, 1960, chap. 1.

Curley, James M.: *I'd Do It Again,* Prentice-Hall, Inc., Englewood Cliffs, N.J., 1957. (By the city's long-time boss.)

Chicago

Banfield, Edward C.: *Political Influence,* The Free Press of Glencoe, New York, 1961. (The Chicago political style.)

Gosnell, H. F.: *Machine Politics: Chicago Model,* The University of Chicago Press, Chicago, 1937.

Gottfried, Alex: *Boss Cermak of Chicago,* University of Washington Press, Seattle, Wash., 1962 (A psychological study of Chicago's boss of the early 1930s.)

Liebling, A. J.: *Chicago: The Second City,* Alfred A. Knopf, Inc., New York, 1952. (An entertaining, though hostile, study.)

Merriam, Charles E.: *Chicago: A More Intimate View of Urban Politics,* The Macmillan Company, New York, 1929.

Meyerson, Martin, and Edward C. Banfield: *Politics, Planning and the Public Interest,* The Free Press of Glencoe, New York, 1955.

Royko, Mike: *Boss: Richard J. Daley of Chicago,* E. P. Dutton and Son, New York, 1970. (By a journalist. Sharply critical of Daley.)

Waters, Harry, and Frank Maier: "Chicago's Daley: How to Run a City," *Newsweek,* Apr. 5, 1971. (A balanced account.)

Wendt, Lloyd, and Herman Kogan: *Big Bill of Chicago,* The Bobbs-Merrill Company, Inc., Indianapolis, 1953. (The biography of Mayor William H. Thompson.)

Cincinnati

Straetz, Ralph A.: *PR Politics in Cincinnati,* New York University Press, New York, 1958.

Dallas

Thometz, Carol Estes: *The Decision-makers: The Power Structure of Dallas,* Southern Methodist University Press, Dallas, Tex., 1963.

Denver

Bridge, Franklin M.: *Metro-Denver: Mile-high Government,* Bureau of Governmental Research, University of Colorado, Boulder, Colo., 1963.

Detroit

Banfield, Edward C.: *Big City Politics,* Random House, Inc., New York, 1965, chap. 3, "Detroit: Balancing Act."

Kornhauser, Arthur: *Attitudes of Detroit People toward Detroit,* Wayne State University Press, Detroit, Mich., 1952.

Mowitz, Robert, and Deil Wright: *Profile of a Metropolis,* Wayne State University Press, Detroit, Mich., 1962.

El Paso

Banfield, Edward C.: *Big City Politics,* Random House, Inc., New York, 1965, chap. 4, "El Paso: Two Cultures."

Fort Worth

Spain, August O.: "Fort Worth: Great Expectations—Cowtown Hares and Tortoises," in Leonard E. Goodall (ed.), *Urban Politics in the Southwest,* Institute of Public Administration, Arizona State University, Tempe, Ariz., 1967.

Houston

McCleskey, Clifton: "Houston: Tripartite Politics," in Leonard E. Goodall (ed.), *Urban Politics in the Southwest,* Institute of Public Administration, Arizona State University, Tempe, Ariz., 1967.

Jersey City

Fleming, T. J.: "City in the Shadow," *The Saturday Evening Post,* 235:80–83, Jan. 6, 1962.

McKean, Dayton D.: *The Boss: The Hague Machine in Action,* Houghton Mifflin Company, Boston, 1940.

Kansas City

Dorsett, Lyle W.: *The Pendergast Machine,* Oxford University Press, New York, 1968.

Gabis, Stanley: "Leadership in a Large Manager City: The Case of Kansas City," *The Annals of the American Academy of Political and Social Science,* 353:52–63, May, 1964. (Post-Pendergast politics.)

Los Angeles

Ainsworth, Edward M.: *Maverick Mayor,* Doubleday & Company, Inc., Garden City, N.Y., 1966. (The story of Mayor Samuel Yorty.)

Banfield, Edward C.: *Big City Politics,* Random House, Inc., New York, 1965, chap. 5, "Los Angeles: Pre (Civil) War."

Brodie, F. M.: "Parks and Politics in Los Angeles," *Reporter,* 32:39–42, Feb. 11, 1965.

Carney, Francis M.: "The Decentralized Politics of Los Angeles," *The Annals of the American Academy of Political and Social Science,* 353:107–122, May, 1964.

Crouch, Winston W., and Beatrice Dinerman: *Southern California Metropolis: A Study in Development of Government for a Metropolitan Area,* University of California Press, Berkeley, Calif., 1963.

Mayo, Charles G.: "The 1961 Mayoralty Election in Los Angeles: The Political Party in a Non-partisan Election," *Western Political Quarterly*, 17:325–337, June, 1964.

Miami

Banfield, Edward C.: *Big City Politics*, Random House, Inc., New York, 1965, chap. 6, "Miami (Dade County): Yes, but . . ."

Sofen, Edward: *The Miami Metropolitan Experiment*, Indiana University Press, Bloomington, Ind., 1963.

Milwaukee

Hoan, Daniel W.: *City Government: The Record of the Milwaukee Experiment*, Harcourt, Brace & World, Inc., New York, 1936.

Schmandt, Henry J., and William H. Standing: *The Milwaukee Metropolitan Study Commission*, Indiana University Press, Bloomington, Ind., 1965.

New Haven

Dahl, Robert A.: *Who Governs?* Yale University Press, New Haven, Conn., 1961.

Talbot, Allan R.: *The Mayor's Game, Richard Lee of New Haven and the Politics of Change*, Praeger Publishers, New York, 1970.

New York

Carter, Barbara: "New York City—Can It Be Governed?" *Reporter*, 30:42–45, Jan. 30, 1964.

Cook, Frederick J., and Gene Gleason: "The Shame of New York," *The Nation*, Oct. 31, 1959, entire issue.

Fitch, Lyle C., and Annmarie H. Walsh (eds.): *Agenda for a City*, Sage Publications, Inc., Beverly Hills, Calif., 1970. (A number of specialists write on issues confronting New York.)

Glazer, Nathan: "Is New York City Ungovernable?" *Commentary*, 32:185–193, September, 1961.

Hamburger, Philip: "That Great Big New York Up There," *The New Yorker*, Sept. 28, 1957, pp. 47–82. (A profile of Mayor William O'Dwyer.)

————: "The Mayor: Profile of Robert F. Wagner," *The New Yorker*, Jan. 26, 1957, pp. 39–67; Feb. 2, 1957, pp. 39–69.

Hapgood, David: *Purge that Failed: Tammany versus Powell*, McGraw-Hill Book Company, New York, 1962.

Hentoff, Nat: "The Mayor," *The New Yorker*, Oct. 7, 1967, and May 3, 1969. (Profiles of Mayor John Lindsay.)

Lowi, Theodore J.: *At the Pleasure of the Mayor: Patronage and Power in New York City, 1898–1958*, The Macmillan Company, New York, 1964.

Makielski, S. J.: *Politics of Zoning: New York, 1916–1960*, Columbia University Press, New York, 1965.

Sayre, Wallace S., and Herbert Kaufman: *Governing New York City*, Russell Sage Foundation, New York, 1960. (Available in paperback.)

Oklahoma City

Mauer, George J.: "Oklahoma City: In Transition to Maturity and Professionalization," in Leonard E. Goodall (ed.), *Urban Politics in the Southwest,*
Institute of Public Administration, Arizona State University, Tempe, Ariz.,
1967.

Philadelphia

Banfield, Edward C.: *Big City Politics,* Random House, Inc., New York, 1965,
chap. 7, "Philadelphia: Nice While It Lasted."
Crumlish, Joseph D.: *A City Finds Itself: The Philadelphia Home Rule Charter
Movement,* Wayne State University Press, Detroit, Mich., 1959.
Gilbert, Charles E.: *Governing the Suburbs,* Indiana University Press, Bloom-
ington, Ind., 1967.
McKenna, William J.: "The Pattern of Philadelphia Politics, 1956–1963,"
Economics and Business Bulletin (Temple University), 16:19–24, Decem-
ber, 1963.
Reichley, James: *The Art of Government: Reform and Organization Politics
in Philadelphia,* The Fund for the Republic, New York, 1959.

Phoenix

Goodall, Leonard E.: "Phoenix: Reformers at Work," in Leonard E. Goodall
(ed.), *Urban Politics in the Southwest,* Institute of Public Administration,
Arizona State University, Tempe, Ariz., 1967.

St. Louis

Banfield, Edward C.: *Big City Politics,* Random House, Inc., New York, 1965,
chap. 8, "St. Louis: Better than She Should Be."
Schmandt, Henry J., Paul G. Steinbricker, and G. D. Wendel: *Metropolitan
Reform in St. Louis,* Holt, Rinehart and Winston, Inc., New York, 1962.

San Antonio

Crane, Bill: "San Antonio: Pluralistic City and Monolithic Government," in
Leonard E. Goodall (ed.), *Urban Politics in the Southwest,* Institute of
Public Administration, Arizona State University, Tempe, Ariz., 1967.

San Diego

Wilcox, Robert F.: "San Diego: City in Motion," in Leonard E. Goodall (ed.),
Urban Politics in the Southwest, Institute of Public Administration, Arizona State University, Tempe, Ariz., 1967.

San Francisco

Bean, Walton: *Boss Ruef's San Francisco,* University of California Press,
Berkeley, Calif., 1952.
Wirt, Frederick M.: "Alioto and the Politics of Hyperpluralism," *Trans*-action,
April, 1970, pp. 46–55. (San Francisco, "Government by Clerks.")

Seattle

Banfield, Edward C.: *Big City Politics,* Random House, Inc., New York, 1965,
chap. 9, "Seattle: Anybody in Charge?"

Toledo

Stinchcombe, Jean L.: *Reform and Reaction, City Politics in Toledo,* Wadsworth, Belmont, Calif., 1968.

Tucson

Joyner, Conrad: "Tucson: The Eighth Year of the Seven-year Itch," in Leonard E. Goodall (ed.), *Urban Politics in the Southwest,* Institute of Public Administration, Arizona State University, Tempe, Ariz., 1967.

Tulsa

Hanson, Bertil: "Tulsa: The Oil Folks at Home," in Leonard E. Goodall (ed.), *Urban Politics in the Southwest,* Institute of Public Administration, Arizona State University, Tempe, Ariz., 1967.

Wichita

Carpenter, Dwight M.: "Wichita: Cowboys, Crises and Tuesday Night Fights," in Leonard E. Goodall (ed.), *Urban Politics in the Southwest,* Institute of Public Administration, Arizona State University, Tempe, Ariz., 1967.

INDEX